IN THE SELF'S PLACE

Cultural Memory
in
the.
Present

Mieke Bal and Hent de Vries, Editors

IN THE SELF'S PLACE

The Approach of Saint Augustine

Jean-Luc Marion

Translated by Jeffrey L. Kosky

STANFORD UNIVERSITY PRESS

STANFORD, CALIFORNIA

Stanford University Press
Stanford, California

In the Self's Place was originally published in French in 2008 under the title
Au lieu de soi © 2008, Presses Universitaires de France.

Ouvrage publié avec le concours du Ministère français chargé de la culture—
Centre national du livre.

This book has been published with the assistance of the French Ministry of
Culture—National Center for the Book.

Printed in the United States of America on acid-free, archival-quality paper

Library of Congress Cataloging-in-Publication Data

Marion, Jean-Luc, 1946– author.
 [Au lieu de soi. English]
 In the self's place : the approach of Saint Augustine / Jean-Luc Marion ;
translated by Jeffrey L. Kosky.
 pages cm. — (Cultural memory in the present)
 "Originally published in French in 2008 under the title Au lieu de soi."
 Includes bibliographical references and index.
 ISBN 978-0-8047-6290-8 (cloth : alk. paper)
 ISBN 978-0-8047-6291-5 (pbk. : alk. paper)
 1. Augustine, Saint, Bishop of Hippo. 2. Self (Philosophy). I. Title. II. Series:
Cultural memory in the present.
BR65.A9M32713   2012
233'.5—dc23

2012002072

In memory of Jean-Marie Lustiger

Hier—das meint diese Hand, die ihr hilft, es zu sein.

Here—that means this hand that helps you to become.

—PAUL CELAN

Contents

Foreword

This book might seem to respond to a necessity manifested long ago in the itinerary of those that preceded it. For, if one starts out from Descartes in order to broach the question of the status of metaphysics, establish its constitution, and mark its separation from Christian theology, how can one not end up returning to Saint Augustine, an obligatory reference, whether it be accepted or denied, for the entire seventeenth century? Yet the necessity, if there was one, was entirely other: the somewhat more precise identification of metaphysics attained by studying Descartes led, beyond the question of his sources, references, and context, to an investigation into the limits of metaphysics and a glimpse of their possible transgression. Now this question is posed more obviously in the terms of phenomenology than in those of the history of philosophy: if one wants to leave behind generalities, that is to say approximations, indeed ideological distortions, it is necessary to discover phenomena, describe them, and recognize those that make an exception, partially or radically, to the objectivity and beingness practiced by metaphysics. This work led only to sketching a phenomenology of givenness, phenomena as given, in particular saturated phenomena, including even the erotic phenomenon, in which Saint Augustine did not yet play a part.

It took chance, then, for this necessity to present itself—more exactly, for Saint Augustine to appear suddenly as the privileged interlocutor and, in a sense, inevitable judge, of the project of accessing phenomena irreducible to the objects and beings of metaphysics. This chance, or rather this fortunate occasion, came from the Conseil scientifique de la "Chaire Gilson," which the Faculty of Philosophy at the Institut Catholique de Paris had set up more than ten years ago, when it did me the great honor of inviting me to deliver the six lectures anticipated for 2004. When it came time to set the theme of this series, I hesitated to take up what had been the theses of my more recent works, in particular *Étant donné* (1996), *De surcroît* (2001), and especially *Le phénomène érotique* (2003), in the fear of wearying my listeners and boring myself, too. I preferred, therefore, to risk another course: read and interpret the *Confessions* of Saint Augustine in a resolutely nonmetaphysical mode, by using to this end the major concepts that I had just elaborated in a logic of radically phenomenological intent. The stakes of this project were in my eyes twofold. First, it would test the hermeneutic validity of the concepts givenness, saturated phenomenon, and the gifted, by applying them to a reference text, supposedly well known yet remaining highly enigmatic. Next, it would enter more deeply into this aporetic work, whose strangeness increases to the measure of the efforts made to appropriate it—whether one translates ever again anew by imposing on it each time the more or less conscious prejudices of impassioned choice, contemporary fashion, or ideological rectification; or one buries the brilliant kernel in a coffin of precise but peripheral information, so as to prudently protect oneself from it by keeping it at a distance. For the problem of reaching the heart of the *Confessiones* resides—at least this was the hypothesis—in the absolute inadequacy of the point of view, or rather, in situating Saint Augustine within the metaphysical conditions of thought, which are still essentially our own. The entire question then became, quite quickly, to approach the site from which Saint Augustine thinks, so as to find there what he tries to think: the itinerary of an approach to the place of self—to the place of the self, the place most foreign to he who, proximally and for the most part, I am, or believe myself to be.

As soon as these lectures were delivered, in the winter of 2004, I understood that the ambition and the difficulty of their attempt demanded of me a work far more vast. In the first place they demanded my reading, as far as possible, the Augustinian texts in their own language, not in ours. By this I do not mean merely Latin (though *this* Latin in and of itself, in the virtuosity that so to speak uproots it from all previous Latin, gives one to think, at least as much as the languages supposed to be by nature the best for thinking) but especially the lexicons that our spontaneous metaphysics is forever imposing on us. To succeed in this, I was obliged to renounce resting on already available translations. This was necessary, first, to maintain coherence when passing from one work to another and, next, because however illuminating they might appear and useful they might remain to us, most of the time they do not avoid the uncontrolled and almost unconscious importation of the concepts of metaphysics into a language that is not only rhetorical and Roman (a double handicap in the eyes of those who, in this case, do not think farther than the end of their prejudices) but, above all, is irreducible to the lexicon of metaphysics.[1] I was therefore obliged to take the risk of producing a new translation of each text cited and to impose on the reader by preceding my translation in each case with the text of the original Latin.

Second, it was necessary to lose myself in the hardly virgin forest of the immense commentary on Augustine, so as to orient myself in the (good and bad) aporiae and commonplaces, so much has the stratification illuminated and at the same time hidden for centuries the text of Saint Augustine, by opening on it larger and larger and also more numerous points of entry, but also closing access to its center—be it only by suggesting that at bottom there is none. I therefore had to take up the entire work from its beginning, to free myself for something like the redaction of a new thesis (and the last). In this task of sometimes despairing slowness, I realized quite quickly that the outcome would be at best approximate: somewhat ignorant and surely incomplete but, above all, falling incommensurably short of the terrifying gravity of the project undertaken by Saint Augustine—of his advance toward God, more exactly of his harsh discovery that, in fact, God always advances from all eternity toward me, and therefore also of the abyssal deconstruction of self that must be consented to in order to receive this *self* finally from God. Moreover, without this feeling of profound inadequacy, no reader of Saint Augustine has the slightest chance of ending up with even the least result—the reason why the most exact investigations can understand nothing about it, while the thinkers who are apparently most distant often succeed in doing so, be it only in a brief and isolated remark.

To execute this plan, or, more exactly, to proceed with it to the point of admitting why there is no great sense in imagining that one could execute it fully, I received as much help as possible. First, Philippe Capelle agreed to offer me the delay required for transforming the sketch of six lectures into a more ambitious book, extending his generosity so far as to approve my publishing it in the series "Épiméthée," rather than the one he himself directs at PUF. I would like to acknowledge him here. Next the Université Paris-Sorbonne and the CNRS granted me a long posting with "Études augustiniennes" in the framework of the "Laboratoire d'études sur les monothéismes" (UMR 8584—CERL), directed by, respectively, Vincent Zarini and Philippe Hoffmann. Their cordial welcome at Ville-juif and the library of the Institut à l'abbaye de Saint-Germain-des-Prés made me, by chance, ascend into the illustrious train of French erudition, which, ever since the founding of the *Bibliothèque augustinienne*, has dominated the field of Augustinian studies. Finding oneself thus in the tutelary shadow of great forerunners, like P. Solignac encountered in the aisles of the defunct library "des Fontaines" at Chantilly in the time of my theses on Descartes, who punctuated the advance of this large project under the firm but kind control of G. Madec, constitutes a somewhat frightening honor, one not tempered by the authorities of P. Brown, W. Beierwaltes, K. Flasch, or J. J. O'Donnell (especially when one dares sometimes to dispute things with them). Finally, and as always, my students helped me by constraining me to work for them and by enduring my studies and my hesitations: those at the Université Paris-Sorbonne, as well as those at the University of Chicago, the Johns Hopkins University, and the University "La Sapienza" (Rome), particularly T. Alferi, R. Calderone, A. Guiu, K. Hefty, J. Manoussakis, and E. Tardivel. I also owe as usual, great thanks to V. Carraud (who reread my text and allowed me to correct it a little), J.-L. Chrétien, M. Fumaroli, J.-Y. Lacoste, C. Romano, H. de Vries, and especially to D. Tracy.

Chicago-Lods
March 2008

Bibliographic Note

I will always cite, for obvious reasons that will nevertheless be justified, the Latin text of Saint Augustine, immediately followed by a new translation. When possible, I give the reference to the edition published in the *Bibliothèque augustinienne* (*BA*), a French series begun by Desclée de Brouwer (Paris, 1947) and continued by the Institut des etudes augustiniennes (chapter, section, volume, page). When that is not possible, either because the texts have not appeared in the current state of the series or because they are there only partially, as with the *Commentary on the Gospel of John*, I give the reference to *Patrologiae Cursus Completus, Series Latina*, edited by J.-P. Migne, 221 vols. (Paris, 1844–64) (chapter, section, *PL* tome, column). For the other Fathers I cite the *PL* or *PG* (*Patrologiae Cursus Completus, Series Graeca*, edited by J.-P. Migne, 161 vols. [Paris, 1857–66]) and, in some cases, the edition of the work in the collection *Sources chrétiennes* (Paris: CERF, 1961).

The immensity of the secondary literature makes impossible even a selective attempt at it. The available apparatus was used, beginning with the *Bulletin augustinien.* I will mention, among the titles read, only those whose usefulness for my interpretation rendered them indispensable. Informed readers will often see what I owe to the standard reference works.

Readers are also advised to keep in mind that different English translations of the Bible (as with those into any other language) are based on different Latin and Greek translations of it and may number certain lines differently. Notably, the Latin Vulgate numbers the Psalms differently than do the texts that serve as the basis for many English translations.

Translator's Note

In the course of talking about the various ways people spend their time and fill their days, my daughter, Claire, asked me the other day if I liked translating: "Do you enjoy it?" I first had to acknowledge the wisdom of her question, especially when it is a question of translating a book about Augustine; then I had to answer her seriously, responding with a firm "yes." But I could only answer that "yes" because of those others whose presence around and with me, even in the distance, makes a place where this work can be enjoyed. First, and above all, Jean-Luc Marion, for generously offering me this charge and giving along with it the knowledge, the vision, and the encouragement needed to make good of it. The burden has been uplifting, a refreshing labor that allows for beginning again with new thoughts to pursue, new projects to follow, and new places to seek. Kevin Hart provided valuable insight, educated opinion, and frequent, but gentle, prodding when prodding was needed. The final product benefited from conversations at a seminar organized by Thomas Carlson at the University of California, Santa Barbara, on the topic of Jean-Luc Marion's reading of Saint Augustine. In addition to Tom's own counsel, Emmanuel Falque also offered words that made for a better work. I thank both of them.

Lexington, Virginia
September 2011

A few notes about the rendering of various terms might be in order at the outset, though I hesitate to do so. A translator should never try to control the interpretation of the book translated; the act of translation already does enough of that. I offer these notes as an indication that decisions were made, not as an explanation of terms themselves. Since every word and phrase translated always comes from a decision, these notes could only be partial; there are undoubtedly many other terms that readers would like to have explained or justified. I prefer to leave it to them and their interpretations to confirm (or not) the decisions I have made.

The title: The French title of the book is *Au lieu de soi*. With *In the Self's Place* I mean to say "instead of the self," "in that place over there where the self is found," and "in that place which is the self." The reader will see why. The French subtitle of the book is *L'approche de saint Augustin*. In the phrase "The Approach of Saint Augustine," awkward to be sure, one should hear the ambiguity of the genitive *of*: both how Saint Augustine approaches the place and how we approach Saint Augustine.

L'adonné: I have rendered this term as I did in Marion's *Being Given: Toward a Phenomenology of Givenness*: "the gifted." This should be taken in the sense of having a talent for . . . (for converting the given into the seen) but also as a substantive made from the passive form of the verb *to gift*. This latter sense is meant to convey that the self, too, happens originarily in and through a givenness in which I receive myself at the same time as and along with the given. What is lost in "the gifted" is the sense of the ordinary French *(s')adonner*, which means something more like "to give oneself over" and is used to describe an addict, a devotee, or someone who applies himself seriously, as to study. The gifted, receiving himself at the same time as the given, is, like the addict and perhaps the devotee, one who cannot live without that on which he depends. That sense of dependency is removed from my rendering.

Répons: I have also rendered this term as I did in *Being Given*: "responsal." According to the *Oxford English Dictionary*, *responsal* refers to a liturgical responsory, but it also has meanings that extend beyond the liturgical.

Autrui: This term is being written as "the other." It should be understood as a personal other as opposed to the generic, indeterminate otherness of *autre*. *Autrui* is a term familiar to readers of Emmanuel Levinas, where translators often render it "the Other." I have not capitalized it for fear that doing so would lead it to be taken too quickly as referring to God, a reference that most often is not the case here. This choice, of course, opens the opposite risk—that "the other" might be taken as anything other (animal, mineral, personal, etc.), which is not the case when "the other" renders *Autrui*.

Differer: Chiefly occurring in Chapter 5, the word means both "to differ" and "to defer." When readers see these words in English, they should be aware that they both render *differer*.

Être: I have used "Being" for *être* to distinguish it from *étant*, "being."

Esprit: The French term is used for what English would say as either "mind" or "spirit." I have used *mind* most frequently, but it should not be forgotten that this is a rendering of the French *esprit*, which evokes more than just the mental sense of mind. I have occasionally used *spirit* where it seemed appropriate. In some cases one might want to consider the Latin original of Augustine, which appears in the text. Marion uses *esprit* to render both Augustine's *mens* and his *anima*, which scholars concur is not equivalent to *l'âme* or "the soul." Matters grow more complicated as the Latin *spiritus* is also rendered as *l'esprit*.

Dilection: I use the unusual English term, indeed obsolete in most nontheological circles, *dilection*. For obvious reasons it was important to adopt a term that could distinguish and then relate the various loves (*charité*, *eros*, *dilection*, etc.) and love (*amour*) discussed by Marion in his reading of Augustine.

Distraction: The term is crucial to Chapter 5, where Marion proposes it as a French translation of Augustine's *distentio*. Marion uses the term in two senses simultaneously: pulled asunder (a sense heard in the etymology of *dis-traction*) and in the sense of diverted attention and loss of focus (a sense heard in the everyday use of *distraction*). I use the English cognate *distraction*, which has the same etymological sense and the same everyday sense.

The verbs Marion uses to describe *decision*, especially in Chapter 4 but throughout, pose special difficulties. Marion uses *décider* to describe the decision about something or some matter, but he also uses the pronominal verb *se décider* to suggest the way in which my self is at stake in the decision, sometimes even going so far as to write *se décider soi-même*. I have most often rendered the conjugated form of *se décider* as "I am decided." This has the disadvantage of introducing being ("am") precisely where Marion says it is not at issue, but it has the advantage of signifying something like resolution ("I am decided" in the sense that "my mind is made up," which might be a very good translation of Marion in many cases) while avoiding the active voice, as if the decision that makes up my mind (and therefore gives myself to me) is one that comes over me, graciously, rather than one for which I take initiative. When Marion seems to want special emphasis on the *se* of the pronominal verb, as when he writes *je me décide moi-même*, I have at times said "I myself am decided" or "I am myself decided" in order to suggest that the decision gives me myself.

IN THE SELF'S PLACE

§1. The aporia of Saint Augustine

Confessio itaque mea, Deus meus, in conspectu tuo, tibi tacite fit et non tacite.
My confession, my God, beneath your gaze is made unto you by keeping silent
and by not keeping silent.
—Augustine, *Confessiones* X, 2, 2, 14, 142[1]

There is a difficulty specific to the reading of Saint Augustine, so
much does he appear at one and the same time unavoidable and inaccessible.

He is unavoidable because ever since he came on the scene, nobody
has been unaware of him; nobody has neglected him. This is the case for
his work and for his thought, as it was for his ordination and his rise to
the bishopric; it was enough that he appear and that he speak for everybody to experience the evidence of his intellectual and moral authority.
That he immediately confronted, indeed attracted, the most resolute
opponents in the Church (during his lifetime and again and again over
the centuries), as well as the most extreme adherents, that he was obliged
to assume quite quickly the role of arbiter in the social life and politics of
his Africa—all of this resulted directly from this stature and only anticipated his role as permanent and ever reactualized reference point in the
history of thought. The greatest Christian theologians have laid claim
to him, in the name of the most rigid orthodoxy, as well as to authorize
sometimes heterodox innovations. Catholics and Protestants divide in
both claiming fidelity to his teachings, while the Eastern Churches have
often indicated their irreducibility to either by a virulent, though little
argued, anti-Augustinian polemic. One could make of him equally the
witness to the original faith and the inventor of the supposed driftings of
modernity. Even those, indeed especially those, who separate themselves
from him make no end of always laying claim to his patronage. Every
Christian has an assessment of Saint Augustine, and every adversary of
the Christian faith has his, too. But this fascination holds not only in

the history of theology and in the entire spectrum of Christian communities; it is also at work in the history of philosophy. The medieval emergence of the separation between theology and philosophy happens in direct relation with Augustinian thought, often invoked as an Aristotelian counterpoint, but also sometimes favoring the autonomy of certain philosophical truths (in noetics, for example). Ever since Descartes, Saint Augustine finds himself frequently invoked as the protector of the *novatores* against Aristotelianism. Of course, even the Enlightenment can be read as having an ambivalent relationship with Saint Augustine: the criticism of the theology of grace and its ecclesiastical implications (Voltaire, d'Holbach, et al.), the revision of subjectivity on the basis of the primacy of *affectus* (Rousseau, et al.). Finally, though sometimes under cover of Pascal (in France) or Luther (in Germany), Saint Augustine gets set up as a central interlocutor, either first adversary to be deconstructed or powerful ally of deconstruction, for all the moderns, even including Nietzsche, Husserl, Heidegger, and Wittgenstein[2]—so much so that the greatness of a thought is measured by the quality of its Augustinian quarrel. The result of all this is that nobody can claim as his or her own the resolution of Etienne Gilson: "We have therefore felt, like so many others, the need to go back to the source and study the Augustinism of Saint Augustine himself, so as to be better able to understand that of his successors."[3]

Inaccessible—Saint Augustine appears so as soon as one tries seriously to "go back to the source." Indications of this difficulty are not hard to find: the contradictory roles that the interpretive tradition always seems to make him play; the habit of selecting anthologies that dismantle the works so as to rebuild a system; reconstituting particular treatises to the detriment of wholes constructed by the author; assuming the lack of unity or poor composition of the greatest treatises (not only the *Confessiones* but even *De Trinitate*). One could multiply the rubrics and the examples. In fact, these are symptoms of a single but fearsome aporia: can one take a single, that is to say unitive, point of view on the immense continent of Saint Augustine? The enormous mass of the texts[4] would demand of the perfect reader the competence of a historian and a philologist but also of a historian of philosophy, equally well versed as a historian of dogma and theology, of a biblicist who would also be a rhetorician, etc., to whom the effort and the erudition accumulated over the centuries would give access to all these points of view. But, in reality, we have to choose from all of them in order to find the ideal but indispensable point of view from which the fragments would become a whole, the point of view that was, at least in any given moment, that of Saint Augustine—and no longer that of a discipline and a specialist of this discipline who has mastery over a selection of texts, indeed over some section taken out of the work. Now this demand, already difficult to assume when faced with any author worthy of the name, becomes almost unbearable here because the three points of view that one might wish to adopt everywhere else turn out, in the case of Saint Augustine, to be impracticable.

The point of view called, lacking anything better, historical (social and political histories, history of ideas, literary history, etc.) has benefited in recent years from an extreme and no doubt legitimate privilege. It obtained indisputable and definitive results—as much concerning the African roots of the doctrinal quarrels (in particular, Donatism) and the expanded responsibilities of the Episcopacy (and in particular that of Saint Augustine) as concerning liturgical life, the teaching and interpretation of biblical texts, and so forth. No one can ignore them or dispense with them. But it remains all the more remarkable that these same outcomes always permit different, indeed opposed, interpretations. This is illustrated perfectly by the two conclusions reached successively by as faithful and reliable a historian as Peter Brown when he passes from the first to the second edition of his biography of Saint Augustine: the *retractio* inverts or, at least, radically corrects his conclusions about nothing less than freedom, sexual morality and the theology of marriage, the handling of Donatism, and the response to Pelagianism. As he himself recognizes with a laudable probity, the evolution of his results comes as much from his own lowering of his ideological cautions as from obtaining new information.[5] And this evolution of the interpreter himself becomes in the end an even greater clue as it is the case of an author and a *corpus* broaching precisely the question of the conditions of the decision, of the affects that cannot not provoke it, and of the so to speak erotic interest that motivates it. The Augustinian doctrine of truth, desire, and the will renders the ambition to treat it solely with the resources of positive and objective information unrealistic and empty.[6] In the same sense the very long and rich debate about the supposed Neoplatonism of Saint Augustine, even when conducted by scholars as eminent as P. Courcelle, no longer appears today as decisive as it appeared at its beginning. This is not to say that the question is without interest but that it seems less central if not marginal: first, because Saint Augustine does not use the fundamental concepts of any of the Neoplatonisms (be it only because God is identical with neither the One, nor a Principle, nor even the Good); second, because one author can influence another without passing through explicit readings; and finally, because it behooves us to take seriously his own judgment, unambiguously negative, on these doctrines.[7] The privilege long granted to the question of the supposed Neoplatonism of Saint Augustine (and the Fathers of the Church in general) testifies perhaps as much to the preoccupation of the age and its interpreters as to an evident characteristic of he who had his roots rather in the practice of the *Enarrationes in Psalmos*.[8] Once again, the approach of Saint Augustine, by virtue of the radicality of the spiritual decisions he is trying to carry out and to theorize, forbids us from pretending to exclude them or neutralize them. The interpreter can neither maintain the pose of the impartial spectator nor fall back on the false modesty of a factual investigation, by imagining that his inevitable presuppositions will not be disclosed at one moment or another.[9] Nobody can leave intact from frequenting an author who wants only to speak from the point of view of Christ and demands it so insistently from his reader. It remains, of course, legitimate to study this or that Augustinian theme by trying to remain, as much as one can, in a perfect neutrality, and some excellent results can even follow from that. But these results will never concern the thought nor the question nor even the care of Saint Augustine *himself*; sometimes they even risk rendering these all the more inaccessible as they cover them over with other questions, indeed with correct answers to nevertheless foreign questions. In all cases these results will manifest negatively the necessity of at least trying *to approach* the point of view of Saint Augustine himself.

   Could all of this be about adopting a philosophical point of view? Some have not hesitated to consider Saint Augustine a pure philosopher, to the point that Fénelon even claimed he was the accomplishment of Cartesianism: "If an enlightened man collected in the books of Saint Augustine all the sublime truths that this Father scattered throughout as if by chance, this extract, made carefully by design, would be far superior to Descartes' *Meditationes*, even though these *Meditationes* are the greatest work of the mind of this philosopher."[10] But besides the fact that Descartes and Pascal refuse this patronage in advance,[11] it could come from, at best, only an "extract, made by choice." And, in fact, the philosophical appropriations of Augustinian theses or themes always proceed by selecting texts, often the same ones, always purged as much as possible of their biblical environment and their theological implications, obviously in opposition to the explicit declarations of Saint Augustine himself. Such is the case with the discussions of time in book XI of the *Confessiones*;[12] those about *memoria* in book X;[13] those about signs, in particular in book I, 8, 13;[14] those about the supposed anticipations of the *cogito*; those on the pair *uti/frui* in *De doctrina christiana*; those concerning the weakness of the will; etc. In all these cases, some of which are very famous, it appears clearly, as we will see again and again, that the philosophical recoveries of Augustinian arguments not only do not conform to the point of view of Saint Augustine but most often contradict it explicitly. The position of the philosophical rereaders consists, in the least naive of cases, in not taking up the analyses of Saint Augustine except as material worth being used better than he himself did or containing precursors still unfortunately formed in an imprecise and deceptive theological gangue in need of being elevated to a conceptual level by neutralizing them with an at best "methodological" atheism. In other words, the very attention that the philosophers pay to the texts, more exactly to *certain extracts* of the Augustinian texts, offers the best proof that Saint Augustine does not proceed as a philosopher and that the philosophical point of view was never his own.

The paradox is even stronger coming from the other side. For it is not only the interest that the philosophers take in him that denies Saint Augustine the status of philosopher, but the theologians themselves evidence great defiance toward claims of his philosophical insufficiency—or at least those theologians who assume that theology can and must rest on a philosophy that would be appropriate to it, that is to say absolutely *non*theological. We find a magnificent example of this interpretive tendency in the contributions of a colloquium organized for the fifteenth centennial of Saint Augustine's death by l'Académie Saint-Thomas (23–30 March 1930). Assuming an Augustinian philosophy, the only question to arise concerned its relation to Saint Thomas Aquinas, understood as the model and norm of a correct articulation of philosophy and theology, the first being sure of its pure nature by reason alone, the second rationalizing the supernatural by the science of the revealed. Even Etienne Gilson evoked an Augustinian philosophy in these proceedings ("The Idea of Philosophy in Saint Augustine and in Saint Thomas Aquinas"), while M. Grabmann investigated the Augustinian (and biblical) principle "If you do not believe, you will not understand" more as a problem than as a shape of the intellect ("De quaestione 'utrum aliquid possit esse simul creditum et scitum' inter scholas Augustinismi et Aristotelico-Thomismi medii aevi agitata"). It fell to R. Garrigou-Lagrange to pose frankly the question that was decisive in the eyes of all: did Saint Augustine succeed in correctly separating nature from the supernatural ("De natura creata per respectum ad supernaturalia secundum sanctum Augustinum")? In other words, did he succeed in distinguishing philosophy from theology ("utrum specifice distingueretur ex parte objecti formalis [philosophia] a theologia")?[15] Garrigou-Lagrange suggested that, despite it all and in a sense, he *almost* succeeded in doing so. In other words, Saint Augustine suffered from a philosophical insufficiency, at least from a certain sense of philosophy—a sense in which it conforms to the system of metaphysics.

Here comes to light the third and chief reason why a philosophical point of view does not permit an approach to Saint Augustine: his very understanding of *philosophia* contradicts in advance and head-on the interpretation, obvious for us, of philosophy as metaphysics. Taking up Saint Paul's warning (and the New Testament *hapax*)—"Be on guard lest someone deceive you with philosophy, διά τῆς φιλοσοφία, and the empty seduction following human tradition, according to the elements of this world and not of Christ" (Colossians 2:8)—Saint Augustine rejects the *philosophical* (Greek and therefore Ciceronian) uses of philosophy in order to retain only the most literal sense: "Amor putem sapientiae nomen graecum habet philosophiam, quo me accendebant illae litterae" (The love of wisdom bears in Greek the name philosophy, and in my reading [of Cicero's *Hortensius*], that [alone] ignited my ardor). That alone, in opposition to those it seduces, because they cover their errors with this great name, flattering and honorable, "magno et blando et honesto nomine colorantes et fucantes errores suos" (*Confessiones* III, 4, 8). Loving wisdom can mean for a Christian only loving God: "verus philosophus est amator Dei" (the true philosopher is he who loves God).[16] In short, philosophy is carried out only in the love of God, or else it is opposed to it and constitutes only an imposter. In this sense philosophy such as Saint Augustine understands it is opposed to philosophy in the sense of *metaphysica*. In this sense, too, one can indeed say that Saint Augustine lacks a philosophy in the commonly accepted sense: "It is clear, all the same, that this conception of philosophy does not correspond with *what men commonly call* 'philosophy,' that is to say with a rational knowing tending to the synthetic explanation of the real."[17] We therefore have to conclude—from the use of Augustinian texts by the philosophers, from the hesitancies of the modern theologians vis-à-vis his imprecision, and above all from his own sense of *philosophia*—that Saint Augustine never admits, when conducting his thought, a point of view that is philosophical in our sense of the term.

Should one conclude from this, by process of elimination and with the most innocent of all likelihoods, that he adopts a *theological* point of view? This response, in fact, seems untenable, too, for several reasons. First, if one sticks to the uses of the term, which are rare anyway, one will not let oneself be led astray by its minimalist definition: "theologia, quo verbo graeco significari intelligimus de divinitate rationem, sive sermonem" (theology, Greek term by which we mean to signify a reasoning or a discourse on divinity).[18] This speech or this reasoning does not in any way concern what the moderns will name *theologia*, in either of its senses, which are, moreover, exclusive: either the understanding of Revelation, or *theologia rationalis* as one of the parts of *metaphysica specialis*, itself framed by *metaphysica generalis* (or *ontologia*).[19] The Augustinian sense of *theologia* concerns much *less*, since it takes up the threefold division of the term by Varro: "Deinde illud quale est, quod tria genera theologiae dicit esse, id est rationis quae de diis explicatur, eorumque unum mythicon, alterum, physicon tertium civile" (*De civitate Dei* VI, 5, 1, 34, 64)—in other words, *theologia* or the poets' discourse on divinity, that of the *philosophi*, and that of the city.[20] This threefold division forbids making Saint Augustine the "theologian" of any of these three *theologiae*. This is because he eliminates two of them: first, that of the fables and the poets (whose ridiculous or immoral stories seem clearly unworthy of divinity); and, second, that of the city (which is purely political, reflecting the ideological pretensions of each city). There remains therefore only "theologia rationalis, quae non huic tantum [sc. Varro], sed multis philosophis placuit" (*De civitate Dei* VII, 6, 34, 140). This text is about that part of philosophy—physics, or more exactly, cosmology—that defines what in nature, in fact in the regular movements of the heavens, can give a certain visibility to the gods. And paradoxically, since philosophers alone reach this narrow but real rationality ("non cum quislibet hominibus . . ., sed cum philosophis est habenda conlatio" [*De civitate Dei* VIII, 1, 34, 228–30]), Christian thought (what we today call theology) can have discussions only with the philosophers, in no way with the other "theologies" of the pagans (by default, theologies of rationality).[21] Thus, in the strict sense, that is to say, in the sense that he himself intended, Saint Augustine does not do, except quite tangentially, a theologian's work.[22] Rigorously speaking, he would do the work of a philosopher, in the strict sense of *amator Dei*, and so the discussion concludes: "verus philosophus est amator Dei" (*De civitate Dei* VIII, 1, 34, 230).

Thus, neither historical investigation nor philosophy nor even theology open access to the point of view from which Saint Augustine understood himself; without that, a reader can, at best, only understand him partially, at worst, take him for another, indeed mis-take him. In fact, this aporia has nothing new or surprising about it, and even though they formulate it in terms that are too conventional and narrow, the best interpreters have seen it and admitted it perfectly. Gilson, for example: "One never knows if Saint Augustine is speaking as a philosopher or as a theologian."[23] Or Karl Jaspers: "It is often asked if Augustine is a philosopher or a theologian. This division does not count for me. He is well and truly both in one, not one without the other."[24] Or as G. Madec sums it up: "It is widely admitted that Augustinian teaching lends itself poorly to the distinction of philosophy and theology."[25] But must we admit, in consequence, that the lack of a decision between theology and philosophy comes as a failure, or by a lack of precision, and deplore it? Couldn't we rather suppose that he did not decide to admit this distinction? As if in passing, Gilson has an excellent formulation: Saint Augustine is to be found "on a plane which might be termed trans-philosophical."[26] How to think *trans-philosophically*, if not perhaps also *transtheologically*, at least in the ordinary sense? Heidegger, at the beginning of his first treatise on time, tells us that he will not speak theologically and therefore not philosophically either:

"nicht theologisch . . ., aber auch nicht philosophisch."[27] In fact, he was reproducing, without knowing it, the position of Saint Augustine, who was unaware *in advance* of a distinction that Heidegger would attempt to discuss *afterward*—the distinction between philosophy and theology (and *a fortiori* between the *theologia* drawn from the scriptures and the *theologia* as *metaphysica specialis*). This very distinction supposes the interpretation of both the one and the other term within the framework of metaphysics, not only its name (of which he was perfectly unaware) but, above all, its concept and system (which will be imposed only after him). It could be that Saint Augustine, who does not pose the question of Being, nor even that of being, who therefore does not name God in terms of Being nor as the being par excellence, who does not speak the language of the categories of being nor starting from the first among them, οὐσία, who does not investigate a first ground nor seek it in any *subject* whatsoever (whether one understands it as a substrate or as an ego), does not belong to metaphysics, neither explicitly nor implicitly. It could just as well be that he does not even belong to theology, in the sense that, with the vast majority of the Greek Fathers, it tries to speak *of* God, *of* principles, *of* the creation of the world, *of* the creation of man, *of* the incarnation, *of* the Holy Spirit, just as the Greek philosophers treat *of* nature, *of* the soul, *of* the world, *of* the categories, *of* the city, and even *of* the divine. For Saint Augustine does not so much speak *of* God as he speaks *to* God. In short, I assume the hypothesis that Saint Augustine was brilliantly unaware of the distinction between philosophy and theology because he does not belong to metaphysics.

It therefore behooves us to read him from a point of view that is at least negatively identifiable: from a nonmetaphysical point of view and, therefore, as our contemporary utopian, we who are trying to think from a postmetaphysical point of view. He would guide, in advance and without intending it, our hesitant steps by having thought *before* this *after* which we are trying to pass—metaphysics and possibly the very horizon of Being.

To develop and, if possible, to verify this hypothesis, I will have recourse to the figure of thought that strives most clearly, at least in its intention, to transgress metaphysics. In particular, I will try to employ the operative concepts of the phenomenology of givenness in order to assess whether they permit a more appropriate, coherent, and correct reading of the Augustinian texts. Thus, one could hope for a reciprocal trial: testing the nonmetaphysical status of Saint Augustine in and through a better intelligibility when he is interpreted according to the terms of a phenomenology of givenness, but testing also just how far the nonmetaphysical character of this phenomenology runs. To this end my attempted reading will call for what Saint Augustine himself called for, or enacted spontaneously: not employing the lexicon of the categories of being, not *a fortiori* importing the concepts of modern metaphysics, in one or the other of its states—in short, not speaking the language of metaphysics.

Confessio or Reduction

§2. What praise means

The point of departure most often decides the point of arrival, for the target depends on the aim and the aim on the sight and the angle of the shot. The exercise of thought makes no exception to this rule; it even makes it all the more imperative, since, in this case more than in any other, nobody can turn back once out of the gate or take back the shot once fired. And, for that matter, there is no second chance at a first beginning.

Now (as we will see little by little) the *Confessiones* do not take place in any site known or defined before them. According to the evidence (provided that one sticks to precise terms), they are not inscribed within a metaphysics, still less within a *metaphysica* even *specialis*, the definition of which, even just the notion of which, they would know nothing about. But this absence of philosophical determination does not lead them toward a theological determination, if one means by "theology" a speculative discourse *about* God, as modern usage would have it. For if their text treats of almost everything, and therefore of nothing precisely, it never busies itself with the object of one of the classical treatises of dogmatic theology—neither with the divine unity nor with a trinitarian god, no more with Christology than with the sacraments, the Church than last things. In other places it certainly will fall to Saint Augustine to write as such *about* the Trinity and the city of God (though it remains to be seen if he treats them as one speaks *about* and *on the subject* of the one and the other, or rather by becoming himself the subject submitted to what he evokes). In others it falls to him to comment on the book of Genesis, the Psalms, and the Gospel of John (but commenting is not equivalent to treating a question, for the interpreter must, or should, always first let him- or herself be interpreted by the text, which no longer has anything like an object or a subject). Here, however, in the *Confessiones*, something else is going on: Saint Augustine does not comment on the text, does not treat any object, for, it could be said, he does not *treat* anything at all. Even when he comes around to analyzing the will, time, truth, the first verse of Genesis and even the vicissitudes of his turning around to God (what is called a bit too quickly his conversion), he never broaches them for themselves, as autonomous and objifiable questions, but always inscribes them within a first-person narrative. And this narration itself constitutes the problem: who speaks, about what precisely, and to whom? Confronted with the difficulty of responding to these questions, the most common and (we will see) the most inadequate solution consists in falling back on something apparently obvious, by assigning the *Confessiones* the status of an autobiography, without worrying anymore about the *autos*, the *self,* of the question.

How are we to break free of this aporia? From what place are we to define the point of departure and therefore what is at stake in the *Confessiones*? If it is about neither philosophy nor theology, must we have recourse to autobiography (itself too indeterminate to be reassuring), indeed "mysticism" (final recourse of the interpreter who no longer wants to understand anything)? One senses that this would be just a trompe l'oeil, without any real relevance. But it could be that the aporia is born from the very formulation of the question. That is, wanting to assign a site to the *Confessiones* already supposes a conviction: that they need a starting point outside themselves and prior to them; in other words, that they cannot themselves offer the starting point on the basis of which they would be delivered. For what is proper to a starting point consists precisely in that it starts by starting from itself and that nothing else precedes it. But then would the *Confessiones* give to themselves their own starting point? Would they assign to themselves their place and their goal? If this was the case, they should say it clearly and at the outset. As is often the case when real difficulties are at issue, an indication of a solution comes from a commentary on scripture."'Quoniam cogitatio hominis confitebitur tibi et reliquiae cogitationis sollemnia celebrabunt tibi.' Prima 'cogitatio'; posteriores 'reliquae cogitationis.' Quae est 'cogitatio' prima? Unde incipimus: bona illa 'cogitatio' unde incipies confiteri. Confessio adjungit nos Christo. Jam vero confessio ipsa, id est prima 'cogitatio,' facit in nobis reliquias cogitationis. . . . Prima 'cogitatio' confessionem habet" ("For man's thought will confess you and the rest of this thought will solemnly celebrate you." First, at first, a "thought"; then, afterward, the rest of this "thought." What is the first "thought"? That from which we take our starting point: good is the thought from which you begin to confess. Confession joins us to Christ. For confession itself, namely the first "thought," already performs in us the rest of thought. . . . The first "thought" possesses the confession).[1] Here confession (and in the sense of *confessio*) appears as first thought, *prima cogitatio.* The first thought does not think that it thinks; still less does it think of itself as a *self,* but it thinks insofar as it confesses: thinking amounts to thinking in the more originary mode of confession of . . ., toward . . ., for . . .—an other instance besides myself, besides the *self.* In the beginning is the *confessio,* first *cogitatio* and therefore first place.

This first place, the thought of confession, *confessio* as first *cogitatio*—could it give the *Confessiones* their starting point? This seems to be the case, if two conditions are admitted. First, and at the outset, the principle that for Saint Augustine *confessio* is twofold, confession of sins and confession of praise: "Confessio enim, non peccatorum tantum dicitur, sed et laudis" (Confession is not said only of sins, but also of praise).[2] It follows that praise fully operates the *confessio.* Next, one must give serious consideration to the opening of book 1: "'Magnus es, Domine, et laudabilis valde; magna virtus tua et sapientiae tuae non est numerus.' Et laudare te vult homo, aliqua portio creaturae tuae" ("You are great, O Lord, eminently worthy of praise: great your strength and your wisdom without number." And to praise you, this is what man, one of the parts of your creation, wants) (I, 1, 1, *BA* 13, 272). Thus, praise launches the *Confessiones;* or rather, as praise emerges with *confessio* and puts it into operation, we should conclude that *confessio* constitutes the first thought of the *Confessiones,* their place and therefore their starting point.

There is more; for this text is still more astounding, and in several ways. First of all, it is the citation of a psalm, or more exactly the combined citation of several psalms,[3] all of which are focused on a single point: God, "great" by definition, since he passes beyond all number and all measure (strictly speaking, incommensurable and immense), draws one to praise him and deserves that one praise him. In other words, the approach of God can happen only by praise, according to an analytic and necessary connection: if it is a matter of God, then it is from the outset a matter of praising [him], for if praise is not called for, then it is no longer a matter of him, God. Praising does not designate one speech act among others, one that would be equally applicable to God and other similar targets. Praising offers the sole way, the sole royal road of access, to his presence. Next, the composite citation of the Psalms holds as an injunction for whoever wants to draw near to God, since the second part of the text responds to him: man, one part among others in the creation, wants very much to praise God; he, too, indeed he first of all. This consequence can in fact be understood as an endorsement of the first part of the citation, which in retrospect does indeed appear as an injunction. The opening lines of the *Confessiones* are therefore articulated in a demand (that God give himself for praise), then in a response (in fact man praises him, as does all creation). At the same time, the possibility of a hermeneutic difficulty is outlined: if he who does not praise cannot approach God and if the *Confessiones* want to approach God, then any reader who would refuse to praise would by that very refusal be blocked from understanding and even reading the *Confessiones*. The hermeneutic obstacle would therefore stem from a properly spiritual refusal.[4] This will not be the only case of what in fact is practiced as a rule. Finally, this insistence on praise and its function as originary hermeneutic place of the *Confessiones* should not be surprising, provided, at least, one observes that the same citation of Psalms that opens them also sets the tone for their articulation in book XI: "Numquid, Domine, cum tua sit aeternitas, ignoras quae tibi dico, aut ad tempus vides quod fit in tempore? Cur ergo tibi tot rerum narrationes digero? Non utique ut per me noveris ea, sed affectum meum excito in te et eorum qui haec legunt, ut dicamus omnes: 'Magnus Dominus et laudabilis valde'" (Can it be in any way, O Lord, since eternity is yours, that you do not know what I say to you or that you see temporally what happens in time? Why then do I tell you a list of so many things? Not, to be sure, so that you might learn them from me, but I bestir toward you my affect and that of my readers, so that we all might say, "Great is the Lord, and eminently worthy of praise!") (XI, 1, 1, 13, 270). Here the praise (and the citation) is extended from the *ego* to the community of readers, or at least of those who accept the call to praise. It is carried out in a church. There is more: this citation returns, in almost the same form, as a conclusion of the entire work and therefore of its journey toward God: "Laudant te opera tua, ut amemus te et amamus te, ut laudent te opera tua" (They praise you, your works, so that we would love you, and we love you so that your works would praise you) (XIII, 33, 48, 14, 516). From now on, praise comes not only from "one of the parts of creation" but from all of creation in its entirety. The praise, which at the beginning is sung by the narrator and in the middle is extended to include the community of believers, is in the end carried out on the scale of all creation. Praise therefore constitutes the starting point of the *Confessiones* and comes from them in such a way that they can end by carrying it out completely.

That praise can constitute a place, therefore, the place for the hermeneutic of the *Confessiones*, should not be surprising. First of all, one text explicitly assimilates it to a city, of which one becomes a citizen only by carrying out, in truly believing it, this very praise, which consists only in saying this—that God certainly is worthy of praise: "Haec est civitas, in monte posita, quae abscondi non potest, haec est lucerna quae sub modio non osculatur, omnibus nota, omnibus diffamata. Non autem universi cives ejus sunt, sed illi in quibus 'Magnus Domine et laudabilis valde'" (This is the city at the top of the mountain, which cannot be hidden; the light, which cannot be hidden under a basket, known to all, spread everywhere. Not everybody is a citizen of it, only those in whom we find "Great is the Lord, and eminently worthy of praise!").[5] Next, praise, which belongs analytically to God, also defines analytically the heart of man: "De radice cordis surgit ista confessio. . . . Hoc est enim confiteri dicere quod habes in corde" (This confession springs from the bottom of my heart. . . . For confessing is nothing other than saying what you have on your heart) (*Commentary on the Gospel of John* XXVI, 2, *PL* 35, 1607). The *Confessiones* are defined in the same way that they are launched: by a confession of praise. It remains to determine what praise means.

The mere fact of praising, provided it is considered correctly, already means a lot. For praise defines by itself a precise and complex language game. It seems somewhat straightforward to say that one can only confess a praise: in order to truly praise what one praises, it is obviously necessary to praise it openly, with an opening that is not only public, before all, but also intimate, with all one's heart, in both cases without reserve or reservation, all the way to the bottom. A praise that would remain unconfessed simply would not be one. Now this rule counts first and above all for God. For, in contrast to all the other cases in which it is always necessary to measure the degree to which the candidate for my praise deserves it (for it never deserves it absolutely), in the case of God the question is by definition no longer posed (if not, it would not be God, but an idol), such that here praising and therefore confessing this praise has nothing optional about it. It is fitting, indisputably, to praise God and to confess before him this praise simply because he is God. If I did not feel this obligation irresistibly, if it depended therefore on my decision to praise or not, that would signify that in fact it is no longer a matter of God but of another myself, more or less dominating, more or less comparable, therefore commensurate to myself—in any case, not God. God, if he reveals himself, reveals himself before being praised, and the praise is deduced from God by his definition, *Deus laudandus.* "Magnus es, Domine, et laudabilis valde" should be understood, let me repeat, as an analytic judgment: you are God; therefore you are great; therefore you are to be praised. This is not a platitude because the greatness of God defines the incommensurability (*sine numerus*) between the greatness of God and the tiny narrowness of all the created, in particular of "aliqua portio creaturae tuae . . . circumferens mortalitatem suam" (that portion of the created which carries its mortality with it wherever it goes). If I do not praise, I would lack not only respect for the creator, I would lack not only God as such, but I would lack first of all myself. Inversely, if I praise and therefore confess God as such, I also recognize myself as such, as creature that can truly neither speak to him as coequal nor say anything whatsoever about him, but that admits him. It logically follows that the incommensurability between God and myself, his creature, portion of his creation, implies that my praise toward him will have no end:

"Magnus es, Domine, et laudabilis valde." Quantum dicturus erat? Quae verba quaesiturus? Quantum conceptionem conclusit in uno "valde"? Cogita quantum vis. Quando autem potest cogitari, qui capi non potest? "Laudabilis est valde; et magnitudinis ejus non finis." Et ideo dixit "Valde," qui "magnitudinis non est finis": ne forte incipias velle laudare, et putes te laudando posse finire, cum magnitudo finem non potest habere. Noli ergo te putare eum, cujus magnitudinis finis non est, sufficienter posse laudare.

"Great is the Lord, and eminently worthy of praise!" How many [words] will it take to say it? Which words will seek him out? Which concept will capture him in this simple "eminently"? Think it as much as you want. But when can you think what you cannot grasp? "Eminently worthy of our praise, and his greatness has no end." It calls "eminently," he whose "greatness has no end," lest you not begin wanting to praise because you think that you can finish praise, while his greatness can have no end. Do not imagine therefore that you have the power to praise sufficiently he whose greatness has no end. (*Commentaries on the Psalms* 144, 5, *PL* 37, 1872)

Praise speaks with a word that predicates nothing of God, but confesses him without end, because, faced with his infinity, *it does not remonstrate with him.*

The originally unequal posture of praise is made explicit and intelligible in the principle that justifies and likewise saves it: "fecisti nos ad te et inquietum est cor nostrum, donec requiescat in te" (you made us for, in view of, and in the direction of yourself, in such a way that our heart knows no rest so long as it does not rest in you) (I, 1, 1, 13, 272). Once again what launches the *Confessiones* will return so as to conclude them: "id, quod tu post opera tua 'bona valde,' quamvis ea quietus feceris, requievisti septimo die, hoc praeloquatur nobis vox libri tui quod et nos post opera nostra ideo 'bona valde,' quia tu nobis ea donasti, sabato vitae aeternae requiescamus in te" (from the fact that you rested at the end of your "eminently good" works [even though you did them while remaining at rest], the voice of your book said to us in advance that we too, after our works, "eminently good" [in that you gave them to us], should rest in the Sabbath of life eternal in you) (XIII, 36, 51, 14, 522). The whole of the *Confessiones* is thus framed by the double utterance of a single principle, one that we could safely say comes from physics but is applied to the spiritual life (and corrected by it): "Corpus pondere suo nititur ad locum suum. Pondus non ad ima tantum est, sed ad locum suum. Ignis sursum tendit, deorsum lapis" (A body is pushed by its weight toward its place. This weight is not just borne downward toward the bottom but toward its [proper] place). Weight can even lift up toward the heights that whose proper natural place is elevated. For example, oil, even covered by water, will always rise above it, and inversely, the water will always end up sinking below the oil. In both cases, "ponderibus suis aguntur, loca sua petunt" (they are borne by their [respective] weights and tend toward their [respective proper] places). Bodies therefore find their rest only when they find themselves ordered to their places in conformity with their weight: "Minus ordinata inquieta sunt: ordinantur et quiescunt. Pondus meum amor meus; eo feror, quocumque feror" (those less in order remain restless; put them in order and they will find their rest. As for me, my weight, it is my love: wherever I am carried, I am carried there by it) (XIII, 9, 10, 14, 440).[6] In the case where I praise God, that is to say, where I address my words to him inasmuch as I love him, my weight leads me to him as to my proper place. Praising him therefore means that I rise into my place, that I go back up there from where I am and toward him from whom I come. The word of praise does not say God, even in his eminence, so much as it refers to him and returns to him—*as the word that ascends.*

And yet, even having reached this point, we are still missing the essential. For to speak with praise implies, beyond the nonremonstrance and the ascent, that first of all I speak *to* God, even before saying anything whatsoever *about* God. Indeed, it means that I speak *to* God without saying anything *about* God, because I no longer predicate anything whatsoever about him. The radical difference between these two language games cannot be overemphasized. Speaking *to* God (as in the case of confessing praise par excellence) demands that the word spoken be referred to what it intends, the eminence that does not speak, therefore referring the locutor to his interlocutor, or more exactly passing from the rank of locutor (in relation to God) to the rank of interlocutor (he whom God approaches as *interloqué*). In contrast, to speak *of* God amounts to speaking a word measured by and starting from the locutor, who is precisely not God; it thereby amounts to submitting God to the conditions of the utterance, in fact the predication of he who speaks. If speaking *of* God consists in predicating something or inscribing him in a class and under a concept, then such a "god" falls to the rank of one object among others, and that about which I speak immediately has nothing to do with that which God could give us to think. To speak *of* God: all things considered, this is a contradiction in terms. But there is more: to speak *of* God also implies being able to speak *to* an other than myself (or to myself as another, "me solum adloquendo") in such a way that God remains, between us, one other among all the other others, of whom we can, you and I, speak as a third, an *ille*. Now, in the role of this third, God is lowered not merely to something *about* which I can say something (τί κατά τινὸς), but especially to this *ille* that I am going to exclude, or rather that is of itself going to be excluded from the dialogical space by assuming the status of a mere excluded third, of an object in the absence of which *ipse* (I myself) and *iste* (you yourself, this other myself), we are going to speak *to ourselves* by speaking *about* him. To speak *of* God would mean in the end speaking *of* him but *without*, indeed *against*, him. Philosophy does not prohibit itself from doing so, nor, for the most part, does theology. In opposition, speaking *to* God, as the confessing praise does, implies first of all turning one's face *to* God so that he can come over me, claim me, and call me starting from himself, well beyond what I could say, predict, or predicate of him starting from myself alone. Wittgenstein saw it perfectly: "'You can't hear God speak to someone else, you can hear him only if you are the *interloqué* (der Angeredete).'—That is a grammatical remark."[7] In the word spoken in praise, the dialogical space puts God and myself into relation. Emmanuel, but backwards: God with me, provided that I speak *to him, myself* toward him.

It follows that the *Confessiones* offer only the appearance of a text *about* God (strictly a text of theo-*logy*), one that would treat him in the way that a philosopher writes *about* the world, *about* the heavens, *about* the city, or *about* virtue, in the manner common to so many theologians.[8] The *Confessiones* are intended to be set forth as, and in fact are set forth as, a praising text, a praise become text, more exactly a text that gives itself to be read as it was written—performance of praise, text to praise, which utters (and consigns) an uninterrupted appeal *to* God. It is, par excellence, a text *unto-God*. In an extraordinary rupture with the metaphysical mode of speech as the predication of something *about* something,[9] praise no longer pretends to say anything *about* God but signifies precisely that I am saying nothing *about* God, or rather it signifies *to* God that I acknowledge him alone as God, by saying it to him and by acknowledging myself a non-god. From now on, each time that the praise is repeated throughout the *Confessiones* (and it will be repeated incessantly, to the point that readers will have their fill of it), Saint Augustine will therefore say and say again, to be convinced of it himself, what he says *to* God, who has no need to learn it from anybody: God, you, you are God, name of God.[10] Hence, confession and praise truly make but one, since praising God amounts to recognizing him as such, without saying anything *about* him, therefore exactly to confessing him as such. "Et ideo inde coepit 'Confitemini Domino et invocate nomen ejus.' In laude enim intelligenda ista confessio, sicut est 'Confiteor tibi, Pater, Domine coeli et terrae' (Matthew 11:25). Praemissa enim laude, invocatio sequi solet. . . . exaudit quippe invocantem, quem laudentem videt; laudentem videt, quem probat amentem" (And therefore he [the psalmist] begins with "Confess the Lord and invoke his name." This confession must be understood in the praise, as it is [said], "I confess you, Father, Lord of heaven and earth" (Matthew 11:25). For once the praise is offered up, the invocation customarily follows. . . . Seeing that he praises him, God answers the one who invokes him; and he sees that whoever has felt his love for him praises him) (*Commentaries on the Psalms* 104, 1, *PL* 37, 1390).

Praise goes even still farther beyond: it does not imply only that my word is said *to* God (and renounces saying anything *about* him); it also supposes that my word is already received and heard by he whom it confesses. "To confess God" means, at bottom, wanting to reach him as he who already hears our appeal. But the confession could not hope that God hear its appeal if it did not already know that in some fashion or another he spoke the word first, before and in order that the word might be offered to him, that he called upon it before and in order to provoke it: "Dominus Deus, noster alloquens et consolans nos" (Lord God, who calls upon us and consoles us) (*Commentaries on the Psalms* 26, 2, 1, *PL* 36, 199). The praise, originarily an interlocutor that calls upon God because more originarily always already called upon itself, says nothing, but addresses itself, as *the word that brings about an encounter*.

§3. Citation and responsal

These remarks having been made, we can finally go on to what is essential. If praise confesses God as God by finding support on its having been heard by God, therefore on the call by God that this hearing already implies, shouldn't we ask: this word that I say *to* God but that is preceded by the hearing and the call of God, do I, with regard to it, have initiative, proprietorship, control? In short, do the words that I say in praise come from me or from him whom I praise? To be sure, I say these words, and that obviously counts as the fact of my praise. But am I, for all that, their author or initiator? Most certainly not. That is, saying a word *to* implies already that its addressee, in one way or another, it matters little, rises up and imposes himself, precisely because he already incited the interlocution and, in this way, renders possible the praise that I then desire to render to him. Of myself, reduced to my dumb solitude, I could not yet say anything *to* anyone, if no one had not already interpellated me. Reciprocally, what interlocutor could appear to me without the space of a reference *to* having already opened, which it presupposes in order to be understood? Predication does not permit it since it remains indifferent to the one who says it and to the one who hears it, and since it must if they are to be able to exchange roles in such a way that their intersubjectivity guarantees the objectivity of scientific discourse. But then why and how does the praise that confesses succeed, if it does succeed? What essential opening of its mode of speaking arranges a separation (a difference, a distance) in which the duality of call and response, of praise and its hearing, can be unfolded? In short, how does the praise that confesses permit an encounter?

Here, finally, appears the greatest strangeness of the speech set forth in the *Confessiones*, such as it is uttered from their first words: "'Magnus es Dominus et laudabilis valde'" ("Great are you, O Lord, eminently worthy of praise").[11] The double quotation marks indicate, when we cite this text, a double citation: the reader who cites Saint Augustine cites him citing the scriptures. This observation is not trivial, since it indicates that with the words cited initially it is not a matter of words said *by* Saint Augustine but of words first said *to* Saint Augustine by the very one *to* whom the confession now *re*says them—words said in the beginning by God, who was first to say his word, or rather who said the first word, as he created the world by it. The word that opens the *Confessiones*, like that which closes them (and like all those that run throughout them), has the status of a citation; that is to say, it resays an other word, anterior and more original to it than itself. Saying therefore wants to resay the word of the other, with a resaying that does not repeat the first utterance but renders it audible to us afterward for the first time. This is first of all an anthropological rule: speaking (and learning to speak) consists first and in fact always in resaying what one heard said. Accordingly, no linguistic innovation (in style, vocabulary, even thought) is excepted from the essential anteriority of the already said but rather comes from it and rests in it. This is also a rule set explicitly by Saint Augustine in the *Commentaries on the Psalms*:

Voces istae Psalmi quas audivimus et ex parte cantavimus, si dicamus quod nostrae sint, verendum est quemadmodum verum dicamus; sunt enim voces magis Spiritus Dei, quam nostrae. Rursum, si dicamus nostras non esse, profecto mentimur. Non enim est gemitus nisi laborantium; aut omnis ista vox, quae hîc sonuit, plena doloris et lacrymarum, potest esse ejus qui numquam potest esse miser? . . . Itaque utrumque verum est, et nostram esse vocem, et nostram non esse, et Spiritus Dei esse vocem, et ipsius non esse. Spiritus Dei vox est, quia ista nisi illo inspirante non diceremus; ipsius autem non est, quia ille nec miser est, nec laborat.

These words of the Psalm that we heard and just sang in part, if we say that they are ours, we should be careful about the way in which they are said in truth; for they are more the words of the Holy Spirit than they are ours. Again, if we say that they are not ours, surely we are lying. For they are complaints and bespeak great trials: how else could these words, which here are resonant with sorrow and tears, come from he who cannot be unhappy? . . . Thus both are true, that these words are ours and that they are not, that they are from the Holy Spirit and that they are not his. It is the word of the Holy Spirit, for we would not say these things if it did not inspire us with them; but they are not his words because he himself knows neither unhappiness nor suffering.[12]

What I say I do indeed say in my name, because I say it in my condition and from my own situation; but the words to say it do not come to me from myself without another putting them into my mouth. What I say and what I mean (my intentionality) belong to me, but that I say it and how I say it (my syntax and my performance) come over me from an other (*autrui*). My speaking believes itself to have the initiative, and in a sense it really does; but it receives it more than it takes it; it has simply been ignorant of it for a long time because it has not yet heard, in the sound of what it utters, the silent staging that in advance renders it possible. The *confessio* will have no other function than to teach my speech little by little the call from which it comes, without knowing it, as a response. The spoken word is enacted in a chiasmus, where my initiative, second as a response still deaf to its question, and a call, so absolutely anterior that it takes a lifetime to finish hearing it for the first time and *as* the first time, cross each other. Whence this conclusion: my word (that which I say in the mode of originary resaying) consists in the word given to me by God in the scriptures, from then on repeated and declined according to my suffering. The scriptures therefore do not record a dead word of God *about* himself but deliver the silent word that, in advance (in the immemorial advance of a creation), renders possible my own living word. My word will learn to speak by repeating, as response, the words of the call always already silently carried out in the scriptures.

From their very first lines, the *Confessiones* validate this rule: "Quaeram te, Domine, invocans te et invocem te credens in te: *praedicatus* enim es *mihi*. Invocat te, Domine, fides mea, quam *dedisti mihi*, quam *inspirasti mihi* per humanitatem Filii tui, per ministerium *praedicatoris* tui" (Let me seek you, O Lord, by invoking you, and let me invoke you by believing in you. For you *addressed me in advance.* Let my faith invoke you, O Lord, my faith that you *gave to me*, that you *inspired in me* through the ministry of your Son, through the ministry of *he who spoke in advance*").[13] The advance of this word—which is consonant with the antiquity of the *pulchritudo tam antiqua*—is carried out in the scriptures. But the scriptures themselves remain inaccessible, as Saint Augustine experienced at great length during his Manichean and Neoplatonic periods. They must therefore be opened through the intermediary of the sent apostle (in this case by the hermeneutic of Saint Ambrose); but the apostolic envoy draws his possibility from the sending of Christ, who himself implies the eternal antiquity of the Father, an envoy who appears only to him whom the Spirit illuminates. For ultimately it is a matter of a hermeneutic apparatus inscribed finally in the Trinity. This is established all the more noticeably as Saint Augustine applies it to himself, as much a writer as a witness: "Neque enim dico recti aliquid hominibus, quod non a me tu *prius* audieris, aut etiam tu aliquid tale audis a me, quod non *mihi tu prius dixeri*"

(I say nothing correct to men that you did not hear me say to you *first*, and you hear nothing correct said by me which *you did not first say to me*) (X, 2, 2, 14, 142). The first to hear was in fact first of all also the first to speak, in a sense the sole one. In other words I can predicate nothing *of* God *to* other men, if I do not first say it *to* God (who validates it to me by hearing it) because more essentially I say nothing *to* God (and *a fortiori* nothing *of* God) that was not first said *by* him *to* me. Scripture precedes my own writing and permits citation, or rather permits me my writing *as citation*, such that the word said silently to me by the other precedes the uttering that I carry out and that follows from it. Whether it falls silent or speaks, my word always responds to the word, silent or written, of God. Not only does the scripture of God precede my live word, which repeats it,[14] but my word becomes live only in and through resaying the originally living saying of the Word of God.[15] Praise is therefore carried out as a word resaid, which responds by resaying what it first heard, in short as *the word of the responsal.*

Thus the originary word of God, that which I cite in order to speak to him in turn, resounds as always already emitted and given, in short, as essentially a call. That the call come from the scriptures by citation still remains undetermined (is it I who speaks? is it something else? is it an other?) changes nothing in this instance, be it only because this indetermination characterizes every call, the more it radically determines me. Well before the *Confessiones*, the opening of the *Soliloquia* had described this quite precisely: "Volventi mihi multa ac varia mecum diu, ac per multos dies sedulo quaerenti memetipsum ac bonum meum, quidve mali evitendum esset, ait mihi subito, *sive ego ipse, sive alius quis extrinsecus, sive intrinsecus,* nescio; nam hoc ipsum est quod magnopere scire molior" (While I was turning over and over again in myself many various things, searching for myself and my good or what evil to avoid, suddenly someone spoke to me: *was it myself, an other outside of myself or indeed an other inside me, I do not know. For that is what I am trying very hard to know*).[16] Praise, which speaks by citation, ends up being identified with a *call*.[17] The one who praises—me, you, or us—is only responding to the prior call of God, which we read in the scriptures and to which we respond possibly as the last, in response, after the fact, by citing it. The opening of the last book of the *Confessiones* makes this unquestionably manifest:

Invoco te in animam meam, quam *prae*paras ad capiendum te ex desiderio, quod inspirasti ei: nunc vocantem te ne deseras, qui *priusquam* invocarem "*prae*venisti" et institisti crebescens multimodis vocibus, ut audirem de longinqo et converterer et vocantem me invocarem te. . . . et *prae*venisti omnia bona merita mea . . . quia et *priusquam* essem tu eras, nec eram cui praestares ut essem, et tamen ecce sum ex bonitate tua *prae*veniente totum hoc, quod me fecisti et unde me fecisti.

I invoke you into my soul, which you are *pre*paring to receive you by the desire that you yourself inspired in it: now that it invokes you, do not abandon it, you who, *before* it invoked you, were calling out from "ahead of me" (Psalm 58:18)[18] and insisting by words ever more insistent, so that I would hear you from afar and turn around and invoke you, you who were provoking me. . . . and you were moving *ahead* of my goods and merits . . . because you were *before* I could be, and I was not even there for you to give me being, and yet see, by your goodness which *went before me*, I am all that you made me and *whence* you made me. (XIII, 1, 1, 14, 424)[19]

Like the gifted, I must receive even myself at the same time as the gifts that I receive because I do not precede them but come from, just as they do, an immemorial instance—from a call without any preliminary. Nobody calls without already responding to a more ancient call: "Vocata invocat Dominum" (*Commentaries on the Psalms* 5, 2, *PL* 36, 83).

Concerning this complex apparatus constitutive of a word laid hold of by the Word, therefore also of my call perceived by citation, the best example is found in Saint Augustine himself. That is, the celebrated episode of his so-called conversion is organized around the characteristics that we just saw at work in the word of praise. One might even suggest that the centrality of this event stems as much from its personal significance for the converted as from the fact that it is the paradigmatic accomplishment of praise and the perfect illustration of the reprisal of a word set forth to the extent it is called by the Word.[20] The story opens with the admission that I speak only before God but that my faults prevent me from speaking *to* God, in such a way that they literally cut off my every word (VIII, 11, 28, 14, 64). I can no longer even speak by myself since I no longer have any self available to me, who breaks down in "controversia in corde meo non nisi de me ipso adversus me ipsum" (a controversy in my heart over nothing other than myself against myself) (VIII, 11, 27, 14, 62). And yet, despite anxiety to the point of tears, the cut-off speech is suddenly reborn in abundance: "multa tibi dixi" (I said many things to you) (ibid.). How can that happen? Solely because at this precise moment Saint Augustine no longer says his own words but *cites* the Psalms 6:4, and 78:5, 8: "'Et tu, Domine, usquequo? Usquequo, Domine, irasceris in finem? Ne memor fueris iniquitatem nostrarum antiquarum'" ("And you, Lord, how long? How long, Lord, will you last in your anger to the end? Keep not alive the memory of our former iniquities") (VIII, 12, 14, 65). He thus begins to respeak only by citing—which is to say that he again takes up the spoken word only by letting himself be taken (and therefore given) by the Word. This reversal, here still implicit, becomes at once explicit, since this first address, therefore praise by reprisal of the Word, is immediately articulated with the hearing of a voice: "Et ecce audio vocem" (And lo, I hear a voice) (VIII, 12, 29, 14, 64). Now, this voice imposes itself as a call, precisely and paradoxically because, like every call, it remains at first anonymous—is it a song, a girl's voice or that of a boy? "Nescio" (I do not know) (VIII, 29, 14, 66).[21] But, as with every call, its crystallization occurs at the moment when he takes it upon himself and for himself: "Statimque mutato vultu intentissimus cogitare coepi . . . repressoque impetu lacrymarum, sur-rexi nihil aliud interpretans divinitus mihi juberi, nisi ut . . ." (Instantly, my face changed and I began to think very intensely . . . and holding back the upswell of tears, I stood up, interpreting this as nothing other than a divine order suggesting . . .) (ibid.).[22] But what does the call so recognized as such by Saint Augustine say? Nothing but this: "Tolle, lege" (Take it, and read it); in this case read Romans 13:13–14: "Not in rioting and drunkenness, not in chambering and wantonness, not in fighting and envy, but wrap yourself in the Lord Jesus Christ and do not become a purveyor of the flesh in concupiscence." Once again the extraordinary hermeneutic situation of confession and praise is accomplished: my word, taken (in hand, so as not to be lost) by the Word, can and need say only what the Word said at the outset and therefore can only cite it in such a way as to make it its most intimate responsal. But what the Word says to my word is nothing other than that very thing—take this Word and read it; read it by taking it for oneself and therefore by receiving it as a call. "Quid autem, ut converteris, posses, nisi vocaveris?" (What could you do for your conversion, except to be called?) (*Commentaries on the Psalms* 84, 8, *PL* 36, 1073).

Put otherwise, conversion consists first only in using the biblical text as my sole and proper word (speaking by citation of an other). Next, the word cited says only this: citing, speaking by citing, the aforesaid, finally recovering the word by the Word interposed. The content and the goal of conversion coincide in the singular return of my word in and through the Word. This hermeneutic recovery is enough to accomplish the psychological conversion—or better the entire theological μετανοία. The entire structure instituted at the opening of the *Confessiones* is verified in the very conversion of Saint Augustine, paradigm of confession and praise. Thus, conversion counts as *ratio occurrendi* of praise and praise as *ratio intelligendi* of conversion. Both the one and the other operate the same and single *praise as the hearing of a call.*

§4. *Confessio* divided and doubled

The final step remains to be taken, where the entire construction of the *Confessiones* is decided: to conceive how praise is itself practiced as confession to the point of being identified with it. For we had juxtaposed them until now, without having clearly established their mutual connection.[23] Now, in fact, Augustine articulates the one with the other, indeed inscribes the one within the other. Very often, the praise that confesses God as "eminently worthy of praise" is duplicated in the confession of my wretchedness, confession that, in books II through IX, even runs ahead of the confession of praise and subordinates it. For example, "Deus meus, ego tamen confiteor tibi dedecora mea 'in laude tua'" (My God, I want to confess to you my disgrace "in praise for you" [Psalm 105:47]) (IV, 1, 1, 13, 408). Or, "'Accipe sacrificum' confessionum mearum de 'manu linguae' meac, quam formasti et excitasti, ut confiteatur nomini tuo. . . . Sed te laudet anima mea, ut amet te et confiteatur tibi miserationes tuas, ut laudet te" ("Receive the sacrifice" [Psalm 50:21] of my confessions by the "hand of my tongue" [Proverbs 18:21] that you formed and stirred to confessing your name. . . . But let my soul praise you so as to love you and confess your mercies to you so as to praise you) (V, 1, 1, 13, 462). And "Taceat laudas tuas, qui miserationes tuas non considerat, quae tibi de medullis meis confitentur" (He does not utter your praises, he who does not take into consideration your mercies [shown toward him], which from the very marrow of my bones do confess you) (VI, 7, 12, 13, 542). Or again: "Deus meus, recorder in gratiarum actione tibi et confitear misericordias tuas super me" (My God, I want to remember in acts of giving thanks to you and to confess your mercies [poured out] over me) (VIII, 1, 1, 14, 8). Or finally: "Accipe confessiones meas et gratiarum actiones" (Accept my confessions and acts of thanksgiving) (IX, 8, 17, 14, 102). How are these two moments connected? No doubt praise and confession of faults go together, for at least two reasons. One is negative: my finitude (creation) and my wretchedness (sin) forbid me from celebrating God as "eminently worthy of praise" if I do not acknowledge both as posing an obstacle to giving thanks (which they shun by their very fact). The other is positive: they attest, contrary to what they intend, the incommensurable distance between myself and God, distance in which alone praise can be deployed. But why name praise and the admission of faults with the same term *confession*? Is it a mere homonym, or does the same concept truly join them?

The question is even more pressing since the pre-Christian use of *confessio* knows only its juridical sense of an admission of guilt. As a consequence, it always implies a negative evaluation—be it that of madness: "As for me, I count as *confessio* every word pronounced against oneself. And the law does not order me to seek the cause for which someone admitted it (*confessus sit*). Moreover, such is the nature of every *confessio* that he appears mad who makes an admission about himself (*de se confitetur*). A madness drives him—drunkenness, error, sorrow, some torture or other. But nobody speaks against himself except under some constraint."[24] Or that of "shame in the admission" (*in confessione*).[25] The Christian usage reverses this juridical acceptation by constructing the sense of a glorious admission, not a shameful one, the voluntary proclamation of faith in Christ. Tertullian, as often, offers a brilliant exposition of this new glory of *confessio*:

And Christians, what of the like do they seek? Nobody has shame, nobody repents, except of his past. If he is dishonored, he is glorified by it; if he is dragged away, he does not resist; if he is accused, he does not defend himself. Questioned, he admits and confesses (*confitetur*); if he is condemned, he is glorified in it. What then is this evil in which the very nature of evil is lacking? In that you yourselves judge from elsewhere contrary to the form of the judgments. For the wicked that are brought to you, if they deny the evidence, you force them to confess (*confessionem*) by torture. But the Christians, who confess (*confessos*) spontaneously [their faith], you submit them to torture so that they might forswear it.[26]

Confessio therefore has nothing despicable about it when the faith of Christians is at issue, since they do not make their admission out of fear but freely, to the point that one tortures them not in order to have them make an admission (*confiteri*) but to make them *not* confess this faith (*confessio fidei*). The confession of faith of Christians thus offers the sole case of a testimony against oneself that nevertheless remains free and therefore honorable. As a result it becomes possible to join under the same term, in Latin as in Greek, the (shameful) admission of sins (but before God, the sole judge) and the confession of faith: "This act, better and more often expressed by the Greek word ἐξομολόγησις, is that by which we confess our fault to God, not that he does not know about it, but insofar as confession disposes us to satisfaction, from it is born penitence, and penitence appeases God. Thus ἐξομολόγησις teaches man to prostrate himself and humble himself, renewing the relation and inciting mercy."[27] Tertullian thus makes the Latin *confiteri* coincide with the double biblical usage of ἐξομολόγησις: on one hand the confession of faith or praise,[28] on the other the admission of sins. The two terms end up overlapping but with a different starting point, since *confessio* is said more commonly first of the admission of sins while ἐξομολόγησις is applied first of all to praise or the proclamation of faith.[29] In any event the doubling quickly becomes an established given, as Hilary of Poitiers attests: "We find that it is necessary to practice *confessio* in two senses: one is the confession of sins, as in the desert of Jordan sins were confessed; but the other is the praise of God, as there where the Lord says to the Father 'I confess you Lord, Father.'"[30]

It now becomes possible to understand Saint Augustine's strategy: he ratifies the previous doubling of *confessio* but so as to erect it into the principle of every one of the words he speaks: "Confessio certum gemina est, aut peccati, aut laudis. Quando nobis male est in tribulationibus confiteamur peccata nostra; quando nobis bene est, in exsultatione justitiae confiteamur laudem Deo; *sine confessione tamen non simus*" (And confession is twofold, either of sin or of praise. When things go poorly for us, in these tribulations we confess our sins; when they go well, in the exaltation of justice, we confess the praise of God. But *never are we without confessing*) (*Commentaries on the Psalms* 29, 19, *PL* 36, 225). *Confessio* unites the admission of sin (which I am) and the praise of glory (that God is) so well that it defines the permanent state of the Christian, confessing man, who thinks first by confessing. In other words, "Confessio quidem *duobus modis* accipitur in scripturis. Est confessio laudantis, est confessio gementis. Confessio laudantis ad honorem pertinet ejus qui laudatur; confessio gementis ad poenitentiam pertinet ejus qui confitetur. Confitentur enim homines cum laudant Deum; confitentur cum accusant se. Et nihil dignius fit lingua" (Confession is understood in two ways in the scriptures: the confession of those who praise, and the confession of those who groan. The confession of those who praise pertains to the honor of he who is praised; the confession of those who groan pertains to the penitence of those who are confessing. For men confess when they praise God, and they confess when they accuse themselves. And there is nothing more worthy that can be said) (*Commentaries on the Psalms* 94, 4, *PL* 37, 1218). Man before God cannot not confess—his only remaining question is to know in what way he will do it.[31] Moreover, the two senses, or, more exactly, the two actions of *confessio*, must be considered as a single linguistic act, the one becoming the condition of the other, like two faces of one and the same address: "Affectum ergo nostrum patefacimus in te confitendo tibi miserias nostras et misericordias tuas supra nos" (We lay bare to you our affect in confessing to you our wretchedness and your mercies [poured out] over us) (XI, 1, 1, 14, 270). I can praise God only if I discover myself already a beneficiary of his mercy, therefore only if I acknowledge myself first a sinner against him. Therefore, even before confessing my sin, in fact, it is my finitude I must confess, so as to praise God on that basis: "Confitetur altitudini tuae humilitas linguae meae, quoniam tu fecisti caelum et terram" (The humility of my tongue confesses your greatness, that it is you who made the heaven and the earth) (XII, 2, 1, 14, 344). In any case I can praise God as God only if I name him as such, but I can name him as such only if I also denominate myself as such. As a result, *confessio*, beyond its double and strict language game, describes my situation even before God: the issue is no longer what I say to him, but what I am before him—how I carry myself (*Haltung*) and find myself (*Befindlichkeit*) before him.[32]

There is, moreover, a wonderful passage that puts to work, with one stroke, the entire logic of the *confessio* (X, 2, 2, 14, 142). In the first place I see that *confessio* defines me, situates me, and that I dwell in it; like it or not, I cannot remove myself from it: "Et tibi quidem, Domine, cujus 'oculis nuda est' abyssus conscientiae, quid occultum esset in me, etiamsi nollem confiteri tibi? Te enim mihi absconderem, non me tibi" (And as for you, "in whose eyes all is laid bare" [Hebrews 4:13], what would be hidden in me, even if I did not want to confess it to you? For I would be hiding you from myself, but I would not hide myself from you). I can elude confession, in the sense of hiding myself from myself and even hiding God from my eyes, but I will never be able to elude God. For he is so much "interior intimo meo" (more within me than the most intimate within me) (III, 6, 11, 13, 382), that he is always with me, even when I am not with him—"Mecum eras et tecum non eras" (X, 27, 38, 14, 208). It certainly depends on me not to see God, but surely not not to be seen by him. Even the refusal to confess constrains me to a confession despite myself, and if I have the choice to orient my confession, I do not have the option of dispensing with it: "sine confessione non simus" (*Commentaries on the Psalms* 29, 19, *PL* 36, 225). For I do not say my confession; I am my confession. I say it only because I am it, and I am truly only what I confess: "Tibi ergo, Domine, manifestus sum, quicumque sim. Et quo fructu tibi confitear, dixi" (For you, Lord, everything in me is manifest, whatever I might be. The fruit of my confession, I said it unto you) (X, 2, 2, 14, 142). Second, what remains therefore is only to decide in what way I am going to confess, or rather how I am going to advance in confession ("Procede in confessione, fides mea . . ." [XIII, 12, 13, 14, 444]). In fact, I confess according to what I am, when I take upon myself the point of view that God has of me: "Cum enim male sum, nihil est aliud confiteri tibi, quam displicere mihi; cum vero pius, nihil est aliud confiteri tibi, quam hoc non tribuere mihi. . . . Confessio itaque mea, Deus meus, in conspectu tuo tibi tacite fit et non tacite" (When I am wicked, confessing to you is nothing other than being displeased with myself, but when [I am] good, confessing to you is nothing other than not attributing it to myself. . . . Consequently my confession, my God, happens "beneath your eyes" [Psalm 95:6], silently before you and yet not in silence) (X, 2, 2, 14, 142). Confession always amounts to turning around toward God, indirectly first by directing upon oneself the very gaze of God, then directly by directing upon God himself my finally free gaze. "Initium operum bonorum confessio est operum malorum. Facis veritatem et venis ad lucem" (The beginning of good works is the confession of wicked works. Do the truth and you

come to the light) (*Commentary on the Gospel of John* XII, 13, *PL* 35, 1491).[33]
Third, *confessio* becomes the unique voice of the spirit, which no longer
even needs to speak to perform it. It can fall silent in sounds, provided it
cries out in affect ("Tacet enim strepitu, clamat affectu" [X, 2, 2, 14, 142],
since it coincides exactly with it. *Confessio* flows and passes like the breath
of the spirit, the air man breathes: "Respiro in te paululum, cum 'effundo
super me animam meam in voce exultationis et confessionis'" (I breathe
a little in you when "I pour out my soul over myself in a cry of joy and
confession" [Psalm 41:5]) (XIII, 14, 15, 14, 450).

   Confessio is therefore not reducible to a language game or just one
speech act among others; it defines, in the end, the activity of every word,
when it is a question of saying myself as such, that is to say before God. For
I cannot accomplish the one without the other, and it is *confessio* precisely
that ties both the one to the other—the admission and the praise—as two
sides of one diction and a single text. In fact, *confessio* does not so much
come up in the *Confessiones* as the *Confessiones* themselves find a position
and a place in *confessio*.

§5. Coherence by *confessio*

   This result permits us to broach the question of the coherence of the
text of the *Confessiones* with some chance of at least posing it correctly.
This coherence is certainly not self-evident since it has so often been cast
in doubt—and in at least two ways. In the first of these the coherence
of each book is contested, in a selective reading that reduces them to an
anthology of choice morsels, either literary (the tales of his youth, often
called autobiographical) or philosophical (the will, memory, time) or even
theological (grace, scriptural exegesis, creation, etc.). This reading no longer pays any attention to the real composition of each book but finds
in them pretexts for a disciplinary investigation or the confirmation of a
polemical, most often anachronistic, thesis.[34] In the second way the coherence of the whole of the thirteen books is contested, by supposing them to
be poorly composed. Most often, the first nine are made into one group
opposed to the last three, with book X, the most theoretical, sometimes
held apart.[35] Now both these objections are born from the same misunderstanding about *confessio*: first, a misunderstanding of the way that it, and

it alone, structures each of the books by opening and closing them; next, a misunderstanding of the way that it stitches together the two sections of the whole (I–IX and X–XIII) by repeating the first *confessio*, still individual, in a second *confessio* that is collective and, in fact, ecclesial. Thus can it be confirmed that if the *Confessiones* not only proffer a confession but are accomplished *as* a *confessio*, they remain unintelligible so long as this viewpoint is missing or so long as one tries to impose another on them, according to the fashion of the times.

Concerning the coherence of the architecture of each book, one primary, absolutely obvious, fact should make it evident from the outset: almost all the books of the *Confessiones* open with a *confessio*. Just begin with the first words of the first among them: "'Magnus es, Domine, et laudabilis valde'; 'magna virtus tua et sapientiae tuae non est numerus.' Et laudare te vult homo, aliqua portio creaturae tuae" ("Great art thou, Lord, eminently worthy of praise" [Psalm 47:2]; "Great is your strength and your wisdom without number" [Psalm 146:5]. And to praise you is what man wants, one part of your creation) (I, 1, 13, 272). The same goes for the opening of IV, 1, 1: "Inrideant me arrogantes et nondum salubriter prostrati et elisi a te, Deus meus, ego tamen confitear tibi dedecora mea 'in lauda tua'" (Let the arrogant mock me, those whom you have not yet, my God, knocked down and crushed in order to save them, but let me confess to you my shameful doings "to your praise!" [Psalm 68:6]) (13, 406–8). Then in V, 1, 1: "'Accipe sacrificium' confessionum mearum de 'manu linguae meae' quam formasti et excitasti, ut 'confiteatur nomini tuo.' . . . Sed te laudet anima mea ut amet te et confiteatur tibi miserationes tuas ut laudet te" ("Receive the sacrifice" [Psalm 50:21] of my confessions by the "hand of my tongue" [Proverbs 18:21] that you made for me and stirred "to confess your name" [Psalm 53:8]. . . . But let my soul praise you so that it might love you and confess to you your mercies so that it might praise you) (13, 462). And, in the same terms, VIII, 1, 1: "Deus meus, recorder in gratiarum actione tibi et confitear misericordias tuas super me" (My God, let me remember with thanksgiving and confess your mercies poured out over me) (14, 8). Or again IX, 1, 1: "O Domine . . . 'sacrificabo hostiam laudis'" (O Lord . . . "I will sacrifice an offering of praise" [Psalm 115:17]) (14, 70). And again X, 1, 1: "volo eam [veritatem] facere in corde meo coram te in confessione" (I want to do the truth in my heart before you in a confession) (14, 140). Likewise, XI, 1, 1: "ut dicamus omnes 'magnus Dominus et laudabilis valde'" (so that we all may say, "You are great, Lord, and eminently worthy of our praise" [Psalm 47:2]) (14, 270, taking up again precisely the citation that was used in I, 1, 13, 272).[36] And also XII, 2, 2: "Confitetur altitudini tuae humilitas linguae meae" (The humility of my tongue confesses it to your greatness [Romans 14:11]) (14, 344). And finally, concluding the whole, XIII, 1: "Invoco te, 'Deus meus, misericordia mea'" (I invoke you, "my God, my mercy" [Psalm 58:18]) (14, 424). It must therefore be set down as a fact, still no doubt awaiting an explanation, that praise and confession open (nearly) each and every book, because they render it possible by giving it its theological place.[37]

This already weighty fact should be all the more decisive as *confessio* does not just open (almost) each book of the *Confessiones*, but also concludes (almost) all of them. Here is how book I ends: "Gratias tibi, dulcedo mea et honor meus et fiducia mea, Deus meus, gratias tibi de donis tuis" (I offer you thanks, O my sweetness, my honor, and my confidence, my God, I offer you thanks for your gifts) (I, 20, 31, 13, 330). Book III closes thus: "Confiteor tibi, Domine, recordationem meam, quantum recolo; . . . .propero ad ea quae me magis urguent confiteri tibi" (I confess to you, Lord, what I remember, insofar as it comes back to me. . . . I am hurrying on to what is more pressing that I confess to you) (III, 11, 20; and III, 12, 13, 400, 402). The same goes for IV, 16, 31: "Sed sic eram nec erubesco, Deus meus, confiteri tibi in me misericordias tuas et invocare te" (But I was indeed that way, and I do not blush, my God, in confessing to you your mercies shown to me and in invoking you) (13, 458). In VII, 21, 27 as well: "Hoc illae litterae non habent. Non habent illae paginae vultum pietatis hujus, lacrimas confessionis, 'sacrificium tuum, spiritum contribulatum, cor contritum et humiliatum'" (These books [those of the Neoplatonists] do not have that. Their pages do not have the face of this piety, nor the tears of confession, nor "your sacrifice [which you love]," "a spirit beaten-down, with contrite and humble heart" [Psalm 52:19]) (13, 640). The same goes, exemplarily, for the end of the story of the conversion: "Gaudet . . . exultat et triumphat et benedicat tibi qui 'potens es ultra quam petimus et intelligimus facere'" (She [Monica] rejoices, exults and triumphs and blesses you, you who "are powerful beyond our asking and our comprehension" [Ephesians 3:20]) (VIII, 12, 30, 14, 68). And in the closing of IX, 13, 37 Augustine asks that the memory of Monica be kept "in multorum orationibus per confessiones quam per orationes meas" (by the confessions [made] in the prayer of many, rather than by my own prayers) (14, 138). Let us note that even the more theoretical books do not make an exception to this use. Book X, 43, 70 also ends with a praise: "'et laudabunt Dominum qui requirunt eum'" ("and they will praise God, those who seek him" [Psalm 21:37]) (14, 268).[38] The aporia of time itself will lead to a praise, moreover a redoubled one: "Qui intelligit, confiteatur tibi, et qui non intelligit, confiteatur tibi" (He who understands, let him confess you; and he who does not understand, let him [too] confess you) (XI, 31, 41, 14, 342). In book XII, 32, 43 submission to the Spirit in the reading of scriptures stems from the *fides confessionis meae* (14, 422). Finally, and above all, the long prayer that completes book XIII and closes all the *Confessiones* (XIII, 38, 53, 14, 524)[39] opens with a praise universalized or, more exactly, extended to the entire universe: "Laudant te opera tua, ut amemus te, et amamus te, ut laudent te opera tua" (Your works praise you so that we might love you, and we love you so that your works might praise you) (XIII, 33, 48, 14, 516).[40] Thus *confessio* does not operate simply as the condition of possibility and theoretical site for the *Confessiones* but also becomes their sole end and singular accomplishment. The *Confessiones* in their entirety come from *confessio* and lead to it.

We should therefore conclude that each book is coherent, opened by and concluded with a double *confessio*. The *Confessiones* say infinitely more than the fragments the philosophers, theologians, or historians (whether they be historians of dogma, theology, or spirituality) most often pull out of them; or in each and every case the sections that they claim as their own ("useful" to them, "usable" by them) are inscribed, more essentially, within the arc that leads from one confession to another, an arc for which they count less as keystone than as what the *confessio* supports with a double prayer. Considering the confessions that frame each book of the *Confessiones* as a literary ornament or a pious convention already makes for a massive misreading, but there is one more grave: imagining that the theoretical statements scattered throughout the *Confessiones* are not found amidst prayer, indeed, that they dispense with it. Of course, one can always not want to see. But then one should not be surprised to no longer comprehend. Whence a sure interpretive criterion: a reading of the

Confessiones that does not take into account their constitution by *confessio* is worth nothing.

§6. Unity by *confessio*

It now falls to us to consider the coherence of the whole of the thirteen books and the difficulty, or at least the apparent difficulty, raised by the supposedly poor composition. As we saw, the question arises from the fact that one might believe it possible to divide the *Confessiones* into two or three parts, according as one separates them into an autobiographical sequence (from birth in sin to conversion: books I–IX), a philosophical analysis of subjectivity (book X), and, finally, a theological exegesis of the first verses of Genesis (incomplete and approximate: books XI–XIII). Of course, this division *can* be conceived and, in fact, was. But the question lies elsewhere: *should one* proceed to such a cutting up of the work? Isn't it possible that Saint Augustine himself saw the difficulty of unifying the *Confessiones*? Couldn't it be that he himself at least attempted a response? Wouldn't it be appropriate, before arguing for or against the unity of the *Confessiones*,[41] to see if Saint Augustine himself did not respond or at least did not attempt a response to the question of their unity? Now there is at least one text, perfectly authorized since it comments on the work after the fact, in which Saint Augustine himself defines the intention and coherence of the *Confessiones*:

The thirteen books of my *Confessiones praise* God [as] just and good for my wicked and my good actions, and they bestir the intelligence and affect of man (*humanum intellectum et affectum*) to go toward him. In the meantime, in what concerns me myself, they produced this effect when I was writing them, and they still produce it when I [re]read them. Let others see for themselves what feelings these books inspire in them; at the very least I know that they have pleased and will continue to please many brothers many times over. From the first book to the tenth, they were written concerning me; in the final three, concerning the holy scriptures, beginning with "In the beginning, God made the heaven and the earth," and continuing on till the Sabbath rest.[42]

Now we have to understand how this text, far from weakening, actually confirms the unity of the *Confessiones*.[43] It calls for two remarks. First, indisputably, it admits a caesura between books X and XI, a caesura that opposes "me" (*de me*) and the scriptures as two themes of the same work. Next, it introduces another caesura, this time between "me" again (*me*) and the other, or rather a plural other (*alii, multi fratres*), as two types of readers. What meaning is to be granted to these two divisions? Don't they give their blessing to those who assert a lack of unity of the *Confessiones*?

Let us consider first the caesura between two themes in the two sets of books (I–X and XI–XIII). It should be observed that it does not stop the two books that begin each set (and them alone) from resting on the same citation: "'Magnus es, Domine, et laudabilis valde'" ("Great art thou, O Lord, and eminently worthy of praise") (Psalm 47:2).[44] What can be concluded from this? At the very least this: if there are two beginnings to the *Confessiones*, both begin with a *confessio*, in fact with the same exact one; therefore the second beginning *re*begins what the first had already begun, and the two sets of the *Confessiones* accomplish twice the same thing—confessing. And, for that matter, the commentary in the *Retractiones* also indicates that the praise ("Deum laudant"), even if it bears on me ("malis et bonis *meis*"), is developed throughout all thirteen books ("libri tredecim . . . laudant"). The question is now transformed: it is no longer a matter of opposing two sets, indeed two independent sections of the *Confessiones*, but of understanding how the second beginning (which sets off again from the scriptures) can resume the very one undertaken by the first beginning (which sets off from myself). Without getting ahead of ourselves, we can nevertheless have a foretaste of the task common to the two sets: Since books I through X run up against the strangeness of the ego to itself, such that it forbids it to access itself in and through the *cogitatio* ("Factus eram ipse mihi magna quaestio" [I had become a great question for myself]),[45] couldn't it be that books XI through XIII, which treat the creation of the world and end up at the paradox of the creation of man (sole creature not to be created "secundum genus, sed . . . 'ad imaginem et similitudinem nostram'" [according to his kind . . ., but "unto our image and likeness"]),[46] thereby respond to the first question? The enigma of man to himself (books I–X) would be repeated then, but positively in virtue of his likeness to nothing other than God himself, without intermediate definition, by immediate likeness to the incomprehensible itself (books XI–XIII). The same praise would apply then starting from the question without response, next starting from the response without definition. Praise suffers no more from a question without response than from a response without definition, since it does not try to know man or to speak of him (no more than it speaks *of* God), but to bring man to speak *to* God. Not to explain God to man or man by God, but that man *explains himself* with God. Now, this explication with God, the same praise, therefore one and the same *confessio* carries out as much in the *quaestio magna* without answer as in the *similitudo* without definition. Thus, the first caesura attests all the more the unity of the *Confessiones* in terms of *confessio*.

Let us now consider the second caesura, this time between myself and others, between *me* and *alii*. To be sure, it opposes "me," the author, to the others, my readers. But this opposition is at once relieved by a more profound similarity between us: I find myself, me too, playing the role of a reader, over whom also the reading of the *Confessiones* had and continues to have an effect, the same as the one it had and continues to have on its readers (at least some among them, if not all). In fact, *me* and the *alii* distinguish ourselves from each other only by playing the same role: that of readers affected by their reading. The fact that myself, and myself alone, played the role of author does not dismiss me, quite the contrary, from also taking on that of reader, like any one of the *alii*. Why can we share the role of reader, while, from a literary point of view, I keep the privilege of author? Evidently because this privilege and the caesura that it leads to disappear or are nullified before our community of readers. But how? In two ways: first, I remain the author only inasmuch as I precede the readers (myself included), but I do not, for all that, constitute the beginning of speech or writing, since here, as we have seen, I always speak second, inasmuch as I respond to the prior word of God, and write belatedly, inasmuch as I cite the scriptures. My infinite secondariness in relation to the spoken or written word of God subverts my tiny authority as an author in relation to my readers. The literary gap disappears, therefore, in the common distance of the created from the Creator. Next, and consequently, the same text, whose scribe I was, exercises the same function regarding me as regarding the *alii*: bestirring the same *affectus* of *confessio toward* God in me as in the others, that is to say my readers. But note that this does not mean evoking or convoking these readers in order to judge Augustine's confession, its veracity, sincerity, etc.; they can think of it (literarily or dogmatically) what they want; that matters little and remains their business (*ipsi viderint*). But, at bottom, the issue is knowing if the literary act of Augustine (his *confessio*) reaches them or not, such that they share, or not, the *intellectus* and the *affectus* of the *confessio* and can repeat it for themselves. Some of them can do so (*scio*), and that is enough.

One question remains: do we find in the text of the *Confessiones* confirmation that the *confessio* of its actor/author has been expanded to the collectivity of its readers? As such, the collectivity of men is not accorded any particular authority. But collecting the votes and the admiration of the public is not the point because it is not a question of literature. The point instead is to associate the *alii* with the *confessio* of the author, which begins only in book IX, after Augustine's conversion, more exactly after the ecstasy at Ostia, even more exactly after the death of Monica. Why at this moment? Because up until his conversion, Augustine could not claim to associate his readers with the confession of his own faults *committed by him*, while after this conversion and the ecstasy, he can offer it to his readers to associate with the positive graces *received by him* and having become public in the eyes of all. He asks it now of his readers, as if off the cuff to his friends: "Et nunc, Domine, confiteor tibi in litteris, legat qui volet et interpretetur, ut volet" (And now, Lord, I confess to you in writing; let he who wants, read and interpret as he will) (IX, 12, 33, 14, 132). With what are the readers associated? With the prayer on behalf of the first others (*alii*) of Augustine: his dead mother and even his father. The author is not trying to win approval but to sustain an *affectus* for the sake of God and his neighbor (the others than myself). But under what heading are they to be associated? Under the heading not only first of readers but of brothers in the liturgical community: "Et inspira, Domine meus, Deus meus, inspira servis tuis, fratribus meis, filiis tuis, dominis meis, quibus corde et voce et litteris servio, ut quotquot haec legerint, meminerint ad altare tuum Monnicae, famulae tuae, cum Patricio" (And inspire, my Lord, my God, inspire your servants, my brothers, your sons, my lords, that I serve in my heart, my voice, and my writings, so that each time they read these pages they are reminded of your altar Monica, your servant, and also of Patrice) (IX, 13, 37, 14, 136–38). The others, those who read, intervene neither in the role of censors nor as amateurs but as brothers in a community that crosses time and space because it is defined first of all as liturgical. Thus the literary act, too, takes on a radically liturgical standing since it aims to sustain for the readers (in the same way as for the author) the initial *confessio*: "Volo 'eam [sc. veritatem] facere' in corde meo coram te *in confessione, in stilo* autem *meo* coram multis testibus" (I want "to do the truth" (John 3:21) in my heart and before you in *confession*, but also with *my pen* before a multiplicity of witnesses) (X, 1, 1, 14, 140). Writing again amounts to confessing, this time across space and time, not oneself, but God: "etiam hominibus coram te confiteor per has litteras adhuc, quis ego sim, non quis fuerim" (I confess before men even with these writings, who I am and not who I was) (X, 3, 4, 14, 146). Starting with book X, the praise becomes definitively always plural because the *confessio* becomes communitarian, through the liturgy to be sure but also through the community of readers, as if the liturgy was extended to reading. Thus Saint Augustine carries out his confession for the sake of God also beneath our eyes, without any indiscrete complaisance, but so that we ourselves might end up carrying out the *confessio*. And, as the author does not ask of his reader literary approval, but, through this, an entrance into communion with he whom the author confesses, God, the reader discovers that he does *not* in the final analysis play the role of ultimate interlocutor, just as the author does not hold the role of originary author. The interlocutor attests himself in he whom the author and the reader confess, the invoked, God, who spoke first and to whom every word ends up returning.

Thus, the two successive parts of the *Confessiones*, far from weakening its unity, demonstrate it: what is going on is not merely a matter of collectively beginning again the *affectus* toward the at first individual *confessio*, nor merely of extending the *confessio* to the communal liturgy, but of pursuing it across the times through the community of readers united to the *confessio* of Saint Augustine—united by it and for it. We thereby arrive at a firm conclusion: the *confessio* does not give the *Confessiones* only their title but also their constitution and their logic.[47]

§7. The model and alterity

Confessio now plays its full role: it provokes (§§2–3), organizes (§4), and unifies (§§5–6) the *Confessiones* through and through. But since this unity of the collection of books implies, starting with book X, a collective repetition (by the readers, therefore by us) of the at first individual *confessio* (that of Augustine) launched in book I, it necessarily follows that the *Confessiones* mobilize not two interlocutors (ego and God) but three (ego, *alii*, and God) or, rather, since one among them proves to be collective (*alii*), three functions of interlocution. Thus is put in place a system, a complex one for that matter, of relations that are now to be described. The relations of one term to another prove each time double and reciprocal.

The first relation remains strictly internal to the ego, which is defined at once by the ascending relation toward God according to the *confessio laudis* and by the descending relation of the *confessio peccati*, the first requiring the second as its condition of possibility, the second pardoning the first (§4). The second relation, this time intersubjective, relates man and man: the ego relates itself to the *alii* as to witnesses of its double *confessio*, which now is repeated: "in stilo autem meo coram multis testibus" (also in writing before many witnesses) (X, 1, 1, 14, 140). The author remains fundamentally one who confesses but this time confessing through means other than the living word, in writing. It follows that he also maintains a double relation with his readers. First of all, a centrifugal relation, which sets before them inseparably his *confessio peccati* (his youthful transgressions, his falling prey to the Manichean ideology, his resistance to the call, etc.) and his *confessio laudis* (for the mercies and *mirabilia* shown to him). But this relation aims at a goal that, this time, passes beyond, and by far, the *ego* alone: one does not justify oneself before the public by pleading one's case and winning the sympathy of readers but by naked exposure of sins and especially of the pardon that annuls them, awakening in the readers too an intelligence and love (*humanus intellectus et affectus*) directed to God. Literary success (pleasing, *placere et placuisse*) keeps its importance, be it only so as to retain the attention of the *alii*, but its necessity is always subordinate to its function as means—means to lead the *alii* toward the same double confession that Augustine addresses to God. Whence a second relation, this time centripetal: the readers can (and must) offer an appreciation of the text of the *Confessiones* such as they read it; but in the final analysis this appreciation does not consist in forming a literary opinion of the text or a spiritual judgment about its author; they can of course conceive these, but that is not important ("quid sentiant, ipsi viderint"), neither to Augustine the individual *nor to themselves*. The only thing that is important is their decision about the *confessio* carried out by the author, or rather their own decision, before the *confessio* of the author, to operate *or not*, for their own account and in the solitude of their face-to-face with God, a similar *confessio*. The readers do not have to respond to the author about their literary enjoyment, nor about their psychological sympathy, but to God about their own confessing *affectus*, occasioned by the *Confessiones*. The *Confessiones* thus appear in their basic function: a machine to make a confession made by each of its readers by inciting in them the human *intellectus* and *affectus* for God. As between the author and God, so too between the author and his readers a question and response is set up—with one essential difference, however: if the question (centrifugal) indeed comes from the author who confesses toward his readers, the response (centripetal) no longer refers them to the author but leads each of them back directly to God: the response asked for by the author does not ask of the reader that he or she respond to the author (for example, to pity him, to approve him, to acquit him, to admire him, etc.) but to respond directly to what God asks; it asks for the accomplishment of a double *confessio*. A third relation necessarily flows from the second. It establishes (or attempts to establish) between God and the *alii* (the readers) a relation analogous to the first relation, between the ego and God, but this time a direct relation, which no longer passes through the ego and which is set forth in perfect independence from that of the ego toward God (as with that of the *alii* toward the ego). This last relation, too, is double: a *confessio laudis* of others ascending toward God, preceded by a *confessio peccati* descending before God. But, in contrast with the two previous ones, the third relation is inaccessible to the *Confessiones*: always written from the point of view of the author ego, they can neither describe it nor say it in the place of the *alii*. That is, the last relation remains, first of all, inaccessible to the ego, who does not enter into it and does not have to enter into it, not because of some solipsism but because the relation of others to God concerns only the other and God and would no longer be *their own*, if I could get mixed up in it, however little.

With this triple (double) relation between the ego, the *alii*, and God, the model of *confessio* is at last laid out completely in its function and all its dimensions, letting appear the so very particular logic of the *Confessiones*. Three remarks still need to be made, each of which concerns one

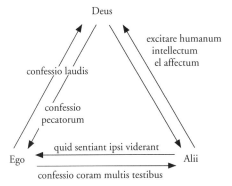

of the three relations and which set definitively the status of the entire undertaking.

I have established that the first relation, that of the ego to God, defines the *Confessiones* so radically that not only does the ego not speak *about* God but it doesn't say anything, not even about itself, except in speaking first and radically *to* God—more exactly in responding to him by repetition of the initial word that God dispensed to the ego in advance. In this way *confessio* (of praise as well as repentance) is not the specification of a word that man would first possess and could then, when the case arose, use in a dialogical mode so that, if he wanted to, he could use it, among other uses, to "dialogue with God."[48] It constitutes rather the original form of every possible word, which right away is carried out as *responsal to*, first, God so that it could be, next, extended as a word *to* an other other besides God, then distended as a word *about* something. It follows that Saint Augustine's entire project aims at retrieving, behind the appearance of the word *about*, the reality of the word *to* (as response *to*, therefore *to* God)—in short, it aims at going back from λόγος to *confessio*. Hence, it goes without saying that the ego could not, particularly not in the *Confessiones*, have as its intention to say something *about* itself or *for* itself to anybody whatsoever, since it aims only at saying itself *to* God by responding to him. And, saying itself thus *to* God, it can hope to respond *for* itself by responding *to him*—in short, end up seeing itself from the point of view God has on him and no longer from his own proper viewpoint. It must therefore be concluded that, contrary to the dominant take on them,[49] the *Confessiones* should not, above all, be read as an *auto*biography.[50]

That is, if they narrate and revisit the lifestory of the ego ("de malis et bonis *meis*"), they do so with God as their viewpoint ("Deum laudant") and precisely not the narrator. In fact, the real issue is to abandon this point of view—in which the sinner is ignorant of himself as such and therefore does not know God, and which in fact constitutes sin itself, in order to see oneself as God alone sees us: as *lovable*, however deformed we might have let ourselves become. Of course, the narrator tells his story, but he does not describe himself as joyful and lighthearted. He tells his story only in order to end up observing and admitting not only that he is displeased and disappointed with himself but that he does not even know himself, absolutely does not comprehend himself. He does not comprehend himself in his past (books I–IX): "factus eram mihi magna quaestio" (I became a great question to myself) (IV, 4, 9, 13, 422); nor in his present (book X): "mihi quaestio factus sum" (I have become a question for myself) (X, 33, 50, 14, 232); nor even in his future (books XI–XIII), since those who see the good see in the Holy Spirit and not by themselves: "non ipsi, sed Deus videt, quia bonum est" (it is not they, but God who sees that it is good) (XIII, 31, 46, 14, 512). As soon as the *Confessiones* as a whole do nothing else but operate and manifest this decentering of the ego in God, what greater misreading could there be than to suppose a narrator who would claim to know the essence and the identity of the character narrated, while the *confessio* consists precisely in admitting the contrary? Far from pretending to be a subject supposed to know, the ego supposes that God alone knows him, himself, this ego. And the confessing ego does not even ask to know for himself what God knows about him but simply to say himself *to* God, he and his readers: "*cui* narro haec? Neque enim tibi, Deus meus, sed *apud te* narro haec generi meo, generi humano. . . . Et ut quid hoc? Ut videlicet ego et quisquis haec legit cogitemus, 'de quam profundo clamandum' sit ad te" (*to whom* am I telling this? For it is not to you, my God, but it is *in your sight* that I am telling these things to those of my kind, the human race. . . . And why is that? Assuredly so that myself and whoever will have read them will direct our thoughts "from the bottom of the depths out of which we cry" [Psalm 129:1] toward you) (II, 3, 5, 13, 338). No more than it is a matter of saying something *about* God is it a matter of saying something *about* oneself. It is only a matter of saying oneself *to* God, or rather (for he already knows me better than I do, without my needing to teach him anything whatsoever, I who in fact know nothing about it) of saying *in God's sight* my ignorance of myself. In short, it is not an *auto-* but a *hetero-biography*, my life told by me and especially to me from the point of view of an other, from close to the privileged other, God.[51] Saint Augustine tries to say himself and to see himself no longer from his own *side* but *from beside God*. Such a decentering can be carried out only by abandoning one world and winning an other world (the great world, the true world, that beside God)—winning, always partially and therefore ever to be resumed, from the point of view of this other; abandoning, always partially and therefore ever to be resumed, too, my ownmost—precisely thanks to a word making *confessio* of sins (which appear only from the point of view of an other) and *confessio* of praise (which presupposes the prior exteriority of an other). Since this double *confessio* thus gives, and it alone, access to the ἕτερον, the other, or rather to the ἕτερος, the personal other, we should no longer speak of autobiography but, strictly speaking, of heterobiography. Or still more precisely, since this access to the ἕτερος opens only to the *confessio laudis*, to the glorifying praise, *doxology*, we should speak of a *heterodoxology*, indeed of a *heterodoxy*—a praise confessed by the gifted, who is decentered toward God by being ex-centered from himself, a praise that comes to me from elsewhere (from a word given to me in advance) and that leads me back there(by the repetition carried out by my responsal). Thus, I find myself cited *to* God by citing the word of God.

The second relation, that of the ego to the *alii* (the others as the readers), is no more self-evident than the first and calls for another remark. It, too, is appropriately understood according to the requirements of the *confessio*, such as it governs the *Confessiones*. Now, about this text, one can ask, as with every other, what it is doing, that is to say, what it says and means. To be sure, it describes first of all things of the world, the events of Augustine's life, other characters (Patrice, Alypius, Monica, Ambrose, etc.), places (Thagaste, Carthage, Rome, Milan, Cassiciacum, etc.), and it discusses theories (in particular, Manicheanism, skepticism, the *libri platonici*, etc.). All these cases are examples of locutionary acts, formulating propositions endowed with meaning, using significations and predicating something about something. On this level of language are posed only difficulties that erudition and a sound hermeneutic suffice to resolve. But, more essentially, the *Confessiones* say what they do, or more exactly do what they say; for the real assertions (bearing on things) always depend on speech acts or performative utterances, which say nothing other than themselves but which, from the mere fact of saying it, accomplish it. When I (myself, the speaker) say, "I praise," I actually praise, in whatever manner, even poorly or roughly. To believe, all you have to do is say, "I believe"; to regret, say, "I regret"; to admit, say, "I admit"; and so forth. My words as illocutionary acts represent nothing and predicate nothing about nothing because what they say, they do. Also, as we have already seen, when a commentator sticks only with those sections that appear to be purely theoretical and excludes the passages of prayer, praise, repenting, and so forth, he or she misses the most important issue of *Confessiones*, which does not consist in saying what one thinks but in doing what one says. It follows that the truth of this perlocutionary word does not rest on the truth (at least in the sense of the adequation of the mind to the thing, *Wahrheit*) but on the will to say the truth (veracity or sincerity, *Wahrhaftigkeit*).[52] Reading the *Confessiones* consists neither in enjoying them nor in investigating them but in reading them as they were written—by *doing* what they say.

Nevertheless, beyond the linguistic description and performance, the *Confessiones* practice another language game. As we have seen, Augustine insists on the fact that they aim first to develop not only an *intellectus* but also an *affectus* oriented toward God. First, they develop the *affectus* of the author himself (following his own conversion) when he was writing them, then each time that he rereads them ("hoc in me egerunt, cum scriberentur, et agunt, cum leguntur"); finally they do this in the other readers: "affectum meum excito in te et eorum, qui haec legunt . . . affectum ergo nostrum patefacimus in te confitendo tibi miserias nostras et misericordias tuas" (I excite my affect toward you as well as that of my readers . . . for we manifest to you our affect toward you by confessing to you our miseries and your mercies) (XI, 1, 1, 14, 270).[53] Everything happens as if the *Confessiones*, far from being the result of a literary act (what one calls, with so ill-suited a term, a "creation"), wanted only to push and orient toward God their readers *and even their author*, as if he were dispossessed of all the authority he might have as their producer, so as humbly to become one among all those who have to make their *confessio*. Written neither to describe nor to demonstrate nor to instruct, but to provoke confession, the *Confessiones* tend only to produce an effect, or rather an *affect*, upon the interlocutor, understood as each reader. This intention is defined exactly as a perlocutionary act, such that it "produces certain consequential effects upon the feelings, thoughts, [and therefore] actions of the audience, or of the speaker, or of other persons: and it may be done with the design, intention, or purpose of producing them."[54] For, as Saint Augustine highlights clearly, the *Confessiones* are not so much about what he can say (even about himself), for he is ignorant of himself: "minus mihi in hac re notus sum ipse quam tu" (in this matter, I am less known to myself than you are [by me]) (X, 37, 62, 14, 254). And especially, supposing him to know himself, he would obviously have nothing to teach God: "Cur ergo tibi tot rerum narrationes digero? Non utique ut per me noveris ea" (Why am I telling you all these things? It is obviously not so that you can learn them from me) (XI, 1, 1, 14, 270). In fact, he does not recount them so as to inform God but so as to associate the others (the readers) to his own praise and *confessio*: "And if something in me is pleasing to you, praise here with me he whom I wanted to be praised on my account." Augustine does not speak so as to say to the other something about something (about God, as if God entered into the ranks of *things*), nor even so as to say something *to* God (as if he did not know the information); rather he speaks *to* the other so as to make him speak *to* God (by associating him with my word of confession *to* God). It is no longer a question of speaking to do (illocutionary act) but of speaking (and writing) to make it be done (perlocutionary act)—namely, to make God praised by the readers and not by myself alone. "Take, I say, any book of the *Confessiones* that you want: here look at me, so as not to praise me for more than I am; here, in my case, do not rely on others but on me; here, be attentive, and see who I was in myself by myself. And if by chance something in me is pleasing to you, praise here with me he whom I wanted to be praised on my account but not myself."[55] Make God praised by the other, by others, across time—this intention confers on the writing and the rhetoric, too easily condemned or poorly celebrated, their real seriousness, that of a provocation to *confessio*. The *Confessiones* most certainly do not constitute a text *about* God but rather a text *to* God, on condition of also understanding it as a text *intending that* all its readers also praise and confess God. It is not a case of a pure and simple written but, as an *illocutionary written*, of a literary performance, accomplishing a theological act.

Now it becomes possible to consider the third and final relation at stake in the model: that of the *alii* to God. This relation remains in principle and in two ways inaccessible to the ego, who does not have access to the one any more than to the other. For the other remains an other to me only inasmuch as I do not have access to his soul (put otherwise, to the flux of his consciousness), which remains his own only on this condition. As for God, by definition no one has ever seen or known him. But these two alterities, each inaccessible in itself, do not keep separate but, in a certain way still to be specified, stage each other reciprocally. How does the other appear to me, seeing as in fact he does indeed appear to me, be it only to make me sense that I do not know him as such? These two questions find the beginning of a response only if they tie together, each to the other, their respective aporiae. Most certainly, the other does not appear to me, not in that he does not appear to me at all—to the contrary, he appears to me as well as, indeed better than, any other object; but to be more precise, he does not appear to me as an object, possessed, utilized, fabricated, possibly destroyed, in this case available to be put to death. He will appear as a genuine other only if I apprehend him exactly as what I cannot use, possess, or kill. How does this manifestation occur? If and only if I do not see *the other* as a façade that I could destroy, but as a face, that silently says to me "Thou shalt not kill." Whence comes this injunction? Not from the poor face that I have perhaps already reduced to silence, or that does not know what it should say, but from my unconditioned responsibility toward him (to the point that it is still pressing even if I transgress it). It comes to me from the third, from the witness in relation to whom my gaze at the other sees itself gazed at and thus submitted to the injunction. The other appears to me, therefore, as such (and not as object), when he appears to me not only or first of all at the end of my own intentionality (which always remains objective intentionality), but starting from another intentionality, that of the third. The other appears to me, if he appears to me, as an other besides me sees him; he does indeed appear to me but only from a point of view other than mine, therefore as a second order other—an other different from the other for me.

In the context of the *Confessiones* that means that every other (the *alii*) appears to me from the viewpoint of God and becomes accessible to me only in this detour through God. The constant proximity of his friends (Alypius, etc.) or his masters (Simplicius, Saint Ambrose, etc.) around Saint Augustine indicates all the more that nobody can do anything whatsoever for him: they can only follow his journey from afar, only encourage or reprimand him from a distance, but never directly help him, because they have no access to him—with one exception: his mother, Monica, who alone knows how to see her son from the point of view of God. The text insists on this, almost overbearingly. For example, during the sojourn in Carthage, Monica hears, in a dream, an angel say to her that her son will return to her: "Ubi esset illa, ibi esse et me" (There where she was, there too I [Augustine] am). And Monica tells it to her son, who prosaically understood the opposite (that his mother would end up retrieving him, which was anyway abundantly so): "Non enim mihi dictum est: 'Ubi ille, ibi et tu,' sed 'Ubi tu, ibi et ille'" (What was told to me was not: "There where he is, you too will be," but "There where you are, he too will be") (III, 11, 20, 13, 400). Now where is Monica found? Evidently, but solely from the point of view of God, in the place where her son is found with her, while from the point of view of Monica herself, he is not found there. That she must pass from her point of view to that of God so as to reach her son, she learns again from a response given to her worries: "dedisti alterum responsum" (you [God] gave her another answer) (III, 12, 21, 13, 402) through the intermediary of a second order third (a bishop): "Sed, inquit, sine illum ibi. Tantum roga pro eo Dominum: ipse legendo reperiet quis ille sit error et quanta impietas" (But, he says, leave him there where he is. Only pray to the Lord: he will find by reading what is his error and his great impiety) (ibid.). This access to her son given by the third will be accomplished during the final conversion of Saint Augustine, where "exultat et triumphat et benedicebat *tibi* . . . quia tanto amplius *sibi a te* concessum *de me* videbat, quam petere solebat" (she [Monica] exults and triumphs and blessed *you* . . . because she saw granted *to her by you* much more *about me* than she was accustomed to ask) (VIII, 12, 30, 14, 68). No ambiguity: the ego (here, Monica) can of itself go toward the other (here, Augustine), but the third (here, God) offers to it access to the other—the third gives to me a grant concerning the other; it grants to me my only access to the other. The meaning of the adieu paid to Monica (at the end of book IX) now becomes perfectly clear: this time it falls to others among the faithful, contemporaries of Saint Augustine or future readers, to have access to Monica in turn through the prayer said to the third, God, "ut quod *a me illa* poposcit extremum uberius *ei* praestetur in multorum orationibus per confessiones quam per orationes meas" (in such a way that what *she* asked ultimately *from me* might be granted *to her* all the more abundantly by the prayers of the many through these *Confessiones* than by my own) (IX, 13, 37, 13, 138). The other becomes visible, even for me, in the light projected upon him or her by the gaze of God and not my own.[56]

Saint Augustine thus anticipates the phenomenological doctrine, now widely admitted, of the third but immediately inverts it. First, here the role of the third falls to God and no longer to a worldly instance.[57] Next, this third, God, who would seem infinitely more distant from the ego than any *alter ego*, should, to assure its mediation, advance more than any other other. And, in fact, God does become closer to me than the other to whom he alone nevertheless gives me access: "Magis enim novit dilectionem qua diligit, quam fratrem quem diligit. Ecce jam potest notiorem Deum habere quam fratrem" (He knows the love by which he loves better than the brother whom he loves. And so God can be more known than the brother himself) (*De Trinitate* VIII, 8, 12, 16, 62). The entire undertaking of the *Confessiones* tends to establish precisely God as the closest, more interior to me than my own interiority, and consequently more interior to the other than himself. Whence the paradox that our strangeness to each other yields to the double intimacy of God to each of us. Between the other and ego there is God, but between ego and God no other assures the mediation, since no mediation is required.

The *confessio* therefore secures the three relations and modifies them essentially. It thus becomes a complete literary model.

§8. The variations of the model

Having reconstituted the complex model of *confessio* as it is practiced by the *Confessiones*, and as it organizes them, it becomes possible to confirm its rigor, by comparing it with the variations that it undergoes (and permits) in subsequent authors.

This comparison first calls for a remark. The *confessio*, as Saint Augustine practices it in the *Confessiones*, demands of its readers that they not yield to curiosity. With the term *curiositas* a vice is surely understood—the pleasure taken in knowledge sought for itself, whatever its object or pretext might be, even without use or finality. But this vice, beyond its strict moral sense, threatens the functioning of the literary model and compromises its theological intention. According to *curiositas*, I know only so as to enjoy an object, or, more exactly, I consume objects to know only in order to enjoy, therefore to enjoy myself and thus remain what I was, my own place and my own end to myself. And so, even when reading the vicissitudes of the life of an other (that of Saint Augustine), a curious reader will still enjoy only himself; therefore he will never be able to accomplish what is at stake in the *Confessiones*: to receive, through the reading, the *affectus* of the author for God and, by association, to confess, him too, God. He will not be able to do so because he will not want to do so, for the "genus humanum profunde curiosum" (the profoundly curious human race) (XIII, 20, 28, 14, 474) wants to know everything precisely in order *not* to correct itself: "curiosum genus, ad cognoscendam vitam alienam, desidiosum ad corrigendam suam" (a race curious to know the life of others, lazy about correcting its own) (X, 3, 3, 14, 144). Either my curiosity is a detour toward the life (therefore the faults) of others solely to permit me not to see my own; or else it buries me so deep in my own that it forbids me from seeing them from another point of view besides my own, condemns me to not seeing them as God sees them, to not seeing them in God, therefore to not seeing God through them. In short, immersed in *curiositas*, the reader reads the *Confessiones* without recognizing the model: he annuls the *confessio* by reading the *Confessiones*. And the majority of modern readers (even the most knowledgeable or the most devout) remain essentially curious. But they must be granted an excuse: the most notable retrievals of the Augustinian project, Montaigne and Rousseau, have deformed the model and, willingly or not it matters little, missed the point.[58]

Montaigne makes clear his intention ("To the Reader") by resuming the Augustinian terms exactly: he works according to the model mobilized by the ego ("myself that I portray"), the "reader," and God.[59] Yet the departures from the *Confessiones* stand out all the more. Not that the relation to God is missing, as is often rashly said, for the final essay, "Of Experience," closes (and with it the whole of the *Essais*) with a praising reference toward

God: "She [my soul] measures the extent of her debt to God for being at rest in her conscience and free from other inner passions." This obligation responds to the grace come from God, which it confesses: "As for me, then, I love life and cultivate it just as God has been pleased to grant it to us." The praising confession is carried out unambiguously in the acknowledgment of God, who imposes on us, as a "commission," that we manage all that was given to us in living scrupulously: "There is no part unworthy of our care in this gift that God has given us . . . and the creator has given it [the charge to humanity to guide one another according to God's condition] to us seriously and sternly."[60] The departure comes rather from the absence—better, from the refusal of the confession of faults, which "Of repentance" holds up as a positive thesis: "I do not teach; I tell," without correcting or regretting anything, because "if I had to live over again, I would live as I have lived. I have neither tears for the past nor fears for the future."[61] It follows that the ego neither can nor should recount its life with the intention of rehabilitating it (it assumes and appropriates it as absolutely its own), therefore without having any intention of provoking in its reader even the tiniest *affectus* of a *confessio peccati*, something it not only does not want to feel or make felt but disapproves of. Next, the ego's reconciliation with itself ("It is myself that I portray. My defects will here be read to the life, and also my natural form, as far as respect for the public has allowed") is not accomplished this time through divine intervention but in an immediate encounter of the ego with all the readers. Being in effect "myself the matter of my book,"[62] I become the place (interchangeable moreover in "each man") where "the entire form of the human condition" is manifest. Like all authors, Montaigne "communicates," but, at least this is what he pretends to do, he is communicating himself and the self of all, "my universal being."[63] As a result, even if the author (ego) can lead his readers (*alii*) to praising confession, he cannot, for all that, make them begin with a *confessio peccatorum* that he himself denies. The one and the others regard each other mutually, in a mimetic nonrivalry but also noninvolvement with any third: the praising confession remains but without provoking conversion nor even demanding it. The *confessio* disappears halfway, since the gap between the ego and the other, in being abolished, nullifies what is at stake in our respective separations from God. A universal Adam, after the Fall but without repenting, praises a God whom it does not have to make up its mind to resemble. The *confessio* remains between us, without reuniting us to God.

Rousseau's explicit reference to Saint Augustine is so patent as to be provocative, be it only by the title chosen.[64] The distortion of the game played by the three protagonists of the *confessio* only seems more evident with the stunning opening of book I. At least one of the three terms remains unambiguously, or rather imposes itself: to wit, the ego: "I am forming an undertaking which has no precedent, and the execution of which will have no imitator whatsoever. I wish to show my fellows a man in all the truth of nature; and this man will be myself." *I* constitute at once the subject and the object of the project. But the consequences of this imposition diverge at once from the use that Montaigne makes of them (and of course *toto caelo* from Saint Augustine). On one hand, far from the ego striving to fix in itself the "universal being" of "human nature," that is to say far from trying to neutralize itself in an everyman in which each could recognize himself and see himself for the first time; in short, far from the ego imposing on itself the ascesis of making itself the mirror of the humanity of the other man, in the case of each of its readers (*alii*), it claims against him a singular exceptionality: "I am not made like any of the ones I have seen; I dare to believe that I am not made like any that exist." Whence a strange claim on the part of the ego, one contradictory in several senses: I know myself perfectly; I want to absorb all human-ity into myself; I am different from all the others; and I alone remain innocent. The delirious expansion of the ego goes so far as to lay claim to innocence but this is a second order claim: of course, "I have shown myself as I was, contemptible and low . . .," but I said it "with . . . frankness"; "I have unveiled my interior as Thou hast seen it Thyself [Eternal Being]."[65] I am innocent, the innocent absolved, not because I have never done evil but because I admit every evil that I have ever done. I am bad, but, in confessing it, I acquit myself without reserve. In short, the hypertrophy of the *confessio peccatorum* merits acquittal and even ends up dismissing the immense innocence of the ego not only from all conversion but even from any *confessio laudis* whatsoever. Whom would he praise, if not himself, who is made innocent by himself?

There follows, on the other hand, a thoroughly empty conflict between the ego and the readers (the *alii*, all other men), who become guilty not so much of having committed faults (I too have committed them, and even the most enormous), as of not having admitted them as perfectly as I did. The *Confessions* have *here* as their sole objective to pass the burden of *confessio peccatorum* from the ego (relieved of admitting because he did so perfectly) to the readers (and the other *alii*)—in short, all the other men. They operate finally only to condemn the *alii* and make them praise the ego. The *affectus* remains, which they always try to provoke in the readers, but this time in opposition to them and to the benefit of the ego—they aim to make it such that nobody remains innocent, that no one else can any longer ever say, "*I was better than that man.*" The ego becomes the innocent par excellence, in short, puts on the figure of Christ. At the end of such a prodigious and monstrous reversal of the terms of the Augustinian *confessio*, what role remains for God? None other than that of the "sovereign judge" who summons the tribunal ("assemble around me the countless host of my fellows"),[66] listens ("let a single one say to Thee, if he dares"), and sees ("I have unveiled my interior as Thou hast seen it Thyself"),[67] so as to finally acquit the ego. Or, more exactly, the role that remains for God is to condemn Rousseau's readers (the *alii*) to confess their faults in a *confessio peccatorum* with regard to Rousseau, so as to end up at a *confessio laudis* to the great glory of Jean-Jacques. God is effaced or, at least, lowered to the function of a guard, a clerk, a procurator (unless the ego itself plays this role), and above all an executioner. In fact, God disappears completely and the *Confessions* can be summed up as a dialogue to the death between the ego and the readers, in which what is at stake consists in *not confessing*, neither one's sins nor God. Victory, of course, will fall to the one who *took* the opportunity to *have* a word of his own. But, in the *confessio* it is, as far as having a word goes, only a matter of receiving and rendering it.[68]

These two variations of the model of the *confessio* will suffice here to validate *a contrario* its functioning in the *Confessiones* of Saint Augustine. *Confessio* does not work without the distance between the ego and the *alii* and without the *confessio peccatorum* (Montaigne). It also does not work without the distance of the ego to God and without the *confessio laudis* (Rousseau); it is in such a case devalued into a death sentence for the innocence of others or of the singular. Inversely, *confessio* opens a space where the ego and its readers enter not only into a dialogue between themselves but especially into a place, where the charity of God can reach them. The model of the *confessio*, in fact, brings about a reduction of the natural attitude, which permits coming to the question of God, namely love. It therefore operates as an erotic reduction.

2

The Ego or the Gifted

§9. The appearance of a *cogito*

Confessio does not consist only or first in an act (even of language or even a performative) but in a disposition (indeed, being put at the disposition) on the part of the one confessing to the confessed. In *confessio* the ego finds its condition and therefore also its place: it becomes itself precisely in the measure to which it responds to a call always already issued, but never entirely received, with praise (of the holiness of God) and, inseparable from it, an admission (of faults which conspire against the holiness of God). Must we conclude from this or expect that I myself, now in the situation of double *confessio*, can succeed in taking possession of my own place and accede to myself? The question cannot be avoided, ever since the *Soliloquia* placed the ego with regard to God, as all that wisdom desires to know: "Deum et animam scire cupio / Nihil ne plus? / Nihil omnino" (I desire to know [what are] the soul and God. / Nothing else? / Absolutely nothing else). The difficulty consists less in the knowledge of the two terms of desire ("nunc autem nihil aliud amo quam Deum et animam quorum neutrum scio" (but in fact I love only God and the soul, about both of which I know nothing))[1] than in the comprehension of their relation. Here access to God is but one with the soul's access to itself because, more radically, my access to myself passes, in the disposition of *confessio*, through the access to God, who precedes me. So how could I know myself if that implies first knowing God? Saint Augustine offers no assurance that I can but, in fact, doubts it very much. He does not ask of God the knowledge that he has of myself (that remains incommunicable to me on principle) but precisely my knowledge by myself (however still impracticable by my own means). And he asks it in a prayer, from which will arise all the conceptual research to come: "Potestas nostra, ipse est. / Itaque ora brevissime ac perfectissime, quantum potes. / Deus semper idem, noverim me, noverim te. Oratum est" (Our power, it is [God] himself. / Pray then as briefly and perfectly as you can: / God, who always remains identical, make it such that I know myself, make it such that I know you. Hark, my prayer is offered).[2] But a wish and a prayer are not enough, or not yet, to assure a knowledge of self by self, still less a knowledge that would be certain. To reach that, a strict conceptual argument is needed, one that would permit reaching the self itself on the basis of the self. That is to say, an argument comparable to that which, since Descartes, is understood by the name of the *cogito*: "I am thinking, therefore I am." Namely, a "truth, so solid and secure,"[3] in that it would open an access of the self to itself in and through thought. The exercise of thought would suffice for me to enter into the place where my self is found.

This doctrinal comparison with Saint Augustine seems all the more inevitable since, in Descartes's lifetime, it already seemed obvious to many. As early as 1637, according to Descartes's own testimony, his friend and correspondent Mersenne had on his own compared the thesis of the *Discourse on the Method* with a text from Saint Augustine's *The City of God*: "Nulla . . . Academicorum argumenta formido dicentium: 'Quid si falleris?' Si enim fallor, sum. Nam qui non est, utique nec falli potest; ac per hoc sum, si fallor" (There is nothing to fear from the arguments of the Academicians who ask: "And if you are deceived?" For if I am deceived, I am. That is, he who is not cannot in any way be deceived; and, in that way, I am if I am deceived).[4] Above all, in 1641, at the time of the publication of the *Meditationes*, Arnauld, whose Augustinian erudition can hardly be contested, immediately confirmed the parallel, basing it, this time, on a passage in *De libero arbitrio*: "Quare prius abs te quaero, ut de manifestissimis capiamus exordium: utrum tu ipse sis. An fortasse metuis, ne in hac interrogatione fallaris, cum utique si non esses, falli omnino non posses?" (Also I would ask you first to begin with the most manifest things: yourself, are you? Lest you perhaps fear to be deceived on this question, whereas, if you were not, you absolutely could not be deceived?)[5] The authority for such a comparison seems so strong to Arnauld that, having become in the meantime a convinced Cartesian, he does not miss the occasion to confirm it in 1648, during his second correspondence with Descartes, this time by citing *De Trinitate*:

Mentem nosse se etiam cum quaerit se, sicut jam ostendimus. . . . Cum se mens se novit, substantiam suam novit; et cum de se certa est, de substantia sua certa est. . . . Nec omnino certa est, utrum aer, an ignis sit, an aliquod corpus, vel aliquid coporis. Non est igitur aliquid eorum: totumque illud quod se jubetur ut noverit, ad hoc pertinet ut certa sit non se esse aliquid eorum de quibus incerta est, idque solum esse se certa sit, quod solum esse se certa est.

The mind knows itself even when it seeks itself, as we have shown. . . . When the mind knows itself, it knows its substance; and when it is certain of itself, it is certain of its substance. . . . It is not absolutely certain if it is made of air, of fire, some body, or something of the corporeal. It is therefore nothing of all that, and all that it is necessary for it to know can be summed up in this: that it be certain of not being any of the things about which it is not certain, and that it be certain of being only that which it is certain to be.[6]

To these parallels others could be added. In particular, the short version of the argument that Descartes draws directly from doubt, without passing through the *cogitatio* (in the formulation "*dubito ergo sum*, vel quod idem est, *cogito, ergo sum*"),[7] offers a nearly exact echo of the certainty of doubt itself such as it is formulated by other Augustinian texts: "Quandoquidem etiam si dubiat, vivit; si dubitat unde dubitet, meminit; si dubitat, dubitare se intelligit; si dubitat, certus esse vult; si dubitat, cogitat; si dubitat, scit se nescire; si dubitat, judicat non se temere consentire oportere" (Even if he doubts, he lives; if he doubts the origin of his doubt, he remembers; if he doubts, he understands that he doubts; if he doubts, he wants to be certain; if he doubts, he thinks; if he doubts, he knows that he does not know; if he doubts, he judges that he need not consent imprudently).[8] Before so many parallels, shouldn't we consider the case closed and admit, with the majority of interpreters, that Saint Augustine already produced, at least in a still hazy outline, the Cartesian argument for the *cogito*? Doesn't Descartes himself seem, for that matter, to validate with "great satisfaction" this lofty ancestry?[9]

Yet it behooves us to doubt that Saint Augustine anticipated the Cartesian *cogito*—for at least two reasons, with the expectation that in the end a third will be discovered, which is by right first.

From the outset we will observe that Saint Augustine does not reach the ego by certifying its being through the exercise of its *cogitatio* but by certifying its life by the exercise of doubt even about this life: "Potesne, inquam, nobis dicere aliquid eorum quae nosti? Possum, inquit. / Nisi molestum est, inquam, profer aliquid. Et cum dubitaret: Scisne, inquam, saltem te *vivere*? / Scio, inquit. / Scis ergo habere te *vitam*, siquidem *vivere nemo nisi vita* potest. / Et hoc, inquit, scio" (Can you, I asked, say to us one of the things that you know? / I can, he says. / If it is not too much trouble, I say, tell us something. And as he was in doubt, I asked him: do you not know at least that you *live*? / I know it, he says. / You know therefore that you have *life*, since nobody can *live except by life*. / That I know, he says).[10] As for Descartes, doubt here yields before the evidence that it denies and assures with the same move and at the same time. But, here, the issue is, in contrast to Descartes, the evidence of life or, more exactly, of the life in me, different from me, but without which I would not be, nor be myself. This radical divide is developed quite clearly by a text from his mature writings:

Quantum rerum remanet quod ita sciamus, sicut nos *vivere* scimus? . . . Quoniam certum est etiam eum qui fallitur *vivere*. . . . Sed qui certus est de *vitae* suae scientia, non ea dicit "Scio me vigilare," sed "Scio me *vivere*": sive ergo dormiat, sive vigilet, *vivit*. Nec in ea scientia per somnia falli potest. . . . Mille itaque fallacium visorum genera objiciantur ei qui dicit "Scio me *vivere*": nihil eorum timebit, quando et qui fallitur *vivit*.

How many things are left that we know as we know that we *live*? . . . For it is certain that even he who is deceived *lives*. . . . But he who knows with certain science that he *lives* does not say: "I know that I am awake," but "I know that I *live*": therefore whether he sleeps or wakes, he *lives*. And dreams cannot deceive him in this knowledge. . . . One can therefore pose all sorts of fallacious visions as objections to the one who says "I know that I *live*": but he will never fear any of them, since even he who is deceived *lives*.[11]

Thus appear several differences between Saint Augustine and Descartes: first, certainty does not bear so much on being as on life; next, it is not based so much on the institution of the *cogitatio* as essence of the *res cogitans* as it is on the performative contradiction of a living doubt. What do these differences have in common? The second indicates that whereas, for Descartes, the experience of self-contradicting doubt attests to the certainty of the act of thinking in such a way that the *ego* finds in it its essence as *res cogitans*, in contrast, for Saint Augustine, doubt does not assure the mind of any essence, which it could perform at will, but assigns it to life, unshakable and inevitable but uncontrollable. Now, it falls to life to determine also the first difference: for Descartes, certainty ends up at *esse*, more exactly at *esse* as first of all mine, in first person, *sum*; there is an indisputable being, unshakable, and this is precisely me, *ego*. In contrast, for Saint Augustine, certainty ends up at life, from which I certainly do draw my being but which I am not myself primarily, even though I only am through it. For—and here is the chief point—no living thing *is* its own life; every living thing lives through the life that it is not and does not possess, not through itself. Nobody lives by himself. Saint Augustine says it literally: "*vivere nemo nisi vita* potest" (nobody can *live except by life*).[12] What is proper to the living consists in that it does not possess its own life but remains a tenant of it. "To live" means "to live for the time being" because, more essentially, by a proxy—by virtue of the proxy that life accords the living. In this sense, if it turns out certain that I live, I possess the certainty of living only in the precise instant of my present life, without any guarantee of still living in the following instant, precisely because the instant literally is not. Therefore, I am certain that I live, without ever being certain that I am inasmuch as living. If life certainly constitutes my essence, then it becomes certain that my existence is not a certainty for me, except in the instant. And the fact that this instant is prolonged changes nothing about the basic observation: I am not *my* life, but I live by proxy from life. "To live" means the certainty of not having the certainty of living again, or rather of having the certainty of not living by oneself—living gives only the certainty of dying. Only the Living par excellence lives from itself.[13] We see now that these two differences, in fact, make just one: there where Descartes accomplishes the ego's appropriation to itself (its thought assuring it of itself in its being as *res cogitans*), Saint Augustine assigns the *mens* to its life (by the contradiction of doubt) only to expose it to this very life; now, this life, by definition not belonging to me as mine, I can only expose myself to it as that to which I belong, more myself than me and for the sake of which, from this moment, I disappropriate myself of myself. The same act of *cogitatio* thus provokes two opposite results: in one case the appropriation of the ego to itself, in the other case the disappropriation of the *mens* to itself.

A second reason to doubt that Saint Augustine anticipates the Cartesian *cogito* confirms this first one: Descartes himself recognized his distance from Saint Augustine. Against the purported evidence for the comparison and against the prestige of such an authority, he himself sometimes claimed unambiguously,

I am obliged to you for drawing my attention to the passage of St. Augustine relevant to my *I am thinking, therefore I exist*. I went today to the library of this town [Leiden] to read it [*De civitate Dei* XI, 26], and I do indeed find that he does use it to prove the certainty of our existence. He goes on to show that there is a certain likeness of the Trinity in us, in that we exist, we know that we exist, and we love the existence and the knowledge we have. I, on the other hand, use the argument to show that this *I* which is thinking is *an immaterial substance* with no bodily element. These are two very different things.[14]

Of course, one could hold that Descartes himself also ends up recognizing in the *res cogitans* "a certain likeness of the Trinity."[15] Yet it remains indisputable that he means first to establish it as a *res intellectualis* and *intelligens*,[16] so as to find in it a first principle so very first that it even precedes the knowledge of God: "I took the being or existence of this thought as my first principle, and from it I deduced very clearly the following principles. There is a God."[17] To be sure, both arguments are about connecting thought and being, no longer with regard to God (as in the tradition issued from Aristotle), but now also with regard to the finite mind, soon to be named the subject. Yet one begins with the ego so as to deduce from it existence, even that of God, as if on the basis of a first principle different from this very God, while the other is about an assurance, by doubt and its contradiction, of the *mens*, for the sake of seeking outside it its condition of possibility, life. This opposition cannot be hidden: it is played out between self-appropriation by the equivalence of thought with being (essence inasmuch as existence) and self-disappropriation of a living of a life *other* than itself. Two philosophers, at least, saw this perfectly. Blondel first: "Is there a more serious misreading than that which discovers his [Saint Augustine's] influence in the Cartesian *cogito*? . . . Augustine never would have dreamed of setting up its thinking as a 'cornerstone,' of positing it as absolute and in the absolute, of making the mind such as we know it a sufficient and separable substance."[18] And, of course, Heidegger: "Descartes blurred Augustine's thoughts. Self-certainty and the self-possession in the sense of Augustine are entirely different from the Cartesian evidence of the '*cogito*.'"[19]

Having established this fundamental opposition beneath the appearance of one and the same argument, what remains is to measure its import and understand what is at stake in it.

§10. The anonymity of the ego

One point thus seems established: at no time does Saint Augustine succeed (nor even attempt, as Descartes will) in assuring the ego of its existence or assigning it *cogitatio* as essence (*res cogitans*). Why this recoil before what appears to us today as undeniable evidence? Or else was Saint Augustine missing certain elements needed to validate the argument?

The *cogitatio* was evidently not missing, since it falls to him to have, first of all, definitively established its conceptual usage, on the basis of a somewhat hazy etymology for that matter: "Quia tria cum in unum coguntur, ab ipso coactu cogitatio dicitur" (For when these three terms [memory, vision, and will] are collected into just one, this collection is called *cogitatio*).[20] Nor was *esse* missing, seeing as he clearly indicated that the mind is certain only of that alone that it is certain to be—"certa sit, quod solum esse se certa est."[21] What then is or would be missing in Saint Augustine such that he could not write *ego cogito, ergo sum* like Descartes?[22] If he was not missing the *cogitatio* nor *esse*, he could only have been missing the *ego* itself—this *ego* that, for Descartes, sustains the two other terms that manifest it only because, more essentially, they presuppose it straightaway, as early as the doubt; to the point that the *cogitatio* is so identified with the *ego* as its very act that it ends up disappearing in it, finally emerging alone, but imperial, in its being without any more mention of it: *Ego sum, ego existo*.[23] The *ego* is missing from Saint Augustine, at least in the Cartesian sense of "ego ille, quem novi" (this ego here that I have come to know),[24] seeing as he knows it only as a question, and a question concerning an unknown essence: "Quis ego et qualis ego?"

(*Confessiones* IX, 1, 1, 14, 70). And the reason for this questioning goes without saying: for him, access through the *cogitatio* to being (or rather to life) does *not* permit acceding to myself and especially not to identifying myself by an essence. In other words the fact that *my* access to *my* being through *my* thought is imposed indisputably does not imply that I have, in this being through thought, the least access to myself in the figure of an *ego* known by itself. Saint Augustine is perfectly willing to admit the argument that connects thought to being; he even inaugurates it and will impose it upon posterity (including Descartes); but he refuses to let this same argument produce and consecrate any *ego* known by itself. Not that he anticipates the objection to come in metaphysics, an objection that is vulgar by dint of repeating that what exists is not myself because "it thinks in me," without myself being at issue; he does not contest that, myself, I think and that through this I am certainly. But he contests or, rather, observes that, when I think and am (or think that I am), I do not take possession of myself as an *ego* that would say *I myself*[25] or that would say itself an *I myself*—and thus would know its essence.

But then what am I taught by the certainty (still uncontested) that I am inasmuch as I think? It teaches me that in thinking, I am put at a distance from myself and become other than *I myself*, that in thinking, I do not enter into possession of any *myself* that could exactly and truly say itself in saying *I*, that the more I think myself (and the more I am by thinking), the more unknowing I become of who I am and alienated from myself. In a word, access to my Being in and through my thought, far from appropriating me to myself as for Descartes, for Saint Augustine exiles me outside of myself. I have no other *ego* besides my division itself with my *self*. In entering the terrain into which the alliance of thought and Being introduces me, I do not discover *myself* nor discover myself as a *myself* assured of self, but I see that I escape myself because I myself exceed myself—that I am this very excess of myself over *myself*. The *cogito*, supposed to appropriate me to myself as a *myself*, expels me from myself and defines me by this very exile. I am therefore paradoxically the one who in thinking knows that he is not (belonging to) himself, does not know his essence and can never say (himself), rigorously, *myself*.

Saint Augustine describes this exile often and clearly, showing thereby that the supposed *cogito* reveals that I am a *quaestio mihi*, a question to myself—that I am myself as this question. Once, he feels himself having become to himself a great question—"factus eram mihi magna quaestio" (*Confessiones* IV, 4, 9, 13, 422)—at the death of a friend. This childhood friend had shared a life and its joys with him—up until the moment of his falling into a great agony. During this agony, moribund and unconscious, he receives baptism; but surviving by a remission, far from denying this so to speak involuntary baptism, as Augustine hoped, he lays strong claim to it and in the end dies baptized. Why does this mourning provoke, more than just sorrow on account of the other, an unintelligibility to himself? No doubt because the friend, "dimidium animae meae" (part of my own soul), keeps a part of myself, which his death amputates, such that I take on with horror a life that I do not want to live partially "nolebam dimidius vivere" (IV, 6, 11, 13, 426). But no doubt there is more: the half-a-life that the death of my friend leaves to me had in fact already escaped me from before his decease, since, in his agony, he had, through baptism, changed his life by receiving it this time from the Immortal himself; consequently, this life already escaped me by dint of a life that remained absolutely foreign to me. The death of the friend deprives me of my own life, but his new life still more. Such an escape of myself out of me (for it is precisely the *self* that lets life escape) leaves me without *myself*, as one remains without voice. And this is not just a provisional state, one that would result from a passing event, like a simple crisis. It concerns an ordeal as repeated as is temptation, or rather as the five modes of temptation that, in adding themselves up in each other and constantly intervening on me, define the permanent status of my condition. If "oneri mihi sum" (I am a burden for myself), this results from the fact that "'temptatio est vita humana super terram' sine interstitio" ("the life of man on this earth is an ordeal" [Psalm 30:10], without the least respite) (*Confessiones* X, 28, 39, 14, 210).[26] Saint Augustine analyzes in detail at least two cases of the exile that they suggest and of the *quaestio mihi*, the question to myself, that they repeat.

First the case of one of the concupiscences of the flesh, sexual desire. I can from now on (now that I am converted and a bishop, editing the *Confessiones*), he argues, resist it without trouble, so lacking in strength is it as long as I remain vigilant ("mihi vigilanti carentes viribus"). In other words, as long as I remain myself, being and thinking (being because thinking), true child of the *cogito*, sexual temptations will remain without effect, even though the images that would incite them still remain alive "adhuc vivunt in memoria mea" (*Confessiones* X, 30, 41, 14, 212). Yet it happens that as soon as I fall asleep, not only do I greet them without showing any resistance, but sometimes I even let myself go so far as to actually take pleasure in them ("non solum usque ad delectationem, sed etiam usque ad consensionem"). Therefore, at the very moment when these images become *weaker* because they offer nothing real ("dormienti falsa . . . vigilanti vera"),[27] the erotic dreams, though involuntary, do not allow for me to take the step to action, such that I am not *he who* I am precisely *because* I am certain in thought *that* I am (in dreaming because I think). The supposed *cogito*, by admitting me into my existence without fixing for me an essence, therefore, alienates me from myself: "Numquid tunc ego non sum, Domine, Deus meus? Et tamen tantum interest inter me ipsum et me ipsum intra momentum, quo hinc ad soporem transeo vel huc inde retranseo!" (At this moment am I not myself, O Lord, my God? And yet a gulf intervenes, separating me from myself, between the moment when I pass into the torpor of sleep and that when I come back!) (X, 30, 41, 14, 214).[28] This difference, if it manifests itself in time, is not itself defined temporally, or else it refers to a scission of the ego temporalized, so to speak, after the fact. For the scission arises in general as soon as the ego, in this case the mind (*animus*), attempts to determine itself by itself: "Imperat animus corpori et paretur statim: imperat animus sibi, et resistitur. . . . Imperat animus, ut velit animus, nec alter est nec facit tamen. Unde hoc monstrum?" (The mind gives a command to the body and the body obeys it immediately. The mind commands itself, and there is resistance. . . . The mind commands the mind to will and there is no other but it itself, and yet it resists. Whence this monster?)[29] The monster (*monstrum*—put otherwise, the phenomenon beyond the norm that is to be shown, *demonstrare*) consists in that the mind refractory to the mind that gives it a command is *not* an other, different, but remains one and the same mind, the sole mind—namely, a mind that it itself cannot even command itself. What is the meaning of this failure of command, except that this mind has not mastered itself and is not such that could take itself into hand—in other words, comprehend itself? The supposed *ego* manifests itself by demonstrating the contradiction in it of its equality to itself. From the beginning A is *not* A; *I* am not *myself.*

We should not restrict, crudely, the demonstration of the supposed *cogito* as a *monstrum* solely to erotic dreams (in fact, mere examples of the temptations linked to the sense of touch). It is repeated almost in the very same terms in the case of one of the temptations linked to the sense of hearing. As is well known, Saint Augustine had discovered the greatness of the Christian faith, in fact for the first time, in Milan, while listening, on one hand, to one of the sermons of Saint Ambrose disclosing to him the spiritual sense of scripture and, on the other hand, to the liturgical songs penetrating him deeply, in particular in the prayer of the Psalms. This experience, musical to be sure (and therefore of importance for the author of a *De musica*), had an especially powerful spiritual effect: entering into the prayer of the community of believers and becoming an agent of the liturgical mysteries.[30] An ambiguity, however, quickly insinuates itself: does the emotion born from singing these hymns come from what these songs say to God as praises ("moveor non cantu, sed rebus quae cantantur") or only from the songs themselves in their strictly musical beauty? Augustine came to suspect that to the contrary "me amplius canus, quam res quae canitur, moveat" (what gave me my emotion was more the song than the things sung).[31] This is not just a case of a beautiful soul's exaggerated scruples but of a very real and very disturbing suspicion. I do indeed differ from myself, to the point of losing all knowledge of *myself*, not only in the experience of my failings (erotic desire, weakness of will) but even in the experience of my highest exaltations (in this case my communion in liturgical prayer). Even in this apparently pure joy, I am deceiving myself; I do not know what I am really doing; I do not comprehend myself, in any case no more than in my erotic dreams. The pretended heights of "religious experience" change nothing: "mihi quaestio factus sum" (I have become, in fact, for myself a question) (X, 33, 50, 14, 232).[32] Even when it prays, the ego differs from its *myself*, or rather self-differs and is therefore not appropriated to any *myself*.

What is unadvisedly named the "Augustinian *cogito*,"[33] therefore, leaves the ego in exile between its existence (certain) and its essence (unknown). Man's ignorance of himself cannot be overcome by a more exact investigation or by a more profound interiority. The contrary is true: the more the certainty of existence permits the mind to enter into its being, the more the endless traversing of this field leaves it inaccessible to itself, unknown, impenetrable, like an abyss: "Grande profundum est ipse homo" (Man himself, what an immense abyss) (IV, 14, 22, 13, 446). Saint Augustine can say without any incoherence, on one hand, that "homo sibi ipse est incognitus" (man is [to] himself unknown) and, on the other hand, that "[mens] se ipsa nihil sibi possit esse praesentius" (nothing can be more present to the mind than itself),[34] for the certainty of existence does not imply knowledge of the essence any more than knowing *that* I am tells me *who* I am—and even if my ego consists in Being. The supposed *cogito* does, indeed, introduce me into Being, but it leaves me there with unknown essence, in-between, knowing myself without self-knowledge: "Quid ergo dicemus? An quod ex parte [mens] se novit, ex parte non novit? . . . Non dico totum scit, sed quod scit tota scit" (What shall we say? That the mind knows itself in part, and does not know itself in part? . . . I do not say that it knows all of itself [entirely], but that what it knows it knows in its entirety) (*De Trinitate* X, 4, 6, 16, 130). What the certainty of my existence offers to me is summed up in the consciousness of my anonymity. I am, therefore I remain, what I am but without essence, without identity, without name even. I am, but just enough to sense that I am not myself, or rather that this existence that I am is not myself; or that this existence, which leaves me without essence, opens for me no access to myself, entangles me in it and holds me to the separation of myself. Being holds me but so as to hold me back from acceding to this *self* that is not said or given in being.[35]

This anonymity weighs so heavily on the analysis of the ego that it even sometimes leads to a forced reading of a passage from Saint Paul: "Tu enim, Domine, dijudicas me, quia et si 'nemo scit hominum, quae sunt hominis, nisi spiritus hominis, qui in *ipso* est,' *tamen* est aliquid hominis, quod nec ipse scit spiritus hominis, qui in *ipso* est, tu autem, Domine, scis ejus omnia, qui fecisti eum" (You, O Lord, you judge me because if "nobody among men knows the things of man except the spirit of man which is in him" [1 Corinthians 2:11], *nevertheless* there is something of man that even the spirit of man, which is in him, does not know, but you, Lord, you know all the things that you have done) (X, 5, 7, 14, 150). Saint Augustine's thesis consists in citing Saint Paul saying that only the mind of man knows man so as to correct him by adding that, in one case, that of the essence of man, the mind of man himself does not and that therefore God alone knows it, in his role of creator of all things, therefore also of man. In other words the essence of man, which remains inaccessible to man, resides in the secret of God. Now the text of 1 Corinthians 2:11 does not lead to this conclusion (an unknowable essence of man, except for God alone). Provided one does not truncate it too quickly (as Saint Augustine does), it has an entirely different intention: just as only the spirit of man knows what is in man, so, too, only the Spirit of God knows what is in God. Therefore, since we have received this spirit, we can know God (1 Corinthians 2:11–12). Augustine's interpretation clearly, intentionally then, betrays the Pauline text: while Paul wants to establish, by an analogy between the spirit of man and the Spirit of God, that man can know the gifts of God, the commentator, Augustine, would like to establish, to the contrary, that far from *us* having knowledge of the gifts of God through the Spirit of God poured out into us, not only do we know nothing of these gifts, but inversely *God alone* knows man, which his own spirit cannot. How to justify this divergence, however provisional?[36] Evidently, by the necessity of defending and illustrating in Pauline terms, even deformed, the radical and decisive paradox of man's anonymity to himself, despite the pretended *cogito* or rather *by virtue* of its limits.

The ego, therefore, does not know itself, but in this unknowing, it can dwell—because it is and exists in it with an anonymous certainty. It knows itself certainly to be and to exist but so as to sense all the more evidently that this Being and this existence, no more than the thought that assures it of them, do not give it to itself or give a *self* to it. Its certain existence does not qualify it in its own regard but immobilizes it and fixes it by forbidding it all access to a self—to its self, now without essence, without definition, therefore without the ipseity of a *self.* The Augustinian ego finds itself imprisoned outside itself, being just enough to conceive that its *self* will remain inaccessible to it and that anyway it *is* not it, for the anonymous being of the hypostasis cannot by definition reach, still less name, the slightest ego. In this sense we must give up speaking of an Augustinian ego since never will I see myself as *ego ille.*

§11. The dimensions of *memoria*

This imprisonment of myself outside itself appears so paradoxical that one might want to seek a supplemental argument that confirms it. This argument is presented in the case of *memoria*—on condition that we do not fall back too quickly onto what metaphysics commonly means by this term. That is, from the beginning, Saint Augustine radicalizes its signification: *memoria* does not so much designate one faculty of the mind among others as it constitutes this mind itself and, so to speak, absorbs it: "animus est ipsa memoria" (the mind is this very memory); "ego sum qui memini, ego animus" (It is I who am [the one] that remembers, myself, the mind).[37] And, in effect, I do not simply have memory, but (in contrast with other faculties) I am identically my memory, since "ibi reconditum est quiquid etiam cogitamus" (here is where all we think is gathered and kept).[38] To the point that consciousness or at least self-thinking thought is said and carried out in memory of self: "tamen [mens] noverit se tanquam ipsa sit sibi memoria sui" ([the mind] knows itself inasmuch as it itself is for it(self) memory of itself); in other words: "mentem semper sui meminisse" (the mind always had the memory of itself).[39] Shouldn't we conclude from this that the permanent possibility of a *memoria sui* compensates, so to speak, for the impossibility of the *cognitio sui (cogitatio sui)* by restoring the ego's access to itself, to *the self*? But this is only an appearance. In fact, memory, understood precisely as *memoria sui*, not only gives the ego no access to itself but renders unquestionably manifest the impossibility, on principle, of such access. "Magna vis est memoriae, nescio quid horrendum, Deus meus, profunda et infinita multiplicitas; et hoc animus est, et hoc ego ipse sum. Quid ergo sum, Deus meus? Quae natura sum?" (Great is the power of memory, my God, its depth and infinite multiplicity possess I know not what fearful things. And this is the mind, and this is what I am, myself. What then am I, my God, of what nature am I?) (*Confessiones* X, 17, 26, 14, 186). The aporia of my ego stems (here quite precisely) from the fact that my own *nature* (my *quid*, my quiddity—in other words, my essence) remains radically inaccessible to me, and all the more so as the fact (my existence) of my mind is imposed incontestably. *Memoria* affords me, in so many ways, the ordeal of self only so as to convince me of my inadequacy to my self: "Magna ista vis est memoriae,

magna nimis, Deus meus, penetrale amplum et infinitum. . . . Nec ego
ipse capio totum, quod sum. Ergo animus ad habendum se ipsum angustus est, ut ubi sit quod sui non capit? Numquid extra ipsum et non in
ipso?" (Great is this power of memory, my God, a vast and infinite secret
chamber. . . . And myself I do not grasp all that I am. My mind is not of
sufficient scope to possess itself, and so where is that which it does not
grasp of [its] self? Or else [is this place found] outside itself and not in it?)
(X, 8, 15, 14, 166). *Memoria* accomplishes and consummates definitively in
it the inaccessibility of the *ego ille* that I am. Remembering, even myself,
means that there is no transition possible between the fact of myself and
my nature, my essence, my ipseity. This should not be so surprising, for
despite what one could expect, *memoria* is characterized by two paradoxical properties: on the one hand, it encompasses infinitely more than what
my *cogitatio* can conceive; on the other, it ends up finally by *not* remembering itself.

Detailed review of its prerogatives confirms this. With *memoria* it
is, of course, and first of all an issue of the faculty of bringing back to
mind what, among all that I have thought, I wish to think again: "Ibi
reconditum est, quidquid etiam cogitamus. . . . Ibi quando sum, posco,
ut proferatur quidquid volo, et quaedam *statim* prodeunt, quaedam
requiruntur *diutius*" (Here, when I am in it, I demand that what I want
should be brought forward, whatever it might be, and some things come
immediately; others take *a longer time*) (X, 8, 12, 14, 162). Memories are
at issue, therefore, images of objects absent, but always already perceived
and therefore always available to return over a more or less long term:
"rerum sensarum imagines illic *praesto* sunt cogitationi reminiscenti eas"
(images of things sensed that are there *available to* the thought that recalls
them) (X, 8, 13, 14, 164). And moreover "cum dico, *praesto* sunt imagines
omnium quae dico ex eodem thesauro memoriae" (when I say [them], the
images of the things that I say are *available to me*, taken from the same
treasure house of my memory) (X, 8, 14, 14, 166), "in memoriae sane mea
praesto sunt imagines [rerum]" (images of things are *available to me* in my
memory) (X, 15, 23, 14, 180). In this sense *memoria* functions as a living
memory, which treats only what has not been forgotten because it has not
gone far off: "haec omnia *rursus quasi* praesentia meditor" (I meditate on
all these things *again almost as if* they were present things) (X, 8, 14, 14,

166). Memory, in fact, remains a memory of the still present, so much so that it remembers especially what is most present to it, namely itself first of all: "Cum memoriam memini, per se ipsam sibi *praesto* est ipsa memoria" (When I remember memory, the memory itself is through itself available to itself) (X, 16, 24, 14, 182) since in effect "sui quoque meminit animus" (the mind also remembers itself) (X, 25, 36, 14, 206). But if the memory, like the mind, also remembers itself, precisely because it makes but one with it and assures its self-consciousness, it therefore does not yet pass beyond the field of the conscious, of what remains present to it, therefore of the present itself. Memory thus has the strange condition of not functioning except in regard to what I have *not* forgotten: "Ibi reconditum est, quidquid etiam cogitamus . . . et si quid aliud commendatum et repositum est, quod nondum absorbuit et sepelivit oblivio" (Here all that we think is stored . . . and all that is commended to it and deposited there, provided that forgetfulness has *not* yet absorbed and buried it) (X, 8, 12, 14, 162). Memory therefore remembers all that I have not forgotten, in a word, all except what I forgot, "*praeter* illa, quae oblitus sum" (X, 8, 14, 141–64). In short, this first memory serves only if one does not need it.

This interpretation of memory as, so to speak, a tautological faculty should not be surprising: it is a consequence authorized by Aristotle, among others. If one sticks to the division of roles in the three moments of the vulgar conception of time—in which the present stems from the field of sensation, the future that of hope, leaving to memory the past[40]—then either memory treats the past as sensation treats the present, that is to say as an available being and one that remains, or it treats it as hope treats the future, as a being not (yet) available but a mere possible. But both processes turn out to be absurd in the case of the past: if it is no longer available and remaining, it is no longer anymore a possible. Memory is in charge of an unavailable, but more than a possible, since it was already available. Thus the metaphysical interpretation of memory as simply rememorizing and reproductive misses the essence of *memoria*.

A more radical conception of *memoria* such as it was practiced by Saint Augustine must therefore be ventured, one that discloses other functions and other recesses. For if it contains previous sensations and perceptions in the form of images (X, 8, 13), it very quickly shows itself to accomplish other functions. First, it composes and reorganizes the images of the past out of the resources of the *mens* itself (X, 8, 14). Next, in the case of theoretical knowledge (the "liberal arts" rather than the modern "sciences"), it goes even farther in welcoming not only images of things but the things themselves ("nec eorum imagines, sed res ipsas gero" [X, 8, 15, 14, 168]; "in memoria recondidi non tantum imagines [rerum], sed ipsas [res]" [X, 10, 17, 14, 170]). That is, the "things themselves" of theory cannot be known as images of things of the world since they are not found there. If, therefore, these things appear without duplicating anything whatsoever in the world, it must be that they reside elsewhere, in the mind, of course, in *memoria*. Hence, it also falls to *memoria* to encompass the act of the *cogitatio*, inseparable from the mind. This is so of course first because remembering supposes thinking,[41] but especially also because *cogitare* supposes a repetition of comparisons and collections (*cogere, colligere*) of terms to synthesize, therefore a temporality contained, maintained, and thoroughly covered in both senses "ut denuo nova excogitanda sint indidem iterum (neque enim est alia regio eorum) et cogenda rursus, ut sciri possint" (they must again be extracted by thought as if new [so as to lead them back] once again toward the same [place] (for they do not have another) and they must be collected again so as to be able to know them) (X, 11, 18, 14, 172ff.). For Saint Augustine the *cogito*, therefore, does not encompass *memoria* as one of its many modes (imagination, sensation, will, understanding, etc.); rather *memoria* encompasses all the *cogitatio* because it alone assures to it the unity of its flux by temporalizing it. With a radicality seen neither by Aristotle nor by Descartes, Saint Augustine here anticipates Kant.

This is eminently the case for the *memoria* of numbers (X, 12, 19) and that of the affections of the mind (X, 14, 21). Though at first glance it appears to concern two extremes, on one side the most abstract of objects, on the other the most passive flux of thought, they have it in common to be kept only "quasi remota inerior loco, non loco" (as if removed to a more interior place, which is [however] not a place) (X, 9, 16, 14, 168). Here *memoria* does not retain past thoughts so much as it contains, without temporal difference, all the utopic knowledges of the world: numbers, abstract idealities, lived experiences of consciousness, their flux, the changes of this flux, the combinations of imaginary objects, and finally, and above all, the *cogitatio* itself.[42] Memory keeps safe all knowings, or rather all knowings remain even if we do not think them, and this remaining without place is named precisely *memoria*: "memoria tribuens omne quod scimus, etiamsi non inde cogitemus" (attributing to memory all that we know, even if we do not think on its basis) (*De Trinitate* XV, 21, 40, 16, 530). *Memoria* thus appears as the place of what does not have place, the place of all the thoughts that are not of the world.

Sometimes it even seems to offer a place to the truth that is least accessible to my thought: myself. That is, Saint Augustine sometimes introduces a highly paradoxical concept of self-memory. In particular, when he must confront the formidable contradiction of two equally rational demands: on one hand one can only love what one knows; on the other each of us loves (and desires) the beatitude that we have never experienced and therefore do not know (see below, Chapter 3, §16). How to explain the fact that we can in the case of our beatitude love with desire what we do not know with even the slightest clear idea? How to name an unconscious knowledge of what it knows—in other words, without knowledge of what it knows? One final hypothesis can be imagined, even though it seems like an oxymoron: "An aliquem finem optimum, id est securitatem et beatitudinem suam videt, per quamdam occultam memoriam, quae in longuiqua eam progressam non deseruit" (Unless it [sc. the mind] sees an excellent end, that is to say its security and its beatitude, by some hidden memory, which did not abandon it when it strayed so far) (*De Trinitate* X, 3, 5, 16, 128). But this hypothesis makes the difficulty all the greater, more than it resolves it. For how to explain the memory *in me* of what I never had or knew? How to explain that I keep in *my* memory *my* beatitude, without properly having a complete and exhaustive memory of *myself*? In short, how could the memory of my beatitude perdure without a comparable self-memory, a memory of *the self*? ("Sed cur memoria beatitudinis suae potuit, et memoria sui cum ea perdurare non potuit?" [ibid.]). Now then, it might behoove us to admit that *memoria* is deployed with total security beyond the limits of the self. In this way the anonymity of the ego would assume a new figure: I am of an in fact certain existence, without however the slightest access to my essence nor to my ipseity, and this crisis can last my whole lifetime, for it finds its place (and its nonplace) in my *memoria*. I can still love what I know nothing about and therefore endure my existence without essence because what I know nothing about, my *quaedam memoria occulta* at once preserves for me and hides from me. And since I am my *memoria*, I therefore become hidden from myself.

§12. The immemorial

The question of *memoria* only now begins to be posed as such, now that it appears as what hides me from myself or, more exactly, as what takes charge in me of the essence that escapes me—my own, an interior hiddenness, a hiddenness to myself, a placeholder in me of interiority, an interiority of hiddenness. Contrary to the ordinary doctrine of the philosophers (Greeks, but also Descartes) who would like to have it that the wise man owes nothing to memory because he would be liberated from his body, Saint Augustine insists not only that "res aliquas sapientis memoriae custodiri" (the wise man should keep things with his memory) but that often this memory is nothing like a slave obeying the mind ("obtemperat mihi") since it often rises up and tramples it ("in aliis rebus ita sese erigit, ut ejus sub pedibus miser jaceam" [in other matters, it arises in such a way as to cast me, miserably, beneath its feet]).[43] Like the body (in fact here the flesh), *memoria* subverts the ego and strips it of access to itself (and to the *self*), alienates it essentially from its essence. *Memoria*, therefore, displays an essential ambivalence: it renders absence present but also keeps absence absent. It implies, as such and by definition, not only sometimes obeying (*obtempere*) the mind by putting at its disposition what it had lost, but *also* resisting it (*sese erigere*) by hiding from it what it lost (indeed, we will see, by hiding from it the very fact of having lost it). The radicality of this Augustinian break from the common metaphysical determination of memory cannot be underestimated. For, if *memoria* passes beyond the limits of what in the *cogitatio* remains accessible to the mind—in short, if it crosses the frontier of consciousness—just where does it convey me outside myself? This raises the question of knowing "quanta et quam multa memoria nostra contineat, quae utique anima continentur. Qui ergo fundus est, qui sinus, quae immensitas quae possit haec capere [. . .]?" (how many things our memory contains and what size they are, all things that are not less completely contained in the soul. What fund, what breast, and what immensity can contain that?) (*De quantitate animi* V, 9, BA 5, 244). To where does *memoria* extend itself so exceedingly far, or, rather, to where does it extend *me* myself beyond what I can think, that is to say outside of myself?

Saint Augustine proves this unthinkable expansion of the domain of *memoria* by emphasizing that *memoria* is not limited to conserving past things, an obvious point that metaphysics established with ease, but also bears on thought's presence to itself. "Quapropter, sicut in rebus praeteritis ea memoria dicitur, qua fit ut valeant recoli et recordari; sic *in re praesenti*, quod est sibi mens, memoria sine absurditate dicenda est, qua sibi praesto est ut sua cogitatione possit intelligi" (This is why, just as we call memory in things past that by which we can recall them and remember them, so too can we say without absurdity that there is a memory *in the present thing* that the mind is to itself, by which it can at its own disposition comprehend itself by its own thought).[44] The present itself, even and especially the present understood in the radicality of the self-presence of *res praesens, quae est mens*, governs *memoria* because it, too, must recall itself. Differance, which shifts thought from its presence and therefore from its *self*, is stigmatized perfectly here and confronted as such, but it is not frozen in the mere report of an intuitive deficiency or the empty denunciation of the illusions of immediacy. It opens onto the paradox of *memoria*, which keeps secret the self. But, in keeping it secret (in withdrawing it from the grasp of the ego), it could also be that it secretes it still more powerfully.

Before arriving at this point, let us confirm that the present itself depends on *memoria* by considering the privileged example of reading, that is to say of the text, therefore of writing really put to work. To listen or read, it is not enough to listen or to read; one must also remember the sounds or letters. Failing that, the past present to hear and read can only pass immediately, therefore pass away and become a past, without our having (had the time to have) heard or read anything at all—more exactly, without our having retained anything, without having kept the memory of anything. We can maintain our present only if we *retain* it through *memoria*; we maintain it (so that it does *not* become a past) only by retaining it through *memoria* (so as to stay not passed away). What makes us lose our present (time) does not stem from a shortage of present perception but from the deficiency in the present of *memoria*. "Verius itaque dixerimus, cum tale accidit, 'non meminimus' quam 'non audivimus'" (We should therefore say when such a thing arrives: "We no longer remember," rather than "we did not hear"). Only the application of memory makes sensation into a perception, therefore renders the present to its presence ("adhibita memoria sensui corpori" [*De Trinitate* XI, 8, 15, 16, 202]). The present loses its supposed (metaphysical) autarchy, since it now depends on *memoria*, now liberated from the παρουσία of οὐσία.[45]

But the scope and primacy of *memoria* goes to the point of paradox, when it comes to reign over the future itself. The example comes from the recitation of a text and, here again, from the choral chant (no doubt the ecclesial chant heard in the church of Milan), *dictis et canticis*, which speaks about memory, *memoriter*. But why not rather say that we speak and sing by seeing in advance, by foreseeing in each moment what it will be necessary to say in the following moment? "Et tamen ut praevideamus, non providentia nos instruit, sed memoria. Nam donec finiatur omne quod dicimus sive canimus, nihil est quod non provisum prespectumque proferatur. Et tamen cum id agimus, non dicimur providenter, sed memoriter canere vel dicere; et qui hoc in multis ita proferendis valent plurimum, non solet eorum providentia, sed memoria praedicari" (And yet, to foresee, it is not foresight that guides us, but memory. For until we have finished saying or singing, nothing has been uttered that was not foreseen and anticipated. And yet when we do so, we do not say that we sing or speak from foresight but from memory; and those who are especially good at saying many things are not normally praised for their foresight, but their memory) (*De Trinitate* XV, 7, 13, 16, 454). In fact, this is not about just the memory that makes me retain (return to the present) what I will have to say or sing in the following instant. It is also about the passage of this moment itself, so that it stays united between its beginning (which stays retained instead of flying away at once) and its end (which imposes itself in advance and attracts without yet being acquired). Take this example: "Dicturus sum canticum, quod novi; antequam incipiam in totum expectatio mea tenditur, cum autem coepero, quantum ex illa in praeteritum decerpsero, tenditur et memoria mea, atque distenditur vita hujus actionis meae in memoriam propter quod dixi et in expectationem propter quod dicturus sum" (I am going to sing a psalm that I know. Even before beginning, my expectation tends toward the totality [of the psalm], but after I have begun, as what I remove from it passes into the past, my memory will in turn tend and my active life be distended into memory of what I said and expectation of what I am going to say) (*Confessiones* XI, 28, 38, 14, 336). The anticipatory expectation not only must pass within and be transformed into *memoria*, but with it alone my sounds are dispersed into meaningless atoms, if *memoria* does not retain and contain them in *one* story or *one* song. Here *memoria* functions as a retention, which assures the present moment its duration in its entirety by retaining its three ecstases, so that they can each play with or against one another. It alone assures a time to the moments because it illuminates time by giving to it what it does not have, a space: "memoria, quod quasi lumen est temporalium spatium" (memory, which is like the light of the space of the times).[46] *Memoria* passes beyond the reach of the *cogitatio* because, like the originary impression of time, it precedes it and makes it possible—not just *like* the originary impression since it operates precisely *in the role of* originary impression: that from which come the ego and its *cogitatio*, in an originary and radical passivity.

But the retreat of the mind and its secret, the *abditum mentis* (*De Trinitate* XIV, 7, 9, 16, 368), sinks still farther. For *memoria* does not recall only what I could have forgotten; it sometimes also recalls the fact of forgetting itself. Reminding me of a lost thing does indeed make me retrieve it, but, above all, it tears it from oblivion. Memory retrieves for me the forgotten thing by making me also forget my own forgetting. Memory and forgetting surely do move in inverse proportion, the one growing as the other diminishes. Yet there is also another situation, that in which I remember having forgotten, without for all that remembering what I forgot. Forgetting could not become an ordeal for the mind if it did not remain still present to it, if it itself disappeared into forgetting. For, if forgetting let itself be forgotten, it would no longer concern the mind in any way, which would have forgotten it. To experience forgetting, one must not have forgotten it, as one can forget a thing. Oblivion is therefore not some thing, but a possible modality of each thing. And to not forget forgetting, it must be retained by the memory itself, "memoria retinetur oblivio." In other words, "cum vero memini oblivionem, et memoria praesto est et oblivio" (when I have a memory of forgetting, memory is available to me, but so too is forgetting).[47] The choice of memory is no longer limited to the alternative of either recovering the forgotten by annulling forgetting or losing its trace to the point of forgetting about forgetting. A third possibility arises: keep the memory of oblivion as such. But that is a contradiction, a double one at that. Not only must *memoria* take into its charge its contrary, but above all it must also renounce reducing anything and everything whatsoever to consciousness. In effect, in the case of forgetting as forgotten, it manages the forgotting without anything forgotten and this forgetting (forgotten) no longer offers anything that could become a memory. *Memoria* no longer remembers anything because it no longer works on a forgotten being but on forgetting without being, oblivion, a something neither passed nor absent nor present.

But if *memoria* does not remember, properly speaking, anything whatsoever, why still name it a memory, still make it into memory and not forget it? Or, would we have to go so far as to say that memory bears on that of which I can no longer have any consciousness, therefore on the unconscious?[48] The answer is undoubtedly no, be it only because the concept "unconscious" presupposes that of "consciousness," which can itself appear only on the basis of Descartes's *ego ille*,[49] therefore in strict contradiction with what Saint Augustine thinks with the term *ego* (or *mens*). It seems more appropriate to stick with the ultimate paradox of *memoria*: it keeps the memory of that which it cannot by definition remember, oblivion, the immemorable par excellence.[50] *Memoria* therefore bears on the immemorable or, with more sobriety, on what Levinas thematized with the name *the immemorial*. It is not a matter of "a weakness of memory" but of what "reminiscence could not recuperate," definitively "irrecuperable," because "it was never present" and will remain forever "a past that passes on the present," which will never become present again because it never was, according to an "antecedence prior to all representable antecedence."[51] *Memoria*, such as Saint Augustine develops it to its extreme, no longer concerns what was present to my mind in the past and could become so again in the future—in the literal sense, the *re*-presentable as re-*presentable*—but what in me remains inaccessible to me and uncontrollable by me (what I forgot, my forgetting of what I forgot, and even my forgetting of this forgetting itself), and which, despite or *because* of this, governs me through and through. It is indeed a matter of this: without *memoria* I am not, but with it, which by definition I do not comprehend, I do not comprehend myself—I have no presence to myself, and I forget *myself*. The aporia of the ego itself, taken in the anonymity without ipseity of its existence, now finds its title and its place: *memoria* precisely of the immemorial.

The aporia of the ego to itself (the *quaestio magna mihi*) is therefore repeated and culminates in the aporia of *memoria*, understood not as the faculty for the restoration of suspended representations but as the experience of the immemorial. Whence the observation that "factus sum mihi 'terra difficultatis et sudoris nimii'" (I have become to myself "a land of difficulty over which I toil and sweat" [Genesis 3:17]) (*Confessiones* X, 16, 25, 14, 184). The citation refers to the earth where Adam and Eve will be exiled once they are chased from the original paradise; but in this context the exile becomes an interior exile. I become for myself the very place of my exile outside myself, since the most intimate in me, *memoria*, not only can just as easily *not* remember me as remember me (memory manages forgetting, which implies forgetting of forgetting itself), but in the final analysis it bears on the memory of what was never present nor represented to me—the immemorial. I inhabit a place, myself, where I do not rediscover myself, where I am not at home, where I am not myself. Exiled from the inside, I am not there where I am. I am without myself, late and lagging behind myself. *Memoria* thus leads to forgetting, and this radical forgetting manifests the facticity of the ego: "We do not repeat the being we have been; we do not take ourselves over [assume ourselves] in our facticity. What we are—and what we have been is always contained in this—lies in some way behind us, *forgotten*. Expecting our own can-be to come from things, we have forgotten the factical Dasein in its having-been."[52] Heidegger's suggestion here lets us read the rest of Augustine's analysis with all its force: "Ego sum qui memini, ego animus. Non ita mirum, si a me longe est quid quid ego non sum. Quid propinquius me ipso mihi? Et ecce memoriae meae vis non comprehenditur a me, cum ipsum me non dicam praeter illam" (It is I who remember, I the mind. There is nothing surprising in the fact that what is not me should remain strange to myself. But what is closer to me than myself? And yet, the power of my own memory escapes my comprehension even though without it I could not call myself myself" (ibid.). The contradiction of the noncomprehension of what comprehends me most intimately and without which I could not conceive myself, *memoria*, is exposed in the contradiction of its unthinkable (void) object: the memory of forgetting. Forgetting, I cannot remind myself of

it, properly speaking, since it effaces that which it lays hold of (the forgotten), but neither can I say that I forgot it since I know perfectly well *that* I
forgot, even if I forgot *what* I forgot. "Et tamen quocumque modo, licet sit
modus iste incomprehensibilis et inexplicabilis, etiam ipsam oblivionem
meminisse me certus sum, qua id quod meminerimus obruitur" (And yet,
in whatever way it might be, however incomprehensible and inexplicable,
I am certain of remembering forgetting itself, this forgetting that ruins
what we remember) (ibid., 14, 186). The interpretation of memory no longer as the faculty that restores the past in a re-presentation but as *memoria*
of forgetting, of the forgetting of forgetting, and finally of the immemorial ends by admitting that in fact if this *memoria* defines me to such
a point that my mind (*animus, mens, cogitatio*) cannot be conceived or
experienced without it, and if this *memoria* turns out "profunda et infinita
multiplicitas . . . varia, multimoda *vita* et immensa" (a profound and infinite multiplicity . . . a life changing and manifold without measure) (X,
17, 26, 14, 186), then not only must we face up to the stupor ("Multa mihi
super hoc oboritur admiration, stupor apprehendit me" [Great astonish-
ment came over me; a stupor seized me] [X, 8, 15, 14, 166]) and the fright
("nescio quid horrendum . . . profunda et infinita multiplicitas" [its profound and endless multiplicity, what a fright!] [X, 17, 26, 14, 186]), but
we must also, and above all, draw the following conclusion, strange but
unavoidable: if *memoria*, which contains the secret of my mind (*abditum
mentis*), goes beyond what my *cogitatio* and my *mens* comprehend, then I
will have to think beyond my own thought if I ever want to think myself.
If "nec ego ipse capio totum, quod sum. Ego animus ad habendum se
ipsum angustus est" (Myself, I do not grasp myself entirely. For my mind
is too narrow to contain itself) (X, 8, 15, 14, 166), then I must think myself
by thinking beyond myself.

§13. What desire thinks

Memoria thus renders aporetic, on principle, all self-knowledge since
it demonstrates that the *mens'* path to itself is lost in the immemorial. The
mens knows now that it extends beyond what it will ever know of itself.
But the aporia contains more than an interdiction and already offers a
way out. For if *memoria* imposes on the *mens* that it endlessly outrun itself

in pursuit of its own withdrawal, it would have to be admitted that the *mens* can outrun itself. At issue would be the ego transgressing its being or rather its *life*: "Quis est ille super caput animae meae? Per ipsam animam meam ascendam ad illum. Transibo *vim* meam" (Who then is it who is found above the summit of my soul? I will ascend unto him through my very soul. I will go across my own vitality) (X, 7, 11, 14, 160). Or: "Transibo et hanc vim meam, quae memoria vocatur" (I will go across even this vitality which is mine and is called memory) (X, 17, 26, 14, 188). But how to transcend one's own vitality? If this is not just an absurdity, isn't self-transcendence reducible to a rhetorical hyperbole, one without conceptual import, not to mention a "mystical" extravagance? Let us look at it a bit more closely. We saw that the *mens* knows itself certainly to be (in fact, to live) because it cannot doubt that it is thinking; it therefore is as, and as long as, it is thinking itself. But what would it be if it were thinking without thinking *itself*? For Saint Augustine this is not just a matter of a mere hypothesis but of a disposition of the *mens* that he already practiced during his last and highest prayer, the one with Monica at Ostia. At a certain moment, but still not the last, it could happen that "et ipsa anima sileat et transeat se *non se cogitando*" (the soul itself falls silent and surmounts itself *not thinking itself*) (IX, 10, 25, 14, 118). Let us note three points here. First, even if the *mens* does not think itself, it still thinks—which is what enables it to certify its existence; the argument of the *cogito* absolutely does not demand that I think myself but that I think something in general, indeed anything, no matter what. Next, in not thinking itself, the *mens* no longer inquires into *its* essence, does not fall back on the existential privilege of the *cogitatio* in favor of the search for the essence of the *cogitant*—in short, is free of self. Finally, the *mens* becomes what it knows because it loves it and therefore wants to identify with it, the result being that if it thinks an other besides itself, possibly *supra caput ejus*, it will become it, since it loves it. In short, as soon as the *mens* frees itself enough to think by thinking another besides itself, it can pass beyond its own (non) essence and become, by thinking another, other than itself. Let me insist once again that for Saint Augustine it is about a practice, an act, and a deed, as is witnessed by the story of Ostia: "erigentes nos ardiore affectu in id ipsum praeambulavimus gradatim cuncta corporalia et ipsum coelum, unde sol et luna et stellae lucent super terram, et adhuc ascendebamus *interius cogitando* et loquendo et mirando opera tua, et *venimus in mentes nostras et transcendimus eas*, ut attingeremus regionem ubertatis indeficientis" (lifting us up with a more ardent affection toward "it itself" [Psalm 121:3], we went by degrees through all corporeal things and even the heavens out of which the sun, the moon, and the stars shine down on the earth; we rose *by thinking* and speaking *more intimately*, and admiring your works, we *came to our own souls and we transcended them*, to reach the region of endless abundance) (IX, 10, 24, 14, 116).[53] I am because I think, but not because I think myself. And, as *memoria* forbids me from thinking myself and refers me to the immemorial, what is left to me is only thinking in the mode of this reference beyond myself.

The question now takes the form of a clear paradox: if the *mens*, which exists certainly inasmuch as it is thinking, cannot however think itself in its essence because it exceeds itself in its role as *memoria*, how will it be able to reach its ipseity? In other words, how could the ego enter into itself, into its *self*, when it neither can nor should pretend to enter into possession of its essence since it itself passes beyond its own measure? *Memoria* opens me onto an immemorial that I cannot, by definition, rejoin but one without which I will never be myself. The sole path from self (existence) to self (essence) would consist, for the *mens*, in rejoining the immemorial by a thought that itself transcends itself. The contradiction seems obvious: the intrinsic finitude of thought cannot self-transcend without deluding itself or dissolving itself. The finitude of thought in me cannot think the immemorial; it forbids me from hitting upon myself.

No doubt this is so—at least if the immemorial has to be reached only by thought, and by thought exercising an intentionality that I will set forth on the basis of myself heading in the direction of this immemorial, as if it were a matter of aiming at an objective, an object, or a worldly being. But the immemorial is nothing like an objective, an object, or a being and belongs no more to the world than to space. Without object, unworldly and utopic, the immemorial does not escape just our finite thought but in fact *all* thought inasmuch as thought is intentional. Does it remain, for all that, definitively unthinkable? Again the answer is without a doubt "yes"—at least if thought must always be exercised intentionally on the basis of an ego heading toward its objective: object or being. But it nevertheless remains that thought, when it does not comprehend what it would like to aim at, can at least still think itself on the basis of what it cannot comprehend, but which comprehends it. For this, it would be necessary to substitute for strictly intentional thought a "great thought," which would admit no longer aiming intentionally at anything whatsoever, but which would know how *to let* what it thinks come to it, weigh on it, and be exercised over it.

Such a thought is enacted and becomes weighty as a desire. Desire in effect enjoys a privilege that intentionality by definition ignores: desire is something I can neither aim at nor attain by deciding on my own; I can at best and sometimes await it, desire it, or rather let it become desirable. For, contrary to appearances, desire does not arise first from me so as to aim at its object but is enacted in or rather over me, weighs on me, and invades me, even if I neither comprehend nor possess its supposed object, or rather precisely *because* I do not possess it, attain it, or even comprehend it. Desire is imposed on me of itself, at its initiative, and never at mine. I cannot decide to desire even if desire can make me decide to do my all to fulfill it. And desire does not impose on me because I comprehend it and have authority over it but, to the contrary, because it imposes itself *on me* from above with all its authority, which, most of the time, I do not truly know. Moreover, my desire is born and lived very often from my impossibility of knowing and comprehending the nonobject, which imposes itself all the more on me, in that it imposes always thinking of it, even when I do not comprehend it. Let me be more specific: Of course, it is not enough that I do not comprehend (a nonobject) for me to desire; for what I do not comprehend, I can desire only *sometimes*—when, precisely, it makes itself desirable, therefore on condition that it knows how to incite my desire and that it merits it. Or rather, as it never falls to the desirer to decide to desire and as desire alone decides its birth (and its death), I desire only what has the power, the prestige, and the dignity to inspire this desire in me. Obviously, then, desire comes to me as from elsewhere, therefore from beyond myself.

Thus specified, the privilege of desire grows even stronger: desire, in imposing itself on me, individualizes me. Objective intentional thought of objects does not succeed in identifying me since, by rule, anyone other than me should be able to think the object that I thought, for my epistemological primacy over the object is endorsed only so long as I constitute it according to the rules of objectification, to which I must submit like any other subject enacting universal rationality. The rationality of the object should universalize me so as to validate me, and therefore it leaves me anonymous. By contrast, desire identifies me: it and I appear face-to-face, without any object or universal rationality serving as a screen standing between us. Desire is enacted over me so immediately that it mirrors for me the first image that I will ever have of myself. More than mirror, it serves for me as idol. For the desire to which precisely I respond, no other besides me answers to. If another seems able to answer it in the same way as I do, either he would not in fact respond to it exactly as I, and we would have to admit two desires in reality quite different, or else he would become effectively an other myself, be it only in a collective identity provoked by one and the same collective desire. In the final analysis, what exercises a desire over me is something I receive and respond to in person, as such. My desire—or more exactly, that to which I respond and commit myself—knows better who I am than my (intentional) thought ever will. My desire prepares for me the ipseity that I will never comprehend but that, in advance, comprehends me. The assurance of my essence, which does not follow from certain knowledge of my existence, does indeed befall me but from elsewhere than my own intentional thought, starting from an unshakable alterity, that of my own desire. For it does not come from me but imposes itself on me.

With great brilliance Saint Augustine put this arrangement to work, for he was able to see and to mark a desire so unconditional that every interlocutor without exception should recognize it as his. He borrowed its formulation from Cicero: "cum vellet in *Hortensio* dialogo ab aliqua re certa, de qua nullus ambigueret, sumere suae disputationis exordium 'Beati certe,' inquit, 'omnes esse volumus'?" (as he would like to take as the point of departure for his argument in his dialogue *Hortensius*, a certainty beyond all discussion, he says: "To be happy, this is certainly what we all want").[54] As the reading of this text played, according to Saint Augustine's own repeated and insistent declarations, a decisive role in his discovery of God, it can be inferred that this discovery, for him first of all, consisted in becoming conscious of the unconditioned desire in him for beatitude, as seems to be witnessed by the *Confessiones*: "Nonne ipsa est vita beata, quam omnes volunt et omnino qui nolit nemo est? . . . Nota est igitur omnibus, qui uns voce si interrogari possent, utrum beati esse vellent, sine ulla dubitatione velle responderent. Quod non fieret, nisi res ipsa, cujus nomen est, eorum *memoria* teneretur" (Is it not the happy life itself that everyone wants? And is it not impossible to find anybody who does not want it? . . . It is therefore known to all, those who, supposing that one were to ask them if they want to be happy, would no doubt respond in one voice that they do. This would not happen if their *memory* did not retain for them [for their mind] the thing itself, from which the name comes) (*Confessiones* X, 20, 29, 16, 194, 196). In fact, the earliest texts, which follow the conversion, identify its moments, and prepare its recapitulation by the *Confessiones*, make a massive appeal to this radical argument. These begin with an entire treatise dedicated to the blessed life written as an echo, no doubt quite consciously, to that of Seneca. "Beatos esse nos volumus, inquam. Vix hoc effunderam, occurrerunt una voce consientes" (To be happy, this is what we want, I say. Barely have I said it than they all with one voice admit it) (*De vita beata* II, 10, 4, 238). There is a consensus: it is not possible to doubt the will every man has to live happy. One should even doubt that it is possible to find a single man who wants to live without the least hope for the slightest possibility of finally experiencing something like the blessed life. The desire for beatitude is not added on, as an option, possibly taken or not, to the desire to live; the connection between wanting-to-live and the desire for beatitude turns out to be analytic *a priori*.

We understand better now why Saint Augustine had substituted life for being. Being cannot go beyond itself and precisely for that reason lets the *mens* stray between the existence that it certifies for it and the essence that it steals from it, to the point that in this very in-between beatitude appears not only unattainable but even out of the question. It is not self-evident to Being—and therefore to beings—that it should *also* be *good*, because *good* does not in and of itself belong, any more than goodness, to what Being permits saying of beings. Accordingly, to evoke an τοῦ ἀγαθοῦ ἰδέα, Plato must suppose it beyond essence, ἐπέκεινα τῆς οὐσίας.[55] In contrast, since life does imply in and of itself that the living receive it from elsewhere and can lose it, therefore that it live in the intrinsic incompleteness of an opening, it is set forth in the horizon of a desire. Life, inasmuch as opening come from elsewhere, does not possess itself any more than it defines itself; it is received and lost, therefore desired, desirable, and offered as desirable in the form of the *happy* life. Being does not permit or forbid beings anything but to be, without promising or assuring them anything more than the presence of a permanent time (thus I can imagine myself possessing it and effectuating it as long as and as often as I want it). Life (precisely because I do not possess it but receive it from elsewhere) gives itself only on condition that I receive it in each instant, therefore without stop or limit, in the situation in which I desire it also and necessarily as *happy*. Being gives only Being (because it, in fact, does not give it), while life gives life, therefore gives it happy (because it can only give itself). When life is substituted for Being, it is already a matter of beatitude, intrinsic to desire and therefore unknown by Being that neither desires nor could desire.

There is more. The strength of the argument for such a desire for *beata vita* in all men stems no doubt from the fact that not one among them would ever deny it—but especially so from the fact that this universal acquiescence happens without any theoretical knowledge, by concept or representation on the part of the *mens*, of what the *vita beata* implies or of what it consists. To the contrary, the desire for beatitude appears all the more certain as it is not preceded or sustained by any certain theory of what it desires. This contradiction between desire (certain) and its object (uncertain) constitutes the very heart of the argument.

Quid igitur? An dicendum est etiamsi nihil sit aliud beate vivere quam secundum virtutem vivere, tamen et qui hoc non vult, beate vult vivere? Nimis quidem hoc videtur absurdum. Tale est enim ac si dicamus: et qui non vult beate vivere, beate vult vivere. Istam *repugnantiam* quis audiat, quis ferat? Et tamen ad hanc contrudit necessitas, si et omnes beate velle vivere verum est, et non omnes sic volunt vivere, quomodo solum beate vivitur.

What now? Am I to say that though living happy is nothing other than living virtuously, nevertheless even he who does not want it [to live virtuously] wants to live happy? This would be as if we were saying that even he who does not want to live happy wants to live happy. That truly appears too absurd. Who would ever want to listen and bear this (*theoretical*) *contradiction*? And yet, necessity constrains us to do so, since it is true that, on one hand, everybody wants to live happy and, on the other, everyone does not want to live in the sole way in which one can live happy. (*De Trinitate* XIII, 2, 7, 16, 284)

The argument drawn from the universality of the desire for beatitude seems contradicted by the fact that the means of attaining the virtuous life are rejected by the majority of those who claim loudly and clearly that they want happiness. Yet the truth of the two terms of this contradiction must be maintained: the end remains true, even though the refusal of the good is incontestably called for. But the contradiction is not one, for it results from a conflict in which at least one of the two terms has no theoretical status: the universal desire for beatitude does not rest on any theoretical knowledge, of whatever sort, of the nature of beatitude, of which nobody has any experience. Rigorously considered, only the refusal to live according to virtue would rest on arguments (utilitarianism, cynicism, egoism, skepticism, etc.). As for desire, it adapts well to its theoretical nullity since it is set forth *as desire*. The theoretical contradiction does not affect it since it is exercised according to a strictly *erotic* certainty, which needs only to desire but not to theorize the object of desire or know it. The principle of desire therefore contradicts the theoretical contradiction because it passes beyond, in the name of paradox—and of paradox in the erotic reduction—every theoretical presupposition. Desire knows and thinks the *vita beata* (in fact, it alone can reach it) but without having any theoretical representation of it and, above all, without having the slightest need for one. And in fact, beatitude does not appear to he who desires it in the field of the *cogitatio*, of the *mens* and therefore of comprehension, but in that of *memoria*. To the question "utrum in *memoria* sit beata vita" (whether the blessed life is found in *memory*) comes the response, "Quod non fieret, nisi res ipsa, cujus hoc nomen est, eorum *memoria* teneretur" (That would not happen if the thing itself, for which it is the name [beatitude], was not something men held in *memory*) (*Confessiones* X, 20, 29, 14, 194, 196). The desire for the happy life is something with which we are familiar without knowing or comprehending, for it inhabits us like the immemorial, the closest and farthest away, inasmuch as it happens in and through our desiring.

§14. *Vita beata* as principle

The *vita beata* or rather the unconditioned universality of its desire now assumes the rank of principle, therefore of first principle (for, strictly speaking, only the first deserves the title). The texts that establish this are too numerous to list, but they converge on the same principle:

Beatos esse se velle, omnium hominum est. . . . Beatos esse se velle, omnes in corde suo vident, tantaque est in hac re naturae humanae conspiratio, ut non fallatur homo qui hoc ex animo suo de animo conjicit alieno; denique omnes id velle nos novimus. Multi vero immortales se esse posse desperant, cum id quod omnes volunt, id est beatus, nullus esse aliter possit: volunt tamen etiam immortales esse, si possunt.

To want to be happy, this is a fact for all men. . . . That they want to be happy, they all see it in their heart, and so common is the aspiration of human nature on this point that a man who supposes it of another on the basis of his own soul takes no risk of being wrong. Finally, we know that we all want it. To be sure many despair of being able to be immortal, but all want to be immortal, if possible.[56]

The desire for beatitude is so deserving of the dignity of principle that it must be admitted unconditionally and unreservedly, even if the result of this is the desperate frustration of not being able to reach it, since immortality escapes us. We prefer (or rather we should, for there is no other choice) the sadness of not being able to reach beatitude (by immortality) over renouncing the desire for it. This implicitly rejects and disqualifies the pretention of the pagan sage to (being able to) renounce his desires, or at the very least his desire for eternity. Nobody can remove himself from the desire for beatitude that nobody can satisfy. There is as much illusion and lying in claiming to fulfill this desire as in pretending to extinguish it. This in-between defines the sole honest condition of man, whose instability now becomes the sole constant. The desire for beatitude is indisputable: "Omnis autem homo, qualiscumque sit, beatus vult esse. Hoc nemo est qui non velit, atque ita velit, ut prae caeteris velit; imo quicumque vult caetera, pro hoc unum vult" (Every man, whoever he might be, wants to be happy. There is nobody who does not want this and who does not want this above all else. Moreover, whoever wants other things wants them only for the sake of happiness). What can be disputed, however, is the means toward this sole end, means all the more varied as they intend by any means this sole necessity:

Diversis cupiditatibus homines rapiuntur, et alius cupit hoc, alius illud: diversa genera sunt vivendi in genere humano; et in multitudine generum vivendi alius aliud eligit et capessit; nemo est tamen quocumque genere vitae electo, qui non beatam vitam cupiat. Beata ergo vita, omnium est communis possessio; sed qua veniatur ad eam, qua tendatur, quo itinere perveniatur, inde controversia est. Quid est hoc, ut, cum omnibus non placeat quaecumque via, omnibus placeat beata vita?

Men are seized by very different desires: one desires this, the other that. Very different are the ways of living among the human species, and from among the multitude of these ways of living, each chooses something other and embraces it. There is, however, nobody, whatever way of life he chose, who does not desire a happy life. The happy life, this is their common good; but which way to go to get there, which way leads there, here is where the dispute arises. But then, how does it happen that while they do not agree about the way, they all do agree about the happy life?[57]

Here again the contradictions remain obvious and insurmountable so long as one persists in considering the desire for beatitude as a *theoretical* first principle—for one cannot assume a desire without the means of its accomplishment as a principle of knowledge, still less as a ground of action. But this very objection dissolves as soon as one takes seriously that what this principle is about is the *desire* for beatitude, not knowledge or possession of it. The *vita beata* assumes and deserves the status of principle insofar as it is *desire*, not knowing or comportment. It is not inscribed within the *cogitatio* nor even in the *mens*; it exceeds them both to the point that it is the *mens* and the *cogitatio* that are inscribed within the *vita beata*. Beatitude governs the ego and, in a sense, grounds it because it precedes it as the objective of its desire. The *mens* remains ignorant of the *vita beata* inasmuch as it thinks it, but it knows it insofar as it desires it. And, as this very desire does not belong to it, but comes to it from the *vita beata* of which it is ignorant, the *mens* comes from what it does not know and precedes it. We therefore should not speak here of a desire (or of a love) *for* the principle but of a principle of desire—or, better, desire as principle.

That is, with the principle, desire for the *beata vita* shares the privilege: doubt, come before it, stops and instantaneously collapses. It stops and collapses no longer before the act of a particular thought, which implies an existence, but before the universal impossibility for any man of wanting to live without desiring his happy life. More clearly, nobody can live without wanting to live, and nobody can want to live an unhappy life;

even if we confront a life deprived of the characteristics commonly connected to happiness (ascesis, sacrifice, intentional dispossession, indeed perversion), this condition always becomes from a certain point of view desirable to it inasmuch as a paradoxical, but resolute, access to the happy life. The performative contradiction privileged by the argument from the Cartesian cogito (I cannot think anything at all, even think that I am not, without necessarily already being, therefore I am) recedes behind another contradiction, one more radical because it does not suppose any performance of thought, but the pure facticity of desire: nobody can accept living a life without beatitude, or at least without the possibility of beatitude: "censesne quemquam hominum non omnibus modis velle atque optare vitam beatam? / Quis *dubitat* omnem hominem velle?" (Do you think that even just one man can be found who does not want or desire with all means available the happy life? / Who *would doubt* that every man wants to be happy?) (*De libero arbitrio* I, 14, 30, 6, 194). From the impossibility of doubting it, follows the possibility of being certain about it: "Beate *certe* omnes vivere volumus; neque quisquam est in hominum genere, qui huic sententiae, antequam plene sit emissa, consentiat" (*It is certain* that we all want to live happy; and in the entire human species there is nobody who does not agree with this proposition, even before we have finished saying it) (*De moribus Ecclesiae Catholicae et de moribus Manicheorum* I, 3, 4, BA 1, 140). The principle is therefore formulated positively in a certain proposition: "Omnium *certa sententia* est, qui ratione quoquo modo uti possunt, beatos esse omnes homines velle" (It is a *certain proposition* for all those who can use their reason in the slightest little bit that all men want to be happy) (*De civitate Dei* X, 1, 34, 422). It is therefore a certainty, leading to a *certissimum*[58] knowledge that takes the place of the Cartesian *inconcussum*.[59] For the *cogitatio* that knows is substituted the desire that wants; for the being that I could provoke is substituted the life that I can only receive; for the impossibility of thinking (oneself) without being is substituted the impossibility of wanting to live a nonhappy life. The same reason becomes, from theoretical, practical, and the same thought finds its principle only at the price of desiring. For the *inconcussum* is desire, therefore a lack, not self-possessed knowledge. And therefore an *inconcussum* thinking itself only while not knowing itself, which does not know itself in producing itself on the basis of itself, but in receiving itself from the one who excited it as desire. For the *vita beata* does not mark an exception to the reception of life but consecrates it.

We must now confront the paradox of such a principle, first and unshakable, which can be thought only by the name of unconditional desire for a beatitude that we do *not*, by experience and perhaps by definition, have—in other words, an absolutely certain principle but one that we can never confirm. "Mirum est autem cum capessendae atque retienendae beatitudinis voluntas una sit omnium, unde tanta existat de ipsa beatitudinie rursus varietas atque diversitatis voluntatum, non quod aliquis eam nolit, sed quod non omnes eam norint. . . . Quomodo igitur ferventissime amant omnes, quod non omnes sciunt? Quis potest amare quod nescit? . . . Cur ergo beatitudo amatur ab omnibus, nec tamen scitur ab omnibus?" (It is a wonder that while one finds among all men one and the same will to lay hold of and to keep beatitude, there exists a variety and diversity of wills aiming at it—not that somebody does not want it, but all do not know it. . . . How then do all love so passionately what all do not know? Who can love what he does not know? . . . Why do all love beatitude when all do not know it?) (*De Trinitate* XIII, 4, 7, 16, 280ff.). Here we spot the paradox (*mirum*) of a knowledge by desire that does not know, neither intentionally nor representationally, the thing that it desires, be this only because this desire does not concern a thing in the world. Now, how are we to explain that what we do not know we still desire, think, and in this sense might even know? In fact, "nonne ipsa est beata vita, quam omnes volunt et omnino qui nolit nemo est? Ubi noverunt eam, quod sic volunt eam? Nimirum habemus eam nescio quomodo" (Isn't it the happy life that everybody wants and that absolutely nobody does not want? Where did they learn about it so as to want it? For we do indeed have it, but I do not know how) (*Confessiones* X, 20, 29, 14, 194). There is a quasi knowledge, proper to beatitude—or, more exactly, to the desire for beatitude—which is knowing without comprehending or representing, literally just enough for desiring it. This knowledge, not theoretical but practical, erotic even, which does not know how it knows what it knows—Saint Augustine attributes it precisely and once again to *memoria*. "Quaero utrum in memoria sit beata vita. Neque enim amaremus eam, nisi nossemus" (I am asking if the happy life might not be found in memory. For we would not love it, if we did not know it) (ibid.) This implies that when we know in the mode that permits loving what cannot be represented, we remember, in the sense of a memory of what was never present, in the sense of the immemorial.

Of course, this must be made more specific: we do not remember the happy life as we remember our father (whom we have seen, but cannot see again, in this life at least), or as we remember Carthage (which we could have seen and could see again, barring a geological catastrophe). The *vita beata* is not something we have ever seen, and there is nothing that assures us that we will ever experience it. We have no memory of it, not even like the idealities (mathematical, logical, etc.) that subsist only in our mind but remain always accessible there, because the *vita beata* subsists nowhere, not even in our mind, and is not any more accessible there than anywhere else. "Non sane reminiscetur beatitudinis suae [homo]: fuit quippe illa et non est, ejusque ista penitus oblita est; ideoque nec commemorari potest" (Man [in a state of sin] no longer remembers his beatitude; it was and is no more; it has fallen into deep oblivion for him; he can no longer remember it) (*De Trinitate* XIV, 15, 21, 16, 400). I do not have *memoria* of the happy life as if I had forgotten it after having known it, as if it were still memorable, a memorial, a memory that it depends upon me to have and recollect. To the contrary, I appeal to *memoria* in order to accomplish a mode of thought that knows indubitably what it can neither represent nor aim at intentionally. That is, *memoria*, already identified as the thought that knows what theoretical consciousness can neither see nor say, coincides with the universal and unconditioned desire for the *beata vita*, which forces itself upon the thought of all men without, at least for the great majority of them, their having the slightest conception of it. If *memoria* bears on the immemorial, and if the *vita beata* forces itself upon us without our knowing where this principle comes from, then *memoria* appears as the place of the *vita beata* and the path of desire.

Memoria as instance of the immemorial thereby establishes itself as the sole proper place of the *vita beata*, desired without our knowing it, thought without our thinking it. "Nescio quomodo noverunt eam, ideoque habent eam in nescio qua notitia, de qua satago, utrum in memoria sit, quia, si ibi est, jam beati fuimus aliquando" (I do not know how they knew it, their having I know not what notion of it, and I ask whether it is not in the memory that it would be found because if it was found,

then we would already have had happy days). Beatitude inhabits us uncon-
sciously, and its desire governs us like an immemorial. For this reason I
seek to know if the happy life is not found in memory: "quaero, utrum
in memoria sit beata vita. Neque enim amaremus eam, nisi nossemus"
(I seek to know if the happy life is found in memory. For we would not
love it if we did not know it) (*Confessiones* X, 20, 29, 14, 194). The common rule that connects knowledge to love remains valid, but in the case
of the desire for the happy life, it functions in an inverse sense: I do not
desire beatitude because I would first know it (for, at least in the mode of
representation, I do not know it), but from the incontestable fact that I
desire it unconditionally, it is necessary to infer that I know it, though in
an exceptional way—in a knowledge without concept or representation,
but desiring. Since nobody can deny that he feels (to the point of suffering
from it) this desire for the happy life, it is necessary to admit that he knows
it in some way or another, even though we do not know how we know
it. This is called knowing in memory: "quam se expertus non esse nemo
potest dicere, propterea reperta in memoria recognoscatur" (this thing
that nobody can deny having experienced is therefore acknowledged to be
found in memory) (X, 21, 31, 198ff.). In other words the *vita beata* precedes
us as an immemorial.

In the place where Descartes claimed to have reached, with the performance of the *cogitatio*, the existence of the ego, but also knowledge
of its essence, Saint Augustine experiences that the performance of the
cogitatio reaches only certainty of existence and attests the inaccessibility
of its essence. He therefore substitutes for it the indisputable fact of the
unconditioned and universal desire for the *vita beata*, perfectly known
(like an essence) but whose actual possession (existence) remains perfectly problematic. We must now weigh the consequences of this inverted
arrangement.

§15. The gifted, more than the ego

The two opposed characteristics that define the absolutely certain
desire for an absolutely unknown *vita beata*, as contradictory as they seem,
nevertheless permit us to determine the new *inconcussum* more precisely.

First, the *vita beata*, although or rather *because* it remains unknown as such, supposes an anchor in the truth: "Quisquis igitur ad summum modum per veritatem venerit, beatus est" (Whoever reaches the supreme measure through truth is happy) (*De vita beata* IV, 34, BA 4, 382). Or else: "Aeterna igitur vita est ipsa cognitio veritatis" (Eternal life consists therefore in the very knowledge of the truth) (*De moribus Ecclesiae Catholicae et de moribus Manicheorum* I, 25, 47, BA 1, 206). Obviously this cannot be a mere reprise of the theme "the beatitude of the sage," happy because he contemplates noetically the true, since here, paradoxically, the *vita beata* remains unknown to the desire that nevertheless postulates it. It concerns therefore, at the very least and to put it somewhat provisionally, a truth accessible in another mode than the noetic: "Haec est vera dilectio, ut inhaerentes veritati juste *vivamus*" (This is true dilection, *to live* justly while standing in the truth) (*De Trinitate* VIII, 7, 10, 16, 58). The truth at issue here gives itself to know, but above all to inhabit, as a place where we can stand and steadfastly so, in such a way that dwelling there is in the end equivalent to loving, indeed to loving it. One sees at once that in order to situate the *vita beata* (still unknown) in the truth, much more is needed than to know it through contemplation in the noetic face-to-face. It is necessary to love it and identify with it, that is to say live from it. That the truth becomes *life* even implies that the one is not possessed (nor produced) any more than the other. I am therefore obliged to describe more carefully the here implicitly accomplished transformation of the essence of truth when it becomes the place for the *vita beata* and because it first becomes the soil where *life* is planted (see Chapter 3, §§20–21).

A second determination confirms the now not exclusively noetic character of truth, at least when it gives its place to the *vita beata*—joy, or rather the joy of enjoyment: "Illa est igitur plena satietas animorum, haec est beata vita, pie et perfecte cognoscere a quo inducaris in veritatem, qua veritate perfruaris, per quid connectaris summo modo" (This consequently is the fullest satisfaction of souls; this is the happy life, to know piously and perfectly he who leads you to truth, of which truth you rejoice, through which you are connected in the highest mode) (*De vita beata* IV, 35, 4, 284). Joy and enjoyment become the sensible index of truth because here truth no longer offers only information to know but opens as a territory to enter, a state of life to enjoy. Truth, it need not so much be contemplated as enjoyed: "Beata quippe vita est *gaudium* de veritate" (The happy life consists in rejoicing *to enjoy* truth) (X, 23, 34, 14, 202). Or else: "beata vita, quae non est nisi *gaudium* de veritate" (the happy life which can be reduced to the joy of *enjoying* truth) (*Confessiones* X, 23, 34, 14, 202). Here again, the understanding of truth, not only as the place of beatitude but as an enjoyment and a joy, supposes a still more radical swerve in its essence.

Hence a third consequence: since God is but one with truth, but a truth that is convertible with charity (and eternity)—"o aeterna veritas et vera caritas et cara aeternitas!" (oh eternal truth, true charity and charitable eternity!) (VII, 10, 16, 13, 616)—it must be concluded that the joy enjoying the happy life resides only in divine truth, in true God. "Quomodo ergo te quaero, Domine? Cum enim te, Deum meum, quaero, vitam beatam quaero. Quaeram te, et vivit anima mea. Vivit enim corpus meum de anima mea et vivit anima mea de te" (How will I seek you, Lord? For when I seek you, my God, I seek the happy life. I seek you and my soul lives. For my body lives of my soul and my soul lives of you) (X, 20, 29, 14, 192). This does not dogmatically close the search, by collapsing the transcendental orientation of the ego, for example, into the supreme being, substituting God for the *vita beata*. It concerns, rather, taking seriously the consideration that since I am not by definition my life, still less my happy life, I can only receive it without producing it, nor even conceiving it: "Quomodo ergo quaero vitam beatam? Quia *non est mihi*" (How then can I seek the happy life? Because it is *not mine*) (X, 20, 29, 14, 194). Life, *a fortiori* the happy life, is not possessed; therefore it is received. From whom and from what, if not God? "Haec est religio christiana, ut colatur unus Deus, non multi dii; quia non facit animam beatam nisi unus Deus. Participatione Dei fit beata."[60] For as with the *vita beata vita*, so with God nobody has seen him, nobody knows him, but nobody can remove himself from him, be it only as a question or a desire.

This chain of determinations imposes a radical reversal on the figure of the ego. For, if my happy life, for which desire constitutes me as myself without possible compromise, can be reached only in a truth that I neither know nor am, since it belongs in the end to God, then I am powerless before what I want most essentially. We even have to go so far as to say that I am not what I am if I limit myself to being only what

I know and what I have power over, the *cogito, sum*. Not only does the gap between what I desire (the *beata vita*) and what I am able to will as measured by what I know ("What can I hope for?") become a yawning chasm, uncrossable, but it also becomes my most evident and definitive characteristic. Not only does the (certain) desire for the (unknown) happy life condemn the fantasized attempt at self-equality (the principle of identity A = A being accomplished in the self-identity of the self to itself), but it also disqualifies the horizon within which such an equality even became thinkable—the horizon of the thinkable, the representable, the comprehensible in the sense of the noetic deploying the face-to-face of the ego subject before its object double. In establishing that desire wants and intends beatitude (and redefines truth in terms of its enjoyment), Saint Augustine opposes head-on Aristotle's thesis—that desire intends and wants first only to know (Πάντες ἄνθρωποι τοῦ εἰδέναι ὀρέγονται φύσει—"All men by nature desire to know")[61]—and anticipates the thesis that he will inspire literally in Pascal: "All men seek happiness. This is so without exception."[62] But if the ego must now be recognized as he who originally desires, then it must take the measure of this originary desire and admit that, more originally than as *cogitans*, it is put in play as *amans*, lover. And, for the lover, the question never consists in deciding to love or not but always and only in orienting oneself in terms of desire, in determining what he loves: "Nemo est qui non amet: sed quaeritur quid amet. Non ergo admonenur ut non amemus, sed ut eligamus quid amemus" (There is nobody who does not love. The only question is what does he love. We are not summoned to not love, but to decide what we love).[63] I am, certainly, but inasmuch as I love (and desire the *vita beata*). The *lover* loves so radically that loving decides everything about him and first of all his being. Accordingly, to reach himself, he does not have to master an οὐσία (supposedly his own, though he perhaps does not have one), but reach what he loves; and to know himself, he does not have to be preoccupied with knowing *himself* but with knowing (or at least identifying) what truly is decisive for him—namely, what he loves in truth. More intimate to me than any equality of the *self* to itself thus turns out to be the distance of the lover to what he loves. Whoever travels this distance knows himself because he knows the other *self* who resembles him more than himself—a self more him than he himself.

To travel this distance of the *self in the self's place*, it is first necessary that it open. Now it opens according to a simple rule: "melius quod interius" (the better is the more interior) (*Confessiones* X, 6, 9, 14, 156). And more precisely, "interior est caritas" (the more interior is charity) (*Tractatus in epistolam Ioannis* VIII, 9, *PL* 35, 2041), which means that distance opens according to the viewpoint of charity, perfectly coherent with the reference of the *mens* to what it loves. Such a rule is obviously marked first by the negative effects provoked by its ignorance and contempt: "Exterius enim conantur ire, et interiora sua deserunt, quibus interior est Deus" (Men strive to go to the more exterior and abandon the more interior within them, to which God is even still more interior) (*De Trinitate* VIII, 7, 11, 16, 60). The distance from the ego to the self's place opens inside the self, not toward the exterior, for this interior alone opens onto what the lover loves. But the interiority in me of what I love does not, for all that, belong to me, as if I kept myself behind closed doors, since the *vita beata* remains immemorial to me, unknown like all that I love wholeheartedly. The interior is constituted by charity, quite possibly the charity in me; therefore it is not imprisoned in my immanence: the interior remains no more in me than what I love remains my own. Almost immediately there follows a positive sense of my distance in the self's place. If God occupies, as most interior axis and highest of causes ("intimo ac summo causarum cardo" [*De Trinitate* III, 9, 16, 15, 304]), the place of the *vita beata*, therefore the place of my desire, then he (and he alone) reveals my final and originary place: "Neque in his omnibus, quae percurro consulens te, invenio tutum locum animae meae nisi in te" (In all that I travel while consulting you, I find no secure place for my soul, unless in you) (*Confessiones* X, 40, 65, 14, 258). Thus is accomplished the change of place: if I am (what, therefore) there where I love, then that becomes my *self* more interior to me than my private ego. Now what I love is named God; therefore, I find myself there. Put otherwise: God appears as the place of *self* that I want and have to become. To the initial question: "Et quis est locus in me, quo veniat in me Deus meus?" (And what is the place in me where my God can come into me?) (*Confessiones* I, 2, 2, 13, 274), finally comes the response: "Tu autem eras interior intimo meo et superior summ meo" (But you were more interior [to me] than what is most inward in me and higher than the most high in me) (III, 6, 11, 13, 382). The paradox, which is marked first by comparatives that surpass the superlatives, indicates a place that I discover neither outside me nor in me, because it finds *me* in a *self* not belonging to me but to which I belong and in which I must finally arrive. God surpasses me with his absolute alterity only inasmuch as, by the very distance that it opens, he defines what I love, therefore what identifies me in my *self*: "tu enim altissime et proxime, secretissime et praesentissime" (you, [who are] highest and nearest, most secret and most present) (VII, 2, 2, 13, 524), "omni secreto interior, omni honore sublimior" (more interior than any secret, more sublime than any honor rendered) (IX, 1, 1, 14, 73), "et interior omni re, quia in ipso sunt omnia, et exterior omni re, quia ipse est super omnia" (both more interior to each thing [than itself], because everything is in it, and more exterior to each thing, because it is above all).[64] And thus I am not from myself nor in myself because I am no longer essentially who I am but what I love—my distance to the place of [my] *self* is defined by my distance to what I love. The *cogito, sum* is carried away toward the *interior intimo meo*.

This does not mean only or first that I am not an *ens per se*, or that I am an *ens creatum*, for it is not a question of making an ontico-ontological determination, not even an inverted or contradicted one. The issue is my mode of manifestation to myself. In fact, crossing the distance from myself to the self's place, I *happen upon and to* myself: "Ibi *mihi et ipse occurro* meque recolo" (Here [in memory, in the immemorial] *I happen upon myself*, and I am recalled [to myself]) (*Confessiones* X, 8, 14, 14, 166). In other words I myself happen to the degree that I advance into the distance where I see my *self* so to speak come upon me. I happen as he who *receives himself* at the same time as what he receives and precisely so as to be able to receive it—the gifted [*l'adonné*]. The Augustinian texts recognize it and describe it without the slightest ambiguity. A commentary, for example, on the basic argument of 1 Corinthians 4:7 ("What have you that you have not received?") insists that "qui videt non sic glorietur, quasi non acceperit non solum quod videt, sed *etiam ut videat*" (he who sees is not glorified as if he had not received not only what he sees, but *also the very fact of seeing*) (VII, 21, 27, 13, 638). For it is a matter of receiving not only the gift received but at the same time, and from the same donation, the *self* that receives it: "priusquam essem, tu eras, *nec eram cui praestares ut essem* et tamen ecce *praeveniente* totum hoc quod me fecisti et unde me fecisti" (before I ever was, you were, and *I was not yet anything whatsoever to which you could give it to be* and yet, see! I am on account of your goodness *which occurs in advance, before all* that you did for me and from which you made me) (XIII, 1, 1, 14, 424). From the outset the creation of the ego is thought in the figure of the gifted: "Deus autem nulli debet aliquid, quia omni gratuito praestat. Et si quisquam dicet ab illo aliquid deberi meritis suis, *certe ut esset, non ei debeatur. Non enim erat cui deberetur.* . . . Omnia ergo illi debent, primo quidquid sunt, in quantum naturae sunt" (Now God owes nothing to anybody, because he gives all gratuitously. And if someone says that God owes him anything whatsoever for his own merits, *it is at least certain that he does not owe it to him for his being there* [to merit it by his own merits]) (*De libero arbitrio* III, 16, 45, 6, 410). I have nothing—better, I *am* nothing—that I did not first receive, beginning with the very *self* who receives. The ego comes from the given *self,* and not the *self* from the ego's self-consciousness. From this distance of the given to self from the self there obviously follows a still more radical separation of the ego from what gives it to itself and gives the *self* to it. Distance that can be understood, to put it in terms of space, as a gap in which I remain on the outside of my own center, cut off by God: "intus enim erat, ego autem foris" (for the light was inside, but me, I was outside) (VII, 7, 11, 13, 604). Distance that can also be understood in terms of time, as a gap in which I would always already be late for what gives me to *self:* "*Sero* te amavi pulchritudo *tam antiqua et tam nova, sero* te amavi! Et ecce *intus* eras et ego *foris* et ibi te quaerebam et in ista formosa quae fecisti, difformis inruebam. Mecum eras et tecum non eram" (*Late* have I loved you, beauty *so ancient and so new; late* have I loved you! Look, you were *inside* and I was *outside,* and I sought you there and, rushing headlong into the beautiful things that you made, I became deformed. You were with me, and I, I was not with you) (X, 27, 38, 14, 208).[65] Come up against the *nearest* (*propinquor*),[66] I can enter into the distance that opens me in the self's place.

It goes without saying that one can, that one even should, here think other determinations of the ego by its distance in the *self's* place: "I is an Other," of course, and "*the being which in every case we ourselves are is ontologically that which is farthest—das Fernste.*"[67] But this should happen only on condition of not collapsing the distance opened by Saint Augustine into mere figures of alienation, even and especially not by declining it according to the *Seinsfrage*. For here the other not only is named God, but this God also names me myself for the first time, inasmuch as he knows and dispenses my *self* more than *I* ever could. In all cases we must be cautious about the homage Husserl rendered, by a misreading, to Saint Augustine. In citing, as the final words of his *Cartesian Meditations*, "Noli foras ire, in te ipsum redi; in interior homine habitat veritas" (Do not go out; turn into yourself; the truth resides in the interior of man),[68] he wanted to endorse the claim that man finds truth in his interiority and therefore should not seek it outside, in the world. But Saint Augustine, in this text, does not ask merely that we quit the exterior (the world) for the interior (subjectivity, transcendental or not) but that we transcend the interior itself for the superior (and the more interior than my most inward). He goes on, without leaving the slightest ambiguity: "et si tuam naturam mutabilem inveneris, *transcende et teipsum. Sed memento cum te transcendis, ratiocinantem animam te transcendere.* Illuc ergo tende, unde ipsum lumen rationis accenditur" (and if you found your mutable nature, transcend also yourself. But remember that when you transcend yourself, *you transcend your rational soul.* Direct yourself therefore toward the point from which the rational light shines). For the inner man does not constitute the dwelling place of truth, since, in contrast, he inhabits himself in He who opens truth to him: "ipse interior homo cum suo inhabitatore . . . conveniat" (the inner man himself is found with he who inhabits him).[69] Truth dwells in the inner man but not in the sense that the inner man would have truth in him, since in fact it dwells rather in he who is invited and invited the truth into him: "Non omnino essem, nisi esses in me. An potius non essem, nisi essem in te" (I would not even be if you were not in me. Or rather I would not be, if I was not in you) (*Confessiones* I, 3, 3, 13, 276).

I am not when and each time that I decide to be by deciding to think. I am each time that, as lover and as gifted, I let the immemorial come over me, as a life that does not belong to me and that, for that very reason, inhabits me more intimately than myself.

Truth, or the Saturated Phenomenon

§16. The demand of the *vita beata*

The blessed life, or, more exactly, the *desire* for the blessed life, desire as the mode of thought of he who becomes a lover, thus turns out to be the principle of the search, more radically than I myself. The *certum et inconcussum quid* that was Descartes's goal does not reside, for Saint Augustine, in the self-certainty of the ego thinking "ego sum, ego existo" but in the unconditional desire for the *vita beata*. A twofold divide separates them: desire without possession rather than possessive certainty, and *life* (as happy life) rather than being. But this desire, at least if one understands it as such, has its own rigor and imposes its own demands. Obviously, it is a question of desire for God: "Et ipsa est vita beata, gaudere ad te, de te, propter te" (Enjoying joy for your sake, from you, and on account of you, that is the happy life itself) (*Confessiones* X, 22, 32, 14, 200). But such a desire for God makes itself felt only because it rests on the *true* God, for only a desire for truth permits a true desire: "Beata quippe vita est gaudium de veritate" (Joy [enjoying] in the truth, that is the blessed life) (*Confessiones* X, 23, 33, 14, 200). To establish itself as ultimate and originary desire, therefore as true desire, the desire for the *vita beata* supposes that I enjoy the truth in it. "Haec est beata vita, pie perfectque cognoscere a quo inducaris in veritatem, qua veritate perfruaris" (This is the blessed life: to know with perfect piety he who leads you to the truth, which truth you enjoy) (*De vita beata* IV, 35, 4, 284). God appears as "highest and more inward truth" (summa et interiora veritas) (*De vera religione* XX, 38, 8,

72) and thus, on this condition alone, fulfills the desire for eternal life: "Aeterna igitur vita est ipsa cognitio veritatis" (For eternal life is the very knowledge of the truth).[1] The joining of beatitude and truth—which, in fact, demands nothing less than God—becomes the knot and the nut of desire. But it remains to be understood. For one question arises here unfailingly: if truth governs the desire for the blessed life, to the point that true desire must be equivalent to a desire for the true, can we avoid desire falling under the control of theory, which would organize even the ethical and the will?

Heidegger spotted the difficulty in the lecture that his 1921 course devoted to book X. Shouldn't Saint Augustine's sense of truth be "understood as existentially *related* to the *vita beata*" but signify "at the same time, the invasion of Greek philosophy" (*der Einbruch der griechischen Philosophie*) within the Christian project of the Augustinian *confessio*?[2] Consider this passage: "Quomodo ergo te quaero, Domine? Cum enim te, Deum meum, quaero, vitam beatam quaero. Quaeram te, ut vivat anima mea. Vivit enim corpus meum de anima mea et vivit anima mea de te" (How then am I to seek you, oh Lord? For when I seek you, I am seeking the happy life. Let me seek you [then], so that my soul might live. For my body lives of my soul, and my soul lives of you) (*Confessiones* X, 20, 29, 14, 192). Now, does it go without saying, Heidegger asks, that the same *how/quomodo* applies to the search for the *vita beata* as for God? For if phenomenology is first of all an investigation into the *how* of phenomena, it must distinguish modes of phenomenalization belonging to each phenomenon. But how would two phenomena as different as the *vita beata* and God manifest themselves in the *same* mode; how would they make themselves accessible in the *same* way? Is the soul's relation to God limited to copying the body's relation to the soul? This becomes an all-the-more pressing question, since the passage that immediately follows will put an even greater emphasis on it: for whether the *vita beata* gives itself to be construed in memory or intended in desire (*appetitus*) or possessed in reality makes no difference at all, in the end, since it is absolutely certain at the very least that all men, in one way or another (in one *quomodo* or another), know it: "Quod eos velle certissimum est. Nescio *quomodo* noverunt eam ideoque habent eam in nescio qua notitia" (That all want it is very certain, but I remain ignorant of *how* they know it in such a way as to possess it in I know not what knowledge) (X, 20, 29, 14, 194). It is uncontestable that Saint Augustine not only does not worry about the difference between the ways different phenomena phenomenalize themselves differently (God, the *vita beata*, and its different modes of access), but that this very ignorance of the *how* even becomes for him an argument for establishing the absolute certainty of the desire for *vita beata*. Whatever the variety of phenomena, the certainty of the universal desire for beatitude is equally established, precisely because it does not depend on differences in their mode of phenomenalization. The less I know how (*nescio quomodo*) phenomena phenomenalize themselves, the more I know that they make themselves accessible. Here there is no search for modes of phenomenalization that would define the modes of access to the phenomena, that is to say the modes of intentionality they would require. This deficiency has an obvious consequence: "The search and, above all, the search for God, have become problematic! Thus, the question turns into a general *theory* of access, which is missing authentic existential rigor: *Vita beata* = *vera vita beata* [the true happy life] = *veritas* [truth] = God. How do I search for this? For this, I must have, somehow, the *vita beata* according to its essence, according to its meaning. And how do I have that?" And therefore: "Does Augustine seek this radically? No, he remains at the same time within the classifying consideration of frameworks, and also within the dominant organizing that corresponds to this.—Greek . . . , 'catholic.'" And, in fact, the phenomenal indetermination of the modes of access to the *vita beata* and to God lead to considering them as objects and therefore as objects of knowledge (*Objektwissen*),[3] in the sense that for Plato virtue is known and taught, and for Aristotle beatitude is acquired by theory. Thus "the tradition is not, or not entirely, destroyed."[4] In other words, Saint Augustine would not have the phenomenological means to achieve his speculative goal; the irreducibility of the first principle to knowledge (and first of all to self-knowledge), benefiting the desire for the *vita beata*, is disqualified, or at least impeded, by the still theoretic and therefore objectifying status of the access to God. If eternal life consists literally in the very *knowledge* of the truth ("Aeterna . . . vita est ipsa *cognitio* veritatis"),[5] then beatitude remains the object of a knowledge, therefore the knowledge of an object.

This objection (a theorizing of the *vita beata* by knowledge of the truth), however powerful it might be (and in a sense it is), nevertheless rests on a presupposition: that Saint Augustine maintained a definition of truth that was itself theoretic, as a truth first of all to be known; and besides, how could he have presupposed otherwise, since philosophy had always understood it so? Unless, precisely in the case of the *vita beata*, truth tacks in the direction, for Saint Augustine, of a nontheoretic sense, extratheoretic even. In this sense one could argue the inverse: if truth defines desire and can become its final consummation, then it would be necessary that *this* truth *of desire* not let itself be confined to the domain of theory, at least in its most narrow sense. It would have to be understood as a truth that is not exhausted in its theoretic function but can also give itself to desire as much as, indeed infinitely more than to, knowledge. To achieve this, the primacy of desire (for the happy life) would have to be founded not on knowledge, that is to say on certain knowledge of a being, but on the primacy of this desire alone—that is to say, on the assurance *without object* yet possessed of desire as such. In other words it would be necessary that the *vita beata* institute itself as truly first principle, that is to say without any previous theoretic condition—without anything to know or make known.

There are at least three arguments that lead me to say that this was, indeed, Saint Augustine's project. The first highlights a fact so obvious that one might overlook it: the *vita beata* rests only on itself, or rather on the desire that it universally provokes, because it does not presuppose the availability of any present object of desire—not even in the form of God. To be sure, Saint Augustine links God inseparably to the *vita beata*, but he does so without any phenomenological confusion since God does not appear here as one being among others, nor for that matter as a being. *Here* there is no presupposition of any sort of proof for the existence of God, which would establish an ontic foundation for the desire for the *vita beata* (as the desire to enjoy eternal existence in God). What is more, *here* there is not even the slightest attempt to define anything remotely like the essence of God, which would provide at least the security of a rationality for the object of desire. Accordingly, this God without established existence or certified essence does not even bear the status of a being, supreme or otherwise, still less that of Being itself, *ipsum esse.*[6] Put otherwise, there is no need, in order for the desire for the *vita beata* to be deployed universally and unconditionally, to be assured of God as a being, whose essence would guarantee its existence, still less as an object, that would be subjected to an intentional aim. Of course, God is surely implied in the desire for the *vita beata* but without that implying that he fixes its foundation thanks to his properties as being par excellence. Everything happens, by contrast, as if the universal necessity of the desire for the *vita beata* was enough to assure access to God, without first having to inscribe him within the horizon of being, with the rank of privileged being. Desire does not have to know its object (not even God as Being or a being) in order to desire in it the *vita beata*.

This is confirmed by a second argument in the shape of a paradox. As we have already observed, a contradiction governs the desire for the *vita beata*:

Quid igitur? An dicendum est etiam si nihil sit aliud beate vivere quam secundum virtutem vivere, tamen et qui hoc non vult, beate vult vivere? Nimis quidem hoc videtur absurdum. Tale est enim ac si dicamus: et qui non vult beate vivere, beate vult vivere. Istam *repugnantiam* quis audiat, quid ferat? Et tamen ad hanc contrudit necessitas, si et omnes beate velle vivere verum est, et non omnes sic volunt vivere, quomodo solum beate vivitur.

And so, do we have to say that, although living happily is nothing other than living virtuously, still, even he who does not want it [to live virtuously] wants to live happily? This would be like saying that even he who does not want to live happily wants to live happily. That is truly too absurd: who would ever listen to and bear this [*theoretic*] *contradiction*? And yet, necessity compels us to do so, since it is true that, on one hand, everyone wants to live happily and, on the other, everyone does not live in that way which, alone, can let him live happily.[7]

In fact, it is possible to want and desire the happy life, without also accepting the conditions for acquiring it—namely, to live in truth according to virtue, in other words, according to truth. Would that lead to a contradiction between desire (for the happy life) and truth (which grounds it)? Of course. But then how are we to understand that in fact it still remains possible not to desire the conditions (truth) for what one desires (happy life) in an obvious logical contradiction? One response alone seems acceptable: our desire can completely contradict the conditions for the acquisition of the object of desire since this desire is not governed by logic—or, at least, not by logic in terms of theory. A theoretic contradiction (between the conditions of the object and desire), even a patent one, does not in any way affect the desire for the *vita beata* because this desire does not rest on any theoretic condition but, like a fact of practical reason, imposes itself by itself, unconditionally. Desire survives logical contradiction because it does not depend on any theoretic condition.

A third argument comes from what could appear, at first glance, like a very strong objection to the thesis of a truth in a nontheoretic sense. Saint Augustine posits in principle that nobody can love what he is ignorant of and therefore that knowledge precedes love, by rendering it possible. "Sed quis diligit quod ignorat? Sciri enim aliquid et non diligi potest: diligi autem quod nescitur, quaero utrum possit. Quia si non potest, nemo diligit Deum antequam sciat" (But who loves what he is ignorant of? For one can know something without loving it; but whether one can love what one does not know is what I am asking myself. Because if one cannot, nobody loves God before knowing him) (*De Trinitate* VIII, 4, 6, 16, 38). But he admits, in the manner of all serious theologians, that God remains as such unknowable. Would he have to conclude from this that nobody can love God since nobody knows him? Obviously he does not end up at this dead end because he introduces a correction to the first principle: it is necessary to know in order to love, but "ab utroque enim notitia paritur, a cognoscente et cognito" (knowledge is born from each of the two terms, the knower as much as the known).[8] It follows that the knowledge of what is at issue in loving can be born also (and perhaps first *especially*) from the knower, even at a distance from the known. This is the case with desire: "Qui appetitus, id est inquisitio, quamvis amor esse non videatur quo id quod notum est amatur, hoc enim adhuc ut cognoscatur agitur; tamen ex eodem genere quiddam est" (This desire, or rather this search, though it does not seem like a love in the sense that one knows what one loves, for here one is still working to know, is nevertheless something of the same kind). How are we to understand the fact that desire, which does not know what it desires, would be *of the same kind* as love, which knows what it loves? Because desire (to know what it desires) gives birth to the very thing it desires: "Partum ergo mentis antecedit appetitus quidam, quo id quod nosse volumus quaerendo et inveniendo, nascitur proles ipsa notitia" (There is a certain desire that precedes the fruit of the soul; in seeking and finding what we want to know, this fruit is born, knowledge itself) (*De Trinitate* IX, 12, 18, 16, 108, 110). Desire does not here presuppose the knowledge of what it loves but precedes it, and it precedes it because it begets it. And, here, this is about nothing less than the reciprocal immanence of the soul, knowledge and love, as image of the Trinity itself. One should not be surprised, therefore, to find that the begetting by desire of that toward which it tends without, however, knowing is sometimes put in strict parallel with the situation of the *vita beata* endowed with the status of immemorial in *memoria*: "Ubi oportet ut dicam quomodo eam quaero, *utrum per recordationem*, tanquam eam oblitus sim oblitumque me esse teneam, *an per appetitum* discendi incognitam, sive quam numquam scierim, sive quam sic oblitus fuerim, ut me nec oblitum esse meminerim" (It behooves me here to say how I go about seeking it [the happy life]: *whether it be by remembering*, as if having forgotten it and [at least] retained that I forgot it, *or else by desire* to learn an as it were unknown thing, be it because I never knew it or because I forgot it in such a way that I do not even remember having forgotten it).[9] These two assignations, as different as they might be (in *memoria* and in *appetitus*), have one essential point in common: they are excepted from the exclusively theoretic (or theoretical) mode of the *mens*, now practiced by an ego understood as lover.

Thus it becomes possible to resist Heidegger's objection. At the very least, Saint Augustine does not found access to the *vita beata* on theoretic knowledge of the essence or existence of God nor even access to God in general on a knowledge of theory. First, because God does not at all enter into play as a being, not even a privileged one. Next, because desire for the happy life survives the theoretic contradiction between the end and the means of reaching it. Finally, because desire does not always depend on knowledge but begets it of itself or has recourse to the immemorial. Knowing, therefore, does not constitute in any way for Saint Augustine a "general *theory* of access"—access to the *vita beata* no longer passes through theory, even though it does pass through truth. Must we conclude then that truth itself is not reducible to theory—more exactly to its theoretic interpretation?

§17. Dual-action truth

How are we to understand truth, when it is no longer reduced to its theoretic interpretion? This question sounds strange only so long as one thinks that a truth determined by desire could only blur the evidence of the true with the arbitrariness of its obscure and reasonless aspirations. Of course, if one assumes that desire does not know what it desires or why it desires it, one would have to conclude that it does not reach truth, nor even respect it, but that it lowers it to the rank either of a phantasm to be realized or an obstacle to transgress. But truth, in the nontheoretic sense, is perhaps not equivalent to a deficiency of unveiling, as if one no longer saw clearly and distinctly what it let fade away into the hypnotic fog of a gaze that no longer sees anything by dint of intending the void. It is characterized rather by its excess. Preserving all its evidence, which it sometimes delivers as clearly and distinctly as a strictly theoretic truth, truth deploys it to so great an extent, or rather what truth puts into evidence is imposed with such power, that he who should receive it can also, sometimes or even most often, not be sufficient for it. Truth does not reveal itself in a nontheoretic sense, but this is not because it would lack evidence but because its excess of evidence opens a new question—in fact, a new ordeal. I do not mean the ordeal of seeing its evidence and noting its proof but the ordeal of bearing the power of the evidence, in which the proof itself is unveiled in itself as an ordeal for me, who encounters it, who must bear it with his gaze, and who could resist it—or not. Truth in the theoretic sense is enacted in the true and the false, which not only can (in principle) be distinguished uncontestably but, above all, do not compete with one another. For who would prefer the false to the true? In theory, but also in practice, the true is always worth more than the false, and nobody is deceived about that, whatever his or her intentions might in the end be. Even to do evil, knowing the true and defying the false is important, such that truth in the theoretic sense governs the false and the evil as well as the true, and remains morally neutral and indifferent. In contrast, in its nontheoretic sense, truth provokes a difference and bars neutrality, for it always imposes a choice on the one who receives it and undergoes it. This choice does not always belong to ethics (though it does sometimes come from it), for whoever receives the manifestation of a truth confronts, first and above all, the choice of whether (and how) to respond to it: either by the ordeal of bearing its excess, at the risk of finding himself affected, modified, altered; or by dodging this excess, at the price of a retreat before the evidence, of a retreat far from the true, from the darkling. The excess of its (theoretic) evidence leads truth to provoke two contrasting effects in the one who must undergo it and who, in fact, undergoes it as an ordeal. These two effects no longer belong to theory, without yet belonging to ethics, but point toward an authority still to be identified.

This double action of truth in excess was described by Saint Augustine in perfectly precise terms in a text that is as decisive as it is unique: "Cur autem 'veritas parit odium' et 'inimicus eis factus est homo tuus verum praedicans,' cum ametur vita beata, quae non est nisi gaudium de veritate, nisi quia sic amatur veritas, ut, quicumque aliud amant, hoc quod amant velint esse veritatem, et quia falli nollent, nolunt convici, quod falsi sint? Itaque propter eam rem oderunt veritatem, quam pro veritate amant. Amant eam lucentem, oderunt eam redarguentem" (Why is it that "the truth gives birth to hatred" and "the man who belongs to you and proclaims the true becomes their enemy" [John 8:40 and Galatians 4:16], when [everyone] loves the happy life, which is nothing other than to enjoy truth? Is it not because [everyone] loves truth in such a way that [all] those who love something else [besides this very truth] want for this other thing that they love to be [also] the truth, and, as they do not want to suffer any illusions, they do want [any the more to admit] to be deceived? This is why they hate truth, out of consideration for the thing they love instead and in the place of the truth. They love the light insofar as it illuminates [them], but hate it insofar as it accuses [them]).[10] One and the same truth therefore provokes two effects: love, but also (and here the decisive point arrives) hatred. Far from producing its effect just in theory, it provokes it even in the practical sphere. That is, truth is not limited to manifesting to me this or that thing over which I could now exercise judgment; rather, by manifesting this state of things with perfect evidence, truth forces me to make a decision regarding it, for or against its evidence, and in accordance with my decision—to accept or refuse the evidence—truth flies back in my face, and my in-principle theoretic judgment about its evidence turns back against me, or rather makes me turn back against myself, my own judgment: I love it, or I hate it. Truth does not accomplish just a judgment about the state of things, but, by the same token, it exercises a judgment about myself, for if in refusing or accepting the evidence, I do not change the world of things, at least I change myself by setting for myself a radical mode of attunement, love or hate. Paradoxically enough, more essentially than a judgment about things (true or false), more essentially even than the manifestation of the phenomenon by itself, the truth produces a verdict about myself, according as I can accept it or can only reject it—love it or hate it. In this sense my relation to the truth does not fall ultimately under the jurisdiction of theory but practice.

At least a certain sort of practice. Truth is no longer defined merely by the two values of truth (the true and the false) but ultimately by the two effects (and two modes of attunement) produced in me by its evidence. Either acceptance of the truth, when it shines, or rather when nobody offers opposition to what it shines, when nobody represses it and wants to remove himself from it—*veritas lucens*. Or rejection of the truth, which does not lead to extinguishing or obfuscating it—since nothing can put up a screen to the light, which embraces all things, royally and irresistibly—but only to attempting not to see it, or even, since one cannot not see it, to attempting not to see *oneself* illuminated by it; repressing the light does not mean casting a shadow on it (with what shadow?), nor hiding from it (in what night?), but hiding from oneself the fact that one cannot hide from it—*veritas redarguens*. These two effects come from the same evidence of the true, which therefore incites the rejection that refuses as well as the acceptance that lets it shine. "Nam etiam sol iste et videntis faciem illustrat, et caeci; ambo pariter stantes, et faciem ad solem habentes, illustrantur in carne, sed non ambo illuminantur in acie; videt ille, ille non videt; ambobus sol praesens est sed praesenti soli unus est absens" (The sun illuminates the face of the sighted as well as the face of the blind. Both alike stand and, facing the sun, are illuminated by it in their flesh, but their sight is not illuminated. The one sees; the other does not. The sun is present to both, but one is absent from the sun, alone present).[11] Hence, not only can truth impose itself in proportion to its evidence (the more the evidence is manifest, the more truth is set forth), but it can also be rejected in proportion to this same evidence (the more the evidence is manifest, the more truth is obscured, *the less* it is set forth). Now, there are some cases in which one refuses the truth precisely *because* it is manifest with more evidence. For truth touches and affects first the one who sees it and who, being unable to obscure its flash, can only choose between accepting or repressing it, loving it or hating it. Still more than its self-disclosure and self-withdrawal, it belongs to the essence of truth that I remain always free to reject its evidence as such, though without being released from the necessity of undergoing it, be it only by repressing it through its very own rebound. For it "questions my own facticity and existence."[12]

The repulsive effect of truth, which duplicates its more commonly admitted attractive effect, is not just a marginal issue. There is no short-age of texts describing it.[13] For example, just before the conversion: "Tu autem, Domine, inter verba ejus *retorquebas* me ad me ipsum, auferens me a dorso meo, ubi me posueram, dum nollem me adtendere, et constitue-bas me ante faciem meam, ut viderem, quam turpis essem" (It was you, my Lord, who, through these words [those of Ponticianus, recounting the conversions of the *agentes in rebus*], *turned me back* to myself, lifting me up from behind myself, where I had put myself so as not to have to look myself in the face, and who put me face-to-face with myself so that I saw how ugly I was) (*Confessiones* VIII, 7, 16, 14, 42). Here the truth *redarguens* disconcerts me, by making me face it, which means phenomenally that it first makes me face myself, therefore face my own judgment, which itself exercises truth over me. The state of continual temptation, at first glance insurmountable, is described in the same terms: "Ideoque consideravi languores peccatorum meorum in cupiditate triplici et dexteram tuam invocavi ad salutem meam. Vidi enim splendorem tuum corde saucio et *repercussus* dixi: quis illuc potest? '*Projectus* sum a facie oculorum tuorum.' Tu es veritas super omnia praesidens. At ego per avaritiam meam non amittere te volui, sed volui tecum possidere mendacium" (I considered the languors of my sins in their triple lust [the concupiscences of sensing, knowing, and the glory of the world], and I called on your right hand to save me. For I saw your splendor with a wounded heart and, *pressed back* [by this shock], I said: who can reach you? 'I was *rejected*, cast far from the face of your gaze' (Psalm 30:23). You are truth that presides over all things, but I myself, following my greed, I did not want to lose, but I wanted to possess at the same time as you lying) (X, 41, 66, 14, 260). The contrary of truth is not found simply in error or falsehood but in lying: wanting to keep, in addition to the true, the false, because one loves it as much as, indeed more than, the true.

What is more remarkable, the permanent temptation happens to be described (at the end of *Confessiones* X) in almost the very same terms as the first moment that follows the conversion (in the opening of *Confessiones* X): "Et tibi quidem, Domine, cujus 'oculis nuda est' abyssus humanae conscientiae, quid occultum esset in me, etiamsi nollem confiteri tibi? Te enim mihi absconderem, non me tibi. Nunc autem quod gemitus meus testis est displicere me mihi, tu *refulges*, et places et amaris et desideraris, ut erubescam de me et *abjiciam* me atque eligam te, nec tibi nec mihi placeam, nisi de te. Tibi ergo, Domine, manifestus sum, quicumque sim" (And for you, my Lord, "to whose eyes is laid bare" [Hebrews 4:13] the abyss of human conscience, what would remain hidden in me, even if I did not want to confess it to you? I would be hiding you from myself, but I would not be hiding myself from you. But now that my groaning witnesses my displeasure with myself, you *turn back* onto me your light, you become a pleasure to me, you become loved and desired by me, so that I am embarrassed about myself and *reject* myself in favor of choosing you, you yourself, and so as not to be pleasing to myself nor to you, except by following you. For whoever I might be, I am manifest to you, my Lord) (X, 2, 2, 14, 142). Here the light of God floods every man, therefore accuses him by manifesting his sin, and this manifestation cannot be obscured, even if it is denied. For *accusing*, here, should first be understood in the optical sense (rare in modern English, though more common in today's French and in older forms of English) according to which the light accuses the depth and the lines of what it strikes, a sense used from time to time by painters. The divine light does not persecute or indict but simply radiates—which is all it has to do to bring to evidence every deformity, therefore my own, me who am sinner. The choice, therefore, does not consist in either letting oneself be accused by the light or not letting oneself be accused, since the light by definition accuses. The choice consists either in identifying myself with what in me is accused and therefore, in this case, will accuse me or else in detaching myself from what in me accuses me and excluding it from myself. In this case the light will no longer accuse me but will spill back over me (*refulgere*) as what I can then love and desire. For since I can appear only in one sole light, that of God, bearing the truth thus done over me means bearing the sight of my sinner's deformity. Bearing it does not mean making it mine, however, nor letting myself be reducible to it; rather, it means not denying my deformity and, by admitting it, finding myself at once free from it. In recognizing it, I am detached from it, and in seeing myself in its light, I appear to myself illuminated by it. In short, to not hate the light, it must be loved more than oneself, at least more than the self, whose traits it accuses. If, in contrast, I love myself, however deformed, more than the light that accuses me, then I will have to hate it, since it will continue to accuse me, and I will also have to love myself as deformed. And in this way I will end up hating myself as much as I hate the truth.

§18. Hatred of truth

The two effects of truth now established, we need to understand this quite particular determination of truth as either to love or to hate. On the surface there is no difficulty admitting it is appropriate to love the truth, while the mere hypothesis of hating it seems absurd, almost insane. Isn't it always worth more to know the truth than to remain ignorant of it, and, in the end, who would prefer remaining in error? One can, of course, wonder if it is better to remain ignorant of an unpleasant truth than to know it or to hold as true good news that is false rather than be disabused of one's illusion, but that remains tangential. And yet, considered a bit more closely, the love of truth might not be any more self-evident than the hatred that one bears it; for, on principle, the true gives itself to knowing, not loving or hating, and there is no need for it to inspire such desires. Or else, if it must give itself to loving, this would not be inasmuch as true (for the understanding) but inasmuch as desirable (for the will). In this respect perhaps it will become lovable or hateable but exactly in the measure to which, each time it manifests itself, it would appear *by excess* as agreeable to the one who already knows it. The true sometimes incites love, sometimes indifference, sometimes even hatred, not in proportion to its truth but solely to its interest. Do we have to conclude from this that the truth would become hateable and therefore lovable only from a viewpoint essentially different from that of the true and the false? Without a doubt, we do, except if, in a sense still to be determined, the truth could, *as such*, make itself loved or hated; in other words, if the truth could make itself loved or hated not because he who first knew it could *then* desire it or refuse it by his optional commentary but because knowing it would *intrinsically* imply either loving it or hating it. In this case love could open, as a condition of its possibility, truth—love making truth, instead of (as in common usage) truth making (the possibility of) love. This would also imply in turn that hatred renders truth impossible, refuses it, and buries it. But which truth—which mode of truth—could be thus determinable by love and hate? Quite obviously, it must be the one that assumes them as the very conditions of its own possibility. The question then becomes: which truth can be disclosed only to the one who loves it and must be covered for the one who hates it? Or, in other words, before what truth does love serve to unveil and hate to cover?

Hatred of truth as a theme[14] does not originate with Saint Augustine; it admits at least two other sources. One, profane, comes from Terence, in his *Andria*: "Obsequium amicos, veritas parit odium" (Flattery begets friends, but truth hatred).[15] Cicero consecrates it by commenting on this line, "I do not know how or why, but what my friend says in his *Andria* is true: 'Flattery begets friends, but truth hatred.' Painful is friendship, when it gives birth to hatred, which is the poison of friendship; but flattery is all the more painful because he who proves indulgent of sins lets his friend stick his neck out first."[16] The other, biblical, comes from John 8:40: "Now you want to kill me for having told you the truth that I heard from God?" This perhaps echoes Proverbs 27:5–6: "Fideliora sunt vulnera amici quam voluntaria oscula inimici" (More sure are the wounds of a friend than the fake kisses of an enemy).[17] But these two origins (which sometimes can be confused)[18] do not settle what is fundamental to the question. For these texts leave undetermined the reason and the manner in which love and hatred could decide the truth and therefore fix its conditions.

How can love unveil truth? To understand this, we begin by taking hatred as our foothold—always more simple to conceive because in itself more simple—and ask why, more strangely still, it covers over truth. In the simple intersubjective situation (described by Terence and the Proverbs), hatred of truth means only that all truth is not good to say since it can contravene the interests or intentions of the one who is taught it. Here the hatred is not directed precisely at the information delivered but at the friend who teaches and becomes bearer of bad tidings. At this stage one refuses to see the truth; one denies its evidence; one lies; but one does not yet hate it for itself. It is the witnesses to it that one hates and that one kills. To hate truth directly, another case is called for, one in which the message itself becomes the enemy. The messenger or the witness must no longer be distinguished from the proclamation and the statement; the truth itself must become its own messenger or the messenger become the truth—that is to say, he must incarnate it. Now, it is no longer the case of a mere apophantic utterance about a state of things, transmitted by a supposed friend, but of the person of this friend in the form of a truth concerning me. Hatred (therefore also love) of the truth supposes that he who announces it to me coincides with what he announces, this very truth. Strictly speaking, hatred can *truly* be directed against the truth only if it is directed against a witness who dares to say: "I am the way, the truth, and the life" (John 14:6). Hatred (and love) of the truth can be addressed only to he who claims to incarnate the truth. It proves therefore epistemologically Christological, therefore theological. For it alone can both advise me and itself constitute the advice, verify and say what it verifies. The theme now poses an absolutely new question: not only does it ask if truth can provoke the hatred of the one who teaches it but, above all, if the truth that God teaches me about myself can make me hate, in this truth, God himself.

To respond to this question, we must first understand how the mode of manifestation of what Saint Augustine here names truth can provoke hatred (and for that matter also love). But since it is a question of a mode of manifestation, it is a question of phenomenality. It behooves us, then, to sketch a phenomenology of hatred, starting from the phenomenon, from *this* phenomenon of truth.

§19. Evidential excess

If this truth incites hatred in the very degree to which it manifests itself, it owes this no doubt to its mode of manifestation. This mode of manifestation is characterized, we will see, by the excess in it of intuition. I will describe it by distinguishing four stages.

The first stage consists precisely in the *excess* of evidence in which truth manifests itself. A text describes this figure exactly: "vidi enim splendorem tuum corde *saucio* et *repercussus* dixi: quis illus potest? 'Projectus sum a facie oculorum tuorum'" (I saw your splendor with a heart *wounded* and *repelled* [by this shock]. I said, who can reach it? "I was rejected far from the face of your sight" [Psalm 30:23]) (*Confessiones* X, 41, 66, 14, 260). The evidence wounds and is attested by the sorrow that it provokes. Wound and sorrow do not result here from a prior fault or sin but from the disproportion between the intensity of the intuition dispensed and the resistance of he who finds himself exposed to it, without being able to perceive anything adequately. And this suffering is first of all described as a physical pain: "Et sensi expertus non esse mirum quod . . . oculis ageris odiosa lux, quae puris amabilis" (And I understood by experience that there is nothing so surprising in the fact that the [same] light that pure eyes can love should be odious to sick eyes) (VII, 16, 22, 13, 626). And when it is a matter of explaining why the crowd cannot recognize Christ, that is to say see him as such—in short, believe what it sees and believe its own eyes—Saint Augustine refers to the same sickness in the eyes, ophthalmia, after exposure to an excess of light: "Turbs turbata est. Unde? A veritate. Turbam lippitudinis turbavit claritas lucis. Oculi enim non habentes sanitatem non possunt ferre luminis claritatem" (The crowd was maddened. Where did that come from? It came from truth itself. What maddened the crowd struck with ophthalmia was the very clarity of the light. For eyes that are not healthy cannot bear the clarity).[19] Thus is specified the first figure of intuitive excess: the experience of a pain and a powerlessness still spiritually neutral—what John 16:12 formulates with a simple observation: "I still have many things to say to you, but you are not yet equal to bearing them."

But the second stage does not stay on the level of neutrality; it determines it as a *refusal of the ordeal* of this excess. Saint Augustine defines it by combining the conclusion of Plato's myth of the cave and the Johannine description of bedazzlement. It involves a pain but one that befalls a weakness struck in return: "et pervenit [sc. ratiocinans potentia] ad id quod est in ictu trepidantis aspectus. Tunc vero 'invisibilia tua per ea quae facta sunt intellecta' conspexi, sed aciem figere non evalui et *repercussa* infirmitate *redditus* solitis non mecum ferebam nisi amantem memoriam" (and [my rational power] arrived at that which is, in the blink of a trembling eye. Then I truly saw "your invisible works made intelligible by what you made" [Romans 1:20], but I did not have the strength to fix my aim to it and, *sent back* in my weakness, I *returned* to my petty old habits, keeping in me only a loving memory) (VII, 17, 23, 13, 628ff.). This frank description of a failed contemplative ascent closes the purely philosophical attempts from which the Mediator is absent. It makes all the greater an impression as it describes its *success*. In fact, I could, for an instant, see the invisible through the visible, conforming to the promise (or program) of Saint Paul, but precisely lacking strength (*non evalui*), I could not reside within this vision, where I remained only for an instant; I lacked the intentionality. I therefore returned to the prior, habitual, empty situation. The decline from the contemplative ascent results from a weakness of the intention and leads back, as for Plato, into the usual obscurity of the cave. What remains is only to at least acknowledge that what sends me back far from God stems precisely from the violence of his splendor: "Cum te [sc. aeterna veritas et vera caritas] primum cognovi, tu assumsisti me, ut viderem esse quod viderem et nondum me esse qui viderem. Et *reverberasti* infirmitatem aspectus mei *radians in me vehementer* et contremui amore et horrore" (When I first knew you [eternal truth and true charity], you took me up so as to make me see that there was something to see, but that I was not yet there to see it. You *reflected back* onto itself the weakness of my gaze, *shining violently upon me*, and I trembled with love and horror) (VII, 10, 16, 13, 616). Once again, I tremble and find myself sent back again into my own obscurity only by the violence of the light, whose excess overwhelms me. The pain, which makes the attempts at a gaze yield, attests the splendor that it flees.[20] Thus the second figure of excess leads from the simple pain to the refusal of the suffering by the decidedly attested and detested weakness of the gaze. The evidence of truth not only makes whoever approaches it suffer but sends back, rejects, and pushes down whoever pretends to see it, or even desires to see it.

A third stage follows. Since the radiance of truth provokes a suffering, there will be some *relief* in removing oneself from it. "Alii vero ipso quem videre vehementer desiderant, *fulgore feriuntur*, et eo non viso saepe in tenebras, *cum delectatione* redeunt" (Some *become struck by the flash* of what they eagerly desire to see, and, as they did not see it, it is often with *pleasure* that they return to their darkness).[21] This pleasure comes from the relief of slipping away from truth, even if one must, to succeed, repudiate it: "Quod qui prius volunt facere [sc. aspectum dirigere in id quod videndum est] quam mundati et sanati fuerint, ita *luce reverberantur veritatis*, ut non solum nihil boni, sed etiam mali plurimum in ea putent esse, atque ab ea nomen *veritatis* abjudicent, et cum *quadam libidine et voluptate miserabili in suas* tenebras. . . refugiant" (Those who want to do it [sc. direct their gaze toward what must be seen] before being washed and purified will find that *the light of truth repels them* such that they think that it contains not only nothing good, but even evil, to the point that they will deny it the very name *truth* and flee to the shelter of their darkness *with a sort of desire and miserable pleasure*).[22] After the pain before truth comes the pleasure of fleeing it, but this pleasure itself would remain unbearable if it had to keep an awareness of the truth that it fled, or more exactly the awareness that what it flees remains the truth, it alone. Consequently, flight before truth must itself be justified by denying truth its very status as truth. Thus is put in place an inverted logic of truth: the evidence saturates the manifestation of truth, which therefore submerges and repels the intention. By contrast, this intention withdraws, curses the truth, disqualifies it, and in the end hates it. Thus arises a hatred not first moral but purely phenomenological—a powerlessness to bear by phenomenalizing the evidential excess of truth, which it ends up recusing—so as not to want to see what it nevertheless sees.

The fourth stage, strictly speaking the first to actually exercise a hatred of truth, bears on a *choice*. For the excess of its manifestation, which makes truth an ordeal, leads to a choice: either flee it so as to avoid its pain, or confront its pain so as to see it. The spectator's choice, or rather the necessity that he or she choose, which forbids one from remaining an indifferent spectator, results from the constitutive ambivalence of saturation. Saint Augustine left it to his mother, Monica, to explain this: "Deum nemo non habere, sed eum qui bene vivit, habet propitium, qui male, infestum" (There is nobody who does not have God; but he who lives well has him as favorable, while he who lives badly has him as enemy). Every man possesses God, but every man who possesses God does not receive from him the *vita beata* because it is necessary that God be favorable to him. How does God show himself favorable or hostile? In fact, the alternative does not come from God but from man—according as his way of living puts him in agreement with God or not: "Qui bene vivit, habet Deum, sed propitium; qui male, habet Deum, sed adversum" (He who lives well has God, God favorable; he who lives badly has him too, but hostile).[23] For the question does not concern access to God (who does not live in and through him?) but the mode of this access—more exactly, the mode by which each manages the disproportion of this access. The manifestation of God in truth (of truth inasmuch as God alone makes it) can only surpass the capacity of sight, therefore impose a suffering, which stems from the discrepancy and renders it manifest. This conflict between the gaze and what it can[not] see obliges me to choose: either refuse the truth so as not to have to bear it and to remain what I now am, or accept it and make it incumbent on me to become other than what I now am. In the first case, to protect oneself from the truth, one prefers to defend falsity itself: "Sed duo sunt quae in errore hominum difficillime tolerantur: praesumptio, priusquam veritas pateat; et, cum jam patuerit, praesumptae defensio falsitatis" (But in the error of men there are two perfectly unbearable things: presuming something before truth unveils itself; and, once it is unveiled, defending the presumed falsity) (*De Trinitate* II, 1, 1, 15, 182). And the defense of falsity becomes a defense *against* truth. In the second case, to stand steadfast before the evidential excess, one accepts accusation by the truth, so as to be able to confess it: "Ad ipsum fuge confitendo, non ab ipso latendo: latere enim non potes, sed confiteri potes" (Flee toward him by confessing instead of hiding from him; for you cannot hide, but you can confess).[24]

Thus, he alone can see the truth who confesses it—that is, he who, in order to carry out the praising confession, accepts confessing his own faults. If I do not accuse myself (and thus liberate myself) of my faults, truth will not be able not to accuse them in me by its light, and I will not be able not to hate it. Truth and falsity uncover, in the final analysis, a question of love and hate: "Quomodo enim diligent Patrem veritatis, qui haberent odio veritatem? Nolunt enim sua facta damnari, et hoc habet veritas ut talia facta damnuntur; tantum igitur oderunt veritatem, quantum oderunt suas poenas, quas talibus irrogat veritas" (For how will they love the Father of truth, those who will have hated the truth? They do not want to see their acts condemned, while it is the truth's task to condemn such acts. Consequently, they hated truth exactly inasmuch as they hated the pains that the truth exacts of them).[25] Thus, hatred of truth only inverts the first hatred, that each bears for himself and his own faults. As a result, hatred of truth attests self-hatred and therefore the self's own self-contradiction. The more I see those who love God, "tanto exsecrabilius me comparatum eis oderam" (the more, finding myself execrable by comparison, I hated myself) (*Confessiones* VIII, 7, 17, 14, 42).

It is necessary, therefore, at the end of these four stages (excess, refusal of the ordeal, relief, and the choice) to be decided about the truth: either deny its evidence and hide from it, or admit its radiance by confessing it. So long as I refuse to choose, I will contradict in myself the desire for the happy life; I will therefore contradict myself: "et *differebam* 'de die in diem' vivere in te et non *differebam* quotidie in memet ipso mori: amans beatam vitam timebam illam in sede sua et ab ea fugiens quaerebam illam" (and I *deferred* "from day to day" [Sirach 5, 8], *deferring* to live in you, and I did not *defer* dying daily in myself. All the while loving the happy life, I dreaded it there where it is [in you], and while fleeing it, I was seeking it).[26] The contradiction, indicated by my impossibility of choosing for or against truth, attests that knowing the truth is no longer enough, *here*, for admitting it, since, sometimes, the more I know it, the more I reject it. The truth, in the unshirkable excess of its evidence, can make itself seen and accepted only by he who loves it and therefore might also hate it.

§20. Love of truth

These four stages have enabled us only to describe the decision that leads to hatred of the truth. It remains to be understood why one can, indeed inevitably must, at a given moment, come to this hatred. Only then will it become possible to conceive in reverse how love can apply to truth and how that which does the truth becomes the doing of love.

Just as the final evasion of truth consisted, we just saw, in avoiding the choice, the first movement of truth consists in referring me to judgment, in putting me before myself ("retorquebas me ad me ipsum" [you put me again face-to-face with myself]) and putting my decision right in my face: "tu *me* rursus *opponebas mihi* et impigebas me in oculos meos, ut invenirem iniquitatem meam et odissem. Noveram eam, sed dissimulabam et cohibam et obliviscar" (and *you again put me face-to-face with myself;* you thrust me before my own eyes, so that I might discover my iniquity and hate it. I knew it well, but I hid it [from myself], I winked at it, and forgot it) (*Confessiones* VII, 7, 16, 14, 42). For, the truth now no longer consists, at bottom, in a judgment that I would make about some third party (predication), nor in a factual state (the unveiling of a phenomenon), but in a judgment that I must make about myself, such that it becomes for me an ordeal—an ordeal of truth. *The proof of the truth consists in the ordeal of truth.* And therefore nontruth will not consist merely, nor even first of all, in an inadequate statement or a real dissimulation but in the avoidance of this ordeal of truth—in lying. "Volui tecum possidere mendacium" (I wanted to possess, at the same time as having you, the lie) (X, 41, 66, 14, 260). The contrary of truth is now no longer called falsity (with respect to the thing) or error (according to knowledge) but lying (on the part of its recipient). While falsity concerns a statement and error a state of things, lying refers me directly to myself. When I lie, I lie first and always to myself.

It is therefore a matter of describing the originary lie. Now, it does not consist in not desiring the *vita beata*, nor even in not wanting what God manifests and gives, but in desiring them and wanting them in such a way that I dispense with God at the very moment when I appropriate what he dispenses to me. A wonderful text describes this process:

Multa enim per cupiditatem pravam, tanquam sui sit oblita, sic agit. (a) Videt enim quaedam intrinsecus pulchra, *in praestantiore natura quae Deus est.* (b) Et, cum stare debeat ut eis fruatur (c) volens *ea sibi* tribuere, et *non ex illo similis illius, sed ex se ipsa esse quod ille est* (d) avertitur ab eo, moveturque et labitur *in minus et minus,* quod putat amplius et amplius; quia nec ipsa sibi nec ei quidquam sufficit recedenti ab illo qui solus sufficit. (e) Ideoque per egestatem ac difficultatem fit nomis intenta in actiones suas et inquietas delectationes quas per eas colligit; atque ita cupiditate acquirendi notitias ex eis quae foris sunt . . . perdit *securitatem.*

The soul, by a perverse desire and as if forgetful of itself, acts in this way. (a) It sees certain intrinsically beautiful things *in the magnificent nature that God is.* (b) And, while it should stand [in this divine nature] to enjoy these things, (c) wanting to attribute *them to itself,* and [wanting] to be *like him without him, but being on its own basis what he is,* (d) it turns away from him, leaves, and falls lower and lower while believing itself to go higher and higher, because it is no more satisfied with itself than with anything else whatsoever, as soon as it grows apart from he who alone is enough to satisfy. (e) And then its destitution and weariness make it too attentive to its own actions and the troubled pleasures that it gathers. And so the desire to acquire bits of knowledge from external things . . . takes away from it all security. (*De Trinitate* X, 5, 7, 16, 134 [I have added the divisions])

Let us retrace the steps of so precise a phenomenological description. (a) First comes the love of beauty, therefore of the *vita beata,* which remains the undisputed principle, just as the location of this beauty in God remains undisputed—in God, that is to say, outside me. By "beauty," truth itself must be understood, but inasmuch as desired (see below, §22). (b) But love of truth, which desires beauty, does not want to unite with it in such a way as to leave it external and extrinsic, shining with an other brilliance—in short, as the sign of an other than it. The self wants to reach the beauty of the true, but by possessing and assimilating it, therefore by uprooting it from its external site, whereas the self should shine "non sua luce, sed summae illius lucis participatione" (not from its own light, but by participation in this highest light) (XIV, 12, 15, 16, 386).[27] The deviance does not concern the true and the beautiful, which still remain desire's target, but the mode of access to this goal: either by direct possession, as if I could annul God's exteriority, or by participation, in recognizing this irreducible exteriority. It is not a matter of identifying the phenomenon, manifest in truth, but of the mode (the *how*) of its manifestation. (c) The fault is committed most exactly when I want to make myself like God without however becoming so by him and on the basis of him, but by myself only: "non ex illo *similis* illius, sed ex se ipsa." The deviance does not concern, here either, the will to imitate God (it is *always* a matter of becoming like God) but the mode of this imitation: either because God gives it to me or because I acquire it by and for myself. The mode of imitation turns out perverse (wrong-way, way-out) when I pretend to imitate God without God, but by I myself alone, who am not, however, God: "Ita fornicatur anima, cum avertitur abs te et quaerit extra te ea quae pura et liquida non invenit, nisi cum redit ad te. *Perverse te imitantur* omnes, qui longe se a te faciunt et extollunt se adversum te. Sed etiam sic te *imitando* indicant creatorem te esse omnis naturae et ideo non esse, quo a te omni modo recedatur" (The soul fornicates thus, when it turns away from you and seeks outside you limpid purities that can be found only by returning to you. They imitate you *with a perverse imitation* who become strangers to you and stand against you. But even *in imitating you* so, they still point to you as creator of all nature, and there is no place where they can retire in any way far from you) (*Confessiones* II, 6, 14, 13, 354). The fault consists in wanting to imitate God crookedly (*perverse*) by pretending to imitate him *without him*, indeed *against him*: "Incipiens *a perverso appetitu similitudinis* Dei, pervenit ad similitudinem peccorum" (Beginning *with a perverse appetite for likeness* to God, it ends by becoming like only to the beasts).[28] In this way, one could say, the lie is proven: one can use this contradiction in terms because lying does not and cannot produce any frank opposition to the truth, as if it opposed to it a counterpossibility but can do nothing more than turn the truth away, more exactly turn it back against itself: not repudiating the beauty and truth of God, nor contesting its brilliance, but carrying it out without or even against it, appropriating it without receiving it, without having to pass through the reception of a gift. Lying does not dissimulate the truth; it falsifies it—it keeps it such, but by pretending to keep it for itself, indeed to produce it by itself, it pretends to say it, but it wants to say it on its own behalf, as coming from itself: "non quia homo ipse *mendacium* est, cum sit ejus auctor creatorque Deus, qui non est utique auctor creatorque mendacii, sed quia homo ita factus est rectus, ut non secundum se ipsum, sed secundum eum, a quo factus est, viveret, id est illius potius quam suam faceret voluntatem; non ita vivere, quam ad modum est factus ut viveret, hoc est mendacium" (not because man himself would be a lie since his author and creator is God, who is absolutely not the author and creator of lies, but because man was made right in order to live not according to himself but according to him by whom he was made, that is to say to do the will of his creator rather than his own. Not to live in the way of life for which he was made, that is lying).[29] Lying does not invert the truth any more than it obscures it; it just perverts its mode of manifestation by substituting one possessive pronoun for another: "Cum vero malus sum, nihil aliud confiteri *tibi*, quam displicere *mihi*; cum vero pius, nihil aliud confiteri *tibi* quam hoc *non* tibuere *mihi*" (Confessing *to you* when I am bad is nothing other than being displeased *with myself*; but when I am pious, confessing *to you* is nothing other than *not attributing it to myself*).[30] The entire difference depends on the *as* employed by the hermeneutic gaze: does it see beauty as a gift, which makes God visible, or as a good to appropriate so as to become the equal of God—ἁρπαγμὸν τὸ εἶναι ἴσα θεῷ (Philippians 2:6)?

The last two steps finally describe the loss of self prompted by the fact of wanting to appropriate it. (d) This contradiction of desire, when it wants to be self-possessed, arises because the good, as soon as it is possessed, loses by definition the divine infinity and assumes the measure of its possessor, finiteness. The good evaporates precisely because it finds itself possessed, therefore finally lost. "Viderunt quo veniendum esset; sed ingrati ei qui illis praestitit quod viderunt, *sibi* voluerunt tribuere quod viderunt; et facti superbi omiserunt quod videbant, et conversi sunt inde ad idola et simulacra et ad culturas daemoniorum, adorare creaturas et contemnere Creatorem" (They [sc. the philosophers seeking the Creator through creatures] saw where to go, but ungrateful to he who had provided them what they saw, they wanted to attribute *to themselves* what they saw, and, gripped by pride, they forgot what they saw, and they were turned from it to idols, statues, and the cult of demons, adoring the creature and despising God).[31] By refusing the origin of a good, one in fact disqualifies all its intrinsic goodness, and what one ends up possessing already lost all reason for wanting to possess it. (e) From this follows the loss of oneself in proportion to the loss of goodness of the good diverted, to which the soul is stuck ("glutino amoris" [by the glue of love]) and is in the end assimilated: "aliud secum amando cum eo se confudit et concrevit quodam modo" (by loving with oneself something other than oneself, it is confused with it and concretized in it, as one).[32] This is the law of idolatry: I always become what I intend and possess; if I intend less than God, I will become less than him, *therefore less than myself.*

From this we understand better how truth comes to incite hatred. The remaining difficulty resides in the paradox that truth is always again loved, even at the moment when it suffers hatred. That is, when I want to hide a truth that displeases me or harms me, or rather (for can one ever truly hide the truth?) when I try to hide this truth from myself (but can I do so for very long?), or finally when I have no goal greater than to hide myself from the truth, I nevertheless do not repudiate this truth any more than I repudiate myself. To the contrary, I want to keep intact and mutually compatible the truth and myself, without choosing between them: "volui tecum possidere mendacium, sicut nemo vult ita falsum dicere, ut nesciat ipse, quid verum sit. Itaque amisi te, quia non dignaris cum mendacio possideri" (I wanted to possess the lie at the same time as you since nobody wants to say the false to the point of no longer knowing himself what is true. Consequently, I also lost you, because you do not condescend to being possessed together with lies) (*Confessiones* X, 41, 66, 14, 260). The ordeal that truth imposes on me, and that does so contrarily (*redarguens*), consists entirely in the injunction to choose between it and me. I do want to make this choice because I love truth as much as myself. To be sure, I want to keep safe my possession of myself (possibly against God *interior intimo meo*), but I also want to keep it in the truth and even justify it by the truth. At no moment does lying want to rid itself of truth; it wants only to be composed with it, to the point of decomposing it, but without ever assuming falsity as such. The lie—self-possession by oneself, without God—does not deny the truth; it falsifies it, precisely so as to keep at least the appearance of it. And therefore, to save the authority of truth without however renouncing self-possession, the lie tries to qualify as truth this very possession of myself by myself. Far from renouncing the truth, the liar tries to make it such that what he prefers (the idol that he loves) to the truth holds precisely the place of truth: "quicumque aliud, hoc quod amant velint esse veritatem" (they want that truth should be something else [provided] that they love it). Far from refusing truth, the liar wants to lay hold of it because he loves it in his own way. Since he cannot love the real truth, he wants to transform what he loves into apparent truth, so as to oppose truth to truth: "propter eam rem, oderunt veritatem, quam pro veritate amant" (they hate the truth on account of the thing that they love in place of the truth). An additional truth is necessary for me to slip away from the real truth, lacking which the liar would be convicted of lying (of not loving the truth itself but a substitute), something he rightly fears above all else: "quia enim falli nollent, nolunt convinci quod falsi sunt" (because they would not accept being deceived, they did not admit being convinced of deception).[33] Lying still lies in the name of truth, or at least of its feigned truth—lying always lies truly. Even in this lie, more than the counterfeit truth, it is a matter of the truth itself. "Tu es veritas supra omnia praesidens. At ego per avaritiam meam non amittere te volui, sed volui tecum possidere mendacium" (You are the truth, who presides over all things. As for me, in my greed, I did not want to lose you, but I [nevertheless] wanted to possess lies at the same time as you) (X, 41, 66, 14, 260). And therefore, even for lying, a relation to truth must still be maintained—be it only *redarguens*, adverse, and accusing of my attachment to what I myself know quite clearly, thanks to the *veritas lucens*, not being the truth, but the love of a disappearing good that I want to keep in my possession. Far from hating the *veritas redarguens*, I love it still and doubly: first, I love the false good that I prefer to God (whence the first lie); next, I love the *veritas* itself, before which I want to justify my refusal to love God (whence a second lie). Not only does *veritas* appear as an affair of love and therefore of hate, but the hatred of the *veritas redarguens* still witnesses, and radically so, to a love, inverted, of truth.

Self-love to the point of despising God thus exercises an epistemological function: it transforms the falsity of self-love into false truth because it undergoes the *veritas lucens* as an ordeal that impugns it in that it appears to it as a *veritas redarguens*. Of this epistemological function, there is no lack of concrete examples in Saint Augustine. There was, first of all, that of the Manicheans, "superbe delirantes" (delirious with pride).[34] That is, by situating the origin of evil (which is human) in God, they pretended to become wise by attributing to themselves what is God's, or, by a still more perverse blindness, even claimed to attribute to God what came only from them alone.[35] There was next that anonymous, mediocre philosopher who had a response for everything, one drawn from Aristotle's *Categories*, "buccis tyfo crepantibus" (chomping his jaws with pride).[36] There were, finally, and above all, the Neoplatonists, who, like this "immanissimo tyfo turgidum" (man inflated with an absolutely monstrous pride),[37] could not admit the rationality of the scriptures. That is, the reading and interpretation of the scriptures constitute the most perfect example of a truth that remains obscure as long as one does not come to it with love and through love of the truth—of *their* truth, which bears only on love itself (all the rest being figurative). Nowhere does the truth become *veritas redarguens* so much as when the pride of the philosophers, that is to say the arrogance of our reason, confronts the Word of God. As a contrast we can hold up the several rules for interpretation of the scriptures that are set, in book XII of *Confessiones*, by the requirements of charity.

First of all, discussion becomes possible only among those who already admit in principle the truth of what truth teaches ("qui haec omnia, quae intus in mente non tacet veritas tua, vera esse concedunt" [XII, 15, 22–XII, 16, 23, 14, 376ff.]). Next, on the basis of this assumption of the truth of scriptures, it seems legitimate to add to the true sense suggested by the sacred author a second true sense, that of the interpreter— and therefore the legitimacy of several true senses (XII, 18, 27, 14, 384; and XIII, 24, 37, 14, 496). But once this plurality of the true is admitted, how can one choose among several readings and claim, for example, that "non hoc sensit Moysen, quod tu dicis, sed hoc sensit, quod ego dico" (Moses did not think what you say; rather, what he thought is what I am saying)?[38] One can do so, if the demand is that an interpretation be based on the text, and that one abandon it if he does not succeed. But this claim becomes unacceptable if the rivals

amant suam sententiam, non quia vera est, sed quia sua est. Alioquin et aliam veram pariter *amarent*, sicut *amo*, quod dicunt, quando verum dicunt, non jam quia ipsorum est, sed quia verum est: et ideo jam nec ipsorum est, quia verum est. Si autem ideo *ament* illud, quia verum est, jam et ipsorum est et meum est, quoniam in commune omnium est *veritatis amatorum*. . . . Veritas tua nec mea est, nec illius aut illius, sed omnium nostrum, quos ad ejus communionem publice vocas

love their opinion not because it is true but because it is theirs. Otherwise they *would love* partially another, true, just as *I love* what they say when they speak truly not because it comes from them but because it is true, and so it is more theirs because it is true. And so therefore if they *love* it because it is true, then it is both mine and theirs, since it is the common good of all those who *love the truth*. . . . Truth is neither yours nor mine nor someone else's, but all of ours whom you call publicly to communion. (XII, 25, 34, 14, 400)

The truth is characterized by its communicational character (its universality permits its communication, and the communication attests its universality); but there is more because this communicational validity can be received and carried out only by giving rise to a *communio*, which assembles in mutual love those who commune in the same love of truth—always theirs although or *because* each does not claim to possess his own. In contrast with the hatred engendered by *veritas redarguens* ("Cur autem veritas *parit odium*?" [X, 23, 34, 14, 2020]), "in this diversity of true opinions, the truth itself gives birth to concord" (in hac diversitate sententiarum verarum concordiam pariat ipsa veritas) (XII, 30, 41, 14, 416).

Thus, the city of those who know, where the truth conceived and confirmed as interobjectivity of valid and common knowledge is done, here assumes the more radical figure of a communion of those who love the scriptures and who love each other. Or, more exactly, who come to love truth to the point of seeing it in the scriptures (where for so long Saint Augustine, like the philosophers, saw only absurdity) because they love each other reciprocally in a communion of charity. That is, only "Caritas novit eam [sc. lux incommutabilis]. O aeterna veritas et vera caritas et cara aeternitas" (Charity knows the unchangeable light. O eternal truth and true charity and dear eternity) (VII, 10, 16, 13, 616).

§21. Third-order truth

Now the substitution of the desire for beatitude for the desire for knowledge (see above, Chapter 2, §15; and Chapter 3, §16) assumes its full scope. It is no longer a matter of desiring to know, as if knowledge itself moved, if not exhausted, desire (according to Aristotle's founding thesis that "all men naturally desire to know"),[39] but of desiring beatitude (according to the principle that "omnes beatos esse volunt, verum est," or as Pascal translates, "All men seek happiness. There are no exceptions").[40] Truth becomes desirable and desired in the radical sense because rejoicing in it constitutes beatitude, "beata quippe vita est gaudium de veritate." But truth would not permit any enjoyment if it itself were not susceptible of making joy enjoyable, if therefore it were not in the end identified with God himself: "gaudium tu ipse es, et ipsa est beata vita, gaudere ad te, de te et propter te" (the enjoyment of joy is you yourself, and the blessed life itself consists only in rejoicing in view of you, from you, and on account of you) (X, 23, 33, 14, 200). Inversely, if knowledge wants to remain its own end and claims to give rise to desire by itself without opening onto truth, itself understood as that which one *must* enjoy because nothing other permits it, as God therefore, then this pretended love of wisdom would lose all seriousness and be disqualified, at worst as idolatry, at best as a mere quirk, curiosity, "vana et curiosa cupiditas nomine cognitionis et scientiae palliata" (a vain and curious desire, which is cloaked in the name of knowledge and science) (X, 35, 54, 14, 238). But this disqualification of a purely noetic, cognitive, and epistemic conception of truth by designating it curiosity does not escape from the suspicion, ever looming, of obscurantism or barbarism, unless one can lay out a figure of truth whose very essence permits and demands that a desire desire it and, in desiring it, put it precisely into operation as truth. One would therefore have to approach a sense of truth that lets it be defined *as manifestation and covering*, yet on the basis of desire and in view of beatitude—in other words, a sense of truth such that it manifests (itself) *inasmuch as loved* and therefore also covers up (itself) *inasmuch as hated*.

If only to sketch an acceptation of truth as loved or hated, in short of truth as *erotic*, it is necessary to distinguish it from two other senses of truth. I will therefore outline a three-term table. In the first place, one can identify truth as correctness of an assertion. It predicates something of something so as to arrive at the correspondence of the concept with the thing, "adaequatio rei et intellectu," or "die Übereinstimmung der Erkenntnis mit ihrem Gegenstande" (the agreement of knowledge with its object), or else "die volle Übereinstimmung zwischen Gemeintem und Gegebenem als solchem" (the full agreement of the intentional [object] and the given).[41] In this figure truth puts into play not just two terms (the state of things, *res*, and the concept that the mind, *intellectus*, [re]produces of them), but also a third, the adequation itself, which is attested in this very mind, set up in fact and by right as the place where truth is made: "Veritatem proprie vel falsitatem *non nisi in solo* intellectu esse posses" (there can be no truth or falsity in the strict sense except in the intellect alone). Or else: "Truth or illusion is not in the object, insofar as it is intuited, but in the judgment about it, insofar as it is thought."[42] The truth does not so much lead to the thing itself as it leads it back to the knowing mind, which has the power to constitute it by saying it. This is not an aporia but a transcendental condition: I make the truth by rendering possible the adequation between the concept and the thing, that is to say, by making a judgment about it. And thus, since I judge it, I make the truth by setting myself at a distance from it. It does not bear directly on me but on something other than me—on the thing in its states. I make the truth, but it does not make me, since it does nothing directly to me. In this figure I obviously do not have to love the truth for it to be carried out since it is carried out only by me and I remain final judge of it.

To this first figure Heidegger opposed a second: truth as uncovering. "'Being-true' ('truth') means Being-uncovering (*entdeckend-sein*)."[43] For never could the slightest conception "correspond" to the slightest thing (and therefore to the least state of things) if the thing itself did not first offer itself of itself for conception, therefore if it did not manifest itself by uncovering itself. Even the slightest adequation supposes that the understanding *equals* something; but, for it to equal anything whatsoever, something must already be; and nothing would be if a thing did not manifest itself of itself. Therefore logical adequation always rests on manifestation, that is to say the phenomenalization of the thing by itself. "The being meant [by intentionality, *gemeinte*] itself shows itself *just as* it is in itself, which means that it uncovers itself (*sich entdeckt*) in its self-identity, as (*so ist als wie*) it is uncovered (*aufgezeigt*) in the statement."[44] Not only does the thing phenomenalize itself, and phenomenalize itself without reserve (no thing in itself), but above all it phenomenalizes itself without arising from a synthesis or a constitution, solely on the basis of itself. Truth is carried out at the initiative of the thing. For that matter this determination of truth as self-manifestation of the thing so that the statement might say it, but *before* it says it, responds literally to the definition that is finally (and for the first time) strictly phenomenological—namely, the definition that Heidegger had already given to the phenomenon in general as *"that which shows itself in itself,* the manifest—das *Sich-an-ihm-selbst-seigende,* das Offenbare."[45] One can no longer alienate the truth of the thing from the thing itself, in the way that would be imposed with its determination by the correctness of the statement and logical adequation. However, as much as the radicality of this phenomenological revival of the essence of truth is not to be disputed, one of its presuppositions clearly limits its scope. For even and precisely if the thing makes truth by manifesting itself as such on the basis of itself, this truth does not impose itself on me so much as it presupposes me as *Dasein*: "'It gives' Being (not beings) only as long as *Dasein* is."[46] To be sure, truth does not say the being, nor is it equal to it, for it is (and even sets forth) the mode par excellence of Being. However, precisely because it manifests the Being of this being, it depends, like it, on what keeps and preserves both, *Dasein* itself. Truth does not put *Dasein* into question, for the radical reason that *Dasein* itself puts truth into play, as one of its figures. I still remain, in a certain way and by a radical because ontological passivity, truth's condition of possibility. "Being-true as Being-uncovering is a way of Being for Dasein."[47] Thus even understood as self-manifestation of the phenomenon, truth always bears on something other than myself—on the thing as phenomenon of itself. And, if I make (or let be made) the truth, truth does not make me. I have neither to hate it nor to love it but to carry it out or not according as I decide or not, precisely because I decide *for it.*

The possibility, and therefore necessity, of a third figure comes up here, precisely in a possibility heretofore ignored or rather denied—one in which I would not decide the truth (neither as the understanding of predication nor as the *Dasein* of uncovering) but in which I must myself make up *my mind,* deciding *myself,* as it were, in relation to it. I must do so because without such a decision (refusal or acceptance), no manifestation will appear to me. This is the figure of truth in which, in order to manifest itself, truth would have to be loved and in which hatred would suffice to cover up this manifestation, love and hate thereby assuming a resolutely *epistemic* (indeed phenomenological) function, that of making visible and therefore intelligible the manifestation of a phenomenon. That is, when the thing (no matter what thing) manifests itself in an evidential excess (of whatever type of excess might be at issue [see above, §19]), its truth can make itself (seen, unveiled) only as long as I myself can gaze on it—which means keep it under my eyes, endure it, and bear it. But I can do this only inasmuch as I resist it. And resistance, in the phenomenological sense,[48] is practiced in two moments. First, it resists the excess of intuitive evidence, as one resists the intensity of an electrical current, too tense for my finitude; for, in the ordeal of a saturated phenomenon, there always arises the index of my finitude, submerged by the excess. But next and by a rigorous consequence, especially if it is a matter of resisting the holiness of God, saturated phenomenon par excellence, the splendor that manifests itself there can only accuse, by contraposition, the inequality right in my face. And Saint Augustine describes this moment with perfect precision: "Constituebas me ante faciem meam, ut viderem, quam turpis essem, quam distortus et sordidus, maculosus et ulcerosus et videbam et horrebam, et quo a me fugeram non erat . . . ut *invenirem iniquitatem meam* et *odissem*" (You put me right in my face so that I could see my own disgrace, my deformity, and my filth, how defiled I was, and my ulcers, and I saw them and I was horrified, and there was no place where I could flee . . . such that I discovered my iniquity and I *hated* it) (*Confessiones* VIII, 7, 16, 14, 42). From now on, since the light of truth inevitably brings an accusation, only one response remains possible: to love the light even in its excess, although it accuses me, indeed torments me, love its very excess more than the mortal repose of my own darkness. The proof of the true cannot not make me undergo the ordeal of truth. The thing here phenomenalizes itself and manifests itself in truth only by thereby doing the truth upon me myself. And therefore I bear its evidence only in the measure to which I love it more than I suffer from its intensity or from the disgrace that it reveals in me and that I want to keep hidden. Truth can give itself only by doing the truth, even and especially upon me, who receives it. In this figure of truth the issue is therefore no longer only a proposition said or thing seen but, above all, a seer, precisely because he can no longer remain just an impartial spectator who would see from a neutral position, without the reverberation of a light too strong for him crashing over him. Only love gives the resistance sufficient for receiving the blow of truth in its inevitable shock. So is sketched, following Saint Augustine, the *erotic* figure of truth.

Saint Augustine is not the only one to suggest that *veritas* does not manifest itself only to the measure of the correctness of what is said or of the manifestation of what shows itself but in the final instance according to the love that accepts it. Among others, but not the least of them, we find, obviously, Pascal, who lays out quite clearly the epistemological role of love as condition for the possibility of knowledge: "Truth is so obscured nowadays and lies so well established that unless we love the truth we shall never know it."[49] This implies that pretending to know without loving amounts to not knowing in truth, to not even seeing: "What a long way it is between knowing God and loving him!"[50] Reciprocally, if love prevails among the three theological virtues (1 Corinthians 13:13), and if truth discloses itself ultimately to love, then one can obviously say without paradox that "the greatest of Christian virtues [is] namely love of truth."[51] These formulations, which make up a system, in fact respond almost directly to those of Saint Augustine: "Volo eam [sc. veritatem] facere in corde meo coram te in confessione" (I want to do the truth in my heart before your face in a confession) (*Confessiones* X, 1, 1, 14, 140). This same epistemological role of love in relation to truth can also be described negatively, following the thread of hatred, which resists the repercussion, all the more accusing, of the truth:

It [self-love] conceives a deadly hatred for *the truth which rebukes it and convinces it of its faults.* It would like to do away with this truth, and not being able to destroy it as such, *it destroys it,* as best it can, in the consciousness of itself and others; that is, it takes every care to hide its faults both from itself and others, and *cannot bear to have them pointed out* or noticed. . . . For is it not true that we *hate the truth* and those who tell it to us, and we like them to be deceived to our advantage? . . . Telling the truth is useful to the hearer but harmful to those who tell it, *because they incur such odium.*[52]

This, by all evidence, is a literal commentary on *Confessiones* X, 23, 34, from which is taken successively the *veritas redarguens*, the *nolunt convinci quod falsi sunt*, the *oderunt eam*, and the initial citation *veritas parit odium*.[53] Similarly, "contradictions have always been left to blind the wicked, for anything offensive to truth and charity is wrong. That is the true principle."[54] This text holds almost perfectly as a commentary on an Augustinian passage: "Initium operorum bonorum, confessio est operum malorum. Facis veritatem et venis ad lucem. Quid est 'facis veritatem'? . . . Venis ad lucem ut manifestentur opera tua, quia in Deo sunt facta; quia et hoc ipsum quod tibi displicuit peccatum tuum, non tibi displiceret, nisi Deus tibi luceret et ejus veritatem ostenderet" (The beginning of good works is the confession of the bad. Do the truth, and come to the light. What does it mean 'do the truth'? . . . Come to the light to make your works manifest because they are done in God. Because the very fact that your sin is displeasing to you would not displease you if God did not shine for you and show you his truth."[55] In other words for Pascal, as much as for Saint Augustine, "truth apart from charity is not God, but his image and an idol we must not love or worship. Still less must we love or worship its opposite, which is lying."[56]

There is, however, a difficulty validating this comparison. It comes, at least indirectly, from Heidegger. That is, meaning to confirm his analysis of the original character of affection (*Befindlichkeit*), according to which "*Dasein* finds itself always already attuned [*bestimmt, intoné*],"

Heidegger cites and compares two texts, one from Pascal, the other from Saint Augustine.[57] Now, as they are cited, the two texts seem to diverge. In the first, Pascal limits the epistemological condition of charity solely to "divine things" in opposition to "human things": "Thence it comes that while speaking of human things, we say that it is necessary to know them before we can love them, which has passed into a proverb, the saints on the contrary say in speaking of divine things that it is necessary to love them in order to know them, and that we only enter truth through charity, from which they made one of their most useful maxims."[58] Are we to understand that charity and love decide the truth only in one region (divine things), but not in another (human things), where, by contrast, one could stick with the customary priority of knowledge over desire? In contrast, Saint Augustine's text suggests that every truth and the whole truth depends on love as an epistemological condition: "Non intratur in veritatem, nisi per caritatem" (One does not enter into truth, except through charity).[59] In fact, the disagreement only seems to be one. First of all, one could trade the positions. Saint Augustine, to put the citation back into its context (something Heidegger does not do), is here dealing with a matter of biblical exegesis in which he is trying to refute an argument of the Manicheans: to the question of whether the apostles had or did not have the Holy Spirit, he responds by emphasizing that the Church admits that the Holy Spirit is given only by Christ once glorified (John 7:39) and therefore that we, apostles or not, can comprehend the scriptures only through the Holy Spirit "poured out in our hearts" (Romans 5:5). Therefore to enter into truth through charity means entering into the understanding of the scriptures by the Holy Spirit. The "most useful maxim" therefore here concerns "divine things," as in the text from Pascal.

Second, there is no choice to be made between the two hypotheses of love conditioning truth, either in divine things alone or in all cases. Heidegger himself assigns love and hate to "*all* knowing": "What we have set forth here as the in-being of Dasein and characterized in greater detail is the ontological fundament for what Augustine and above all Pascal already noted. They called that which actually knows not knowing but *love and hate*. All knowing (*alles erkennen*) is only an appropriation and a form of realization of something which is already discovered by other primary comportments. Knowing is rather more likely to cover up something which was originally uncovered in non-cognitive com-portment."[60] That is, for *Dasein* as such, as it approaches *every* being (and especially not just *divine* beings, which, far from benefiting from the slightest privilege, fall, in the existential analytic, beneath the blow of "methodological atheism"), knowledge is no longer defined as a theo-retical attitude (in terms of *Vorhandenheit*), but depends first on the more originary affections and dispositions of Dasein—concern, care, fear, anxiety, and so forth. Therefore, the more *Dasein* operates as such, that is to say with *the most* usual (*zuhanden*) beings, the more it "knows" them by handling and using them, according to its affective tonalities, among them love and hate. But this seems also to have been the position Saint Augustine took when he described the variations in the mode of knowledge according to the steps of its progression. "Confugiendum est igitur ad eorum praecepta, quos sapientes fuisse probabile est. Hacte-nus potuit ratio perduci. Versebatur namque, non veritate certior, sed consuetidine securior, *in rebus humanis*. At, *ubi ad divina* perventum est, averit sese: intueri non potest, palpitat, aestuat, inhiat amor, *reverberatur luce veritatis* et ad familiaritatem tenebrarum suarum, non electione, sed fatigatione, convertitur" (Recourse is to be had to the precepts of those who, in all probability, were wise men. Reason can be led to this point. It treated *human things* with the assurance of custom more than with the certainty of truth. But once arrived at *divine things*, it was turned away; it cannot gaze at them; it shudders, it is on fire, it gasps with love; *the light of truth reverberates over it* and it turns back to its customary darkness, not by choice, but out of exhaustion).[61] Hence the problematic of bedaz-zlement, which can in fact be borne only by the courage, endurance, and suffering of love, arises each time that the phenomena to see pass beyond the common use of the faculties. Love must then open (and keep open) the mind to truth, simply because in the case of divine things, it is an issue par excellence of the truth of saturated phenomena—"invisable," unbearable, irregardable, and absolute. But the same love (or the same hatred) should intervene for every other type of saturated phenomenon. For that matter Pascal offers a similar diagnostic in a slightly different form: "Those who do not love truth excuse themselves on the grounds that it is disputed and that very many people deny it. Thus their error is solely due to the fact that they love neither truth nor charity, and so they have no excuse."[62] In all cases it is necessary, in order to continue to see the truth, to want to see it, therefore to love it.

In entirely different registers others have also had recourse to the erotic figure of truth. When Nietzsche postulates that "the will to truth is only a means of the will to power," he does not mean, as some imagine, to submit truth to power, indeed to eliminate it thereby; he is rather trying to think the essence of truth more radically than as a representation or even a manifestation—to think it as what thought thinks only by *creating* it: "The 'truth' is not something that would be [already there], and would be there to be found or discovered—something which is to be created."[63] What does *create* mean here? Obviously *to will*. But what in turn does *willing* mean? Willing *wants* to say, and when the will says, first and essentially, it wills. What does it will? Its own will rising forever in power. Up to what power can the will rise by creating truth? As far as it bears it: "'How much truth does a spirit *bear (erträgt)*, how much truth does it risk *(wägt)?'*—that is what would be for me the appropriate measure of value." And bearing (for example, the "edifying" thought of the Eternal Return) depends only on the scope of the "dionysian yea-saying"—in other words, on love.[64] Wittgenstein, too, retrieves the Augustinian doctrine of truth. When, for example, he opposes to truth not falsity but lying—"You cannot not want to give up your lying and tell the truth"[65]—one can hardly fail to hear an echo of *Confessiones*: "At ego per avaritiam meam non amittere te volui, sed volui tecum possidere mendacium" (But I, in my greed, I did not want to lose you, but I wanted to possess at the same time both you and the lie) (X, 41, 66, 14, 260). Here he does not consider truth in terms of its assertion, therefore in relation to a state of things, but directly in relation to him who says it and who, in saying it, submits to his ordeal. Also he does not here oppose to truth error or falsity, as would be appropriate when it is a matter of what truth says or manifests, but rather lying, as is appropriate when one considers *this* truth, which is understood on the basis of he who utters it—that is, precisely the truth at play in a confession or an admission and that in turn is decided on the basis of something like veracity. "The criteria for the truth of the *confession* [*die Wahrheit des Geständnis*] that I thought such-and-such are not the criteria for a true *description (wahrheitgemässen Beschreibung)* of a process. And the importance of the true confession (*wahren Geständnisses*) does not reside in its being a correct and certain report of a process. It resides rather in the special consequences that can be drawn from a confession (*Geständnis*) whose truth is guaranteed by the special criteria of *truthfulness* (*Wahrhaftigkeit*)."[66] The third order of truth, since it is opposed first of all to lying, should be understood first as sincerity. An unexpected confirmation comes finally from Levinas. Attempting to oppose to truth such as it operates within the horizon of being, therefore as manifestation (in Heidegger's sense, of course), a truth appropriated to ethical obligation (to the point of substitution), Levinas, too, brackets the state of things that words could say in a formalizable and verifiable said. He focuses instead on the pure utterance, considered as an act, that is to say inasmuch as it refers directly to him who says it. "Saying prior to anything said bears witness to glory. This witness is true, but with a truth irreducible to the truth of disclosure, and does not narrate anything that shows itself. Saying is without noematic correlation in the pure obedience to glory that orders."[67] Such a truth does not say any statement and does not concern any state of things in the world. With neither noema nor unveiling, such a truth does not come from ἀγηθεία but occupies itself only with him who says it or, more exactly, is exposed to it. It is carried out directly in its relation with him who says it, bears the Saying of it. The witness does the truth in speaking true, without saying any said. "No said equals the sincerity of the saying, is adequate to the veracity that is prior to the true, to the veracity of the approach, of proximity, beyond presence. Sincerity would then be saying without the said."[68] Truth is understood again as veracity—in other words, as sincerity, the putting to work of the Saying itself, the pure and simple vocal attestation of the witness faced with him for whom he testifies, before and even at the limit without saying anything, with no Said.

Thus is defined a truth of another order. Neither a predication about things, nor the manifestation of the thing, but the event of an evidence, which shows itself only inasmuch as I tolerate its excess. And I can do so only inasmuch as I love it. "Therefore how bitter, and learnt how late, the truth!" (G. M. Hopkins).[69] In other words, "Sero te amavi, pulchritudo" (X, 27, 38, 14, 208).

§22. The truth loved: *pulchritudo*

If truth is now no longer accomplished merely as an assertion (where the mind resides as a third between the thing and predication), nor as a manifestation of the phenomenon by itself (in which the mind remains the condition of possibility), but as an ordeal of evidential excess, which weighs so directly on me that I can bear it only in the measure to which I love it, then it is not accomplished solely nor first of all in theory—precisely because it is necessary to love it in order to bear the knowledge of it. It is therefore necessary that truth be set forth in such a way that it appear as lovable. And, as he defines what we can love precisely as the beautiful ("Num amamus aliquid nisi pulchrum?" [What do we love if not something beautiful?] [*Confessiones* IV, 13, 20, 13, 442]), Saint Augustine thinks the truth inasmuch as lovable with the name *beauty*, and names it as such: "nec amatur quicquam salubrius quam illa prae cunctis formosa et luminosa veritas tua" (there is nothing more salutary to love than the truth more beautiful and more luminous than all the others, yours). No longer the truth that refers me to myself (*redarguens*) because I refuse it, but the one that becomes "dulcis veritas" (sweetly flowing truth) because I let it come, since I love it.[70] But, if truth must be loved to be known, then it is also fitting that the truth can appear in *this* light where love loves and *in the name* of beauty, therefore without a doubt well beyond truth in the theoretic sense of metaphysics. For it is not merely a matter of extricating oneself from the errors that philosophers most often sell under the name of truth ("dicebant 'veritas et veritas,' et nusquam erat in eis et falsa loquebantur" [they were saying "truth, truth!" but it was nowhere in them and they were speaking falsities]); such a movement rightly defines philosophy itself. The issue, then, more radically, is transgressing *even the truths* that could be said by the philosophers, if these truths cannot be *loved* or do not lead to *loving*: "etiam vera dicentes philosophos transgredi debui prae amore tuo, mi pater summe bone, pulchritudo pulchrorum omnium. O veritas, veritas" (I was obliged *to transgress* the philosophers, *even when they spoke truly*, for the sake of preferring your love, my supremely good Father, beauty of all beauties. O truth, truth) (III, 6, 10, 13, 378). The wisdom of the philosophers remains at best a true knowledge but one still not lovable (nor for that matter hateable) and one that must yield to the beautiful truth, itself lovable (or hateable). Beauty here no longer plays the role of a mere transcendental that could be derived from being, at the same level (or almost) as the one, the true, and the good with which it would be counted, precisely because it does not concern the horizon of Being but the question of love—unless it be necessary to say rather that the horizon of Being is resumed, revisited, and revised on the basis of the question that love addresses to it. The love of truth now understood in the strictest sense, that is to say on the basis of the question of love and no longer in another horizon, foreign to it (for example, that of Being), no longer serves for the *definition* of philosophy (in the sense, at least, in which it understands itself), but for *its transgression*. Here love is no longer limited to the role of provisional preparation, by lack or desire, for bringing me into possession of the truth; it is set up as the ultimate and perhaps even the unique operator of my opening *to* truth.

And yet I am slow to love it. I come late to the love of the true inasmuch as beautiful with an inevitable, indeed imprescriptible, delay: "Sero te amavi, pulchritudo tam antiqua et tam nova, sero te amavi! Et ecce intus eras et ego foris et ibi te quaerebam et in ista formosa, quae fecisti, diformis irruebam. Mecum eras et tecum non eram. Ea me tenebant longe a te, quae si in te non essent, non essent" (I delayed in loving you, beauty so ancient and so new, oh how I loved you belatedly! And look, you were within, but I was outside, and that is where I was seeking you, and I rushed, myself deformed, upon those beautiful things that you made. You were with me, and I, I was not with you. These forms kept me far from you, these which would not be if they were not in you) (X, 27, 38, 14, 208). This delay, which fills me with old age or rather old-fashionedness,[71] results entirely and directly from my reticence and even my recoil before the excess of light imposed on me by the truth; it even consists only in my willing blindness before it. I close my eyes so as not to have to suffer its brilliance: "Lux non est absens, sed vos absentes estis a luce. Caecus in sole praesentem habet solem, sed absens est in sole" (The light is not absent, but it is you who are absent from the light. A blind man in the sun does indeed have the sun present; it is he who is absent from the sun).[72] To make up for this delay, one has only to return from absence to presence and expose oneself to bearing the evidence of truth, which can only occur by seeing it *inasmuch* as beauty, therefore finally loving it. Loving beauty does not do away with suffering its radiance, but makes one understand that this suffering results only from the deformity that the light reveals and cannot not reveal in me—me, who am not beautiful, since I am not true, but, with the true, want always also "to possess the lie" (possidere mendacium) (X, 41, 66, 14, 260). This dual action of the truth as beautiful reproduces the doubling of the *confessio*: confessing beauty implies first confessing the sins that hide it from me, or even render it hateable to me, as is explained by the commentary on the verse "Confessio et pulchritudo in conspectu ejus" in Psalm 95:6: "Pulchritudinem amas? Vis esse pulcher? Confitere. Non dixit pulchritudo et confessio, sed 'confessio et pulchritudo.' Foedus eras, confitere ut sis pulcher; peccator eras, confitere ut sis justus. . . . Amamus pulchritudinem: prius eligamus confessionem, ut sequatur pulchritudo" (You love beauty? You want to be beautiful yourself? Make confession. The psalmist does not say "beauty and confession," but "confession and beauty." You were repugnant, make confession to be beautiful; you were a sinner, make confession to be just. . . . We love beauty: let us choose first confession, so that beauty follows).[73] Of course, but the final difficulty remains: how will I ever be able to confess my sins so as to accede to beauty, since, precisely, I hate the confession of my sins, and, as a direct consequence, I hate beauty, too (and prefer my sins to it)? If I must make the movement by confession of sins so as to love beauty, never will I arrive at loving truth, therefore at truth.

Unless beauty takes toward me the step I cannot take toward it. Unless, by the same privilege of beauty, beauty makes me come toward it by attracting me with a seduction strong enough to make me make, as if despite myself, confession of my sins. That, beauty not only can do, but, like the immemorial, which was always already there, the beauty "tam antiqua et tam nova" has never stopped doing. It makes me love it and launches my double *confessio*. Since I cannot come to it, beauty comes to me. Nothing proves this as much as the fact that the very text that begins by stigmatizing my lateness to the truth to love, therefore to truth as beauty, continues by putting onstage the seduction that beauty exercises over me so as to call me to truth: "Vocasti et clamasti et rupisti surditatem meam. Coruscasti, splenduisti et fugasti caecitatem meam. Fragasti et duxi spiritum et anhelo tibi. Gustavi et esurio et sitio. Tetegisti me, et exarsi in pacem tuam" (You called me; you cried and you broke my deafness. You shined and poured out your splendor, and you chased away my blindness. You blew fragrantly; I breathed in your perfume, and I panted after you. I tasted, and I was [now] hungry and thirsty. You touched me, and I burned from it, [even though this be] from your peace) (X, 27, 38, 14, 208). This truly is a seduction scene, in the most straightforward and exact sense: beauty plays like a virtuoso upon the five senses and captures each time him who will become in the end its belated lover.[74] It truly is about the five physical senses, not a spiritual allegory, because the sensible senses exert from the start a spiritual function: they manifest the invisible flesh, or rather the flesh makes manifest in them itself and what the mind senses and sees of the world. There is, therefore, no choice to be made between a literal and a spiritual reading of this seduction, not only because the letter signifies only in the spirit, but above all because the seduction aims at the soul as much as at the flesh—which, for that matter, make just one, me.[75] Truth is indeed manifest as a saturated phenomenon, but when it manifests itself according as it makes itself loved, this saturated phenomenon belongs first of all to the flesh.

We need not fear, therefore, understanding the union of the lover and wisdom with all the eroticism that Saint Augustine employs quite consciously: "Nunc illud quaerimus, qualis sis amator sapientiae, quam castissimo conspexu et amplexu, nullo interposito velamento quasi nudam videre ac tenere desideras, qualem se illa non sinit, nisi paucissimis et electissimis amatoribus suis" (We are now seeking to find out what sort of lover of wisdom you are: wisdom that you desire most chastely to see with your eyes and to hold in your arms without the screen of any veil and as if naked, something it permits only to a small handful of lovers, highly chosen).[76] He is describing a sudden attraction as savage and exuberant as it was slow to come: "Nam et illam singularem veramque pulchritudinem cum viderit, plus amabit; et, nisi ingenti amore oculum infixerit, nec ab aspiciendo uspiam declinaverit, manere in illa beatissima visione non poterit" (For, when [sc. the soul] will see the true and unequaled beauty, it will love it all the more. And unless an immense love fixes its eye upon it, being not turned away from it, it [the soul] will not be able to reside in this blessed vision).[77] As we saw, a vision can endure only insofar as love renders it possible, or rather renders possible bearing its excess. The desire for beauty stays only if love of truth not only endures but still grows ("plus amabit"). For, failing to love more, one ceases to love.

We thus discover the strong coherence of Saint Augustine's journey. The first text that he wrote, the treatise *De pulchro et apto*, later lost, already advanced toward truth by way of its phenomenalization in beauty, *sub specie pulchritudinis*, taking its lead from one single question: "dicebam amicis: 'Nunc amamus aliquid nisi pulchrum? Quid est ergo pulchrum? Quid est pulchritudo? Quid est quod nos allicit et conciliat rebus, quas amamus? Nisi enim esset in eis decus et species, nullo modo nos ad se moverent'" (I used to say to my friends, "What do we love, if not something beautiful? Now, what is it that is beautiful? What is beauty? What is it that attracts us and reconciles us with the things that we love? For, unless there were in them some brilliance and some grace, they would not move us toward them").[78] What still keeps, at this time, the name *philosophy*, as love of wisdom, will become the love of truth as beautiful. And one would even come to find philosophy itself beautiful in turn, indeed more beautiful than all other loves: "Pulchrior est philosophia, fateor, quam Thysbe, quam Pyramus, quam Venus et Cupido, talesque omnimodi amores" (Philosophy is more beautiful, I admit, than Thisby, Pyramus, Venus, and Cupid and all these sorts of loves).[79] Thus is established a doctrine of the love of beauty, a radical *philocalie*. Saint Augustine takes it up consciously from the Greek Fathers but invokes it just as consciously as an essential corrective for *philosophy*, indeed its substitute:

"Philocalia" ista vulgo dicitur. Ne contemnas nomen hoc ex vulgari nomine; nam philocalia et philosophia propre similiter cognominatae sunt, et quasi gentiles inter se videri volunt, et sunt. Quid est enim philosophia? Amor sapientia. Quid philocalia? Amor pulchritudinis. Quaere de Graecis. Quid est ergo sapientia? Nonne ipsa vera est pulchritudo? Germanae igitur istae sunt prorsus et eodem parente procreatae. . . . Non enim philocalia ista unde genus ducat, agnoscit, nisi philosophia.

This is what is commonly called "philocalia." Do not condemn this name on account of it being used colloquially, for philocalia and philosophy are named in almost the same fashion and keep a family resemblance since in fact they are of the same family. What then is philosophy? The love of wisdom. What is philocalia? The love of beauty. Ask this of the Greeks. What then is wisdom if not true beauty itself? The two are indeed sisters, begotten of the same parent. . . . But this philocalia does not know what family it comes from if philosophy does not teach it.[80]

No more than it pertains to a particular field of experience of the world (the entire world falls under its jurisdiction, even in its ugliness and horror) does beauty define a particular domain of philosophy (like a transcendental or like the object of *aesthetics*). It ensures for the world in its totality its mode and therefore first its erotic reduction, in which truth can be known inasmuch as it is loved.

For beauty does not limit the search to itself, confining the investigation to some being supposed to be paradigmatically beautiful, indeed to the enjoyment of itself. Beauty opens and becomes itself a way (*via*), which traverses every creature ("universitatis admirabilis pulchritudo" [the stupefying beauty of the universality (of things)]),[81] proposing it to be seen as its Creator sees it—beautiful, for God saw that all that was "beautiful and good"—and which, at the same time, without removing anything from the creature, but to the contrary *because* it grants it its highest dignity, transgresses it toward the absolute beauty of the true. "Intuens ergo et considerans universam creaturam, quicumque *iter agit* ad sapientiam, sentit sapientiam *in via* se sibi ostendere hilariter, et in omni providentia occurrere sibi: alacrius ardescit *viam* istam peragere, quanto *et ipsa via* per illam *pulchra est*, ad quam exaestuat pervenire" (And therefore, whoever, gazing at and considering every creature, *makes his way* toward wisdom senses that this wisdom manifests itself, joyful, to him on this *path* and comes to him providentially. He burns all the more to pursue his *path* as wisdom, to which he seethes to arrive, makes this *path* itself beautiful to him). Wisdom, namely "pulcherrime omnium, creator omnium" (the most beautiful of all, creator of all),[82] whose beauty defines beatitude: "ineffabilis pulchritudo, cujus plena visio est summa felicitas."[83] The family resemblance between philosophy and philocalia authorizes philosophy to let beauty be charged with phenomenalizing truth, so that the intentionality of love might learn to see it and end by knowing it as loved. Things appear beautiful only in absolute beauty, as they show themselves true only in absolute truth. "Tu ergo, Domine, fecisti ea, qui pulcher es: pulchra sunt; qui bonus es: bona sunt enim; qui es: sunt enim. Nec ita pulchra sunt, nec bona sunt, nec ita sunt, sicut tu conditor eorum, quo comparato nec pulchra sunt, nec bona sunt, nec sunt" (It is you, Lord, who made them, you who are beautiful: they are therefore beautiful. You who are good: they are therefore good. You who are: they therefore are. But they are not beautiful, not good, not even existent like you, their founder, and compared to you, they are neither beautiful nor good nor existent) (*Confessiones* XI, 4, 6, 14, 280).

The last step remains: that I myself become beautiful through beauty itself. "Nondum diligabamus eum: diligendo pulchri efficimur. . . . Anima vero nostra, fratres mei, foeda est per iniquitatem: amando Deum pulchra efficitur. Qualis amor est qui reddit pulchrum amantem? Deus autem semper pulcher est. . . . Quomodo erimus pulchri? Amando eum qui semper est pulcher. Quantum in te crescit amor, tantum crescit pulchritudo; qua ipsa caritas est animae pulchritudo" (We do not yet love it, but in loving it, we become beautiful. . . . For our soul, my brothers, is made ugly by the fact of its injustice. In loving God, it becomes beautiful. What is the love that makes beautiful he who loves [the lover]? God is [to him] always beautiful. . . . How then will we be beautiful? By loving him who is always beautiful. As much as love grows so grows beauty, because charity is itself the beauty of the soul).[84] Access to beauty demands more than access to truth, at least understood in a nonerotic sense. It demands not only that what I know appear and manifest itself as beautiful but also that I who know it accede to it myself in person and therefore that I become (like) what I know—beautiful. Beauty embraces and governs the beautiful and he who loves truth inasmuch as beautiful. For I could not know the truth *inasmuch as lovable and loved* from a distance (supposing that I could do so in the other, nonerotic, senses of truth), precisely since I must love it—in other words, unite myself to it and become what it itself gives to see: beauty. To know truth, then, it is necessary not only that I become myself truthful (and cease wanting also to keep the lie with the true in me) but also that I become beautiful like it. Now my beauty, in the end, is decided according as I love or not the beauty of the true. The question of truth becomes the question of my will to truth—in the sense of my will to love.

Weakness of Will, or Power of Love

§23. Temptation and the fact of self

If one admits, as I have wagered here, that the *Confessiones* must be organized according to the Augustinian model of *confessio*, one cannot not observe the striking succession of three decisive passages in book 10 (the central one, where everything turns upside down, from the ego to the scriptures and from the singular to the plural): first, the *veritas redarguens* (*Confessiones* X, 23, 34 [Chapter 3 above, §§17–19]), then the love of beauty ("Sero te amavi, pulchritudo tam antiqua tam nova, sero te amavi!" [X, 27, 38; Chapter 3 above, §§20–22]), but also, still to be conceptualized, the universal sway of temptation over life in its entirety: "Numquid non 'temptatio est vita humana super terram' sine ullo interstitio?" ("The life of man on earth, is it anything but a temptation" [Job 7:1] without interruption?) (X, 28, 39, 14, 210). Now having seen that the first two themes did not succeed one another by chance (only the love of truth in the aspect of beauty permits enduring the *veritas redarguens* without succumbing to its hatred), we surmise that the universality accorded to temptation is doubtlessly articulated together with the dual-action truth that precedes it. We still have to see in what way: is it a matter of a succession, a consequence, or a resistance?

One can hardly be anything but astonished, at least on first impression, that the theme of temptation comes up again and, in fact, especially *after* the conversion. One cannot but notice, as Saint Augustine admits elsewhere, that conversion does not resolve everything and that, even if baptism erases all faults, the inclination to commit them does not immediately disappear: "Sane ista renovatio non momento uno fit ipsius conversionis, sicut momento uno fiat illa in Baptismo renovatio remissione omnium peccatorum" (To be sure, this renewal does not happen in a single moment, that of conversion, as in baptism renewal by remission of sins is accomplished in a single moment). The renewal that follows conversion is accomplished only "quotidianis accessibus" (by daily advances), "de die in diem proficiendo" (progressing from day to day) (*De Trinitate* XIV, 17, 23, 16, 408–10). In other words, and to remove all ambiguity: "Sic et post baptismum restat vita christiana in temptationibus" (Thus, even after baptism, the Christian life remains mired in temptations) (*Commentaries on the Psalms* 72, 5, *PL* 36, 917). It could even be that temptation does not appear as such, in all its enigma, except once its connection with actual sin has been suspended. For only in this situation does it indeed appear as an unconditioned possibility, which persists precisely as such without having any need of passing into the actuality of a wicked deed. Temptation is already operative entirely within possibility alone and demands nothing more than possibility to operate; it is tempting precisely in opening possibilities. A delay, a belatedness, must be admitted—in short, a differ*a*nce provoked by the conversion itself because it is only produced in ever having to be reproduced, because it only happens in experiencing a resistance, that of the temptations that continue the combat lost by the sins: "his temptationibus quotidie conor resistere" (each day I strive to resist these temptations) (*Confessiones* X, 31, 44, 14, 218). Thus, not only does conversion demand time for my decision toward God to free me from what turns me away from him, but it also produces this time because it requires it and allocates it. My resistance to conversion—put otherwise, conversion as resistance of what I have become to what I used to be—renders me different from myself and therefore makes me defer my coming to God, that is to say my coming to myself, more exactly myself coming to itself. Through this differ*a*nce an arena opens where time plays itself out, or more exactly as we will see, for the time of *distentio*, the time that sin distends and that provokes resistance.

Temptation thereby assumes its proper status: a state of resistance, as much the resistance *to* the conversion of my inclination to sin as the resistance *of* my progressive conversion to this very inclination. In any case it is precisely not a matter of sin but of temptation, which, if it precedes, permits, and possibly produces the sin, is absolutely not identical to it—which, for that matter, is confirmed by the fact that the theme of temptation here comes from a citation of Job 7:1: "Numquid non temptatio est vita humana super terram?" Job, that is, has not sinned, and his unhappiness cannot be understood as a punishment, but it comes upon him solely because God authorizes Satan to tempt him. Disconnected from the actuality of sin, temptation becomes for Job a pure possibility, one that he keeps open as such by stubbornly refusing the counsel of his friends—to once again join unhappiness to sin as effect to cause, so as to put everything again back into effective actuality. Maintained in possibility and exercising itself as this possibility itself, temptation becomes for Job not only the paradoxical occasion for a proof of faith but also an ordeal of self—in short, for a resistance.[1] The distinction between sin and temptation is inscribed in time: while each sin is an act, therefore an event that comes and that goes (even if it lets its trace remain), temptation defines a possibility, therefore a disposition that persists without end, to the point of remaining a sort of *habitus*, even after conversion and baptism—indeed *especially* after conversion and baptism, which provoke so much resistance. Temptation institutes the resistance in time and gives me my time each day: "his temptationibus *quotidie* conor resistere" (I strive *each day* to resist these temptations) (X, 31, 44, 14, 218); "In his ergo temptationibus positus certo *quotidie*" (*Each day*, I am exposed to these temptations) (X, 31, 47, 14, 226); "multis minutissimis et contemptibilibus rebus curiositas *quotidie* nostra temptetur" (our curiosity is tempted *each day* by a tumult of miniscule and contemptible things) (X, 35, 57, 14, 242); "Temptamur his temptationibus *quotidie*, Domine, sine cessatione temptamur. *Quotidiana* formax" (We are tempted *each day* by these temptations, Lord, incessantly we are. A fiery furnace *each day*) (X, 38, 60, 14, 248). Thus, temptation counts out my days. This means not only that not one day passes without my suffering a temptation but also that, for me, time always befalls me as an assault against me, which gives me the ordeal of the possibility of sinning but, above all, through this very possibility, imparts to me an ordeal *of* myself. The time that tempts me tests me, to the point that I undergo myself only in the daily test posed by the daily ordeal of the possibility of sin.

The permanence and universality of temptation become all the more a definition of the *vita humana* as Saint Augustine sometimes adds "*tota*" or related words to the verse from Job 7:1: "vita ipsa mortalium *tota* poena sit, qui *tota* temptatio est, sicut sacrae litterae personant, ubi scriptum est 'Numquid non temptatio est vita humana super terram?'" (the very life of mortals is *in its totality* a temptation, as we hear in the passage from scriptures: "Is not human life a temptation on this earth?") (*De civitate Dei* XXI, 14, 37, 438). Or: "Nunc vero quamdiu 'corpus quod corrumpitur aggravat animam' et 'vita humana super terram *tota* temptatio'" (Now, while "the body that is corruptible oppresses the soul" [Wisdom 9:15] and "human life *in its totality* is temptation") (*De Trinitate* IV, 3, 5, 15, 348). Or again: "*Tota* enim 'vita humana super terram, sicut scriptum est, temptatio est'" (For, as it is written, *in its totality*, "the life of man on earth is temptation") (*Commentaries on the Psalms* 74, 1, *PL* 36, 946). And above all: "Non enim ait scriptura in Job: Temptationibus abundat vita humana; sed ait: 'Numquid non temptatio est vita humana super terram?' *Totam* ipsam vitam temptationem dixit. *Omnis* ergo vita tua super terram plagae tuae sunt" (For scripture does not say in the book of Job: The life of man abounds in temptations, but, "Is not human life on earth temptation?" It said that this life itself [is] *in its totality* temptation. Therefore your troubles last *all* your life on earth).[2] Temptation does not come up just from time to time, punctually as it were, but "sine ullo interstitio" (without respite) (*Confessiones* X, 28, 39, 14, 210), without stop in time, therefore totally and without exception as the constant mark of a *human* life. *Permanent* in time, temptation is proven in its *universal* definition. This means, of course, that the spirit of man finds itself, converted or not, baptized or not, inasmuch as man, radically exposed to the possibility of sinning, in such a way that living in the mode of man is equivalent to the ability to sin. This means, especially, that, in the figure of the possibility of sinning, it is radically exposed to possibility as such.

As universal and permanent determination, temptation confronts life inasmuch as human with possibility as such. For, in it alone appears what each man thinks fundamentally: "Multos interrogant tentationes et tunc apparent cogitationes; multi autem latent" (Many are those who investigate the temptations, and then their thoughts appear; but many hide themselves) (*Commentary on the Gospel of John* XLVI, 5, *PL* 35, 1730). Not only what each man thinks, but what he can bear and, finally, what he is: "Omnis enim temptatio probatio est, et omnis probationis effectus habet fructum suum. Quia homo plerumque etiam sibi ipsi ignotus est, quid ferat, quid non ferat ignorat. Qui ferat, quidve non ferat, ignorat; accedit temptatio quasi interrogatio et invenitur homo a seipso" (Every temptation is in effect an ordeal, and every effect of an ordeal has its fruit. Because man is most of the time ignorant, even about himself, he also does not know what he bears and what he does not bear. Temptation comes upon him as an inquisitor and man finds himself).[3] Temptation, therefore, has the power to make visible what would remain, without it, hidden, in fact invisible *to man himself*: his thoughts, his strength, his own *self*, what he is in himself, but precisely not *to* himself. From where does it get this power of phenomenalization? Evidently from the fact that it confronts each man with the things themselves but with these things in the truth (theirs *and also therefore his own*)—that is to say, exclusively insofar as he comes to desire them or not, to love them or hate them. The decisive point resides here: the *anima* does not relate to the things of the world as to stable beings, accessible and already available, consequently, good to know (*vorhanden*), but as to moving targets of desire, sometimes all the more desired as they are not available and do not stay at hand, precisely because their mere possibility is enough for desire to enjoy them. In turn, the *anima* does not remain equal to itself, in the neutrality of the theoretic attitude (in fact, in the natural attitude of metaphysics), nor does it accede to *itself* as to a permanent object; rather, it appears to itself, without cease, as a pure possibility, which does not know itself except insofar as it is decided, or rather insofar as it has to be decided in the face of temptation, the ordeal of possibility.

Thus, no longer relating to the things of the world as to subsistent beings to be known, but as to possibilities for desiring, no longer relating to itself in and through stable self-knowledge, barred from neutrality by an unceasing temptation, human life finally undergoes the ordeal of itself. Or, more exactly, it experiences itself as the very ordeal of its possibility, of a *self outside self*. In it, nothing has ever been decided once and for all. It is necessary to decide, nevertheless, with nothing else but it itself able to do so in its place. Never decided, always to decide, the *vita humana* has no other state besides its indetermination in determining, its always pending possibility. Saint Augustine names this privilege, for it is one, *mutability*: "*Mutantur* enim atque variantur" (They change and vary)

(*Confessiones* XI, 4, 6, 14, 280), since "inest ei tamen ipsa *mutabilitas* unde tenebresceret et frigesceret, nisi amore grandi tibi cohaerens tanquam semper meridies luceret et ferveret ex te" (there is however in it [created wisdom] mutability itself, which would cast its shadow over it and freeze it if, adhering to you by a great love as to a perpetual noonday sun, it did not shine and burn from out of you) (XII, 15, 21, 14, 374). This mutability should not be mistaken for an ontic determination and reduced to a mere opposition to eternity, according to an all too easily supposed "Neoplatonism" on the part of Saint Augustine.[4] For it concerns nothing less than what Heidegger will identify as facticity, such that it deploys the radical possibility of what he will name *Dasein* but that here operates as the *vita humana*.

Temptation thus imposes on me the possibility, itself inevitable and permanent, of a self-decision. It imposes on me the ordeal of the self as such (the *Selbst*)—as such, that means no longer as an object or even a being of the world but as a mode, a manner and a style of phenomenality proper—mine insofar as I must, by *fait accompli*, always already be decided and, in myself deciding, decide for all myself. In facticity no deed, no being, not even the least bit of the world, but a particular mode of phenomenality is at play—that of the *humana vita*.[5] As a mode, facticity grants it the power to undergo the ordeal of self, certainly a privilege, but always also inseparably in an ordeal—a trouble (*molestia*), a heavy weight (*onus*): "Oneri mihi sum" (I am a weighty burden to myself) (X, 28, 39, 14, 208). For the *vita humana* never undergoes the ordeal of itself (of the self) with a light heart because the ineluctable possibility of having to be decided weighs on it as a burdensome charge, which is imposed without its even being able to accept it. The possibility of being decided has itself never been decided, not even (*especially* not) by me: it weighs therefore on the *vita humana* with all its weight, the weight of a deadweight. The non-decided possibility of deciding without respite (*sine interstitio*) my life—in other words, facticity as my ownmost *how*—weighs more heavily than life itself.

How to interpret this? We owe it to Heidegger, no doubt unique among the moderns, to have taken seriously the weight of the self's burden to itself, of the *onus mihi sum*, by thinking it as facticity: "It is necessary to grasp more sharply this fundamental character in which

Augustine experiences factical life—the *tentatio* [trial, temptation]—in order to understand accordingly *to what extent* [*inwiefern*] the one who lives in such clarity, and on such a level of enactment, is necessarily a burden to himself (*eine Last ist*)."[6] In 1921 Heidegger did not lead this weight back farther than to possibility ("*Possibility* is the true 'burden.' *Heavy!*"), therefore to facticity ("the *tolerare* . . . is born and moves in a characteristic and fundamental direction of factical life, one in which the *tentatio* finds at the same time its sense and motivation").[7] To this degree the weight of the ordeal of self in temptation remains still undetermined. In 1927, by contrast, Heidegger will determine this weight definitively as a burden, this time precisely, of Being: "Being has become manifest as a burden. . . . A mood [*Stimmung*, tonality or attunement] makes manifest 'how one is, and how one is faring' ['wie enim ist und wird']. In this 'how one is,' having a mood brings Being to its 'there.'" "Weighing heavily" (*Lastcharakter*) from now on characterizes not simply the *vita humana* in the face of God, where it is a question of love and hate, but *Dasein* in its Being, where Being itself is at issue.[8] The gain the existential analytic aims at through this interpretation of the *onus mihi* is identified quite clearly: winning an "authentic existential"[9] that philosophy could attain only by recourse to an Augustinian (and therefore *theo*logical) analysis of the *vita humana*. But this overturning has a price, and the violence can no longer be ignored: it makes the aim of the *vita beata* and the truth of the third order, which is to say all that Saint Augustine was seeking, vanish, reducing it to a mere instrument in reasking the question of Being. What served to aim at God, or rather what was set forth only in view of God, therefore rightfully *on the basis of* this horizon, is devalued and neutralized, becoming an analysis that merely prepares for the opening of another horizon, one totally different, that of Being.[10]

We cannot not be astonished by such a diversion of facticity *coram Deo*, nor can we help but wonder if another interpretation of the weight of facticity may remain more legitimate, therefore preferable. But before requalifying it, it is again necessary that it should first be proven possible within the horizon of the *confessio*.

§24. Desire or care

To reach such an interpretation, one must attempt to think such a weight of the self weighing on me ("oneri mihi sum") from a decidedly theological point of view—in other words, for Saint Augustine, from a biblical point of view. This can be done if we refer *onus mihi* to the weight evoked by Christ according to Matthew 11:28, 30: "Venite ad me omnes qui laboratis et *onerati* estis, et ego reficiam vos; . . . jugum autem meum suave est et *onus* meum leves" (Come to me, all you who are labored and carry a heavy weight. I will remake you; . . . sweet is my yoke, light my weight).[11] Only this rapprochement lets us understand the complete argument, from which Heidegger extracts only the three words *onus mihi sum*: "viva erit vita mea tota plena te. Nunc autem quoniam quem tu imples *sublevas* eum, quoniam tui plenus non sum, *oneri mihi sum*" (alive will be my life [once] filled by you. But right now, as you *lighten, relieve, and lift up* him whom you fill, and as I am not full of you, *I am a heavy weight to myself* (*Confessiones* X, 28, 39, 14, 208). Now this argument is not self-evident since it takes on the allure of a paradox: how is it that what is filled is lifted up, while what remains empty weighs itself down on itself? Shouldn't we say, in contrast, that what remains empty weighs less than what is filled? It's of no use to make the correction that here Augustine is talking about the difference between being filled with God (to grow light) or with self (to weigh *oneself* down), for it would still remain to be understood why filled with God means growing light while filled with self (in fact, the void of God, therefore a void) is crushing.

The response to this conceptual problem comes, as is often the case with Saint Augustine, from his exegesis of the biblical text. Provided one takes the time to look at it, which Heidegger does not do (nor do the majority of other modern readers), one will see that he maintains a steady interpretation of Matthew 11:28–30: "Quidquid enim difficile est in praecepto, leve est in amanti. Nec ob aliud recte intelligitur dictum 'Onus meum leve est,' nisi quia dat 'Spiritum sanctum, per quem diffunditur caritas in cordibus nostris,' ut amando liberaliter faciamus, quod timendo qui facit, serviliter facit" (All that is difficult in a commandment is light for him who loves. This is the only way to understand correctly the saying "My weight is light," because "the Holy Spirit by which charity is diffused in our hearts" [Romans 5:5] gives us to do willingly what is done with fear by him who does it slavishly).[12] Or else: "'Jugum enim meum lene est et onus meum leve.' Non enim poterit labor finiri, nisi hoc quisque diligat quod invito non possit auferri" ("My yoke is sweet and my weight light." For only he who loves that of which he cannot acquit himself [by doing it] against his liking can come to the end of a task).[13] The reasoning thus appears limpid: so long as I remain empty of God, that is to say so long as I love neither him nor his will, the requirements of love take on the figure of the Law, which I cannot accomplish by myself, precisely because I do not love; hence, empty of grace, the Law crushes me under a weight that in fact comes from me, reduced to myself alone and hating the demand of God. But, as soon as grace fills me, I love what no longer appears to me exactly as a commandment but as a demand that I love and that, since I love it, I accomplish with all my heart, with a heart finally *light*. The weight weighs me down only insofar as I remain empty—but empty of the love of God or, more exactly, of the love with which Christ alone can fill me. For it is indeed a question of Christ: "'Sarcina mea levis est.' Alia sarcina premit et aggravat te; Christi autem sarcina *sublevat* te; alia sarcina pondus habet, Christi sarcina pennas habet" ("The baggage that I impose is light." Every other weighs you down and crushes you; but that of Christ *lightens you, relieves you, and lifts you up*. Every other weight weighs you down, that of Christ gives you wings).[14] The paradox is clear: the burden becomes light to whoever loves bearing it or rather to whoever loves the one who imposes it on him, but it crushes whoever hates both. In this sense the burden that Christ imposes lightens and relieves the ego of the weight weighing down on it from not only the commandment of the Law, adversarial and impracticable, but, above all, from the decision to remain solely full of self by not loving this burden and him who imposes it—that is to say, the weight of the self reduced to itself alone. I am a weight to myself when I do not love; neither the commandment nor Christ, and therefore in the end not even myself.

The weight of self—more exactly, the weight of *the* self—therefore manifests facticity, the situation in which the *vita humana* always already has to decide about itself before deciding about the things of the world. But this facticity does not decide about itself alone in its Being: the weight is not identified with the Being nor with the nothingness of beings within the world. The weight of the self assigns it to deciding between two burdens: that of the self reduced to itself, the weight of a deadweight, or that which I would love and which would lighten me—precisely the weight of the decision by and for myself. And it is this second weight that is at play in the ordeal of temptation, in which it is not a matter of resisting by oneself solely by insisting all the more on and in oneself but of passing from a crushing passivity to a loving toleration, that is, to "the love that bears all" (I Corinthians 13:7). Temptation teaches one to pass from resistance to toleration by love of the factical weight: "'Numquid est non temptatio est vita humana super terram?' Quis velit molestias et difficultates? Tolerari jubes eas, non amari. Nemo quod tolerat amat, etsi tolerare amat. Quamvis enim gaudeat se tolerare, mavult tamen non esse quod toleret" ("Is not human life on earth temptation?" Who bears willingly the troubles and the difficulties? You order us to bear them, not to love them. Nobody loves what he bears, even if he loves [being capable of] bearing them. For though he rejoices [to be successful in bearing] to bear them, he would nevertheless prefer having nothing to bear) (*Confessiones* X, 28, 39, 14, 210). The question does not consist in bearing or not bearing temptation and the troubles (*molestias*) it imposes; in all cases it must be done, and nobody can evade it. The only question is the manner of bearing them: either by undergoing them and possibly yielding to them (then the evil undergone will render me evil, too), or by undergoing them without yielding to them, by loving the joy that I experience in not yielding to them. "Quis enim pertinens ad Christum non variis temptationibus agitatur, et quotidie agit cum illo diabolus et angeli ejus, ut pervertatur qualibet cupiditate, qualibet suggestione?" (Who, belonging to Christ and concerned by him, is not stirred by various temptations, stirred by the devil and his angels each day so as to be turned away by some desire, some suggestion?) (*Commentaries on the Psalms* 62, 17, *PL* 36, 758). Temptation indeed becomes the permanent and universal condition of the *vita humana*, a facticity, in which a tonality provokes and also results from a decision to be made without respite. But the stakes for someone who belongs to Christ (*pertinens ad Christum*) are essentially different from the stakes for someone who is identified with *Dasein*. In the place where the self in its tonalities (*Stimmungen*) decides about itself in a decision about Being, the self in its temptations decides if it loves or does not love by deciding about Christ.

To this difference a second is added: in opposition to *Dasein* the *pertinens ad Christum* decides without knowing if he will be able to decide and how: "et ex qua parte stet victoria nescio" (and I do not know to which side victory will belong) (*Confessiones* X, 28, 39, 14, 208). For, this decision does not depend on him, since it is about loving and loving must be received. Here an absolutely new principle intervenes: "Da quod jubes et jube quod vis" (Grant what you command, and command what you will) (X, 29, 40, 14, 210). In its radicality it scandalized Julian, bishop of Eclanum, but it is also directly opposed to Heidegger. For this principle postulates that, in the decision that temptation imposes, I can bear the burden by loving him who imposes it on my spontaneous desire only if he gives me to love him more than I hate the burden. I will not love because I will have decided; I will not decide, therefore, because I will have willed it but because I will receive it as a gift: "'et hoc ipsum erat sapientiae, scire cujus esset hoc donum" ("and the knowledge of him from whom this gift came will itself come from wisdom") (ibid., 14, 212, citing Wisdom 8:21). Temptation thus becomes the ordeal of self in which the self learns if it loves what it received as a gift and if it loves this gift more than anything else.

It now becomes possible to consider, albeit only briefly, the temptations and their logic. First, the things that occasion temptation must be specified. It is not a matter of things insofar as they are, more exactly insofar as they remain as such beneath the gaze of the neutral knowledge (*vorhanden*) that would aim only to know them in their present essences. It is a matter of these same things inasmuch as things of use, usual things available for me to use them (*zuhanden*). It is not a matter solely of things that are desirable because usable, in opposition to others that are not usable and therefore not desired, but of all things that desire can always interpret as usable exactly to the degree that they can, all of them, fall beneath the desiring gaze. Things inasmuch as desired, these obscure objects of desire, Saint Augustine will name *libidines*—literally, "desirables"—such as they appear from the point of view opened by the unconditioned desire for the *vita beata*. How do they incite temptation, provoke a decision, and exert the facticity of the *vita humana*? Without even having recourse to the famous distinction between *uti* and *frui* (use and enjoyment of things inasmuch as desired),[15] it suffices here to stick with the conclusion: however desirable the *libidines* appear and might be (if not, would there be a decision to make?), their threat consists in that none of them can claim to grant access to him who gives us to love what he orders. "Nihil eorum esse te inveni. . . . Neque in his omnibus, quae percurro consulens te, invenio tutum animae meae locum" (I found that none of them was you. . . . And in all the things that I run through in consulting you, I do not find the assured place of my soul) (X, 40, 65, 14, 258). The decision consists, when faced with each of the *libidines*, in choosing between loving it for itself or else, through it, loving what gives it, in deciding between loving the gift given or else what renders it possible. But if "amplius placuit donum hominis quam Dei" (we are pleased more with the gift received from man than with the gift given by God) (X, 36, 59, 14, 248), and if I decide to love the *libido* itself, without God, then, left alone and to myself, the weight of the self crushes me: "ita praegravatus animus quasi pondere suo a beatitudine expellitur" (thus, as if crushed beneath its own weight, the mind finds itself cast out of happiness).[16] The temptation consists in enjoying absolutely what merits only use; the resistance to temptation demands enjoying only what serves no other use.

We can now run through the different temptations. Resuming the canonic threefold distinction established in 1 John 2:16, Saint Augustine distinguishes concupiscence of the flesh, concupiscence of the eyes, and *ambitio saeculi*—in other words, the temptations arising through the five senses (through the auto-affection of the flesh), the temptation of *curiositas* (from which Heidegger will get *Neugier*),[17] and the desire for praise. Now, in each of these three temptations the issue is always undergoing the ordeal of self: never is the soul experienced as itself, except in undergoing one of the three temptations, thus being decided in relation to one of the three *libidines*. But, in turn, each temptation leads to the ordeal of self by self, though in the paradoxical mode of an aporia of the self to itself.

Consider first the *libidines* of the flesh (X, 30, 41–53), in terms of touch, taste (gluttony, X, 31, 43–47), smell (in this case not much of a temptation: "odorum non satago nimis" [X, 32, 48]), and hearing (X, 33, 49–50). I will keep for consideration here only touch, one of the least avoidable temptations from which sexual desire proceeds. *Here* it is not a matter of a desire that is so to speak real (that of waking life, always in some sense voluntary or assumed), but of unreal desire (experienced in sleep, without consent). Now, marvels Saint Augustine, as much as I can remain *inconcussus* (unshakable) by real temptation, therefore in principle stronger than it, so too, before the unreal and in principle less-constraining dream, I yield and consent to pleasure. In this situation I become what I do not decide on my own (consenting in irreality to the real pleasure) more so than what I do decide on my own (not consenting really to a possible pleasure). It follows that I am what I do not decide, therefore that I do not decide what I am: "Numquid tunc ego non sum, Domine Deus meus? Et tamen tantum interest inter me ipsum et me ipsum intra momentum, quo hinc ad soporem transeo vel huc inde retranseo!" (Am I, at this moment, not myself, O Lord my God? And yet, there is such a gap between myself and myself, between the instant in which I cross from here to sleep and that in which I return from there to here!) (X, 30, 41, 14, 214). Not only am I not myself and do I not attain my self, but this is not even owing to a default of knowledge or of power to be decided (or to decide about this or that), because now it appears as clear as day that, in this temptation, no decision any longer defines this self; or again that the ipseity of self is neither attained nor any longer accomplished by a decision, nor by the slightest act of will. The self crushes me precisely because I do *not* have access to it.[18]

The temptation that comes from the *libido sciendi*, or the concupiscence of knowing for the sake of knowing, operates first as seeing for the sake of seeing with the eyes (X, 35, 54–58). It puts the *vita humana* under the sway of the things of the world, exterior and foreign to it, inasmuch as perceived and known.[19] In perfect agreement with the doctrine of a truth of the third order, it is necessary to denounce, under the guise of a neutral and disinterested knowledge, a desire to dissipate in things that are not me—solely in order to distract myself from myself with "vana et curiosa cupiditas nomine cognitionis et scientiae palliata" (a vain and curious desire, decked out in the name of knowledge and science) (X, 35, 54, 14, 238). It is not a matter of knowing something real but which would truly bear on me. It is only a question of satisfying the desire to let *oneself* dissipate, each day, in the knowledge of anything whatsoever, even and especially the tiniest and most futile of matters ("in quam multis minutissimis et contemptibilibus rebus curiositas nostra quotidie temptetur" [how many condemnable and miniscule trivialities each day tempt our curiosity] [X, 35, 56, 14, 240]). In curiosity there is not even any longer a real difference between theater, mathematics, and divinatory astronomy (X, 35, 56, 14, 240ff.) because knowing no longer has as its goal to know something or other, but solely to know knowing—still more paradoxically: to know precisely what does not concern me: "quae scire nihil prodest et nihil aliud quam scire homines cupiunt" (things that do no good, men desire to know nothing other than these) (X, 35, 55, 14, 240). The *libido* for the things of the world repeats on the outside what the *libido* of the flesh accomplishes within: putting the self into a crisis vis-à-vis itself.

The temptation of pride—*ambitio saeculi*—repeats and accentuates this aporia but this time in terms of intersubjectivity. The ultimate temptation is born from my desire for the esteem of men, a desire that is so unconditional that I condemn any possible esteem God might have for me: "tertium temptationis genus . . . timeri et amari velle ab hominibus . . . hinc fit vel maxime non amare te nec caste timere" (a third type of temptation . . . wanting to be feared and loved by men . . . from which it follows, more than anything, that one does not love you [sc. God] and that one does not fear you chastely). There is more: not only do we in fact pay more attention to men's judgment of us than to that of God regarding us, but in the desire to obtain the praise of men at any price, not only does one not beg for it by virtue of the (possible) esteem that God could have for us, but one begs for it with such excess that one is ready to claim from men the esteem that they owe only to God: "nos amari et timeri *non propter* te, sed *pro* te" (we are loved and feared *not for your sake*, but *in your place*) (X, 36, 59, 14, 246), and become loved and honored not because of he who made us such as we might possibly merit it, but in his place. Such a masquerade, and one so obvious, should render this temptation perfectly visible and therefore resistible; yet it turns out to be impossible not to yield to it in one way or another. Even the resolute claim to renounce the glory of men (supposing it to be perfect and sincere) can only attract for its part an esteem that is all the more legitimate, which strengthens the temptation all the more (X, 37, 61, 14, 250, 254). I never know therefore if praise touches on me for my own sake or solely for the edification of the others ("non . . . propter me, se propter proximi utilitatem"). That—nothing less than the self that I am in the final analysis—I know it even less than I know God himself: "minus mihi in hace re notus sum quam tu" (in this matter, I am less known to myself than you are to me) (X, 37, 62, 14, 254).

Never has the aporia posed to the ego by the self in it, that is the aporia of care of the self, been so radically exposed, not even in the phrase "Tu autem eras interior intimo meo et superior summo meo" (III, 6, 11, 13, 382). For here I know the *interior intimo meo* (supposed to know me better than I know myself) better than I know the *intimum* in myself.

§25. The will or my ownmost

Facticity, to which the temptations attest, therefore makes evident the self's ownmost, but only as an aporia. This aporia does not, however, leave the self undetermined, to the point that its facticity could not assign it to anything or, what amounts to the same thing, that it could not be conducive to an existential analytic. For the universal and necessary condition of temptation discloses *cura* (which we can legitimately understand as *Sorge*, or care), and *cura* itself is recognized by what it aims at, pleasure, more exactly by that in which it delights, its delectation. "Finis autem curae delectatio est; quia eo quisque curis et cogitationibus nititur, ut ad suam delectationem perveniat. Videt igitur curas nostras, qui scrutatur cor. Videt autem fines curarum, id est delectationes, qui perscrutatur renes" (The end of care is delectation; because each of us endeavors in his care and his thoughts to succeed in his delighting. May he see our cares, he who examines our heart. May he also see the ends of our cares—namely, our delights—he who examines our every nook and cranny) (*Commentaries on the Psalms* 7, 9, *PL* 36, 103).[20] There is only one way to identify care, *cura*: identifying that for which it cares, that is to say, that where it finds (or at least believes it finds) its delights, its *delectatio*. But once that is done, the question is not put to rest, for it still remains to understand how each self decides to assume this or that *delectatio*. And, according to the evidence, this decision rests neither on an objective calculation of interests nor on a pure resolution, since it is carried out in a horizon that is not economic or ontological but strictly erotic, according to what the self can love or believe to love, desire or believe to desire. "'Pes animae' recte intelligitur amor; qui cum pravus est, vocatur cupiditas aut libido; cum autem rectus, dilectio vel caritas. Amore enim movetur, tanquam ad locum quo tendit. Locus autem animae non in spatio aliquo est, quod forma occupat corporis, sed in delectatione, quo se pervenisse per amorem laetatur" (The "striding of the soul" is correctly understood as love—which if it is perverse is named desire or concupiscence, but if it is straight, love or charity. That is, love puts it into motion as that toward which it tends. For the place of the soul is not found in some extension or other, which the form of a body would occupy, but in delectation, that it rejoices in having attained).[21] The factical self of the ego is indeed experienced in temptation; temptation does indeed lead it to be decided according to its care (its *cura*). That for which it takes care has nothing to do with stable beings for theoretical knowledge (*vorhanden*) but everything to do with a useful being (*zuhanden*) where one can find one's delights (*delectatio*). But this *cura* and *delectatio* remain unintelligible without the horizon of love and the erotic reduction that provokes them—and they become perfectly problematic within the horizon of being, where beings admit at best an organization according to the diminished authority of utility, without ever being able to incite *libido, cupiditas*, or, of course, *dilectio. Delectatio* therefore explains *cura* only insofar as it is set forth within a radically erotic horizon. It is not enough to mobilize *cura* and care at the service of beingness for them to become intelligible and remain operative within the pure and simple horizon of Being. It could be that this poaching, by uprooting them from their radically erotic horizon, renders them unintelligible and, essentially, ontologically inoperative.

This is what we find clearly confirmed in the Augustinian interpretation of the will as a mode of love: "Hanc voluntatem non timor, sed caritas habet, 'quae diffunditur in cordibus credentium per Spiritum sanctum'" (This will is not possessed by fear but by the love that "the Holy Spirit spreads in the heart of believers" [Romans 5:5]).[22] The will—or, if one prefers, resolution (*Entschlossenheit*)—does indeed, in the final analysis, *define the self, but in Saint Augustine's terms,* this is because the self is resolved always according as it loves. The paradox of self-will, therefore, is from now on to be formulated in terms of the demands of love. The argument comes up first in the refutation of Manicheanism. Since this ideology, aiming to acquit its clients of evil, had to assert evil's necessary, natural, and substantial character, therefore putting it finally even in God himself, Saint Augustine refutes it by showing that God does not in any way cause evil, which needs no other cause besides my will: "liberum voluntatis arbitrium causam esse, ut male faceremus" (The free decision of [our] will is the cause of our doing evil) (*Confessiones* VII, 3, 5, 13, 584ff.). Or: "Nulla res alia mentem cupiditatis comitem faciat, quam propria voluntas et liberum arbitrium" (No other thing renders the mind servant of desire, except its own will and its free choice) (*De libero arbitrio* I, 11, 21, 6, 178). Or: "Nusquam scilicet nisi in voluntate esse peccatum" (Nowhere is sin to be found except in the will).[23] To be sure, this assignation has as its consequence that I am rendered the one most possibly and probably responsible for evil, but this imputation should not hide the liberation thus accomplished: since evil depends only on a will, and moreover one that is mine, it becomes thinkable, if not possible, to restrain it, indeed to suppress it in me, if not already by myself alone. Seeing myself as responsible for evil amounts to declaring myself potentially free from it.[24] Whence the privilege of the will. Nothing defines the self more than the freedom of its decision; nothing belongs to me more as my own than my will. This is the first knowledge: "Non igitur nisi voluntate peccatur. Nobis autem voluntas nostra *notissima* est: neque enim scirem me velle, si quid sit voluntas ipsa nescirem" (One sins only willingly. Our will is *perfectly known* to us. For I would not know that I was willing if I did not know what my will was).[25] I sin only in willing to (if not, there would not be sin, since there would not be any responsibility). Indeed, I sin (who will seriously deny it?); therefore, my will is absolutely known to me, for I could not will (in fact) if I did not know what the will is (its essence), for the will is but one with the act of willing. And what I know perfectly is something of which I also have perfect certainty in the use, even abusive, that I make of it: "Sublevabat[26] enim me in lucem tuam, quod tam sciebam me habere voluntatem quam me vivere. Itaque cum aliquid vellem aut nollem, non alium quam me velle ac nolle *certissimus* eram et ibi esse causam peccati mei jam jamque advertebam" (What lightened me, relieved me and lifted me up was that I knew I had a will and that I was alive. Therefore when I willed or did not will something, I was *absolutely certain* that there was nobody other than myself who willed or did not will, and I said, for a long time, the cause of my sin lay there [and nowhere else]) (*Confessiones* VII, 3, 5, 13, 586). What wills in me is me and not something else, whose necessity would alienate me from it, just as all the ideologies claim—that at least is entirely as certain as the fact that I live. In other words, I will insofar as I live, and I live insofar as I will. This does not imply that Saint Augustine reestablishes here with the will the *cogito* that he had disqualified in the understanding,[27] since here it is not a matter of knowing *that* I am but *who* I am. What I want manifests my *delectatio*, therefore my *cura* according to my facticity (my temptations)—my willings tell and tell me *which* self is mine. "Interest autem *qualis* sit voluntas hominis; quia si perversa est, perversos habebit motus, si autem recta est, non solum inculpabiles, verum etiam laudabiles erunt. Voluntas est quippe in omnibus; immo omnes nihil aliud quam voluntates sunt" (What is important in a man is this: *which* is his will; for if it is perverse, he too will be perverse in his movements; if it is straight, not only will he not be guilty, but even praiseworthy. For in everyone the will is found or, better, everyone is nothing other than a will) (*De civitate Dei* XIV, 6, 35, 368ff.). What I am, *who* I am, is summed up in my willings, therefore in my will: "Nihil aliud habeo quam voluntatem."[28] The certainty of this perfect knowledge does not contradict the impossibility of the *cogito* or of self-knowledge, since I cannot know what I want, indeed not know that I want it, nor in any way foresee it.

The will, inasmuch as radically erotic instance (*amor, dilectio, cupiditas, libido*, etc.), is the operator of facticity and care in that it wills, in all its willings, only *delectatio*. The will assumes and assures the self itself. Saint Augustine establishes this privilege, on which he will never compromise, from the very beginning. "Non enim posses aliud sentire esse in potestate nostra, nisi quod cum volumus facimus. Quapropter nihil tam in nostra potestate, quam ipsa voluntas est. Ea enim prorsus nullo intervallo, mox ut volumus praesto est. Et ideo recte possumus dicere 'Non voluntate senescimus, sed necessitate;' aut 'Non voluntate morimur, sed necessitate;' et quid alius ejusmodi: 'Non voluntate autem volumus,' quis vel delirus audeat dicere?" (For you can sense that there is nothing else in our power except that when we will, we do. This is why there is nothing so much under our power as our will. It is at our disposition, immediately and without any delay as soon as we want it. This is why we can say correctly that "we do not grow old willingly, but by necessity," that "we do not die willingly, but by necessity," but who would be mad enough to dare say that "we do not will willingly"?) (*De libero arbitrio* III, 3, 7, 6, 336–38). This factual evidence seems so solid that Saint Augustine posits it as a definitively established, legitimate ground.[29] There would be something like a performative contradiction in not being able to will, since to will to will, it suffices to will. For in this case and in it alone, the possibility is equivalent to the actuality, since the will is carried out as a power, therefore in the role of possibility: "Non enim negare possumus habere nos potestatem, nisi dum nobis non adest quod volumus; dum autem volumus, si voluntas ipsa deest nobis, non utique volumus. Quod si fieri non potest ut dum volumus non velimus, adest utique voluntas volentibus; nec aliud quidquam est in potestate, nisi quod volentibus adest. Voluntas igitur nostra nec voluntas esset, nisi esset in nostra potestate" (We can say that we do not have the power only as long as what we will is missing. But as long as we are willing, if the will itself is lacking, it is because we do not truly will it. If therefore it cannot be the case that we did not will while we will, the will is therefore truly there for those who will and nothing is under our power, except what is there for those who will it. This is why our will would not be one if it were not in our power) (III, 3, 8, 6, 340). When the issue is one of having a will (not of willing something other than to will), what I will coincides exactly with the act of willing it, in such a way that it becomes impossible not to actualize what I will, since for that it is enough to will it. Thus, "nihil aliud ei quam ipsum velle sit habere quod voluit" (having what one wants is nothing other than the willing itself) (I, 29, 6, 192). My will is identified with me, to the point that it would become the self itself, this same self, which most often escapes me under other names, under other movements, under the mask of my desires and my temptations. Beneath the multiplicity of facticity, the will alone decides and it decides about the self.

This insistence on the will means that my access and my relation to *veritas* (*lucens* or *redarguens*), therefore that my *vita beata* (in truth or not), do not depend on knowing something but on a decision. Or better, they are known only insofar as they are decided, decided according as I will: "quicumque aliud amant [quam veritatem], hoc, quod amant *velint* esse veritatem. . . . Itaque propter eam rem oderunt veritatem, quam pro veritate amant. Amant eam lucentem, oderunt eam redarguentem" ([All] those who love something other [than this very truth] will that this other thing that they love should be [also] the truth. . . . It is thus that they hate the truth, out of consideration for the thing that they love instead of and in the place of the truth. They love the truth insofar as it illuminates [them], but hate it insofar as it accuses [them]) (*Confessiones* X, 23, 34, 14, 202).[30] The truth of the third order, which manifests itself only as loved, is therefore no longer accomplished except insofar as I am willing, insofar as I will it. In this sense the Nietzschean principle that truth results from the will finds a clear forerunner: more original to the truth than itself is, it turns out, the will to truth. Or more exactly, the will *for the* truth. For it is not a matter of willing it, in the (supposedly plain Nietzschean) sense in which the will to power would establish it starting from and with a view toward its own rise to power, but of letting it itself advance in manifestation, by wanting to support its manifestation and in the measure of this resolution. My will does not take hold of such an authority by force, since it always falls to the truth of the third order to demand deciding about it so as to and even *because* it manifests itself first by this very demand. Only my decision permits a practice of the truth, a practice that is finally genuinely theoretic.

§26. To will, not to will

At the precise moment when the doctrine of the truth of the third order is articulated with facticity, itself accomplished by the will as the resolution by itself of ipseity, there comes to light what Saint Augustine (thrice) names "hoc monstrum" and defines by the paradox that "Imperat animus corpori et paretur statim: imperat animus sibi, et resistitur" (The mind commands the body, which obeys at once; the mind commands itself, and it resists [itself]) (*Confessiones* VIII, 9, 21, 14, 50). In other words the will is felt (and brings the self to feel itself) precisely insofar as it does *not* will—more exactly, is able *not* to will what it wills. When it must decide about anything other than it, it experiences itself as willing and obedient, but when it must decide about itself, it is experienced as not deciding. The relation between the appropriation of the self and the will resolving itself remains, but it begins by inverting itself: there where Heidegger takes it as established that resolution can (and must) in the end come to decide no longer about something other, but about itself, Saint Augustine is astounded by his difficulty, indeed by his impossibility to will and be resolved, as soon as it is no longer a matter of something other than himself. There where Heidegger assumes a possibility and even possibility par excellence, Saint Augustine investigates an impossibility and even the most intimate of impossibilities. In contrast to *Dasein*, which attains its self in anticipatory resoluteness, precisely because it can (and therefore should) appropriate it in the end, the *mens* attains its self first and especially in the powerlessness of its will to decide itself. This paradox (for one should thus translate *monstrum*) structures the entire narrative of the conversion that occupies book VIII of *Confessiones*. As for the question of knowing if this is an empirical account or a literary reconstruction, it remains, despite the fierce and fascinating debates that the question has long sustained, artificial and without solid basis, so long as the structure of the phenomenon related has not been identified and its issue remains not understood—the irresolution of resolution, the indecision of decision as enactment of the facticity of the self.

The structure of this paradox shows up without any ambiguity. There is no doubt that we can (or could) will the good: first because others have indeed done so, either after a long delay, as in the case of Marius Victorinus (VIII, 2, 3–5, 14, 12), or "ex hac hora" (in a timely fashion), as the emperor's agents of public affairs (or *agentes in rebus*) (VIII, 6, 15, 14, 40); second because we, too, perceive clearly and distinctly the truth, now certain: "Et non erat jam illa excusatio, qua videri mihi solebam propterea me nondum contempto saculo servire tibi, quia incerta mihi esset perceptio veritatis: jam enim et ipsa certa erat" (The habitual excuse no longer held for which it seemed I had not yet served you by condemning the world: to wit, because the perception of the truth still remained uncertain to me. For from now on, this very perception was certain to me) (VII, 5, 11, 14, 30). The irresolution that remains can therefore no longer be attributed to the understanding: "Nempe tu dicebas propter incertum verum nolle te abjicere sarcinam vanitatis. Ecce jam certum est" (You do not want to reject the charge of vanity, you said, owing to the uncertainty of the true. Look, now it is certain) (X, 7, 18, 14, 44). I know perfectly at least one indisputable truth: all men want beatitude, without exception, and all agree that it consists in the enjoyment of the truth, *gaudium de veritate*. In the standard situation (that is to say, in the kingdom of metaphysics) this great light in the understanding should also provoke a great inclination in the will fully in possession of itself, which should (can) will in direct proportion to the knowledge of the true.[31] Here precisely is where the paradox comes up: "Imperat animus, ut velit animus, nec alter est nec facit tamen. Unde hoc monstrum? Et quare istuc? Imperat, inquam, ut velit, qui non imperaret, nisi vellet, et non facit, quod imperat" (The mind commands that the mind will; this mind is not something other and yet it does not do it. Whence this paradox? And why? It commands, I say, willingly, since it would not command if it did not will, yet it does not do what it commands) (VIII, 9, 21, 14, 50ff.). The metaphysical rule of the will finds itself suspended, deactivated, and as if bracketed—in short, submitted to the erotic reduction. There no longer subsists any direct connection between the evidence of the understanding and the actualization of the will, between the knowledge of the true and the resolution to enact it. Indeed, they are governed, *in contrast*, by a relation of inverse proportion: I do not want the truth precisely *because* I know it. In other words I hate it. For that matter the narrative of the conversion (*Confessiones* VIII) should, at least at first, be read as that of a *non*conversion, of an obstinate refusal to convert, as it already puts into operation what the doctrine of the truth of the third order will define (*Confessiones* X): the almost insurmountable impossibility of loving the truth and the almost inevitable possibility of hating it, precisely because one can reach it only by loving it: "Cur autem 'veritas parit odium' et 'inimicus eis factus est homo tuus verum praedicans,' cum ametur vita beata, quae non est nisi gaudium de veritate, nisi quia sic amatur veritas, ut, quicumque aliud amant, hoc quod amant velint esse veritatem, et quia falli nollent, nolunt convinci, quod falsi sint? Itaque propter eam rem oderunt veritatem, quam pro veritate amant. Amant eam lucentem, oderunt eam redarguentem" (Why then does "truth give birth to hatred," and why does "the man who serves you and declares the truth become their enemy" [Galatians 4:16], seeing as [everyone] loves the happy life, which is nothing other than rejoicing in the truth? Is it not because [everyone] loves the truth in such a way that [all] those who love something else will that this other thing that they love should be [also] the truth, and, as they do not want to be deceived, they do not want [to admit] that they are deceived? This is how they hate the truth out of consideration for the thing that they love in place and instead of the truth. They love the light when it illuminates [them], but hate it when it accuses [them]).[32] The narrative becomes intelligible only within the context of this phenomenal description. What is at stake is not found in the literary form but in what structures the historic narrative conceptually: the paradox, *monstrum*, of a will that cannot will because it hates the truth to the very degree that it receives its evidence.

This must be specified again: the paradox of the will does not consist in the fact that it would be simply lacking, as a simple "weakness of will," since I do indeed experience its force. What I cannot (or want not to) will, I nevertheless will sufficiently enough to hate it. Hatred of the truth attests that I still will, and even powerfully so, since my will resists the evidence, braces itself on the counterevidence with the energy of a counterwill, stiff-necked and frozen in its obstructed effort. If my will cannot do what it would perhaps will to do (love the truth) but only what it does not will (hate the truth), this does not result from the fact that it is taking on something too great (something no longer falling in its field of action) but, in contrast, from the fact that it takes on the nearest and what, according to good (metaphysical) logic, should offer it the *least* difficulty: the self itself. The lesson of *De libero arbitrio* always holds: "Nemo autem vult aliquid nolens" (Nobody wills something without willing it) (II, 13, 37, 6, 286), and "nihil aliud ei quam ipsum velle sit habere quod voluit" (having what one willed is nothing other than the willing itself) (I, 13, 29, 6, 192). In itself the will benefits from the privilege of not contradicting itself because it always comes back to itself. It does what it wills of its own will and accomplishes the self for this reason alone. But here is the paradox: that the will enjoys this privilege when it wants something other than itself: "Tam multa ego feci, ubi non hoc erat velle quam posse" (So often, I found, it was not the same thing to do and to will) (*Confessiones* VIII, 8, 20, 14, 50)—as is the case when the movements of my flesh (as during this crisis when I tear my hair, fall to my knees, strike my brow, etc.) act on the usual things of the world that are not me. In short, in the majority of cases where it is enough for me to will it to be able to, willing is precisely not equivalent to being able, because my mind (that wills) is not identical with my flesh (that is able, with respect to itself or worldly beings). And if my strengths do not permit me in certain cases to be able to actualize physically what I will of the things of the world, I at least keep intact my power to will to, be it only virtually. I can therefore always will, without a gap from me to me, so long as I will in *the faraway*. But, if I will in *the nearest*, namely, if I will that my will wills what I truly know the best, then it happens that sometimes, indeed most often, I lose the privilege of willing what I will. For the sake of what remains far from me, I keep the privilege that I lose for the nearest. "Et non faciebam, quod et incomparabili affectu amplius mihi placebat et mox, ut vellem, possem, quia mox, ut vellem, utique vellem. Ibi enim facultas ea, quae voluntas, et ipsum velle jam facere erat; et tamen non fiebat, faciliusque obtemperabat corpus tenuissimae voluntati animae, ut ad nutum membra moverentru, quam ipsa sibi anima ad voluntatem suam magnam in sola voluntate per- ficiendam" (And I would not do what I would decide quite amply with an incomparable attunement [*Stimmung*] and that very thing of which I was able as soon as I willed, because provided that I willed, I would will it absolutely. For here is where this faculty, the will, is found, and where the very fact of willing was already done; and yet that did not happen, and my [fleshy] body would obey more readily the slightest will of my soul to move its members than the soul obeyed itself to carry out its great will in its own will) (ibid.). The will can will (in the sense of actualizing by merely willing) all that it wills, except itself. The will, which can do almost all, because it can always will when it is a matter of what is not it, *from far off*, cannot will, when it is a matter of *the nearest*, that is to say of willing to will, of itself willing itself, in short of the self.

A radical suspicion about the will thus arises and forces itself upon us: it is able to will everything and therefore, if its power for actualizing actuality becomes unlimited (which can be imagined conceptually and is being realized factually almost beneath our very eyes), to such an extent that it could be capable of all that it wills, but it cannot itself will itself. The will, as ultimate instance of the self, can, of course, be deployed as will to power, to the point of willing only the increase in power of its very will, in a will to will, which decides in it the Being of beings. But as Nietzsche more than anyone else showed, it cannot decide itself by itself. To pass from nihilism to the great *amen*, it is necessary to await an event that does not depend on it, even though it happens in it. The will, even to power, does not have power over itself, for it cannot always be able to will as it would will, even if it can always will to be able as it can. It often comes over the will that it is not able to be able to will its own will. The only thing to escape from the will is the will itself: "ego suspirabam ligatus non ferro alieno, sed mea ferrea voluntate. Velle meum tenebat inimicus" (as for me, I panted, tied as I was not by shackles imposed by others, but by the shackles of my own will) (*Confessiones* VIII, 5, 10, 14, 28). In other words the will can decide about the things of the world and even about its own flesh infinitely more effectively than about itself. So long as it concerns an other being or what in me remains still other to me, I am able to will. The willing of what is not my ownmost remains always possible for me (even if it is not followed by an effect, sometimes all the more). In contrast, the willing of *the nearest*, therefore of my *ownmost*, turns out most problematic and most difficult. In contrast to Heidegger, Saint Augustine sees that the pretended "authenticity" (which should be understood more exactly as appropriation of self by self) is precisely *not* accomplished with the will and resolution. Supposing that it was necessary for oneself to appropriate one's own *self*, it would not happen by the will, seeing as the will is characterized precisely by a powerlessness over itself that is as radical as its power over what does not fall under the self. Access of self to self does not depend on me, especially not by the simple return to itself of the will, in which I experience by contrast the inaccessible *monstrum* of the *magna quaestio* that I appear to myself.

Temptation bears also on the things of the world (*libido sentiendi*) but, we saw, not uniquely, since the last two, the most fearsome, concern the *libido sciendi* and the *ambitio saeculi*—my curiosity and my pride, which make the things of the world occasions for temptation, which they themselves do not constitute and about which they know nothing. There is not anything that makes me pass from its (legitimate) use to its (illegitimate) enjoyment instead and in place of the truth for the sake of reaching the *vita beata*. I pass from *uti* to *frui* only by a slide of my will, which escapes me and turns me away from what I most desire, to the point of imprisoning me outside my self: "Quippe ex voluntate perversa facta est libido" (To be sure, concupiscence is made from the perverse will) (ibid.). Neither the thing nor the tempter (who does nothing but play on my voluntary servitude) tempts me, but rather my own will, or, more exactly, my will inasmuch as it cannot want what it would want because it can do nothing about itself. I enter into temptation, paradoxically, because I can*not* do *my* own will because my will is not its own, because the will opens no access to my ownmost. Facticity, when care is directed to the will of the self, does not lead to resolution but precisely to *the impossibility of deciding oneself* and therefore of acceding to the self.

§27. Weakness of will

How are we to understand such a powerlessness in willing or, more exactly, in willing to will? Must we oppose a first-order will$_1$ to a second-order will$_2$, the one willing or not willing to trigger the other? Or is it enough to distinguish two wills of the same order in conflict? "Duae voluntates meae, una vetus, alia nova, illa carnalis, illa spiritualis confligebant inter se atque discordando dissipabant animam meam" (My two wills, one old, the other new, the first carnal, the other spiritual, entered into conflict with one another and, in their discord, ravaged my soul) (*Confessiones* VIII, 5, 10, 14, 30). Does this mean a conflict between two independent and opposed wills or a contradiction of the will with itself alone?

Obviously, the hypothesis that there is a conflict of two opposed wills could be authorized officially, seemingly so at least, from the Christological model. Saint Augustine himself describes the final will of Christ as unifying his two wills (human and divine), *de ex duabus voluntatibus una facta*, insofar as he submits the first to the second: "Sed contra voluntatem ipsius evenit aliquid; subjungat se voluntati Dei, non resistat voluntati magnae" (But something happens counter to his own will; he submits himself to the will of God; he does not resist a great will).[33] But this solution implies that the two wills that confront one another (and finally are in accord) remain really distinct, which is possible only on the basis of two really distinct natures (human and divine), which is possible in turn only if they reside in one hypostasis—conditions that are met only in the exceptional case of Christ and are not found in the *monstrum* of any man whatsoever. Such a Christological model would even have, in the context of the always active polemic against Manicheanism, a perverse effect: just as in the case of Christ a distinction of natures results from that of the wills, so too, in the case of the average man, would the principle that "tot sunt contrariae naturae quot voluntates sibi resistunt" (there are as many contrary natures as wills in conflict) (VIII, 10, 23, 14, 54) lead to introducing into me several substances, and therefore to establishing an origin of evil that though in me would not be me: "cum duas voluntates in deliberando animadverterint, duas naturas duarum mentium asseuerant, unam bonam, alteram malam" (observing two wills in deliberation, they assume two natures for two minds, the one good, the other evil) (VIII, 10, 22, 14, 52). Now this is not the case: I do not stand behind one will that would correspond to my nature, faced with another will deployed by a hostile nature, from which I would remain safe. In the conflict of wills all the pain and disorder stems from my finding myself, me, one and the same, with my own and unique nature, in the same moment, at once of two minds: "ego quidem in utroque, sed magis ego in eo, quod in me approbabam, quam in eo, quod in me improbabam. Ibi enim magis jam non ego, qui ex magna parte id patiebar *invitus* quod faciebam *volens*. Sed tamen consuetudo adversus me pugnatior ex me facta erat, quoniam *volens quo nollem* perveneram" (I was no doubt in one and the other [flesh and spirit], but more myself in what I approved [spirit] than in what I disapproved [flesh]. Here, I was not myself, I who was undergoing largely *despite myself* what I was doing nevertheless by *willing to*. But habit, having become more combative with me, it is indeed myself who had so acted, since it is by *willing to* that I had come to what I *did not will*) (VIII, 5, 11, 14, 30). The "violentia consuetudinis" (the violence of habit)[34] results precisely from the fact that the very habit that at this moment contradicts my will also results from my will, from a will no doubt anterior but one that gets its present power from its long past, whose powerful momentum still ruins my today. One should not therefore, in the aporia of man to himself, oppose two wills as two natures but confront the *monstrum* (VIII, 9, 21, 14, 50) of a single will (quite obviously in a single nature) nevertheless in conflict with itself.

Or, we speak of a conflict of wills—reading in this the inner division of the single will playing against itself, removing its strengths from itself so as to be able to contradict itself: "Et ideo sunt duae volunates, quia una earum tota non est et hoc adest alteri, quod deest alteri" (And there are then two wills of the following type: one of them is not complete, and what the one has available to it, the other lacks) (VIII, 9, 21, 14, 52). In other words the other deploys what the first does not put into operation by itself: there are two wills but by division, a will split in two, more exactly, by a *shortage*. In fact, there is only one will, but one that wills only without power and is split into an empty willing (without power) and an uncontrolled power (without willing): "volunt homines et non valent" (Men will and are not able) to will what they will (VIII, 8, 20, 14, 48). This single will wills without having the means for what it wills because it does not will so much as it yields to its desire, because it does not will so much as it lets itself go in desiring: "Ita certum habebam esse melius tuae caritati me dedere quam meae cupiditati cedere; sed illud placebat et vincebat, hoc libebat et vinciebat" (Thus I had the certainty that it is better to give myself over to your charity than to yield to my desire; but even if your charity pleased me and prevailed, desire was agreeable and tied me down).[35] The will wills but without willing with all its heart, without willing wholeheartedly, in short without willing to will: "Sed non *ex toto* vult: non ergo *ex toto* imperat. Nam in tantum imperat, in quantum vult, et in tantum non fit quod imperat, in quantum non vult, quoniam voluntas imperat, ut sit voluntas, nec alia, sed ipsa. Non itaque *plena* imperat; ideo non est, quod imperat. Nam si *plena* esset, nec imperaret ut esset, quia jam esset" (But it does not will *entirely*; therefore it does not command *entirely*. For it commands exactly as far as it wills, and it is the case that it does not command, except exactly as far as it does not will, since just the will gives the command to the will to will, and not to another will, but to itself. This then is what it means that it does not command *entirely*, and it is also why what it commands does not happen. That is, if it were *entire*, it would not command that it be, but it would already be) (VIII, 9, 21, 14, 52).[36] The will wills only halfway, not entirely: "He only *half-willed* to accomplish the act, and that is why the act accomplished left him only half-certain."[37] The question does not consist in a conflict between two real wills that would be opposed as two powers but in the powerlessness of one will that is no longer able truly to will (or not to will) entirely and unreservedly.

The will, when it is no longer a matter of willing a good (or an evil) distinct from it, but of willing its own movement of will, when being able to will its own movement of decision is at issue, *is not sufficient* for willing. "Lex jubere novit, gratia juvare. Nec lex juberet, nisi esset voluntas; nec gratia juvaret, si *sat* esset voluntas" (The law knows how to order, grace to help. The law would not order were it not for the will, but grace would not help if the will was *sufficient*). And also: "*non sufficit sola voluntas* hominis, si non sit etiam misericordia Dei" (*the will is not sufficient*, if there is not also God's mercy).[38] The will is not sufficient for willing, not only because it often lacks the power to accomplish in the world what it wills (power of will) but also because it lacks willpower (power to will)—in other words, the power of willing to will. The intervention of grace, which starts here, never consists for Saint Augustine in opposing itself to the autonomy of my will, by disarming its power or thwarting its choice—be it only because this will of mine manifests itself first and essentially by its insufficiency, its alienation from itself, and its powerlessness. Grace, if it intervenes, can and must do so as a palliative for the insufficiency of the will, restoring it and rendering to it its power to will. Between grace and the will, the relation is not conflictual but one of assistance to an endangered will. The image of a grace that constrains the will and threatens its autonomy presupposes the very thing whose absence makes for the aporia—that the will can of itself will what it wills, that the will secures for itself its own autonomy—in short, that the will *suffices* for freedom. In Augustinian terms there is no conflict between grace and will because without grace there simply is no will. Pelagianism does not constitute a sin of pride but first of all an intellectual fault; it assumes the excellence and even the reality of a faculty whose phenomenological description shows its insufficiency and inconsistency.

If one understands that the will is not sufficient for willing, the *monstrum* is definitively established as a paradox, that of a sickness of the will: "Ego eram, qui volebam, ego, qui nolebam; ego eram. *Nec plene* volebam *nec plene* nolebam. Ideo mecum contendebam et dissipabar a me ipso, et ipsa dissipatio *me invito* quidem fiebat, nec ostendebat naturam mentis alienae, sed poena meae" (It was I who willed, I who did not will; it was I. But when I willed, it was *not fully*, when I did not will, it was also *not fully*. This is why I struggled with myself and dissipated myself, and this dissipation occurred *against my will*, without however manifesting the nature of a foreign mind, but the punishment of mine) (VIII, 10, 22, 14, 54). The will does not will fully, and its powerlessness to will itself (the impossibility of the will to will, of the will to have the will for willing) indicates less a difficulty still to surmount than it diagnoses the disaster of a will that, as such, is defined, in contrast, by the privilege of immediately willing what it wants, from the simple fact that it wants it. Contrary to what philosophy never ceases (and never will cease) to repeat, we do not do evil only out of ignorance but also out of weakness: "Duobus ex causis peccamus; aut nondum videndo quid facere debeamus, aut non faciendo quod debere fieri videamus: quorum duorum illud ignorantiae malum est, hoc infirmitatis" (There are two causes of our sinning: either not seeing what we should do or not doing what we see should be done. The first is the evil of ignorance, the second the evil of weakness).[39] The "sickness of the soul" (*aegritudo animi*) (VIII, 9, 21, 14, 52) consists in the weakness that unplugs, so to speak, the will from itself—so as to make of it a *nill.*

Concerning this malady of the will, which cannot will entirely what it would like to will, the variety of motives for it—original sin (VIII, 10, 22, 14, 54), "*vinculum desideri*" (desire's attachment) (VIII, 6, 13, 14, 34), or "*violentia consuetudinis*" (the violence of habit) (VIII, 5, 12, 14, 32)—is of little importance *here* but remains, in what is essential, secondary and matter for a far more vast inquiry. What is of the highest degree of importance consists in the symptom of this sickness: self-hatred, or, more exactly, the hatred inspired in me by my injustice and therefore by myself inasmuch as unjust. Still more exactly, the hatred of myself who loves me unjustly, by holding for true what I love, rather than loving what gives itself as the true: "sic amatur veritas, ut, quicumque aliud amant, hoc quod amant velint esee veritatem. . . . Itaque propter eam rem oderunt veritatem, quam pro veritate amant" (truth is loved in such a way that men will that all that they love, whatever it might be, should be truth. . . . And thus they hate the truth on account of the thing that they love in place of the truth) (X, 23, 34, 14, 202). I hate the truth because I do not will (or cannot will) this truth as such, and I try, out of weakness, to will in its place what holds the place of truth for me and whose falsity I, in fact, know perfectly well. Hatred of the truth therefore flows directly from the unjust love that I bear for myself by way of my preferred falsity. I will therefore not be able to overcome my hatred of truth except by hating it in me: "videbam et horrebam, et quo a me fugerem non erat . . . et tu me rursus opponebas mihi et impingebas me in oculos meos, ut invenirem iniquitatem meam et *odissem*" (I saw [myself], and I was horrified, and there was no place to which I could flee . . ., and you planted me right before my own eyes, so that I might see my injustice and *hate* it.)[40] It is important to emphasize that here, in contrast to its later avatars (in Nietzsche, in particular, but not Pascal), self-hatred does not bear on the self itself but on the horror inspired in it by its own powerlessness to will the truth, its injustice in wanting falsity in place of this truth. Hatred does not flow from the truth toward the self but is directed against the mode of the self—against its irresolution, its powerlessness to will.

§28. *Vehementer velle*

So described, weakness of will means far more than a lack of will-ing, for the insufficiency goes as far as perversion. Not only can the will not will the truth that it sees and recognizes as such according to its *pul-chritudo*, but it actively prefers a falsity, which it knows in its deformity yet still admits as such. Not only does the will not will truth, but because it loves a nontruth, it actively hates the truth that it should love and that disturbs its love of nontruth. To speak here only of a weakness of the will amounts to hiding what is essential: the will remains still strong enough to at least will negatively, unwilling—in short, to hate truth and to not will it not because it would be ignorant of it or would wrongly identify it but because it recognizes it perfectly as such. Or else, if one still wants to speak about a weakness of the will, this would have to mean a weakness as an inclination *for* lying, which it wants painlessly and for itself, exactly as it has a weakness *for* the hatred that it spontaneously prefers. When Saint Augustine understands the deficiency of the will so radically that it ends up at a perversion of the will into a hatred of truth *as such*, it is a matter of a lie in the strictest sense ("volui tecum possidere mendacium" [*Confessiones* X, 40, 66, 14, 260]), not just ignorance (in the intellect) or a simple weakness (of willing). But then shouldn't such a deficiency of the will be forthrightly opposed to what philosophy ordinarily understands by "weakness of the will"?

We cannot here be expected to take into consideration the entire his-tory of this question or even its contemporary developments. It will suffice to examine quickly three representative examples of "weakness of the will" in order to assess at what point Saint Augustine's doctrine is different from them and even opposed to repeated attempts to reduce the *aegritudo animi* to a benign affection, confined to the therapeutic means of philosophy.

Saint Thomas, when he undertakes to identify the cause of sin (and thus conceives the three temptations according to the same set of topics from 1 John 2:16 that Saint Augustine followed), means to maintain the thesis, explicitly recognized as Socratic (in fact, Platonic and Aristotelian), that "all the virtues are sciences and all the sins ignorance" (*omnes virtutes esse scientias et omnia peccata esse ignorantiae*). He must therefore explain sin first by an obscurity in our knowledge of the good, which would provoke weakness of the will as a mere consequence of this ignorance: "The will never moves toward evil, unless what is not good appears by some reason as good" (*nisi id quod non est bonum, aliqualiter rationi bonum appareat*). The weakness of the will (not being able to will the good and the true) flows from an obscurity in knowledge, more original, but also more known, since it belongs precisely to knowledge, its faculties, and its procedures. Thus led back within the strict limits of the epistemic, the obscurity admits being reduced to a practical syllogism, only poorly constructed. This is either because one knows the universal (for example, that one must not commit fornication), but without coming to see it in the particular (without seeing that this is fornication), the result being that one practices fornication but *without knowing it* (*distractio*). Or it is because one mistakes the universal (assuming wrongly, by *contradictio*, for example, that pleasure is always a good). Or it is because a modification of the body (*immutatio corporalis*: drunkenness, a dream state, seized by passion, etc.) leads to preferring the particular and contradicting the universal.[41] It is therefore not so much the will that fails or wills evil as it is the reasoning that does not correctly define what it should will. Two consequences, exactly contrary to the Augustinian description, follow. First, the decision for evil does not really implicate the decision of the will: "voluntas numquam in malum tenderet, nisi cum aliqua ignorantia, vel errore rationis" (the will would never tend toward evil, were it not for some ignorance or error of reason), and consequently the will properly suffers no deficiency. Next, truth itself, in order to manifest itself in its evidence, demands no decision, not even that of loving or hating it, and it does not put the will in play as condition of phenomenalization but only as a practical consequence of its theoretic evidence.

Kant seems to draw closer to the radicality of Augustine, since in defining "radical evil," he seems to admit a will to evil as such, therefore a radically evil will. And, in fact, for him it is important not to accord "too little" to radical evil by lowering it to the rank of a mere influence of sensibility on decision; sensibility remains in effect morally neutral, and even its powerlessness to assume the universality of the law still leaves us entirely responsible for our choices. For all that, however, Kant is vigilant about not according "too much" to radical evil by making it run so deep as to become an intrinsic corruption of my practical reason, that is, of the power that gives me laws; for in going this far, the stature of all law would be annihilated, and its constraining authority would be impugned, therefore its power to oblige lost. If I could disobey the law as such and repay evil with evil—in short, if I could transgress the categorical imperative with eyes wide open and scorn the "fact of reason" while looking it in the eye—then I would lose all my dignity as a rational mind. Nothing remains any longer, in Kant's eyes, but to admit a middle ground: there is indeed a meanness (*Bösartigkeit, vitiositas*) of the will that does not do the good that it sees as such but clearly prefers to accomplish evil; yet for all that, there is no perversity (*Bösheit, malitia*) of will, as if it succeeded in eliminating the authority of the law in general (obligation, respect) so as to substitute for it the love of *evil as such,* without any other instance coming to combat its sway.[42] Evil, therefore, always results here from the "fragility" or "impurity" of human nature, which does not will what it nevertheless always sees as its obligation, without that implying a "meanness" radical enough for its will to escape from all moral imperative. Thus, evil is not radicalized to the point of intrinsically compromising the will itself or its dependent relation with the moral law. Kant, therefore, maintains, be it only under the title "fact of reason" (the law and practical reason strangely assuming the very facticity of finitude, instead of and in the place of the will and sensibility), the regulation of the will by knowledge. And respect does not intervene as condition of the manifestation of truth, even reduced to *practical* reason; to the contrary, it results from it, as the effect in sensibility of a "fact of reason."

More recently, Donald Davidson has conducted an investigation into the possibility and conditions for a weakness of the will; his attempt does not duplicate either of these two precedents. While Saint Thomas attributed the error as exclusively as possible to faulty knowledge and Kant burdened the will only with a meanness lacking in any perversity by submitting it, at least in principle, to the authority of the law, even when it transgresses it, Davidson introduces another instance in order to pose another question. He asks, in effect, "What is the agent's reason for doing *a* when he believes it would be better, all things considered, to do another thing?" The issue is no longer knowing the good to be desired or accomplished (a matter for the intellect alone) as for Saint Thomas Aquinas, nor the will actualizing the desire or the act (and of its possible irregularity) as for Kant, but the cause or reason that holds the place of cause for the action. Thus Davidson no longer presupposes the knowledge of any good whatsoever, its real or imaginary character, nor the rectitude of the will; the only issue is the connection between these two faculties, whatever it might be; and this connection is identified with the cause or reason of the action—the *causa sive ratio* taking over the question of the action and its morality, so as to integrate it into the common and univocal field of rationality. In fact, the literally metaphysical arrangement of the schema ends up, beneath the appearances of a banality, at a new result: if the agent actually does something other than what he says or thinks (he is obliged) to do, it is because "for that the agent has no reason."[43] If the will does not actually will (to do) what it nevertheless sees in principle as the best (before being done), this is because, in fact, it does not have good or sufficient reasons to will it—or, more exactly, to will it *truly*. The involuntary agent does not will what he would like to will, precisely because he does not know what he wants or why he would want it. The important point consists in this: the weakness does not come from the fact that the will does not will what it knows well (Kant), nor that it wills what it knows poorly (Thomas Aquinas), but that it does not truly will what it does not truly know. It is no longer an issue of a will that is wrong or misguided but of a *false* or bogus will; it is also not an issue of a will rendered insufficient by knowledge that is false or impugned but of a will rendered insufficient by itself, one which does not will *ex toto* but only half wills. It is evident that this is still not Saint Augustine's position, since the weakness of will remains conditioned by the weakness of causes or reasons, therefore still by knowledge. But it is nevertheless a step in the direction of Saint Augustine since the weakness of will this time really does concern the will and not the understanding. Here lacking reasons, the will, which believes it wills the bad rather than the good, in fact is limited to not willing fully, or to not willing at all. From now on, the weakness of the will does indeed concern the will as such.

Saint Augustine's position can now be clarified. Evil—or more exactly, the failure of resolution that chooses the worse and rejects the better—flows first neither from a mistaking of the good nor from a contradiction of the will with itself ("imperat animus sibi et resistitur" [VIII, 8, 21, 14, 50]), nor even from an insufficiency of reasons, but from the perversity of a will that wills evil for the sake of evil, in full knowledge, eyes wide open. Here Saint Augustine is no longer speculating but describing what he experienced directly and in the first person, in the course of a theft committed during his early youth: "Et ego furtum facere *volui* et feci nulla compulsus egestate, nisi penuria et fastidio justitiae et sagina iniquitatis. . . . Nec ea re *volebam* frui, quam furto appetebam, sed ipso furto et peccato. . . . Malitiae meae *causa* nulla esset nisi malitia. Foeda erat, et *amavi* eam; *amavi* perire, *amavi* defectum meum, non illud ad quod deficiam, sed *defectum meum ipsum amavi*" (It is I who wanted to commit the theft, and I did it, driven on by no other need than lack of and distaste for justice and by being fattened on injustice. . . . And I did not even *want* to enjoy the thing that I coveted but to enjoy the theft and the sin itself. . . . My malice had no other cause than this malice itself. It was horrible, and I *loved* it. I *loved* perishing. I *loved* my failings. I did not love that which I had failed but my failing itself) (II, 4, 9, 13, 344–46). The transgression is carried out as such because the good appears to me so evidently that I decidedly condemn it, because the evil appears to me so evidently that I am clearly decided for it. The transgression does not aim to make me enjoy its forbidden object (here, the stolen fruit), which remains a mere pretext, an occasioning cause, but it makes me enjoy the transgression itself, the evil as evil: "Nam decerpta projeci epulatus inde solam iniquitatem, qua laetabar fruens" (I threw away what I had plucked. I tasted from it only the injustice, which I enjoyed with joy) (II, 6, 12, 13, 350). In this sense the evil will wants only to enjoy the evil, therefore wants to enjoy only itself. But this will to will has a price: not willing *anything*, therefore a consequence: willing *nothingness*. Contrary to metaphysics, which will always conceive the evil resolution as a moral fault of the mind (at best a weakness of the will, most often an ignorance of the intellect), Saint Augustine thinks it in an extramoral sense as an *aegritudo animi*, a sickness of the spirit, which can no longer will anything, not even will willing, except to will nothingness.

This doctrine poses two difficulties. First, how can nothingness play the role of a *malitiae meae causa*, therefore of a reason for willing, even for willing evil as such? Next how can we admit that *defectum meum ipsum amavi*, that my fault, my defect, and my failing can be loved, if I can no longer will, therefore love?

For the first difficulty it is necessary to return to the thesis that Saint Augustine alone diagnosed: if I can will what I do not want, this is not a matter of a contradiction of my divided will with itself but of the fact that I do not will truly or *ex toto* what I say or believe myself to will. It is a matter of only a powerlessness to will: the will that wills evil first wills evilly; it finds itself wickedly short in willing—in willing in the strict sense, that is to say "velle *fortiter et integre*, non semisauciam hac atque hac versare et jactare voluntatem parte adsurgente cum alia parte cadente luctantem" (to will, *strongly and completely*, not to turn and twist here and there, a half-wounded will, torn between one part that rises and another that succumbs to the struggle) (VIII, 8, 19, 14, 48). This combat between two wills proves simply that the will no longer resides in a state of willing at all. Its sickness comes from the fact that it no longer has reason or, above all, will to will. Deficiency of cause causes its deficiency. The description of the *Confessiones* thus perfectly anticipates the doctrine of *The City of God*: "Nemo igitur quaerat efficientem causam malae voluntatis; non enim est efficiens, sed deficiens, quia nec illa effectio, sed defectio. Deficere namque ab eo, quod summe est, ad id quod minus est, hoc est incipere habere voluntatem malam" (Let nobody seek out the efficient cause of the evil will; for it is not efficient, but deficient, since this will is not effective but defective. For defecting from what is supremely, so as to fall toward what is less, this is to begin to take on an evil will) (XII, 7, 35, 170). Or else, "malae voluntatis efficiens naturalis vel, si dici potest, essentialis nulla sit causa" (for the evil will there is no natural, or if one can put it this way, essential, efficient cause) (XII, 9, 35, 174).[44] Willing evil requires no cause (efficient, real, natural, essential, etc.) because evil consists in nothing real and because, for the will, it is not equivalent to gaining or producing something at once evil and real (which would constitute a pure contradiction in terms) but in having a bad time willing, in willing evilly, in evil willing—"Deficitur enim non ad mala, sed *male*" (For one does not defect toward evil things, but one defects *by* [turning] *evil*) (XII, 8, 35, 172). The evil will, ultimately, wills nothing evil (for strictly speaking, nothing is evil inasmuch as it is real), but it doesn't will anything; it does not will; it is self-deficient, deficient of the self.

The second difficulty finds, paradoxically, an answer by confirming the response to the first. Why, that is, if the evil will simply does not will at all, does Saint Augustine, at the very moment when he was describing the will to evil for the sake of evil, grant it a cause, indeed nothing less than the love of evil? "Malitiae meae *causa* nulla esset nisi malitia. Foeda erat, et *amavi* eam; *amavi* perire, *amavi* defectum meum, non illud ad quod deficiam, sed defectum meum ipsum *amavi*" (My malice had no other *cause* than this very malice. It was horrible, and I *loved* it. I *loved* to perish. I *loved* my defects. I did not *love* that toward which I was defecting, but my defectiveness itself) (II, 4, 9, 13, 344–46). The first and most simple hypothesis is this: if love causes evil and evil admits only deficient causes, it is necessary that love itself become a deficient cause; but wouldn't it then lose its privileged status in access to the manifestation of truth? Another hypothesis is possible: that the will in this case truly wills evil; for in the episode of the theft of fruit, one has to see that the will truly wills, without hesitation or reserve. Does it will evil by loving it? The text says nothing other than that. How is this to be understood? By admitting that the will succeeds in willing (even evil, for it often wills evil) only on condition of truly willing, *ex toto, fortiter et integre, plena*, that is to say on condition of loving. The perversity of evil resides, we know from experience, not only in that I do it but in that I love it. Out of this scandal a light shines, however: willing, truly willing, whether it be the good or evil, means in the final analysis loving. Loving seems to be the name of the will that wills, of the will reborn from the *aegritudo animi*.

This equivalence between the will truly willing and love—in other words the fact that one wills only when one loves what one wills and to the measure of this love—is a constant doctrine of Saint Augustine beginning with *De libero arbitrio*: "Voluntas qua appetimus recte honesteque vivere, et ad summam sapientiam pervenire" (The will with which we desire to live rightly and honestly in order to reach supreme wisdom) supposes that "*vehementer* velis" (you will it *strongly*) (I, 25, 6, 184). But it will fall to *De Trinitate* to establish definitively the nature of this vehemence: "Et quia non tantum quam doctus sit, consideratur laudabilis animus, sed etiam quam bonus: non tantum quid meminerit et quid intelligat, verum etiam qui velit attenditur; non quanta flagrantia velit, sed quid velit prius, deinde *quantum velit*. Tunc enim laudandus est animus *vehementer amans*, cum quod amat *vehementer amandum* est" (And, as a mind is not considered worthy of praise only for its knowledge but also for its goodness, one pays attention not only to its memory and its intelligence but also to its will; and not merely to the ardor of its willing but first of all to what it wills, then to its *degree of will*. That is, one praises a spirit for the *strength of its love*, when it *loves* what must *be strongly loved*) (X, 11, 17, 16, 152).[45] These two examples of the strength of will as the strength of love lead to the conclusion of the treatise: "De Spiritu autem sancto nihil in hoc aenigmate quod ei simile videretur ostendi, nisi voluntatem nostram vel amorem seu dilectionem, quae *valentior est voluntas*" (In this enigma nothing other appears that seems to resemble the Holy Spirit, except our will, or love or dilection, which is only *a stronger will*) (XV, 21, 41, 16, 532).[46] Between the Holy Spirit and me, the image and likeness play together only in one formal univocity, that of the will. But this will, to will truly, must will strongly, that is to say love. I can will truly, *fortiter et integre*, only if I love. Love does not constitute one of the possible uses of the will but the sole truly efficient (not deficient) mode of the will. It should not be said that the will alone permits loving but that loving alone permits truly willing.

§29. The grace to will

Love does not make up a will like the others, one merely specified by a particular objective and affective modality, but is the sole *valentior voluntas*, the sole truly strong will, in fact the sole will able to will effectively what it knows should be willed—all the other wills remaining *velle* that, in fact, are not willed (and that, in fact, are called *velles* only by antiphrasis). The will can thus be conceived and therefore described only in terms of love and only in the figure of its erotic realization. But, to continue this line of thinking, it could be that the will, inasmuch as love, ends up evidencing characteristics quite different from those that are attributed to the metaphysical concept of will.

The first point is to avoid an initial misreading: if the will becomes itself only in willing to the point of loving, that does not mean that love of the good would permit the will to will truly. For a perfect neutrality permits the *valentior voluntas* to be exercised as much for evil as for good: "Recta itaque voluntas est bonus amor et voluntas perversa malus

amor. Amor ergo inhians habere quod amatur, cupiditas est, id autem
habens eoque fruens laetitia; fugiens quod ei adversatur, timor est, idque
si accederit sentiens tristitia est. Proinde mala sunt ista, si malus amor est;
bona, si bona" (And so the right and straight will is thus a good love, the
twisted will a bad love. Therefore the love that aspires to what it loves is
desire; that which has it and enjoys it is joy. That which flees an adversary
is fear and, if it feels that something happens to it, sadness. Consequently
all these things are evil, if the love is evil, and good if it is good) (*De
civitate Dei* XIV, 7, 25, 374). This is not (as it will become in many of the
subsequent readers of Saint Augustine) an enumeration, indeed a deduction of the passions, even on the basis of love. It is an erotic reduction of
all movements of the mind to motions of the will, itself understood in its
vehemence, that is to say as a love. But, since without love the will cannot
will, and since the will, when it wills, wills just as much (indeed often
much more) evil as good, one has to admit, to explain the will to evil,
nothing less than a love of evil itself. This is the ambivalence of love: it
renders good or evil what it wills according as it itself intends the good or
the evil. "Pes animae recte intelligitur amor, qui cum pravus est, vocatur
cupiditas aut libido; cum autem rectus, dilectio vel caritas. Amore enim
movetur tanquam ad locum quo tendit. Locus autem animae non in spatio
aliquo est, quod forma occupat corporis, sed in delectatione, quo se pervenisse per amorem laetatur" (The stride of the soul is correctly understood
as love, which if it is perverse is named desire or concupiscence, but if it
is straight, love or charity. That is, love puts the soul into motion as the
place toward which it tends. For the place of the soul is not located as if in
some space, which the form of a body would occupy, but in delectation,
where it rejoices to have come by following its love) (*Commentaries on the
Psalms* 9, 15, *PL* 36, 124). When I will, it is absolutely necessary that I love,
for I cannot will truly, except by willing unreservedly, *ex toto*, therefore
by loving; that holds for the will to evil as well as for the will to the good.
To the point that I cannot will evil except by loving what I chose in place
and instead of the good: "propter eam rem oderunt veritatem, quam pro
veritate amant" (the thing for the sake of which they hate the truth, this
was precisely what they love in its place) (*Confessiones* X, 23, 34, 14, 202).
Even if evil perverts love by not loving the good, it cannot, in order to
reach something other than the good, not love. The evil will still renders

homage to love, since it must still love, even in the opposite direction, in order to will the opposite of the good.

If the will is accomplished only to the degree that it goes all the way to love, it must be concluded that love determines me more originally than the will. In other words I am not individualized by what I think intellectually (everybody, or at least others, can think it as well as me) nor by the will alone and its resolution. In effect, if the issue is my will willing something other than itself, it is perfectly possible for others than myself also to will it, provoking mimetic rivalry or a competition of desires, more so than my individuation. And if the issue is the will willing to be decided, willing itself, one can claim to be individualized by self-resolution, but, as we saw, the will cannot do so on its own, except by passing into love, as *valentior voluntas*. It therefore has to be admitted that my individuation exceeds will-power and requires that of love in me. I find myself there where I think, but I think there where my pleasure is found: "Ubi cogitatio, ibi et delectatio est" (*Commentaries on the Psalms* 7, 11, *PL* 36, 104). Put otherwise, I know what I am by discovering that in which I find my pleasure: "talis est quisque, qualis ejus dilectio" (*Homilies on the First Letter of John* II, 14, *PL* 35, 1997). Of course, that in which I find my pleasure is not something I know in advance, as if I could foresee it, or even choose it. I discover it only once the event teaches it to me and discovers it to me. I do not love what I will, or at least what I believe I will. What I will truly I recognize after the fact as what I loved, and what I love I identify after the fact when I enjoy having reached it. Thus it is necessary for me to enjoy what I love in order to know that I loved it and that in fact, knowingly *or not knowingly*, I desired it beforehand. I am always late to the event and the last to know what I love. The will therefore follows what I love, and what I love precedes my will. I do not find myself there where I am, or where I am thinking, but there where I love, I desire and enjoy. The *self's place* precedes where *I* come from. The radicalization of the will into love reverses the advance—the intentional advance of the *I* toward the object of its willing reverts into a delay of the *I* with regard to the place of that which the *self* loves. *The anticipation belonging to resolution yields to the delay of the will inasmuch as it loves.* As much as I will by an intentional advance, so much I love in the delay of desire.

This reversal of the advance into a delay is asserted by Saint Augustine in the form of a theological principle: "*Da* quod jubes et jube quod vis" (*Give* what you command, and command what you will) (*Confessiones* X, 29, 40, 14, 210). This principle incited not only the scandal of Pelagius but Pelagianism itself, and it provoked them quite rightly, as it is necessary, in order to get it, first to admit it, the paradox of a will reversed into love. Let us consider the two examples that justify the intervention of this paradox. First is the issue of liberating oneself from sexual desire, something no will can want truly, except when another gift permits the will to do so: "quia 'nemo enim potest esse continens (ἐγκρατὴς) nisi tu *des*, et hoc ipsum erat sapientiae, scire cujus esset hoc *donum*' (because "nobody can be continent, unless you *give* continence to him, and knowing from whom this *gift* comes is something that itself belongs to wisdom" (Wisdom 8:21) (X, 30, 45, 14, 212). In other words, in the case of continence it goes without saying that the will does not suffice for wanting and that an other love is necessary to it, one that can come to it only from elsewhere. It is necessary that the will let itself be relieved and lifted up by a gift that precedes it and from which it could only proceed. Next is the matter of vanity and the pleasure of flattery, which themselves result from our incurable and unbreakable dependence on the opinion and esteem of others: "Quotidiana fornax nostra est humana lingua. Imperas nobis et in hoc genere continentiam: *da* quod jubes et jube quod vis" (The tongue of men is the furnace in which we are cooked each day. In this domain, too, you order us to continence: *give* what you command and command what you will) (X, 37, 60, 14, 248). As we saw (in §24), I can never extract myself from the will to please men, since the very fact of renouncing this (by making it known or, worse, keeping it secret) reinforces all the more their esteem regarding me and, a still more sure outcome, mine for myself. Here, then, are two impossible wills, one in actual fact (sexual continence)[47] and one in logic (continence with respect to flattery).

The entire force of the paradox resides in opening a possibility at the very heart of this impossibility: what my will absolutely cannot will, God can permit it to will, provided that he *give* it to will it. God can order all the impossibilities possible to the powerlessness of my will, provided that he *give* it also the power for these very impossibilities. In fact, this paradox is sketched out well before the polemics formalized around grace, since from the time at Cassiciacum this demand becomes the rule: "*Jube, quaeso, atque impera quidquid vis, sed sana et aperi aures meas, quibus voces tuas audiam, sana et aperi oculos meos, quibus nutus tuos videam*" (*Order*, I ask you, and *command all that you will*, but cleanse and open my ears so that by them I might understand your words. Cleanse and open my eyes so that by them I see what you are showing me). Why take the risk of asking that one ask no matter what of my will, which I know will not will a great thing? Because the will is now revived and reversed by love and therefore desire and enjoyment precede it: "*Jam solum te amo*, te solum sequor, te solum quaero, tibi soli servire paratus sum, qui tu solus juste dominaris; tui juris esse cupio*" (Now I love only you, I follow only you, I seek only you, I am ready to serve only you, because your dominion alone is just. I desire to be under your jurisdiction).[48] God can ask the impossible of my will, which does not will on its own *ex toto* (and cannot will to will it), because he, more than anybody, can give it to be carried out in a love and to become *valentior* to the point of willing what remains impossible to a will abandoned to itself. The Pelagians' misunderstanding about the paradox "*Da* quod jubes et jube quod vis" obviously stems first from their not understanding the *gift* such that it precedes, conditions, and surpasses the commandment but, above all, from their blindness in the face of the transformation of the will, inevitably powerless before the impossible, into a love tangentially powerful enough to desire this impossible. "*Give* what you command" supposes in fact that given to me is *to love* and *what* I can love—namely, *that which can make me love*. This is formulated literally by a second principle and paradox, which alone renders the first intelligible (and which the Pelagians simply have not seen): "*Da quod amo*: amo enim. Et hoc tu *dedisti*" (*Give* what I love; for I love. And that too [that I love what you give to love] you [also] *gave*) (*Confessiones* XI, 2, 3, 14, 274). And again: "*Da quod amo*: amo enim, et hoc tu *dedisti*" (*Give me what I love*; for I love and that too [that I love what you give to love], you *gave* [to me]) (XI, 22, 28, 14, 316). Thus the will becomes *valentior* and is accomplished *ex toto* by becoming love; but that, too, it receives as what it can neither will nor give itself. To will truly befalls the will only in the advance, as a gift to love—which is also named a grace.

It follows that we cannot will in the real sense without God giving it to us, by giving us to will in the mode of loving, according to an advance to which we come late. This can also be put this way: we will only in response (see above, Chapter 1, §3), and even the possibility of refusing the gift also turns out given. The will (like love more ancient than myself) comes to me like a gift. "Nam si quaeramus utrum Dei *donum sit voluntas bona*, mirum si negare quisquam audeat. At enim quia *non praecedit voluntas bona vocationem*, sed *vocatio bonam voluntatem*, propterea *vocanti Deo* recte tribuitur quod bene volumus, nobis vero tribui non potest quod vocamur; . . . nisi ejus vocatione, non volumus" (If we ask if *a good will is a gift* of God, it would be surprising if someone were to deny it. But because *the good will does not precede the call*, but *the call [precedes] the good will*, we rightly attribute the fact that we will well to *God who calls*, for we cannot attribute to ourselves the fact of having been called; . . . without his call, we simply would not will at all) (*Quaestiones VII ad Simplicianum* II, 12, BA 10, 470). One could find a problem here however. As regards the will, is it the will in general with its indifference that is given to us (the "Possibilitas quippe illa, quam [Deus] dedit, tam nos facit bona posse, quam mala" [The possibility given (by God), such as it makes us have the power for good things as well as evil ones]),[49] or the good will ordered by love ("sic vult homo, ut tam Deus voluntati ardorem dilectionis inspirat, . . . quia, nisi natura esset in qua nos condidit, qua velle et agere possumus, nec vellemus, nec ageremus" [man wills in such a way that God inspires his will with the ardor of love, . . . because if there was a nature, in which we were set up such that we could will and act, then we would not will at all, nor act at all])?[50] But this distinction can itself be disputed because it supposes that the possibility of willing (even evil) arises exclusively from nature without passing through (or for) a gift, while the actuality of the *vehemens in bono voluntas* arises exclusively from the gift without coming by grace. Now, from the strictly Augustinian point of view, this opposition is illegitimate: all of the will, its possibility (still weak) of (not) willing (truly) results as much from a gift as its accomplishment in love. And the reproach he makes to the Pelagians targets precisely the fact that they admit neither the one nor the other as a gift: "Nec alicubi potui reperire, hanc *gratiam confiteri*, qua non solum possibilitas naturalis voluntatis et actionis, quam dicit nos habere etiamsi nec volumus nec agimus bonum, sed ipsa etiam voluntas et actio subministratione Spiritus sancti adjuvatur" (And I could not find anywhere a *confession of this grace* that supports not only the natural possibility of willing and acting, which he says to be ours even if we do not want or do the good, but also the will and action done under the guidance of the Holy Spirit).[51] In fact, precisely because "Dei donum sit voluntas *bona*" (the *good* will is a gift of God) (*Quaestiones VII ad Simplicianum* II, 12, 10, 470), it was necessary first that *all* that rendered it possible, including the mere indifferent possibility of (evilly) willing evil, that is to say by loving it (though evil), come from God as a gift. For the advance of love, which makes the will *valentior*, never arrives to us, in any case, except as a gift.

Whence emerges a final character of the will realized as love: since by definition willing *ex toto* arises from a gift given in advance and one that gives itself only in the advance of the *self* of desire ahead of the *I* of intention, the customary and confused debates about grace and free choice must be revised on the basis of the advance itself—in other words, of my delay to myself (of the *I* to *itself*). There cannot be a conflict between freedom and grace, since without grace (that is to say, its transformation into love) the will cannot will well, since, at bottom, it simply cannot will at all: "Ergo et victoria qua peccatum vincitur, nihil aliud est quam *donum* Dei, in isto certamino *adjuvantis* liberum arbitrium" (Therefore even the victory over sin is nothing other than a gift of God, bringing into this combat his assistance to free choice) (*De gratia et libero arbitrio* IV, 8, 24, 110). Or else: "gratiam Dei . . ., qua voluntas humana non tollitur, sed ex mala mutatur in bonam et, cum bona fuerit, *adjuvatur*" (the grace of God . . ., which does not suppress the human will but changes it from evil to good and, once changed, assists it) (*De gratia et libero arbitrio* XX, 41, 24, 184). The very hypothesis of a conflict presupposes what it is a matter of overcoming or, rather, what has proven ever since the outset unthinkable: for it to be opposed and distinguished from the gift of the advance (of grace), it would be necessary for freedom to function alone and of itself without grace, while it is realized only in becoming, by grace, *valentior*, only in becoming a love. "Ecce quemadmodum *secundum gratiam Dei, non contra eam*, libertas defenditur voluntatis. Voluntas quippe humana non libertate consequitur gratiam, sed gratia potius libertatem" (And it is in this way that the freedom of the will is defended, *according to the grace of God, not against it*. For the will of man does not obtain grace through its freedom, but its freedom through grace) (*De corruptione et gratia* VIII, 17, 24, 306).

There is no dispute about what freedom could accomplish without grace, since without grace freedom attains absolutely nothing, because it cannot will anything. The (good, but above all effective, *valentior*) will does not disappear in grace; it comes from it, starting from this very advance. The best confirmation is found in the fact that in the advance of grace the will not only remains, not only attains its efficaciousness, but is finally imputed officially to us ourselves: "Certum est nos velle, cum volumus, sed ille facit ut velimus bonum. . . . Certum est nos facere cum facimus; sed ille facit ut faciamus, praebendo *vires efficacissimas* voluntati" (It is certain that it is we who will, when we will, but it is God who makes it that we will the good. . . . It is certain that it is we who act, when we act, but it is God who makes it that we act by providing *very efficacious strengths* to the will) (XVI, 32, 24, 164). God does not dispense grace so that we might dispense with willing (as the Pelagians, on one hand, and the extremists proposing double predestination, on the other, seem to suppose) but so that we might be *permitted* to will: "Aguntur enim ut agant, non ut ipsi nihil agant" (For God acts in them so that they act, not so that they themselves do not act) (*De corruptione et gratia* II, 4, ibid., 274). And he permits us to will by giving us to will in the sole efficacious manner, *by loving*: "Quasi vero aliud sit bona voluntas quam *caritas*, quam Scriptura nobis esse clamat ex Deo a Patre *datam*, ut filii ejus essemus" (As if the good will was something other than *charity*, that scripture proclaims to be *given* to us from God through the Father, so that we might be his sons) (*Liber de gratia* I, 21, 22, *PL* 44, 371). God does not give us only the power for what we will (or to obtain it by receiving it), nor even to choose well what we want, but above all to be able to will what we will to will; he gives us what is most intimate in us—our willing to will itself: "Nos ergo volumus, sed Deus in nobis operatur et velle; nos ergo operamur, sed Deus *operatur et operari* pro bona voluntate" (It is indeed we who will, but God operates in us this willing; it is indeed we who operate, but God *operates even this operation* according to his good will" (*De dono perseverantiae* XIII, 33, 24, 676). The resolution that defines and decides the *self* in me belongs to me without, however, coming from me; it comes from elsewhere. God does me the grace of succeeding in willing what I would will to will: "Fit quippe in nobis per hanc Dei gratiam . . . non solum posse quod volumus, verum etiam *velle quod possumus*" (What arrives by this grace of God . . . is not only that we can what we will but that *we will [truly and entirely] what we can [in fact without knowing it or willing it]*) (*De corruptione et gratia* XI, 32, ibid., 342).

It now becomes possible to will what God wills rather than what I on my own believe I will: "Et hoc erat totum nolle, quod volebam et velle, quod volebas" (And the entire affair consisted only in not willing what I willed, but willing what you yourself willed) (*Confessiones* IX, 1, 1, 14, 70). Not of course because I renounce willing what I want but, exactly to the contrary, because I begin to will truly *ex toto*, since I will what is given to me to love.

5

Time, or the Advent

§30. Time and the origin

No more than self-knowledge (Chapter 2), truth (Chapter 3), or desire (Chapter 4) does the aporia of time become part of Saint Augustine's investigation for purely philosophical reasons. Like the previous questions, it rises to the forefront only inasmuch as it is opened and imposed by *confessio* (Chapter 1), the sole theological authority for speaking, therefore also the sole regulator for the apparition of questions to be debated. We therefore ought not be too hasty, as the stubborn commentators, in a caricature of themselves, often are, in isolating, in book XI of *Confessiones*, a philosophical treatise on time and inscribing it into the long line of grand teachings dedicated to this theme—whether we want to hail or assault its inventiveness. In contrast, and precisely because at first glance it does indeed concern time, its definition, and its aporiae, it behooves us to keep this essay within the *confessio*, alone capable of securing for it a place, in the sense that Saint Augustine understands it. For, before looking into the origin of time (or even into the time of the origin) we must deal with the issue of determining the origin of the very *question* of time.

This question arises, in the first lines of book XI of the *Confessiones*, when, after the individual *confessio* of books I through X, Saint Augustine intends to join his readers' drive to his own: "excito in te et [affectum] eorum, qui haec legunt" (I excite toward you also the affection of those who read these lines) (XI, 1, 1, 14, 270). This public, in fact ecclesial, *confessio* can only revive an earlier line of questioning: how could I not only confess whatever it might be to God (who by definition already knows all things), but above all make myself understood in the time of God, in eternity? "Numquid, Domine, cum tua sit aeternitas, ignoras, quae tibi dico, aut ad tempus vides quod fit in tempore" (Could it ever be, O Lord, since eternity is yours, that you would not know what I say to you or that you would see one at a time what happens in time?) (ibid.). This question is not rhetorical but takes seriously the Greek aporia of the gods' knowledge or rather nonknowledge of the vicissitudes of men. Since "Aeternitas ipsa Dei substantia est" (Eternity is the very substance of God) and since "Nos sumus tempora. Quales sumus, talia sunt tempora" (We, we are of the times. Such as we are, so too are the times),[1] God, at least when inscribed in the Greek site of the divine, does not have to know about my life and what I could say to him about it but knows only himself—not out of indifference but because he is not obliged to, nor can he even do so without doing damage to his divinity, which separates him from mortals as eternity is opposed to time. And if eternity has nothing in common with time, then, properly speaking, no *confessio*, neither praise nor an admission, has any meaning, because it has no place where it could ever produce itself. In rigorous philosophy God does not have to respond *to* any *confessio* because he does not have to know *about* it.

Considering it more carefully, this aporia has already silently threatened, or rather, *de jure*, that is to say *philosophically*, it has disqualified the entire *confessio* ever since the beginning of its de facto *theological* deployment. Saint Augustine wrote, up until now, *as if* the *confessio* could pursue its project, while in all metaphysical rigor, it could not, since the gods do not listen to men nor fraternize with them. This impediment could in some ways be ignored by the intrigue of the *interior intimo meo*, with its tacit acosmism; but, as soon as the *confessio* begins to claim to pass beyond the face-to-face of a pure *coram te* and to arise on a public stage, *coram multis testibus* (X, 1, 1, 14, 140) and open up (*patefacimus* [XI, 1, 1, 14, 270]) to all in the world we have in common, the rules of the *cosmos* and its philosophical comprehension impose themselves inexorably.[2] Time, in Greek terms, opens no access to the divine but forbids it. Far from being able to assume unhesitatingly and unreservedly the opposition between divine eternity and the temporality of mortals, such as ancient philosophy established the ironclad distinction, Saint Augustine, like all Christian thinkers, had to confront it as a serious objection and contest it, in order to uphold the then unthinkable paradox that time has to do with eternity, can lead to it or, at least, not forbid access to it, that men who are passing can pass beyond themselves toward God, who is not passing. (This will mean, in fact, an even less acceptable paradox: that God, who is not passing, can pass, himself, among men, who are passing.) In this context the question must be understood in an entirely different way than is customary: book XI of *Confessiones* is not about a definition of time *or* its supposed psychological reduction; *nor* is it about an anticipation of Kant's doctrine of time or an existential precomprehension of its Being. It aims rather to conceive how time is not closed to eternity any more than it is abolished in it—in short, how it could be articulated together with it, without confusion or separation.

   And, in fact, book XI will conclude with a recognition of this almost unthinkable articulation: "Intelligant te ante omnia tempora aeternum *creatorem* omnium temporum et neque ulla tempora esse tibi coaeterna nec ullam creaturam" (Let them comprehend you as the eternal *creator* of all times from before all times and with whom no time nor any creature is coeternal) (XI, 30, 40, 14, 340). There really is an articulation of the time of mortals together with the divine eternal, and it is at play in creation, a concept that is non-Greek par excellence and that will always remain refractory to metaphysics. In fact, the relation between the temporal and the eternal is duplicated in that of the visible world and invisible God: "Visibilium omnium maximus mundus est, invisibilium omnium maximus Deus est" (The greatest of all visible things is the world; the greatest of all invisibles is God). For whoever admits the authority of the scriptures, they will intersect in creation: "Sed mundum esse conspicimus, Deum esse credimus. Quod autem Deus fecerit mundum, nulli tutius credimus quam ipsi Deo. Ubi eum audivimus? Nusquam interim nos melius quam in scripturis sanctis, ubi dixit propheta ejus: 'In principio fecit Deus coelum et terram'" (But that the world is, we see; that God is, we believe. As for the fact that God made the world, what better guarantee for believing it than God himself? Where have we heard it? Nowhere better than in the holy scriptures, where his prophet said: "In the beginning God made the heavens and the earth") (*De civitate Dei* XI, 4, 1, 35, 38). Creation

thus constitutes, de facto and de jure, what is really at stake not only
in book XI, but as we have already seen, in the last three books of the
Confessiones. Among other reasons for that, a most significant one is this:
the interpretation of beings as created makes it possible to inscribe them
all, without exception, inanimate as well as animate, in the theological
place par excellence—*confessio*, this time possible no longer for just one of
us alone but for the cosmic community. That is, the first *confessio*, that,
individual, of Aurelius Augustinus, is not only doubled in a collective *confessio* by his readers and the other believers of the Church, but also in a
quasi-cosmic *confessio* of the creator *by all the created*. More exactly, the
confessio is enacted only when the response of one sole believer (the author)
is confirmed in the response of the community of believers (and of readers), which is in turn ratified by the response of the world, interpreted as
created, to God, himself acknowledged as creator: "Ecce sunt coelum et
terra, clamant quod facta sint; mutantur enim atque variantur. Quidquid
autem factum non est et tamen est, non est in eo quicquam, quod ante
non erat: quod est mutari et variari. Clamant etiam, quod se ipsa non
fecerint: 'Ideo sumus, quia facta sumus; non ergo eramus, antequam essemus, ut fieri possemus a nobis'" (Behold the heavens and the earth are;
they proclaim themselves to have been made; for they change and vary.
Nothing that is without having been made contains anything whatsoever
that was not beforehand—in other words, which changes and varies. They
proclaim also that they did not make themselves: "We are because we were
made; we therefore were not before being such that it would have been
possible to make ourselves") (*Confessiones* XI, 4, 6, 14, 280).[3] From the very
depths of their variations, therefore of their temporality, the things of the
world (under the name of heaven and earth) praise the eternity of God,
acknowledged as their creator, to the point where this proclamation takes
on the status of an authentic *confessio*. Thus, when one asks them about the
beauty that renders them divine, the things confess not being this beauty:
"Et quid est hoc? Interrogavi terram et dixit 'non sum'; et quaecumque in
eadem sunt, idem *confessa* sunt" (And what then is it? I asked the earth
and it answered me: "It is not I; all that is found in the earth *confessed* the
same thing) (X, 6, 9, 14, 154). Above all, when he comments on Psalm
99:14 ("Confessio ejus in terra et coelo"), Saint Augustine specifies clearly:
"Quid est 'Confessio ejus in terra et coelo?' Qua ipse confitetur? Non,

sed qua illum *omnia confitentur*, omnia clamant; omnium pulchritudo quodam modo vox eorum est, *confitentium* Deum. Clamat coelum Deo: 'Tu me fecisti, non ego.' Clamat terra: 'Tu me condisti, non ego'" (What does it mean: "His confession is in the earth and the heavens"? [Would it be] that by which he himself confesses? No, rather that by which *all things confess him*, all proclaim him; the beauty of all things is in some way their voice, the voice of those that *confess* God. The heavens proclaim to God: "It is you who made me, not myself." The earth proclaims: "It is you who established me, not myself").[4] Thus, the hermeneutic of Genesis in books XI through XIII does not endeavor only to interpret the biblical account of the creation of the world but, above all, to interpret the world *as created* and therefore as operating a cosmic *confessio*, in which the temporality of things would at last be articulated, contrary to all (Greek) philosophy, with the eternity of God.

Only this repetition of the first *confessio* by a new navigation across the global world confers on it its final legitimacy and complete phenomenality—that of a *confessio* perfectly ecclesial because it achieves a cosmic liturgy. And so, if one cannot, indeed if one does not want to, endorse a theological understanding of the *Confessiones*, that is to say lead the *confessio* all the way to its ground and its end—creation—the best method is not to read books XI through XIII seriously, and the chief way of doing this is to see in book XI only a treatise on time, one among other treatises on time and, moreover, one that is to be despised owing to the fact that it remains burdened by a rhetorical interpretation of creation according to the first verses of Genesis. But, in consequence also, if one misses this ultimate cosmic exposition of *confessio*, the first remains in turn undetermined; it is devalued into a neutral psychological description, henceforth without theological function and now available for other enterprises, as much literary as philosophical, which have nothing to do with the liturgical intention of Saint Augustine, indeed contradict it head-on.

Let us therefore admit the hypothesis that, for Saint Augustine the question of time can and should be posed only on the basis of creation, so as to be articulated together with eternity. Posed this way, the question of time emerges in an inevitably polemical frame, under the figure of an objection, short but efficacious: if God created the world, what was he doing before creating it? "Quid faciebat Deus, antequam faceret caelum et terram?"[5] Like all serious thinkers, Saint Augustine does not respond directly to this question: he begins by deconstructing it, so as to address what it puts at stake without itself seeing it.

First of all, he deconstructs the primary presupposition of the objection, according to which God would have needed a motive—a reason or a cause—for creating the world: "Qui quaerit quare voluerit Deus mundum facere, causam quaerit voluntatis Dei. Sed omnis causa efficiens est. Omne autem efficiens majus est quam id quod efficitur. Nihil autem majus est voluntate Dei. Non ergo ejus causa quaerenda est" (Asking why God wanted to make the world amounts to asking for the cause of the will of God. But every cause is efficient and every efficiency is greater than what it effects. Now nothing is greater than the will of God. Its cause is therefore not to be sought) (*De diversis quaestionibus LXXXIII* 28, 10, 80).[6] In the case of God the notion of cause does not hold, and the demand for a cause has no legitimacy. In advance Saint Augustine refuses to let causality (already reduced to efficiency) be applied to God, exactly in the sense that he also disqualifies in advance what will become with Descartes the *causa sui*: "Qui autem putat ejus esse potentiae Deum, ut seipsum ipse genuerit, eo plus errat, quod non solum Deus ita non est, sed nec spiritualis nec corporalis creatura: nulla enim omnino res est, quae se ipsam gignat ut sit" (He who supposes a God of such power that he generates himself is all the more deceived since not only is God not such, but no more is any spiritual or corporeal creature; for there is absolutely no thing that generates itself) (*De Trinitate* I, 1, 1, 15, 88). Let me note that this is not a matter of setting limits to the power of God since this impossibility holds for all beings, even those less powerful than him. It is a matter of emphasizing that coming to be does not rest on power turned back onto itself. In other words no more than efficiency governs the way of Being of God does it rule the way of Being of beings that are *insofar as created*.[7] Nothing could be more coherent: the interpretation of beings as created, since it means to read in them a *confessio*, rules out the possibility of reducing the expression of God in them to a causal relation, even an inverted one. Saint Augustine's theological logic liberates itself from the requirements and the pretensions of metaphysical logic.

§31. Differ*a*nce

From the first deconstruction follows a second. For, the very hypothesis that before creating the world God was simply doing nothing[8]—in
other words, the objection of a *vacatio Dei*—contradicts itself by assuming precisely what constitutes the entire difficulty: "inaniter homines cogitare praeterita tempora vacationis Dei, cum tempus nullum sit ante mundum" (what vanity of men, to think a divine idleness in past times, since
before the world there was no time) (*De civitate Dei* XI, 5, 35, 48). How
could God have been wasting time before creating the world, since time
comes with the world, in one and the same creation? There is no more
a *then* (*tunc*) than there is a *now* (*nunc*), and there is a *now* only for the
world and with creation: "Id ipsum enim tempus tu feceras, nec praeterire
potuerunt tempora, antequam faceres tempora. Si autem ante caelum et
terram nullum erat tempus, cur quaeritur, quid *tunc* faciebas? Non erat
tunc, ubi non erat tempus" (Time itself, you made, and the times would
not have been able to pass before you made them. And if there was no time
before the heavens and the earth, how can one ask what you were doing
then? For there was no *then*, there where there was no time) (*Confessiones*
XI, 13, 15, 14, 296). The question manifests its own absurdity, since creating
the world means creating time as well. Time has meaning only in and for
the world, and for that very reason it is not inscribed within it as a worldly
being but discloses itself as the world itself. Time comes *with* the world; it
worlds and *makes* a world: "Quis non videat, quod tempora non fuissent,
nisi creatura fieret, quae aliquid aliqua motione mutaret, cujus motionis
et mutationis cum aliud atque aliud, quae simul esse non possunt, cedit
atque succedit, in brevioribus vel productioribus morarum intervallis tempus sequeretur? . . . Procul dubio non est mundus factus in tempore, sed
cum tempore" (Who does not see that there would not have been time
without there coming to be some creature who changes something by
some movement, movement and change whose terms, which cannot be
simultaneously, yield and succeed each other at longer or shorter intervals,
provoking time? . . . Without a doubt the world was not made in time,
but together with time) (*De civitate Dei* XI, 6, 35, 48–50).[9] If God precedes
the world, he does not precede it temporally. Consequently the world does
not follow him, and it does not proceed from him either: "Nec tu tempore

tempora praecedis: alioquin non omnia tempora praecederes. Sed praecedis omnia praeterita celsitudine semper praesentis aeternitatis et superas omnia futura" (And it is not by time that you precede the times: if not, you would not precede all times. But you precede all past things with all the loftiness of your present eternity and you surpass all futures) (*Confessiones* XI, 13, 16, 14, 296). God anticipates and is in advance of the world in a way not given temporally precisely because God gives time as he creates the world—in an advance without world or time. This means likewise that God's eternity is not itself defined by time because it is not set up in opposition to the time that passes. One can speak with rigor of an eternity that does not pass but only on condition of understanding by that a strictly apophatic approximation, because only that can endure which risks passing, time. And the present, even permanent, remains temporal, therefore created. Strictly speaking, permanence concerns only what temporalizes, therefore the created and, first of all, myself.

A conclusion can be drawn, decisive for all the rest of the research. If time emerges only with the world and in one and the same creation, if the difference between time and eternity can therefore be defined by a temporal belatedness, God's precedence over and above the ego, as well as the world, goes back beyond time. The difference between the ego and God, finitude, therefore, stems from the fact that I alone differ from in deferring myself, because I temporalize. My differ*a*nce is translated temporally, without however consisting in time. My differ*a*nce temporally translates my separation from myself but thus attests my difference from what does not differ from itself. The difference between my differ*a*nce (temporal) vis-à-vis myself and God's in-differ*a*nce (eternal) indicates my *belatedness*, itself intemporal, but multiform, vis-à-vis God. Differing from in deferring oneself, remaining other than oneself and at a distance from oneself, suffices to characterize finitude in myself. Man concentrates creation around himself precisely because, more so than any other creature, he differs from himself temporally: "cum ipse [Deus] sit aeternus et sine initio, ab aliquo tamen initio exorsus est tempora et hominem, quem nunquam ante fecerat, fecit in tempore" (God, though eternal and without beginning, nevertheless made emerge, from some beginning, both time and man—man who had never been previously, he made in time). Temporalization is not just a characteristic of man; it defines him as such, *homo temporalis*, who differs from God in that he differs temporally from himself, is *delayed* behind himself.[10]

This differ*a*nce has *already* been at work in many delays of the ego with regard to itself, without our having been able to see in them the ordeals of temporality, for from the outset *homo temporalis* has been incessantly late. The initial differ*a*nce came up at the beginning, or more exactly before the beginning (see above, Chapter 1), when *confessio*'s word of praise spoke in the mode of a citation, which I can only repeat after the fact (ibid., §3). First of all, my word is addressed to someone who is already there, before me, a fait accompli already; second, it can therefore only take on the status of a response, never a call or a provocation; third, my word can respond only by citing the first word, proffered in advance by God and recorded in the scriptures, well before I say it and even hear it. In all these senses, speaking to God consists first in acknowledging my belatedness: "*prae*dicatus est nobis" (you were said to us *in advance*) (I, 1, 1, 13, 274). This lateness will not disappear with the possible conversion of the listener but will become even more patent, for just as faith comes from listening ("fides ex auditu" [Romans 10:17]), so too: "Quid autem, ut convertereris, posses, nisi vocareris?" (What could you do to be converted, if you were not first called?).[11] The belatedness of the response, which defines the call, but without which this call would remain inaudible, imposes the first differ*a*nce in every word that I believe I say and that, in fact, I hear myself resaying.

A second differ*a*nce of the ego delaying behind itself arises from the immemorial (Chapter 2). If it never experiences itself, paradoxically, so well as in its powerlessness to become present to itself in its *cogitatio* (for "non ego vita mea sim: male vixi ex me, mors mihi fui" [I am not myself my life. I lived poorly on my own. I was a death to myself]) (XII, 10, 10, 14, 358), this is owing to the inaccessibility of its *memoria* in it. "Quid autem propinquus me ipso mihi? Et ecce memoriae meae vis non comprehenditur a me, cum ipsum me non dicam praeter illam" (What then is closer to myself than myself? And look, the strength of my memory remains incomprehensible to me by myself who nevertheless cannot say myself apart from it) (X, 16, 25, 14, 184). Since *memoria* collects my entire *cogitatio*, it must be concluded that I am late with regard to my own *cogitatio*, which becomes other to me. I am alienated from myself because in fact my *memoria* shows itself not to belong to me but to pertain to the unattainable that it conceals and that I reveal, God: "mecum erat memoria tui, . . . sed *nondum* me esse" (the memory of you was with me, . . . but it was I who was *not yet* there) (VII, 17, 23, 13, 626). The third differ*a*nce follows at once, for it consists only in declining the lateness of the self to its *cogitatio* in terms of a lateness of the self to its own desire for happiness, according to a paradox that is all the more striking as it remains no longer theoretic but becomes pragmatic (Chapter 3). I differ from in deferring the most intimate intimacy with myself because I never stop deferring what I desire on principle above and beyond every other object of desire. "*Sero* te amavi, pulchritudo *tam antiqua* et tam nova, *sero* te amavi! Et ecce intus eras et ego foris. . . . Mecum eras et tecum non eram" (*With what a delay* did I love, beauty *so ancient* and so new, *with what a delay*! And look, you were within me and I was outside. . . . You, you were with me, but I was not with you) (X, 27, 38, 14, 208).[12] The delay deepens into a logically inexplicable differ*a*nce, that of the desire that contradicts itself.

But the belatedness that best attests my differ*a*nce from myself is clearly evident in the delay of conversion (Chapter 4). For the will's powerlessness to will (itself) on its own is not just one delay among others, occasional, since the delay is all that is at stake in the ordeal, which is focused on the belatedness itself. The delay in which the will gets bogged down manifests differ*a*nce itself, as the heart become a stranger to the self that I am. That is, "*multi mei anni mecum effluxerunt,* forte duodecim anni, ex quo ab undevicensimo anno aetatis meae lecto Ciceronis Hortensio excitatus eram studio sapientiae et *differebam* contempta felicitate terrana ad eam investigandam vacare" (*so many years had flowed by for me,* twelve perhaps, since the time when, at age nineteen, the reading of Cicero's *Hortensius* had excited in me the pursuit of wisdom, and *I deferred* freeing myself to seek it by condemning earthly happiness). Why or rather how could I thus delay what I desire? By the ever added delay of a moment of time: "et dixeram: 'Da mihi castitatem et continentiam, sed noli *modo*'" (and I said: "Grant me chastity and continence, but *not right now*") (VII, 7, 17, 14, 42–44).[13] In fact, the experience of time as an endless splitting of the present, which disperses and fades away in inconsistent and inconstant instants to the point that no sense, no decision, and no will can any longer be carried out, comes up well before book XI of the *Confessiones* with the story of the (non)conversion related in book VIII. Time, as the flux in which freedom vanishes and consciousness is engulfed, does not appear first in the conceptual analysis of a rigorous philosophy but in the dismaying diagnosis of sin and the powerlessness in which it fixes the will. An extraordinary passage bears witness to this:

Dicebam enim apud me intus: "*Ecce modo* fiat, *modo* fiat," et cum verbo *jam* ibam in placitum, *jam* paene faciebam et non faciebam, sed relabebar tamen in pristina, sed de proximo stabam et respirabam. Et item conabar et paulo minus ibi eram et paulo minus, *jam jamque* attingebam et tenebam; et non ibi eram nec attingebam, nec tenebam, haesitans mori morti et vitae vivere . . . *punctumque ipsum temporis*, quo aliud futurus eram, quanto proprius admovebatur, tanto ampliorem incutiebat horrorem; sed non recutiebat retro, nec avertabat, sed *suspendebat*.

I was, in effect, saying inside myself: "Look, *this is the moment*, the time is *now*," and with this word *now*, I was heading toward what I had decided, I was doing it almost *now*, and I was not doing it; but I did not fall back to the same point as before. I stood at the ready. I took a deep breath, and I made a new attempt, again a little and there I was, again just a little bit, and *now, now* I arrived. I held fast; but no, I was not there, I had not arrived, I did not hold to it, remaining still between dying to death and living to life . . ., and the *very point of time itself* held me in suspense. (VIII, 11, 25, 14, 58–60)[14]

Time—or, more exactly, the diffe*r*ance that disseminates it into untenable *now*s—does not therefore come up as just one more theoretic question in the midst of the philosophic neutrality of available beings, nor as the verbalized trial of a personal, indeed existential, crisis. It reveals itself as the delay of self to itself, to be sure, enacted temporally but unveiled solely within the horizon of the relation to God—or rather of its impossibility.

Correctly interpreting Augustine's exposition of time therefore demands not merely reconstituting the logic of a doctrine of time that is conceptually acceptable and coherent but also (and precisely to succeed in this) thinking it on the basis of its origin and its issue, both of which are theological: the diffe*r*ance that disperses time puts to work, more originally, a delay that defers speaking out, self-knowledge, and the love of truth—in short, conversion—because it disseminates the very decision of the will. If, then, there does turn out to be a philosophical aporia of time, we must learn to see it, also and even first of all, as the symptom of a theological crisis.

§32. The aporia of the present

So, it is only once the question of time is put back into its theological setting, that is, creation ("Omnia tempora tu fecisti et ante omnia tempora tu es, nec aliquo tempore non erat tempus" [You made all times, and you are before all times, without which in no time would there ever be any time] [XI, 13, 16, 14, 298]), that the analysis of time properly speaking really begins. It opens, therefore, with a famous question: "Quid est tempus? Si nemo ex me quaerat, scio; si quaerenti explicare velim, nescio" (What is time? If nobody asks me, then I know; but if I want to explain it to someone who asks me, I do not know) (XI, 14, 17, 298). This formulation would hardly merit its celebrity if it were only a matter of admitting an aporia, provisional or definitive, that many others have also seen. Be it Plotinus: "We think we have spontaneously in our minds, as if by universal intentions of thought and ourselves, on these matters [eternity and time], an evident impression so that we all always name them the same way for everybody. But as soon as we try to go farther and investigate these knowledges a bit more closely, we come to a dead end (ἀπορῦντες) with our conceptions." Or Husserl (commenting on the Augustinian formulation): "Naturally, we all know what time is; it is that which is most familiar. However, as soon as we make the attempt to account for time-consciousness, to put Objective time and subjective time-consciousness into the right relation and thus gain an understanding of how temporal Objectivity—therefore, individual Objectivity in general—can be constituted in subjective time-consciousness—indeed, as soon as we even make the attempt to undertake an analysis of pure subjective time-consciousness—the phenomenological content of lived experiences of time [*Zeiterlebnisse*]—we are involved in the most extraordinary difficulties, contradictions, and entanglements."[15] It should rather be observed that this aporia arises regarding something banal, commonly experienced and accessible to each and all, a banality that turns out, however, to be incomprehensible, one of those "ista et usitata et abdita" (banalities that also wear a profound mask). For: "Manifestissima et usitatissima sunt et eadem rursus nimis latent et nova est inventio eorum" (It concerns the most manifest and most usual things, and yet it is these which hide themselves par excellence, such that discovering them calls for an innovation) (XI, 22, 28, 14, 316).[16] The aporia is not threatening because we lack information about the fact of time, or about the description of its phenomenon (we know nothing more common, more usual), but because we do not succeed in thinking what comes over us with its emergence. And as time constitutes me more than any other thing, the aporia bears directly not only on it (as for *memoria* and *temptatio*, which after all are already radically temporalized), but also on myself, this already para-doxical phenomenon, *hoc monstrum*, that I am to myself, to the point of me becoming an aporia to myself, *mihi magna quaestio.* In other words Saint Augustine does not ask himself the question of time, as if it were, for instance, the "age old crux of descriptive psychology and theory of knowledge."[17] Rather, he confronts, in the aporia of time as the nearest and dearest of usual affairs, the question of what I am—supposing that precisely the question of time bears on my way of *Being.* For it could be that with time something else entirely is at issue besides Being and that it can neither be reached nor described.

The aporia therefore defines time. And it is an aporia that formulates itself quite clearly. Even though we do not understand how, we admit that time is, since, if it were not, it would not be what we experience, the time that passes, or rather the *praeteritum tempus*, the time that just passed, and the *futurum tempus*, the time that is about to pass. By definition, the past is not because it is no longer, and the future is not because it is not yet. But left without past or future, the present would be confused with eternity; therefore, time is time only because the present in it passes into the past, because it ends up no longer being, "ut scilicet non vere dicamus tempus esse, nisi quia tendit in non esse" (such that we will not say in truth that time is, if it did not tend to not be) (XI, 14, 17, 14, 300). Time, therefore, is only by not being truly, and consequently it is only inasmuch as it remains in the present. Yet this present remains temporal (is distinguished from the eternal) only if it persists; and it can persist, be long or short, only by mobilizing the past and the future. A long past permits the present to have persisted a long time; a long future assures the present of having to persist a long time. Except that neither the past nor the future persist, for "quo pacto longum est aut breve, quod non est?" (how would what is not be long or short?) (XI, 15, 18, ibid.). A correction must be made, and it should be said that only what is present can persist for a more or less long time because it alone is. Time persists only as long as it has *not* passed, as it remains present. If presence can persist, this will be through the present, more exactly through the persistence of present time. It remains to be seen "utrum praesens tempus possit esse longum sit" (if present time can persist for a long time) (XI, 15, 19, 14, 302). In short, how does the present succeed in ensuring presence? Apparently, there is no problem, since we were "given the faculty to sense the delays and to measure them (*sentire moras et metiri*)" (ibid.). Yet this faculty is thrown into disarray as soon as one tries to employ it, since every delay can be divided between a present, which alone truly is, and a past (or a future), which is not (or not yet), therefore escapes every measure and all presence. Let us suppose a delay (*mora*) of one hundred years: they cannot all be present together but just one; or rather, even this one cannot be so in its entirety ("Nec annus, qui agitur, totus est praesens . . . non annus est praesens" [XI, 15, 19, 14, 302]). Not even a single day could do any better ("nec unus dies totus est praesens" [XI, 15, 20, 14, 304]) because the more I divide the delay, the more the present is restricted in it, in a reduction that will not stop at the hour, minute, second, or anything divisible: "Si quid intelligitur temporis, quod in nullas jam vel minutissimas momentorum partes dividi possit, id solum est quod praesens dicatur" (If one understands something about time, which cannot be divided into any momentary parts, however miniscule they might be, that, and that alone, will be named the present) (ibid.). Henceforth, of time there will remain only the present.

But this pure present can absolutely not persist, so as to remain indivisible. Therefore, if time remains present only on condition of not persisting for just an instant, the present coincides with the nonpresent, and the disappearance of the present time follows from the definition of the present without space or delay: "Praesens nullum habet *spatium. Ubi* ergo est tempus, quod longum dicamus? An futurum?" (The present has no *space. Where* then is time, that we call long? Would this be the future?) (ibid.). That the present should find refuge in the future, here again, the aporia resurfaces.[18] In fact, the contradiction becomes patent: we sense and measure the delay (*mora*), but there is in fact none, not even a miniscule one: "ita raptim a futuro in praeteritum [sc. praesens] transvolat, ut *nulla morula* extendatur" (the present passes, flying so furtively from the future to the present that it does not span even the time of the slightest delay) (ibid.). The reduction of presence to the present, far from assuring it domination over time, dissolves it in the absence of presence of an absolute non*mora*, literally in the im-*mora*-lity of the present. The im-*mora*-lity of the present always refers presence off to later, according to a ruthless differ*a*nce. If the present moment is never reached, nor ever present, we understand why the moment of decision would find itself, in conversion, always put off until later. The dissolution of the present moment would already defer the moment of decision: the decision would never arrive *now* (*jam, tunc, nunc*), because, besides the weakness of my will, there never was, and there surely never is, in general and on principle (*überhaupt, schlechtin*), *now*, and because the aporia of time consists precisely in the impossibility of fixing the slightest moment persistent enough for a decision to find stable ground: "clamat praesens tempus longum se esse non posse" (the present time proclaims [itself] that it cannot be long) (XI, 15, 20, 14, 306).[19] The aporia of time thus maintains a direct relation with the difficulty of conversion. Must time itself be converted so as to grant the possibility of conversion?

But before pursuing this line of thought, we must better identify the aporia that sustains it. It has two characteristics. First, whatever the historical mediations that connect them might be (or not), Saint Augustine here retrieves precisely the terms of the aporia of time as it was laid out by Aristotle: "Time is not, or else barely and obscurely, οὐκ ἔστι ἢ μόλις καὶ ἀμυδρος,"[20] for it is not composed of beings but of what is no longer or not yet. If it is divided, it is into parts that are not; for, even what in it is, the instant, τὸ νῦν, does not constitute a real and ontic part but remains a mere limit that, precisely because it reaches indivisibility, does not persist and, in this sense, is not any longer. Contrary to what current commentaries say, the Augustinian aporia of time has nothing original about it, since it retrieves that, more original, of Aristotle. It is neither a positive doctrine of Saint Augustine responding to a previous question nor a difficulty that he himself would have discovered but just a simple reformulation of a Greek aporia. If ever Saint Augustine does contribute some new elements, they will serve to address this previous aporia, in no way to pursue it or to confirm it. We must next be more precise about the nature of the difficulty of time according to Aristotle. Far from consisting in the privilege of the present over time and its other dimensions, it shows in contrast that the present persists no better nor any longer than the past and the future. For just as these latter are inasmuch as they are thoroughly not (or not yet or no longer), so, too, the present is finally not any longer, though not by thorough nonbeing as with the two other but by a passage to the limit, to the rank of limit rather, which reduces it to the point of passing to the other side of the present, "nulla morula." This, so to speak, im-*mora*-lity of the present excludes it from presence, therefore from παρονσία and therefore from ούσία.[21] The problem with time, therefore, consists less in its persistence in the present than in its limitless flight or rather its flight to the limit, outside of the present. Everything passes without remainder or remaining to the point that everything comes to pass as if no moment ever stays, one that would persist long enough for carrying out even the slightest resolution of the will.

Time does *not* give time to time nor presence to the present. But we know clearly this lack of time itself, even though by definition we do not receive time from this lack. It is therefore necessary, since we know so well what is going on with the time that we never have, that we *undergo* it, even though we do not comprehend it. If Saint Augustine takes a step forward, it is this: he thinks that time affects us in a sensation so original that it does not even depend on any comprehension we could have of it—in this case, that we could *not* have of it. "Et tamen, Domine, *senti-mus* intervalla temporum et comparamus sibimet et dicimus alia longiora et alia breviora. . . . Sed praetereuntia metimur tempora, cum *sentiendo* metimur. . . . Cum ergo praeterit tempus, *sentiri* et metiri potest, cum autem praeterierit, quoniam non est, non potest" (And yet, Lord, *we sense* the intervals of the times, we compare them among themselves and we call some longer, others shorter. . . . But we measure the times in their passage, when we measure them *by sensing them*. . . . For when time is passing, one can *sense* it and measure it, but once it is past, since it is not, one can no longer do so) (XI, 16, 21, 14, 306).[22] How does it come about that the times, which we can neither comprehend nor define in terms of presence or beingness, we can still succeed in measuring? Evidently because we undergo them (able to sense them, *sentiri potest*) inasmuch as they are not—or more exactly (for "audebit quis dicere metiri posse quod non est?" [will someone dare to say that he can measure what is not?] [ibid.]), inasmuch as they are in passing, passing through, in the midst of passing away (*praetereuntia*). We sense by an originary affection what we do not comprehend and even do not see—namely, the passage itself in the time of the present that its nonpermanence defines.

Would this mean sensing and therefore being able to measure what I do not comprehend and even what I do not see? Doesn't that respond to one aporia (that of time) with another (that of an original sensing without sensation)? Perhaps yes, but the thing itself seems to require or at least permit it according to what Saint Augustine analyzes as "the secret of the anticipatory sensation of future things" (*arcana praesensio futurorum* [XI, 18, 24, 14, 310]). How can I see the rising of the sun when I have not yet seen the sun? I see its aurora—that is to say, the rising "that is not yet there" (*nondum est*); but this absence of sun, the aurora, announces (in the role of cause, advance, anticipation, index—little difference, in fact) its coming as such, "the sun inasmuch as coming" (*sol futurus*)." In fact, in the present instant (more truly, in the instant that lacks a present), two presences overlap: that of the present, the aurora that is not the sun, and that of the sun, which is not present, except as sensed—the sun of which I have a presentiment, the sun *fore-sensed*. The future, too, is therefore perceived in the present, but in the fore-sensed present of the *praesensio futurorum*. What is not seen can be *fore*told and thus *fore*seen "*prae*dici possunt, ex praesentibus qua jam sunt et videntur" (ibid.).

Should we conclude from this a double present—that (in fact unattainable at the limit) of the thing in presence and that too of the original sensing that receives not only presence but above all passed and future absence? In fact, arriving at this paradox is necessary: "Tempora sunt tria, praeteritum, praesens et futurum, sed fortasse proprie diceretur: tempora sunt tria, praesens de praeteritis, praesens de praesentibus, praesens de futuris. Sunt enim haec in anima tria quaedam et alibi ea non video, praesens de praeteritis, memoria, praesens de praesentibus, contuitus, praesens de futuris, expectatio" (There are three times: the past, the present, and the future, but perhaps one would speak more properly to say that there are three times: the present of things past, the present of things present, the present of things to come. For all three are found in the soul, and I do not see where else: the present concerning things past, memory; the present concerning things present, attention; the present concerning things future, expectation) (XI, 20, 26, 14, 312). The thing itself calls for this paradox, which should be preferred to "the customary impropriety" (*abutitur consuetudo* [ibid.]). But how are we to understand that the time of things is doubled by a time in me? Should we think that time is more in me than I am in it, indeed that in the final analysis, it is myself?

§33. The measure of bodily movement

But these hypotheses become meaningful only by relating them to what they contradict. In fact, they are opposed to a thesis that Saint Augustine reports being one he really did hear: "Audivi a quodam homine docto, quod solis et lunae ac siderum motus ipsa sint tempora, et non adnui" (I heard a learned man say that the movements of the sun, the moon, and the stars constitute the times, something I did not admit) (XI, 22, 29, 14, 318). Rather than seeking to ascertain the identity of this man,[23] it seems more useful and possible to attend to the doctrine so transmitted. Even if it no doubt concerns an all-too-summary account of a doubtlessly syncretistic doctrine, one cannot not compare it, with requisite hesitations, to the definition of time set by Aristotle.

Among all the determinations making up this definition, at least two seem in question here. The first is that time consists in a change, and that this change, though it includes also genesis and destruction (in terms of οὐσία),[24] growth (in terms of quantity), and alteration (in terms of quality), is accomplished most often and first of all as displacement in terms of place: "Time seems to be first a movement and change" (δοκεῖ μάλιστα κίνησις εἶναι καὶ μεταβολή τίς ὁ χρόνος).[25] The next questionable determinant is that this displacement can be measured and numbered by the well-ordered discontinuity of a numbering number: "Time is the (numbered) number of movement according to before and after" (ἀριθμὸς κατὰ τὸ πρότερον καὶ τὸ ὕστερον).[26] In other words the regular, but discontinuous, unfurling of *now*s ("now, now" [*jam, jam*]), which isolate at each moment the pure limit of an instant, would produce by cumulative effect the continuousness of the temporal flux. These two determinations obviously awaken two difficulties. First is the difficulty of conceiving how time can be defined by an other besides itself, the here of place, which of itself would already carry with it the variation from which, by abstraction, time would arise. Next is the difficulty of conceiving what equivalence is established between the measured discontinuous and the measuring continuous. Saint Augustine puts them together into one single question: time—for example, the time for which a day persists—does it consist in the movement (of a star) or in the delay (*mora*) required to accomplish it?[27] His examination will lead to disconnecting time from the measure of the change, even in the sense of an absolutely well-ordered displacement (such as that of the stars).

This disconnection is put into operation in the form of a threefold deconstruction. First by absurdity. Take the question of knowing if time is equivalent to the movement of the stars or to the delay (*mora*) set for crossing this movement. Let us suppose that the sun turns around the earth not once per day but twenty-four times (the geocentrism of the argument does not make it any less pertinent). If time measures the movement itself, it should admit twenty-four revolutions, that is to say twenty-four days in one single day. But if time measures the delay, the sun would have to accomplish twenty-four revolutions for just one day to pass. Finally, if it is both that time measures, the impossibilities would double. Next comes a contrafactual, which is provided, strangely perhaps, by the authority of *scripture*. When Joshua asked God to stop the movement of the sun to give him time to finish massacring the Amorites, God granted his wish by having "the sun stand still in the sky and delay its setting for almost a day" (Joshua 10:13), such that "sol stabat, sed tempus ibat, per suum quippe spatium temporis" (the sun remained still, but time ran on across its own temporal space) (XI, 23, 30, 14, 322).[28] Here the argument from authority becomes a perfectly rational argument, one that confirms empirical observation (instead of inverting it, as when it was used to condemn Galileo's heliocentrism): time does not measure the movement of the stars since it continues to pass even if their displacement is suspended. Even when time measures the displacement of the stars and other bodies ("Cum enim moveatur corpus, tempore metior" [For even when a body moves, I measure it by time] [XI, 24, 31, 14, 322]), it does not consist in this very same movement precisely because it measures it ("Aliud sit motus corporis, aliud, quo metimur, quamdiu sit" [The movement of the body is one thing; that by which we measure how long it persists is another] [ibid., 14, 324]). That is, to measure what is displaced, it is first of all necessary that time pass, that in itself it offers the gap of a spacing: "Video igitur tempus quandam esse distentionem" (I see then that time is some sort of drawing apart [*distraction*]) (XI, 23, 30, 14, 322). Time must, therefore, *of itself,* diffract, pull itself apart, and therefore distance itself from itself (*distentio*), as if by an originarily temporalized space (*spatium temporis*), so that it could, next and possibly, measure the gap of a spatial displacement. The displacement does not render possible its temporal measure; rather the distancing of time from itself permits, among other things, measuring spatial displacement.

The disconnect between the measure of movement and that of time results finally from a more refined phenomenological description of what comes to pass when time passes. How do we measure when we measure the passage of time? We have already seen how: we measure by sensing: "Cum ergo praeterit tempus, *sentiri* et metiri potest, cum autem praeterierit, quoniam non est, non potest" (For when time is in the midst of passing, we can *sense* it and measure it, but once it is passed, since it is not, we no longer can) (XI, 16, 21, 14, 306). But why then must we sense, if we want to measure? Because with time we do not measure by counting discontinuous moments but by comparing *in a continuum* longer or shorter durations, and we could not compare them in this way, by counting their continuities, if we did not sense them passing, that is to say if we did not sense the passing of their transitions: "Sed praetereuntia metimur tempora, cum sentiendo metimur" (But we measure times of passage when we measure by sensing) (ibid.). We do not count by adding passed moments (*praeterita*) but by experiencing the respective lengths (durations) of several transitions (*praetereuntia*), passings, passages still in the midst of passing, not already passed or passed beyond. "Cum ergo praeterit tempus, sentiri et metiri potest; cum autem praeterierit, quoniam non est, non potest" (It is in the moment when it passes that time can be measured and sensed, but once it is passed, it cannot be so any longer because it is no longer) (ibid.). Or else: "Metitur ergo, cum praeterit, cum praeterierit, non metitur" (It is measured when it is passing, but once passed, it is no longer measured) (XI, 21, 27, 14, 314). And again: "Quid ergo metior? An *praetereuntia* tempora, non praeterita? Sic enim dixeram" (What then do I measure? Would it not be times *passing and their passage*, rather than times passed?) (XI, 26, 33, 14, 328).[29] Change and even local movement become measurable only if I can measure, that is to say sense, the continuum of their transitions (displacements, passages), this continuum that escapes pure space, ever discontinuous *partes extra partes*. Thus, the properly temporal phenomenon consists no more in spatial movement than in its measure but in the continual transition of its change, a transition that alone temporalizes it. Time does not measure movement but provokes it by producing the transition of the thing toward itself, its passage into another than what it was, its passing beyond, its distancing with respect to itself.

We still have to determine what distances itself, modifies, passes, and passes beyond itself (and finally assures what is assumed too quickly as the evidence of change). It is necessary that some instance remain all along this passage so as to permit measuring its transition. Persisting in the present in the very passage from the future into the past is what Saint Augustine identifies as intention, the present intentionality of the mind: "praesens intentio futurum in praeteritum trajicit" (the present intentionality traverses the future toward the past) (XI, 27, 36, 14, 334).[30] The intentionality, if the letter of this *intentio* can be transcribed thus, renders possible the temporalization of the phenomenon because in it the mind present to itself presents to it its three temporal dimensions. Such a *stricto sensu* intentional presence persists and remains for the purpose of measuring the passage from one temporal dimension to each of the others: "Sed fortasse proprie diceretur: tempora sunt tria, praesens de praeteritis, praesens de praesentibus, praesens de futuris" (But perhaps one speaks properly when one says that there are three times, [but that it always concerns a certain form of the present], the present concerning things past, the present concerning things present, the present concerning things future" (XI, 20, 26, 14, 312).[31] The intentional present is deployed but on the second level, as the condition for the possibility of the past, the future, and *especially* the present, itself on the first level. Such a second order intentional present has nothing to do with a *nunc stans*, not only because it does not bear on or come from an *ousia* or a *substantia* but because it remains present only in order to render possible the dissolution of the present itself and to permit the passage, dissipation, and differentiation of each and every thing. It measures the passage by deferring and differing from itself, by identifying with differ*a*nce, which forever puts off to a better time.

§34. *Distentio animi*

Bringing to light a second order and, so to speak, intentional present depends on a fact, again and again experienced and discussed by Saint Augustine—the fact that we perceive time—or, more exactly, the persistence of the time of a phenomenon—only by memory. If a man "premeditated" (*praemeditando*) the emission of a sound by setting its length, that is to say foresaw its future, "egit utique iste spatium temporis in silentio memoriaeque commendans coepit edere illam vocem, quae sonat donec ad propositum terminum perducatur" (he composed its temporal space in silence and, confiding it to memory, began to emit this sound, which goes on resounding until he arrives at the time foreseen in advance) (*Confessiones* XI, 27, 36, 14, 334). The paradox here stems from the fact that memory intervenes *before* the sound has passed through the present from the future to the past, so as to keep and collect in advance what will then unfold through the three ecstases of time. It's the same with the tiniest temporal unity, the tiniest *spatium temporis*. Take the syllable. "Aut vero vel brevissima syllaba enuncietur, cujus non tunc finem audias, cum jam non audis initium. Porro quippe sic agitur, et expectatione opus est ut peragi et *memoria* ut comprehendi queat quantum potest. Et expectatio futurarum rerum est, praeteritarum vero *memoria*. . . . nec coepti motus corporis exspectari finis potest sine *memoria*" (Or else even the shortest syllable is not uttered, at whose end you now no longer hear its beginning. For what happens there must happen by expectation and is understood by *memory*, insofar as it can be. Expectation bears on things to come, *memory* on things past. And the end of the movement begun by a body cannot be anticipated without *memory*) (*De immortalitate animi* III, 3, 5, 176). One should not think that I begin to hear the syllable with my memory and then hear it by expectation, for each fragment (however minimal it might be) of its *spatium tempus* already persists too long to be held exclusively in one or the other but demands both one and the other. The proof is my impossibility to maintain the slightest fragment of it in the present (*non tunc, cum jam*), which obliges me, in order to perceive its now passing duration, to combine straightaway from the outset expectation and memory. Memory persists as long as expectation and simultaneously with it. Without expectation *memoria* must be mobilized, as I must not be late in expecting, if I want to perceive the slightest present passing now—so little does this now stay put. Doubtless, one can (and even should) legitimately distinguish *memoria* from expectation (*expectatio*) and attention (*contuitus*)—"nam et expectat [animis] et adtendit et meminit, ut id quod expectat per id quod adtendit transeat in id quod meminerit" (for the mind expects, attends, and remembers, in such a way that what it expects passes through that to which it directs its attention toward what it remembers) (*Confessiones* XI, 28, 37, 14, 334, congruent with XI, 20, 26, 14, 312). Yet not only do none of the three terms have any meaning without the two others, but, of the three, *memoria* dominates the two others: "Itemque in auditu, nisi auribus perceptae vocis imaginem *continuo* spiritus in se ipso formaret ac *memoria* retineret, ignoraretur secunda syllaba utrum secunda esset, cum jam prima utique non esset, quae percussa aure transierat" (So too for hearing: if the mind did not form *continually* in itself an image [of the sound] of the voice perceived by the ears, and if it did not retain it with its *memoria*, it could not know that the second syllable is second, since the first would already no longer be there, having disappeared as soon as it struck the ear) (*De Genesi ad litteram* XII, 16, 33, 49, 384). The privilege of *memoria* over the question of time and its other ecstases should not be surprising; it reproduces the sway that it already exercised over the ego's (non)comprehension of itself: "Et ecce *memoriae* meae vis non comprehenditur a me, cum ipsum me non dicam praeter eam" (And behold, I did not myself comprehend the power of my *memory*, while I could not call me myself without it) (*Confessiones* X, 16, 25, 14, 184). The privilege of *memoria* in the determination of the ego does not disappear in the determination of its temporality; it dominates both and projects on them the same shadow of nonknowledge.

A recurring example leaves no doubt about this: the analysis of a verse from a hymn of Saint Ambrose, "Deus creator omnium."[32] Scanning a verse into long syllables (here four: the second, fourth, sixth, and final) and short ones (here the four others) amounts to measuring the time that flows while I recite it, and I measure it by measuring each time an interval (*intervallum metimur* [XI, 27, 34, 14, 330]). How am I to measure this interval since by definition I can finish assessing it only when it is done, such that so long as it is there, I cannot yet measure it, and I will have to measure it only starting from the moment when it is no longer there? This contradiction is one that I rise above since I measure this interval by sensing it. But what does "sensing it" mean? This sensing is carried out by two operations, not just one: "pronuntio et renuntio, et ita est, quantum sentitur sensu manifesto" (I proclaim and reclaim, and so it goes, so long as I sense by a manifest sensation) (XI, 27, 35, 14, 330). In saying the syllable, long or short, I carry out two operations: I *pro*claim when anticipating the end of the sound to be heard, but in order to hear it in its length, however short it might be, I must be able to go back to the beginning or retain it—in short, *re*claim it.[33] But where and how can I thus anticipate by making heard what has not yet sounded (by *pro*claiming) and prolong by making heard again what is no longer sounding (by *re*claiming)? I can do so precisely because anticipation and prolongation are not deployed in the ungraspable present moment but in the "penetrale amplum et infinitum" (X, 8, 14, 15, 166) of my *memoria*, that which, without comprehending it, I am: for "animus [est] etiam ipsa memoria" (X, 14, 21, 14, 178). I therefore do not measure absent presents, nor futures already lost, but times retained by my memory, which *re*claims them for its own. And in this way I measure them inasmuch as I make them become my own: "Non ergo ipsas, quae jam non sunt, sed aliquid in memoria mea metior, quod infixum mane" (I therefore do not measure the things themselves, which are already no longer now, but something that remains fixed in my memory) (XI, 27, 35, 14, 332). *Memoria* alone retains what passes because it *re*claims it for its own in my mind. This *re*claiming constitutes the original sensing, which permits the sole measure.[34]

I therefore do indeed measure time but on condition of always and only measuring "something in my memory," never directly things or their movement. My memory permits me to do so because it plays the role of a second-order present: it, in fact, absorbs all the *spatium temporis*, which it retains, because it alone can *re*claim. In return, it is diffracted and distended in proportion to this *re*clamation. "Video igitur tempus quandam esse *distentionem*. Sed video? An videre mihi videor. Tu demonstrabis, lux, veritas" (I see then that time is some *pulling apart* [*distraction*] I see it [truly], or does it seem to me that I see it? You will show me, you, oh light, oh truth) (XI, 23, 30, 14, 322). What must now be done is to specify what should be understood by *distentio*. The term admits two everyday uses when one speaks of "diffusio maris, distentio aeris" (the extent of the sea, the distance of the air) or of "dimensiones mensium, distentiones horarum" (dimensions of the months, distances of the hours).[35] Should we conclude from this that its application to time is just a metaphor?[36]

At the very least, *distentio* has two precise conceptual determinations. First, it does not relate to perceiving past times (or times yet to pass or remaining without passing), as so many stable objects (though in different modalities), that could be represented as such, that is to say measured and enumerated. It relates to perceiving times that pass, passages, moments passing, literally of keeping track of the passing stream. As we have already seen elsewhere (pp. 209–210), Saint Augustine distinguishes very specifically the past times, now imperceptible and no longer measurable, from times in the midst of passage, the only ones perceptible and still measurable. He poses the question explicitly: "Quid ergo metior? An *praetereuntia* tempora, non praeterita?" (What do I measure? The times passing and passage rather than the times passed?) (XI, 26, 33, 14, 328). His response leaves no doubt: "Affectionem, quam res *praetereuntes* in te [sc. animus meus] faciunt et, cum illac praeterierint, manet, ipsam metior praesentem, non ea quae praeterierunt, ut fieret. Ipsam metior, cum tempora metior" (The affect that things generate in you, my soul, in passing and that remains once they have passed, that is what I measure; it is that very thing that I measure when I measure times) (XI, 27, 36, 14, 332). The aporia of the present, which cannot be measured because it possesses no space ("praesens tempus, quomodo metimur, quando non habet spatium?"), finds its solution in substituting for the unthinkable stable space of the present the presence of the passage itself: "Metitur ergo, cum praeterit, cum praeterierit, non metitur" (It is measured when it is passing; once passed, it is no longer measured) (XI, 21, 27, 14, 314). This passage between moments is not something the things themselves can accomplish since they remain each time in their state at the moment, frozen in their present of the moment, however brief it might be. The passage between two states of a thing or two things can only be recorded in a third, *animus meus*. The passing stream is registered only on what is affected by it, *animus meus*. The passage appears only if it is accompanied by an item slack and distended enough to follow its transition. The mind makes time by itself becoming as passing as the passing stream, whence its *distentio*.

Its second characteristic now becomes evident. If measuring time means measuring the passing stream of things in the midst of passing, this measure can be accomplished only by a discontinuous account that would count successively one interval, then a second, followed by a third, etc. To measure the passage, it is necessary to follow it, but to follow it, it must remain present (on the second level) in proportion as each state of the things yields to the next. For this is needed a contemporaneousness of each of the instants not contemporaneous with one another but only with itself. Now, no counting or enumeration can succeed in this since it adds discontinuous *quanta*. To accomplish this sort of continual self-dilation, what is needed is precisely a self—more precisely, an *affected* self, which measures not by enumerating but insofar as it *senses*. And Saint Augustine (as we have seen [p. 206–207]) clearly assumes this position: the passing stream is not counted; it is sensed. "Sed praetereuntia metimur tempora, cum *sentiendo* metimur. . . . Cum ergo *praeterit* tempus, *sentiri et metiri potest*" (But we measure passing [times], when we measure them by *sensing* them. . . . It is when it is in the midst of passing that time can be *sensed* and measured) (XI, 16, 21, 14, 306).[37] The states of things are temporalized, inasmuch as passing, only to the extent that the mind lets itself be affected, inasmuch as it itself is ever passing passage, and that it is therefore distracted, pulling itself apart from itself: "sicut nota cantantis notumve canticum audientis expectatione vocum futurarum et memoria praeteritarum variatur *affectus sensus*que *distenditur*" (just like one who sings a well-known air or hears a well-known song, for whom anticipation of the sounds to come and memory of the sounds passed makes the *affect* vary and the *sensing distracted*) (XI, 31, 41, 14, 342). The *distentio* implies that I measure by sensing (and not by enumerating or counting) the passing (not passed) times.

But for me to let myself be affected by the passing stream, I must let myself pass first of all; for the present state of things does not pass any more than it persists. I measure the passage of the times only by myself carrying out the times of passage, which the states of things cannot, by themselves, considered only as they remain in the aporia of the present time, make pass. I must myself first pass so that the times can pass inasmuch as passing. I thereby invent the passage by accomplishing it first, that is to say by undergoing it in myself. I perceive time, I temporalize the states of things, only by temporalizing myself. The passing mind does not measure any other passage but its own. Time happens as what distends the mind, if not as what is distended by the mind. Time temporalizes the world only by being first temporalized by and in my mind, which knows the times only by notions that are themselves temporalized, "tempora . . . temporalibus notionibus" (*De civitate Dei* XI, 21, 35, 94). Thus we reach the famous formulation, which takes on the status of a definition: "Inde mihi visum est nihil esse aliud tempus quam distentionem: sed cujus rei, nescio, et mirum si non ipsius animi" (From which it follows that it seems to me that time is nothing other than *distentio*: but of what, I do not know, except that it would be very surprising to me if it were not a *distentio* of the mind itself) (*Confessiones* XI, 26, 33, 14, 326ff.). This definition (really a stage in the middle of the analysis more than a conclusion) is surprising for its prudence and its reserve. More particularly, how are we to comprehend the claim that the *distentio* determines, surprisingly enough (*mirum si*), the human mind without however our knowing the thing that it distends (*cujus rei, nescio*)? One wonders here about something nobody seems to wonder about?

§35. The event of creation

Among the numerous questions raised by the *distentio animi*, some of them remain by and large historical and can therefore receive clear answers.

The first asks if the *distentio animi* does not define time simply by repeating the doctrine of Plotinus. That is, after having defined eternity and the aporia of the present time, up until the discussion of the measure of number in terms of before and after invoked by Aristotle to determine time,[38] Plotinus comes to define time as διάστασις, thinning out and dissipating of life, even of the life of the soul, ψυχῆς [. . .] ζῶη.[39] The comparison is compelling literally, but at the same time, it makes a difference all the more visible: Plotinus means by ψυχὴ the soul of all, of the whole (τοῦ παντὸς for it likewise remains the same ἐν πᾶσι),[40] the universal and cosmic soul, whereas Augustine always speaks of *animus meus*, a spirit, a rational soul, indeed an understanding (more than a vital principle), and always mine, individualized and individualizing.[41] And in this way time does not serve to characterize the world in general (nor a degree of beingness in the hierarchy inaugurated by the One), but man, exactly the creature status that is manifest, par excellence, in him, or more precisely in this man that each time *I* am. For I am not only *in* or *with* time; I am time itself. Rather than as a repetition of Plotinus, the Augustinian determination should be compared with what Gregory of Nyssa meant by διάστημα τοῦ χρόνου.[42] This would put an even greater accent on the properly spiritual dimension (not cosmic or even psychological) of the experience of time.

But a simpler comparison still remains: wouldn't Aristotle himself provide a precedent to the Augustinian definition of time as *distentio animi*? No doubt they are directly opposed when it comes to defining time in terms of the measure of movement, and also with regard to the movement of the things of the world, the stars in particular, and especially with regard to the account of before and after.[43] Yet Aristotle, too, saw that "if some movement is found in the soul, immediately (εὐθὺς ἅμα), it seems, some time is produced."[44] Yet it seems that if time is not temporalized in itself without the soul, then *what* time temporalizes or *what* temporalizing is all about—namely, movement understood as what at each moment time is—*that* does not depend on it at all. Whence a counterargument:

> But the difficulty is knowing if, without the soul, time would be or not. It is not possible that something be numbered, therefore that number be, without something that numbers; for number either is numbered or it numbers. But if nothing other than the soul and the mind of the soul is of a nature to number, then without the soul time is no longer possible. *Except* for what in each moment (ἤ τοῦτο ὅ ποτε ὄν) is time, *since in fact* (οἷον εἰ) it can be that movement is possible without the soul.[45]

Aristotle therefore sticks to the same fundamental position as Plato: time arises only when the mind refers itself (by detailed account or imitation, it matters little) to the world of natural things (the movement of the heavens, the stars, etc.), whereas Saint Augustine understands time as arising from the temporalization that my mind incites by itself, inasmuch as it never ceases to differ and defer, first of all with respect to itself. Neither Plato nor Aristotle nor Plotinus can therefore offer a precedent for Saint Augustine's three fundamental decisions: first, to extract temporality from every natural, extended, physical substrate, so as to assign it first to the mind of man; second, no longer to have it bear on the length of the present or on its persistence in presence (inevitably leading to the aporia of the present, which vanishes and dissolves in itself the entirety of time) but concentrating it on the passage itself of one moment to the other (the passing stream), thereby substituting for the discontinuity of the enumerating numeration the continuity of an originary sensation; and third, since temporalization depends neither on the nature nor on the soul of the world, it in turn determines directly what provokes it, the mind of the *ego*, that it individualizes. These three decisions signify more radically that temporalization, individualized by and for my *mens*, definitively stigmatizes its finitude. Temporalization is equivalent to finitude, not only the finitude of my *mens* but of time itself. From now on time, my own and finite, imitates nothing, especially not eternity or infinity, but it opens the *creatum tempus* (*De civitate Dei* XII, 16, 35, 202) for a decision absolutely proper to me.

A second line of questioning seems to raise a fundamental, and more fearsome, difficulty: does Saint Augustine always maintain the doctrine of time such as he elaborates it in book XI of the *Confessiones*? There is reason to doubt it, seeing as the *distentio animi* sets up a radically "subjective" interpretation of time, almost already Kantian, which would not agree with the theology of history or the exegesis of creation to which Augustine's efforts are directed. To uphold this hypothesis, one could look to arguments found in several other texts.[46] For example: "Ubi enim nulla creatura est, cujus mutabilibus motibus tempora peragantur, tempora omnino esse non possunt" (There where no creature is, whose mobile movements carry out times, the times are absolutely not possible) (*De civitate Dei* XII, 16, 35, 204). It is easy to understand that time remains impossible without the movements of things in the world, thus contradicting the supposedly subjectivist definition of time as *distentio animi*. But it could be that this text suggests nothing of the sort. It might indicate, to the contrary, (1) that it is not a question of defining *time*, as such, but *the times* of things; (2) that these times of things suppose in each moment movements, here called *mutables*, not by a pleonasm but to designate these movements as mutations, therefore passages (by opposition to the decomposed and enumerated intervals)—in short, times of passage; (3) especially that these times get their possibility from a creature, exactly as in *Confessiones* XI: "nullum tempus esse posse sine creatura."[47] But we must also ask what *creatura* means *here*. For the objection supposes that the text of *De civitate Dei* is about a reality of an extramental nature, but does the text of the *Confessiones*, the one we just cited, mean something else? Moreover, what sense could there be in considering *animus meus*, such as it supports the *distentio*, as something other than a *creatura*, in the obvious sense of the term, which does not imply the distinction between extramental and intramental reality? Such a distinction, doubtlessly fraught with anachronism, would in any case be of no importance, since the mind of man, supposing that it remains "intramental" (what does this term mean, anyway?), would remain no less radically created than anything else whatsoever, supposedly "extramental." And what does *created* mean? In both cases it implies the potential to change, to pass from one state to another (and others) by mobile and mutable movements (*motus mobiles*), which affect the *mens* no less, which even affect more than any other thing. And the entire doctrine of *Confessiones* XI, in fact, consists only in this one point. Of course, one can say that "rerum mutationibus fiunt tempora" (the times occur only through the mutations of things) (XII, 8, 8, 14, 356) or that "sine varitate motionum non sunt tempora" (without variation in movements, there would be no time) (XII, 11, 14, 14, 262);[48] but that no more reveals an "objective" doctrine of time than it contradicts a previous "subjective" doctrine of time, for the movements and variations that make up the times are carried out in all creatures and therefore especially in the most exemplarily created of them all: *animus meus*, the human *mens* in me. Neither of the two terms in the alternative opposing these two times has the least pertinence because every thing, as such, is inscribed within time to the very measure of its status as creature. The sole privilege of *animus meus* does not consist in an anachronistic and fantasized "subjectivity" but in its exceptional mutability, which stems from its exceptionally *created* character. Of all creatures, the *mens* of man bears the mark of its creation most profoundly and, for that reason, offers itself, more fragile and friable than any other, to the *distentio* of a temporalization. And if Saint Augustine will now attempt to understand the creation of the world, the heavens and earth as well as all living things, that happens precisely because the determination of time starting from the *distentio mentis* does not forbid but rather permits access to their modes of temporalization. Creation in its entirety is temporalized all the more as the *mens* of man is exposed to the *distentio*.[49]

A final question must be broached, one that is more fearsome because phenomenologically more rigorous. "A fundamental difficulty remains, one which is *the* difficulty of the Augustinian analyses of time. The soul is at once temporalizing and temporalized; but it is temporalized *only inasmuch as it is temporalizing* and on this condition alone." In other words, the *mind* (not the soul, we make this correction because it concerns *animus* more than *anima*) temporalizes the movements of the things of the world according to the ecstases of time owing to its facility for the *distentio*, but this *distentio* itself remains problematic since it spontaneously evokes a temporality armed with its three ecstases and its doubling of the present, without advancing any clear and precise phenomenological subject matter, that is to say without describing really the temporal becoming of this consciousness. "We must hold, in contrast, that the intrapsychic changes *presuppose* the time in which they unfurl and cannot constitute, in turn, the origin of time."[50] The issue here is not the "subjectivity" of temporality nor its "objectivity" as in the previous objection; it concerns its phenomenological extraterritoriality or, rather, its absence of phenomenal ground. Augustinian temporality would produce itself, so to speak, as a sort of *causa sui*, enigmatic and uninvestigated, or rather with an absence of any temporal or extratemporal origin. This immanence of time to the consciousness of time would imply (in anticipation of many other immanences in contemporary philosophy) the impossibility of the event. It would end up stopping us from seeing the sole temporality that radically transcends (in the phenomenological sense) the *mens* and that alone could temporalize it, that of the event. And, in fact, the question is well put: if the *mens* temporalizes itself by temporalizing everything in the world, its autotemporalization does not open it onto any temporal exteriority but assures it a purely immanent temporality, which receives no external or transcendent temporality. The *distentio* temporalizes it but in itself. The event becomes impossible, since it would always be inscribed in a time already triggered without it, though possibly available for whatever will be inscribed therein.

I will attempt to respond to this question only by doing justice to it. I will ask in response if the determination, as yet undecided, of time as *distentio animi* still leaves open a possibility for the event. To do this, it is appropriate to revisit the order of reasons followed by the *Confessiones*. More specifically, book XI struggles toward the *distentio animi* only in between its treatment of two other problems: that of books VIII through

X, which stand astonished by the quasi-impossibility of making the decision to convert (Chapter 4); then that of the books which investigate the
genesis of the world we all have in common. Now these two difficulties
both concern, and in the strictest sense of the term, *events*. First is the
impossibility of the individual event, which should alone decide all that I
am, my ipseity and my identity—the event of my "conversion," as a decision for God. Next is the actuality of the cosmic event, the emergence of
the heavens and the earth, an event always already decided, but in such
a way that it imposes itself as a fact irremediably accomplished, but also
definitively incomprehensible, since it precedes me by a radical facticity,
a saturated phenomenon. In short, two events frame the temporality of
the *distentio animi* like so many saturated phenomena par excellence: the
most proximate being-given (myself in my relation to the other) and the
being-given in totality (the world).[51] These two events *precede* the temporality of the *distentio animi*. The first does so because time imposes
itself as an inevitable question of the incontestable fact of the impossibility
of stabilizing any present moment available for the voluntary decision of
conversion. "Conversion," and first of all in the figure of the impossibility
of willing it, presents itself as a differ*a*nce, which negatively manifests the
event by forever putting it off until later. The *mens* finds itself precisely
and paradoxically temporalized by its very powerlessness to will in time,
by its powerlessness to temporalize itself in the instant of decision. This
event, at once negative and individual, opens the ecstasy of the future.
Another event, collective and cosmic, doubles it by opening the *mens* onto
another impossibility, the irremediable event of the worlding of the world,
which opens toward an immemorial past, always already accomplished,
which attests a facticity over which I can never go back.

Thus, the *distentio animi*, if it does indeed temporalize the passing
stream of the passing moments, in measuring by an original sensation, is
not however temporalized by itself. Its own temporalization comes upon
it as an event. Or rather, it comes upon it, in fact, starting from a twofold event, equally inaccessible, and heading toward either the future (the
decision that had remained until now impossible, "conversion," [Chapter
4]), or the past (which will remain immemorial and impossible to access,
creation [Chapter 6]). These two events emerge from beyond or rather
from beneath the temporalization of the second-level present, the *distentio*

animi, which is experienced as not emerging from itself. It comes upon itself in the shadow of what these two events have in common—creation. I cannot be decided by myself, because I am created and seized by facticity, care, and the *affectiones*. I cannot take control of *my* origin (which precisely does not fall to me, since I come from it) because I arrive in myself in the irremediable delay of my creation, all the more so as it is always a question of *our* creation. This twofold event of creation makes time itself come upon me. The event that lays hold of the *mens* and imposes the *distentio* on it consists in the event *of* time, of *tempus creatum*. This absolute and unconditional event is no longer even named an event but an advent—the advent of time itself.

§36. Conversion of the *distentio*

If the event par excellence consists in the advent of time itself, we understand even better how creation could determine time, as well as the world and the mind of man (see above, §30). But a problem also arises: does the temporalization of man remain univocal and mandatory, like temporality determines the changes of the world in just one way, or can it (must it) be modifiable according as it is related differently to the eternity of God? Put otherwise, does temporalization determine man essentially as such or does it determine only one of his possible modalities?

Doubtlessly making an allusion to the nearly conclusive formulation of *Confessiones* XI ("at ego in tempora dissilui" [but, as for me, I have fallen in time] [XI, 29, 39, 14, 338]), Heidegger makes a strong criticism of him: "'Spirit' does not first fall into time, but it *exists as* the primordial *temporalization* (*Zeitigung*) of temporality. Temporality temporalizes world-time, within the horizon of which 'history' can 'appear' as an intratemporal advent." At first glance Heidegger thus opposes Saint Augustine, by assigning to temporality the status of an originary determination of the existence of *Dasein*, having nothing of the fall or accidental about it. Man is insofar as he *exists*, that is to say temporalizes in a mode that is originary and absolutely his own. Yet Heidegger does not stick with this all-too-simple response but adds: "'Spirit' does not fall *into* time, but factical existence 'falls' as falling *out* (aus) of the primordial and authentic temporality. But this 'fall' itself finds its existential possibility in a mode of its temporalization belonging to temporality."[52] The factic existence of Dasein constitutes, among its numerous possibilities (or better in the role of the possibility that it is), fallenness (decline, *Verfallen*), in which it temporalizes according to the present, "makes present for the sake of the present," and therefore, since the fallen present is characterized by the fact that it does not hold, the fallenness itself does not hold; it never has the time, it never finds the instant—for the decision.[53] Hence, the fallenness, which "falls" (in the existential sense of *Verfallen*), belongs to temporality in such a way that it reproduces, to a degree that must still be specified, the situation in which *animus meus* "falls" in time. Or rather, Saint Augustine says, *in times* (*in tempora*), clearly marking a difference from *time*, in the sense of the temporality that defines me essentially as a creature and that I define essentially by my mind. *Dasein* does not fall into temporality, but it can (perhaps cannot not) fall into the fallenness of an inauthentic temporality. But can't we say as much about the *distentio animi*? It defines the temporal condition of created man as such, but it also stigmatizes evil and dispersion.[54] Thus, far from rejecting it, Heidegger's criticism of the *distentio animi* entices us to reconsider more attentively our examination of it.

This tenacious ambiguity of temporality is seen again in the very indetermination of the translation of *distentio animi*. That is, if you want to stick with an originary existential temporality, you will prefer an equivalent that is as descriptive and neutral as possible: time as *distancing*, *stretching*, indeed *ecstasis*; but if you mean by it a fall or decline, you will not hesitate to speak of a *dissipation*, *slacking-off*, or *diversion*. The impasse is even indicated sometimes by the pure and simple refusal to translate the term, except by itself.[55] This is not just a matter of an index added to confirm, as we have already observed (see above, p. 217), the strange way in which Saint Augustine introduces the phrase *distentio animi* in the course of his discussion: "It appears to me that time is nothing other than a *distentio*: but of what I do not know, except that it would surprise me to find that it is not a *distentio* of the mind itself" (XI, 26, 33, 14, 326). If *distentio* determines, barring the unexpected (*mirum si*), the mind of man, how are we to understand that one does not know the thing that it distends (*cujus rei, nescio*)? Why be surprised if it is indeed the mind of man that it distends? But, if one is still surprised about it, why have already attributed it to man? All these hazy matters suggest once again the real conceptual difficulty: with the *distentio animi*, is it really a matter of defining "the essence of human time in general"[56] or, more exactly, one of the *modes* in which it operates?

The answer to this question begins to dawn when one attends to the real origin of the term *distentio*. Naturally, it draws its origin from the Plotinian διάστασις (see above p. 217), but it achieves full conceptual dignity for Saint Augustine in the commentary on Philippians 3:13–14,[57] which concludes *Confessiones* XI:

Sed "quoniam melior est misericordia tua super vitas" ecce *distentio* est vita mea et "me suscepit dextera tua" in Domino meo, mediatore filio hominis inter te unum et nos multos, in multis per multa, ut per eum "apprehendam, in quo et apprehensus sum," et a veteribus diebus colligar sequens unum, "praeterita oblitus," non in ea quae futura et transitura sunt, sed "in ea quae ante sunt" non *distentus* sed "*extentus*," non secundum *distentionem*, sed "secundum *intentionem* sequor ad palmam supernae vocationis."

But "since your mercy is better than all lives" [Psalm 32:4], behold my life is a *distentio* and "your right hand took hold of me and put me" [Psalm 32:9] in my Lord, the Son of man, mediator between you [who are] one and us [who are] multiple, in the multiple and across the multiple, so that by him "I might grasp he in whom I am grasped" [Philippians 3:12] and, gathering myself together from out of the old days, I might follow the unique, "forgetting things that have passed" [Philippians 3:13], not *distended*, but "*extended*" [Philippians 3:13], not toward the things that are going to come and will pass, but "toward those that are in advance," "I pursue," in no *distention*, but a *tension*, "the garland of the call from above" [Philippians 3:14]. (XI, 29, 39, 14, 338)

The doctrine of the *distentio animi* (which here finds the last of the rare moments when it is mentioned in *Confessiones* XI) is clearly completed when Plotinus's διάστασις is observed and repeated in Saint Paul's ἔμπροσθεν ἐπεκτείνομενος and therefore when the *distentio* is opposed to and based on another disposition, here named *extensio*. This dichotomy must now be understood.

A first point presents itself unsurprisingly: the *distentio* characterizes what is proper to me inasmuch as the most radical of creatures, therefore the most differ*a*nt from itself and the one most distracted from itself: "Ecce distentio est vita mea" (And behold all my life is only this distraction [*distentio*]) (XI, 29, 39, 14, 338). In fact, the *distentio* already governed the dispersion of my willings, that the affections of facticity *distracted* in every sense (in the etymological sense of pulled apart and dispersed; and in the sense of a dispersed or scattered focus or attention): "Si ergo pariter delectent omnia simulque uno *tempore*, nonne diversae voluntates *distendunt* cor hominis, dum deliberatur, quid potissimum arripiamus?" (If therefore one delights together at the same *time* with the others, won't different wills *distract* the heart of man in the midst of deliberating about what we should rather choose?) (VIII, 10, 24, 14, 58). That is, here the distraction of wills by the contradiction of desires among themselves ends up stealing the time for decision—there is never a good time to decide. The *distentio animi* defines time in such a way that not only does it pass (the inevitable passing stream), but it also steals away from the will and becomes ever unavailable to it. In contrast, God is characterized by the absence of *distentio*: "non habens futurum quod expectet, nec in praeteritum tranjiciens quod meminerit, nulla vice variatur nec in tempora ulla *distenditur*" (not having any future to expect, nor any past to go back over so as to remember it, he does not suffer change from any vicissitude and is not *distracted* into any time whatsoever) (XII, 11, 12, 14, 360). God does not admit *distraction*, neither into spaces nor times.[58] But this first point must be at once corrected or, at least, completed. For what is important is not the mere opposition distraction, which is imposed on man by the *distentio animi* and its mode of temporality, and God's exemption from this distraction, but the fact that, *for man himself,* another disposition is offered besides *distentio*. Man, too, can be liberated from *distentio*, and not (as in Neoplatonism and all other metaphysics) by an in fact impracticable imitation of divine eternity but by a disposition that is perfectly practicable because always temporal (though in a temporality that is not metaphysical because eschatological), a disposition here named *extensio*. For this new disposition, nothing less than the reinterpretation of *distentio* by Philippians 3, is needed to make it appear: "non *distensus*, sed 'extentus' [ibid., 3:13], non secundum *distentionem*, sed secundum *intentionem* 'sequor ad palmam supernae vocationis' [ibid., 3:14]" (not *distended*, but "*extended*," "I pursue," not following any *distractions*, but an *extraction*, "the garland of the call from above") (XI, 29, 39, 14, 338).[59] How can the *distentio*, the distraction that dissipates time into change without leaving a moment available for decision, be reversed into an *extensio*, which extracts me from the dispersion by extending me outside myself? What common term permits the door to turn and open on another mode of temporality?

Another commentary on Philippians 3 explains this with great specificity: "Perfectionem in hac vita dicit, non aliud quam 'ea quae retro sunt oblivisci et in ea quae ante sunt *extendi*' secundum *intentionem*. Tutissima est enim quaerentis *intentio*, donec apprehendatur illud quo *tendimus* et quo *extendimur*. Sed ea recta *intentio* est, quae proficiscitur a fide. Certa enim fides utcumque inchoat cognitionem: cognitio vero certa non perficietur, nisi *post* hanc vitam" (The Apostle says that perfection in this life is nothing other than "forgetting things left behind and *tending* toward those that are in advance" by *intentio*. That is, *intentio* is the surest way for he who seeks, until we lay hold of that toward which we tend and *extend by extraction*. But the only right *intentio* is the one that advances by faith. For only the certainty of faith, in some way, inaugurates knowledge, and knowledge is not complete until *after* this life) (*De Trinitate* IX, 1, 1, 16, 74). We could understand this in this way: the *intentio* can be liberated from (or renounce) the distraction of the *distentio*, which dissipates in the passing stream, all the while remaining in temporality (which is maintained in the completion *after* this life), not through the illusion of being frozen in eternity (which remains decidedly proper to God) but by stretching out in *extensio* toward "the things that are ahead (ἔμπροσθεν)," the things of God, going so far as to be extracted from the variations of the world. Common *intentio* can turn us from *distentio* toward *extensio*[60] and convert temporality from one mode to the other, without ever betraying it or its finitude. A translation of *distentio*, in the context of these three terms, now becomes possible, despite the difficulty acknowledged by all. I suggest, beginning with the transposition of *distentio* into a *distraction*, that we speak of *attraction* for *intentio* (thereby removing its exclusively epistemic use in Husserl) and *extraction* for *extensio* (in the sense of a broadening sometimes equivalent to a liberation).[61]

This conversion of a temporality of distraction into a temporality of extraction can be admitted, be it as a hypothesis, only if we can establish a time that makes an exception to the passing stream, a future that does not vanish in its presentification in the passed past, without, for all that, claiming to be eternal. Confirmation of the possibility of such a temporality—that of a perfectly eschatological future, where the future would remain always a still-to-come, ahead of every passage, thus extracted from the passing stream—seems legible in the same commentary on Philippians 3, which ends *Confessiones* XI: "a veteris diebus colligar sequens unum, 'praeterita oblitus' [Philippians 3:13], non in ea quae futura et transitura sunt, sed 'in ea quae ante sunt' non *distensus*, sed '*extentus*' [ibid.], non secundum *distentionem*, sed 'secundum *intentionem* sequor ad palmam supernae vocationis' [Philippians 3:14]" (gathering myself from those old days, I follow the one, "forgetting the things that have passed," not *distracted* but "*extracted*," not toward things that are going to come and that will pass, but "toward those that are before me," I pursue, not with *distraction*, but by means of an *attraction*, "the garland of the call from above") (XI, 29, 39, 14, 338). We should observe here that extraction out of distraction no longer consists in tending toward things that are going to come, *futura* (precisely because they are also going to pass), *et transitura* (since they remain inscribed in the passing flow), but toward those that *remain and will remain* before me (*ea quae ante sunt*). They are not found before me in the sense of what still has to pass without already being passed by but in the sense that they stand before me in and *by* their very advance of me and abide in their advance: they are in advance of me, up ahead of me and from before me. How can I temporalize myself before what will always keep such an advance and, in as much as ever in advance, will never pass? What affection sets me up in this eschatological ecstasy? The response is derived from the disposition or affection (*Stimmung*) of desire, as is indicated by another commentary on Philippians 3:

Nemo retro respiciat, nemo pristinis suis delectetur, nemo avertat ab eo quod ante est ad id quod retro est: currat donec perveniat; non enim pedibus, sed *desiderio* currimus. Nullus autem in hac vita pervenisse se dicat. Quis autem potest tam perfectus esse quam Paulus? Et ait tamen "Fratres, ego me non arbitror adprehendisse; unum autem quae retro oblitus, in ea quae ante sunt *extentus*, secundum *intentionem* sequor ad palmam supernae vocationis Dei in Christo *Jesu*" (Philippians 3:13–14).

Let nobody look back, let nobody delight in his past, let nobody turn away from what is before him toward what is behind. Let him run until he arrives; for we do not run with our feet, but with our desire. But nobody can be said to arrive in this life. Who can be as perfect as Paul? And yet he said: "My brothers, I do not claim to have understood, but forgetting a single thing behind me, *entirely in extraction* toward the things that are before me, I pursue, by means of an *attraction*, the garland of the call of Christ come from on high in Jesus Christ.[62]

Running does not have as its goal attaining what precedes, so as to nullify the advance, but to put me too in the advance itself. To run, I must in effect constantly put myself in a disequilibrium, put myself into the advance itself. And the happiness of running the race consists in remaining permanently in the unbalanced advance, perfectly and continually free from the permanence and stability, which is illusory anyway, of a *nunc stans*. If God inspires the desire in me, it is not first to fulfill it by satisfying it, but to fulfill it by hollowing it with achievements that become so many new beginnings. "Quod autem desideras, nondum vides: sed *desiderando capax* efficeris, ut cum venerit quod videas, implearis. . . . Deus *differendo extendit* desiderium, desiderando *extendit* animum, *extendendo* facit capacem" (What you desire, you do not yet see; but *by desiring it*, you are made *capable* of it such that you might be filled when what you must see will come. . . . God *extends* desire *by deferring it and differing from it*, by desiring he *extends* the mind, by *extending* it he renders it more capable). And, citing Philippians 3, the text concludes that Saint Paul "*extentum* se dixit, et secundum *intentionem* sequi se dixit" (said that he was *tending toward* [*by extraction*] and pursuing [these things] *by attraction*).[63]

Instituted by extraction in desire for the advance itself, I am uprooted from distracted time, time of the undone, time that undoes, time finally of sin (inauthentic, if one really wants to say so, temporality)—that of the *modo, modo, cras, cras, jam et non jam* in which I do not will, cannot will—will not to will. Time thus converted to the advance finally gives me the time for conversion. It does not pass but comes upon me as a possibility, and the last.

6

The Creation of the Self

§37. The opening of the world

The question of time thus arises for Saint Augustine only on the basis of his affirmation of creation, in such a way that it derives its theological status from it. Thus I have wound up thinking time, in the end and at bottom, exclusively as the time of conversion. This means that it is not a question of the time of physical beings any more than it is a question of the time of beings in general, because it is no longer a matter of the time of the closed world but of the infinite site of creation. Or, rather, it is not a matter of the time of what the Greeks called *kosmos*, precisely because it comes from the event of creation, and creation does *not*, for Saint Augustine, pertain to the world but to what he understands, following the biblical nomenclature, as "heaven and earth." For this phrase remains, despite its purported clarity, perfectly aporetic, since we speak, ordinarily, Greek. To this end it should be noted that in his numerous and ever again resumed commentaries of Genesis (none of which, for that matter, I would like to emphasize, bear the expected title *peri . . .*), he speaks only very little, indeed almost never, of the creation of *the world*, as if he came to it, after the rational doctrines concerning the *mens* and God, in the end according to the Thomist, Cartesian, or Kantian order, in the fashion of a rational cosmology.[1] Or, rather, when he turns to a consideration of the things of the world, he immediately sees them, too, inasmuch as created, on equal footing with the *mens*. Now, when the *mens* comes to recognize itself as created, it is confronted with something entirely other than its essence, its existence, and its mode of Being: it finds itself inscribed in the structure of the *confessio*, which precedes it and summons it as an address calls for a response, and a response that already speaks the language of the address itself (Chapter 1), in view of the love of truth, which alone gives access to the *vita beata* (Chapter 3, §§20–22), by way of nothing other than the conversion of time (Chapter 5). By good logic, then, one should infer from this that what we call, a bit hastily, the question of the *world* should, too, be thematized on the basis of creation. Such a "creation of heaven and earth" would repeat and complete the structure of *confessio* by extending it to the totality. It remains the case, however, that we do not know what precisely to understand by *created*, nor even by *creation*, since for us, inevitably caught in a metaphysical and Greek position, creation remains another way, imprecise and cursory, to say the totality of beings—or, more exactly, to not think it. But one can think the totality of beings in two very different ways, as Heidegger lets us see, perhaps against his declared intention.

Nobody has done more than Heidegger to point out the ontological insufficiency of the concept of creation, supposing that it is a matter of a concept. He admits that "creatureness [*Geschaffenheit*] in the widest sense of the production [*Hergestellheit*] of something is an essential item in the structure of the ancient concept of Being,"[2] and he concludes from this that "within the region of created being, of the 'world,' in the sense of *ens creatum*," not only "is every being that is not God an *ens creatum*," but "the production of what subsists [present-at-hand] (*Herstellung zu Vorhandenem*) . . . constitutes the horizon on the basis of which Being is understood."[3] In this way the distinction between the *ens creatum* and *ens increatum* would be a mere translation, deprived of any and all phenomenological justification, of the division between God and all that is not God. It would hide the question of their modes of Being by covering it over with the univocal permanent subsistence (*Vorhandenheit*), itself deprived of any ontological legitimacy. God, bearing the title Creator, would intervene as the most perfect subsistent being, *ens perfectissimum*, instituting, by way of efficient causality, all the other beings, here understood as creatures. The doctrine of creation, whether it belongs to "ancient thought" or to "Christian thought,"[4] is disqualified with the name of *Vorhandenheit* precisely because Heidegger interprets it as taking a position concerning beings, indeed one that would pretend to designate (wrongly) their mode of Being. He even declares this presupposition straightforwardly in a clear, since polemical, text:

Anyone for whom, for example, the Bible is a divine revelation and truth already has the answer to the question: "Why is there something, in general, rather than nothing?" even before it is asked: namely, being, insofar as it is not God himself, has been created by Him. God "is" in the role of uncreated creator. One who stands in the land of such a faith can in a way follow the questioning of our question and participate in it, but he cannot really question without renouncing himself as believer with all the consequences of taking such a step. He can only act *as if*.[5]

In a word, creation offers an inept, or rather in-apt, response, because theologically based, to an ontological question, that it masks and misses.

But how can we not be amazed by the weakness of this objection? In the first place Heidegger assumes here (in 1935), without questioning it, the question "Why is there in general something, rather than nothing?" He does not in any way interrogate the metaphysical status proper to it, which, however, he had acknowledged already in 1929 when he evoked "the fundamental question of metaphysics: 'Why is there something, in general, and not rather nothing?'"[6] That one could and should put into question this question itself *inasmuch as* it remains essentially metaphysical will be confirmed quite clearly by a subsequent text (1949):

[This question] states: "Why is there something, in general, and not rather nothing?" Provided that we no longer think about the truth of Being from within metaphysics in the ordinary metaphysical sense, but according to the essence and the truth of metaphysics, one can also ask here: Whence comes it that beings have primacy everywhere and claim for themselves this "is," while what is not a being, the nothing itself understood as Being, remains forgotten?[7]

Thus, the very question that faith supposedly would not comprehend or would not want to comprehend, far from opening the *Seinsfrage*, could, by contrast (owing to its origin in Leibniz, therefore metaphysics), close it or falsify it by privileging, from the very outset, beings to the detriment of Being, itself reduced to the rank of mere nothingness, or even of *nothing*, more "simple" than Being. Might it be the case that, strangely enough, faith has good reasons *not* to listen to a question that does *not* make the *Seinsfrage* heard but smothers it under the noise of beings?

But there is more. Heidegger takes it for granted that faith, in revolving around the doctrine of creation, pretends to respond to the question "Why is there, in general, something rather than nothing?" He supposes that creation aims to provide a biblical response, however inappropriate, to a metaphysical question—about the provenance of beings. Without this presupposition his objection does not stand even for one minute, but never is it demonstrated nor really stated clearly. Now is it really self-evident that "he for whom the Bible is a divine revelation and truth" seeks in it first and foremost "to possess answers" to "questions"? Even admitting it to be so, is it self-evident that he seeks the answer to *this* precise question, the one that asks, "Why is there in general something, and not rather nothing?" Is it clear that the Bible at any moment whatsoever raises the question *why* with regard to creation? Doesn't creation offer, by contrast, the best example of an absence of any and all *why*—not by lack but by excess? And, for that matter, is it even self-evident that beings are at issue in the creation that remains, like the rose, without *why*? When, then, would the concept, or even only the word, ever appear? Moreover, with what right can one interpret what God creates as a *being*? With what right can one likewise interpret it as a *subsisting* (*vorhanden*) being since what is proper to the created would rather consist in the radical caducity that forbids it from subsisting on its own? The only response consists in the fact that, as Heidegger first recognized, "'God' is a purely ontological term" (*ein ontologischer Titel*)[8] and is therefore in no way the biblical God, "God of Abraham, Isaac, and Jacob," but rather the "God of the philosophers." It could be that Heidegger here translates the theological thesis of creation into a mere answer to an ontological question, with the same degree of arbitrariness (in other words, by leaving the obvious uninvestigated) as does metaphysics (in this case Cartesian metaphysics) when it translates God the Creator into an ontological title. But instead of perversely coupling the biblical doctrine of creation to the metaphysical obsession with the *why*, therefore with the principle of sufficient reason, wouldn't it be more appropriate to liberate it and not make creation into the response, at once forced and inept, to a question that it does not satisfy because it never even tries to? It is no more self-evident, for Christian thought, at least Saint Augustine's, that the question of creation aims to establish the *world* than it is that, for it and for him, it aims to establish beings in their

234 The Creation of the Self

subsistence or whatever other mode of *Being* one can imagine. Hence, it may be concluded, Heidegger's objection to the doctrine of creation is reversed and now appears as a very reliable negative indicator of the path to follow. I will no longer ask if creation responds to the question *why* concerning the world, but inversely I will seek the question to which creation provides a response, since this response does not take on, whatever the case, the guise of a cause, nor a sufficient reason, nor an ontology, still less a cosmology. It could be that creation does not provide any response other than the response itself—in the sense that everything, in heaven and on earth, emerges in the created only precisely for that, *to respond.*

Between creation and response there rules a reciprocal and necessary connection, which is deployed at once in a praise and a *confessio.* Creatures find themselves first in praise. I have already noted the fact that books XII and XIII of the *Confessiones,* which treat the story of creation, open with a confession of praise ("Confitetur altitudini tuae humilitas linguae meae, quoniam tu fecisti caelum et terram" [The humility of my tongue confesses it unto your highness, you made heaven and earth] [XII, 2, 2, 14, 344]) and conclude with a praise ("Laudant te opera tua, ut amemus te, et amemus te, ut laudent te opera tua" [Your works praise you, so that we may love you, and we love you in order that your works may praise you] [XIII, 33, 48, 516]). In fact, the pure and simple acknowledgment of the goodness (therefore also the beauty) of created things is equivalent in actuality to a praise, which no longer need be qualified explicitly as such: "et vidimus, quia bona sunt singula et omnia bona valde" (and we saw that each is [by itself] good and that all taken together are very good) (XIII, 34, 49, 14, 518). The entire "ordo pulcherrimus rerum valde bonarum" (perfectly beautiful order of very good things) (XIII, 35, 50, 14, 520) that concludes all the *Confessiones* completes the initial praise of God *laudabilis valde* (I, 1, 1, 13, 272). But there is even more and even earlier: the first thematic mention of creation, which appears, we saw, as early as book XI of the *Confessiones,* evokes the reading of the text of Genesis in terms that recall Romans 13 during Augustine's personal conversion. That is, at Cassiciacum Saint Augustine hears *tolle, lege:* he hears and therefore takes (VIII, 12, 29, 14, 66), while here he asks to hear and to understand: "Audiam et intelligam, quomodo 'in principio' fecisti 'caelum et terram'" (Let me hear and understand how "in the beginning" *you made "heaven and earth"*) (XI, 3, 5, 14, 278)—which is to say that his conversion, which begins by a reading of the scriptures concerning regeneration in God, is finally accomplished by another reading, concerning my creation by God. Between these two readings, however, a difference is to be noted: the first ends up at an individual conversion, while the second, the one that will interpret the creation of heaven and earth in the first chapters of Genesis, takes under its charge the entire community of readers, who share the same creation and the same community of prayer.

The exegesis of Genesis attempts to comprehend the creation of the plurality of things only by speaking in the name of the community of created men and, among them, that of the believers. As we saw above (Chapter 1, §6), the literary act takes on, with the exegesis of creation, a communal and liturgical status, because it aims to provoke, for the readers as well as for the author, the initial *confessio*: "Volo 'eam [sc. veritatem] facere' in corde meo coram te in confessione, in stilo autem meo coram multis testibus" (I want "to do the truth" [John 3:21] in my heart and in front of you in confession, but also with my pen before many witnesses) (X, 1, 1, 14, 140). Writing, in particular here the exegesis of Genesis, amounts to making *us* confess God "ut *dicamus* omnes 'magnus Dominus, et laudabilis valde'" (XI, 1, 1, 14, 270). The plurality of created things is realized in a confession that is itself plural. In fact, the common confession of believers permits taking charge of created things as so many occasions to praise their creator. And it alone permits such a charge: the things themselves could not give themselves to be seen as created by God—in other words as given by God—if nobody interpreted them as such, as witnesses to the glory of God. The community of believers, of those who confess God in faith, is therefore the sole thing that permits seeing and saying things as created, therefore as not subsisting (non-*vorhanden*) because it alone hears and sees in them the goodness of God: "O si vitia nostra cohibeamus! Quia bona sunt omnia, quia bonus Deus fecit omnia; et laudant illum opera sua, considerata quia bona sunt, ab eo qui habet spiritum considerandi, spiritum pietatis et sapientiae. Undique laudatur Deus ab operibus suis" (O, if only we could contain our vices! [We would see] that all things are good because good God made them all; and all his works praise him provided they are considered as good, [as they are by] he who has the spirit to consider them so, the spirit of piety and of wisdom. Everywhere, God's works praise him).[9] Nothing less than the plurality of believers is needed to interpret the plurality of things as the beauty that refers to God and assigns them, then and only then, the dignity of creatures. For heaven and earth to "proclaim that they themselves did not make themselves" (clamant etiam quod se ipsa non fecerint) (XI, 3, 5, 14, 280), what is needed is that somebody pose to them a strange and not-so-evident question, one that asks if they come from themselves or from elsewhere: "Interrogavi terram et dixit 'non sum'" (I asked the earth, and it replied, "It is not I") (X, 6, 9, 14, 154). But what is even more necessary is somebody who knows how to hear the possible and silent response, "cui sileat omnino—quoniam si quis audiat, dicunt haec omnia 'non ipsa nos fecimus, sed fecit nos qui manet in aeternum'" (somebody who is capable of an absolute silence—for if somebody would listen [truly listen], all things would say: "We ourselves did not make ourselves, but rather he who remains forever" [Psalm 99:3]) (IX, 10, 25, 14, 118).[10] The exegesis of Genesis in fact ends at a hermeneutic, by the community of believers, of heaven and earth as gifts given by God—in other words, the interpretation of the creation story leads to interpreting the world as created.[11] This is possible only by a universalized *confessio* of God, by all believers, with regard to all things, as so many gifts.

Creation appears—or, more exactly, heaven, earth, and all things appear—as created only starting from the *confessio* of the believers, who assume in the flesh (constituting and constituted) the interpretation of creation as praise rendered to God, acknowledged as such because invoked in the figure of the creator. Qualifying heaven, earth, or any other thing with the title *creature* amounts to literally praising in it God's gift, to praising God by acknowledging him as creator. This means that the hermeneutic of creation consists precisely in *not* defining things as beings (still less as beings subsisting in an uninterrogated presence) but in acknowledging them *as* gifts received in the form of creation and offered in the form of praise—and thus whose presence is maintained only in this exchange. In fact, creation and praise reciprocate one another and render each other possible: "Te *laudant* haec omnia *creatorem* omnium" (These things all *praise* you [as] *creator* of all) (XI, 5, 7, 14, 282). In other words the formulation "Laudant te opera tua" (Your works praise you) (XIII, 33, 48, 14, 516) should be understood as a pleonasm, or rather as an equivalence.

"Creation" does not belong to the lexicon of beings, being, or Being but to the liturgical vocabulary, like *confessio* and praise, which alone acknowledge and establish it.

§38. The aporia of the place

Creation does not come at the beginning but after and within praise because it alone can and wants to interpret visible things as endowed with a beginning, therefore as created. There would not be any possibility of seeing the world as heaven and earth created by God if one did not first consent to praising God as God. Praise thus sets forth the *liturgical* condition for the possibility of recognizing creation—even if afterward and almost anachronistically, one can obscure the praise and posit creation as an ontic commencement. But this reversal of the real and primordial liturgical order into a cosmological order reconstituted *a posteriori* remains, even if it is convenient to accept it, a methodological artifice and, as such, is deprived of even the least bit of legitimacy in the eyes of the *confessio*. Creation does not render *confessio* possible, as the ontic place for its enactment, but it itself becomes possible only starting with *confessio*, its liturgical preliminary. In short, in and through its praise of God, *confessio* gives its first place to the creation of heaven and earth, not the inverse. Thus we understand the extent to which the question to which creation responds has nothing ontic or ontological about it. This question asks about the liturgical and therefore theological conditions for the praise of God and considers creation only as an output of the hermeneutic operation of praise—in and through the interpretation of heaven and earth *as* created and *as* silently proclaiming not themselves but God.

It is therefore necessary to begin by fixing the place of creation in praise if one wants later, by derivation, to see creation itself as a place. In fact, from the very opening of the *Confessiones* (in I, 1, 1) the issue has always been to deduce a place starting from praise. For if God gives himself as *laudabilis valde*, as he who is par excellence fit to praise, a question arises: how to praise him seeing as we do not know him and, in fact, seeing as he must first announce himself to us for us to invoke him: "*Prae*dicatus enim es nobis" (You were said to us *in advance*)? We can therefore praise him (say him) only in response to his own announcement of himself (his *pre*diction), such that praising him amounts to calling him upon oneself: "Quaeram te, Domine, *in*vocans te et *in*vocem te credens te" (I want, Lord, to seek you by invoking you and to invoke you by believing in you) (I, 1, 1, 13, 275). But what does it mean to *in*voke or to praise by *in*voking, if not to call God to come into myself, "*in me* ipsum eum *in*vocabo, cum *in*vocabo ipsum"? This coming of God into myself, which turns out to be the sole posture praise can adopt, supposes that I myself have the status of an open place for God to come into; but who am I to pretend to constitute a place when faced with God? "Et quis locus est in me, quo veniat in me Deus meus? Quo Deus veniat in me, Deus, qui 'fecit caelum et terram'?" (And what place is there in me where my God might come into me? In what corner would God come into me, God "who made heaven and earth"?) (I, 2, 2, 13, 274). A contradiction arises here: I have no other place in me besides the one that God made; therefore God cannot come into me without my first coming into him or discovering myself always already in him: I am not a place for God; rather I take place in him. Praise cannot ask God to come into me, since I do not have a place to offer to him, where he would dwell as in his temple. In fact, of place, I have none other besides him, or more simply, besides the place that he himself has set up for me by creating heaven and earth. If praise there must be, it will call for an impossibility—that I come, myself, into his very own place, God—to wit, into God himself. "Et ego, quid peto, ut venias in me, qui non essem, nisi esses in me? . . . Non ergo essem, nisi esses in me, an potius non essem, nisi essem in te, 'ex quo omnia, per quem omnia, in quo omnia'" (And what is it that I imagine I am asking when I ask that you come into me, me who would not be if you were not in me? . . . For I would not be if you were not in me, or rather I would not be if I was not in you, you "from whom all things come, by whom all things were made, in whom all things reside" [Romans 11:36]) (I, 2, 2, 13, 276). Once again creation does not respond to the ontic or ontological question, since it precedes it and, at best, renders it conceivable, but always as a derivative, in a secondary set of considerations. The metaphysical interpretation of creation, in fact, supposes that the question of place has already been resolved and in the basest manner conceivable: as the production of a world of beings by the exercise of an efficient causality. This interpretation quite simply does not see the difficulty, which resides in asking on the basis of what place a praise of the *laudabilis valde* can be set forth. The creation of heaven and earth (once again *not* the creation of the world, nor of beings, especially not subsistent) comes up only in order to respond to the original question, the *confessio*.

The absence in myself of the place for praise by *confessio* is illustrated by at least two aporiae. The first is almost self-evident. Since God created heaven and earth, he is found everywhere where heaven and earth are stretched out; in this sense I find myself from the outset already in him. This does not, however, resolve the difficulty, which by contrast becomes all the more formidable: in finding myself in heaven and earth, which come from him and are in him, I experience how great is the distance separating me from him; for, located in what is of, by, and in God, I do not discover myself exactly in, nor of, nor through God. I must, inversely, notice that God is not contained anywhere, especially not in what he created: "An non opus habes, ut quoquam continearis, qui continues omnia, quoniam quae imples continendo imples?" (Or is it that you have no need that some place contain you, since what you fill, you fill by containing it yourself?) (I, 3, 3, 13, 276). As it seems unacceptable to conclude that one part of God is present in heaven and earth while another would remain outside—seeing as one thereby supposes a univocal spatialization of God in his creation, it must be concluded by contrast that "ubique totus es et res nulla te totum capit" (you are entirely everywhere without anything comprehending you) (I, 3, 3, 13, 278). But then even the creation of heaven and earth, far from opening for us a place to receive God, reveals him as all the more *secretissimus et praesentissimus*, at one and the same time the most secret and the most present (I, 4, 4, 13, 278). Hence, the aporia of the place where and whence God could be praised by our *confessio* imposes its utopia.

This way of crystallizing the difficulty in fixing a place by mere recourse to the creation of heaven and earth refers us to a second aporia: the most pressing and the most evident, since it has, in fact, all along haunted the path we have been traveling, in particular when we were tracking the anonymity of the *ego* and the immemorial (Chapter 2, §12; Chapter 3, §16). The utopia of heaven and earth seems, throughout Saint Augustine's itinerary, like a repetition (in book XII) and an anticipation (in book I) of the most constant utopia, that of the self: the creation of heaven and earth leaves me without place for praise because, more essentially, I know of no place (*ubi*) permitting me to dwell anywhere, much less in myself. If I do not offer a place where God can come, this is not first or only on account of my sin rendering me uninhabitable to his holiness[12] but on account of a utopia constitutive of my finitude, which sin only orchestrates. We have already seen this once before in the gaps that sometimes arise between myself and myself to the point of alienating me from myself. For example, when the pain of losing a friend makes me hate all other things ("oderam omnia"), ones that nevertheless make up my own life ("mihi patria supplicum et parterna domus mihi infelicitas" [my homeland becomes a torture and the house of my father a great unhappiness]), to the point of transforming my own evidence into a question to myself: "factus eram mihi magna quaestio" (IV, 4, 9, 13, 422). Or again when the temptation to prefer, in listening to a song, the musical pleasure over the liturgical praise makes me no longer know who I truly am, that is to say *where* I am truly going with my desire, I discover myself once again outside myself: "mihi quaestio factus sum" (I become for myself a great question) (X, 33, 50, 14, 232). I can appear to myself as so frequent a question only because I do not, in fact, frequent myself—I lack access to myself, there where I truly dwell. My alienation in these crises attests that I do not know where to recover myself because, in fact, I do not have any proper *place*, because I no longer have *place* for myself nor for a *self*.

The same utopia leads me astray in the exercise of *memoria*. In its first sense this faculty offers the *place* par excellence for the mind since, in it, *here*, everything we think is buried ("*Ibi* reconditum est, quiquid etiam cogitamus") in such a way that, *here*, I am even able to make reappear at will what is past ("*Ibi* quando sum, posco, ut preferatur quidquid volo" [X, 8, 12, 14, 162]). I can always therefore, in the normal course of things, encounter myself here ("*Ibi* mihi et ipse occurro meque recolo" [X, 8, 14, 14, 166]). In remembering everything, I dwell in myself; I have a place. But strangely (or, like a stranger), what is proper to my memory, to this *place* more my own than any other, consists also in that I am not always in command of it, since sometimes it dispossesses me of myself and does not come back to me: "Ecce memoriae meae vis non comprehenditur a me" (And look, the strength of my own memory is not something I comprehend) precisely when I do not remember or, worse, do not even remember having forgotten. Hence, I suffer from myself, because I no longer recover myself *here*, because the place is missing precisely there where I find myself, "laboro *hîc* et laboro *in* me ipso" (X, 16, 25, 14, 184). In other words I no longer know *what* I am because I no longer know *where* I am. "Nec ego ipse capio totum, quod sum. Ergo animus ad habendum se ipsum angustus est, ut *ubi* sit quod sui non capiat? Numquid extra ipsum se ac non *in* ipso?" (I do not know myself entirely what I am. The mind is too narrow to contain itself, so narrow that it does not know *where* to find what is its own [place]? Would it find it outside itself and no longer *in* itself?) (X, 8, 15, 14, 166). I do not give *place* to myself.

The utopia runs still deeper. For there is still one place, just one, *where* I know that I find myself, at least *where* I would like absolutely to find myself, but this is the one place that I am incapable of reaching. That is, all men desire beatitude, unconditionally, but no one even knows *where* his knowledge of it comes from: "Nonne ipsa est beata vita, quam omnes volunt et omnino qui nolit, nemo est? *Ubi* noverunt eam, quod sic volunt eam? *Ubi* viderunt, ut amarent eam?" (Isn't it the good life itself that all men want to the point that nobody, absolutely nobody, can be found who does not want it? *Where* then did they know it so that they want it so? *Where* did they see it to love it so?) (X, 20, 29, 14, 194). Not only do I admit as radically my own only the sole *place* that I know I cannot reach by myself, but I do not even know *where* I got the knowledge that I have of it since I absolutely do not know it. I do not even know from *where* it came to me, the *place where* I desire to find myself but *where* I know I cannot find myself.

Now, I who no longer have a place for myself (the *quaestio*), I who no longer give place to myself (*memoria*), I who do not know from where the place of my desire comes to me, I hear it named everywhere, provided that I no longer listen to myself but to heaven and earth *inasmuch as created*. For, if the things of the world remain mute so long as one interprets them as apparently subsisting beings (in fact, even this mindless thick-headedness already demands an interpretation, though it is ignorant of this), they say, in a loud and understandable voice, their place as soon as one succeeds (in fact, accepts) in hearing them as they say themselves, as creatures. At once, "si quis audiat, dicunt haec omnia: 'Non ipsa nos fecimus, sed fecit nos qui manet in aeternum'" (if someone listens, they all say, "We are not made by ourselves, but he, he alone made us, he who remains for eternity" [Psalm 99:3, 99:5]) (IX, 10, 25, 14, 118).[13] By proclaiming in a silent, but piercing, voice that they do not subsist in themselves, that they do not have a *place* in themselves, heaven and earth make plain that they arise from an other place besides their self, and this tacit yet evident acknowledgment is, in fact, already equivalent to praise—that is to say, to the mode of *confessio* that is appropriate for them. But, at the same time, heaven and earth, in proclaiming their utopia, overcome it, in recognizing it, transform it from *quaestio* into response, a response not only to the *quaestio* of their place (the place consists in an other place besides the self), but in general to the possibility of praise. Hence, since the interpretation of heaven and earth as created does not come from them, but from my interpretation of the world as not subsisting in itself and referring to its utopia, creation (its hermeneutic as created) appears as the response to the *quaestio* about my possibility of praise and *confessio*—by no means, once again, a response to the investigation that wants to know why there is something rather than nothing.

The possibility of *confessio* thus opens when the utopia (I no longer have place for myself, I no longer give a place to myself, and I do not know from where the place of my desire comes over me) is no longer fixed in itself, no longer closed on itself, no longer withdrawn as aporia, but itself becomes the response: when the *not-here* appears as an other place, or rather an otherplace, an alteration that displaces the place outside itself, outside even the self, in such a way as to open the *over-there* as my place. "Sed *ubi* manes in memoria mea, Domine, *ubi illic* manes?" (But *where* do you reside in this memory that is called mine, O Lord, *where* do you reside *over there*?) (X, 25, 36, 14, 205). For me (therefore, on the basis of my hermeneutic of the world as created, also for all things), the only *here* is *over there* such that I find myself when I head off for *there where I am not*. The desire for beatitude (therefore desire as such, since desire always desires beatitude) saves me only because it enjoins me to leave—but to leave from what, if not from the self, which clings to its *here*? Toward what in me, if not toward *over there*? Turning to God (which one names, without fully understanding what one says, conversion) designates first of all the exodus from the *ubi* toward an *illic*—which means, of course, that I am only because I arrive in him by praise: "Et ego dico: Deus meus *ubi* es? Ecce *ubi* es. Respiro *in te* 'paululum,' cum 'effundo super me animam meam in voce exsultationis et confessionis'" (And I say, my God, *where* are you? But, look *where* you are: I breathe "a little" *in you*, when I pour out "over myself my soul in a voice that exults and confesses" [Psalm 41:8]) (XIII, 14, 15, 14, 450). But this suggests, above all, that I am in him only because, in the first place, he is in me and that in this way the *illic, over-there*, precedes and renders possible derivatively an *ubi, here*, for me. For me every *ubi* becomes an *illic*, which neither remains nor ever becomes again an *ibi*—I am in my place (*ubi*) only by not remaining in it as in a closed *here*, by forever passing elsewhere (*illic*). "Et ecce intus eras et ego foris, et *ibi* quarebam. . . . Mecum eras et tecum non eram" (And behold you were inside [the place to reside], and I myself was outside, and I sought you *here*. . . . You were with me, but I myself was not with you) (X, 27, 38, 14, 208). The truth resides inside me, but not *in* me, because *I am not inside myself*, because my interior remains exterior so long as I do not become interior to my exterior itself. This reversal of the *here* and *over there* is not equivalent to the presence in me of God or a piece of the divine but indicates that I reach myself only by taking place *over there*—in this case, in God. For I have no place to take place so long as I stubbornly dwell *here*—in other words, stubbornly will that my *ubi* reside where I am, *ibi*: "Non ego vita mea sim: male vixi ex me, mors mihi fui: *in te* revivisco" (I am not myself my own life. On my own, I lived woefully; I was a death to myself. I return to life *in* you) (XII, 10, 10, 14, 358).[14] Life, like the happy life, defines my place, which in both cases is found *over there*.

By converting the place, creation therefore offers, in the form of a hermeneutic of heaven and earth, but also of man, a response to the question of the possibility of praise. With it the aporia of the place becomes, just like a utopia, the very posture of *confessio*.

§39. The site of *confessio*

Creation, therefore, responds to the question of the possibility of *confessio*, and creation gives place to *confessio* by defining *where* those who must do so—in other words, all that is not confused with God—can do so. Creation does not define only what happens to be created but, first of all, that in view of which the created is created—accomplishing a *confessio* by praise of the creator. Creation gives place (*ubi*) to *confessio* by opening the dimensions where the created can direct itself toward the creator of a *here* (*ibi*) turning toward an *over-there* (*illic*). Three such dimensions can be specified, and this enables us to designate the site.

The first dimension opens out toward nothingness on the basis of the earth. More exactly, it is detected as early as the first reading of the verse that comments on the beginning ("In the beginning God created the heaven and the earth") by adding: "And the earth was obscure and empty, *inanis et vacua*" (Genesis 1:2). Or rather, for that is the version of the Vulgate about which he was ignorant (or which he refused), Saint Augustine prefers to reproduce literally the translation of the Septuagint: ἀόρατος καὶ ἀκατασκεύαστος, *invisibilis et incomposita*.[15] This choice does, indeed, seem better since, instead of two redundant terms (giving rise to inevitably loose translations), it lets us distinguish two different characteristics of the earth. First, it appears without form because it remains at bottom unorganized, without structure or composition. If what is at issue is indeed the original, primal earth, truly that of the beginning (*primitus*), then this notion implies logically (*consequenter*) that it is still without form or composition: "ipsa terra, quam primitus facit, sicut Scriptura consequenter eloquitur, invisibilis et incomposita" (*De civitate Dei* XI, 9, 35, 56ff.). Whence the paradoxical consequence that if we are talking about the earth of creation, but of a "creation born and without memory" (Péguy),[16] then it is not a matter of the earth such as we see it, since we now see only forms in it: "non erat talis, qualem nunc cernimus et tangimus. Invisibilis enim erat et incomposita et abyssus erat" (it was not such as we see and touch it today, for it was invisible and not composed; it was an abyss) (*Confessiones* XII, 8, 8, 14, 354). But if it is an issue of an "informitas sine ulla specie" (a formlessness without form) (XII, 3, 5, 14, 348), then it is no longer a question of our earth, but of "informis material" (formless matter) (XII, 15, 22, 16, 376). The earth, such as we know it, would not have been created if, more originally and even though the biblical text does not mention it explicitly, matter had not also been and at the same time. The creation of the earth as formless and without composition implies that of matter. This implication has at least two consequences.

First, if primary matter is created, Augustine's doctrine breaks with the Greek position (from Plato to Plotinus), despite all the similarities one would like to point out, by removing matter from the rank of principle.

Whence an argument that proves decisive, though derivative, against the Manicheans: since *materia* comes, by creation, from God, it cannot constitute a principle of evil, because more essentially it does not constitute any principle whatsoever:

Neque enim vel illa materies, quam ὕλη antiqui dixerant, malum dicenda sit. Nam eam dico, quam Manicheus ὕλην appellat dementissima vanitate, nesciens quid loquatur, formatricem corporum: unde recte illi dictum est, quod alterum deum inducat: nemo enim formare et creare corpora nisi Deus potest. . . . Sed ὕλην dico quandam penitus informem et sine qualitate materiam, unde istae, quas sentimus, qualitates formantur, ut antiqui dixerunt. Hinc enim et silva graece ὕλη dicitur, quod operentibus apta sit, non ut aliquid ipsa faciat, sed unde aliquid fiat.

For even this matter, which the Ancients called ὕλη, should not be called evil. I am not speaking of this ὕλη that Manes, in his demented vanity, not knowing what he was saying, claimed was formative of bodies, from which it was correctly concluded that he was introducing another god, for nobody can form and create bodies except God. . . . But I myself call ὕλη a certain formless matter without quality from which the qualities that we sense take form, as the Ancients said. Hence in Greek the wood to be worked is called ὕλη because it is of service to the workers, not because it itself makes something, but on account of the fact that it is that out of which something is made.[17]

Thus the earth presupposes matter, but matter itself presupposes creation. Therefore matter offers no place, neither to the earth nor to the *confessio*, but it receives itself just like all the other things (even if it does not yet have the rank of thing) in itself for the sake of working *confessio*.

But there is more: since matter has no place in the world and since it gives no place to the world, from where does it get its place? It can get it only from an other instance, still more empty, invisible, and formless than it, yet there is no longer any to be found: "Citius enim non esse censebam, quod omni forma privaretur, quam cogitabam quiddam inter formam et nihil nec formatum nec nihil, informe prope nihil" (I would sooner admit the nonbeing of what had no form than I would think something between form and nothing, neither formed nor nothing, formless next to nothing) (XII, 6, 6, 14, 350). On the hither side of matter, just at the limit of nothing ("illud totum prope nihil erat . . . jam tamen erat"), nearly nullified ("de nulla re paene nullam rem") (XII, 8, 8, 14, 354), is found nothing other than nothing itself; and therefore "fecisti aliquid et *de* nihilo" (you made something even of nothing, out of and *with* nothing) (XII, 7, 7, 14, 352). It is a good idea, in other words, to use the two possible translations of *de nihilo*, for God does not merely create *out of* (*ex*) nothing in such a way as to exit from it and substitute for it being (after nothing comes being); he, above all, created *with* (*de*) nothingness so as to make being with nothingness itself. Nothingness, in the figure of *de nihilo*, does not hold merely the place of starting point for the created (as that from which it would have exited); it also holds the place of its material (as that of which it will always remain woven). The created does not emerge from nothing except by assuming it again at the heart of its very beingness. It should, then, be said, in a transitive sense, that the created *is* its nothingness and that it is so because God gives it to it: the created *is* its nothingness only because it is so *by* God, "*abs te*, a quo sunt omnia" (XII, 7, 7, 7, 14, 352). God, in creating the created, does not abolish nothingness in it, but assigns this very nothing to the created in assuming it as created *by* him. The *de nihilo* is understood and thought together with the *a Deo*. The *a Deo* balances, maintains, and subverts the *de nihilo*. "*De* nihilo enim *a te*, non de te facta sunt, non de aliqua non tua vel quae antea fuerit, sed de concreata, id est simul *a te* creata materia, quia ejus informitatem sine ulla temporis interpositione formasti. . . . Materiem quidem *de omnino nihilo*. . . fecisti" (*With* nothing, not *with* you, that is things were made *by* you, not *with* a matter not created by you or already there, but *with* concrete matter, because you formed the formless in it without the slightest temporal delay. . . . You truly did make matter *absolutely with nothing*) (XIII, 38, 48, 14, 516ff.).[18] In this sense creation does not, strictly speaking, confer Being on the created but permits it to assume its nothingness in order to make it work at the *confessio*. Here what is is not absolutely, as if God remained an optional complement to the act of Being; to the contrary, here what is is only optionally, inasmuch as created and insofar as the *de nihilo* remains thought together with the *a Deo*, therefore is oriented to the *confessio*. The created remains an intermittent being, under contract to time, marching to the beat of a time determined by its praise: "Et inspexi caetera infra te et vidi nec omnino esse, nec omnino non esse: esse quidem, quoniam ab te sunt, non esse autem, quoniam id quod es non sunt. . . . Si non manebo in illo, nec in me potero" (I considered the other things beneath you, and

I saw that they neither are absolutely nor are not absolutely. They are, of course, since they are from you, but they are not, since they are not what you are. . . . If I do not remain in him [God, my good], I will not be able to do it in myself either) (VII, 11, 17, 13, 618). Creation, which presents itself first as an event and an advent (Chapter 5, §35), also sets up a condition—the status of what does not take place in itself but in a nothing that sustains and cuts across an other than itself. In a sense, every created thing says: "Non ergo vita mea sim" (It is not I who am my own life) (XII, 10, 10, 14, 358).

A second dimension can also open a site for the *confessio*, this time in terms of the heavens—or, more exactly, the "heaven of the heavens." That is, from his first reading of the verse "In the beginning God created the heavens and the earth," Saint Augustine read it together with a surprising formulation found in Psalm 113:15–16, which itself already comments on Genesis 1:1: "Domino qui fecit caelum et terram, caelum caeli Domino, terram autem dedit filiis hominum" (Lord who made heaven and earth, the heaven of the heavens belongs to Him; the earth, he gave to the sons of men). There ineluctably follows an investigation concerning place: "*Ubi* est caelum, quod non cernimus, cui terra est hoc omne, quod cernimus? . . . Sed ad illud 'caelum caeli' etiam terrae nostrae caelum, terra est" (*Where* is the heaven that we do not see, by relation to which all that we see is earth[ly]? . . . But, in relation to this "heaven of the heavens," even the heavens of our earth are earth[ly]) (XII, 2, 2, 14, 346). Even if the hypothesis of a τόπος νοητός has a long tradition, it falls to Saint Augustine alone to have elaborated this isolated, indeed marginal, biblical phrase into a concept of great importance. Just as the earth, once reinterpreted as *invisibilis et incomposita*, becomes matter and even the *nihil* of the *de nihilo*, in such a way as to give place for praise, so, too, do the heavens, once overinterpreted as *caelum caeli*, give another place for praise. The difficulty of this place stems from the imprecise, indeed contradictory, determinations, which render it all the more strange.[19] It would seem at first that we are dealing with just an equivalent of the (Plotinian, indeed Aristotelian) νοῦς, since the title of a *caelum intelligibile* (XII, 21, 30, 14, 390) is associated with that of *mens pura* (XII, 11, 12, 14, 360) or *mens rationalis et intellectualis* (XII, 15, 20, 14, 372), sometimes in the same sequence: "caelum intellectuale, *ubi* intellectus nosse simul, non 'ex parte, non in aenigmate, non per speculum, sed ex toto,' in manifestatione, 'facie ad faciem'" (intelligible heavens, *where* the understanding goes together with knowing, not "in part, enigmatically, in a reflection, but totally," fully manifest, "face to face" [1 Corinthians 13:12]) (XII, 13, 16, 14, 366). This makes it seem to be about the place where the knowledge of God becomes manifest and evident (but evidently not adequate). Yet the situation proves to be more complex since this intellectual evidence still comes from the created: the intelligible heavens still remain a *creatura aliqua intellectualis* (XII, 9, 9, 14, 356). They contemplate God as such, without sensible intermediary, but always from the point of view and within the essential limits of the created: "profecto sapientia, quae creata est, intellectualis natura scilicet, quae contemplatione luminis lumen est—dicitur enim et ipsa, quamvis creata, sapientia" (wisdom, which is created, intellectual nature to be sure, but wisdom which is light only by contemplating the light—it too is therefore said to be wisdom, though created) (XII, 15, 20, 14, 372).[20] No gnostic temptation can insinuate itself here, therefore, since the contemplation, even purely intellectual, of God remains marked by the distance of the created from the uncreated, a distance that does not so much safeguard the divine privilege as it maintains the created in its possibility of praising. Thus, *confessio* alone unites with God, not mere knowledge, which remains only a means and a mode of it. Consequently, no distinction seems any longer to institute itself explicitly between the intellects united in this place, establishing hierarchies, for example among men and the angels or among the angels themselves, as if their differences blur here in the single office of *confessio*. This function alone is enough to characterize a common place *where* the intelligent created (human or angelic) praises God inasmuch as intelligible.

We are therefore dealing with a place, but one that embraces indifferently the angelic choirs (celestial hierarchy), the terrestrial church (ecclesiastical hierarchy), the eschatological mass of the elect, and the intelligible heavens, indeed the world of idealities, provided that the *confessio* of God the intelligible is put into operation everywhere by intellectual creatures. Thus this place receives explicitly the title of place par excellence, of *domus tua* and *civitas tua* (XII, 11, 12, 14, 360),[21] that must be understood as the house or the city where God can come and dwell *as* God, without being disfigured, blasphemed, and killed. God can *descend* into the "heaven of the heavens," as one descends upon a city, in order to sojourn or holiday there. For this city should not be understood as God's proper place, his everyday residence, nor the city where he would be at home, but as the sojourn where he lets one come and meet or see him. Thus, these houses and this city do *not* belong to eternity, for the very purpose that we, we men like the other intelligent creatures, might have access to them. The "heaven of the heavens" draws as close as possible to the eternity of God but does not enjoy it, neither fully nor directly. This residence of God does not reside in God, therefore does not share his eternity, *domus Dei, non quidem Deo coaeterna* (XII, 15, 22, 14, 374). Between the "heaven of the heavens" and the eternity of God, things are never so intimate as to reach coeternity, but an exteriority always remains open for participation: "domus Dei non terrena neqe ulla caelesti mole corporea, sed spiritualis et particeps aeternitatis tuae" (the house of God, not terrestrial and not bodily, not even a celestial body, but spiritual and taking part in your eternity) (XII, 15, 19, 14, 370). Yet this intellectual but not eternal place for the praise of the intelligible manifests a new mode of temporality for the creature. For, though not eternal because not coeternal with God ("nec illa creatura tibi coaeterna est" [XII, 11, 12, 14, 360]), the "heaven of the heavens" benefits, if not solely, at least first of all and in the name of the other creatures, from the privilege of not being submitted to time ("nec in illa invenimus tempus" [XII, 15, 21, 14, 374])—at least not to time understood in the derived and devastated mode of *distentio*: "supergreditur enim omnem *distentionem* et omne spatium" (it overcomes all *distension* and space) (XII, 15, 22, 14, 376). The "heaven of the heavens" therefore appears, inasmuch as the place for intelligible praise, as a place free from distraction (from *distentio*). Does its privilege in space therefore bring with it a privilege in time? How to explain this new consideration and formulation?

The text adds that the "heaven of the heavens" is liberated from distraction *and* from space. But why space, since distraction refers in book XI to time? Because, no doubt, distraction is the definition of the time distended by temporal ecstases, ecstases that, themselves obliged to be distended and distending, *spatialize* time, to the point of distending it and dispersing it according to the model of space (see Chapter 5, §36). It must therefore be understood that while all the other creatures are strictly worldly and decline their temporality according to the most widespread and powerful model—namely, space *partes extra partes*—thereby deploying their time only by dispersing it and distending the mind in it, the "heaven of the heavens" makes an exception—precisely and to the degree that it participates in eternity (without however becoming annexed to it), it succeeds, "sine ulla vicissitudine temporum" (without the least variation in time) (XII, 13, 16, 14, 366), in deploying an intentional temporality ("secundum intentionem") (XI, 29, 39, 14, 338). It can do this, however, only by letting itself be affected and taken up by the eternity that it does not possess: "te sibi semper praesente, ad quem toto affectu se tenet, non habens futurum quod expectet nec in praeteritum trajiciens quod meminerit, nulla vice varietur nec in tempora ulla *distenditur*" (holding present to you with all its [creation's] affection, you who always remains present to it, it has no more future to expect, nor past to cross in order to remember, it no longer varies with any change nor is it *distracted* and pulled apart into any times) (XII, 11, 12, 14, 360). The "heaven of the heavens" overcomes the distension of time with an intention only insofar as it tends toward the divine eternity, therefore insofar as it adheres to it—tension by adherence: "*cohaerentem Deo* vero et vere aeterno, ut, quamvis coaeterna non sit, in nullam tamen temporum varietatem et vicissitudinem ab illo se resolvat et defluat" (*adhere to God*, the true and truly eternal, so that without being coeternal with him, it [this sublime creature, the "heaven of the heavens"] is nevertheless never unstuck from him and does not flow out in any alteration or change of time) (XII, 15, 19, 14, 370).

In fact, the privilege of the "heaven of the heavens" explains the situation of all creatures. Distraction (or temporal distension) characterizes them all by virtue of a more essential and all-encompassing, therefore also spatializing, mutability: "quia non *de* ipsa substantia Dei, sed *ex* nihilo cuncta facta sunt, quia non sunt id ipsum, quod Deus et *inest quaedam mutabilitas* omnibus, sive *maneant* sicut aeterna domus, sive mutentur, sicut anima hominis et corpus" (because none of them are made *of* [i.e., *with*] the very substance of God, but *out of* nothing such that *some inherent mutability is still in them*, whether they *settle* like the eternal mansion ["heaven of the heavens"] or change like the soul of man and his body) (XII 17, 25, 14, 380ff.). For all, the one question becomes how to reach a dwelling place where they settle despite their natural (created) mutability. That cannot come about through some new natural immutability (since eternity characterizes the uncreated alone); it will therefore have to happen through a disposition that is not natural but free and decided—an adherence through love: "inest ei tamen ipsa mutabilitas, unde tenebresceret et frigesceret, nisi *amore grandi tibi cohaerens,* tanquam semper meridies luceret et ferveret ex te" (the mutability is still in it ["the heaven of the heavens"], which could make it grow dark and cold, if it does not *adhere to you by a great love,* like a noonday always shining and burning with you) (XII, 15, 21, 14, 374). The creature, following the model of the "heaven of the heavens," should not overcome the distraction of time by trying not to yield to spatial (spatializing, spatialized) changes through a correction of its nature (Manicheanism), nor by a supernatural knowledge (Gnosticism), but by a loving adhesion to God, in which, as an added bonus, it will also find cohesion with itself. This does not mean passing beyond time, so as to pass into eternity, but surpassing the incoherence of distraction in and through love of the divine permanence, in a tension that itself still remains temporal. In this way the "heaven of the heavens" at last, after having been called *domus tua* and *civitas tua,* assumes the, eschatological, name *new Jerusalem,* which descends from the heavens to the earth: "recordans Hierusalem *extento in eam* sursum corde, Hierusalem patriam meam, Hierusalem matrem meam, teque super eam regnatorem" (remembering Jerusalem *stretched out toward it* with all my heart, Jerusalem my homeland, Jerusalem my mother, and toward you who rules over it).[22] In this way the "heaven of the heavens" provides the paradigm for every place of praise for every creature because, though instituted from the first day of creation, it also takes on eschatological status: place for all confessions, therefore place for all the loving adhesions to God's unalterability, arbiter of my confessions, "arbiter inter *confessiones* meas" (XII, 16, 23, 14, 378).

It now becomes possible to see a third dimension of the place of *confessio.* Or more exactly, to advance an interpretation of the concluding books of the *Confessiones* as themselves constituting a place, opening the place par excellence for every word that would like to be said as *confessio.* These three books are, in effect, organized, at least they can be read as being organized, trinitarily: each of them takes up in one of the figures of the Trinity (*Trinitas omnipotens* XIII, 11, 12, 14, 442) one of the ecstases of time.[23] In this sense *Confessiones* XI lays out the present of the past and the immensity of *memoria* in terms of the Father: "Omnia tempora tu fecisti et ante omnia tempora, tu es" (You made all of time, and before all time, you are) (XI, 13, 16, 14, 298). As for *Confessiones* XII, it lays out the present of the present, keeps in its *contuitus* the inaugural now of the creation of heaven and earth: "in Verbo suo sibi coaeterno fecit Deus intelligibilem atque sensibilem corporalemque creaturam" (it is in his coeternal Word that God made the creature endowed with intelligence, sensible therefore and corporeal) (XII, 20, 29, 14, 388) and that "*always* contemplates the face of God" (semper Dei faciem contemplantem) (XII, 17, 24, 14, 380). Finally, *Confessiones* XIII lays out the present of the future, the eschatological *expectatio*, because the Spirit from the beginning watches over our future: "et Spiritus tuus bonus superferatur ad subveniendum nobis in tempore oportuno" (And your good Spirit hovered [over the waters] so that it could come to our assistance when the time comes) (XIII, 34, 49, 14, 518).

"Heaven of the heavens" and creation *de nihilo* therefore attempt to define the place *where*, or more exactly *from where*, the *confessio* can be lifted up. In fact, these places turn out, in the end, to be trinitarian: it becomes possible to praise God as God only if God himself gives the place and time for it. And *where* else would that be except in God himself?

§40. Resemblance without definition

So, the creature's place is not found in itself but always in God, such that the place for the *confessio* of God is determined by and in God, to such an extent that creation consists only in the opening of the place of *confessio*. It is hence a universal rule. What remains for us to understand is how it is specified in the case of man.

The story of creation contains, on the sixth day and in the case of man, several peculiarities. If we admit the story as it is told in the *Vetus Latina*,[24] each created thing was created according to its kind, "secundum genus suum,"[25] in conformity with itself and itself alone. This version even emphasizes the self-identity of the individuation by kind when it adds "secundum similitudinem" (Genesis 1:11), indeed, when it insists "secundum *suam* similitudinem" (Genesis 1:11, 12). The created thing bears a likeness to itself; it resembles itself. In other words the work of creation, which separates and distinguishes in order to open distance (thus setting the conditions for the blessing of the created by God, as well as those for the praise of God by the created), requires referring each creature to itself, such that it resembles nothing other than its own kind, its own species, its own aspect (*species*)—in short, nothing other than itself in its ultimate essence. But, this is not how things go in the case of the creation of man. First, because in the story of his creation, the mention of kind (or of species) disappears: there is no reference of *this* created thing to its own proper essence: "Cur ergo et de homine non ita dictum est 'Faciamus hominem ad imaginem et similitudinem nostram *secundum genus*,' cum et hominis propago manifesta est?" (Why then did he not also say with regard to man: "let us make man in our image and likeness *according to his kind*," since man, too, obviously reproduces [according to his kind]?).[26] This modification does not involve some threat of no longer being able to reproduce (as a consequence of the first sin, for example) since what immediately follows is the blessing of his fruitfulness (Genesis 1:28: "Increase and multiply"). The sole explanation would come from the appearance of Eve, who shows up on the margins and as an exception to the species of the primordial *man*, so to speak. In order to understand this first peculiarity of the story of the creation of man (and woman), a second, still more explicit, one should be considered. In Genesis 1:26 creation no longer happens according to the creature's resemblance *to itself* ("secundum *suam* similitudinem") but according to its resemblance *to an other* besides itself—and, moreover, to an other of maximum alterity, since it is a reference to God: "non jam secundum genus, tanquam imitantes praecedentem proximum, nec ex hominis melioris auctoritate viventes. Neque enim dixisti: 'Fiat homo secundum genus,' sed: 'Faciamus hominem ad imaginem et similtudiem *nostram*,' ut nos probemus, quae sit voluntas tua" (no longer according to a kind, as if we imitated some precedent nearby or lived under the authority of some man better [than us]. For you did not say: "Let man be according to his kind," but: "Let us make man in our image and likeness," so that we might know by the ordeal what your will is) (*Confessiones* XIII, 22, 32, 14, 482). Not only does the phrase *ad similitudinem nostram* literally contradict *secundum suam similitudinem*, but it is also substituted for kind (or species)—that is to say, it holds the place, in the case of man, of any and every definition: "Nec dicis *secundum genus*, sed *ad imaginem et similitudinem nostram*" (You did not say *according to its kind* [ours], but *according to the image and likeness* [yours]) (XIII, 22, 32, 14, 484). Whence this paradoxical consequence: man constitutes a creature par excellence and even particularly excellent, precisely because he does not have a kind or species proper to him, therefore does not have a definition that would appropriate him to himself. Man is defined by the very fact that he remains without definition—the animal properly without property.

This is not just an incidental remark; it concerns what Saint Augustine does not hesitate to name a *mystery*, in the sense of the *magna quaestio* that man becomes for himself (Chapter 2, §10) and also in the sense of a sacrament by which God blesses man by creating him. "Sed quid est hoc et quale mysterium est? . . . Dicerem te, Deus noster, qui nos ad imaginem tuam creasti, dicerem te hoc donum benedictionis homini *proprie* volnisse largiri" (But what is this and what mystery is it? . . . I would say, our God, who created us in your image, I would say that you wanted to grant *properly* to man the gift of your *blessing*) (XIII, 24, 35, 14, 490). However, Saint Augustine hesitates before this conclusion as the issue remains quite subtle. God also encouraged the animals to reproduce; he even blessed the fish of the sea (Genesis 1:22). What then is particular to the blessing of fruitfulness given to man? No doubt precisely that: man alone receives from God a blessing of fruitfulness, while he did not receive a kind or species thanks to which he could naturally reproduce—reproduce *himself from himself.* This means that if man propagates himself over the entire earth to the point of dominating it, he owes this not to his kind or his species (which he does not have), nor to his essence (which remains unknown), but to a direct and ongoing blessing from God. In what does this consist? Evidently in substituting for kind and species the *ad imaginem et similitudinem nostram* in order to hold the place of the absent essence. Thus man does not increase according to his kind, his species, and his essence—that is to say according to himself—but by the blessing come from elsewhere that sets him up from the get-go in the likeness and in the image of an other than himself, God. Man does not increase by an essential and internal law but solely by receiving God's blessing, a blessing that consists only in being disposed according to the image and likeness toward God. Man does not have a proper essence but a reference to an other than himself, who, more intimate to him than himself (than his lacking essence), occupies the essential place on loan to him.

The image, by definition and essentially, can never provide an essence or a definition, which would be obtained by replicating, reproducing, and imitating another essence or definition—all the more so here, as the image concerns that for which man does not, by definition and essentially, have the means to constitute the slightest bit of image: God. Here, and in the case of man more than in that of any of the others, the image remains impracticable; consequently, it has to be thought starting from the likeness (*similitudo*). Obviously man does not bear the image of God as God the Son bears it toward God the Father through the connection of the Spirit, for only the Son *is* the image of the Father, while man is found only *in* the image of God: "Sed quia non omnino aequalis fiebat illa imago Dei tanquam non ab illo nata, sed ab illo creata, hujus rei significandae causa, ita imago est *ut ad imaginem* sit: id est, non aequaliter parilitate, sed *quadam similitudine* accedit. Non enim locorum intervallis, sed *similitudine* acceditur *ad* Deum, et dissimilitudine rededitur *ab* eo" (But because this image of God [man] was not absolutely equal to him, since not born of him but created by him, so as to make this point clear, this image is image *inasmuch as unto the image*—that is, it is not equal to it in a parity of God and man, but approaches it by *some likeness*. It does not draw near *toward* God by degrees of place but by likeness *toward him* and it grows apart by unlikeness *away from him*) (*De Trinitate* VII, 6, 12, 33, 550).[27] It is not a matter of keeping or losing the image of God as a content (as if *created in the image of God* can count as a definition as categorical as *rational animal, animal endowed with language,* or *animal that laughs*), but of referring the image *toward* that *unto which* it is like. The image is not compared to a model, like a visible reproduction is to another visible thing accessible elsewhere: the image is borne only by that which refers itself across the likeness unto an original that remains, as such, invisible and only in the measure to which it so refers itself. The image consists only in the tension of referring itself *to* that to which it means to resemble. It appears only as this movement *toward*, and only this *intentio ad* keeps a likeness. Man bears the image of God instead and in place of kind, species, or essence inasmuch as he resembles Him. But he cannot, except absurdly, pretend to resemble him as a visible image is like a visible model, indeed as an intelligible image is like an intelligible model. This would seem to be the illusion of the Neoplatonists: establishing a positive likeness, one measurable by intervals, between the terms of the likeness. It must be that man resembles God otherwise—which means both in another way and by remaining in alterity. "Sola est autem adversus omnes errores via munitissima, ut idem ipse sit Deus et homo; *quo* itur Deus, *qua* itur homo" (In order to avoid all errors in advance, one thing alone is needed: that the same item be God and man, God *toward* whom it goes, man *through* whom it goes).[28] This means that one must go toward the image through the likeness: man bears the image of God to the degree that he abandons any likeness to himself (*ad suum genus, ad suam similitudinem*) and risks resembling nothing—at least nothing of which he could have any idea or the *species* (ἰδεῖν εἶδος) of which he could see. For man does not resemble God by resembling something visible or intelligible but mostly by resembling nothing visible or intelligible—in short, by resembling no image, especially not some so-called *imago* of God, but in bearing the likeness of the *style* of God. Man is a God, like a Cezanne is a Cezanne, a Poussin a Poussin—without anything behind or beside them that would be Cezanne or Poussin visible as themselves apart from the painting. No, the paintings of Cezanne and Poussin appear as such, without any other visible mark or signature, but still as paintings that bear all over the inimitable style of Cezanne or Poussin. As a Cezanne is a Cezanne, then, or a Poussin a Poussin, man is a God. He appears as God-made, as a God if he admits bearing God's style, letting his own particular features be suppressed so that its provenance might come forward. Man is a God only as he returns from where he comes, to his most intimate other.[29]

We should not be misled into assimilating the image to a content of the likeness, for it provides less a content than a container, in the sense of a place where the likeness is at play in its varying degrees: "Ergo intelligimus habere nos aliquid *ubi* imago Dei est, mentem scilicet atque rationem."[30] Of course the rational mind offers the place for the likeness, but it does not offer its content. One can draw up a table of the images that offer a place in the rational mind of man for a likeness with the Trinity: considering this mind as a whole (*De Trinitate* IX), the triad mind, knowledge, and love (*mens, notitia, amor*) refers to the Trinity; considering man in his relation to the world, one sketches the Trinity with two other triads: first (according to XI, 2, 2–5), the thing seen, sight, and the intention that connects the one to the other (*res, visio, intentio*); second (according to XI, 3, 6–7), memory, interior vision, and the will (*memoria, visio, voluntas*); finally, and especially, one can privilege the triad of memory, understanding, and will (*memoria, intelligentia, voluntas*) following *De Trinitate* X, 11, 17.[31] This last figure specifies the place of the best likeness: "Ecce ergo mens meminit sui, intelligit se, diligit se: hoc si cernimus, cernimus Trinitatem; nondum quidem Deum, sed jam imaginem Dei" (Look, the mind remembers itself, understands itself, loves itself: if we see that, we see the Trinity; not yet God, of course, but already the image of God).[32] But these triadic analogies disclosing an image of the Trinity do not display it in themselves as their stable content but solely in the degree to which they refer this content to God himself. A major text specifies this:

Haec igitur trinitatis mentis *non* propterea Dei *est imago*, quia sui meminit mens, et intelligit ac diligit se; sed quia *potest etiam* mcminisse, et intelligere, et amare a quo facta est. Quod cum facit, sapiens ipsa fit. Si autem non facit, etiam cum sui meminit, seseque intelligit ac diligit, stulta est. Meminerit itaque Dei sui, ad cujus imaginem facta est, eumque intelligat atque diligat. Quod ut brevius dicam, colat Deum non factum, cujus ab eo capax est facta, et cujus particeps esse potest.

And therefore this final trinity of the mind *is not the image* of God inasmuch as the mind in itself remembers itself, understands itself, and loves itself, but because it *can also* remember and understand and love he by whom it was made. If it does that, it becomes itself wise. But if it does not do so, it is stupid, even when it remembers itself, understands itself, and loves itself. To put it briefly, let it worship the God not made, of whom it was made capable and in whom it can participate.[33]

To be sure, the three faculties make an image of God; however, it is neither the three faculties themselves, nor their reciprocal organization, nor even their possible and distant similarity to the three persons of the Trinity that does so—as the majority of commentators seem to say again and again—but rather their possibility of referring to God as he who can make them play among themselves the likeness of the trinitarian game of persons in it. The faculties offer a mere place, which becomes a visible and reliable image of the Trinity only to the degree that they receive (in the sense of *capacitas*) participation in the Trinitarian communion and, thus, play trinitarily, as if by derivation, among themselves. They appear as images only to the degree of their likeness, therefore tangentially, by changing degrees, measured by their participation. "Non sua luce, sed summae illius lucis participatione sapiens erit. . . . Neque enim participatione sui sapiens est [Deus], sicut mens participatione Dei" (It [the mind of man] will not be wise by its own light, but by participating in this great light. . . . For God is not wise by participating in himself, as in contrast the mind [of man] is wise by participation in God).[34] What makes the image (pure place and simple possibility of similitude) a likeness does not stem from some status, a property, or an essence of this image but from the movement, from the tension and the *intentio*, toward God, therefore from the degree of participation allowed by the *capacitas*. In this sense the absence of a proper definition becomes for man the negative condition of the likeness toward God but a negative that must forever be increased and confirmed. Not only is man defined by his never-fixed likeness with God rather than by a fixed definition; but he is defined by this very absence of definition: it is proper to him not to appropriate himself or be appropriate to himself; it is proper to him *not* to resemble himself because that which he does resemble, God, does *not* coincide with his essence, nor with any essence whatsoever, because, God resembling nothing worldly, man too resembles nothing in this world. There is man only without properties and therefore without definition. To the question "quid sit homo?" (what is man?) hasn't Saint Augustine at least once answered that he does not have to answer: "Nec nunc definitionem hominis a me postulandum puto" (I think that a definition of man cannot be asked of me now).[35]

The essential indefinition of man should be understood as a privilege. Lacking the power, lacking any obligation to be circumscribed, does indeed constitute a privilege—indeed the privilege of God according to the prohibition against "making any graven image, nothing that resembles what is found in the heavens" (Exodus 20:4), nothing therefore that would pretend to represent God by comprehending him. Would man therefore also find himself "in the heavens"? To be sure, first by becoming a nonresident alien (by participation), if not official citizen, of the "heaven of the heavens." But also in the sense that—and this is the decisive paradox— what counts for God (that no name, no image, and no concept can pretend

The Creation of the Self   259

to comprehend him) also counts for man; neither one nor the other admits either kind, species, or essence. Man remains unimaginable, since formed in the image of He who admits none, incomprehensible because formed in the likeness of He who admits no comprehension. Strictly speaking, man resembles nothing since he resembles nothing other than Him whom incomprehensibility properly characterizes. Or again, if God remains incomprehensible, man, who resembles nothing other than him (and especially not himself), will bear the mark of his incomprehensibility. In other words, man, without kind, species, or essence, delivered from every paradigm, appears without mediation in the light that surpasses all light. Of this borrowed incomprehensibility, his face bears the mark precisely inasmuch as it reveals itself as invisible as the face of God.[36] Man differs radically from every other being in the world by an insurmountable difference—one no longer ontological but holy. He no longer differs as the rational animal, *ego cogitans*, the transcendental I, absolute consciousness, the "valuating animal as such,"[37] or even as "the lieutenant of nothing" (*Platzhalter des Nichts*),[38] still less as the "shepherd of Being" (*Hirt des Seins*),[39] but as the icon of the invisible God, εἰκὼν τοῦ θεοῦ τοῦ ἀοράτου (Colossians 1:15)—exactly as by participation in the image and likeness of the incomprehensible icon of the invisible. His invisibility separates man from the world and consecrates him as holy for the sake of the Holy.

In coming to this conclusion, Saint Augustine inscribes himself within an ongoing tradition of Christian theology, whose argument was formalized by Gregory of Nyssa:

The icon is perfectly an icon only so long as it is missing nothing of what is known in the archetype. Now, since incomprehensibility of essence (τὸ ἀκατάληπτὸν τῆς οὐσίας) is found in what we see in the divine nature, it must necessarily be that every [icon] keeps in it too a likeness with its archetype. For if one understood the nature of the icon, while that of the archetype transcended comprehension, the contrary character of what we see in them would betray the deficiency of the icon. But since the nature of our mind, which is according to the icon of the Creator (ὃς κατ᾽ εἰκόνα τοῦ κτίσαντος), escapes knowledge, it keeps exactly its likeness with its lord by keeping the imprint of the incomprehensibility [set] by the unknown in it (τῷ καθ᾽ ἑαυτὸν ἀγνώστῳ).[40]

Knowing man, therefore, demands referring him to God inasmuch as incomprehensible and therefore establishing by derivation his incomprehensibility, with the title image and resemblance. Augustine, too, came to this conclusion. While Saint Paul, for his part, posited that no one "among men knows the secrets of man, except the spirit of men in him" (1 Corinthians 2:11) and thereby assumed that man understood the secrets of man, Augustine is quick to posit the contrary: "tamen est aliquid hominis, quod nec ipse scit spiritus hominis, qui in ipso est, tu autem. Domine, scis ejus Omnia, quia eum fecisti" (and yet there is something in man that not even the spirit of man itself knows, which is [nevertheless] in him, but you, oh Lord, you know all of him [man], for you made him).[41] Starting from this self-non-knowledge nevertheless known by another, God alone, the operation of *confessio* must necessarily be launched, or rather the duality constitutive of a doubly oriented *confessio*, toward my ignorance of myself and toward the knowledge of myself by another: "Confitear ergo quid de me sciam, confitear et quid de me nesciam, quoniam et quod de me scio, te mihi lucente scio, et quod de me nescio, tamdiu nescio, donec fiant 'tenebrae meae' sicut 'meridies' in vultu tuo" (I will confess therefore what I know of myself, and I will also confess what I do not know about myself, since even what I know of myself is because you illuminate me that I know it, while what I do not know of myself I remain ignorant of as long as my *shadows* do not become *like a noonday* [Psalm 89:8] before your face).[42] Man differs infinitely from man, but with a difference that he cannot comprehend and that, provided he intends to save it, he ought not comprehend.

In this way we verify again the principle that guides every itinerary toward oneself and toward God (for there is but one): "Interior intimo meo, superior summo meo" (*Confessiones* III, 6, 11, 13, 382). But we know now that the aporia of *magna mihi quaestio* coincides with the solution: the indefinition of man.

§41. *Pondus meum*

The indefinition of man, this privilege, implies that I do not reside in any essence but that, on the contrary, I resemble what has no semblance, God, without shape or εἶδος, indescribable, incomprehensible, invisible—in other words, that I resemble nothing. Or, more exactly, that I *re*semble, that I semble by way of reflection, like the glittering light of the light that illuminates, I appear as the *re*port of the rapport *to the* likeness of God, *ad similitudinem Dei*. I appear each time myself according as I move up (or down) the invisibly graded scale of my likeness, of my proximity or separation from the invisibility of God, whose invisible accomplishment I reflect more or less in the visible. What remains to be understood is by what scale I could travel from one degree to the other of this *re*semblance and if I could, in the end, should there be one, find a stable point in a visible reflection of the invisible. Managing this instability constitutes the ultimate, and the most disturbing, risk in the march toward this outside oneself, lacking which I will never become who I am. If I have to cross the resemblance and dwell in it, which momentum and drive can lead me there?

To go farther, we must go back to our point of departure, to the *confessio*. It has, since the beginning, put into operation the principle of rest and restlessness: "Et tamen laudare te vult homo, aliqua portio creaturae tuae. Tu excitas, ut laudare te delectet, quia fecisti nos *ad* te et inquietam est cor nostram, domec requiescat in te" (And he wants to praise you, man does, this tiny portion of what you have created. You excite him to love and praise you because you made us *unto* you, and our heart knows no rest so long as it does not rest in you) (*Confessiones* I, 1, 1, 13, 272). The way and the question open, therefore, with the observation of my restlessness—literally, my disequilibrium: so long as I rest in myself, I do not hold steady nor hold myself together. I cease to vacillate only if I find a place outside myself in God. I cannot not want (and love) to find my repose in God because I cannot settle in myself, or in anything else, if I do not *settle* myself in God. With perfect coherence the final moment of the *confessio* describes, in three successive passages, only the three actors of this rest: the one that completes creation, the one in which creation took place as a place of rest for the created, and, finally, the very rest in which creatures should end, if they admit an end, by settling as if in their own place. "Quamvis ea [sc. opera tua] *quietus* feceris, *requievisti* septimo die, hoc praeloquatur nobis vox libri tui, quod et nos post opera nostra ideo 'bona valde,' quia tu nobis ea donasti, sabbato vitae aeternae *requiescamus* in te" (Though you made your works while remaining *restful, you rested* on the seventh day, your book told us in advance that we, too, after our works (which are "very good," since it is you who gave them to us), in the Sabbath of eternal life, we will find our *rest* in you) (XII, 36, 51, 14, 522).

Put otherwise: "Etiam tunc enim sic *requiesces* in nobis, quemadmodum nunc operaris in nobis, et ita erit illa *requies* tua per nos, quemadmodum sunt ista opera tua per nos" (For then, too, you *will rest* in us, as now you work in us, and then this *rest*, yours, will be in us, as your actions are yours through us) (XIII, 37, 52, 14, 522). And finally: "Post illa [sc. quaedam bona opera nostra] nos *requituros* in tua grandi sanctificatione speramus. Tu autem bonum nullo indigens bono, semper *quietus* es, quoniam tua *quies* tu ipse es" (After them [some of our works, good ones], we hope to *rest* in your great sanctification. But you, who have no need of any good, you are always *at rest*, because you are unto yourself your own *rest*) (XIII, 38, 53, 14, 522ff.). God alone holds himself at rest because he alone holds himself in himself, such that everything that does not hold itself in God but remains in itself (willingly or not) cannot settle there, therefore does not settle at all or come to remain anymore at rest. God alone gives rest, because he alone has it. And he alone has it because he alone is it. And everything else, all the way until the ends of his creation, takes place (happens and is found) only in this rest. Creation, originarily eschatological, consists only in giving place to this coming of each creature into the place of its rest. This place, for man without definition, is found in nothing less than in the rest of God himself: "Nam et in ipsa misera inquietudine . . . satis ostendis, quam magnam rationalem creaturam feceris, cui nullo modo sufficit ad *beatam requiem*, quidquid te minus est, ac per hoc nec ipsa sibi" (For even in our unhappy restlessness . . . you show sufficiently how great you made your rational creature, since nothing less than you will suffice for its *rest*, not even itself to itself) (XIII, 8, 9, 14, 438). Short of God, man does not find himself, or find where he is.

Now, and this is a remarkable fact, the text that I just quoted, the one that defines the "heaven of the heavens" as *place* where one settles in the Spirit ("requiesceret in spiritu tuo") and shows that man can find rest in nothing less than God ("magnam rationalem creaturam feceris, cui nullo modo sufficit ad *beatam requiem*, quidquid te minus est") goes on to show how to measure the proximity or distance of each man with regard to this place: "Corpus pondere suo nititur ad locum suum. Pondus non ad ima tantum, sed ad locum suum. Ignis sursum tendit, deorsum lapis. Ponderibus suis aguntur, loca sua petunt. Oleum infra aquam fusum super auqam attolitur, aqua supra oleum fusa infra oleum demergitur: ponderibus suis aguntur, loca sua petunt. Minus ordinata inquieta sunt: ordinantur et quiescunt. Pondus meum amor meus; eo feror, quocumque feror" (The body strives with all its weight toward its place. The weight does not push only down, but toward its place. Fire tends toward the higher, the stone toward the lower. They are [both] put into motion by their [respective] weight, [but] they seek their [own] places. The least ordered things remain without a place to settle: as soon as they recover their order, they settle down at rest. My weight, it is my love; wherever I take myself, it is my love that takes me there) (XIII, 9, 10, 14, 440). This argument looks limpid as well as decisive, for it does not say merely that "anima . . . velut pondere amore fertur quocumque fertur" (the soul, wherever it takes itself, takes itself there by love as by a weight)[43] but specifies also, and above all, that it is ultimately for the soul a matter of its will: "Voluntas. . . ponderi similis est" (The will . . . resembles a weight).[44] The details of this have yet to be understood precisely.

The point of departure for this argument does not concern, it is worth noting, the question of love but the strictly physical problem of the cause of local motion. On this issue Aristotle reasons in this way: "If each of the simple bodies has by nature a certain type of movement, for example fire upward and earth downward and towards the center, it is clear that the void cannot be the cause of motion."[45] To this distinction between movements up and down, he also adds the possible distinction, for each of them, between those that follow nature and those that contradict it (κατὰ φύσιν καὶ παρὰ φύσιν)—in other words, by force or by nature (ἢ βίᾳ ἢ κατὰ φύσιν).[46] But it is doubtless wise, here and elsewhere, not to exhaust oneself in identifying the supposed Greek sources of Saint Augustine by arbitrarily offering erudite readings; it is enough to stick with Cicero, the common and most credible mediator:

The earthy and moist parts are borne by themselves and by their weight (*suo pondere ferantur*) in perpendicular angles toward the earth and the sea, while the two other parts, fire and animate, in contrast with the two previous ones which are borne by their gravity and their weight (*gravitate ferantur et pondere*) toward the central place of the world, are raised (*rursum subvolent*) in straight lines toward the celestial place, be it because their own nature desires higher things (*ipsa natura superior appetente*), or be it because they are pushed, by virtue of their lighter nature, by the heavier parts.[47]

Indisputably, Saint Augustine assumes as such this principle for the explanation of locomotion—as a physical theory. Several texts testify to this: "Lege naturae cedunt pondera minora majoribus, non modo cum ad proprium locum *suo sponte nutu feruntur*, ut humida et terrena corpora in ipsius mundi medium locum, qui est infimus, rursus aeria et ignea sursum versus; sed etiam cum aliquo tormento aut jactu aut impulsu aut repulso, eo quo sponte *ferrentur*, vi aliena ire *coguntur*" (According to a law of nature, the less heavy weights yield to the heavier, not only when *they move them-selves* toward their proper place [in this way, the moist and earthly bodies tend toward the place at the center of the world, which is the lowest, while, inversely, the airy and fiery bodies tend upward], but also when *they are compelled to move* in another direction besides that which they would follow *of themselves*, by some mechanism, disturbance, attraction, or repulsion).[48] He even attaches enough authority to this "law of nature" that he will rely on it as something like an experimental test in narrative form:

Pondera gemina sunt. Pondus enim est impetus quidam cujusque rei, velut conan-tis ad locum suum: hoc est pondus. Fers lapidem manu, pateris pondus; premit manum tuum, quia locum suum quaerit. Et vis videre quid quaerat? Subtrahe manum, venit ad terram, quescit in terra: pervenit quo tendebat, invenit suum locum. Pondus ergo illud motus erat quasi spontaneus, sine anima, sine sensu. Namque si aquam mittas super oleum, pondere suo in ima tendit. Locum enim suum quaerit, ordinari quaerit; quia praeter ordinem est aqua super oleum. Donec ergo veniat ad ordinem suum, *inquietus motus* est, donec teneat locum suum.

There are two kinds of weight. For weight is the impetus of any thing whatso-ever insofar as it strives toward its [proper] place: such is weight. Take a stone in your hand; you feel its weight; it presses your hand, for it seeks to reach its place. And do you want to know what it is thus seeking to reach? Withdraw your hand, it goes to the earth and settles there. It has arrived there where it tended; it has found its place. Therefore this weight was a quasi-spontaneous movement, with neither soul nor sensation. For if you throw water on oil, the water tends by its weight to go downward. It tends, that is, toward its place; it seeks to put itself in order; for water above oil, this is not in order. So long as it has not returned into its order, *movement does not settle and come to rest*, until such time as it has arrived in its place.[49]

The "laws of nature" (almost in the modern sense) abide so firmly that Augustine will even mention them as objections to the possibility of miracles: "Ac per hoc, *inquiunt*, quoniam terra abhinc sursum versus est prima, secunda aqua super terram, tertius aer super aquam, quartum super aera caelum, non potest esse terrenum corpus in caelo; momentis enim propriis, ut ordinem suum teneant, singula elementa librantur" (And consequently, *they say*, since, in ascending from lower to higher, earth comes first, then the water above the earth, third is the air above the water, and fourth comes the heavens above the air, a terrestrial body cannot be found in the heavens; for these different moments balance each of the elements, such that they [each] find their proper order).[50] Up until this point there has been nothing innovative on the part of Saint Augustine; he simply assumes a doctrine that was widely accepted at his time—to the point that one could even legitimate it theologically by the authority of the Book of Wisdom 11:21: "Omnia in mensura et numero et pondere disposuisti" (You arranged all things in order, measure, and weight), with the immense legacy that this verse is known to have.[51] It is thus still only a matter of the laws of local motion and, in a restricted sense, of the laws of the world.

In fact, the innovation only starts when Saint Augustine no longer deals with a place in the world (neither physics, nor nature, nor local motion) but the *place* of he who *confesses*. How, it will be asked, can one pass from the laws of local motion to the place of confession? By an unforeseen tactical reversal: the laws of local motion will be elevated, transposed, and overtaken at the level of the rules of love; *pondus*, its tensions and its movements, will be displaced into the movements and intentions of *amor*. Saint Augustine undertakes this by bringing the formulation of Cicero (more so than those of Aristotle) together with one from Virgil: "Trahit sua quemque voluptas" (Each is led by his own pleasure).[52] Still more surprising, he introduces it, in fact, in order to comment on a verse from the Gospel of John, "Nemo venit ad me, nisi quem Pater attraxit" (Nobody comes to me, if the Father has not attracted him) (John 6:44), in which he tries to explain how the Father, even if he attracts someone toward the Son, does not compel him and does not contradict his will, even though attracted:

Quomodo voluntate credo, si trahor? Ego dico: parum est voluntate, etiam voluptate traheris. Quid est trahi voluptate? "Delectare in Domino, et dabit tibi petitiones cordis tui." Est quaedam voluptas cordis, cui panis dulcis est ille caelestis. Porro, si poetae dicere licuit "Trahit sua quemque voluptas," non necessitas, sed voluptas, non obligatio, sed delectatio, quanto fortuis nos dicere debemus trahi hominem ad Christum, qui delectatur veritate, delectatur beatitudine, delectatur justitia, delectatur sempiterna vita, quod totum Christus est?

How do I believe willingly if I am attracted into belief? As for me, I say: you are only slightly led by your will, but [much more] also by pleasure. What does it mean to be attracted by pleasure? "Take pleasure in the Lord, and he will give you what your heart asks" [Psalm 36:4]. There is a certain pleasure of the heart for whomever the bread from heaven is sweet. For that matter, if a poet could say: "each is led by his own pleasure," not necessity but pleasure, not obligation but delight, how much more so should we say that the man is led toward Christ who takes pleasure in the truth, who takes pleasure in beatitude, who takes pleasure in justice, who takes pleasure in life without end, all things that Christ is entirely?[53]

The breakthrough and the boldness consists in calling on Virgil to interpret John 6:44, so as to complete and correct Cicero (and Aristotle). Local displacement (φορά)—in other words, arrival in the proper place—no longer results only from a physical weight but also from pleasure's inclination, which triggers in the heart the same spontaneity that gravity unleashes in the body. For what takes up and displaces the role of weight in the spirit does not come from (at least not first of all) "the weight of glory" (Βάπος δόξης) in Saint Paul's sense,[54] but from *delectatio*. By *delectatio* we must understand the fact not of taking pleasure (according to the ignoble expression of today) but of *receiving* it: "Delectatio quippe *quasi* pondus est animae. Delectatio ergo ordinat animam. 'Ubi enim erit thesaurus tuus, *ibi* erit et cor tuum': *ubi* delectatio, ibi thesaurus; *ubi* autem cor, *ibi* beatitudo aut miseria" (It is therefore pleasure that is *something like* the weight of the soul. For pleasure puts the soul in order. "There where your treasure will be, there too will be your heart" (Matthew 6:21): *there where* your pleasure is, *there* is your treasure; *there where* your heart is, *there* is beatitude or misery).[55] Love is set forth according to a logic as strict as motion and, therefore, can be understood as rigorously as it.

A comparison between motion and love is thus established, one that ends up at an analogy of proportion, according to which what weight is to the body desire is to love. Sometimes the terms correspond strictly without admitting any difference: "Amant enim requiem, sive piae animae, sive iniquae; sed qua perveniunt ad illum quod amant, plurimae nesciunt; nec aliquid appetunt etiam corpora ponderibus suis, nisi quod animas amoribus suis" (For all souls love rest, the pious as well as the unjust; but by which path to reach what they love, most of them know not at all, and bodies too seek nothing with their weight, except what souls seek with their loves).[56] But more often the terms respond to one another while maintaining a gap, for differences remain. First, this is because the relation between desire (for pleasure) and love serves as a paradigm for the relation between natural weights and bodies, and not the other way around, as common sense doubtlessly would expect: "Si essemus lapides aut fluctus aut ventus aut flamma vel quid hujus modi, sine ullo quidem sensu atque vita, non tamen nobis deesset *quasi* quidam nostrorum locorum atque ordinis appetitus. Nam *velut* amores, corporum momenta levitate nitantur. *Ita* enim corpus pondere, *sicut* animus amore fertur, quocumque fertur" (If we were only stones, waves, winds, a flame, and something of this sort, without any sensation or life, we would not however be deprived *of some sort of appetence* in our motions and their [right] order. For, *just like loves*, the pressings of bodies strive on by their lightness. That is, *just as* the spirit is borne by its love wherever it is carried, *so too likewise* the body by its weight).[57] Motion follows weight, like desire follows love, to the point that the loving drive of the desiring soul becomes the paradigm for movements, even in things.

The drive of love in its desire does not serve as paradigm just for inanimate nature but even with regard to all the reasonable spirits; even men and the angels see their hierarchy modified according as the weight of love follows the law of nature or that of justice: "Sed tanutm valet in naturis rationalibus *quoddam veluti* pondus voluntatis et amoris, ut, cum ordine naturae angeli hominibus, tamen lege justitiae boni homines malis angelis praeferantur" (But it holds among rational natures *like some sort* of weight of the will and of love, which makes it such that, if, according to the order of nature, one should prefer angels to men, nevertheless, according to the law of justice, one should prefer good men to bad angels).[58] When the desire deployed by love is at issue, weight loses the characteristics that it had when only the weight of a body is considered: concerning love, weight weighs even without nature, indeed against it, to the point of becoming a free or voluntary weight, which weighs there where it wills: "Qui motus si culpae deputatur . . . non est utique naturalis, sed *voluntarius*; in eoque similis est motui quo deorsum lapis fertur, quod sicut iste proprius est lapidis, sic ille animi: verumtamen in eo dissimilis, quod *in potestate* non habet lapis cohibere motum quo fertur inferius; animus vero dum non vult, non ita movetur" (But if one assigns blame to it . . ., this movement is no longer natural but *voluntary*. It is like the movement that carries the stone downward, in that it belongs properly to the mind, like its own to the stone; but it is also unlike it, in that the stone does not have the *power* to contain the movement that bears it downward, while the mind does not move thus unless it wills to).[59] Love may indeed be explained as a weight, provided that we mean a free weight: free first from the constraints of matter, second from the limits of nature, and therefore, in the end, perfectly voluntary.

Saint Augustine therefore corrects the model of physics that explains local movement by the weight of bodies—not out of a concern to spiritualize or to edify but in order to adapt the paradigm of *pondus* to the theoretical requirements that love imposes on it. For in the case of love *pondus* must become voluntary and therefore set itself free from natural (and material) determinations, since it implies freedom in two ways: First, nobody can love except voluntarily; even if freedom does not always signify the choice of decision, a lover without freedom inevitably becomes a patient, indeed, soon enough a sick soul. Second, love supposes choosing some end for its love rather than another; consequently, the freedom of love necessitates splitting its weight and accordingly opposing one weight to another in order to do justice to the choice between two loves. There will be at least two loves and two weights: "Amores *duo* in hac vita secum in omni tentatione luctantur: amor saeculi et amor Dei; et horum *duorum*, qui vicerit, illuc amantem tanquam pondere trahit" (*Two* loves contend with one another during this life at each temptation: the love of the world and the love of God; and the one of these *two* loves that emerges victorious will transport the lover as by a weight).[60] Love splits according as the desire of the soul, that is to say its weight, pushes it upward or downward. Love is so determinative of weight, and so loosely bound to the material sense of a bodily displacement, that Saint Augustine does not hesitate to assign it the upward movement as well as the habitual (physical) movement downward.

If weight can still make something fall, this fall is no longer physical, since it makes the soul fall and also brings about spiritual falls: "Mane si potes: sed non potes; *relaberis* in ista solita et terrena. Quo tandem *pondere,* quaeso, *relaberis,* nisi sordium contractrum cupiditatis visco et peregrinationis erroribus?" (Settle, if you can; but you cannot; you will *fall back* into your earthly habits. *Under the weight of what weight,* I ask you, *will you fall back,* if not that of the filth you have acquired through the clinging of your desire and the erring of your errors?)[61] And therefore, faced with this weight that can make one fall in spirit, in spirit, too, can another weight operate, one that brings an ascent: "Quomodo enim oleum a nullo humore premitur, sed disruptis omnibus exsilit et supereminet: sic et caritas non potest premi in ima; necesse est ut ad suprema emineat" (As oil is compressed by no other liquid, but escapes them all and wraps around them, so, too, charity cannot be pressed down to the bottom. It must necessarily rise up and dominate).[62] Here the paradox that appeared earlier finds the logic that structures it: I am to myself a weighty burden when I remain empty of God, who relieves me and lifts me up toward him, as soon as he fills me: "Nunc autem quoniam quem tu imples, *sublevas* eum, quoniam tui plenus non sum, oneri mihi sum" (But now, since you *lift up* the one whom you fill, seeing as I am not filled with you, I am to myself a burden).[63] Filled with God, I undergo the impact of a weight oriented upward, while filled (in fact, stuffed) by myself alone, I undergo a weight oriented downward. Grace, in other words, the love come from God with the aim of returning me to him, exerts a *counterweight,* a weight that ascends, an uplift and an upbraiding. "Cui dicam, quomodo dicam de *pondere* cupiditatis in abruptam abyssum et de *sublevatione* caritatis? . . . Neque enim loca sunt. . . . Affectus sunt, amores sunt, immunditia spiritus nostri *defluens* inferius amore curarum, et sanctitas tui *attolens* nos superius amore securitatis" (To whom and how should I speak of the *weight* of cupidity [that leads] toward the sudden abyss and of the charity that *uplifts?* . . . It is not about places. . . . These are the affects, loves, the impurity of our spirit *plummeting* lower through love of its cares and your holiness *lifting us up* higher by love of assurance) (X, 7, 8, 14, 436). Love, like the weight from above, which comes from there and leads back, lifts us up toward our place, which is defined precisely by the fact that there and there alone we can settle: "In dono tuo requiescimus: ibi te fruimur. Requies nostra locus noster. Amor *illuc attolit nos*" (It is in the gift that you give that we find rest: here we enjoy you. Our rest, our place. *Here, up to here,* your love *lifts us*) (XIII, 9, 10, 14, 438). That weight not only could relieve us and lift us toward the heights, but in fact does so first and essentially when the issue is my proper place, this paradox imposes itself and ceases to appear surprising. The bottom line is that the ground always attracts—rather than grounds—precisely because it shows itself above, attracts from on high, weighs on us *from above.* Consequently, Christ constitutes the ground par excellence, the "fundamentum fundamentorum," insofar as he comes from on high, like the heavenly Jerusalem descends from the heavens, descends like the "heaven of the heavens:" "Etenim origo fundamenti hujus summitatem tenet; et quemadmodum fundamentum coporae fabricae in imo est, sic fundamentum spiritualis fabricae in summo est" (And therefore the origin of this ground stands at the summit; and just as the ground of the corporal construction is found below, so is the ground of the spiritual construction found at the summit).[64]

I find my place only there where I truly want to dwell. And I truly want to dwell only there where my love pushes me, transports me, and leads me, as a weight leads, transports, and pushes. This weight must be known in order to know what I freely want. "Sed vis nosse qualis amor sit? Vide quo ducat. Non enim monemus ut nihil ametis, sed monemus ne mundum ametis, ut cum qui fecit mundum, libere ametis" (But do you want to know which love it is? See where it leads you. For we are not warning you to love nothing, but not to love the world so that you might love freely with he who made the world).[65] I am the place where I confess, but I rest in this place only because my love pushes and settles me there like a weight. But it is a voluntary weight, since through it I love. And if I love there, I am there as in my self.

§42. The univocity of love

Love weighs, therefore, and with a weight that rises as well as falls, because it exerts a pressure, which pushes only of itself. It is not, however, a wild impulse, since the lover can always decide its direction and modify it, by his will or at least *also* by his will. It is not a pure will, perfectly at the disposition of the lover, since he can never suspend this pressure, reducing it or annulling it. At best, he can direct it, without extricating himself from it. Neither is it a *conatus in suo esse perseverendi* since it is not here a matter of *being* but of loving, possibly all the way to the point of suspending being in oneself, nor is it a matter of being *in-self* but of passing into an other, indeed of becoming other than oneself. As this unconditional and irreversible weight before which no indifference or ataraxy has any meaning, because it always pushes, from the outset and forever from *behind* me, with a pressure that makes me myself more than I make me myself, love is established as the ultimate condition for the possibility of the self. Absolute and unconditioned transcendental, love operates in such a way that no condition of possibility can impose any limits on it, nor therefore any impossibility. Its irreversible anteriority precedes me, in such a way that it imposes on me a nonnegotiable facticity—not only because all facticity, by definition, fixes and establishes me in myself without my having anything to say about it or any negotiation with it, but especially because inasmuch as it is a weight of love, this facticity, which concerns me right to the ground, in a certain sense no longer belongs to me. It no longer depends on me since it refers me to what I love, therefore to what I am *not* (and will perhaps never be) and what governs me by attracting me *elsewhere*, because it pushes me *from elsewhere* than myself. The facticity of love fixes and assigns me, like all facticity, but in operating as love, it does not assign me to myself, nor does it fix me to myself, since it consists precisely in sending me off into an irrecuperable *elsewhere*. The sole possibility opened to me by the pressure of the *pondus amoris* resides simply in the determination of this *elsewhere*, in no way in its suspension (indifference) nor in its appropriation to myself ("authenticity," to render, poorly, *Eigentlichkeit*). Love weighs on myself like the sky at the horizon, not that it oppresses me with a lid of anxiety but because it discloses to me an opening that will never be closed again: the opening onto the unshirkable, absolute, inalienable, but still always undetermined, possibility of deciding to love, of *having to* love whatever comes, whatever I might want, and whether I want it or not. This horizon, the never-impossible possibility of loving, is never closed, never goes on vacation. "Habet tamen omnis amor vim suam nec potest vacare amor in anima amantis; necesse est ducat" (All love has its strength, and love cannot take a vacation in the soul of the lover; in all things necessary, it leads).[66] In other words:

Ipsa dilectio vacare non potest. Quid enim de quoquam homine etiam male operatur, nisi amor? Da mihi vacantem amorem et nihil operantem. Flagitia, adulteria, facinora, homicidia, luxurias omnes, nonne amor operatur? Purga ergo amorem tuum; aquam fluentem in cloacam, converte ad hortum; quales impetus habebat ad mundum, tales habeat ad artificem mundi. Num nobis dicitur: Nihil ametis? Absit. Pigri, mortui, detestandi, miseri eritis, si nihil ametis. Amate, sed quid ametic videte. Amor Dei, amor proximi, caritas dicitur. Cupiditas refrenetur, caritas excitetur.

Love cannot go on vacation. For what is it that is at work, even poorly, in any man whatsoever, if not love? Give me [an example of] a love on vacation, one which is doing nothing. Wicked deeds, acts of adultery, crimes, homicides, indulgence in luxuries, what is it that does these things if not love? Purify therefore your love; water flows toward the sewer; turn it toward the garden. Those very movements that you make toward the world, turn them toward he who made the world. Have we been told to love nothing at all? No, of course, not. You would be inert, dead, cursed, miserable if you loved nothing. Love therefore, but watch carefully what you love. The love of God, the love of the neighbor, these are called charity. Check [in yourselves] desire [cupiditas], but excite charity.[67]

Not only does the question never consist in to be or not to be, for it only concerns loving, but the question of love never consists in loving or not loving since as ultimate possibility, it demands of me, with neither break nor vacation, that I love no matter what. The question and ultimate possibility oblige me to decide on the subject of what I love—since in every case, whether I want to or not, whether I know it or not, I will love. "Nemo est qui non amet. Sed quaeritur quid amet. Non ergo admonemur ut non amemus, sed ut eligamus quid amemus" (There is nobody who does not love. But one must seek out what one loves. We are not asked not to love, but to choose what we love).[68] There is nothing optional or facultative about love; it predestines us absolutely (*schlechthin*), with an irrecusable, inexcusable, and irremediable possibility. All that's left is to decide how and what to love.

Such a transcendental determination of love implies that, formally at least, it is put into practice in the same way and according to the same logic, however different its object and occasions appear. Whatever I love, I always love for the same reasons and in the same fashion, which vary no more than love itself ever ceases to love—*dilectio vacare non potest*. But this univocal universality can be contested and, in fact, was by Anders Nygren, more so than by any other. He observes, rightly, that "the difference between Caritas and Cupiditas is not one of *kind*, but of object. By kind, Caritas and Cupiditas, Love of God and love of the world, correspond most closely." Consequently, for Nygren "love is a longing indifferent in itself, whose quality is determined by the object to which it is directed."[69] But he objects that ἔρως and ἀγάπη cannot coincide and are opposed as a Greek concept (Platonic and Neoplatonic) to a biblical concept (from the New Testament), term for term: The first defines a movement from low to high, human toward the divine, desire to save one's life, desire for the good, which supposes its value already established, in opposition to a movement from high to low, of God toward man, by pure grace, at the risk of losing his life, without acceptance by anybody, and which establishes value. There results a "difference of kind." I will not here dispute this thesis itself (in fact, untenable) but will limit myself to examining the conclusion Nygren draws from it: the Augustinian project consists in identifying these two contradictory concepts in a third, named *caritas*; in other words, "the meeting of the Eros and Agape motifs produces a characteristic third which is neither Eros nor Agape, but *Caritas*."[70] All the while straining to find the textual arguments to support his rash conclusion, he does not hesitate to conclude that *caritas* so understood has no Christian legitimacy but imports like contraband a Neoplatonic conception: "Indeed we might say that, *for Augustine, Neoplatonic Eros has become the means of discovering Christian Agape*."[71] The strangeness of this reasoning leaps right out at you: charity would not come to Saint Augustine from the revelation of Christ but from Neoplatonism, which in turn would have made him understand that love played a central role in this very revelation. In short, to find love in the New Testament, Saint Augustine would have had to learn its centrality from a well-known Neoplatonic concept, *caritas*! My own project does not demand refuting this inept argument but only assessing if the univocity of love leads Augustine to aporiae and incoherencies that excessively distort biblical revelation.

One piece of evidence should, at the outset, be recalled: the univocity of love in no way forbids Saint Augustine from indicating required distinctions among the modes in which it is put into operation. First, and above all, is the separation between two modes of love, so distinct that they are opposed term for term: "Duae sunt amores, mundi et Dei; si mundi amor inhabitet, non est qua intrat amor Dei; recedat amor mundi et habitet Dei" (There are two loves—one of the world, the other of God.

If the love of the world inhabits you, there is no longer a point of entry for the love of God. Let the love of the world be withdrawn, and the love of God make its home in you). Or else: "Fecerunt itaque civitates duas amores duo, terrenam scilicet amor sui usque ad contemptum Dei, caelestam vero amor Dei usque ad contemptum sui. Denique illa in se ipsa, haec in Domino gloriatur" (The two cities make up two loves: the earthly city, the love of self to the point of contempt for God; the heavenly city, the love of God to the point of contempt for self. And, finally, the former is glorified in itself, the latter in its Lord).[72] This splitting of love into two opposed modes can and should be made more precise by using two distinct concepts. Either, desire (*cupiditas*) can be opposed to *dilectio*: "Quapropter non est praecipue videndum in hac questione, quae de Trinitate nobis est, et de cognoscendo Deo, nisi quid sit vera *dilectio*, imo vero quid sit dilectio. Ea quippe dilectio dicenda est, quae vera est; alioquin *cupiditas* est; atque ita cupidi abusive dicuntur diligere, quemadmodum cupere abusive dicuntur, qui diligunt" (For that, one need not consider anything [other] in this question, [which is posed to us] concerning the Trinity and knowledge of God, except what is the true *dilection*, or even what is dilection. For it is the true [alone] that must be named dilection; otherwise it is *desire* [*cupiditas*]; and then one speaks imprecisely about those who desire when one says that they love by dilection, just as one speaks imprecisely of those who love by dilection when one says that they desire) (*De Trinitate* VIII, 7, 10, 16, 58). Or else, this same desire (*cupiditas*) can be opposed to *caritas*: "Quae est radix? Caritas; hoc enim dicit apostolus: 'Ut in caritate radicati et fundati.' Quomodo enim 'radix omnium malorum cupiditas,' sic radix omnium bonorum caritas est" (What is the root? Charity, for the apostle Paul says, "[Let God give it to you to dwell in Christ] rooted and grounded in charity" [Ephesians 3:17]. Just as "desire [*cupiditas*] is the root of all evil" [1 Timothy 6:10] so too is the root of all good charity).[73] Their shared opposition to *cupiditas* also permits him to sometimes assimilate one to the other, *dilectio* and *caritas*: "Quid vero aeternum est, quod aeternitate animum afficiat, nisi Deus? Amor autem rerum amandarum, caritas vel dilectio melius dicitur" (What then is eternal, that could affect the spirit with eternity, if not God? But the love of things to be loved [truly] is better named charity or dilection). Put otherwise: "Nihil aliud est caritas quam dilectio" (Charity is nothing other than dilection).[74] There is so little a lack of precision that Saint Augustine even emphasizes that Latin has two terms, *caritas* and *dilectio*, to render the one Greek word ἀγάπη: "Caritas alia est divina, alia humana: alia est humana licit, alia illicita. De his tribus caritatibus vel dilectionibus, duo enim nomina habet apud Latinos, quae graece ἀγάπη dicitur, quod Deus donaverit dicam" (With regard to these three dilections or charities, there are among the Latins two words to say the Greek ἀγάπη, what God, I say, gave to us).[75] In the Augustinian lexicon there is no confusion to speak of, still less a hidden forced reading of texts: *cupiditas* falls under love (*amor*), but is distinguished very clearly from the love of God and the things of the heavens, which can be described as either *dilectio* (taking the profane term that designates benevolent love) or as *caritas* (when it is a matter of what the Holy Spirit sows in our hearts, according to Romans 5:5).

Let us therefore pose the question in terms other than those chosen by a groundless and insignificant polemic. This question aims to understand how love remains univocal in the role of transcendental horizon all the while being perfectly capable of being distinguished in different modes. Part of the difficulty no doubt comes from an all-too-quick reading of the celebrated distinction between two loves produced by the two cities: "amores duo, . . . scilicet amor sui *usque ad* contemptum Dei, . . . vero amor Dei *usque ad* contemptum sui" (two loves, . . . namely, love of self *to the point of* contempt for God; . . . and love of God *to the point of* contempt for self" (*De civitate Dei* XIV, 28, 35, 464). In fact, it's not a matter of an exclusive opposition, where one love would entirely disqualify the other, but of a radical passage to the limit ("usque ad") of each of these two loves: thinking that if one loves the world, one must hate God, or the inverse. For the parallel between the two loves does not hold all the way until the end, or rather it all depends on what one means by to the point of, *usque ad*. If loving oneself (or rather wanting *in vain*, stubbornly and imaginarily, to love oneself) indeed ends up blocking one from loving God, inversely loving God, provided that such love is love for him and unreserved first, permits one to love *also* both oneself and one's neighbor. God is not jealous about our love for self or for the neighbor or for any creature; he makes it possible, and he alone can do so: "Caritatem voco motum animi ad fruendum Deo propter ipsum *et se atque proximo propter Deum*; cupiditatem autem, motum animi ad fruendum *se et proximo et quolibet corpore* non *propter Deum*" (I call charity the movement of the spirit [that carries it] to enjoy God for himself *and the self and the neighbor* in view of God; and desire [concupiscence] the movement [that carries it] to enjoy self and neighbor and any body whatsoever otherwise than in view of God).[76] Here the question does not bear on whether the enjoyment of oneself, one's neighbor, or any body whatsoever is licit but of knowing first if that is even possible, then if that would be detrimental to the love of God. These two lines of questioning have just one response: enjoyment is possible only of God, who alone does not disappoint, because he alone stays in place (privilege of immutability) and alone offers the good without reserve, inasmuch as "ipsum bonum . . . bonum omnis boni."[77] Consequently, pretending to enjoy another thing, one that cannot offer the absolute good, whether it be myself, others, or some other body, leads to the disaster of *cupiditas*: disappointment, then hatred of oneself, others, and this very body itself. But reciprocally, to enjoy God—in fact, the sole enjoyment possible—renders possible at the same time, by extension and with reference to it ("propter Deum"), enjoying all the rest, since this rest constitutes precisely a gift of God. Whence the possibility and even the promise that if I enjoy *only* God for himself, all the rest can become lovable, no longer by *cupiditas* but well and truly by *caritas*. An extraordinary and fascinating text says this in so many words:

Quod verbum [mentis] amore concipitur, sive creaturae, sive Creatoris, id est, aut naturae mutabilis, aut incommutabilis veritatis. Ergo aut cupiditate, aut caritate: non quo non sit amanda creatura, sed *si ad Creatorem refertur amor, non jam cupiditas, sed caritas erit*. Tunc enim est cupiditas, cum propter se amatur creatura. Tunc non utentem adjuvat, sed corrumpit fruentem. Cum ergo aut par nobis, aut inferior creatura sit, inferior utendem est ad Deum; *pari autem fruendem*, sed *in* Deo. Sicut enim te ipso, non *in te ipso frui* debes, sed *in* eo qui fecit te; sic etiam illo, quem diligis, tanquam te ipsum. Et nobis ergo et fratribus *in* Domino fruamur.

This [mental] word is conceived by love, either of the creature or of the creator, that is to say changeable nature or unchangeable nature. Therefore either by desire or by charity: not that creatures should not be loved, but *if this love is referred to God, it is [already] no longer desire, but charity*. For it is when one loves creatures for themselves that it is desire. This then is why desire no longer helps he who [only] uses it, but it corrupts he who enjoys it. Since creatures are either equal to us or inferior, the inferior must be used for the sake of God; *the equal must be enjoyed*, but *in* God. For just as you must, yourself, *enjoy yourself*, not *in* yourself, but *in* him who made you; and likewise for him whom you love [by dilection] as yourself. And therefore let us enjoy ourselves and our brothers *in* God. (*De Trinitate* IX, 8, 13, 14, 98)

Therefore, it's not a question of two parallel or opposed loves but of two modes of the same love: creatures, myself or my brother, can therefore be loved, and even loved *with enjoyment*, provided that they come to be loved *in* the enjoyment of God: the *propter Deum* (which should be understood more as *in view of God* rather than as *with God as the motivation*) becomes *in Deo*, a place and the place for all enjoyment, the enjoyment of God and therefore in it of every other thing.

The univocity of love thus permits converting *cupiditas* (which wants to enjoy without ever succeeding in it) into *caritas* (which alone permits enjoyment because it alone enjoys God, the sole *enjoyable*). This conversion no doubt also concerns, though in a manner less visible, *dilectio* and *amor* in their ordinary usages since it is played out in the will. For the two cities, like their loves, are distinguished in terms of the mode of our will, never in terms of a distinction of their own natures. Here is their definition: "duas societates angelicas inter se dispares atque contrarias, unam et natura bonam et voluntate rectam, aliam vero natura bonam et voluntate perversam" (two angelic societies, different and opposed each to the other, one of good nature and upright will, the other of good nature but perverse will) (*De civitate Dei* XI, 33, 35, 138). The nature given by God, and therefore always good, does not constitute the difference, which comes from the will alone. Evil comes from the hypostasis, not the essence, contrary to all Manicheanism and Neoplatonism. It even becomes possible to sketch a table of dispositions (*Stimmungen* rather than *affectus* or passions) of the spirit, deduced entirely from the permanent primacy of love in them: "Recta itaque voluntas est bonus amor et voluntas perversa malus amor. Amor ergo inhians habere quod amatur, cupiditas est, id autem habens eoque fruens laetitia; fugiens quod ei adversatur, timor est, idque si accederit sentiens tristitia" (It follows that good love is the upright will while the perverse will is bad love. Love that aspires to possess what it loves defines desire [*cupiditas*], that which enjoys it is called joy; that which flees from what is opposed to it defines fear, and if it feels what comes over it, sadness) (*De civitate Dei* XIV, 7, 2, 35, 374). In all cases it is an issue of love, univocal, declined by its modes, intrigues, and wills. It is never about not loving nor loving only God, but of knowing how to love each and all in the appropriate mode, God and the gifts of God: "Non te prohibet Deus amare ista, sed non diligere ad beatitudinem; sed approbare et laudare ut ames Creatorem" (God does not forbid you from loving these things, but he does forbid you from loving them by dilection in view of [believing that you are] finding beatitude there. Approve them and praise them so as to love God) (*Commentary on the Epistle of Saint John* II, 11, *PL* 35, 1995).

The univocity in which the different modes and names of love are imbricated is confirmed by three paradoxes, concerning, respectively, self-love, love of neighbor, and love of God. First of all, the obvious paradox that loving oneself becomes possible only for him who first and above all loves God: "Qui ergo se diligere novit, Deum diligit: qui vero non diligit Deum, etiam si se diligit, quod ei naturaliter inditum est, tamen non inconvenienter odisse se dicitur, cum id agit quod sibi adversatur, et se ipsum tanquam suus inimicus insequitur" (He who knows how to love himself [by dilection] loves God; he who, on the contrary, does not love God, even if he loves himself [by dilection], something he received by nature, it is not inappropriate to say about him that he hates himself since he is opposed to himself and persecutes himself as if he was his own enemy) (*De Trinitate* XIV, 14, 18, 16, 392). That is, in terms of the previous argument he forbids himself access to the place *in Deo*, the one and only place where enjoyment becomes in general possible—in this case the enjoyment of oneself. "Nescio quo enim inexplicabili modo quisquis semet ipsum, non Deum, amat, non se amat; et quisquis Deum, non seipsum amat, ipse se amat. Qui enim non potest vivere de se, moritur utique amando se; non ergo se amat qui ne vivat se amat. Cum vero ille diligitur de quo vivitur, non se diligendo magis diligit, qui propterea non se diligit, ut eum diligit de quo vivit" (I do not know how to explain it, but whoever loves himself and not God does not love himself; and whoever loves God and not himself loves himself. For one who cannot live from himself alone dies radically in loving himself—in effect, he does not [truly] love himself who loves himself so as not to live. While he who loves [with dilection] that from which he lives, in not loving himself [with dilection] loves himself more [with dilection] since he does not love himself [with dilection] so as to love [with dilection] he from whom he lives) (*Commentary on the Gospel of Saint John* CXXIII, 5 *PL* 35, 1968). To love oneself successfully, it is better to love that from which one lives than to love oneself directly, which one knows very well one cannot live from. Direct love of self dies of a great contradiction, one for that matter seen perfectly by him who decides for it: I know that I am not enough for myself, neither ontically as *causa sui* nor erotically as *amor sui*, such that I can scarcely even give myself my own death; but most often I prefer to die from and by virtue of myself than to live elsewhere than myself. There are those men for whom the evidence of God is the worst news, since they see it as a threat depriving them of the sole thing that they aim to give themselves—the autonomy of their death. This argument, besides its obvious conclusion, therefore provides a derivative result: the love of self, far from contradicting the love of God, therefore far from harming charity, calls for it and results from it.

A second paradox confirms the convertibility of each of the modes of love in the univocity of its concept: the love of others. Examining the declaration, as celebrated as it is deceptive: "Dilige et quod vis fac" (Love [with dilection] and do what you will) provides the occasion to see this. This declaration does not sanction any action or attitude whatsoever under the cover of the good intention of loving, which would excuse everything. It instead tries to set a strict rule for interpreting acts among men, according to a hermeneutic of love—that which love makes possible as *Grundstimmung* of man as lover. Consider this line of questioning. If a man punishes another, does that always deserve reprobation? If a man, on the contrary, coddles another, approbation? No, not if in the first case it is a father correcting his son, or if in the second, it is a trafficker luring his potential slave. There is, then, a criterion permitting one to see through appearances: does each want the good of the other—put otherwise, does he love the other? "Non discernuntur facta hominum, nisi de radice caritatis. Nam multa fieri possunt quae speciem habent bonam, et non procedunt de radice caritatis" (There can be no discrimination of the acts of men, except by charity, which is their root. For they can do many apparently good actions, which do not take root in charity). They must be discriminated, therefore, "ad discipinam dictante caritate" (according to what charity teaches), by performing in each case what can be called a reduction to charity: an action is worth what it reveals once it has been led back from its appearance in the natural attitude (sociological description, police statement, account of different facts) to its reality in charity. Hence a principle of discrimination: "Semel ergo breve praeceptum tibi praecipitur: Dilige et quod vis fac: sive taceas, dilectione taceas; sive clames, dilectione clames; sive emendes, dilectione emendes; sive parcas, dilectione parcas; radix sit intus dilectionis, non potest de ista radice nisi bonum exstitere" (Once a short precept was prescribed to you: love [with dilection] and do what you will. If you keep silent, keep silent with dilection; if you speak loud and strong, speak with dilection; if you chastise, chastise with dilection; if you are merciful, be merciful with dilection. Let at bottom the root [of your actions] be dilection; from this root nothing can grow but the good).[78] The precept therefore means, in the final analysis, once the reduction has been made: love and do therefore all that you will, provided that it is for the sake of love and with love; put otherwise: love, provided that in every action you love. This is not a morality of intention (as in Kant) but a morality of action reduced to dilection.[79] Is it, for all that, a tautology? No, since besides the fact that the reduction leads appearances back to the reality from which they arise, the criterion of charity ("de radice caritate") passes through and is transcribed in *dilectio* ("radix sit intus dilectione"). It must be understood: act as you will, provided that you love, and love as you will, provided that this be with dilection or charity. By their equivalence, two parallel texts confirm this convertibility. One states the criterion of reduction according to love in terms of *dilectio*: "Tenete ergo *dilectionem*, et securi estote. Quid times ne male facias alicui? Quis male facit ei quem *diligit*? *Dilige*, non potest fieri nisi bene facias" (Hold fast to *dilection* and you will be safe. Why do you fear to do wrongly to someone? Who does wrong to him whom he loves with *dilection*? Love with *dilection*, it can only happen that you will do good). The other states it in terms of *caritas*: "*caritas*, de qua nihil mali potest procedere" (*charity*, from which nothing bad can proceed).[80] To stick to the main point, we can conclude that love for the other, here more exactly for the neighbor, authorizes the passage, with univocity maintained, from *caritas* to *dilectio* and back.[81] Nothing but the erotic reduction itself is at issue.

One final paradox remains and a final evidence for the univocity of love: the case of loving God. Confirming the pertinence of the question, there is a text in the *City of God* that deals explicitly with the question of the univocity of the words designating love: "nonnulli arbitrantur aliud esse dilectionem, sive caritatem, aliud amorem. Dicunt enim dilectionem accipiendam esse in bono, amorem in malo" (some have claimed that *dilectio* and *caritas* are one thing, and love another. For they say, *dilectio* should be used for good moments, and love in bad ones). Recalling that this opposition is not found in the profane literature ("Sic . . . nec ipsos auctores saecularium litterarum locutos") and that the philosophers admit "amorem . . . erga ipsum Deum" (love even with regard to God), Saint Augustine holds that "scripturas nostrae religionis non aliud dicere amorem, aliud dilectionem vel caritatem" (the scriptures of our religion do not say that love is one thing, *dilectio* or charity another). To prove this, he bases himself on the account of Peter's final mission in John 21:15–18. That is, Christ's first two questions to Peter ("Do you love me?") use ἀγαπᾶν, correctly translated by *diligere*, while Peter answers twice ("Lord, you know that I love you") with φιλεῖν, correctly translated by *amare*. One could then, if one follows the supporters of an equivocity between *dilectio* and *amor*, argue that Christ repeats his question a third time so that Peter might finally understand that it is appropriate to respond with ἀγαπᾶν to a question that asks ἀγαπᾷς με. Now what happens is entirely the opposite: not only does Peter's final response, the one held to be the best, maintain φιλεῖν (therefore *amare*), but in raising the question, Christ, too, uses for the first time this very same φιλεῖν (therefore *amare*), abandoning ἀγαπᾶν (therefore *diligere*).[82] Shouldn't we conclude from this that when the issue is committing oneself fully to Christ and assuming the mission of pastor of his Church, *amare* is more appropriate than *diligere*, contrary to current usage, which accords *dilectio* a gratuity and disinterestedness that is rejected for *amor*? At least, one might suppose he has found an argument for it here: "Ubi demonstratur unum atque idem esse amorem et dilectionem" (Where it is proven that *dilectio* and love are one and the same).[83] At the very least God does not condemn one for loving him with love, as well as with charity or *dilectio*.

Thus is defined the univocity that permits love to admit, without diluting itself, the plurality of its meanings and modes. This plurality would be of no importance if it did not serve in turn to articulate the singular playing field of love. And this field itself would in the end hardly be important at all if it did not play for me a life-or-death function: defining

my place. For love is indeed defined as a place, or rather defines my place
for me: "Duo sunt amores, mundi et Dei: si mundi amor habitet, non est
qua intret amor Dei. Recedat amor mundi et habitet [amor] Dei; melior
accipiat *locum*. Amabas mundum, noli amare mundum . . .; et incipit
habitare jam caritas, de qua nihil mali potest procedi" (There are two
loves, one of the world and one of God. If love of the world should come
to dwell [somewhere], there is no longer [a place] through which God can
enter. Let the love of the world withdraw and the love of God come to
dwell; let the better occupy the *place*. You used to love the world, love it no
more . . .; and let charity begin to inhabit you, that from which nothing
vile can proceed). Let us note the essential point: according to my love,
dwelling varies. But for me it is not a question of changing my dwelling
but of changing in me the dweller who comes to take place in me: charity
takes place in me by occupying me in place of the world. It gives me to
make me its place, to give place to it. "Facietis *locum* caritati venienti, ut
diligatis Deum. Quia si fuerit *ibi* dilectio mundi, non *ibi* erit dilectio Dei"
(Give [a] *place* to the charity that comes, so that you love God. For if *here*
there was love of the world, *here* there will not be a love of God). I find my
place according as charity takes place in me, or not. Thus am I as I am
because I am there where I love: "talis est quisquis, qualis ejus dilectio est"
(each is such as his love).[84]

§43. In the self's place

We can now reconstruct the path Saint Augustine's thinking took
in quest of the self.

Here is the first moment: the question of acceding to oneself never
consists in proving my existence but in testing my identity: "Quis ego et
qualis ego?" (And as for me, who am I and what *ego*?) (*Confessiones* IX, 1,
1, 14, 70). My existence and my access to it are, in fact, only too well guaranteed by my facticity; for this guarantee, doubtlessly certain, nonetheless
does not procure for me any assurance—or better, it assures me only the
place where I suffer the ordeal and painfully discover that *I do not know*
who I am nor what self falls to me as my own: "Factus eram ipse mihi
magna quaestio" (I myself became a great question to myself) (*Confessiones*
IV, 4, 9), and "Mihi quaestio factus sum" (To myself I become a question)

(X, 33, 50, 14, 232). Because I know, in my facticity, that I am, I above all know, indeed I uniquely know, that I do not know myself radically (see Chapter 2 §10 and §12). The aporia—I do not know who I am, I am not myself—becomes my place, but it is a place where the self stays inaccessible to me. Therefore my self becomes a nonplace, mine, more myself than every accessible place. The second moment consists in measuring the aporia of this nonplace: "*Ubi* ergo eram, quando te quaerebam?" (*Where* therefore was I when I was seeking you?) (V, 2, 2, 13, 464). If I am nowhere, then setting out from where can I begin a search? I, in fact, do find myself nowhere, in no place from where I could find one—placeless like a stateless person who, in losing his land, ends up losing also his self. "Ego mihi remanseram infelix *locus, ubi* nec esse possem, nec inde recedere. *Quo* enim cor meum fugeret a corde meo? *Quo* a me *ipso* fugerem? *Quo* non me sequerer?" (I remained for myself a *place* of unhappiness, *where* I could not settle, and from *where* I could not leave. Toward *where* could my heart flee my heart? *Where* could I take flight from myself? *Where* would I not always follow myself?) (IV, 7, 12, 13, 428). For Saint Augustine has the lucidity or courage (something often lacking in the moderns) to not "tell stories": if I do not have a place to take place because I have no access to myself, to the self, I cannot any the more go elsewhere to find another one, new, and perfectly my own, since I do not even have a point of departure, a place to leave. Only he could leave who already resides in himself as at home in his own place; without a place to oneself at the outset, without a point of departure, nobody can change place or self. I therefore cannot flee myself or localize myself, myself who departs from nowhere.

The third moment turns out to be decisive precisely because it does *not* consist in resolving, and therefore dissolving, the aporia but calls for it to be posited and thought as such. If I am neither in myself as a self identical to itself nor outside myself as departing from self, but indeed without a place, I can at the very least conclude from this that the question of my place cannot find a response through myself, who does not have a place. If, therefore, something like a self remains possible for me, I will never find it in my own nonplace but solely there where a place is found, even if it is not situated in my own domain. This place without me, before me, but only thus *for* me, who remains essentially outside and foreign to it, God alone is found there. As creator of the heavens and the earth, he alone opened the possibility of places for whoever differs from him and therefore also from itself. Or rather differing from God consists in receiving a place, which can therefore open outside God only on the basis of taking place, for the propriety of appropriating in a locality, more exactly of *localization*, that alone can be allotted to another by him who remains absolutely in a place because he remains himself to the point of taking place in himself, God. The aporia—my utopia, the fact that I have no place to take place, therefore no access to myself, to a self that is mine—is not dissolved but becomes the very thing that I must stare in the face, conceive and finally inhabit. I am this self that has no other place but to remain outside the place, which, elsewhere and already, is nevertheless found open. My place is defined as nonplace and not as an other place, as what remains out of place, that is to say more within me than myself.[85] For my nonplace leaves me not only outside of myself, but in alienating me, it also closes to me every possible interior: "Intus enim erat [lumen]; ego autem *foris*" (The light was inside, but I was *outside*) (VII, 7, 11, 13, 604). "Ecce intus eras et ego *foris*. . . . Mecum eras et tecum non eram" (And behold, you were on the inside, and I was *outside*. . . . You were with me, and I was not with you) (X, 27, 38, 14, 208). The aporia of the place from now on becomes the very thing that must be inhabited as a place. It is a paradoxical place but a paradox in which I nevertheless find my sole possible place. "Tu eras interior intimo meo et superior summo meo" (You were more inside than the most intimate in me, and higher than the highest in me).[86] What I am is not found in myself but in a place that is characterized in a twofold way. On one hand, as place, it is found to be more me than myself, therefore more in myself (or myself in it) than myself, who am out of place (except in it). On the other hand, as the place that escapes me absolutely, as the interior I lack, it turns out to be above the highest I can grasp. What is most intimate to me, my place, is found elsewhere than in myself, superior. I therefore find my intimate place only outside myself. If truly "*ibi est locus* quietis imperturbabilis, *ubi* non deseritur amor, si ipse non deserat" (*the place* where I might come to rest without any more disturbance *is there where* love is not abandoned, provided that it itself does not abandon) (IV, 11, 16, 13, 436), then the self finds its place—in other words, itself—only there where it loves, according to the principle that "talis est quisquis, qualis ejus dilectio est" (each is such as his love).[87] Thus, I become myself (oneself) only in going toward an other and by finding in it my first place.

The ego is not itself therefore by itself—neither by self-apprehension in self-consciousness (Descartes, at least in the common interpretation) nor by a performative (Descartes, in a less commonly accepted reading), nor by apperception (Kant), nor even by autoaffection (Henry) or anticipatory resoluteness (Heidegger). The ego does not even accede to itself *for* an other (Levinas) or *as* an other (Ricoeur); rather, it becomes itself only *by* an other—in other words by a gift; for everything happens, without exception, as and by a gift: "Ista omnia Dei mei dona sunt. Non mihi ego dedi haec" (But all these things are gifts of God to me. For I did not give them to myself) (*Confessiones* I, 20, 31, 13, 328). I undergo the ordeal of myself (of selfhood) when I reduce each thing to the given in it. And I know that I am performing this reduction correctly when I reach in each thing what I *cannot myself give to myself*; the given thus reduced to the nongivable provides absolute and irrefutable testimony to the ordeal of the exteriority of the self's place. What is it that comes over me really, that is to say as given? What I know I cannot myself give to myself: "Haec est tota scientia magna, hominem scire quia ipse per se nihil est; et quoniam quidquid est, a Deo est et propter Deum est. 'Quid habes, quod non accepisti? Si autem et accepisti, quid gloriaris quasi non acceperis?'" (This is all of knowledge and the greatest: that man knows that he is by himself nothing; and that all that is is from God and for God. "What have you that you have not received? And if you have received it, why do you glorify yourself in it as if you had not received it?" [1 Corinthians 4:17]).[88] This is a famous verse but one whose use, always significant and crucial in the Augustinian text, is not limited to the debates about grace with the Pelagians. Or rather, grace not being limited to a particular domain of the debate but encompassing the entire horizon (creation, which defines the horizon, constituting the first grace and making possible all the others), the verse "What do you have that you have not received (τί δὲ ἔχεις ὃ οὐχ ἔλαβες)?" avails itself of the universal validity of an erotic reduction of experience in general to the given, including, and especially, the attempt to determine the self. Understood rigorously, this principle does not reduce to the status of gift received only all that I receive (being, being-good, life and eternal life, etc.), but also me who receives. And if the first of the gifts consists in the very possibility of receiving one, then it is necessary that the self receive itself as a gift. But, in this case, the ego discovers itself received like one of its other gifts, contemporaneous with, not anterior to, its other gifts, not preceding them, still less conditioning them. Here we must unmask the willed illusion that pretends there must already be a preceding ego to receive the gifts and that, therefore, it itself does not fall under the jurisdiction of the gift nor happen itself as a gift as given as the others, because it would render them possible. Just the contrary must be acknowledged: since it receives each thing as a gift, it is necessary that the ego itself come from a second-order gift, or rather that it receive itself first and on the most basic level, before the other gifts or exactly by accompanying them. Just as the *I think* in Kant accompanies every other thought, the ego accompanies every other gift and, *for that very reason*, must find itself given absolutely, unconditionally, and primordially. The reduction of each and every thing to the given implies obviously that the ego, so reduced, is reduced first to the rank of given—first gift, absolute and without remainder, unconditioned and thoroughly so. The reduction to the gift includes first of all the self.

The self comes over me like a given, which I receive at the same time as all the other givens. What receives itself at the same time as what it receives can be named the gifted.[89] God gives place to what cannot yet receive because it is not yet there, not having by itself and for itself either a *here* or a *there*, either *self* or *Being*. For it belongs to the first gift, to the gift of origin (and deserves this title precisely for that reason), to give to what cannot yet receive, since it still has not yet found itself given. Saint Augustine describes the gifted with the greatest precision: "priusquam essem, tu eras, *nec eram, cui* praestares ut essem" (before I was, you were, and *I used to not be, such that to me* you conferred being) (XIII, 1, 1, 14, 424); "ut serviam tibi et colam te, ut de te *mihi* bene sit, a quo *mihi* est, *cui* bene sit" (so that I might serve and worship you, in such a way that it might come *to me* from you to be good, from you from whom it comes *to me* to be *he to whom* Being good comes" (ibid., 426). God gives the first gift by definition to him who still does not exist, *et non existentibus*. That God is with me before I am with him ("qui mecum est et *priusquam tecum sim*" [X, 4, 6, 14, 150]) goes beyond the question of grace and concerns that of my *esse* and my self, be it only because all is grace. The question of my Being falls under the gift, before ontology fixes and freezes it in an illusory permanence. "Deus autem nulli debet aliquid, quia omni gratuito praestat. Et si quisnam dicet ab illo aliquid deberi meritis suis, certe *ut esset, non ei debebatur. Non* enim *erat cui* deberetur" (God owes nothing to anybody because he gives all things gratuitously. And if by chance someone should happen to say that something is due to his own merits, at the very least it is certain that *it is not owed to him for having been so.* For there is not *anybody to whom* that would have been due).[90] I become myself by receiving myself originarily from elsewhere—oneself not only by an other but coming from an other, oneself from elsewhere. In the self's place is found elsewhere than the self, from where alone, as an other-self, more self than myself, the self can receive itself.

If I discover myself essentially given, too, a gift given even before anybody could receive it (and especially not itself), this paradox is the result of the paradox of the absolute gift in God and responds to it. For following a radical analysis on the part of Saint Augustine, God, in the person of the Spirit, is defined so absolutely as and by the gift that he does not even have to become, so to speak, given (*datum, donatum*) and therefore received to be accomplished already from the outset and forever as gift (*donum*), since he is already as such and by definition given, even though nobody yet can be found to receive him: "An eo ipso quo *daturus* erat eum [Spiritum sanctum] Deus, *jam donum* erat *et antequam* daretur. . . . An semper procedit Spiritus Sanctus, et non ex tempore, sed ab aeternitate procedit; sed quia sic procedebat ut esset *donabile, jam donum* non erat, et *antequam esset cui* daretur? Aliter enim intelligitur cum dicitur *donum*, aliter cum dicitur *donatum.* Nam *donum* esse potest *et antequam detur*" (Was he [the holy Spirit] already a gift even before he was given, on account of the fact that God meant to give him? . . . Or is it that the Holy Spirit is always proceeding, not in time but from [all] eternity? But if he processes in such a way that he would be *givable,* wasn't he *already a gift, even before anyone could be found to whom he could be given*? For *gift* is to be understood otherwise, *gift given* otherwise, too. For there can be a gift *even before a given*). Put otherwise: "In tantum ergo donum Dei [Spiritus Sanctus] est, in quantum datur eis quibus datur. Apud se autem Deus est, *etsi nemini detur*, quia Deus erat Patri et Filio coaeternus *antequam cuiquam daretur*" (But for himself he is God, *even if he is given to nobody* [outside of God], because there was God coeternal in the Father and the Son *before giving himself to anyone*).[91] Just as and because God is seen always already as a gift giving and giver without any condition, even that of its reception by some receiver outside God (and who, in all cases, could by definition never receive it as and as much as it gives itself— namely, with an excess lacking all measure), so, too, and consequently I find myself, me, always already given (gifted with and recipient of myself), even before having received reception of it. I have originarily the rank of gifted, given to oneself before being able to receive even one's proper self. In the self's place I receive reception of me from elsewhere than myself. The aporia of the self, therefore, never disappears—it is received as the horizon of my advance toward the immemorial.

Addition: *Idipsum,* or the Name of God

§44. The question of the names of God

No Christian theologian can remove himself from the question of the names of God. Whether he deals with it explicitly (as in the tradition that runs from Gregory of Nazianzus to Dionysius and John of Damascus) or implicitly (as all[1] the defenders of orthodoxy against Arianism) matters little, provided that he faces the difficulty as such—naming the unnameable, and naming it *as such.* Now, since by definition the unnameable cannot be named by *a* name, it is fitting, before taking any other steps, to admit that all names are in a sense suitable to God, since precisely none can name him adequately. The endless proliferation of divine names constitutes the first and indispensable step in their institution.

Even though he is not considered a major theoretician of the divine names, Saint Augustine does not dispense with them. "Deus vero *multipliciter* quidem dicitur, magnus, bonus, sapiens, beatus, verus, et *quidquid aliud* non indigne dici videtur" (God is surely said in multiple ways, [as] great, good, wise, happy, true and [as] all that seems to be said without indignity).[2] This formula has a remarkable aspect: it not only enumerates the names, but it states the principle of their enumeration and its indefinition. Since no name says God *as such,* then all are suitable, each in its way, for naming him, provided only that they name him with dignity. But how to decide about this dignity? How far does it extend, and, above all, what hierarchy does it establish between the names that it multiplies?

These questions arise clearly in the great and solemn invocation of God and his names that opens the *Confessiones*:

Summe, optime, potentissime, omnipotentissime, misericordissime et justissime, secretissime et praesentissime, pulcherrime et fortissime, stabilis et incomprehensibilis, immutabilis, mutans omnia, numquam novus, numquam vertus, innovans omnia et "in vetustatem perducens superbos et nesciunt" [Job 9:5]; semper agens, semper quietus, colligens et non egens, portans et implens et protegens, creans et nutriens et perficiens, quaerens cum nihil desit tibi. . . . et quid diximus, Deus meus, vita mea, dulcedo mea sancta, aut quid dicit aliquis, cum te dicit? et vae tacentibus de te, quoniam loquaces muti sunt.

Very great, very good, very powerful, absolutely all powerful, very merciful and very just, very secret and very present, very beautiful and very strong, stable and incomprehensible, without change and changing all, never new, never old, making all things new and "leading to their old age the prideful who know nothing" [Job 9:5]; ever acting and ever at rest, collecting but without need, sustaining and fulfilling and protecting, creating and nourishing and achieving, seeking while nothing is lacking. . . . And what have we just said, my God, my life, my holy sweetness, or what has he said who says something about you? And yet, woe to those who keep quiet about you because they remain silent in their very babbling.[3]

This remarkable text shows, first of all, with the most exact precision, the characteristics by which any speculative theology worthy of the name is recognized: (a) The divine names are said both by the positive way (cataphasis, predication) *and* by the negative way (apophasis, denegation). (b) But neither the apophasis nor the cataphasis have validity on their own because God surpasses the denegation as much as the predication. (c) It is therefore necessary to pass to another order of utterance, a new play of language: no longer to say or to deny something (the names) of something (God), since neither the one nor the others admit the status of thing, but to say *to* God the names according to which *we* can aim at him, positively or negatively; and this play operates only in praise, which invokes (in the vocative) God *as* such or such. Without this last way, which neither names nor denies him, but which denominates, we do not know, as Saint Augustine explicitly concludes, what we are saying when we say whatever it might be *concerning you* (*de te*).[4] Concerning God, it is not enough to speak of him, either to say something about him or even to deny something about him, because it is necessary only to speak *to him*, and therefore to speak in the mode of praise. The *Confessiones* therefore open with a praise: "'Magnus es, domine, et laudabilis valde. . . .' Et laudare te vult homo, . . . et tamen laudare vult te homo" ("You are great, Lord, and truly worthy of praise. . . ." And man wants to praise you, . . . and nevertheless man wants to praise you).[5] And they likewise conclude with a praise: "Laudant te opera tua, ut amemus te, et amemus te, ut laudent te opera tua" (Your works praise you so that we might love you, and we love you so that your works might praise you).[6] One will note that this praise is redoubled and radicalized: praise praises God precisely insofar as and in the title of praiseworthy and even praiseworthy par excellence, *laudabilis valde*. All the more so as, to accomplish this praise of the praiseworthy, a citation of scriptures is used, that is to say of the word given by him who it is a matter of naming in praising him. In this precise sense the *Confessiones* constitute, from beginning to end, an immense treatise of speculative theology.

One observes also, in the list of names chosen for this praise, two other decisions. Right away it is clear that no unique name suffices to name God. This is so, in the first place, obviously because one praises him *as . . .*, and such an *as . . .* forbids a univocal nomination and lays out a gap, such that it forbids ever pretending to seize even the slightest univocal conceptual definition. Next, and especially, each and every name is insufficient because in this case it concerns God, who, by definition, escapes all definition, in effect is praised as *incomprehensibilis*. "Si enim quod vis dicere, si capisti, non est Deus. Si comprehendere potuisti, cogitatione tua decepisti. Hoc ergo non est, si comprehendisti; si autem hoc est, non comprehendisti" (If what you want to say you grasp, it is not God. If you could comprehend it, your thought deceived you. It is not that, if you comprehended it; and if it is that, you have not comprehended it).[7] The impossibility of comprehension not only points out a factual impossibility but also defines the field and the conditions of access to Him who, without incomprehensibility, would disappear from thought: "Sic enim sunt incomprehensibilia quaerenda, ne se existimet nihil invenisse, qui quam sit incomprehensibile quod quaerebat, potuerit invenire. Cur ergo sic quaerit, si incomprehensibile comprehendit esse quod quaerit, nisi quia cessandum non est, quamdiu in ipsa incomprehensibilium rerum inquisitione proficitur et melior meliorque fit quaerens tam magnum bonum, quod et

inveniendum quaeritur, et quaerendum invenitur? Nam et quaeritur ut
inveniatur dulcius, et invenitur ut quaeratur avidius" (For incomprehensible things are to be sought in such a way that he who finds that what he
seeks is incomprehensible does not think he has found nothing at all. Why
then seek in this way, if he comprehends that what he seeks remains incomprehensible? Because he ought not cease to seek, so long as he is progressing
in the search [even] for incomprehensible things and becoming better and
better by dint of seeking so great a good, [this good] that one seeks in order
to find, but that is found only in order to be sought. For one seeks it in
order to find it with all the more pleasure, and one finds it in order to seek
it all the more avidly).[8] Incomprehensibility requires the use of an endless number of names, because it qualifies them, paradoxically, by opening
for them a proper site. Ignorance thus becomes, strictly, a knowledge, the
sole one appropriate to the incomprehensibility because it comes from it as
from its Spirit: "Est ergo in nobis quaedam, ut ita dicam, docta ignorantia,
sed docta Spiritu Dei, qui adjuvat infirmitatem nostram" (There is found
in us therefore so to speak a learned ignorance but learned from the Spirit
of God, who comes to the aid of our weakness).[9]

In the context of so long a praise, one observes a second decision: not
only is God not defined here by Being (whatever figure one assigns it), but
the very term *Being* never appears.[10] Nevertheless, the majority of commentators do not hesitate to hold that Saint Augustine defines God by *esse*—in
other words, ends up at the "discovery of God-Being," of "God, absolute
Being," or at "a theologic ontology," indeed at one "of the Christian ontolo-
gies of Being."[11] Is there an incoherence on the part of Saint Augustine
himself, who would have failed to harmonize the primacy of Being in God
and his denomination by the divine names? Or is there rather an ongoing
difficulty among his modern readers, who do not hesitate to maintain, even
in the case of Saint Augustine, the denomination of God within the horizon
of Being, indeed of the metaphysics of beings as being?

§45. The common response

It cannot be contested that sometimes Saint Augustine explicitly
links God to Being. He does so with at least three arguments.

The first has a scriptural authority: Saint Augustine takes up the tradition that, since Origen, privileges the name that God gives to Moses: "Sum qui sum," according to Exodus 3:14.[12] Among the many uses of this verse we can privilege one of those that most clearly assigns to it an avowed philosophical import: "cum ad sanctum Moysen ita verba Dei per angelum perferantur, ut quaerenti quod sit nomen ejus . . . respondeatur: 'Ego sum qui sum' . . . tanquam in ejus comparatione, qui vere est quia incommutabilis est, ea quae mutabilia facta sunt non sint, vehementer hoc Plato tenuit et diligentissime commandavit" (When the words of God come to Moses by way of the angel, such that to his question *what was his name*, . . . he answered: "I am who I am" . . ., as if, by comparison with him, who is truly because he is without change, the changing made things were not, Plato held that adamantly and recommended it strenuously).[13] The formulation of Exodus 3:14 becomes all the more a proper name, Saint Augustine emphasizes, as no attribute completes the tautology: "Non ait et ibi: ego sum Deus; aut: Ego sum ipsius populi liberandi propagator; sed hoc tantum: *Ego sum qui sum*" (He does not say here: I am God, nor does he say: I am the maker of the world; nor: I am the creator of all things; nor: I am the guide for the liberation of the people; he says only: *I am who I am*).[14] The tautology of Being becomes, in its very strangeness, if not something like the proper name, at least the name par excellence of God: "Quae vero proprie de Deo dicuntur, quaeque in nulla creatura inveniuntur, raro ponit Scriptura divina; sicut illud quod dictum est ad Moysen: *Ego sum qui sum* et *Qui est misit me ad vos*. Cum enim esse aliquo modo dicatur et corpus et animus, nisi proprio quodam modo vellet intelligi, non id utique diceret" (For about the things said properly of God and which are not found in any creature, the divine scripture rarely talks, as for instance what it says to Moses: *I am who I am* and *He who is sent me to you*. As Being is said in a certain sense both of the body and of the soul, scripture would not have spoken thus if it did not want to be understood in some special sense).[15] Yet because a biblical name is here at issue, even if it takes on an ontological sense by attraction to Plato or Aristotle, this argument could be insufficient for imposing Being itself (in the philosopher's sense) as a divine name.

This is no longer the case when Saint Augustine pushes the denomination by proclamation of Being to the point of an extreme formulation, where the second *is* becomes a substantive, functioning as attribute of a first verb *is*: "bonum est, quidquid aliquo modo est: ab illo enim est, qui non aliquo modo est, sed est *est*" (everything that is in one way or another is good; for it is by that which is not in a certain manner, but which is *is*).[16] Incontestably, God is here identified with Being—at least he is, and he alone, the fact of Being, such that the fact that he is his fact of Being defines him in his particularity. This identification is sometimes strengthened by the redoubling of *esse* into *ipsum esse*: "Considera igitur, quantum potes, quam magnum bonum sit *ipsum esse*, quod et beati et miseri volunt" (Consider then, as much as you can, what great good is *Being itself*, [since it is] he who is wanted by the happy as well as the unhappy).[17] In other words: "sic sum quod sum, sic sum *ipsum esse*, sic sum cum *ipso esse* ut nolim hominibus deesse" (thus am I what I am, thus am I Being itself, thus am I with *Being itself* in such a way that I do not want for it to be missing from men).[18] There is no doubt but that *ipsum esse* appears, here especially, as the goal sought by the desire of those who are not themselves, or as the figure of the *Sum qui sum*, when it gives itself to the desire of the rest of the things that are not God. But what shows itself as desired falls into the realm of Being, of Being itself.

There is more: The first doubling (of *est* into *ipsum esse*) is repeated in a second, this time of *ipsum esse* into *idipsum esse*: "Nam Deum ergo diligere debemus, trinam unitatem, Patrem et Filum et spiritum Sanctum, quod nihil aliud dicam esse, nisi *idipsum esse*" (We should therefore love God, triune unity, Father, Son, and Holy Spirit, that I will say to be nothing other than this, that he is *Being itself*).[19] Or again: "Cum ab ea [sc. immutabilis res, veritas] est aversus [sc. animus], *idipsum esse* minus habet" (And when the mind turns away from it [sc. the truth, the unchangeable thing], it possesses less of *Being itself*).[20] Even better, Being itself is an essential characteristic of He who is sayable only with the name of Exodus 3:14.

From this it seems that we should conclude that this *ipsum esse* (backed up by *idipsum esse*) not only permits but even requires a sort of Thomistic interpretation *avant la lettre*: the name *Who is* could not be imposed as the "most proper name of God" (*maxime proprium nomen Dei*) if first of all Being itself did not guarantee its essence ("essentia Dei est ipsum esse ejus").[21] Why not think, like Dominique Dubarle, that, "during the Middle Ages, Saint Thomas Aquinas judged it wise to nuance Saint Augustine's locution *ipsum esse* by saying of God that he is the *ipsum esse per se subsistans*, explaining the idea, already present in the Augustinian understanding of *ipsum esse*, of the independent subjectivity of the divine Being"?[22] Why not suggest with Maritain that "such texts . . . contain *virtually* the entire Thomist doctrine of the divine names and analogy"[23] and therefore that, with Saint Augustine, the most appropriate name of God is said *ipsum esse*, as *idipsum esse*?

§46. Translating *idipsum* by attraction

This conclusion must, however, be contested—not by disputing the authenticity of the Augustinian uses of *ipsum esse* or *idipsum esse* but because we must look into the relation of these terms to another term, the one Saint Augustine prefers to use when denominating God, *idipsum*: "*idipsum* quod Deus est, quidquid illud est" (that itself which is God, whatever that might be).[24] Now, this is indeed the term most proper to Saint Augustine since it also comes up in two absolutely decisive places. First it is used to designate nothing less than that toward which he casts his intention in the contemplation at Ostia, the first summit of his experience of contemplative prayer: "erigentes nos ardiore affectu in *idipsum*" (with ever more burning affections, raising ourselves higher toward that [sc. the thing] itself).[25] Next, because this is not only the formulation of a private experience, one finds exactly the same intending designation in the liturgical (communitarian and public) praise of the *Sanctus*: "Itaque, tu Domine, qui non es alias aliud et alias aliter, sed *idipsum* et *idipsum* et *idipsum*, 'sanctus, sanctus, sanctus, Dominus Deus omnipotens'" (And therefore, you, O Lord, who are not here another and there otherwise, but *the same thing itself* and *the same thing itself and the same thing itself* [in other words,] "holy, holy, holy").[26] Before any other consideration, a few observations are in order: (a) It is clearly a question of a praise name—in this case, the highest, that of the triple *Sanctus*; we should not therefore see in it a determination of God (positive or negative, it matters little), but according to the evidence, a denomination in the strictest sense. (b) The syntagma *idipsum* is translated, without difficulty, by *that itself* [*cela même*]: a demonstrative pronoun (*cela*), supported by an adverb (*même*);

as such, it does not define, nor even name, what it is limited to indicating, precisely because it indicates it and such an indication does away with defining what one is indicating. It is a pure deictic: it shows, but signifies nothing. It can therefore be applied to all names—or, more exactly, use them all so as to pass beyond them—by marking that, whatever it might be that a name can signify, it signals toward that which no name will ever be able to name. As radical deictic, *idipsum* can therefore practice and permit only a strict denomination. (c) Consequently, attributing a fixed signification to *idipsum* is an absurdity and a logical mistake, which demotes the denomination *as . . .* to the rank of a nomination, at once impracticable and illegitimate. Consequently, just as *idipsum* forces itself upon us as indisputably the central term (for my private praise, as for that of the liturgical community), so, too, does it turn out to be difficult to translate. That is, no signification is fitting to a deictic. One can barely understand it as something like an indication of . . ., an orientation toward . . ., less as a thing than as the *that itself* of the thing, whatever it might be. I will therefore understand *idipsum* as the thing itself, or that selfsame *itself* of the thing (understood in the characteristic imprecision of *thing*).

Now the majority of translators do not seem to see this singularity nor its function in speculative theology, since most often they translate *idipsum* by "être même" or "Being itself."[27] And this is not just a case of absent-mindedness; it is customary usage. There is no dearth of other examples of unconscious substitution. I will limit myself to calling up just a few. *Confessiones* IX, 4, 11, "et clamabam in consequenti versu clamore alto cordis me: 'O in pace! O in id ipsum!' . . . tu es id ipsum valde, quia non mutaris," which one should translate: "'O in peace, O in the itself,' [Psalm 4:9] . . . you are the thing itself, you who do not change," becomes in fact: "Oh! in *Being* itself . . . you are *Being* itself, unchangeable," or else: "Oh! Dans *l'être* même . . . tu es toi, cet être même par excellence."[28] Or else *Confessiones* XII, 15, 21: "Unde ita est [sc. mens] abs te, Deo nostro, ut aliud sit plane quam tu et non *idipsum*"—in other words: "Whence it [sc. the soul] is through you, our God, such that it is entirely other than you, and not the thing itself"—is transformed into: "un être tout autre que toi, et non l'*être* même" or "it is not *Being itself.*"[29] And again, when *Confessiones* XIII, 11, 12 attempts to define "illud, quod supra ista est" (literally, "what is above these things") as "sibi notum est et sibi sufficit incommutabiliter *idipsum*" (*the thing itself* that is known to itself and sufficient unto itself without change), it is translated such that "l'être immuable [the unchangeable Being]" is defined as "*L'Être* même," or as "the ultimate Being," indeed as "Being-Itself."[30] How are we to explain this constant wrong reading, which ends up as a misreading of what is most basic? It is evident that *idipsum* signifies first and simply "the same, the same thing."[31] And if, by some chance, one absolutely must cling to substantifying it, it would be rendered rigorously as the "identical."[32] There would be no difficulty, then, in translating it, if one really wanted to translate the text itself; but in fact, an *other* text is translated, one added on top of Augustine's and combined with his. Here is a symptomatic example (*Confessiones* I, 6, 10): "tu facis nos, Domine, cui esse et vivere non aliud atque aliud, quia summe esse ac summe vivere *idipsum* est. Summus enim es." There is no problem translating this passage simply as: "you made us, Lord, you for whom to be and to live are not one thing and another thing, because to be supremely and to live supremely are *the same thing*. For you are supremely." But it happens that, after having correctly translated the explicit text ("the highest degree of Being and the highest degree of life, those are one"), one goes on *to add* another text, an implicit one at that: "You are in effect *Being* at the highest degree," there where we find only: "You are in effect supremely."[33] How are we to explain the fact that *Being* [*Être*] is added to the simple Latin *summus es*? From the fact that one is not translating just the *idipsum* that is written, but an implicit text, a text that one reads spontaneously in its place: *ipsum esse*. In fact, the translator has so strong an understanding of *idipsum* as *ipsum esse* that when, under the constraint of the obvious grammar, he can no longer successfully translate it without rendering it literally (*the same thing, the same*, without ontological determination), he does not hesitate, so as to maintain *ipsum esse* at all costs, to insert it into the following phrase, where it surreptitiously reinvests the invocation of God with an ontico-ontological determination: "You are in effect *Being*."

These slippages and distortions are not the result of chance, still less of the carelessness of the translators, who are everywhere else excellent. They come rather from an overscrupulousness, not philological to be sure, but conceptual, so much does the Thomist decision about the most proper name of God determine their comprehension of the Augustinian denomination that they take it to be irreducible and for that very reason make corrections. What is more, they do so with full awareness and a clean conscience, as one of the best admits without ambiguity: "It is by design that I left in the translation the Latin term *Idipsum*. As will be seen, this is the *technical* term equivalent to *Ego sum qui sum* and to *Qui est* of Exodus, the term that, *taken in the metaphysical sense*, defines God as he defines himself: Being in the full sense, unchangeable Being, eternal Being. The best translation therefore seems to be this *Being itself*."[34] It cannot be said any better: what leads to translating *idipsum* as if it were *ipsum esse* does not come from the text or from the teaching of Saint Augustine but from its interpretation[35] in the "metaphysical sense." The entire question now becomes knowing, first, what *metaphysics* could mean here, since, according to the evidence, Saint Augustine is unaware of its use and significance (as were, for that matter, all the philosophers who preceded him); next, identifying which subsequent *metaphysics* can serve as paradigm and with what legitimacy; and finally, asking on this occasion if what is always named too quickly *the* Thomist position tolerates or requires being granted the status of *metaphysica*, or if one should go farther ahead into modernity to find its genuine paradigm;[36] then finally and especially, if the retrospective application of this "metaphysical" interpretation to the *idipsum* (and therefore to the Augustinian denomination of God) can claim any authority whatsoever. In fact, beneath the inoffensive appearance of something approximating a scholastic translation, indeed a piously neo-Thomist one, a radical bypassing of Saint Augustine's intention is at work, one that substitutes a metaphysical concept of Being (and, for that matter, one that is largely problematic from the point of view of metaphysics itself) for a radically biblical and decidedly apophatic denomination.[37]

Such a confusion cannot not show itself to be as imprudent as impudent, since "Being/*esse*" designates precisely what the two formulae, on the one hand Thomas's *ipsum esse* and, on the other, the *idipsum* of Saint Augustine, do *not* have in common—hence, *esse* is precisely what is lacking to *idipsum*. To the contrary, the question consists in knowing if it is still necessary for the denomination *idipsum* (precisely without *esse*) to be "taken in the metaphysical sense" or if, in contrast, it should not be so taken.

§47. The silence of *idipsum*

Now there is one very pertinent argument for suspending the metaphysical interpretation of the formula *idipsum*: its biblical provenance. That is, with *idipsum* it is even less a matter of what metaphysics means by Being as it comes directly from a citation of Psalm 121:3, a psalm of ascent that celebrates the entry into Jerusalem with a greeting: "Hierusalem quae aedificaris est civitas / cujus participatio idipsum."[38] This translation owes its strangeness only to the fact that it transcribes literally the version of the Septuagint: ἧς ἡ μετοχὴ αὐτῆς ἐπὶ τὸ αὐτὸ, a verse that describes the solidity and the coherence of Jerusalem so as to conclude that taking part in it, participating in it (becoming literally a resident alien of this city), constitutes the thing itself—what one desires, what has to be reached. And therefore, by isolating τὸ αὐτὸ, which he translates as *idipsum*, Saint Augustine succeeds in establishing literally the determination of "the thing itself in which we must participate" as ultimate denomination of God. And "idipsum quod Deus est" (that itself that God is)[39] becomes the "thing itself" that God is, "Deus . . . idipsum est."[40] Far from being a "misreading,"[41] this Augustinian formulation is authorized on the basis of a literal biblical exegesis as a rigorous denomination of God, without imposing any other determination on him, especially not an ontico-ontological or metaphysical one. This use of *idipsum* emerges from a tradition *more* ancient, because biblical, than the *ipsum esse*, which in the modern commentaries buries it. *Idipsum* is not equivalent to *ipsum esse* but resists it in advance and dismisses it.

To specify these characteristics of *idipsum*, it is fitting to refer to the central text, the Commentaries on the Psalms 121.[42] I will identify four moments, which will be so many specifications. First moment: "Quid est *idipsum*? Quomodo dicam, nisi *idipsum*? Fratres, si potestis, intelligis *idipsum*. Nam ego quidquid aliud dixero, non dico *idipsum*" (What is *idipsum* [the thing itself]? How will I say this, if not by saying *idipsum*? My brothers, if you can, understand *idipsum*. For, whatever else I say, I do not say [the signification of] *idipsum*). *Idipsum* therefore remains radically and definitively apophatic, says no essence, and reaches no definition. If it indicates God, it does so only by its own powerlessness to say him. All its privilege as most appropriate name comes, for *idipsum*, paradoxically from its patent void of signification, which frees for it the possibility of denominating without pretending to define. Whence a second moment: "Conemur tamen quibusdam vicinitatibus verborum et significationum perducere infirmitatem mentis ad cogitandum *idipsum*. Quid est *idipsum*? Quod semper eodem modo est, quod non modo aliud, et modo aliud est. Quid est ergo *idipsum*, nisi quod est? Quid est quod est? Quod aeternum est. Nam quod semper aliter atque aliter est, non est, quia non manet; non omnino non est, sed non summe est" (Let us try then to bring the weak gaze of our mind, by some approximative words and meanings, so far as to think *idipsum*. What is *idipsum*? What always is in the same way, which is not sometimes one way, sometimes another. What then is *idipsum*, if not that which is? What is that which is? That which is eternal. For that which is ever otherwise and otherwise is not because it does not remain; not being absolutely, but it is not supremely). On the basis of its definitive apophasis, *idipsum* can nevertheless still be defined, though by a definition that is precisely negative. It is in a mode that is neither ours nor that of any creature. It is in the mode of that which does not change. What here makes the difference between *idipsum* and everything that is not the thing itself does not reside in Being (or non-Being) but in the opposition among the ways of Being (the *how* of the being)—mutable or immutable. *Strictly as such*, Being does not suffice to characterize *idipsum*, as if it could be reduced without remainder to an *ipsum esse*. It characterizes it only inasmuch as it is the horizon within which the criteria of immutability is imposed: *esse est nomen incommutabilitatis*.[43]

It is only third that we come to Exodus 3:14:

Et quid est quod est, nisi ille qui, quando mittebat Moysen, dixit illi: *Ego sum, qui sum?* Quid est hoc, nisi ille, qui cum diceret famulus ejus *Ecce mittis me; si dixerit mihi populus: Quis te misit?, quid dicam ei?*, nomen suum noluit aliud dicere quam *Ego sum qui sum*; et adjecit et ait: *Dices itaque filiis Israël: qui est misit me ad vos. Ecce idipsum: Ego sum qui sum; qui est, misit me ad vos.* Non potes capere: multum est intelligere; multum est apprehendere.

And what is that which is, if not he who, when he sent Moses, said to him: *I am who I am?* What is this, if not he who, when his servant said: *See, you are sending me; and if the people ask me: Who sent you?, what should I say?*, did not want to say another name besides *I am who I am*; and he added and said: *Tell the children of Israel: He who is sent me to you.* And see [what is signified by] *idipsum: I am who*

I am; he who is sent me to you. You cannot grasp it; there is much to understand, much to grasp.

One sees first of all that Exodus 3:14 comes into play only after *idipsum* and following its apophasis, in such a way that the latter, far from being identical to it or fading into it, encompasses and gives its meaning to *Sum qui sum*. Consequently, we see above all that *Sum qui sum* no longer admits being translated into *ipsum esse*, which would make of Being the most proper name of God, and therefore no longer works to establish the "metaphysics of Exodus," by fading into *ipsum esse*. Rather *Sum qui sum* indicates the divine immutability opposite all the rest that fall into nullity: "Et quis magis est, quam ille qui dixit famulo suo Moysi *Ego sum qui sum* et *Dices filiis Israël: qui est, misit me ad vos*? . . . Et ideo sola est incommutabilis substantia et essentia, qui Deus est, cui profecto ipsum esse. . . maxime ac verissime competit" (And what is greater than he who said to his servant Moses: *I am who I am* and *He who is sent me to you*? . . . And so alone is immutable the substance and essence that is God, to which it is proper with a supreme truth to come forward as Being itself).[44] Thus, immutability, not Being, designates the difference of God, with an immutability that is marked by the *equivocity* of Being, without measure between it and all the rest.

There follows, finally, a fourth moment, still more surprising, since it attributes Exodus 3:14 not only to God the Creator but also to Christ, not only to the *Filius invisibilis* but, indeed, to the *Filius visibilis*,[45] to the kenotic God: "Quid enim debes tenere? Quod pro te factus est Christus, quia ipse est Christus; et ipse Christus recte intelligitur: *Ego sum qui sum*, quo modo est 'in forma Dei.' Ubi 'non rapinam arbitratus est esse Deo,' ibi est *idipsum*. Ut autem efficiaris tu particeps in *idipsum*, factus est ipse prior particeps tui, et 'Verbum caro factus est' ut caro participet Verbum" (What must you hold [as true]? That he became Christ for you, because he is himself Christ; and Christ himself is understood correctly [as] *I am who I am*, in the mode in which he is 'in the form of God' [Philippians 2:6]. There where 'he did not consider it his property to be equal to God [ibid.]' is precisely where he is *idipsum*. Thus, in order that you might partake of *idipsum*, he himself first partook of you, 'and the Word became flesh' [John 1:14], so that the flesh might partake of the Word).[46] To be sure, this text establishes a relation, so characteristic of Augustinian exegesis, between Exodus 3:14, "Sum qui sum," and John 8:27 (or 12:19).[47] But this relation itself presupposes that the immutability of the mode of Being of God can pass into the mutability of the mode of Being of humanity, assumed by Christ. If such a paradox can be thought, if therefore *idipsum* can be incarnate by paying the price of kenosis and if it can give itself in partaking of man, then it becomes clear that, for Saint Augustine, the function and characteristic of *idipsum* are not governed by Being, at least in the sense that metaphysics will understand Being in its ontology, but by the charity of God. It is because he first reestablished the *Sum qui sum* (and therefore also *ipsum esse*) in its originally soteriological signification that Saint Augustine can deploy it in its most extreme reaches in the figure of the humble servant. There is *idipsum* for us, there where the "form of God" takes on the "condition of a slave," in Christ the Savior.[48]

The most proper name of God, *idipsum*, is therefore characterized as apophatic, marking its transcendence by the privilege of immutability, interpreting *ipsum esse* on the basis of *Sum qui sum* (and not the inverse) outside the horizon of Being, but in the perspective of divinization by Christ. This radically biblical exegesis confers on it therefore a radically theological status, to the point that *idipsum* is equivalent to the *Sanctus*: "idipsum et idipsum et idipsum, sanctus, sanctus, sanctus Deus omnipotens."[49]

§48. *Sum qui sum*, or immutability

The essential point now resides in the status and the function of immutability. For, taken up in *idipsum*, Augustinian *esse* puts itself at the service of immutability. When *esse* comes up to denominate God, it designates him immediately as immutable: "Esse, nomen est incommutabilitatis."[50] The difference between the immutable and the moving becomes an *indirectly* ontological difference, that of the ways of Being of beings,[51] and organizes being as a whole on the basis of a distinction as originary, indeed more originary—the distinction of the created and the Creator. "Cum enim Deus summa essentia est, hoc est summe sit et ideo immutabilis sit, rebus quas ex nihilo creavit, esse dedit, sed non summe esse, sicut ipse est" (For since God is supreme essence, that is to say since he is supremely and therefore immutably, he gave Being to the things that he created from nothing, but not supreme Being, in the way that he himself is). The hierarchy of beings ("naturas essentiarum gradibus ordinavit" [he arranged the natures according to degree of essence])[52] is translated into and read in the levels of the hierarchy of immutability rather than in strictly ontological terms. Faced with the *Ego sum qui sum*, everything happens as if that which was not absolutely, that is to say immutably, even in being finally was not: "*tanquam* in ejus comparatione, qui vere est quia incommutabilis est, ea quae mutabilia sunt non sint" (*as if* by comparison with that which truly is, because it is immutable, the changing things were not).[53] We thus arrive at the point where *idipsum* can sometimes be designated directly by immutability, without passing through a determination coming from Being. "Et tu es *idipsum* valde, quia non mutaris" (And you, you are radically the thing itself, because you do not change).[54] Or else: "non sunt *idipsum* quod Deus, et inest quaedam multiplictas omnibus" (they [sc. created things] are not the same, like God, and a certain mutability inhabits them).[55] Or else: "*idipsum*, id est naturam incommutabilem" (the thing itself: to wit, immutable nature).[56] And finally: "*In idipsum* qui sit, nisi quod mutari non potest? (*In the thing itself*, what is it if not what cannot change?)[57] God names himself, then, *Sum qui sum* because he first attests himself unchanging, and not the contrary. There where, in the system of metaphysics, eternity follows from the Being of God, among other properties, here the divine difference in face of the world is marked at the outset by immutability, which originarily determines their difference in ways of being, and therefore Being. *Aeternum* determines *esse*, and not the inverse. Saint Augustine's procedure no longer gives rise to any doubt: Exodus 3:14 does not lead to *ipsum esse*, nor therefore to a "metaphysics of Exodus," because, in contrast, it is understood on the basis of the *idipsum* of Psalm 121. *Idipsum* permits thinking the difference between God and his creation without passing through an ontic difference, without inscribing it within the horizon of Being.

There remains a difficulty, nevertheless, for at least one text in the Augustinian corpus clearly seems to interpret the distance between the eternity of God and the mutability of creatures according to the lexicon of Being:

Aeternitas ipsa Dei substantia est, quae nihil habet mutabile; ibi nihil est praeteritum quasi jam non sit; nihil est futurum, quasi nondum sit. Non est ibi nisi:

Est; non est ibi: Fuit et erit; quia et quod fuit, jam non est; et quod erit, non-dum est; sed quidquid ibi est, nonnisi est. Merito sic misit Deus famulum suum Moysen. Quaesivit enim nomen mittentis se. . . . *Ego sum.* Quis? *Qui sum.* Hoc est nomen tuum? hoc est totum quod vocaris? Esset tibi nomen *ipsum esse*, nisi quidquid aliud, tibi comparatum, inveniretur non esse vere? . . . Magnum ecce *Est*, magnum *Est!* Ad hoc homo quid est? Ad illum tam magnum *Est*, homo quid est, quidquid est? Quis apprehendat illud esse? quis ejus particeps fiat?

Eternity is the very substance of God, who has naught mutable. Here nothing is [in the] past as if it were no longer now. Nothing is [in the] future, as if it were not yet. Here there is nothing else but *Is*; here there is not *Was* or *to come*, because what was is no longer and what will be is not yet; but all that which is here is and nothing other. It is fitting, then, that God sent his servant Moses thus. For the latter asked the name of what was sending him. . . . *I am.* [I am] who? *Who I am.* Is this your name? Do you call yourself thus without more? [But] *Ipsum esse* would this be your name, if we did not find that no matter what else, compared to you, would not truly be? . . . How great is this *Is*, this great *Is*! Before that, what is man? Before this so great *Is*, what is man, whatever he might be? Who will apprehend this Being? Who will partake of it?[58]

Shouldn't we see here, contrary to the preceding discussion, (a) that *ipsum esse* replaces *idipsum*, which is absent, when interpreting *Ego sum qui sum*; (b) that eternity, which here is substituted for immutability, holds the rank of *substantia*, despite the reticence of *De Trinitate*; (c) that a new term appears as privileged divine name, *Est*; (d) that the eternity of this *Est* is described in terms of the three dimensions of time, itself understood in the lexicon of Being, as to come, present being, already past? Don't we find here, indisputably, the conditions for a perfectly and exclusively onto-logical reading of Exodus 3:14? What then would remain of the originality that we supposed for the *idipsum*?

Now, far from this text contradicting the thesis being argued here, it turns out that it provides, on a more attentive reading, the crucial experi-ence that validates it. That is, far from permitting a rapprochement of Saint Augustine and Saint Thomas Aquinas on the reading of Exodus 3:14, it serves as occasion for a partisan of "the metaphysics of Exodus" as authoritative as Etienne Gilson himself to oppose the two head-on. And that happens at least twice. In the first case, in his *Introduction à l'étude de saint Augustin*, he bases himself on the principle "aeternitas ipsa Dei substantia" in order to oppose the two doctrines:

Augustinian proofs for God's existence would be understood incorrectly if one tried to interpret them in the same sense as the proofs of St. Thomas Aquinas. The "ways" to God do not follow the same paths in the two doctrines because their terminal points, like their starting points, are not the same. It is true that they have the same God in view, and He is the same god with the same name, but whereas St. Thomas will try especially to prove the existence of a supreme *Esse*, or subsistent act of existing, St. Augustine wanted above all else to stress the obligation which the mind has of explaining the spurious *esse* known in experience by a supreme *Vere Esse*.[59]

Let me note that it is not certain that the points of departure and the divine names are exactly the same nor, above all, that Saint Augustine intends *Vere Esse* in the slightest.[60] Gilson's thesis clearly illustrates the ontological *in his eyes* insufficiency of Saint Augustine, who, even when he does not reduce, *ipsum esse* to *idipsum*, as is the case here, would not reach "supreme *Esse*." This antagonism is confirmed quite explicitly in what remains Gilson's fundamental text, *Le thomisme*. Here, the same principle, "Aeternitas, ipsa Dei substantia est," drawn from the same text of Saint Augustine, is invoked as the clearest proof of "the ultimate limits of his ontology," by opposition to Saint Thomas's principle, "Deum est suum esse," which "marks clearly the decisive progress attained by his ontology." In effect, by maintaining for Being "that variable value which it always has in an ontology of essences," Saint Augustine proves unable to "bridge the gap between the Being of essence and the Being of existence," that is to say of entrusting *ipsum esse*, itself understood as an *actus essendi* (here understood as "existence"), with guarding the immutable transcendence of God.[61] But at no moment does Gilson ask himself about the legitimacy of speaking of ontology in the case of Saint Augustine (nor, indeed, for Saint Thomas), who not only was unaware of the word (which appeared some ten centuries later) but would never even have had the use for it, since for him *Sum qui sum* doesn't even belong to an investigation into being. And that is so not because "Augustine's philosophy lagged behind his theology"[62] but because, by contrast, his philosophy was but one with his theology, to the point of making no difference between the one and the other: "verus philosophus est amator Dei" (the true philosopher is he who loves God).[63] The ontological insufficiency that Gilson and, with him, so many others attribute to Saint Augustine, in fact, attests that one should not stubbornly impose an ontico-ontological hermeneutic on a thought that is claimed by a wholly other horizon than that of metaphysics, with something else entirely at stake besides the *Seinsfrage*. For even when he sometimes uses *ipsum esse*, never does Saint Augustine trouble himself about Being. It could be that he, with many others for that matter, makes an exception to the rule set perhaps unwisely by Gilson: "There is but one God and this God is Being, that is the cornerstone of all Christian philosophy."[64] For Saint Augustine, Christian par excellence and who thinks, does not think God as Being—so as not to make of Being a god.

Conclusion

§49. Oneself as inclusion

Thus is accomplished the movement that I make toward myself. But can it even be said that *I* make it toward *myself*? Rigorously speaking, Saint Augustine does not speak in this way and does not say as much. First, if he sometimes uses *ego*, he never uses it as a substantive, in the way inaugurated by Descartes: if I knew myself to be an *ego* and if I knew what *ego* meant, I would no longer be a *magna quaestio* for myself (*Confessiones* IV, 4, 9, 13, 422), and I would already have attained my essence or, at least, enough certainty to no longer worry about it. Next, is it really I myself who makes this movement, as if I had the initiative to launch it, the strength to cross it, and especially the anticipated knowledge of the itinerary? If I go through the trouble, wouldn't this be rather because it inspires me in advance? Last of all, arriving at the finish line, isn't it still a matter of asking and receiving—"sic, sic accipietur, sic invenietur" (XIII, 38, 53, 14, 524)? Finally, and especially, is it really about *myself*, or is the movement not launched precisely because I know neither if I have a *self* nor if I am a *self*, nor what that means, a *self*? And, if the movement led me somewhere, wouldn't this be precisely to the point of understanding this—that if I ever reach such a self, this self, which will indeed be myself, will not be for all that *from* me, as it will not be *the one* that is my own, even if it will be mine. This self, that I am, I am not it permanently, and I would not need so absolutely to move toward it if I did not find myself first of all outside it, this *self*, therefore outside myself, as it is without myself: "Intus enim erat, ego autem foris" (It was inside, but myself, outside) (VII, 7, 11). The movement becomes possible and unconditionally necessary in the very degree to which the more I advance upon it, the more it manifests that I am not myself my own self, more precisely that I do not of myself have access to, nor possession of, this *self* itself; but that it harbors and reveals more myself than I am, than I can by myself, that there is more me in me, than what I can be by myself. The self, which is myself, I, me the *ego*, am not it; I do not know by myself. No *I* is *self*, still less by itself, and especially not me.

I is an other, evidently. The problem consists in knowing *which* other. And also if it can give me access to it, who is the sole *self* that remains for me, the sole *self* that would be myself, even if it is not through me, the sole *self* that would be mine, even if it is not the one proper to me. It was therefore necessary to cross this originary separation of the *ego* from *itself* and, for that, first of all to enter it, therefore dive into it in all its depths. The moments of our itinerary are confined to recording the successive theses of the inclusion of the *ego* in the place of the *self*.

The first thesis (Chapter 1) holds that *confessio* does not constitute just one speech or language act among others but originally structures all speaking and every linguistic performance; for the principle that the call is heard only in the response implies in turn that some utterance (at least, if not all of them) already constitutes a response, which thus attests a prior word, even if it remained silent. And the *confessio* belongs to this type of utterance, since it carries out this reference in two ways: by the admission of faults *to* God and by praise *toward* God; indeed three times, since the two first are carried out by citing biblical words, that is to say giving in response what was received in call. Thus, *confessio* (and therefore the *Confessiones* that is entirely organized by it, as the *Confessiones* themselves organize the entire work) opens the space where the *ego* (and soon enough the *alii*, other believers and readers as well) find themselves *before* and already *in the house of* (*apud*) God. Making the *ego* appear by leading it back (reduction) to itself, the *confessio* makes it appear in and through (its) relation to God, whom it confesses as the other of reference. This is enough to define this reduction, the *confessio*, as an *erotic reduction*.

The second thesis (Chapter 2) establishes that the certainty of my existence, obtained by the performance of thought (act or primal sensing, it matters little here), far from making me accede to my essence (for example, as *res cogitans*, indeed transcendental *I* or "evaluative animal") manifests all the more the inaccessibility of my essence: the more I exist, the more I understand that I do not know my essence, that by definition my essence escapes me. And it does so not only negatively, as in metaphysics, where the essence once defined drops to the rank of object and an empirical *me*, but positively, because my thought grows deeper or rather is poured forth into the chasm of *memoria*, which exceeds me like an unconscious and precedes me like an immemorial. Without essence and taken over by *memoria*, the *ego* (precisely because thinking) can in no way pretend to the rank of first principle. To be sure, it performs, knows, and appropriates its existence but so as to lose its *self* therein. This *self*, by contrast, it sees reappear in the desire for beatitude, that nobody can not admit, since no *ego* can deny being able to live only on condition of desiring to live happy. But this *self* of desire, the *ego* can aim at it only paradoxically, in the negative mode of what it cannot perform by itself, cannot know by itself, nor, of course, appropriate by itself. Nothing better signals the gap between the *ego* and *self* than the desire for beatitude, which defines the *self* precisely as what the *ego* cannot attain by itself, still less have in itself. The *ego* finds itself addicted to beatitude. It is *given over* to beatitude in that it could not receive it except by receiving itself from it as its *self*.

The third thesis (Chapter 3) indicates that the desire for beatitude, which now plays the role of a first principle displaced within the practical order and in this way remains valid even without one being able to complete it, know it, or appropriate it, is imposed nevertheless only because I desire it precisely, therefore because I love it. Now, in order that what I love can give me the blessed life, it is necessary that what I love without knowledge or possession remains at least true. Whence the situation of a truth to love—in other words, toward which I can no longer orient myself except through my desire and in the measure to which this desire loves it. Now, being such that I cannot not love and that, whatever happens, I love, the entire question resides in *deciding* what I love. Always loving, I often love another thing besides the truth—a falsehood, therefore, mine and familiar, about which I must, if I want to love it, convince myself that it does indeed hold the rank of truth, while most often I know perfectly well, or at least I suspect when alone with myself, that it is a falsehood. Henceforth, loving the truth will imply not only entering into the separation of the true and the false beloved but also *deciding* to pass from the latter to the former, to change loves out of love, precisely, for the true, preferred to the false. As *saturated phenomenon*, the truth to love therefore demands a *decision*, which puts to the test the *ego's* resistance inasmuch as *gifted*.

The fourth thesis (Chapter 4) confirms the difficulty and the conditions of the decision. Decision puts the *ego* into operation in the figure of the will, which corresponds exactly to the displacement of the first principle from the *cogitatio* to *desire* (for beatitude). The will appears, then, as the irreducible kernel of the *ego*, what cannot be distinguished from it and coincides absolutely with it, always remaining at its disposition (*praesto est*). And yet the description should, in contrast, record that, if the will can formally decide everything about the world and its own body (without consideration, of course, for the means of materially effecting what it chooses formally), it cannot decide about itself—if it wills to will, if it wills this rather than that, if it wills unreservedly or only halfway. Nothing resists the will, except itself. Consequently, it can will itself only by willing powerfully (*vehementer*), which is possible only in the erotic situation of the *advance*—the movement of the lover who is decided about loving, without sufficient reason and without other cause besides the love itself, by advancing into the field where nobody has yet responded to his decision to love. Only the erotic *advance* can surpass the resistance that the saturated phenomenon arouses and the weakness of the will provokes.

The fifth thesis (Chapter 5) makes clear that the time—or, more exactly, temporality—of the *ego* does not refer to it alone, nor even just to finitude. It signals, as its first marker, the condition of the creature: the created is temporalized inasmuch as created, and the question of time itself begins with the *advent* of the created. The aporia of time in Greek philosophy (that it is divided even in the present instant but that the instant itself never remains in presence) comes from the misrepresentation of creation and from the illusion of time ascending to eternity, be it only by imitation. One must, by contrast, root temporality in the *distentio animi* so as to recognize there the very place of the gap between the *ego* and *self.* Thus the differ*a*nce or delay of the *ego to self* does not consist in temporality but provokes it and stages it. The *distentio animi* describes, more than time, the time of sin, in which the *ego* is late to its *self*, as beforehand certain existence was to the desire for beatitude, the will to the strength of love. To the *distentio animi* of a time of the loss of self by self, we must oppose the crossing of the distance of the *ego* to *self*, the traversal of the *regio dissimilitudinis*, and the movement across differ*a*nce. Ipseity in becoming. If the question is one of intention and image: "quantumcumque se *extenderit* in id quod aeternum est, tanto magis inde formatur *ad* imaginem Dei" (*De Trinitate* XII, 7, 10, 16, 230).

The sixth and final thesis (Chapter 6) addresses the question of *place*. Creation, as is already the case with temporality, its symptom, designates the gap not as differ*a*nce but as distance, therefore properly place. But in contrast to the place that Greek philosophy locates in nature (more exactly, in the nature of each thing) as its natural place, Saint Augustine understands place in distance—the distance of desire to beatitude, of love to truth; in short, the differ*a*nce of the *ego* to the *self*. Place is defined by the ascent of the *ego* toward that which it loves and which defines it more intimately than the most intimate in it. *Place* is defined as what the *ego*, instead of resting in its natural position (its natural place), attains as the veritable *place of self*: what it loves by itself. For I am what I love, since I put in this place all that I am, what I love offers me in return the self's place. And if I succeed in loving nothing of myself but God, God will appear to the *ego* the self's place. And consequently, as God remains by definition inaccessible, in the sense that, each time that he gives himself and in the very measure to which he gives himself, he appears as forever infinitely in advance and beyond that to which I have drawn near, the self's place in God can become only the movement of an incessantly ongoing tension. Never will I find the *self's place as an essence*, because an absolute and infinite place can only draw near to the infinite and unbounded. My place, never will I attain it as to a finite essence since it is found unto the image and in the image of the infinite. But of the infinite, I will not become in any way the image, because no image can bind in it the absolute. Therefore, my place in God that I love will be accomplished *unto the image* (*ad imaginem*) endlessly referred to the infinite, endlessly liberated from all ties so as to freely advance in the infinite that nothing binds.

The *ego's* advance to the self's place permits it finally to know itself as such—namely, as he who bears the stigmata of the place where he rediscovers himself by discovering what he loves, the incomprehensible.

An et inventus forte quaerendus est? Sic enim sunt incomprehensibilia requirenda, ne se existimet nihil invenisse, qui quam sit incomprehensibile quod quaerabat, potuerit invenire. Cur ergo sic quaerit, si incomprehensibile comprehendit esse quod quaerit, nisi quia cessandum non est, quamdiu in ipsa incomprehensibilium rerum inquisitione proficitur, et *melior meliorque fit* quaerens tam magnum bonum, quod et inveniendum quaeritur, et quaerendum invenitur. Nam et quaeritur ut inveniatur dulcius, et invenitur ut quaeritur avidius.

Unless, even once one has found it, it still must be sought? But this is how one must seek incomprehensible things, such that he who could find how incomprehensible is what he was seeking does not imagine himself to have found nothing. Why then seek in this way, if one understands that what one is seeking remains incomprehensible? If not because one must not stop [seeking] as long as one is advancing in the search for incomprehensible things and as long as *one is becoming ever better* from the fact of seeking so great a good, that one is seeking to find it, but that one finds it also in order to seek it still. That is, one seeks it so as to find it with all the more sweetness just as one finds it so as to seek it more ardently. (*De Trinitate* XV, 2, 2, 16, 422)

In this case the seeker comes after what he is seeking, which therefore precedes him; therefore, he can only find it. But as the sought-for infinitely precedes the seeker, the latter can only seek it forever without end, all the more so as he never ceases to find it. Between seeking and finding, the relation is reversed as a consequence of the reversal of the relation between receiving and asking. If I receive before being able to ask, then I will find before finishing the seeking. And as I am (myself, *ego*) that which I seek (the *self's* place), since I am what I love, it follows that I will never cease coming to the *self's* place, to the degree that I bury myself in the incomprehensible into whose image I understand myself. There where I find God, all the more as I continue to seek him, I find myself all the more myself as I never cease to seek that of which I bear the image. In the self's place there is not a shape of consciousness, nor a type of *subjectum*, but that unto which the self is like and refers.

Notes

1. This silent retranslation of Augustinian thought into the language of metaphysics when one translates from Latin to French never appears so clearly as in the case of the name of God, such as I analyze it in Chapter 7.

THE APORIA OF SAINT AUGUSTINE

1. Péguy seems to have commented on this passage literally: "But what is proper to confession, to which it is becoming evident I am inclined, is to show willingly invisible sites and to say above all what should be kept silent. On the other hand, it is certain that there is not reality, without confession, and that once one has tasted of the reality of confession, all other reality, every other attempt appears just literary. And even false, fake. Since so incomplete" (*Victor-Marie, comte Hugo*, ed. R. Burac, *Œuvres en prose complètes* [Paris, 1992], 3:165).

2. There are, of course, many others, including H. Arendt, *Liebesbegriff bei Augustin: Versuch einer philosophischern Interpretation* (Berlin, 1929) [*Love and Saint Augustine* (Chicago, 1996)]; H. Jonas, *Augustin und das paulinische Freiheitsproblem* (Göttingen, 1930); K. Jaspers, *Augustinus* (Munich, 1976) [*Plato and Augustine*, in *The Great Philosophers*, vol. 1 (San Diego, 1962)]; P. Ricoeur, *Temps et récit*, vols. 1 and 3 (Paris, 1983 and 1985) [*Time and Narrative*, vols. 1 and 3 (Chicago, 1984 and 1988)]; J. Derrida, *Circumfession* (Paris, 1991) [in *Jacques Derrida: Circumfession* (Chicago, 1993)]; J.-F. Lyotard, *La confession d'Augustin* (Paris, 1998) [*The Confession of Augustine* (Stanford, 2000)]. See also E. Stump and N. Kretz, eds., *The Cambridge Companion to Augustine* (Cambridge, 2001); and G. B. Matthews, ed., *The Augustinian Tradition* (Berkeley, 1999).

3. E. Gilson, *Introduction à l'étude de saint Augustin* (Paris, 1928), vii.

4. Confronting the mass of a *corpus* that surpasses by a large margin even that of Husserl and makes Saint Thomas appear to practice a form of shorthand, we should not, or rarely—as is ordinarily the case, for example, for many of the Greek Fathers and Saint Bernard—remove the supposedly apocryphal texts but *add* them: for example, the *Sermons* reattributed by F. Dolbeau (*Augustin*

d'Hippone: Vingt-six sermons au peuple d'Afrique (Paris, 1996); and the *Letters* recovered by J. Divjak (*Epistulae ex duobus codicibus nuper in lucem prolatae*, in *Corpus Scriptorum Ecclesiasticorum Latinorum* [hereafter *CSEL*], vol. 88 [Vienna, 1981]); then *Letters 1*-29** (Paris, 1987).

5. See Peter Brown, *Augustine of Hippo: A Biography* (Berkeley, 1967¹, 2000²).

6. See P. Courcelle, *Recherches sur les "Confessiones" de saint Augustin* (Paris, 1950¹, 1968²); following P. Henry, *La vision d'Ostie: Sa place dans la vie et l'œuvre d'Augustin* (Paris, 1938); and, of course, the works of P. Hadot. Along the same lines, one should not neglect the new working tools provided by computer technology; see, e.g., R. H. Cooper, L. Ferrari, P. Ruddock, and J. R. Smith, *Concordantia in libros XIII Confessionum S. Aurelii Augustini* (based on the text of the Skutella edition, 1969) (Hildesheim, 1991); or G. Vigini, *Le Confessioni di Sant'Augustino*, vol. 3, *Indice* (Milan, 1994). But the edition of *Confessions* annotated by J. J. O'Donnell, whose commentary based on these automated results is now indispensable, does not escape the common problems of some debatable theological decisions in the more recent works; see *Augustine: Confessions*, 3 vols., text and commentary by J. J. O'Donnell (Oxford, 1992). The rule holds for St. Augustine, as for all other major authors, but no doubt even more in his case: nothing can dispense with digitized lexicology, but this decides nothing, except negatively.

7. I am following here the position of E. von Ivanka, *Plato Christianus: Übernahme und Umgestaltung des Platonismus durch die Väter* (Einsiedeln, 1964).

8. So long as one has not gone back from Saint Augustine's conceptual argument to the exegesis of the biblical verse or verses that support it—in other words, so long as one has not gone back to the *Enarrationes in Psalmos* and the other scriptural commentaries—the interpretation lacks solid ground. This was demonstrated, through very different means but in an exceptionally clear way, by A.-M. Bonnardière (for example, *Biblia augustiniana: Le livre de la Sagesse* [Paris, 1960]; and, under his direction, *Saint Augustin et la Bible* [Paris, 1986]); and J.-L. Chrétien, *Saint Augustin et les actes de parole* (Paris, 2002).

9. An excellent confirmation *a contrario* of this is found in E. R. Dodds, "Augustine's *Confessions*: A Study of Spiritual Maladjustment," *Hibbert Journal* 26 (1927–28): 459–73, which is inexplicably reprinted in *The Hunger of the Heart: Reflections on the "Confessiones" of Augustine*, ed. D. Capps and J. E. Dittes (West Lafayette, IN, 1990). His unfailing intelligence, which is equaled only by the profound vulgarity of his interpretation, a vulgarity elevated by the thoroughly Oxonian offhandedness of this erudite Hellenist (from Birmingham), rehearses the vexing list of all the misreadings that are to be overcome—beginning with the assessment of this text as a *moribund masterpiece*; the text has, however, survived its reader. See a trenchant refutation by Paul J. Archambault, "Augustine's *Confessions*: The Use and the Limits of Psychobiography," in *Collecteana Augustiniana: Augustine: "Second Founder of the Faith,"* ed. J. C. Schnaubelt and F. Van Fleteren (New York, 1990), 83–99.

10. *Lettre sur divers sujets concernant la religion et la métaphysique: Lettre IV, sur l'idée de l'infini et sur la liberté de Dieu de créer ou ne pas créer*, in *Œuvres*, ed. J. Le Brun (Paris, 1997), 2:785. For once, Arnauld would have approved, who used to define Saint Augustine as "accerrimi vir ingenii, nec in Theologia modo, sed etiam in Philosophicis rebus plane mirandus" (a man of the sharpest intellect and a remarkable thinker, not only on theological matters but also on philosophical ones) (*Œuvres de Descartes*, edited by Charles Adam and Paul Tannery, 11 vols. [Paris, 1983], VII, 197 [hereafter AT]; English trans. in *The Philosophical Writings of Descartes* 2:139).

11. See Chapter 2, §9 below.

12. K. Flasch, in his otherwise excellent collection, *Was ist Zeit? Augustinus von Hippo: Das XI Buch der "Confessiones": Historisch-philosophisch Studie. Text-Über-setzung-Kommentar* (Frankfurt, 1993), provides the best example, which summarizes and discusses all the previous ones, including J.-T. Desanti, *Réflexions sur le temps (Variations philosophiques I)* (Paris, 1992); and F.-W. von Hermann, *Augustinus und die phänomenologische Frage nach der Zeit* (Frankfurt, 1992).

13. See, e.g., G. Wills, *Saint Augustine's Memory* (New York, 2002).

14. A text privileged by Wittgenstein, *Philosophische Untersuchungen*, vol. 1, §1, *Werkausgabe* (Frankfurt, 1984 [English trans., 2e]). See the critique of M. F. Burnyeat, "Wittgenstein and Augustine *De Magistro*," in *The Augustinian Tradition*, ed. G. B. Matthews (Berkeley, 1999), 286–303. See also, more generally, B. D. Jackson, "The Theory of Signs in St. Augustine's *De doctrina christiana*," *Revue des études augustiniennes* 15 (1969): 9–49.

15. See the *Analecta Hebdomadae Augustinianae-Thomisticae* (Turin-Rome, 1931) for all articles and p. 224 for the last citation.

16. *De civitate Dei* VIII, 1, 34, 230. See "Ipsi eis erant philosophi, hoc est amatores sapientiae . . . non secundum homines, sed secundum Deum" (There were among them the philosophers, that is to say those who love wisdom . . . not according to men, but according to God) (XVIII, 41, 36, 628). And "Obsecro te, non sit honestior philosophia Gentium quam nostra, Christiana, quae una est vera philosophia, quandoquidem studium vel amor sapientiae significatur hoc nomine" (I beg you, do not honor the philosophy of the pagans more than ours, Christian, which is the sole true philosophy, inasmuch as one intends by this name the study or love of wisdom) (*Contra Julianum* IV, 14, 72, *PL* 44, 774). See "una verissima philosophiae disciplina. Non enim est ista hujus mundi philosophia, quam sacra nostra meritissime detestantur, sed alterius intelligibilis" (a most true teaching of philosophy. Not of the philosophy of this world, that our holy mysteries rightly detest, but that of another intelligible world) (*Contra academicos* III, 19, 42, 4, 198). And "Nam ne quid, mater, ignores hoc graecum verbum, qui 'philosophia' nominateur, latine 'amor sapientiae' dicitur. Unde etiam divinae Scripturae, quas vehementer amplecteris, non omnino philosophos, sed

philosophos hujusmundi evitandos atque irridendos esse praecipiunt" (To omit nothing, know, mother, that the Greek word that names "philosophy" is said in Latin "amor sapientiae" [love of wisdom]. From which it comes that the holy scriptures that you espouse so strongly, do not demand absolute avoidance and condemnation of the philosophers but only of the philosophers of this world) (*De ordine* I, 11, 32, 4, 356). This radical formulation will still be admitted for a long time after Augustine, by Abelard ("principibus hujus philosophiae christianae tam in veteri quam in novo populo studia sunt exorta" [*Sermon* 33, *PL* 178, 585]), as well as by Saint Bernard ("in christiana utique philosophia" [*De consideratione* III, 4, 15, *PL* 182, 767]); and this will be so at least until Erasmus.

17. F. Van Steenberghen, introduction to *Bibliothèque augustinienne* (Paris, 1949), 1:28–29 (my emphasis), but this is in fact *against* what he holds as *common*.

18. This passage, from *De civitate Dei* VIII, 1, 34, 230, echoes a definition of *sapientia* offered by Cicero: "Sapientia esse rerum divinarum et humanarum scientiam cognitionemque" (*Tusculanes* IV, 26, 57, ed. J. E. King [Cambridge, MA, (1927[1]), 1996[8]], 392); and "Illa autem sapientia, quae principem dixi, rerum est divinarum et humanarum scientia, in qua continetur deorum et hominum communitas et societas inter ipsos" (*De officiis* I, 43, 153, ed. W. Miller [Cambridge, MA, 1911[1], 1975[10]], 156, or ibid., II, 2, 5, 172). The standard list was established by G. Madec, *Saint Augustin et la philosophie* (Paris, 1996), in particular chapter 2, which, in what is essential, I am following.

19. On the contrasting senses of theology as *metaphysica specialis* in opposition to the *theologia* of Revelation see my own brief considerations in "Théo-logique," in *Encyclopédie philosophique*, vol. 1, *L'univers philosophiques* (Paris, 1989); and in Jean-Luc Marion, *Etant donné: Essai d'une phénoménologie de la donation* (Paris, 1996[1], 2005[3]), 104 (English trans., 71); as well as Olivier Boulnois, *Duns Scot: La rigueur de la charité* (Paris, 1998), chap. 3. For a more encompassing history of the constitution of metaphysics in *metaphysica generalis* and *metaphysica specialis* (including *theologia rationalis*) see Jean-Luc Marion, *On Descartes' Metaphysical Prism* (Chicago, 1999), chap. 1; and the collection of J.-F. Courtine, *Suarez et le système de la métaphysique* (Paris, 1990), based on the works of H. Reiner, "Die Enstehung und ursprüngliche Bedeutung des Namens Metaphysik," in *Zeitschrift für philosophische Forschung* (1954); and E. Vollrath, "Die Gliederung der Metaphysik in eine *Metaphysicis generalis* und eine *Metaphysica specialis*," in *Zeitschrift für philosophische Forschung* (1962); then *Die These der Metaphysik. Zur Gestalt der Metaphysik bei Aristoteles, Kant, und Hegel* (Wuppertal, 1969). I broached the Heideggerian background of this question in my *God Without Being* (Chicago, 1991), chaps. 2 and 3.

20. Varro, *Antiquitatem rerum humanarum et divinarum libri I–II*, I, frags. 10, 14, 23, 28, and 29 (ed. A. G. Condemi (Bologna, 1965), 9, 10, 14, 16, and 17, reproducing *De civitate Dei* VIII, 1; VII, 6; VI, 5; and VI, 6). Even the formulation "[theologia] naturali, quae philosophorum est" (*De civitate Dei* VI, 8, 2, 34, 86)

refers to the discourse on divinity based on nature, that is to say cosmology, such as Varro understands it and obviously does not in any way whatsoever anticipate *metaphysica specialis* (against what G. Madec leads us to believe in *Saint Augustin et la philosophie* [15]).

21. This point was strongly emphasized by J. Ratzinger, among others, in "Vérité du christianisme?" in *Christianisme. Héritages et destins*, ed. C. Michon (Paris, 2002), 306ff.

22. Let me mention, for posterity, that there is no dearth of "professional" theologians who grant only reluctantly the title of theologian (if only amateur) to Saint Augustine:

> Consequently, the word that is appropriate to characterizing his work is less *science* or *theology* than "*wisdom*." From the viewpoint of *technique*, Augustine was surpassed in the Middle Ages and still more in our times. But one cannot say as much of the religious sense, of this loving contemplation of the divine truth, of this *wisdom*, in a word, for which his work remains an inexhaustible source.
>
> This simple remark allows us to answer an objection that one sometimes hears. After the systematizations elaborated by the great scholastics, is it not *backwards* to favor a reading of the Fathers, even if it is Saint Augustine? Their writings, so interesting for history, wouldn't they be *regressive* for thought? . . . If the Fathers had for providential mission to establish faith on its revealed bases, the *theologians* had that of fixing its *metaphysical* bases and frames: speculative theology, direct inheritance of scholasticism, constitutes an *immense progress* over the ancient methods. It is necessary, however, to acknowledge in the latter a merit that scholasticism, in its very effort at necessary abstraction, was obliged to neglect *a little bit*: direct contact with *life*. (F. Cayré, introduction to *Bibliothèque augustiniennes* [Paris, 1949], 1:12–13 [my emphasis])

Each word would deserve a lengthy commentary, so marked is it by arrogance, blindness, and deep theological unintelligence.

23. Gilson, *Introduction à l'étude de saint Augustin*, 9.

24. K. Jaspers: "Man sagt wohl, ob Augustinus Philosoph oder Theologe sei. Solche Scheidung gilt für uns nicht. Er ist noch beides in einem, eines nicht ohne das andere" (*Augustinus*, 63–64 [English trans., 101]).

25. Madec, *Saint Augustin et la philosophie*, 15.

26. Gilson, *Introduction à l'étude de saint Augustin*, 41n2 (English trans., 9).

27. Martin Heidegger, *Der Begriff der Zeit* (1924), in *Gesamtausgabe* [hereafter *GA*] (Frankfurt, 1975–), 64:108.

CHAPTER 1

1. *Commentaries on the Psalms* 75, 14, *PL* 36, 965. This verse comes from Psalm 146:7, translated by the Vulgate "Canite Domino in confessione." It is also interpreted by the *Commentary on the First Epistle of John* IV, 3, *PL* 35, 2006, but solely in the sense of *confessio peccatorum*.

2. *Commentaries on the Psalms* 144, 13, *PL* 37, 1878—with the anticipation of a more detailed demonstration in §4 below.

3. Sticking with the Vulgate, this citation combines Psalm 47:2: "Magnus Dominus et laudabilis nimis"; Psalm 95:4: "quia magnus Dominus et laudabilis nimis et magnitudinis ejus non est finis"; and Psalm 144:3: "Magnus Deus et laudabilis nimis."

4. In other words the hermeneutic "as" depends on a more originary "as," which will not however be qualified here as existential or phenomenological but spiritual—unless one supposes that phenomenology, in its depths, can itself become a matter of spirituality (this will be the wager of Chapter 3 below).

5. *Commentaries on the Psalms* 47, 2, *PL* 36, 533. See the confirmation that follows: "Quid est hoc? 'Magnus Dominus et laudabilis valde, in civitate Dei nostri, in monte sancto ejus'; nec potest esse laus ejus, nisi in sanctis ejus. Nam qui male vivunt, non eum laudant; sed etsi praedicant lingua, blasphemunt vita" (What is this? "Great is the Lord and eminently worthy of praise, in the city of our God, on the holy mountain!" There cannot be praise for him, except among his saints. For whoever lives wickedly does not praise him; even if you preach him with your language, you blaspheme him by your life) (ibid., 10, *PL* 36, 540).

6. On this essential rule see below, Chapter 6, §41, p. 263.

7. Wittgenstein, *Zettel*, §717 (see *Werkausgabe* 8:443 [English trans., 124e (modified)]).

8. In this the Fathers, Greek as well as Latin, who write treatises *De Trinitate* (Cyprian, Hilary), *De carne Christi* (Tertullian), *De mysteriis* (Hilary, Ambrose), *De sacramentis* (Ambrose), περί ἀρχῶν (Origen), περί ἁγίου πνευμάτος (Basil), περί ἀνθρωποσέως τὸν Λόγου (Athanasius), etc., repeat, in a certain fashion, the theoretic posture of the Greek philosophers. This was not always the case, however, since the apostolic and even apologetic Fathers practiced either preaching (toward actual or potential believers) or apology (toward the pagans) and thus addressed themselves *to* (men, to be sure, more often than *to* God) more so than they spoke *about* (God). No doubt, in other places, Saint Augustine practiced the word *about*, but always and fundamentally starting from the word *to*, as should be proven sufficiently by the eminent role of the prayers, confessions, and invocations in all these apparently theoretic texts.

9. This predication also implies the primacy of the theoretical use of language over its pragmatic use, however more original and comprehensive, in conformity with the phenomenologically inevitable sway of *Vorhandenheit* over *Zuhandenheit*.

10. S. Poque points this out quite clearly: "The XIII books of the *Confessions*, we know, were not formally addressed by their author to possible and foreseeable readers, but to God alone. Now, since from the first to the thirteenth book, Augustine addresses himself to God, one will perhaps find some interest in seeing the terms of these invocations highlighted" ("L'invocation de Dieu dans les *Confessions*," in *Collecteana Augustiniana Mélanges T. J. van Bavel*, ed. B. Bruning, M. Lamberigts, and J. van Houtem [Leuven, 1990], 927–35). Along the same lines J. J. Goux evokes an "absolute vocative": "Augustine explicitly does not address me; he has turned his face toward the unknown. He speaks to someone and on behalf of someone that I do not see" (*Tel Quel*, 21 [Paris, 1965], 67–68). It has been noted that of the 453 paragraphs of the *Confessiones*, 381 include addresses to God and more than 500 invocations to God (in particular in books I and IX). This has not prevented some from seeing nothing: "Such a God Neoplatonism could not provide. Plotinus never *gossiped* with the One, as Augustine *gossips* in the *Confessiones*" (Dodds, "Augustine's *Confessions*: A Study of Spiritual Maladjustment," 471). Noting some obvious points would have made it possible to avoid the vulgarity of this supposedly *British* spirit: first, that praising and confessing are by no means gossip, except for one who does not practice them and has no idea what they mean; next, that one can by definition no more speak *to* the One than play music and dance before the god *causa sui* of metaphysics (Heidegger, *Identität und Differenz*, *GA* 11:77 [English trans., 72]).

11. *Confessiones* I, 1, 1, 13, 272. We find moreover exactly the same situation in the very last words of the *Confessiones*, which cite, in the form of praise, Matthew 7:8: "a te petatur, in te quaeratur, ad te pulsetur: sic, sic 'accipietur, sic invenietur, sic aperietur'" (Let it be asked of you, let it be sought in you, let it be knocked for on your door: so, so [alone] "will it be received, found, opened") (XIII, 38, 53, 14, 524; the Vulgate reads, "Omnis enim qui petit accipit, et qui quaerit invenit et pulsanti aperietur"). Even more: citation thus does what it says, since it manifests precisely the anteriority of the word of the invoked to that of the one invoking, who does nothing more than repeat it and ends up saying what he was seeking. In repeating the biblical text, the confessant proves the fact that it suffices to ask to find, to knock to make open—all was *already* there, *already* available. Again it was necessary that the latecomer perceive himself from the gift already given because given in advance—"Sero te amavi, pulchritudo tam antiqua et tam nova" (Late did I love you, beauty so ancient and so new) (X, 27, 38, 14, 208).

12. *Commentaries on the Psalms* 26, 2, 1, *PL 36*, 199. Another version of the same argument: "Ergo 'In Deo laudabo sermones meos'; si 'in Deo,' quare 'meos'? Et 'in Deo,' et 'meos.' 'In Deo' quia ab ipso; 'meos' quia accepi. Ipse voluit meos esse qui dedit, amando eum cujus sunt; quia ex illo mihi sunt, mei facti sunt" (Therefore "In God I will praise my words"; but if it is "in God," why say "mine"? In fact, they are as much "in God" as "mine." "In god" because they come from

him; "mine" because I received them. He Himself, who gave them to me, wanted that they be mine, in loving him to whom they were given; because they came from him to me, they have become mine) (*Commentaries on the Psalms* 55, 7, *PL* 36, 651).

13. *Confessiones* I, 1, 1, 13, 274 (my emphasis). The entirety of this text should in fact be read as a commentary on the celebrated verse of Psalm 21:27, which it cites: "'Quomodo autem invocabunt, in quem non crediderunt? Aut quomodo credunt sine *praedicante*'" ("How will they invoke him in whom they will not have believed? Or how will they believe without anybody who preaches to them, *saying it to them in advance*?") (ibid.). Not only does this text say that every word that is sayable *to* God comes from the originary word said *by* God, but it says it by citing this very word, which says that every word that is mine (invoking, believing) is a citation (of he who *pre*-dicts or speaks *in advance*), such that what is said coincides absolutely with the means of saying it. One can compare this with *Sermon* 59, 1, 1: "Missi sunt ergo *prae*dicatores, *prae*dicaverunt Christum. Illis *prae*dicantibus populi audierunt, audiendo crediderunt, credendo invocarunt. Quia ergo rectissime et verissime dictum est 'Quomodo invocabunt, in quem non crediderunt,' ideo *prius* didicistis eum invocare, in quem credidistis" (Some were sent who *pre*-dicted and preached Christ. These *pre*-dictors, speaking *in advance*, the people heard; having heard them, they believed; in believing, they invoked. Therefore because it was said truly and rightly: "How will they invoke he in whom they will not have believed?" you therefore *first* learned to invoke he in whom you believed) (*PL* 38, 387). Or *De libero arbitrio* II, 2, 6: "Nisi enim et aliud esset credere, aliud intelligere et *primo* credendum esset quod magnum et divinum intelligere cuperemus, frustra *propheta* dixisset 'Nisi credideritis, non intelligetis.' . . . *Jam* credentibus dicit 'Quaerite et invenieritis,' nam neque inventum dici potest quod incognitum creditur, neque quisquam inveniendo Deo fit idoneus, nisi *ante* crediderit quod est *postea* cogniturus" (For if believing and comprehending were not two different things, and if it was not necessary *first* to believe what we desire to comprehend of the great and the divine, the *pro*phet would have said in vain: "If you do not believe, you will not understand" [Isaiah 7:9, according to the Septuagint]. . . . To the people who *already* believed, he says: "Ask and you will receive" [Matthew 7, 8], for one cannot call received what one believes without knowing it, any more than one can become apt to receive God, if one does not *first* believe what is *then* known) (*BA* 6, 216–18).

14. J.-F. Lyotard: "In true sacrifice, the confession gives back to him who first gave and gives forever" (on *Confessions* V, 1 [in Lyotard, *The Confession of Augustine*, 26]).

15. And if "the Psalmic text itself becomes . . . Augustinian text," then "one could almost go so far as to say that the *Confessions* are an immense psalm seeded throughout with the theses of the rhetorician" (P. Cambronne, notes to his

translation, in *Les Confessions précédées de dialogues philosophiques*, in *Œuvres I* [Paris, 1998], 1370). It is not a matter of theses, however, but of responses to the Psalms themselves, written to be sure by a rhetorician, but one who would think like a theologian. In other words, "Totus ergo textus psalmi est oratio" (The entire text of the psalm is therefore a prayer) (*Commentaries on the Psalms* 5, 18, *PL* 36, 89)—and reciprocally, every prayer could indeed come down to a reprise of a psalm or the Psalms.

16. *Soliloquia* I, 1, 1, *BA* 5, 24. To be sure, Saint Augustine makes no mistake about the question of the necessary mediations by which the word of the originary call comes over me: either by syllables or by private revelation or by another corporeal mode. But in all cases God spoke: "Quid ergo ex his omnibus factum sit, ad liquidum comprehendere non valeamus, verum tamen certissime tenamus et dixisse hoc Deum" (Of all these hypotheses we might not be able to say clearly which one is the case, but nevertheless let us hold it most certain that it is God who said this word) (*De Genesi ad litteram* IX, 2, 3, *BA* 49, 94).

17. K. Kienzler, in "Der Aufbau der *Confessiones* des Augustinus im Spiegel der Bibelzitate," *Recherches augustiniennes* 24 (1989), showed convincingly that the biblical citations not only ground Augustine's speech but also secure the unity of all the books in one single whole; see also G. Knauer, *Psalmenzitate in Augustinus Konfessionem* (Göttingen, 1955).

18. See other examples of such a *precedence* of the call in terms of mercy: "'Misericordia mea,' quid est? Totum quidquid sum, de misericordia tua est. Sed promerui invocando te? Ut essem, quid feci? Ut essem, qui invocarem, quid egi? Si enim egi aliquid ut essem, jam eram antequam essem. Porro, si omnino nihil eram antequam essem, nihil te promerui ut essem" ("[God] my mercy," what is that? [That means] all that I am, whatever it might be, it comes from your mercy. But did I not win a merit in advance by invoking you? But what did I do, to be? To be he who invokes you, what act did I do? For if I did some act, any act whatsoever, in order to be, I was before being. What is more, if I most absolutely was not before being, I merited nothing in advance of you in order to be) (*Commentaries on the Psalms* 58, 2, 11, *PL* 36, 713). Likewise: "*Praecedit* enim bona voluntas hominis multa Dei dona, sed non omnia: quae autem *non praecedit ipsa*, in eis est *et ipsa*, nam utrumque legitur in sanctis eloquiis, et 'Misericordia ejus praeveniet me,' et 'Misericordia ejus subsequitur me.' Nolentem *praevenit* et velit, volentem sequitur ne frustra velit" (The goodwill of man *comes before* many gifts of God, but not all, and among those that *it does not precede* is *itself*. For we read these two things in holy scriptures: "My mercy *will precede* you" [Psalm 22:6] and "His mercy will follow" [Psalm 22:6]. It *precedes* he who does not will and he wills; it follows he who wills and he does not will in vain) (*Enchiridion* IX, 32, *BA* 9, 162).

19. See also: "*Veritas*, ubique *prae*sides omnibus consulentibus te simulque responnes omnibus. . . . Liquide tu respondes, sed non liquide omnes audiunt"

(Truth, you *pre*side everywhere for all those who consult you and at the same time you answer all. . . . You answer clearly, but all do not hear clearly) (*Confessiones* X, 26, 37, 14, 206). "Coepisti, ut desinamus esse miseri in nobis et beatificemur in te, quoniam *vocasti* nos" (You began in such a way that we might not be unhappy in ourselves and become happy in you, since you *called* us) (*Confessiones* XI, 1, 1, 14, 270); "Ecce *vox* tua gaudium meum, *vox* tua super affluentiam voluptatum. Da quod amo, amo enim et hoc tu dedisti" (See, your *voice* is my joy, your *voice* above the rising flood of pleasures. Give what I love, for I do love. And it is you who gave it to me to love) (*Confessiones* XI, 2, 3, 14, 274).

20. On this decisive point see the excellent observations of F. J. Crosson in his "Structure and Meaning in St. Augustine's *Confessions*," in *The Augustinian Tradition*, ed. G. B. Mathews, 27–38 (Berkeley, 1999). Crosson emphasizes that *here* par excellence Augustine is taken to task by the anterior word of God and verifies in his own case the general status of the *confessio*.

21. This "Nescio" corresponds exactly to that of the *Soliloquia* I, 1, 1, *BA* 5, 24. For the *Soliloquia* do not in any way unfold the solipsistic soliloquy of a mind speaking to itself (according to an almost universally common misreading), but strive to regain and reopen, starting from an ego encapsulated in itself, the space—first anonymous and undecided—of the call and response, of my word received and rendered to the Word. The *Confessiones* explore this restoration more deeply by grounding it on the resaying of the scriptures by my own word, then reappropriated to itself.

22. The fact that Saint Augustine here repeats the move of St. Anthony during his conversion, judging that what he read was said specifically about him ("tanquam sibi diceretur quod legebatur"), and that, just as significantly, Alypius, reading a little while later the following verse (Romans 14:1), would immediately take it as a call specifically for him: "'Infirmum autem in fide recipite.' Quod ille ad se retulit" (ibid.), far from diminishing the authenticity of the tale, reinforces it, by manifesting the permanence of the rules of the singular logic of confession, followed to the letter even in individual conversions.

23. On this point see the essential article by J. Ratzinger, "Originalität und Überlieferung in Augustinus Begriff der *Confessio*," *Revue des études augustiniennes* 3 (1957): 375–92, whose results are taken up by A. Solignac in the introduction to the *Confessiones* (*BA* 13, 9ff.). See also the analysis of J.-L. Chrétien: "The word *confessio* refers to speech acts that are at once distinct and inseparable: confession of faith, confession of sins, confession of praise. But before describing them and thinking about them, it is important to measure the unique scope of *confessio*, which, in a sense, is not numbered among the other speech acts. . . . In effect, confession, before being a word of faith that could be distinguished from others and compared with others, forms the *very opening of the dimension* in which the words of faith become possible. . . . Confession is in effect

nothing other than the human response to the call of God" (Chrétien, *Saint Augustin et les actes de parole*, 121–22).

24. Pseudo-Quintillian: "Ego . . . confessionem existimo qualemcumque contra se pronuntiationem. . . . Immo ea natura est nobis confessionis, ut possit videri demens qui de se confitetur. Furore impulsus est: alius ebrietate, alius errore, alius dolore, quidam quaestione. Nemo contra se dicit, nisi aliquo cogente" (*Declamationes*, 204, ed. C. Ritter [Leipzig, 1884], 122–234).

25. Cicero: "O patrem sapientem! Qui quod praemii solet esse in judicio reliquerit, quod turpitudinis in confessione, id per accusationem filii susceperit" (*Opera*, ed. J. G. Baiter and C. L. Kayer, vol. 4 [Leipzig, 1862], 330).

26. Tertullian: "Christiani vero quid tale consequuntur? Neminem pudet, neminem poenitet, nisi tantum pristinorum. Si denotatur, gloriatur; si trahitur, non subsistit. Si accusatur, non defendit; interrogatus, confitetur; damnatus gloriatur. Quod hoc malum est, in quo mali natura cessat? In quo ipsi etiam contra formam judicandorum malorum judicatis. Nam nocentes quidem perductos, si admissum negent, tormentis urgetis ad confessionem. Christianos vero sponte confessos tormentis comprimitis ad negationem" (*Ad Nationes* I, 1–2, *PL* 1, 630). Saint Augustine appears to remember this paradoxical argument: "Torqueantur christiani, donec negent quod christiani. Cum antea solerent confessi percuti, ad hoc postea torqueantur ut negarent; et cum omnis reus tamdiu torquebatur, quamdiu neget, christianorum confessio torquebatur, negatio dimittebat" (Whereas beforehand one struck them because of what they had confessed, later they were tortured on account of denying it; and as one tortures the guilty as long as he denies it, one used to torture the confession of Christians and relent upon their denegation) (*Commentaries on the Psalms* 90, 2, 2, *PL* 37, 1161).

27. Tertullian: "Is actus, qui magis graeco vocabulo exprimitur et frequentatur ἐξομολόγησις est, qua dilectum Domino nostrum confitemur, non quidem ut ignaro, sed quatenus satisfactio confessione disponetur, confessione poenitentia nascitur, poenitentia Deus mitigatur. Itaque ἐξομολόγησις prosternandi et humilificandi hominis disciplina est, conversationem injugens, misericordiae illicum" (*De poenitentia* IX, 2, *PL* 1, 1354).

28. For example in Matthew 11:25, Luke 10:21, Acts 19:18, and Romans 14:11 and 15:9, orchestrating among others 1 Timothy 6:12: "confessus es bonam confessionem (ἐξομολόγησας τὴν καλὴν ὁμολογίαν) coram multis testibus. Praecipio tibi coram Deo, qui vivificat omnia, et Christo Jesu, qui testimonium reddidit sub Pontio Pilato bonam confessionem (καλὴν ὁμολογίαν) ut serves mandatum sine macula irreprehensibile usque in adventum Domini nostri Jesu Christi."

29. Following Matthew 3:6 or Mark 1:5 and John 5:16. Origen: "Confession ἐξομολόγησις means the act of giving thanks and praise. It even covers the confession of faults" (*In Psalmos* 135, 2, *PG* 12, 1653–55). And Saint Jerome, commenting on Psalm 34:18, "Confiteor tibi in ecclesia magna," emphasizes that

"confessioque in hoc loco non pro paenitentia, sed pro gloria et laude accipitur" (*Letter 75*—to Augustine, *PL* 24, 395).

30. Hilary of Poitiers, meditating "Confiteantur tibi populi, confiteantur tibi populi omne": "Invenimus enim confessionem *duplici ratione* esse tractandam: esse unam confessionem peccatorum, ubi in deserto Iordanis confitebantur peccata sua; esse etiam laudationis Dei, ubi Dominus loquitur ad Patrem 'Confiteor tibi Domine, Pater.' Prima ergo illa et superior confessio peccatorum esse credenda est, maxime quae praedicationi propheticae atque apostolicae connectitur; sequens haec laudationis Dei intelligenda est populorum, deinde omnium, i.e. gentium" (*In Psalmos*, 66, 6, *CSEL* 22 [Vienna, 1891], 273ff.). See also his commentary on Psalm 6:6, "In inferno autem, quis confitebitur tibi?": "Confessioque in hoc loco non pro paenitentia, sed pro gloria et laude accipitur" (*In Isaiam prophetam* 11, 39, *PL* 24, 409).

31. See also: "Multis autem jam locis sanctarum scripturarum insinuavimus *confessionem* etiam pro laude poni" (We suppose that in many passages of the scriptures *confession* is also used for praise) (*Commentaries on the Psalms* 78, 17, *PL* 36, 1020). Or else: "In aeternum laudabo te, quia diximus esse confessionem et in laudibus, non tantum in peccatis. Confiteor ergo modo quod tu fecisti in Deum, et confitiberis quid tibi fecerit Deus. Quid fecisti? Peccata. Quid Deus? Confitenti iniquitatem tuam dimitti peccata tua, ut ei postea laudes ipsius confidens in aeternum, non compungaris peccato" (I will praise you eternally because, we said, there is a confession in praises, not only in sins. Confess then only what you have done toward God and you are confessing what God did for you. What have you yourself done? Sins. And God [what has he done]? He has remitted your sins because you would confess your injustice, so that next you praise him eternally with perfect confidence instead of fighting against him with your sin) (*Commentaries on the Psalms* 29, 22, *PL* 36, 226). And also: "Confitemur ergo sive laudantes Deum, sive accusantes nos ipsos. Pia est utroque confessio, sive cum te reprehendis, qui non es sine peccato; sive cum illum laudis, qui non potest habere peccatum" (We confess therefore either by praising God or by accusing ourselves. Both confessions are pious, either when you rebuke yourself, you who are not without sin, or when you praise he who cannot have sin) (*Sermon* 67, 1, *PL* 38, 433). But Saint Augustine needs to highlight the duality of *confessio* all the more as his listeners, conforming to Latin usage, hear it most often as only the admission of sins and ignore the praise in it. There is no shortage of texts that denounce this one-sided view: "Sed prius commemoro vos confessionem in scripturis, cum confitemur Deo, *duobus modis* dici solere, vel peccatorum, vel laudis. Sed confessionem peccatorum omnes noverunt; laudis autem confessionem *pauci* advertunt. Nam ita nota est confessio peccatorum, ut in quocumque scripturarum loco auditum fuerit 'Confitebor tibi Domine,' aut 'Confitebimur tibi,' continuo ad pectus tunendum; usque adeo non solent homines intelligere confessionem esse nisi

peccatorum" (But first I would remind you that confession is used in scriptures in two ways, confession of sins and confession of praise. But, if all know the confession of sins, *few* [among you] know the confession of praise. The confession of sins is so well known that when, in some corner of scriptures, we find "I will confess unto you Lord," or "We will confess you" (Psalm 137:1) at once, owing to this ordinary comprehension, your hands are quick to strike your breast, so habituated are we to conceive confession as of sins" (*Commentaries on the Psalms* 137, 2, *PL* 37, 1174). Or: "*Duobus* autem *modis* confessio intelligitur, et in peccatis nostris et in laude Dei. In peccatis nostris nota est confessio, et ita *nota omni populo,* ut quando auditum fuerit nomen *confessionis* in lectione, sive in laude dicatur sive de peccatis dicatur, currant pugni ad pectus. *Notum* est ergo nomen confessionis de peccato; confessionem in laude quaeramus" (Confession is understood in *two ways,* of our sins, but also of the praise of God. Of our sins, we know confession well, it is even *so well known* by all the people that, when one hears in a reading the word *confession,* whether it concerns praise or sins, the hands rise to the breast. There we know the name of confession of sins, but it is the confession of praise that we seek) (*Commentaries on the Psalms* 141, 19, *PL* 37, 1844). Likewise: "Confessio enim non peccatorum tantum dicitur, sed et laudis; ne forte ubicumque auditis confessionem putetis jam non esse nisi peccati. Usque adeo enim hoc putatur, ut quando sonuerit de divinis eloquis, continuo sit consuetudo pectora tundere. Audi quia est laudis confessio" (Confession is said not only of sins but also of praise, and accordingly you should not think, each time that you hear *confession,* that it is only about sin. For we think this way to such a point, when we hear it in the words of God, we are in the habit of at once striking our breast. Listen, for there is also a confession of praise) (*Commentaries on the Psalms* 144, 13, *PL* 37, 1878). Or finally: "Confessio aut laudantis est, aut poenitenis. Sunt enim *parum eruditi,* qui cum audierint *confessionem* in scripturis, tanquam nisi peccatorum esse no possit, continuo tundunt pectora, velut jam moneantur confiteri peccata" (Confession bears either on praise or sins. They are familiar with just a small thing, those who upon hearing *confession* in the scriptures, as if it concerned only sins, at once strike their breast, as if they had been asked to confess their sins) (*Sermon* 29, 2, *PL* 38, 186).

32. Heidegger said nothing other than this: "Augustine communicates all phenomena [by carrying himself] in the posture of the *confiteri* [to confess], standing within the task of searching and of having God (dass Augustin alle Phänomene mitteilt in der Haltung des *confiteri,* in der Aufgabe des Gott-Suchens und Gott-Habens stehend)" (*Phänomenologie des religiösen Lebens, GA* 60:283 [English trans., 214]). That is equivalent to "sine confessione tamen non simus" (we are never without confession) (*Commentaries on the Psalms* 29, 19, *PL* 36, 225; see p. 29 above).

33. Similarly: "Quomodo ergo distinguis vota quae reddis Deo? Ut illum laudes, te accuses; quia illius est misericordia, ut peccata nostra dimittat. Nam

si vellet pro meritis agere, non inveniret nisi quod damnaret. . . . Quanta ergo illius laus, quanta misericordia, confiteamur, utique laudantes. . . . Confitere itaque peccata tua, quo magis desperabas de te propter iniquitates tuas. Tanto enim major laus est ignoscentis, quanto major exaggeratio peccata confiten-tis" (How do you distinguish the vows that you offer to God? To praise him, accuse yourself; for it is precisely his mercy that remits our sins for us. For if he wanted to act according to the merits, there would only be condemna-tion. . . . Let us confess, therefore, simply by praising, whether it be his praise or his mercy. . . . Confess then all the more your sins as you do not despair of yourself on account of your iniquities. For the praise of him who pardons grows in the measure of the enormity of he who confesses his sins) (*Commentaries on the Psalms* 94, 4, *PL* 37, 1219). In *this* sense confession of sins precedes (in time as well as condition of possibility) the confession of praise, for I cannot praise, I, a sinner, without first acknowledging myself as such, therefore confessing my sins: "Confitere ergo, et invoca: confitendo enim mundas templum quo veniat invocatus. Confitere, et invoca. Avertat faciem a peccatis tuis; non avertat a te; avertat faciem ab eo quod tu ipse fecisti; non avertat ab eo quod ipse fecit. Te enim ipse fecit; peccata tua ipse fecisti. Confitere ergo et invoca" (Confess [sc. your sins] and invoke [sc. praise]. By confessing, you in effect cleanse the temple where he whom you call can arrive. Confess and invoke. Turn your face away from your sins; do not turn it away from yourself. Turn your face away from the sins that you yourself did; do not turn it away from what he himself did. For he himself did it for you, but your self did your own sins. Confess therefore and in-voke) (*Commentaries on the Psalms* 74, 2, *PL* 36, 947). But precisely in the role of condition of possibility, confession of sins is ordered to the confession of praise, as its dark, yet not *a contrario*, narthex.

34. One can only share the harsh diagnosis made by J. J. O'Donnell concern-ing the common rules for the nonreading of the *Confessiones*: choose to ignore all that does not matter to us; be indignant when what is said contradicts what does matter to us; pass over in silence as naive what we deem such; treat with conde-scension what we find interesting but overcome by our modernity (as with time and memory, for example); privilege what confirms our interpretive prejudices; etc. (O'Donnell, *Augustine: Confessions*, vol. 1, *Introduction and Text*, xix).

35. H.-I. Marrou: "Augustine composes poorly" (*Saint Augustin et la fin de la culture antique* [Paris, 1938[1], cited according to the edition of 1958[4]], 61–67, 73–75, with, it is true, a retraction in 1949[2] [665–72]). Marrou was not alone, but was followed by, among others, H. U. von Balthasar in *Augustinus. Bekenntnisse. Nachwort und Anmerkungen* (Frankfurt, 1955), 213n1; M. Pellegrino, *Le Confes-sioni di Sant'Augustino* (Rome, 1956), 130; then by A. Solignac, who (supposing a chronological gap between books I through IX and X through XIII and even an early dissemination of the first) admits only "a unity more *internal* than logical"

(*Introduction à BA* 13 [Paris, 1962], 20, 48, and 53); and by A. M. Kotzé, who considers the first books as an anti-Manichean propaedeutic (*Augustine's "Confessions": Communicative Purpose and Audience* [Leiden, 2004]). On the different arguments in favor of the unity of the *Confessiones* see the elaboration offered by F. Van Fleteren, in A. D. Fitzgerald, ed., *Augustine Through the Ages: An Encyclopedia* (Grand Rapids, 1999).

36. This is insisted upon quite rightly by W. Stiedle, "Augustinus *Confessiones* als Buch," in *Romanitas-Christianitas: Untersuchungen zur Geschichte und Literatur der Römanischen Kaiserzeit. Johannes Staub zum 70. Geburtstag gewidmet*, ed. G. Wirth (Berlin, 1982), 440, finding a strong argument for the unity of the entire *Confessiones*.

37. Is this conclusion invalidated by the absence of a *confessio* in books II, III, VI, and VII? Certainly not; indeed, to the contrary, these books in effect treat the periods of maximum distance from God, where precisely such a *confessio* of praise remains impossible, lacking the least *confessio* of repentance. For sin consists finally more in the negation (or lack of consciousness) of the fault than in the fault itself. And in the place of and instead of *confessio*, these books testify to an obsession with sin, indeed by sin. Thus in the opening of book II, 1, 1: "recordari volo transactas foeditates meas et carnales corruptiones animae meae" (I want to call back to mind the foul doings of my past and the carnal corruptions of my soul) (13, 332). Thus in book III, 1, 1: "Veni Carthaginem, et circumstrebat me undique sartago flagitiosorum amorum" (I came to Carthage and everywhere around me crackled the cauldron of shameful loves) (13, 362). As well as in VI, 1, 1: "Ambulabam per tenebras et lubricum, et quaerebam te foris a me et non inveniebam 'Deum cordis mei'" (I was going through the shadows and across slippery terrain, and I was seeking you outside myself and not finding "the God of my heart") (Psalm 72:26) (13, 514). Or finally VII, 1, 1: "et ibam in juventutem, quanto aetate major, tanto vanitate turpior" (I entered into adulthood, and the more I grew the more vile was I made by my emptiness) (13, 576). In all these cases *confessio* therefore does not mark an exception to its constitutive role but confirms it: it shines by its absence, which the sinner's own blindness to himself alone forbids.

38. Here is a perfect example of a citation of a citation, as highlighted above (see §3).

39. It is achieved, moreover, by a barely modified citation from Matthew 7:7–8: "sic 'sic accipietur, sic invenietur, sic aperitur'" (so, "so shall we receive, so shall we find, so shall the door open") (14, 524). As with the first word of the *Confessiones*, the last consists in a citation of the words of God.

40. Here again there are some exceptions: four books conclude neither with a praise nor a confession. Yet one can in each case make some conjecture as to the reason for this absence. In book II Augustine finds himself in the "regio egestatis" (II, 10, 18, 13, 360), just as, in book III, he reaches the "depths of hell"

(in profunda inferi) of Manicheanism, there where God had shown pity for someone who *had not yet confessed,* "nondum confitentem" (III, 6, 11, 13, 382). In book V, 10, 19, confession appears to be blocked by the skeptical principle that "de omnibus dubitandum est" (13, 498). Finally, how would *confessio* have been possible at the moment of the break with Adeodatus's mother, an unjustified break of a communion, which for that matter leaves him a wreck ("cor ubi adhaerebat, concisum et vulneratum mihi erat et trahebat sanguinem" [VI, 15, 25, 13, 570])? These books are missing a final confession not through negligence or forgetting but because in each case Augustine finds himself in a situation of *not being able* to confess.

41. By arbitrarily choosing the criteria, as K. Grotz shows in *Die Einheit der "Confessiones": Warum bringt Augustinus in den letzten Büchern seiner "Confessiones" eine Auslegung der Genesis?* (Tübinger, 1970), which suggests a good thirty or so hypotheses.

42. *Retractiones* II, 6: "*Confessionum* mearum libri tredecim et de malis et de bonis meis Deum, *laudant* justum et bonum, atque in eum excitant humanum intellectum et *affectum.* Interim, quod ad me adtinet, hoc in me egerunt, cum scriberentur, et agunt cum leguntur. Quid de illis alii sentient, ipsi viderint; multis tamen fratribus eos multum placuisse et placere scio. A primo usque ad decimum *de me* scripsi sunt, in tribus caeteris de Scripturis sanctis ab eo, quod scriptum est 'In principio fecit Deus coelum et terram' usque ad sabbam" (*BA* 12, 460). It should be noted that, of the only two repentings that the author admits, one, the most important, concerns the description of the pain provoked by the loss of a friend: this brilliant paradox (I fear my death because it would make my lost friend die a second time) sins because it does not reach the dignity and the seriousness of a true *confession*: "mihi quasi declamatio levis quam gravis confessio videtur" (ibid.). In short, the *Confessiones* would here be lacking a *confession.*

43. Based on the commentary of the *Retractiones,* G. Bardy concludes that, despite the distinction of parts he finds in the *Confessiones,* "this argument is far from being decisive and it remains more probable that the *Confessiones* constitute a collection redacted from one sole spring" (*BA* 12, 578). A reason for this probability must still be found.

44. The same opening by the same citation appears in I, 1, 1, 13, 272 and XI, 1, 1, 14, 270.

45. *Confessiones,* IV, 4, 9, 13, 422.

46. *Confessiones,* XIII, 22, 32, 14, 482.

47. "The highest unity of the *Confessiones* is in confession." I can do nothing more than subscribe to this thesis from P. L. Landsberg, "La conversion de saint Augustin," *Supplément à la Vie spirituelle* (1936): 33–34.

48. This phrase, if you really think about it, is equivalent to a blasphemy, without speaking of its pragmatic incoherence. In this sense Deleuze's remark that in philosophy one never *dialogues* extends to *theo*logy.

49. G. Misch, all the while seeing the swerve from the third to the second person in order to speak *to* God, maintains, however, against all good sense, that it is an issue of an *auto*biography (*Selbstbiographie*): "In Augustine, there appears for the first time this cultural form known as autobiography, which will blossom in the 18th Century" (*Geschichte der Autobiographie* [Berne, 1907], 3:646, 641). This judgment has been authoritative. J.-M. Leblond follows it: "They [the *Confessiones*] obviously [?] contain an autobiography" (*Les conversions de saint Augustin* [Paris, 1950], 5); P. Courcelle, too, all the while seeing the difficulty: "Augustine deliberately [?] sacrificed the end of his autobiography so as to broach more quickly the more theological matters; he never found the leisure to finish this collection" ("Antécédents autobiographiques des *Confessiones* de saint Augustin," *Revue de philologie* 31 (1957): 23–51; A. Solignac remains in the same straits: "Is this, properly speaking, an autobiography? Most certainly [?] Augustine narrates and wants to narrate his own life. But the question is already posed, does autobiography make up, in Antiquity at least, a sufficiently determined 'genre'" (*BA* 13 [Paris, 1962], 44). One will not be surprised to hear the habitual smugness and triviality of E. R. Dodds: "I invite [the reader] to envisage this book, on the one hand, as the earliest example of a well-defined and very curious literary genre, the introspective autobiography; on the other, as the intimate record of a neurotic conflict. These two aspects are, of course, complementary" ("Augustine's *Confessions*: A Study of Spiritual Maladjustment," 460). As the one is false (no *auto*biography), the second could be too (but one would have to take oneself to be neurotic to decide). One should be surprised, too, to see that more genuine philosophers did not see the problem. For instance, Hannah Arendt: "Although the confession of his life had but little psychological significance for Augustine, it is *nevertheless* the case that he is the forefather of the modern autobiographical and psychological novel" (*Le concept d'amour chez saint Augustine*, p. 183). Would she simply be following the opinion of her *Dissertationvater*, K. Jaspers? "Augustine writes the first genuine autobiography and concludes his work with a retrospective glance" (*Augustinus*, 63 [English trans., 101 (modified)]).

50. "The *Confessiones* therefore is no autobiography, and not even a partial autobiography. It is the use of Augustine's life and confession of faith in God as an illustration of his theory of man" (J. J. O'Meara, *The Young Augustine* [New York, 2001], 18).

51. The merit of having ventured the neologism falls to G. Lettieri: "l'autobiografia agostiniana é stata interpretata come *eterobiografia*" (*L'altro Agostino: Ermeneutica e retorica della grazia della crisi alla metamorfosi del De doctrina Christiana,*" [Brescia, 2001], 522 [my emphasis]).

52. Wittgenstein notes, in a closely related sense, that the truth of *Geständnis*, the confession of an admission, resides solely in its *Wahrhaftigkeit*, never in its description: "The criteria for the truth of the *confession* that I thought such-and-such are not the criteria for a *description* (*Beschreibung*) that conforms to the truth (*wahrheitgemässen*) of a process. And the importance of the true confession does not reside in its being a correct and certain report of a process. It resides rather in the special conclusions which can be drawn from a confession whose truth is guaranteed by the special criteria of *truthfulness* (*Wahrhaftigkeit*)." (*Philosophische Untersuchungen*, Part II, 1:466 [English trans., 189e (modified)]).

53. This precise use of *affectus* in XI, 1, 1 confirms literally, in advance, its role in the retrospective examination of the *Retractiones* II, 32: the *Confessiones* want to incite the movement toward God of whoever reads them, including their author. The stories and the arguments are submitted, like the literary seduction that they exert, to this radically theological goal.

54. J. L. Austin, *How to Do Things with Words* (Cambridge, MA, 1962), 101. See also "What Cannot Be Said: Apophasis and the Discourse of Love," in Jean-Luc Marion, *The Visible and the Revealed* (New York, 2008), 101–18.

55. This comes from a cover letter to the *Confessiones*, which had just been completed: "Et si quid in me placuerit tibi, lauda ibi mecum quem laudari volui de me. . . . Sume inquam etiam libros, quos desiderasti, *Confessionum* mearum: ibi me inspice, ne me laudes ultra quam sum; ibi non aliis de me crede, sed mihi; ibi me attende et vide qui fuerim in me ipso per me ipsum. Et si quid in me placuerit tibi, laude ibi mecum quam laudari volui de me" (*Epistula* 231, 6, *PL* 33, 1025).

56. This explains the fact that the other, seen from the point of view of God, can appear different from, indeed contrary to, what one would expect from the point of view of the ego. Hence the apparently ill-intended description of Alypius as a thief (IV, 9, 14, 13, 548ff.), which he is not, or the reprimand for mourning a friend denounced as idolatry: "O dementiam nescientem diligere homines humaniter" (What madness it is that knows not how to love men humanly) (IV, 7, 1, 13, 426).

57. This third is named, in Husserl, the world, which guarantees intersubjectivity in and through the object constituted in common (it would therefore be better to speak of an inter*obj*ectivity). It becomes the group-in-fusion in Sartre, the flesh for Merleau-Ponty, life for Michel Henry. The same holds, in a sense, for Levinas, not only because the third, anonymous and indeterminate, appears straightaway, at the same time, and along with the face of the other, but because the other becomes this face only by annulling his empirical visibility to the benefit of the invisible and silent word ("Thou shalt not kill"). See my study "Le tiers ou la relève du duel," in "Le tiers," ed. M. M. Olivette, special issue, *Archivio di filosofia* 84, nos. 1–3 (2007).

58. The rapprochement of Saint Augustine, Montaigne, and Rousseau can be authorized at least by Chateaubriand: "Montaigne and Rousseau gave us their *Confessions*. The first mocked the good faith of his reader; the second displayed shameless turpitude in setting himself, even in the judgment of God, as the model of virtue. It is in the *Confessions* of Saint Augustine that we learn to see man as he is. The saint does not confess to the earth, but to the heavens; he hides nothing from he who sees all" (*Génie du christianisme* III, 4, 2, ed. M. Regard [Paris, 1978], 853). I will not broach the question here, in fact an essential one, of knowing if and how far the *Mémoires d'outre-tombe* are written not only into the literary tradition of the *Confessiones* (which can hardly be disputed) but, above all, into the model of *confessio* (something it would be unwise to exclude). It could be that Chateaubriand is more incomparably Augustinian than Montaigne and Rousseau, just like Descartes and Proust, for that matter.

59. Montaigne, *Les essais*, ed. P. Villey (Paris, 1965), 1:3 (English trans., 2).

60. "De l'expérience," in *Les essais* 3:13.1112, 1113, 1114 (English trans., 854, 854, and 855–56). See also "Oh, how much am I obliged to God that it was his pleasure that I should receive all I have directly from his grace" ("De la vanité," in ibid., 968 [English trans., 739], citing almost literally 1 Corinthians 4:7). On the citations and paraphrases of Saint Paul in the *Essais* see V. Carraud, "L'imaginer inimaginable: Le Dieu de Montaigne," in *Montaigne: Scepticisme, métaphysique, théologie*, ed. V. Carraud and J.-L. Marion (Paris, 2004), 137–71, esp. 142ff.

61. "Du repentir," in *Les essais* 3:2.806 and 816 (English trans., 610 [modified] and 620). See: "As for me, I may desire in a general way to be different; I may condemn and dislike my nature as a whole, and implore God to reform me completely and to pardon my natural weakness. But this I ought not to call repentance, it seems to me, any more than my displeasure at being neither an angel nor Cato" (813 [English trans., 617]). One could, however, temper this apparent refusal of repentance. First, no censure from Rome ever stigmatized this point (see J.-R. Armogathe and V. Carraud, "Les *Essais* de Montaigne dans les archives du Saint-Office," in *Papes, princes et savants dans l'Europe moderne: Mélanges à la mémoire de Bruno Neveu*, ed. J.-L. Quentin and J.-C. Waquet [Paris, 2007], 79–96). Next, he does not refuse *confessio peccatorum* as such, seeing as it is clearly assumed, even with a reference to the *Confessiones*: "I confess myself in public, religiously and purely. Saint Augustine, Origen, and Hippocrates have published the errors of their opinions; I, besides, those of my conduct. I am hungry to make myself known, and I care not to how many, provided it be truly" ("Du repentir," 5.846ff. [English trans., 643]). Finally, even the refusal of repentance seems to insist on the facticity of the faults, done without hope of cure ("The deed is done, from here on out" [ibid., 804]) but not on any regret for having committed them.

62. "Au lecteur," in *Les essais*, 1:3 (English trans., 2).

63. "Du repentir," 2.805 (English trans., 611 [modified]). See my interpretation of these texts in "Qui suis-je pour ne pas dire *ego sum, ego existo?*" in Carraud and Marion, *Montaigne.*

64. The rapprochement of Rousseau and Augustine is validated by, among others besides Chateaubriand, G. Gusdorf, *La découverte de soi* (Paris, 1948), 18–24; and P. Courcelle, *Les "Confessions" de saint Augustin dans la tradition littéraire: Antécédents et postérité* (Paris, 1963), 459ff., who remarks that Rousseau's *Confessions* "are however the exact antithesis of those of Augustine," owing to the complete absence of Christ and the praise of God, among other reasons. He refers to D. Nisard: "As much as the beginning of the *Confessions* of J. J. Rousseau leaves me suspicious of all that he will say, so the first words of the *Confessions* of Saint Augustine inspire me with confidence" (*Histoire de la littérature française* [Paris, 1877⁶], 4:451).

65. Rousseau, *Confessions*, in *Œuvres complètes*, ed. B. Gagnebin and M. Raymond (Paris, 1959), 1:5 (English trans., 5). "Rousseau sees himself as God himself," is the wise diagnosis of A. Harle, "Augustine and Rousseau: Narrative and Self-Knowledge in the Two *Confessions*," in Mathews, *The Augustinian Tradition*, 265 (see also his *The Modern Self in Rousseau's "Confessions": A Reply to Saint Augustine* [Notre Dame, 1983]).

66. This must obviously be understood as "the host" not of "my fellows" but of "my un-fellows."

67. Rousseau, *Confessions*—Rousseau supposes that God does only what he himself already does perfectly: know himself. In Augustinian terms this is a double mistake: first because the ego does not have access to itself, and next because God rightly does what he himself cannot do, know it and himself. See the excellent analyses by E. Dubreucq: "God or the reader are [in Rousseau] only witnesses of this unveiling," while, for Saint Augustine, "the unveiling is not performed by the 'I' narrator for one of the addressees and in the presence of God, but by the divine 'you' in the act of this 'I' and in the presence of the third person of the addressee" (*Le cœur et l'écriture chez saint Augustin: Enquête sur le rapport à soi dans les "Confessiones"* [Lille, 2003], 215, 237).

68. "I am forming an undertaking which has no precedent, and the execution of which will have no imitator" (Rousseau, *Œuvres complètes*, 5 [English trans., 5]). About this demented declaration two things at least are certain: the undertaking has a precedent, even if it unhinges it (Saint Augustine), and it will have countless imitators (including Céline and the late Sartre).

CHAPTER 2

1. *Soliloquia* 1, 2, 7, *BA* 5, 36. Compare this to the definition of philosophy in terms of a "duplex quaestio: una de anima, altera de Deo. Prima efficit ut

nosmetipsos noverimus, altera ut originem nostram"—(twofold question: one concerning the soul, the other about God. The first makes us know ourselves, the second our origin) (*De ordine* II, 18, 47, *BA* 4, 444).

2. *Soliloquia* II, I, 1, *BA* 5, 86. Saint Bernard will reverse the formula: "In hac nimirum duplici consideratione spiritualis viri meditatio tota versatur. Orans denique sanctus quidam 'Deus, inquit, noverim te, noverim me.' Brevis oratio, sed fidelis. Haec enim est vera philosophia et utraque cognitio prorsus necessario ad solutum: ex priore siquidem timor concipitur et humilitas, ex posteriore spes et caritas" (The entire meditation of a spiritual man is found to be contained in this assuredly twofold consideration. In the end it takes a saint to say: "Make me know you, make me know myself." This prayer is brief but faithful. Such is the true philosophy, and these two knowledges are absolutely necessary for freed thought: and if the first makes us conceive of fear and humility, the other makes us conceive of hope and charity) (*Sermo de divinis* V, 5, *Sancti Bernardi Opera*, ed. J. Leclercq and H. Rochais, vol. 6.1 [Rome, 1970], 104).

3. *Discours de la méthode*, AT VI, 32, 19 (English trans., 2:127 [modified]).

4. *De civitate Dei* XI, 26, *BA* 35, 114. The text continues: "Quia ergo sum si fallor, quo modo esse me fallor, quando certum est me esse, si fallor? Quia igitur essem qui fallerer, etiamsi fallerer, procul dubio in eo, quod me novi esse, non fallor" (Therefore, because I am if I am deceived, how could I be deceived about my being, as soon as it is certain that if I am deceived, I am? Consequently, because I, I who was deceived, even if I was deceived, I would not be deceived since it is beyond doubt that I know that I am). Curiously, the first letter from Mersenne is lost to us, but Descartes attests to it in three letters in response: "Some time ago, you drew my attention to a passage from St. Augustine concerning my *I am thinking therefore I exist*, and I think you have asked me about it again since then. It is in the Book Eleven, chapter 26 of *De civitate Dei*" (*To Mersenne*, December 1640, AT III, 247, 1–3 [English trans., 3:161]), referring to "the letter in which you quote the passage from St. Augustine" (*To Mersenne*, 19 October 1638, AT II, 435, 19–20 [English trans., 3:129]), namely the "passage from Saint Augustine" received 25 May 1637 (AT I, 376, 19–20). Even Gilson accepted the comparison: "No doubt we shall never know to what extent Descartes may have been influenced directly or indirectly by St. Augustine or the Augustinian tradition. Besides, it would be unwise to overlook the original elements in the Cartesian *Cogito*. But the similarity of the two doctrines is quite evident even to one who does not compare the texts in detail" (*Introduction à l'étude de saint Augustin*, 55 [English trans., 43]). *Even*, or shouldn't we say *especially*, to whoever does not go too deeply into an examination of the texts?

5. *De libero arbitrio* II, 3, 7, *BA* 6, 220. Cited by Arnauld, *IVeme Objectiones* (AT VII, 197, 23 and 198, 11), who comments: "V. C. [Descartes] idem pro totius suae philosophiae principio statuisse, quod statuit D. Augustinus, acerrimi vir

ingenii, nec in Theologia modo, sed etiam in Philosophicis rebus plane mirandus" ([He] has laid down as the basis for his entire philosophy exactly the same
principle as that laid down by St Augustine, a man of the sharpest intellect and
a remarkable thinker, not only on theological topics but also on philosophical
ones) (197, 26–27 [English trans., 2:139]).

6. *De Trinitate* X, 10, 16, *BA* 16, 150. This time the comparison no longer bears
on the demonstration of the ego's existence (in AT VII, 25, 5–13, which corresponds to *De civitate Dei* XI, 26) but on the definition of its essence (AT VII,
26, 24–28, 22), setting aside, too, the hypothesis that it is *corpus, aer,* or *ignis* (27,
19, 20, and 21). Arnauld comments: "Quae de mentis a corpore distinctione dis-
seruisti, certa, clara, perspicua, divina mihi videntur, atque, ut veritate nihil an-
tiquius, eadem fere a S. Augustino, toto pene libro X *De Trin.*, sed maxime ca-
pitulo 10, luculenter esse disputat non sine magna voluptate percipi" (What you
have shown concerning the distinction of the mind and body appears to me certain, clear, limpid, and divine, and as nothing is older than the truth, I found,
not without great pleasure, that Saint Augustine discussed it in almost the same
terms in almost the entirety of book X of *De Trinitate,* but above all in chap. 10)
(*To Descartes,* 3 June 1648, AT V, 186, 9–13).

7. *The Search for Truth,* AT X, 523, 24–25, or in a bit more developed form:
"Quando quidem itaque dubitare te negare nequis, et e contrario certum est te
dubitare, et quidem adeo certum, ut de eo dubitare non possis: verum etiam est
te, qui dubitas, esse, hocque ita etiam verum est, ut non magis de eo dubitare
possis. / Assentior hic equidem tibi, quia, si non essem, non possem dubitare. /
Es igitur, et te esse scis, et hoc exinde, quia dubitas, scis" (You cannot deny that
you have such doubts; rather it is certain that you have them, so certain in fact
that you cannot doubt your doubting. Therefore it is also true that you who are
doubting exist; this is so true that you can no longer have any doubts about it.
/ I quite agree with you on that point, because if I did not exist, I would not be
able to doubt. / You exist, therefore, and you know that you exist, and you know
this just because you are doubting) (ibid., 515, 15–22 [English trans., 2:409–10]).

8. *De Trinitate* X, 10, 14, 16, 148.

9. *To Mesland,* 2 May 1644: "I am grateful to you for pointing out the places
in St. Augustine which can be used to give authority to my views. Some other
friends of mine had already done so, and I am pleased that my thoughts agree
with those of such a great and holy man. For I am not the kind of person who
wants his views to appear novel; on the contrary, I make my views conform with
those of others so far as truth permits me" (AT IV, 113, 12–21 [English trans.,
3:232]). Yet in the *IVeme Responsiones* (AT VII, 219, 6–10) Descartes prefers not to
argue on the basis of this authority so as to let *rationes meae* present themselves by
themselves. Concerning this unsolvable issue, see the classic works of G. Rodis-
Lewis, "Augustinisme et cartésianisme" (*Etudes augustiniennes* [1955], included

in *L'anthropologie cartésienne* [Paris, 1990]); H. Gouhier, *Cartésianisme et augustinisme au XVIeme siècle* (Paris, 1978); and despite some gaps, Z. Janowski, *Index augustino-cartésien: Texts et commentaire* (Paris, 2000) (with a good recounting of the history of the problem), included in and developed as *Augustinian-Cartesian Index: Texts and Commentary* (South Bend, IN, 2004).

10. *De vita beata* II, 7, *BA* 4, 232.

11. *De Trinitate* XV, 12, 21, 16, 478. See "Si dubitat, vivit" and the surrounding context, *De Trinitate* X, 10, 14, 16, 148. See also: "Imo nescire se dicunt, quod nescire non possunt. Neque enim quisquam sinitur nescire se vivere: quandoquidem si non vivit, non potest aliquid vel nescire; quoniam non solum scire, verum etiam nescire viventis est" (They [sc. certain philosophers] say they do not know what they cannot not know. For it is not permitted to anybody not to know that he lives—since if he did not live, he could not even not know something; that is, it is not only knowing but also not knowing that requires a living) (*Enchiridion* VII, 20, *BA* 9, 142).

12. *De vita beata* II, 7, *BA* 4, 232. And: "Vivit enim corpus meum de anima mea et vivit anima mea de te. Quomodo quaero vitam beatam? Quia non est mihi" (My body lives from my soul and my soul lives from you. How do I ask for the good life? For it is not mine) (*Confessiones* X, 20, 29, 14, 192).

13. One should refer, on this major point, to the powerful analysis of Michel Henry: "No livings are possible except within Life." Accordingly, "the ego comes into itself only in the coming into self of absolute Life and in the process of its eternal self-generation." Life therefore is not in possession of itself but receives itself as a gift: "this gift is that of Life—the extraordinary gift through which a person who by himself would be nothing (particularly not any self) instead, comes into himself in life, . . . thus as a living and as a Self" (Michel Henry, *C'est moi la vérité: Pour une philosophie du christianisme* [Paris, 1996], 139, 190, 178 [English trans., 109, 150, 141]).

14. *To Colvius*, 14 December 1640, AT III, 247, 1–248, 11 (English trans., 3:159). He concludes: "In itself it is such a simple and natural thing to infer that one exists from the fact that one is doubting that it could have occurred to any writer. But I am very glad to find myself in agreement with St. Augustine, if only to hush the little minds who have tried to find fault with the principle" (248, 1–7 [English trans., ibid.]). Elsewhere Descartes emphasizes that the banality of the principle ("hoc tritum: *Cogito, ergo sum*") should not hide its power since "ex his et Dei existentiam et reliqua multa demontrarim" (*VI Objectiones*, AT VII, 551, 9–12). See also the remark that Saint Augustine "does not seem to use it in the same way as I do" (*To Mersenne*, 25 May 1630, AT I, 376, 20–21).

15. For example, AT VII, 51, 15–52, 9; and AT VII, 56, 26–57, 25. I tried to lay out this paradox in *Questions cartésiennes II*, chapter 1, §6 (Paris, 1996 [English trans., 23ff.]).

16. *Meditationes V and VI*, respectively AT VII, 71, 7; and AT VII, 78, 25 (English trans., 49 and 54).

17. Preface to the French edition of *Principles of Philosophy*, AT IX-2, 10 (English trans., 1:184). Pascal, who obviously saw the difference, here takes Descartes's side (as almost always in philosophical matters), insisting on the "difference . . . between writing a word by chance without making a longer and more extended reflection on it, and perceiving in this word an admirable series of conclusions, which prove the distinction between material and spiritual natures, and making of it a firm and sustained principle of a complete metaphysical system, as Descartes has pretended to do" (*De l'art de persuader*, in *Œuvres complètes*, ed. L. Lafuma [Paris, 1963], 358 [English trans., 414]). On this complex position assumed by Pascal, in a sense opposed to Saint Augustine and siding with Descartes, see V. Carraud, "Le véritable auteur du *cogito*: Traits d'anti-augustinisme," in *Pascal: Des connaissances naturelles à l'étude de l'homme* II, 1 [Paris, 2007], 65ff.

18. "Le quinzième centenaire de la mort de saint Augustin (28 août 430)," *Revue de métaphysique et de morale*, no. 4 (1930); repr. in *Dialogue avec les philosophes* (Paris, 1966), 165.

19. *Phänomenologie des religiosen Lebens*, GA 60:298 [English trans., 226], insisting, of course, on the relation of the *mens* to the Trinity in *De Trinitate* XI.

20. *De Trinitate* XI, 3, 6, BA 16, 174. Varro's formulation, "Cogitare a cogitando dictum: mens plura in unum cogit, unde eligere possit" (*De lingua latina*, ed. P. Flobert [Paris, 1985], 22), also finds an echo in *Confessiones* X, 11, 18: "cogitando quasi colligere" (14, 172). See *Confessiones* VII, 1, 1, 13, 576; *De Trinitate* X, 5, 7, 16, 134 and XIV, 6, 8, 16, 364.

21. *De Trinitate* X, 10, 16, 16, 150. That *esse* remains, at bottom, in the case of the *mens*, understood on the basis of life and not *substantia* obviously does not forbid it from intervening explicitly in the argument.

22. Descartes, *Principia philosophia* I, §7, AT VIII, 7 (English trans., 1:195).

23. Descartes, *Meditatio II*, AT VII, 25, 12 (English trans., 2:17). On the primacy of this formulation, which leaves out precisely the *cogitatio*, in what is always called, a bit hastily, "the *cogito*," see my studies in *Sur la théologie blanche de Descartes* II, §16 (Paris 1981¹, 1991²), 370ff.; and *Questions cartésiennes II* I, 1, §§3–4, 12ff. (English trans., 8ff.).

24. Descartes, *Meditatio II*, AT VII, 27, 30 (English trans., 2:18 [modified]). The complete text, "Novi me existere; quaero *quis* sim ego ille quem novi," indicates that from here on out, it is a matter of determining the essence of the *ego*, after having secured its existence (and, in fact, the *res cogitans* and the explication of its modes will follow, 28, 20–23). We should also take note of the *ille* (as in 25, 14: "quisnam ego ille, qui jam necessario sum," and in 49, 13–14: "ego ille, qui jam sum," which should be translated "this *I*, that I am," as Luynes once does in AT

IX-1, 21, 41: "I seek what I am, me whom I recognized to be") being used to designate the *ego* (instead of the more expected *ego ipse, myself,* as in VII, 51, 22ff.).

25. Leibniz, *Systéme nouveau de la communication des substances,* ed. Gerhardt, *Philosophische Schriften* IV, 473 and 482. On this point see my study "The Egological Deduction of Substance," in Marion, *On Descartes' Metaphysical Prism,* chap. 3, §13.

26. The citation comes from Job 7:1, but the Vulgate reads "Militia est vita hominis super terram." The addition of "sine interstitio" comes from Saint Augustine, confirming the interpretation that Heidegger gives to this verse: *tentatio* defines the existential condition of *Dasein* (see below, Chapter 4, §23).

27. And here it is reason itself that is put into question: "Ubi est *ratio,* qua talibus suggestionibus resistit vigilans et, si res ipsae ingerantur, inconcussus manet?" (Where then is *reason* found, by which it [*ego . . . sum*] resists such suggestions when it is awake such that it remains unshakable when the very same things come upon it) (*Confessiones* X, 30, 14, 214). For Descartes, *ratio* does not vary because it is but one with the univocal power of the *cogitatio,* such that the *esse* of the *ego sum* remains unchangeable and the same, whether I am dreaming or awake (see my essay "Does Thought Dream?" in Jean-Luc Marion, *Cartesian Questions* [Chicago, 1999]). For Augustine, who never imagines an *ego* reduced without remainder to the existing *cogitatio* but considers the entire *humana vita,* the *ego* (*mens*), all the while continuing to be even in dreams because it continues to think, undergoes, from the point of view of sexual temptation (in fact the facticity of a *Stimmung*), considerable factic variation. The *cogitatio* manifests, in its very permanence, not only that I am always, but especially that I am no longer myself, that I am altered in an other *myself,* who is no longer the *ego.*

28. On this distance of self from self see Heidegger's analysis, *Phänomenologie des religiösen Lebens,* §13b, *GA* 60:212ff. (English trans., 157ff.). This separation of ourselves from ourselves (our word, our speech), which distinguishes us from God, also makes possible, derivatively, the separation of communication with the other: "Inter animum autem nostrum et verba nostra, quibus eundem animum extendere conamur, plurimum distat. . . . Quid enim aliud molimur, nisi animum ipsum nostrum, si fieri potest, cognoscendum et percipiendum animo auditoris inferre, uti nobis quidem ipsi maneamus nec recedamus a nobis, et tamen tale judicium quo fiat in altero nostra notitia proferamus?" (Between our mind and the words we speak, by which we try to reach out of our mind, resides a great distance. . . . For what else are we trying to do if not to transport, as far as possible, our own mind to the mind of the listener so as to make him know and perceive it in such a way that, all the while remaining in us and without our having to leave ourselves, we still issue a judgment so that the other knows something of us?) (*De fide et symbolo* III, 4, 1, *BA* 9, 26).

29. *Confessiones* VIII, 9, 21, *BA* 14, 50. As we will see in Chapter 4, the impossibility for the will to will itself constitutes the essential and founding result of the impossibility of converting *oneself.* From this ordeal stems the scission of *myself,* divided by its powerlessness to master what is most intimate to it, the will—whose shifting sands modern metaphysics, since at least Descartes (AT VII, 57, 15–58, 14), has stood firm about erecting into a final foundation.

30. See *Confessiones* IX, 7, 15, 16, 98.

31. *Confessiones* X, 33, 50, 14, 230. One finds elsewhere the criticism of those who sing loudly in church all the while going in the same spirit to the circus, the market, and live it up (*Commentaries on the Psalms* 30, 3, 10; and *Commentaries on the Psalms* 48, 2, 10, *PL* 36, respectively 240 and 563).

32. The translation should not only avoid becoming a platitude (rendering *quaestio* by *problem*, which some do) but take advantage of the difficulty in rendering *factus sum* so as to insist on the pure facticity of this situation.

33. It is regrettable that this linguistic commodity, which disseminates a fundamental misreading, finds disciples even among the best intentioned commentators. Cartesians of the seventeenth century left a large inheritance, from P. de Labriolle (in *BA* 5, 402), J.-F. Thonnard (*BA* 6, 517–18), and J. Agaësse (*BA* 16, 681) to M.-A. Vannier, "Les anticipations du *cogito* chez saint Augustin," in *San Agustín: Homenaje al Profesor Jaime García Álvarez en su 65 aniversario,* ed. R. Lazcano (Madrid, 1957); G. B. Mathews, *Thought's Ego in Augustine and Descartes* (Ithaca, 1992); or E. Bermon, *Le cogito dans la pensée de saint Augustin* (Paris, 2001).

34. *De ordine* I, 1, 3, *BA* 16, 128. See also "quasi possit mens in mente non esse?" (as if the mind could not be in the mind?) (X, 4, 16, 16, 132); "quid tam menti adest, quam ipsa mens?" (what could be more present to the mind than itself?) (X, 7, 10, 16, 140); "Quid enim tam in mente quam mens est?" (For what is as much in the mind as the mind itself?) (X, 8, 11, 16, 142).

35. If, in Levinas's terms, "consciousness is a rupture of the anonymous vigilance of the *there is*" (*Le temps et l'autre* [1947[1]; Paris, 1991[4]], 31 [English trans., 51]), then there would be no Augustinian consciousness, at least in the sense of self-consciousness.

36. I say provisional, since this same passage from 1 Corinthians 2:11–12 will be interpreted, this time correctly, in *Confessiones* XIII, 31, 46, 14, 512, but in such a way as to reinforce the thesis of the unknowability of the human essence (see below, Chapter 6, §40, p. 259–260). The first level of interpretation is found again elsewhere in *De diversis quaestionibus LXXXIII,* 51, 4 (*BA* 10, 138) and especially in the *Commentary on the Gospel of John* 32, 5:

> Animus enim cujusque proprius est spiritus ejus: de quo dicit Paulus apostolus "Quis enim scit hominum quae sunt hominis, nisi spiritus hominis, qui in ipso est?" Deinde adjunxit "Sic et quae Dei sunt, nemo scit, nisi spiritus Dei." Nostra nemo scit, nisi spiritus noster. Non enim novi quid

cogitas, aut tu quid cogito: ipsa sunt propria nostra, quae interius cogitamus; et cogitationum uniuscujusque hominis, ipsius spiritus testis est. "Sic et ea quae Dei sunt, nemo scit, nisi spiritus Dei." Nos cum spiritu nostro, Deum cum suo: ita tamen ut Deus cum Spiritu suo sciat etiam quid agatur in nobis, nos autem sine ejus Spiritu scire non possumus quid agatur in Deo. Deus autem scit in nobis et quod ipsi nescimus in nobis.

The spirit of each is to him his own. In this regard the apostle Paul writes: "Who among men knows the things of man, except the spirit of man which is in him?" And adds: "Thus, nobody knows the things of God, except the Spirit of God" (1 Corinthians 2:11). What is ours, nobody knows it, except our own spirit. For I do not know what you are thinking, nor you what I am thinking. The things that we think within are proper to us, and the sole witness of the thoughts of each man is his own spirit. "Thus nobody knows the things of God, except the Spirit of God." We know ours by our spirit, God his own by his Spirit—but in such a way that God knows also by his own Spirit what happens in us but we cannot know without his Spirit what happens in him. But God knows in ourselves what we ourselves do not know about it. (*PL* 35, 1644).

Only the final phrase retains something of the forced interpretation of *Confessiones* X, 5, 7, while the rest of the commentary respects the obviated reading reestablished in XIII, 31, 46.

37. *Confessiones* X, 14, 21 and X, 16, 25, *BA* 14, 178 and 184. See "ipsam memoriam vocantes animum" (we call mind the memory itself) (X, 14, 21, *BA* 14, 178). About memory J.-F. Lyotard says rightly that "memory *is* the mind itself" (*La confession d'Augustin*, 70 [English trans., 46–47]).

38. *Confessiones* X, 8, 12, 14, 162. See Heidegger: "the *memoria* is certainly nothing outside consciousness but is consciousness itself" (*Phänomenologie des religiösen Lebens*, *GA* 60:186 [English trans., 136]). And R. Teske: "In memory Augustine also encounters himself and recalls himself ("Augustine's Philosophy of Memory," in *The Cambridge Companion to Augustine*, ed. E. Stump and N. Kretz, 151).

39. *De Trinitate* XIV, 6, 8 and 7, 9, *BA* 16, 364 and 366.

40. Aristotle, *On Memory and Remembering* 1.449b27. Saint Augustine sometimes admits this context: "Haec igitur memoria quaecumque de motibus animi tenet, qui adversus passiones corporis acti sunt, φαντασίαι vocantur; nec invenio quid eas latine malim vocare" (All that this memory retains of the movements of the mind that it accomplished counter to the passions of the body are called, in Greek, φαντασίαι, and I can find in Latin no better term) (*De musica* VI, 11, 32, *BA* 7, 428).

41. As the *res cogitans* comprises and permits all its modes. But for Descartes *memoria* is not directly part of the *modi cogitandi*; rigorously speaking, it is only

part of it indirectly, by the intermediary of the *imaginans quoque* (AT VII, 28, 22), or *imaginans etiam* (34, 20), according to the Aristotelian model.

42. This reconstituted list (no doubt not exhaustive) could be compared to the list drawn up by Husserl of all that is included in givenness (*Gegebenheit*) inasmuch as givenness in thought (*Die Idee der phänomenologie*, Husserliana 2:74 [English trans., 59]).

43. *De ordine* II, 2, 7, *BA* 4, 372 and 370. As G. P. O'Daly showed ("Memory in Plotinus and Two Early Texts of St. Augustine," *Studia Patristica* 15 (Berlin, 1984) against K. Winkler ("La théorie augustinienne de la mémoire à son point de départ,") *Augustinus Magister* (Paris, 1954), 1:511–19, Saint Augustine here criticizes the position of Plotinus (*Enneads* 4.3.25), held in the dialogue by the character of Licentius.

44. *De Trinitate* XIV, 11, 14, *BA* 16, 386. Sometimes *memoria* even bears *first of all* on the present, more than on the past: "Primum ergo videndum est non nos semper rerum praetereuntium meminisse, sed *plerumque* manentium; . . . posse dici earum etiam rerum, quae nondum interierunt memoriam" (It must be seen before all else that we do not always remind ourselves of things that are past, but *the majority of the time* of those that remain; . . . one can speak of memory even of things that are not yet past) (*Letter 7*, 1, 1, *PL* 33, 68). By "those [things] that remain" he means, for example, Carthage (still standing despite it all), in opposition to Patrice (deceased); but one can even more understand every present moment of thought, presupposed by every other worldly being thought.

45. This was seen quite clearly by E. Gilson: "The Platonic recollection of the past gives way to that Augustinian memory of the present." And "association with the past ceases to be an essential characteristic of the memory. Since the soul remembers everything present to it even though unaware of it, we can say that there is a memory of the present which is even far more vast than the memory of the past" (*Introduction à l'étude de saint Augustin*, 100, 137 [English trans., 75, 102]). In fact, this excess of memory even intervenes, we saw, from before the question of the present, with the investigation into the thought of self. As for saying that Saint Augustine wants "to extend memory beyond the limits of psychology to metaphysics" (ibid., 139 [English trans., 103]), although the intention is admirable, the phrasing is unfortunate. The limits of psychology result directly from metaphysics, which sets them. And to extend *memoria* thus to the present (and to the future), without limiting it to the past, implies *contesting* the autonomy of the present by imposing on it an exterior and anterior condition of possibility.

46. *De musica* VI, 8, 21, *BA* 7, 404. See: "Ita ratio invenit tam localia quam temporalia spatia infinitam divisionem recipere; et idcirco nullius syllabae cum initio finis auditur. In audienda itaque vel brevissima syllaba, nisi memoria nos adjuvet, ut eo momento temporis, quo jam non initium, sed finis syllabae sonat,

maneat ille motus in animo, qui factus est cum initium ipsum sonuit; nihil nos audisse possumus dicere" (Thus, reason has discovered that all the spaces, local as much as temporal, admit an infinitesimal division and therefore that one does not hear the end of any syllable with its beginning. That is, in hearing even the shortest of syllables, we could not say we heard anything if at the moment of time when there no longer sounded the beginning but the end of the syllable, memory did not help us to keep in mind the movement that was produced when the beginning sounded) (ibid., 7, 402).

47. *Confessiones* X, 16, 24, 14, 184 and 182. The same analysis continues in ibid., X, 20, 29, 194, which distinguishes between the forgetting of what one still retains in the mind, the forgetting that has forgotten what it lost but knows that it has lost something, and the forgetting that is totally forgetful, even of itself. A. Solignac finds the problems "exceedingly subtle" and reproaches Augustine for "contriving to materialize forgetting, to consider it as a thing" (*BA* 16, 563ff.). Let us note, however, that not only did Heidegger recognize that "the characteristic of forgetting is that it forgets itself. It is implicit in the ecstatic nature of forgetting that it not only forgets the forgotten but forgets the forgetting itself" (*Grundprobleme der Phänomenologie*, §20, *GA* 24:411 [English trans., 290]), but also that it could be, in contrast, that here Saint Augustine extricates himself in advance from the dichotomy between material memory (involuntary) and intellectual memory (voluntary)—a dichotomy that in Descartes, for example (but also many others), makes the very concept of memory disappear by rendering unintelligible its facticity and its ambivalence (to remember and *not* to remember) and therefore the contingency of the *mens*.

48. P. Agaësse suggests "something of a preconscious awareness, or at least a non-reflective one" (*BA* 16, 606), but E. Gilson has no hesitations about the word: "the only modern psychological terms equivalent to Augustinian *memoria* are 'unconscious' or 'subconscious'" (*Introduction à l'étude de saint Augustin*, 194 [English trans., 299n110]). L. Cilleruelo attributes to *memoria* a content that is "oscuro, implicito, impreso, arcano, habitual, *inconsciente*" ("La 'memoria Dei' segun San Augustin," *Augustinus Magister*, 1:5. See "¿Por qué 'memoria Dei'?" *Revue des études augustiniennes* 10 (1964); and "Pro memoria Dei," *Revue des études augustiniennes* 12 (1966). See the reservations of G. Madec in *Revue des études augustiniennes* 9 (1963); then Madec, *Saint Augustin et la philosophie*, 87ff.

49. *Conscientia* does not appear in the *Meditationes*, but it does in the *IIIeme Responsiones*: "Sunt deinde alii actus, quos vocamus cogitativos, ut intelligere, velle, imaginari, sentire, etc., qui omnes sub ratione communi cogitationis, sive perceptionis, sive conscientiae conveniunt" (AT VII, 176, 16–19, but especially *conscius* in the *IIeme Responsiones*, AT VII, 160, 8, 14, etc.). See also *Principia philosophiae* I, §9: "Cogitationis nomine, intelligo illa omnia, quae nobis consciis in nobis fiunt, quatenus eorum in nobis conscientia est" (AT VIII-1, 7) and originally in French: "as

for the principle by which I claim to know that the idea I have of something *non redditur a me inadaequata per abstractionem intellectus*, I derive this principle purely from my own thought or awareness" (*To Gibieuf*, 19 January 1642, AT III, 474, 9–12 [English trans., 3:201 (modified)]). The traditional claim to attribute the invention of the French *conscience* to Coste's translation of Locke's *An Essay Concerning Human Understanding*, 2:28 (still maintained by E. Balibar, "L'invention européene de la conscience," in *John Locke: Identité et différence* [Paris, 1998]), should be revisited (see the reformulation by G. Olivo in *Descartes et l'essence de la vérité* [Paris, 2005], 320n2, following G. Rodis-Lewis, *Le problème de l'inconscient et le cartésianisme* [Paris, 1950], 39; and G. Rodis-Lewis, *L'œuvre de Descartes* [Paris, 1970], 240).

50. According to the excellent phrasing of Lyotard, *La confession d'Augustin*, 53 (English trans., 33).

51. Emmanuel Levinas, *Autrement qu'être ou au-delà de l'essence* (The Hague, 1974), 49, 33, 48, 112, 13, 157 (English trans., 38, 26, 38, 88, 11 [modified], 122). This does not, by the way, contradict Heidegger: "This forgetting is not nothing, nor is it just a failure to remember; it is rather a 'positive' ecstatical mode of one's having been" (*Sein und Zeit*, §68, 339 [English trans., 388]).

52. Heidegger, *Grundprobleme der Phänomenologie*, §20, *GA* 24:411 (English trans., 290).

53. On this transcendence by the crossing of all things, including the self, see:

> Cogita corpus: mortale est, terrenum est, fragile est, corruptibile est; abjice! Sed forte caro temporalis est? . . . Transi et ipsa [sc. corpora]! Et quomodo, inquies, transeo caelestia corpora, quando ambulo in terra? Non carne transis, sed mente. Abjice et ipsa! . . . Sine dubio melior est animus quo ista omnia cogitasti, quam ista omnia quae cogitasti. Animus ergo spiritus est, non corpus: transi et ipsum. . . . Magna ergo res est animus. Sed quomodo dico, *est*? Transi et ipsum; quia et ipse animus mutabilis est, quamvis melior sit omni corpore. . . . Transi ergo et animum tuum! Effunde super te animam tuam ut contingas Deum.

> Think of the body: it is mortal, earthly, fragile; it is corruptible. Reject it! But perhaps it is a temporal flesh? . . . Cross through even these bodies! And how, you will ask, do I cross through the celestial bodies, I who walk on earth? Not with your flesh, but with the mind you cross through. Reject also these [celestial] bodies! No doubt, the mind by which you thought of all these things is better than all the things that you thought. The mind, that is, is spiritual and not the body: cross through also the body! . . . The mind is a great thing. But *is*, I ask, in what way? Cross through it too. Because even the mind remains mutable, even though it is better than any body whatsoever. . . . Cross through even your mind! Stretch out your soul over your head so as to touch God. (*Commentary on the Gospel of Saint John* XX, 12, *PL* 35, 1562–63)

Similarly: "Quaero ego Deum meum in omni corpore, sive terrestri, sive caelesti, et non invenio; quaero substantiam ejus in anima mea, et no invenio; . . . Ibi enim domus Dei mei, super animam meam" (As for me, I seek my God in all bodies, celestial or earthly, and I do not find him there. I seek his substance in my soul, and I do not find it there. . . . For, look, the dwelling place of my God is found above my soul)' (*Commentaries on the Psalms* 41, 8, *PL* 36, 469).

54. *De Trinitate* XIII, 4, 7, *BA* 16, 282. The loss of the *Hortensius* has made it such that the authority on which Saint Augustine here rests is known to us only by its citation (become *Fragment* 28 in J. C. von Orelli, *M. T. Ciceronis opera quae supersunt omnia* [Zurich, 1861], 4:982). Of course, Cicero formulated this principle in other texts: *Contra academicos* I, 5, 21–26, 22 (Loeb ed., 19:430ff.); *De natura deorum* I, 20, 53; and *Tusculanes* V, 10, 28 (see M. Testard, *Saint Augustin et Cicéron* [Paris, 1958], esp. 1:19–39; and M.-P. Folet, "Cicero, Augustine and the Philosophical Roots of the Cassiciacum Dialogues," *Revue des études augustiniennes* 45 [1999]: 51–77). Seneca had followed: "Vivere, Gallio frater, omnes beate volunt, sed ad pervidendum, quid sit quod beatam vitam efficiat, caligant" (*De vita beata* I). The theme obviously goes back also to Aristotle, *Nicomachean Ethics* 1.1.1094a1 (Πᾶσα τέχνη καὶ πᾶσα μέθοδος, ὁμοίως δὲ πρᾶξίς τε καί προαίρεσις ἀγαθοῦ τινός ἐφίεται δοκεῖ). See on this tradition R. Holte, *Béatitude et sagesse: Saint Augustin et le problème de la fin de l'homme dans la philosophie ancienne* (Paris, 1962), esp. chaps. 17 and 18. To such a point that philosophy itself is redefined as exclusively the search for blessedness: "Quando quidem nulla est homini causa philosophandi nisi ut beatus sit; quod autem beatum facit, ipse est finis boni; nulla est igitur causa philosophandi, nisi finis boni: quamobrem quae nullum boni finem secatur, nulla philosophiae secta dicenda est" (Man has in effect no other reason to philosophize, except to be happy. Now, what makes us happy is itself the end of the good. Consequently there is no other reason to philosophize except the end of the good, and this is why one should not call it a philosophical school if it does not seek the end of the good) (*De civitate Dei* XIX, 1, *BA* 37, 48).

55. *Republic* 6.509b.

56. *De Trinitate* XIII, 20, 25, 16, 338. In effect, the desire (impossible to realize) for immortality results, as desire for the means, from the desire (this one absolutely inevitable) for the end, beatitude—accordingly, the pain of failing at immortality attests again, indirectly and by default, the principial character of the quest for beatitude: "Cum ergo beati esse omnes homines velint, si vere volunt, profecto et esse immortales volunt: aliter enim beati esse non possent. Denique et de immortalitate interrogati, sicut et de beatitudine, omnes eam se velle respondent. Sed qualiscumque beatitudo, quae potius vocetur quam sit, in hac vita quaeritur, imo vero fingitur, dum immortalitas desperatur, sine qua beatitudo esse non potest" (Since all men want to be happy, if they truly want it, they want

also to be immortal; for otherwise they could not be happy. Finally, if they are also asked about immortality, as [they are asked] about beatitude, they all will respond that they want it too. But they seek in this life some small version of beatitude, or rather forge an illusion of it, while they despair of attaining immortality, lacking which they could not have beatitude either) (*De Trinitate* XIII, 8, 11, 16, 294).

57. *Sermon* 306, 2 and 3, *PL* 38, 1401.

58. "Ita vellent beati esse: quod eos velle *certissimum* est" (that they want to be happy, as it is very certain that they want it) (*Confessiones* X, 20, 29, 14, 194). See: "si interrogari [homines] possent, utrum beati esse vellent, *sine ulla dubitatione* velle responderent" (if one could ask men if they want to be happy, they would respond *without any doubt* that they do want it) (ibid., 196). And: "Quid est hoc? Si quaeratur a duobus, utrum militare velint, fieri possit, ut alter eorum velle se, alter nolle respondeat; si autem quaeretur, utrum esse beati velint, uterque se statim *sine ulla dubitatione* dicat optare" (How does it happen that if you ask two men whether or not they want to serve in the army, it can happen that one responds he wants to while the other does not want to; but if you ask them if they want to be happy, both will say *without any doubt* that they do wish for it) (ibid., X, 21, 31, 14, 198).

59. On this Cartesian term, as rare as it is famous, see "minimum quid invenero quod certum sit et inconcussum" and "ut ita tandem praecise remaneat illud tantum quod certum sit et inconcussum" (AT VII, 24, 12 and 25, 23). It appears already in *De libero arbitrio* II, 2, 5: "Deum esse. Etiam hoc non contemplando, sed credendo inconcussum teneo" (God is. Even without contemplating this, it is something that I hold by faith as unshakable) (*BA* 6, 214). In contrast, what is lacking in the ordeal of temptation is precisely the *inconcussus* in me (see *Confessiones* X, 30, 41, 14, 214).

60. *Commentary on the Gospel of Saint John* XXIII, 5, *PL* 35, 1585. See: "Ut enim homo se diligere nosset, constitutus est ei finis, quo referret omnia quae ageret, ut beatus esset; non enim qui se diligit aliud vult esse quam beatus. Hic autem finis est adhaerere Deo" (So that man might know how to love himself, an end has been established for him to which is referred all that he would do to be happy [for whoever loves himself wants nothing other than to be happy]. This end is to cleave to God) (*De civitate Dei* X, 3, 34, 436).

61. Aristotle, *Metaphysics* 1.1.980a1. One could, by contrast, say that the *Nicomachean Ethics*, in postulating that Πᾶσα τέχνη καὶ πᾶσα μέθοδος, ὁμοίως δὲ πρᾶξίς τε καὶ προαίρεσις ἀξαθοῦ τινός ἐφίεται δοκεῖ (Every art, every project, as well as every action and every intention, seems to desire some good [1.1.1094a1]), already presupposed what in fact constitutes the difficulty: if these postures intend a good and even desire it, how are the theoretic and desire

articulated together in them? Does desire bear on knowing or on what know-ing makes known to us? And if it bears on both, does it do so in the same sense?

62. Pascal, *Pensées*, §148 (*Œuvres complètes*, 519 [English trans., 74]).

63. *Sermon* 34, 2, *PL* 38, 210.

64. *De Genesi ad litteram* VIII, 26, 48, *BA* 49, 82. We thus encounter again what this forced commentary of 1 Corinthians 2:11 wanted to demonstrate: "Plus noverat artifex quid esset in opere suo, quam ipsum opus quid esset in semetipso. Creator hominis noverat quid esset in homine, quod ipse creatus homo non noverat. . . . Homo ergo nesciebat quid esset in se, sed Creator hominis noverat quid esset in homine" (The artist knew what was found in his work better than this work knew what was found in it. The creator of man knew what was found in man, something man himself did not know. . . . And therefore man did not know what was in him, but the creator of man knew what was in man) (*Commentary on the Gospel of Saint John* X, 2, *PL* 35, 1475).

65. See: "Lux non est absens, sed vos absentes estis a luce. Caecus in sole prae-sentem habet solum, sed absens est ipse soli" (It is not the light that is absent but you who have absented yourselves from the light. In the presence of the sun the blind man truly does have the sun, but it is he who has absented himself from the sun) (*Commentary on the Gospel of Saint John* III, 5, *PL* 35, 1398). The unbeliev-ers are sometimes defined by their lateness, by being outdated, by their conser-vatism: "ecce pleni sunt vetustatis, qui nobis dicunt" (here they are, full of their decrepitude, which they speak to us) (*Confessiones* XI, 10, 12, 14, 290). Courcelle has insisted on this lateness with regard to God (see *Recherches sur les "Confessio-nes" de saint Augustin*, 441ff.).

66. "Tibi laus, tibi gloria, fons misericordiarum! Ego fiebam miserior et tu *propinquior*. Aderat jam jamque dextera tua" (Praise to you, to your glory, source of mercies! Me, I became more unhappy, but *you, more close*. Already, already, it was there, your right hand) (*Confessiones* VI, 16, 26, 13, 570).

67. Rimbaud, *Lettre à Izambard*, 13 May 1871, in *Œuvres complètes*, ed. A. Adam (Paris, 1972), 249 (English trans., 371 [modified]); and Heidegger, *Sein und Zeit*, §63, 311, 11 (English trans., 359 [modified]) (referring to "Das Dasein ist zwar on-tisch nicht nur nahe oder gar das nächste—wir *sind* es sogar selbst. Trotzdem oder gerade deshalb ist es ontologisch des Fernste" (Ontically, of course, Das-ein is not only close to us—even that which is closest: we *are* it, each of us, we are ourselves. In spite of this, or rather for just this reason, it is ontologically that which is farthest) (§5, 15, 25–27 [English trans., 36]). Chance is not at play, but an obvious necessity in the fact that it is in order to comment on "Factus sum mihi terra difficultatis" that Heidegger specifies "Das ontische Nächste und Be-kannste ist das ontologische Fernste" (That which is ontically closest and well-known is ontologically the farthest) (ibid., §9, pp. 43, 37; see also §5, 15, 25–27; and *Wegmarken*, *GA* 9:333, 343, 344). The entire question resides in knowing if

the closest should first be called *ontic* and if (even in this case) its enigmatic anonymity can be overcome *ontologically* or if the aporia of the *self* does not call for
an other instance besides the ontological difference, however one understands it.
J. J. O'Donnell refers to, besides Rimbaud, Nietzsche, *Zur Genealogie der Moral*,
Preface, §1 (see O'Donnell, *Augustine: Confessions*, 3:180). Kant, Hegel, Freud,
and some others are likewise appropriate, for what is important is not the distance but its horizon.

68. *De vera religione* XXXIX, 72, *BA* 8, 130, cited at the very end of the
Cartesianische Meditationen, §64, Husserliana 1:183. See another version of
the same argument: "Quare vis loqui, audire non vis? Semper foras exis, intro
redire detractas. Qui enim te docet intus est; quando tu doces, tanquam foras
exis ad eos qui foris sunt. Ab interiore enim audimus veritatem et ad eos qui
foris a nostro corde sunt, loquimur. . . . Non ergo amemus magis exteriora,
sed interiora: de interioribus gaudeamus; in exterioribus autem necessitatem
habemus, non voluntatem" (Why do you want to speak and not to listen?
You always go out, and chafe at returning inside. Now he who teaches you
is found inside. When it is you who are teaching, you go so to speak outside
toward those who are there. . . . Let us not love the exterior but rather the
interior: let us rejoice and enjoy the interior; let us place in the outside only
what necessity and not our will imposes on us) (*Commentaries on the Psalms*
139, 15, *PL* 37, 1560).

69. *De vera religione* XXXIX, 72, *BA* 8, 130. The entire text should be at issue, from which Husserl abstracts this short citation. In fact, Saint Augustine
here maintains what is his constant doctrine: "Ille autem, qui consulitur, docet,
qui in interiore homine habitare dictus est Christus, i.e. incommutabilis Dei virtus atque sempiterna Sapientia" (He whom we consult teaches, he who is said to
dwell in the inner man, Christ, that is to say the immutable strength of God and
his eternal wisdom) (*De Magistro* XI, 38, *BA* 6, 102).

CHAPTER 3

1. *De moribus Ecclesiae Catholicae et de moribus Manichaeorum* I, 25, 47, *BA* 1,
206ff. Or: "Haec est autem vera dilectio, ut inhaerentes veritati juste vivemus"
(For this is true love, to live in justice, being attached to the truth) (*De Trinitate* VIII, 7, 10, 16, 58). Or else: "Quisquis igitur ad summum modum per veritatem venerit, beatus est. Hoc est animo Deum habere, id est Deo frui" (Whoever
came by way of the truth to the highest mode is happy. This, for the soul, is to
have God, to enjoy God) (*De vita beata* IV, 35, 4, 282).

2. Heidegger, *Phänomenologie des religiösen Lebens*, *GA* 60:201 (English trans., 148).

3. Ibid., 192–94 (English trans., 141–42 [modified]). The abbreviated formulation is indeed found in the manuscript: "Griechisch . . . 'katholisch.'" It is

necessary, of course, to respect the ambiguity: Augustine remains too Greek, in the sense that he keeps a universal position (καθόλου) regarding the difference in the phenomenalizations, but yields to it all the more when, following the un-interrogated "catholic" theology, he maintains, by recourse to a "universal exten-sion," the equivalence of the happy life and God.

4. "Tradition—nicht, bzw. nicht ganz destruiert!" (*GA* 60:193 [English trans., 141 (modified)]). The reproach is constant: Saint Augustine destroys the "Greek," objectifying, metaphysical approach but not entirely; he remains "still Greek" (257 [English trans., 193]), "not radically existential, but Greek" (247 [English trans., 185 (modified)]). The ambivalence of this approach, which at once plays Saint Augustine against the Greeks and condemns him for not completing their "destruction," will continue in *Sein und Zeit*. It has not yet been studied with the attention it deserves.

5. *De moribus Ecclesiae Catholicae et de moribus Manichaeorum* I, 25, 47, *BA* I, 206ff.

6. See below, Chapter 7.

7. *De Trinitate* XIII, 4, 7, 16, 284.

8. Ibid., IX, 12, 18, 16, 108. Should we hear an echo of Aristotle: "The act of the sensible and that of the sensing are one and the same, αὐτὴ μέν ἐστι καὶ μία" (*On the Soul* 3.2.425b25–26; see also 3.5.430a20 and 3.7.431a1)?

9. *Confessiones* X, 20, 29, 14, 194. See: "Sed quaero utrum in memoria sit beata vita. Neque enim amaremus eam, nisi nossemus. . . . Quod non fieret, nisi res ipsa, cujus hoc nomen est, eorum memoria tenetur" (I am asking if the happy life is found in memory. For we would not love it if we did not know it. . . . This would not occur if our memory did not contain the thing itself, for which it is the name) (ibid., 194–96).

10. *Confessiones* X, 23, 34, 14, 202. See also: "Accusat Deus peccata tua; si et tu accusas, conjugeris Deo. Quasi duae res sunt, homo et peccator. Quod audis homo, Deus fecit; quod audis peccator, ipse homo fecit. Oportet ut *oderis* in te opus tuum, et *ames* in te opus Dei. . . . Sit ante te quod non vis esse ante Deum. Si autem post te feceris peccatum tuum, retorquet illud tibi Deus ante oculos tuos; et tunc retorquet, quando jam paenitentiae fructus nullus erit" (God ac-cuses your sins, and if you too accuse them, you will be united with God. It is as if there were two things [in you]: the man and the sinner. What you understand by a man is what God did; what you mean by sinner is what the man himself did. You should *hate* your own work and *love* in yourself that of God. . . . Put before yourself what you would not like to see put before God. For if you put your sin behind you, God will thrust it back before your eyes; and he will thrust it back before your eyes at a moment when repentance will no longer bear fruit) (*Com-mentary on the Gospel of John* XII, 13, *PL* 35, 1491).

11. *Commentary on the Gospel of John* XXXV, 4, *PL* 35, 1659.

12. Heidegger, *Phänomenologie des religiösen Lebens*, §10, GA 60:201 (English trans., 148 [modified]).

13. Cicero had already described this repulsion, not of course with regard to truth but with regard to the birth of philosophy among the Latins: one must work at it but knowing full well that it will attack and reject: "eamque non adjuvemus, nosque ipsos *redargui* refellique patiamur." Those will not bear it well, who are committed, by tradition, habit, or interest, to keeping preconceived opinions, that they themselves cannot demonstrate ("certis quibusdam destinatisque sententiis quasi addicti et consecrati sunt eaque necessitate constricti, ut, etiam quae non probare soleant, coguntur constantiae causa defendere"). By contrast, those who seek truth, or at least stick to what is close to it, will accept, without fighting back, being refuted and, without acrimony, finding themselves refuted by it ("nos, qui sequimur probabilia . . . et refellere sine pertinacia et refelli sine iracundia parati sumus") (*Tusculanes* II, 1, 5, ed. J. E. King [Cambridge, MA, 1945²], 150–52). This use is found in the passage: "Nam tu, Deus *verax*, improbas eos et *redarguis* atque convincit eos" (For it is you yourself, veracious God, who reproves them, *impugns* them and convinces them of error [the Manicheans]) (*Confessiones* VIII, 10, 24, 14, 56).

14. Or, by contrast, of the truth that gives birth to love: "Concordiam pariat ipsa veritas" (Let the truth itself give birth to concord) (*Confessiones* XII, 30, 41, 14, 416).

15. Terence, *Andria* 1.1.68, a verse cited first in *Confessiones* X, 23, 34, 14, 202. J. J. O'Donnell (*Augustine: Confessions*, vol. 3, *Commentary on Books 8–13*, 194) refers to other occurrences in the form of a proverb in A. Otto, *Die Sprichwörter und sprichwörtlichen Redensarten der Römer* (Leipzig, 1989¹, Hildesheim 1962²), s.v. *veritas*, 2 (Ausonius, Lactantius, Rufinus, etc.).

16. Cicero, *De amicitia* 24.89, ed. W. Falconer (Cambridge, MA, 1923¹, 1996¹²), 196.

17. Lemaitre de Sacy's translation does not hesitate to say that "the wounds left by one who loves are worth more than the deceptive kisses of one who hates." See also Galatians 4:16: "Ergo inimicus vobis factus sum, verum dicens vobis" (Have I then become your enemy in speaking the truth to you?) John 8:40 and Galatians 4:16 are combined in the second citation made by the very same text of *Confessiones* X, 23, 34, 14, 202.

18. Thus the preface to *De civitate Dei* cites in the same trajectory and as equivalents Proverbs 3:34 (taken up for that matter by 1 Peter 5:6 and John 4:6) and the *Aeneid* 6.853: "Rex enim et conditor civitatis hujus, de qua loqui instituimus, in scriptura populi sui sententiam divinae legis aperuit, qua dictum est 'Deus superbis resistit, humilibus autem dat gratiam.' Hoc vero, quod Dei est, superbae quoque animae spiritus inflatus adfectat amatque sibi in laudibus dici: 'Parcere subjectis et debellare superbos'" (The king and founder of this city, about which we have decided to speak, has disclosed in the scriptures of his people the sentence of

the divine law in which it is said that "God resists the proud, but shows grace to the humble." But, this which is God's prerogative has been claimed as its own by the spirit that inflates the proud soul of man and loves to hear it said in its own praise, "it spares the submissive and subdues the proud") (*De civitate Dei, Praefatio*, 33, 192). The proud soul who wants to appropriate the law of God (favor those who submit, knock down the proud) is here Rome: "Tu regere imperio populos, Romane, memento / (Hae tibi erunt artes), pacisque imponere morem, / parcere subjectis et debellare superbos" (*Aeneid* 6.851–53).

19. *Commentary on the Gospel of John* XXX, 2, *PL* 35, 1633. *Lippitudo*, "inflammation of the eyes," can be translated by *ophthalmie* in French (see F. Gaffiot, *Dictionnaire*, s.v. "lippitudo," p. 914) or *ophthalmia* in English (see *Oxford English Dictionary*, s.v. *ophthalmia*).

20. This is confirmed by the *Commentary on the Gospel of John* XVIII, 11, *PL* 35, 1542–43. When we want to turn ourselves toward the light, "rursus quasi *reflectimur* pondere nostro ad ista consueta, tales sumus quales lippientes, cum producuntur ad videndum lumen, si forte antea visum omnino non habebant, et incipiunt eumdem visum per diligentiam medicorum utcumque reparare" (we are again *reflected* [bent back] by our own weight toward our habits; we are all like the opthalmiacs, when they are led to see the light, if they saw absolutely nothing beforehand, and begin to reestablish their vision by the care of doctors). The doctor, therefore, cares for them and tries to lead them once again to see the light. But "cum viderint, fulgore ipso *reverberantur* quodammodo, et respondent medico demonstranti: 'Jam jam vidi, sed videre non possum.' Quid ergo facit medicus? Revocat ad solita et addit collyrum" (once they saw, they were *reverberated* in some way by the very flash [of light] and, to the doctor who shows them the direction, they respond: "I just saw this very moment, but I cannot see." What does the doctor do? He sends them back to their old habits and gives them some eyedrops). And the same goes for the faithful: "erexistis cor vestrum ad videndum Verbum, et ipsius luce *reverberati* ad solita recedistis, rogate medicum ut adhibeat collyria" (you set up your hearts to see the Word, and *struck backwards* by his very light, you were sent back to your habits; ask a doctor, now, to apply eye drops). The question in its entirety consists in knowing how to make good use of the pain, which appears when we want to uproot ourselves from custom. For one must suffer to see.

21. *Soliloquia* I, 13, 23, *BA* 5, 72, which continues: "Quibus periculosum est, quamvis jam talibus ut sani recte dici possint, velle ostendere quod adhuc videre non valent. Ergo isti exercendi sunt prius, et eorum amor utiliter *differendus* atque nutriendus est" (To these, whom one can indeed say to be healthy, it is still dangerous to want to show what they cannot bear. They must therefore be trained first, and their love, which must be nourished, should usefully be delayed).

22. *De quantitate animae* 33, 75, 5, 382. See also: "In ista Trinitate quo missi sunt apostolic, videamus quod videmus, et quod mirum est quia illi non vident; non

enim vere non vident, sed ad id quod facies eorum ferit, *oculos claudant*. . . . Ergo, dilectissimi, videamus quod videre illi nolunt, non quod videant, sed quod se videre *doleant*, quasi clausum sit contra illos" (In this Trinity by which the apostles were sent, we see what we see and how astonishing is it that they do not see; not that they do not really see, but that they *close their eyes* to what smacks them in the face. . . . Therefore, beloved, let us see what they do not want to see, not because they do not see it but because what causes them pain to see closes up, as it were, before them) (*Commentary on the Gospel of John* VI, 6, then 9, *PL* 35, 1427 and 1429). The importance of this text resides in the fact that the impossibility of vision does not result from a fault or a weakness but from a decision about God himself.

23. *De vita beata* III, 19 and 21, 4, 256, 258. This ambivalence in the access to God according to the dispositions of man is based on 1 Corinthians 11:28–29. It is confirmed by "quam [sc. Sapientiam] quidem omnis rationalis anima consulit; sed tantum cuique panditur, quantum capere propter propriam, sive malam sive bonam voluntatem potest" (Wisdom is consulted by every rational soul, but it opens to each of them only insofar as each can receive it, according to its own will, be it good or ill) (*De Magistro* XI, 38, 6, 102).

24. *Commentary on the First Epistle of John* VI, 3, *PL* 35, 2021. See another development of the same argument: "Multi enim delixerunt peccata sua, multi *confessi* sunt peccata sua; quia qui *confitetur* peccata sua et accusat peccata sua, jam cum Deo facit. Accusat Deus peccata tua; si et tu accusas, conjungeris Deo. . . . Oportet ut oderis in te opus tuum, et ames in te opus Dei. Cum autem coeperit tibi displicere quod fecisti, incipiunt bona opera tua, quia accusas mala opera tua. Initium bonorum operum, *confessio* operum malorum. Facis veritatem et venis ad lucem. . . . Quia et hoc ipsum quod tibi displicuit peccatum tuum, non tibi displaceret *nisi Deus tibi luceret* et ejus veritatem tibi ostenderet" (Many are those who loved their sins, many those who *confessed* their sins; because he who *confesses* his sins and so to speak accuses them, he does it with God. God accuses your sins; if you too accuse them, you are joined with God. . . . It behooves you, then, to hate in yourself your own doing and to love in yourself God's work. When what you have done will have begun to displease you, your good works will begin because you accuse your bad works. The beginning of good works is the *confession* of the bad. Do the truth and you will come to the light. . . . For the very fact that your sin was displeasing to you would not have been displeasing to you had God not illuminated you and had his truth not shown itself to you) (*Commentary on the Gospel of Saint John* XII, 13, *PL* 35, 1491).

25. *Commentary on the Gospel of Saint John* XC, 3, *PL* 35, 1860.

26. *Confessiones* VI, 11, 20, 15, 560. See: "Quid ergo adhuc suspendor infelix, et cruciatu mirabili *differor?* Jam certe ostendi mihi nihil aliud me amare, siquidem quod non propter amatur, non amatur. Ego autem solam propter se amo sapientiam" (Why then did I still stay in suspense and will I *defer* with an astonishing

sorrow? It is now surely shown to me that what one does not love for itself, one simply does not love. And as for me, what I love for itself is only wisdom) (*Soliloquia* I, 13, 22, *BA* 5, 70).

27. See: "te *ipso*, non in te *ipso* frui debes, sed in eo qui fecit te" (you should enjoy *yourself*, not however *in yourself*, but in he who made you) (*De Trinitate* IX, 8, 13, 16, 98).

28. *De Trinitate* XII, 11, 16, 14, 240.

29. *De civitate Dei* XIV, 4, 1, 35, 362. See also: "Haec igitur trinitas mentis non propterea Dei est *imago*, quia sui meminit mens, et intelligit ac diligit se: sed quia potest etiam meminisse et intelligere et amare a quo facta est" (Therefore the trinity of the mind is not an *image* of God because it remembers itself, understands itself, and loves itself, but because it can *also* remember, understand, and love he who made it) (*De Trinitate* XIV, 12, 15, 16, 386). The character of image does not stem from the pure and simple trinitarian structure of mental operations but from their common orientation toward him from whom they bear, by creation, the likeness.

30. *Confessiones* X, 2, 2, 14, 142. See another exchange of pronouns: "Sed unaquaeque anima tanto est pietate purgatior, quanto *privato suo* minus delectata, legem universalitatis intuetur, eique devote ac libenter obtemperat. Est enim lex universalitatis divina sapientia. Quanto autem amplius *privato suo* gaudet et *neglecto Deo*, qui omnibus animis utiliter et salubriter praesidet, *ipsa sibi* vel aliis, quibus potuerit, *vult esse pro Deo, suam* potius *in se* vel in alios, quam *illius [Deus]* in omnes diligens potestatem, tanto est sordidior, tantoque magis poenaliter divinis legibus, tanquam publici servire cogitur" (Now every soul is of a piety all the more pure as, taking pleasure less in what is proper to it, it keeps before its eyes the law of universality and submits to it willingly and with devotion. The law of universality is the wisdom of God. But the more it enjoys what is proper to it and, *neglecting God*, who presides over all souls, seeing to their interest and health, *wants to be taken for God*, either in its own eyes, or in the eyes of others, if such a thing can be, preferring more *its own* power to *that* of God who loves them all, the more it degrades itself and feels weighing on it, as a punishment, the constraint of the divine laws which protect that interest of all) (*De diversis quaestiones LXXXIII*, 79, 1, 10, 344).

31. *Commentary on the Gospel of John* II, 4, *PL* 35, 1390.

32. *De Trinitate* X, 8, 11, 16, 142.

33. *Confessiones* X, 23, 34, 14, 202.

34. Ibid., III, 6, 10, 13, 378. Or else: "non solum ignorata, sed falsa tam vesana superbiae vanitate diceret [sc. Faustus]" (V, 5, 8, 13, 474).

35. See "sibi tribuendo quae tuae sunt, ac per hic student perversissima caecitate etiam tibi tribuere quae sua sunt" (ibid., V, 3, 6, 13, 470).

36. Ibid., IV, 16, 28, 13, 454.

37. Ibid., VII, 9, 13, 13, 608.

38. Ibid., XII, 25, 34, 14, 398. See the same question in XII, 14, 17 and the response that follows in XII, 15, 18, 14, 366ff.

39. *Metaphysics* 1.1.980a1.

40. *De Trinitate* VIII, 7, 10, 6, 284; and *Pensées*, §148, *Œuvres complètes*, 519 (English trans., 74).

41. Thomas Aquinas, *De veritate*, q. 1, a. 1; Kant, *Critique of Pure Reason*, B 82, Ak. A III, 79 (English trans., 97); and Husserl, *Logische Untersuchungen*, VI, §39 (Tübingen, 1921²), 121 (English trans., 263 [modified]).

42. Descartes, *Regulae ad directionem ingenii* VIII, AT X, 396, 3–4 (English trans., 1:30); and Kant, *Critique of Pure Reason*, B 350 ("Wahrheit und Schein sind nicht im Gegenstande, sofern er augeschaut wird, sondern nur im Urteil über denselben, sofern er gedacht wird," Ak. A III, 234) (English trans., 297).

43. *Sein und Zeit*, §44, 219 (English trans., 262).

44. Ibid., §44, 218 (English trans., 261 [modified]).

45. Ibid., §7, 28 (English trans., 51). And therefore phenomenology has no other goal and definition than "to let that which shows itself be seen from itself in the very way in which it shows itself from itself" (Das was sich zeigt, so wie es sich von ihm selbst her zeigt, von ihm selbst her sehen lassen) (§7, 34 [English trans., 58]).

46. "Sein—nicht Seiendes—'gibt es' nur, sofern Wahrheit ist. Und sie *sit*, nur sofern und solange Dasein ist" (*Sein und Zeit*, §44, 230 [English trans., 272 (modified)]).

47. "Wahrsein als entdeckend-sein ist eine Seinsweise des Daseins" (*Sein und Zeit*, §44, 220 [English trans., 263]). See also: "Die Erschlossenheit ist eine wesenhafte Seinsart des Daseins. *Wahrheit 'gibt es' nur, sofern und solange Dasein ist.* Seiendes ist nur *dann* entdeckt und nur *solange* erschlossen, als überhaupt Dasein *ist*" (Disclosedness is a kind of Being which is essential to Dasein. *"It gives" truth only insofar as Dasein is and so long as Dasein is.* Beings are uncovered only *when* Dasein *is*; and only as long as Dasein *is*, are they disclosed) (ibid., 226 [English trans., 269 (modified)]). It should, however, be checked if and how far, when Heidegger developed these analyses in "On the Essence of Truth" (a seminar given in 1930), he maintained still more firmly this quasi-transcendental function or if he did not try to overcome it: "existent freedom as essence of truth is not man's property; rather man ex-ists as the property of this freedom and only in this way founds a history" (*Wegmarken*, GA 9:191 [English trans. in *Basic Writings*, 129 (modified)]).

48. See some suggestions in *De surcroît: Etudes sur les phénomènes saturés* (Paris, 2001), chap. 2, §5, and chap. 3, §1 (*In Excess: Studies in Saturated Phenomena* [New York, 2004]).

49. *Pensées*, in *Œuvres complètes*, §739, 596 (English trans., 256 [modified]).

50. Ibid., §377, 546. (English trans., 137).

51. Ibid., §979, 469 (English trans., 350).

52. Ibid., §978, 636ff. (English trans., 348–49). Cf. "There is a lot of difference between not being for Christ and saying so, and not being for Christ and pretending to be. The former can perform miracles, but not the latter, for it is clear in the case of the former that they are against the truth but not in that of the others, and so the miracles are clearer" (ibid., §843, 610 [English trans., 290]).

53. See my translation of *Confessiones* X, 23, 34, above, §17, p. 109.

54. *Pensées*, §962, 632 (English trans., 340).

55. *Commentary on the Gospel of Saint John* XII, 13, *PL* 35, 1491.

56. *Pensées,* §926, 622 (English trans., 318 [modified]).

57. *Sein und Zeit*, §29: "dass das Dasein je schon immer bestimmt ist" (134, 19–20 [English trans., 173 (modified)]), and 139n1 (English trans., 492nv).

58. See Pascal, *De l'art de persuader*, in *Œuvres complètes*, 355 (English trans., 406). (I commented on this thesis in *On Descartes' Metaphysical Prism*, §25. Heidegger refers, though vaguely, to "Vgl. *Pensées*, a.a." In fact, as indicated by a note in §1, p. 4 (English trans., 489), he uses the Brunschvicg edition, *Pensées et Opuscules* (Paris, 1897¹, 1912⁶), 169, without mentioning the real title of the passage. These enigmatic suggestions have to be completed by a previous remark: "Scheler first made it clear, especially in the essay 'Liebe und Erkenntnis,' that intentional relations are quite diverse, and that even, for example, love and hatred ground knowing. Here Scheler picks up a theme of Pascal and Augustine" (*Metaphysische Anfangsgründe der Logik*, §9, *GA* 26:169 [English trans., 134]).

59. *Contra Faustum* XXXII, 18, *PL* 42, 507. The conclusion must also be read: "Probamus etiam ipsum [sc. Spiritum Sanctum] inducere in omnem veritatem, quia non intratur in veritatem, nisi per charitatem: 'Charitas autem Dei diffusa est, ait apostolus, in cordibus nostris per Spiritum Sanctum qui datus est nobis' (Romans 5:5)."

60. He goes on: "What Augustine identifies as love and hate and only in certain contexts specifies as Dasein's truly cognitive mode of being we shall later have to take as an original phenomenon of Dasein" (*Prolegomena zur Geschichte des Zeitbegriffs*, §20, *GA* 20:222 [English trans., 164–65]). We should note, too, that as early as 1921, Heidegger understood the "sero te amavi [pulchritudo tam antiqua et tam nova]" of *Confessiones* X, 27, 38, 14, 208 as a "level of factical life" in general (*Phänomenologie des religiosen Lebens*, §11, 204 [English trans., 150]).

61. *De moribus Ecclesiae Catholicae et de moribus Manichaeorum* I, 7, 11, *BA* 1, 152. *Consuetudo* no doubt alludes to probable knowledge had from the opinion of the most wise, according to Aristotle's precept (*Topics* 1.1.100b22–25).

62. *Pensées*, §176, 523 (English trans., 84).

63. *Posthumous Fragments*, 7 [24] and 9 [91], in Nietzsche, *Sämtliche Werke: Kritische Studienausgabe*, ed. Colli-Montinari, 8:1.311, and 8:2.49.

64. Ibid., 16 [32], 8:3.288. On these points see my analysis in Jean-Luc Marion, *The Idol and Distance* (New York, 2001), §§5–6.

65. *Vermischte Bemerkungen*, in *Werkausgabe* (Frankfurt, 1984), 8:504 (English trans., 39 [modified]).

66. *Philosophische Untersuchungen*, II, *Werkausgaben*, 1:566 (English trans., 222).

67. *Autrement qu'être*, 184 (English trans., 145). In "Vérité du dévoilement et vérité du témoignage," an early version of chapter 7 of *Autrement qu'être ou au-delà de l'essence*, we already find an anticipation of this very page: "This witnessing belongs to the very glory of the Infinite. . . . The glory of the infinite is the subject's exit out from the dark corners of the *as-for-myself*, which—like the bushes in Paradise where Adam hid after his sin, hearing the voice of God . . . offered a way out in the assignation from the other" (see E. Castelli, ed., *Le témoignage* [Paris, 1972], 107).

68. *Autrement qu'être*, 183 (English trans., 143).

69. *The Oxford Authors: Gerard Manley Hopkins*, ed. C. Phillips (Oxford, 1986), 68.

70. *Confessiones* II, 6, 13, 13, 352; and IV, 15, 27, 13, 454. H. U. von Balthasar showed definitively the decisive function played by *pulchritudo* in Augustinian theology (*Herrlichkeit*, 2, *Fächer der Style* [Einsiedeln, 1962], chap. 3 [English trans., *The Glory of the Lord*, vol. 2]. I am entirely in his debt. Since then, see C. Harrison, *Beauty and Revelation in the Thought of St. Augustine* (Oxford, 1992); and J. Kreuzer, *Pulchritudo. Vom Erkennen Gottes bei Augustin. Bemerkungen zu den Büchern IX, X, and XI, der Confessione* (Munich, 1995).

71. "pleni sunt vetustatis suae" (*Confessiones* XI, 10, 12, 14, 290).

72. *Commentary on the Gospel of Saint John* III, 5, *PL* 35, 1398.

73. *Commentaries on the Psalms* 95, 7, *PL* 37, 1232.

74. It should be noted that hearing comes up as the first of the senses, in opposition to the platitudes often heard about the primacy (obviously Greek and metaphysical) of sight. This primacy is verified with the voice, at first anonymous, that said "tolle, lege!" (*Confessiones* VIII, 12, 29, 14, 66; commented on in Chapter 1, §6) and thereby shattered his deafness for the first time. Such a voice does not only open access to the joy of truth, therefore to the *vita beata*; it already fully accomplishes it: "Ecce vox tua gaudium meum, vox tua super affluentiam voluptatum" (Behold, your voice is my joy, your voice [that rings out] higher than the inrushing of pleasures) (XI, 2, 3, 274).

75. Another text confirms this seduction game: "Nunc autem quod gemitus meus testis est displicere me mihi, tu refulges et places et amaris et desideraris, ut erubescam de me et abjiciam me atque eligam te et nec tibi nec mihi placeam nisi de te" (But now that my moaning testifies that I am displeased with myself, you, you shine out, you are pleasing, you are loved, you are desired, to such a

point that I am embarrassed about myself and choose you and am never pleasing, either to you or to myself, except on account of you) (*Confessiones* X, 22, 14, 142).

76. *Soliloquia* I, 13, 22, *BA* 5, 70. J. J. O'Donnell, who makes the comparison, finds the seduction in the second part of *Confessiones* X, 27, 38 "erotic, but much less explicitly [so]" than the possession described in the *Soliloquies* (see O'Donnell, *Augustine: Confessions*, 3:197). But isn't seduction *always* more erotic than possession? See also the surprising qualification of the "lumen honestatis et gratis amplectendae pulchritudinis" (the light of honesty and of a beauty that is embraced without paying for it) (*Confessiones* VI, 16, 26, 13, 572), that the French translation of *BA* waters down passably by rendering it as "that must be embraced with a disinterested goal." In fact, it truly is about embracing without even paying, in a bold extension of the eschatological feast in which one will eat and drink without having to pay anything.

77. *Soliloquia* I, 7, 14, *BA* 5, 52.

78. *Confessiones* IV, 13, 20, 13, 442. On *De pulchro et apto* see Testard, *Saint Augustin et Cicéron*, 49–66.

79. *De ordine* I, 8, 21, *BA* 4, 336.

80. *Contra academicos* II, 3, 7, *BA* 13, 70.

81. *Enchiridion* III, 10, 9, 118.

82. *De libero arbitrio* II, 17, 45, 6, 302; and *Confessiones* II, 6, 12, 13, 350. It is in this context, obviously, that we must understand how beautiful things achieve beauty itself: "pulchra trajecta per animas in manus artifciosas ab illa pulchritudine veniunt, quae super animas est, cui suspirat anima mea die ac noctes" (for the beautiful things that pass through souls in order to arrive in artful hands come from this very beauty, which surpasses the souls and toward which my soul pants "day and night" [Psalm 1:2]) (*Confessiones* X, 34, 53, 14, 236).

83. *Enchiridion* I, 5, 9, 108.

84. *Commentary on the First Epistle of John* IX, 9, *PL* 35, 2051.

CHAPTER 4

1. Saint Augustine's translation says *temptatio* following the Septuagint πειρατήριόν, while the Vulgate is content with "Militia est vita hominis super terram." Saint Augustine's commentary clearly validates this sense: "Temptationem vero dicit tanquam stadium certaminis, ubi vincit homo vel vincitur" (For it says temptation for the stage of combat when man is victor or vanquished) (*Annotations to Job* VII, 1, *PL* 34, 832). Following the Vulgate, the question is not one of knowing if Job's innocent petition is just but of understanding that it rests on the distinction between sin and temptation. For Job it is all about resisting the temptation to accuse God, as one bears a conscription, a service in the army,

which is identified with one's entire life. One can clarify this debate by taking into account D. Marion, *L'homme combatif* (Paris, 1980).

2. *Commentaries on the Psalms* 122, 7, *PL* 37, 1635. J. J. O'Donnell (*Augustine: Confessions*, vol. 2, *Commentary on Books 1–7*, 200) cites and discusses other texts in this sense but without seeing the implication of this addition.

3. *Commentaries on the Psalms* 55, 2, *PL* 36, 647. See "Qui enim non tentantur, non probantur, et qui non probatur, non proficit" (ibid., 69, 5, *PL* 36, 870). The discussion concerning the usefulness of temptation in *De Genesi ad litteram* (XI, 4, 6–6, 8, *BA* 49, 238–42) remains removed from possibility as such. In contrast, the doctrine of temptation responds to the question of self-knowledge, inaccessible otherwise, as other texts make quite clear. For example: "'Tentavit, inquit, Deus Abraham.' Sed ergo ignarus est Deus rerum, sic nesciens cordis humani, ut tentendo hominem inveniat? Absit: non ut ipse discat, sed ut quod in homine latet aperiat" ("God tempted Abraham" [Genesis 22:1]. But then is God unaware of some things, and does he not know the human heart, since he finds it by tempting it? Far from that being the case, this is not done so that God might learn something but so that what there is in man might be disclosed) (*Sermon* 2, 2, *PL* 38, 28). And: "tentatione Deum non id agere, ut ipse aliquid cognoscat quod ante nesciebat, sed ut ipso tentente, id est interrogante, quod est in homine occultum prodatur. *Non enim sibi homo ita notus est, ut Creatori*; nec sic aeger sibi notus, ut medico. . . . Quia *nescit se homo*, nisi in tentatione discat se" (With temptation God does not act so as to know what previously he did not, but by becoming himself the tempter, that is to say inquisitor, [he makes it happen that] there comes to light what in man had remained hidden. *For man does not know himself as his Creator knows him*, nor do the sick know themselves as their doctors do. . . . Because *he does not know himself*, it is by temptation that man learns to know himself) (*Sermon* II, 3, 3, *PL* 38, 29).

4. J. J. O'Donnell (*Augustine: Confessions*, 2:30) makes the highly relevant point that it is not about eliminating the passions and *mutabilitas* but, contrary to every Neoplatonic schema, deciding *mutabiliter*, at the heart of the unsurpassable mutability of the created, of facticity itself.

5. Heidegger, commenting on *Confessiones* X, saw this perfectly and said, "The *molestia* is not a piece of object—a region of being, present in some sense of the theoretical objectification of nature (*vorhanden*)—but it designates a *How* of experiencing, and precisely as such a How, it characterizes the How of factical experiencing" (*Phänomenologie des religiösen Lebens*, GA 60:231 [English trans., 172]). See "[*Tentatio*] is not something that happens, but an existential sense of enactment, a How of experiencing" (ibid., 248 [English trans., 186 (modified)]).

6. GA 60:206 (my emphasis) (English trans., 152 [modified]). Same prudence even farther along: "*Inwiefern* die *Tentatio* ein echtes *Existenziel*" (ibid., 256). The phrase "Oneri mihi sum" is cited only on pp. 205 and 250.

7. *GA* 60:249 (see perhaps also 242) and 206 (English trans., 186 [modified] and 152 [modified]).

8. *Sein und Zeit*, §29, 134: "Das Sein ist als Last offenbar geworden. . . . Die Stimmung macht offenbar 'wie einem ist und wird.' In diesem 'wie einem ist' bringt des Gestimmtsein das Sein in seinem 'da.'" See *Lastcharakter des Daseins*, §29, 134–35.

9. With the reservation of a doubt: "Es gilt, diesen Grundcharakter, in dem Augustin das faktische Leben erfährt, die *Tentatio*, schärfer zu fassen und daraus dann zu verstehen, *inwiefern* der in solcher Helligkeit und Vollzugsstufe Lebende sich selbst notwendig ein Last ist" (*GA* 60:206).

10. C. Sommer has accurately qualified this tactic as "de-theologization" (*Heidegger, Aristote, Luther: Les sources aristotéliciennes et néo-testamentaires d'"Etre et temps"* [Paris, 2005], 31 and passim).

11. The comparison is justified by the citation of Matthew 11:28–30 in the pending exposition of the temptation of curiosity in *Confessiones* X, 36, 58, 14, 246 (cf. *De Trinitate* IX, 9, 14, 16, 100).

12. *Commentaries on the Psalms* 67, 18, *PL* 36, 823.

13. *Commentaries on the Psalms* 7, 16, *PL* 36, 107.

14. *Commentaries on the Psalms* 59, 8, *PL* 36, 719. *Sarcina* (equivalent of *onus* as another translation of φορτίον) designates the soldier's pack. We see here the same *sublevare* as in *Confessiones* X, 28, 39, 14, 208. Another reference to Christ in: "Durum jubet [sc. avaritia], levia jubeo [sc. Christus]: onus ejus grave, sarcina mea levias est. Noli velle ab avaritia possideri" (The order that greed gives is hard, mine light. Want not that it should take possession of you) (*Commentaries on the Psalms* 128, 4, *PL* 37, 1691).

15. On *uti/frui* see the canonic text in *De doctrina christiana* I, 3, 3–I, 4, 4; see also Holte, *Béatitude et sagesse*; O. O'Donovan, "*Usus* et *fruitio* in Augustine, *De doctrina christiana* I," *Journal of Theological Studies* (1992): 361–97; and Madec, *Saint Augustin et la philosophie*, 77ff.

16. *De Trinitate* XII, 11, 16, 16, 242.

17. Curiosity (*Neugier*) comes explicitly from Augustinian *curiositas*: *Sein und Zeit*, §36 (p. 171, note citing *Confessiones* X, 35, 54), does nothing else but confirm *Phänomenologie des religiösen Lebens*, §14b, *GA* 20:223, 225. To *curiositas* is opposed *studiositas* (*De utilitate credendi* IX, 22, 8, 256).

18. A similar conclusion—the crisis of the self in temptation—appears in the description of the *libido* of hearing: "in [Dei] oculis mihi quaestio factus sum" (X, 35, 50, 14, 232). See the analysis in Chapter 2, §10 above.

19. Saint Augustine here emphasizes a privilege of sight, but it is negative: besides playing its own role as vision, vision is also a double for all the other senses, since we say *see* with regard to what we hear, taste, smell, or touch: "*videri* enim

dicuntur haec omnia" (X, 35, 54, 14, 238). But this privilege becomes a burden, since, in fact, it is no longer about a sense but a temptation that uses them all.

20. Heidegger rightly cites this text (*GA* 60:207) as a sketch of factical life, but he completely omits an analysis of *delectatio* as such, still less in its intrinsic relation with *amor*. This permits him to *neutralize cura*, so as to employ it in the *Seinsfrage*, but it also makes him lose not only the Augustinian argument but, especially, the erotic horizon proper to *cura* (therefore no doubt to *Sorge* itself), which thereby becomes unintelligible or, at least, greatly weakened.

21. *Commentaries on the Psalms* 9, 15, *PL* 36, 124.

22. *Commentaries on the Psalms* 77, 10, *PL* 36, 991.

23. *De duabus animabus contra Manichaeos* X, 12, 17, 88.

24. The countless criticisms of the Augustinian doctrine of sin ought not lose sight of this point and, especially, not reestablish, unknowingly (or even knowingly), ideologies comparable to Manicheanism.

25. *De duabus animabus contra Manichaeos* X, 14, 17, 90. This knowledge is so clear that it is formulated in terms of the principle of contradiction: "Ita quidem invitus et volens unus animus simul esse potest; sed unum et idem nolle simul et velle non potest" (One and the same mind can at the same time will and [act] despite itself, but it cannot will and not will the same thing at the same moment) (ibid.).

26. *Sublevare* again, as in "quem tu imples, sublevas eum" (*Confessiones* X, 28, 39, 14, 208). I maintain the same translation as above (p. 153). The certainty of enjoying a free will, even experiencing it as evil, constitutes a first liberation. Whence the absurdity of opposing grace to freedom of choice, since freedom itself comes over me as a gracious gift: "non omnibus naturis dedit voluntatis arbitrium" (*De Genesi ad litteram* VIII, 23, 44, 49, 76). And: "Nam si quaeramus utrum Dei donum sit voluntas bona, mirum si negare quisquam audeat" (For if one asks if a good will is a gift of God, it would be surprising if someone were to deny it) (*Quaestiones VII ad Simplicianum* II, 12, 10, 470). See below, §29.

27. This would be a strictly Cartesian project. See my sketch "Notes sur les modalités de l'*ego*," in *Chemins de Descartes*, ed. P. Soual and M. Veto (Paris, 1997) (first delivered at Actes du Colloque "Descartes," organized by l'Université de Poitiers [November 1996]).

28. *Soliloquia* I, 1, 5, *BA* 5, 34. It is not a question of a "*good* will" (as P. de Labriolle translates *ad loc.*) but of the will as such, good or bad (which, by the way, sounds paradoxically more Kantian than this gloss).

29. Even the difficulty of the all-seeing omnipotence of God could not put it into question, be it only by reference to the case of desire for beatitude. God can foresee that I desire beatitude, without this knowledge preventing me from desiring it freely. "Sed dico, cum futurus es beatus, non te invitum, sed volentem futurum" (But I say that when you will be blessed, you will be so by having wanted it, not against your inclination) (*De libero arbitrio* III, 3, 7, 6, 338).

30. This permits us to understand *De Magistro* XI, 38: "Ille autem qui consulitur, docet, qui in interiore homine habitare dictus est Christus, id est incommutabilis Dei Virtus atque sempiterna Sapientia: quam quidem omnis rationalis anima consulit; sed tantum cuique panditur, *quantum capere propter propriam, sive malam, sive bonam voluntatem, potest.* Et si quando fallitur, non fit vitio consultae veritatis, ut neque hujus, quae foris est lucis vitium est, quod corporei oculi saepe falluntur, quam lucem de rebus visibilibus consuli fatemur, ut eas nobis *quantum* cernere valemus, ostendat" (He who teaches is therefore he whom one consults, Christ of whom it is said that he dwells within the man, that is to say, the unchangeable Virtue of God and his eternal Wisdom, consulted by every rational soul, but which opens to each *only insofar as it can receive according to its own will, be it bad or good.* And if a soul should happen to be deceived, the fault does not lie with the truth consulted, no more than if the bodily eyes are often deceived, the fault lies with the external light, that we admit consulting so that it might show us visible things *insofar as we are able to see them*) (6, 102ff.).

31. Descartes: "ex magna luce in intellectu magna consecuta est propensio in voluntate, atque ita tantomagis sponte et libere illud credidi, quanto minus fui ad illud indifferens" (from a great light in the intellect there follows a great inclination in the will such that I believed it all the more freely [sc. that I exist] as I was less indifferent to it) (*Meditationes de prima philosophia* IV, AT VIII, 59, 1–4 [English trans., 41 (modified)]).

32. *Confessiones* X, 23, 34, 14, 202. See Chapter 3, §17, p. 109.

33. *Commentaries on the Psalms*, respectively, 93, 19, and 100, 6, *PL* 37, 1206 and 1287.

34. "Lex enim peccati est violentia consuetudinis, qua trahitur et tenetur etiam *invitus* animus eo merito, quo in eam *volens* inlabitur" (The law of sin is the violence of habit, which drags and holds the spirit itself *against its liking*, something it does indeed deserve, seeing as it falls into it *by willing it*) (VIII, 5, 12, 14, 32).

35. *Confessiones* VIII, 5, 12, 14, 32. "But the one was pleasing and bent me to it; the other attracted me and tied me to it" (E. Tréhorel and G. Bouissou, *BA* 14, 32) is better than "But on one side, charm and fascination [?], and, on the other, complaisance and fetters" (P. Cambronne, *Les Confessions précédées de dialogues philosophiques*, 937).

36. Opposite *BA* 14, I translate "non est, quod imperat" in the obvious sense of *non est id quod imperat*, "what it commands does not happen," and therefore I understand "imperat ut esset" simply as "commanded that it [what it wills] be" without adding a reflexive, as if it commanded itself. This, more sober, reading of the text, is justified conceptually, too: the immediacy of the will to itself (according to *De libero arbitrio*) makes it impossible, and for that matter useless, that it will itself to the second degree; as soon as it wills, it wills and commands entirely.

The difficulty of finding oneself in a situation of having to will to will already indicates an anomaly of the will that Saint Augustine will elsewhere diagnose immediately as a sickness of the spirit.

37. Bergson, *La pensée et le mouvant: Essais et conférences* (Paris, 1934), 66.

38. *Letter 177, PL* 33, 766; and *Enchiridion* IX, 31, 9, 162. See also: "ad vitam vero
tenendam voluntas *non sat est*, si adjutoria sive alientorum, sive quocumque tuta-
nimum desint" (to maintain itself in life, the will *is not sufficient* without the help
of food and other necessities) (*Enchiridion* XXVIII, 106, 9, 296).

39. *Enchiridion* XXII, 81, 9, 250. In contrast we read in Plato: "Simonides was
not so irreverent as to praise those who do not do evil willingly (ἑκὼν), as if there
were none who did evil willingly (ἑκόντες): 'As for me, I am thoroughly convinced that there is nobody, among wise men, who would assert that there is any
man whatsoever who would do wrong and dishonorable and wicked things willingly (ἑκόντα), for everybody knows well that doers of dishonorable and wicked
deeds do them against their will (ἄκόντες)'" (*Protagoras* 345d).

40. *Confessiones* VIII, 7, 16, 14, 42. Or "tanto exsecrabilius *me* comparatum eis
[sc. the other converts] *oderum*" (VIII, 7, 17, 14, 42). This reversal of one hatred
into another (a hatred of the hatred of truth) does nothing but recover one of the
possible definitions of *confessio*: "Cum enim malus sum, nihil aliud confiteri tibi
quam displicere mihi: cum vero pius, nihil est aliud confiteri tibi quam hoc non
tribuere mihi" (For when I am wicked, confessing to you is nothing other than
being displeased with myself; but when I am pious, confessing to you is nothing
other than not attributing it [being pious] to myself) (X, 2, 2, 14, 142; see above,
Chapter 1, §4).

41. *Summa Theologiae*, Ia IIae, q. 77, a. 2, resp., and the example *ad* 4. The correct syllogism (No fornication is permitted / This is a fornication / Therefore this
is not permitted) is thus transformed into an incorrect syllogism (Pleasure is to
be sought [contradiction of the universal, replaced by a particular] / This is not
a fornication [distraction as to the nature of the universal] / Therefore this is to
be sought). See also *De malo*, q. 3, a. 7: science merely in *habitus* (and not in act)
can lack by distraction the universal as such, and *passio*, defined as "fortis circa
aliquod particulare," can also contradict the universal; the modifications of the
body proper can end up at the same result. It can be doubted that one can commit fornication *without knowing it* and smile at the hypothesis.

42. Kant, *Religion Within the Limits of Reason Alone*, I, 2, Ak. A, t. 6, 29.

43. Donald Davidson, *Essays on Actions and Events* (Oxford, 1980), 42.

44. See: "cum efficientes non sint, ut dixi, sed deficientes" (since they are not
not efficient, but, as I said, deficient) (XII, 7, 35, 170). "Hoc scio, naturam Dei
numquam, nusquam, nulla ex parte posse deficere, et ea posse deficere, quae ex
nihilo facta sunt. Quae tamen quanto magis sunt et bona faciunt (tunc enim aliquid faciunt) causas habent efficientes; in quantum autem deficiunt et ex hoc mala

faciunt (quid enim tunc faciunt nisi vana?) causas habent deficientes" (What I know is that the nature of God can never, anywhere or in any part, be deficient and that what can be deficient are things made from nothing. Which, nevertheless, the more they are and do good works [for they do indeed do something], the more they have efficient causes; but the more they prove defective and in consequence the more they do evil works [and what do they do other than vain and empty things?], the more they have deficient causes) (XII, 8, 35, 172). And again: "malorum [causam] vero ab immutabili bono deficientem boni mutabilis voluntatem" (the cause of evils is only the will for a changing good, which itself defects from a permanent good) (*Enchiridion* VIII, 23, 9, 148).

45. See also: "Voluntas autem tantam vim habet copulandi haec duo, ut et sensum formandum admoveat ei rei quae cernitur et in ea formatum teneat. Et si tam *violentia* est, ut *possit vocari amor*, aut cupiditas, aut libido, etiam caeterum corpus animantis *vehementer* afficit" (The will has such strength to couple these two terms [sc. the body and the image of the thing] that, in order to form the meaning, it applies it to the thing seen and maintains it formed in it. And if it is violent enough that one can name it a love, a desire, or a concupiscence, it then powerfully affects all the rest of the body that animates it [sc. of the flesh]) (XI, 2, 5, 16, 172).

46. This definition of love by the will, or more exactly of the full will *as love*, will find a remarkably faithful echo in William of St. Thierry: "bonae voluntatis vehementia amor in nobis dicitur" (strength of will in us is called love) (*De contemplando Deo*, §18). Or: "Nihil enim est aliud amor quam vehemens in bono voluntas" (Love is nothing other than a will strong in the good) (*De natura et dignitate amoris*, §6). Or: "Voluntas in hoc filia gratiae est. Gratia eam generat, gratia lactat, gratia nutrit ac provehit et a perfectum usque perficit; hoc est caritas, id est magna et bene affecta voluntas fiat" (The will is in this child of grace. Grace engenders it, grace nurses it, it nourishes it and leads it to perfection, which is to say it becomes charity—in other words, a great and most affected will) (*Speculum fidei*, §14). And finally: "magna enim voluntas ad Deum amor est" (Love is nothing other than a great will toward God) (*Epistula ad fratres de Monte Dei*, §104). Saint Francis de Sales is quite clearly inscribed within this tradition: "The will governs all the other faculties of the human mind, but it is governed by its love, which makes it what it is; . . . thus sacred love is a miraculous child since the human will cannot conceive it if the Holy Spirit does not spread it in our hearts; and as it is supernatural, it must preside and reign over all the affections, even over the understanding and the will" (*Traité de l'amour de Dieu*, I, 6, in *Œuvres*, ed. A. Ravier [Paris, 1969], 367). On the relation between the will, freedom, and love (of God) see my sketch "L'image de la liberté," in *Saint Bernard et la philosophie*, ed. Remi Brague (Paris, 1993).

47. That sexual desire remains radically uncontrollable is emphasized by many texts: "Quod adversus damnatum culpa inoeboedentiae voluntatem libido

inoeboedentialiter movebat, verecundia prudenter tengebat" (Modesty hid out
of a sense of shame what concupiscence set on fire with disobedience, defying
the will which had been punished for its own revolt) (*De civitate Dei* XIV, 17,
BA 35, 430). This disobedience is doubled into two contraries: not only can't I
hold myself back from desiring, but sometimes I cannot set myself to desiring:
"Sed neque ipsi amatores hujus voluptatis sive ad concubitus conjugales, sive ad
immunditias flagitiorum, cum voluerint commoventur; sed aliquando importu-
nus est ille motus poscente nullo, aliquando autem destitutit inhiantem, et cum
in animo concupiscentia ferveat, friget in corpore" (But the very ones who love
this pleasure, whether it be in the conjugal bed or in the impurities of depravity,
do not bestir themselves at will; but this movement sometimes imposes itself on
them when they do not ask for it, sometimes it is missing from him who aspires
to it, and when concupiscence warms the mind, the body remains cold) (XIV,
16, 35, 426).

48. *Soliloquia* I, 1, 5, *BA* 5, 32 (twice). In this same dialogue it happens that
the character Augustine, in a demand made of the character Reason, formulates
a mistaken version of this principle: "Impera quaevis dura, quaelibet ardua, *quae
tamen in mea poteste sint*, per quae me quo desidero, perventurum esse non du-
bitem" (Command of me things as hard as you will, as arduous as you will, *but
which still remain within the limits of my power*, by which I do not doubt but that
I will succeed in what I desire) (I, 14, 24, 5, 74). In fact, the "Jube quod vis et da
quod jubes" concerns precisely what does *not* remain "in mea potestae" but in
that of the love that renders it *valentior*.

49. *Liber de gratia* I, 17, 18, *PL* 44, 369. See: "Sed plane illa possibilitas
utriusque radicis est capax" (For this possibility has the capacity for two roots) (I,
20, 21, *PL* 44, 370). And: "possibilitas ad utrumque valere" (a possibility to exercise itself in both directions) (I, 25, 26, *PL* 44, 373).

50. Ibid., I, 6, 7, *PL* 44, 363ff.

51. Ibid., I, 34, 37, *PL* 44, 378. The Pelagians' attempt to divide the phenomenon of the will into possibility, will, and actualization (*posse/velle/esse* or *possi-
bilitas/voluntas/actio*) and to limit the giftedness to one of these moments, so as
to detach the others from it, suffers not only from the failing of heresy but, first
of all, from a phenomenological fault: it does not help describe the phenomenon
and, by contrast, burns it up, dissolves it (ibid., I, 47, 52, *PL* 44, 383ff.).

CHAPTER 5

1. Respectively *Commentaries on the Psalms* 101, 2, 10, *PL* 37, 1311; and *Sermon*
80, 8, *PL* 38, 498.

2. On the ignorance of the gods see the excellent collection assembled by J.-C.
Bardout and O. Boulnois, *Sur la science divine* (Paris, 2002).

3. The same proclamation appears in *Confessiones* IX, 10, 25: "quoniam si quis audiat, dicunt haec omni: 'Non ipsas nos fecimus, sed fecit nos qui manet aeternum'" (for if one tries to hear them, all these things say: "We ourselves did not make ourselves, but he who remains eternally made us'" [Psalm 99:3]) (14, 118—curiously enough this theme is not taken up in *Commentaries on the Psalms 99, PL* 37, 1271ff.). Elsewhere, a praise is carried out by inanimate creatures as well as the animate: "Undique laudatur Deus ab operibus suis. . . . Laudant coeli, laudant angeli, laudant sidera, laudant sol et luna, laudant dies et noctes, laudat quidquid germinat de terra, laudat quidquid natat in mari, laudat quidquid volitat in aere, laudant omnes montes et colles, laudant frigora et aestus; et caetra omnia quae Deus fecit, audistis quia laudant Deum" (From all corners of the world, God is praised by his works. . . . The heavens praise him, the angels praise him, the stars praise him, the sun and the moon praise him, the days and the nights praise him, all that grows from the earth praises him, all that swims in the sea praises him, all that flies in the air praises him, all the mountains and all the hills praise him, the freezing cold and the burning hot praises him; and you hear all things made by God praising God) (*Commentaries on the Psalms* 128, 5, *PL* 37, 1691).

4. *Commentaries on the Psalms* 148, 15, *PL* 37, 1946. It should be noted that the Vulgate reads "Confessio ejus *super* coelum et terram," while the *Vetus Latina* says "*in terra et coelo*," thus opening the possibility that confession is made *in* the heavens and the earth in the sense that it would rise *on the basis* of them.

5. *Confessiones* XI, 10, 12, 14, 290. This type of question comes from a Manichean context: "cui bono mundum fecerit, qui non erat indigens?" (for what purpose did he make the world, he who was lacking nothing?) (*De ordine* II, 17, 46, 4, 440ff.), or: "quaerunt [sc. Manichei] 'In quo principio?' et dicunt: 'si in principio aliquo temporis fecit Deus coelum et terram, quid agebat antequam faceret coelum et terram? Et quid si placuit subito facere quod numquam antea fecerat per tempora aeterna?'" (they ask: "In what principle?" and they say: "If God made the heavens and the earth in a temporal principle, what was he doing before making the heavens and the earth? And what if he decided suddenly to make what he had never made in eternal times?") (*De Genesi contra Manicheos* I, 2, 3, *BA* 50, 160). But the Neoplatonists are also at issue (*De civitate Dei* XI, 4, 2, 35, 40–44); as is Cicero: "Cur mundi aedificatores repente extiterint, innumerabilia saecula dormierint?" (Why did the makers of the world arise suddenly after having been asleep for so many centuries?) (*De natura deorum* I, 9, ed. H. Rackham [Cambridge, MA (1933¹), 1972], 24); and Lucretius: "Quidve novi potuit tanto post quietos / Inlicere ut cuperent vitam mutare priorem?" (What novelty could after so much [time] incite the blessed in repose to want to change their previous life?) (*De natura deorum* V, 168–69, ed. A. Ernout [Paris, 1948], 57). An echo of the objection can already be heard in Saint Irenaeus, who found it an embarrassment: "Ut puta: si quis interrogat: Antequam mundum faceret Deus? dicemus quoniam ista

responsio subjacet Deo. Quoniam autem mundus hic factus est ἀποτελεστικῶς a Deo, temporale initium accipiens, Scripturae nos docent; quid autem ante hoc Deus sit operatus, nulla Scriptura manifestat." (It is thought that if someone asks, "what was God doing before the heavens and the earth?" we would say the answer is left to God. For that the world was made by design, receiving a beginning in time, is something the scriptures teach us; but as for what God was doing before that, no scripture reveals it) (*Adversus haereses* II, 28, 3). So, too, Origen: "Sed solent nobis objicere dicentes: si coepit mundus ex tempore, quid antea faciebat Deus quam mundum inciperet?" (They are in the habit of objecting to us: if the world began in time what was God doing before he began the world), with a weak response: "Nos vero consequenter respondebimus . . . dicantes quoniam non tunc primum, cum visibilem istum mundum faecit Deus, coepit operari, sed sicut post correptionem hujus erit alius mundus, ita et antequam hic [mundus] esset, fuisse alios credimus" (But we, we will answer coherently . . . by saying that God did not begin to make only when he made this visible world, but that just as there will be another world after the disappearance of this one, so too before this world was, we believe that there were others) (*On First Principles* III, 5, 3). On this point see E. Peters, "What Was God Doing Before He Created the Heavens and the Earth?" *Augustiniana* 34 (1984): 53–74. In the immense bibliography concerning the Augustinian doctrine of time, I am basing my own position on the recent collections of E. P. Meijering, *Augustin über Schöpfung, Ewigkeit und Zeit: Das elfte Buch der Bekenntnisse* (Leiden, 1979); Flasch, *Was ist Zeit?*; and N. Fischer, "'Distentio animi': Symbol der Entfluchtigung des Zeitlichens," in *Die "Confessiones" des Augustinus von Hippo: Einführung und Interpretationen zu den 13 Büchern*, ed. N. Fischer and C. Mayer (Freiburg, 2004).

6. See: "Si enim habet causam voluntas Dei, est aliquid quod antecedat voluntatem Dei, quo nefas est credere. Qui ergo dicit, quare fecit Deus coelum et terra, respondendum est ei, quia voluit. Voluntas enim Dei causa est coeli et terrae et ideo major est voluntas Dei quam coelum et terram. Qui autem dicit, quare voluit facere caelum et terram, majus aliquid quaerit quam est voluntas Dei: nihil autem majus inveneri potest" (*De Genesi contra Manicheos* I, 2, 4, *PL* 34, 175). To claim to go back behind the will of God (to assign it a reason or a cause) amounts to the absurdity of pretending to surpass God himself: "Neque enim voluntas Dei creatura est, sed ante creaturam, quia non creatur aliquid, nisi creatoris voluntas praecederet. Ad ipsam ergo Dei substantiam pertinet voluntas ejus" (That is, the will of God is not a creature [of God], but before creatures, since nothing is created unless the will of the creator precedes it. His will belongs therefore to the very substance of God) (*Confessiones* XI, 10, 12, 14, 292).

7. One can read here the exact inverse of Spinoza's position: "Eodem sensu quo Deus dicitur causa sui, dicitur etiam causa omnium rerum" (in the same sense that God is said to be self-caused [*causa sui*] he must also be said to be the

cause of all things" (*Ethica* I, §25, sc. [English trans., 49]). Lacan gives credit, rightly, to Saint Augustine for having here dismissed the very hypothesis of the *causa sui* (see *Des-noms-du-Père, séminaire 1963* [Paris, 2005], 76–78). On the difficulty of (even) introducing into metaphysics the thesis of the *causa sui*, see my own *On the Ego and on God: Further Cartesian Questions* (New York, 2007), chap. 8: "The *Causa Sui*: First and Fourth Replies."

8. "Scio, quod nulla fiebat creatura, antequam fieret ulla creatura" (I know there was no creature before there were any creatures) (*Confessiones* XI, 12, 14, 14, 294).

9. Or: "Omnia tempora tu fecisti et ante omnia tempora tu es, nec aliquo tempore non erat tempus" (You made all times and before all times, you, you are, and there is no time where there were no times) (*Confessiones* XI, 13, 16, 14, 298). And again: "nullum tempus esse posse sine creatura" (no time is possible without creatures) (XI, 30, 40, 14, 340).

10. *De civitate Dei* XII, 15, 35, 196. The translation of the first passage in *BA* 35 completely misses the equivalence of the creation of the times and that of man ("he wove the fabric of time starting from a beginning and in this time he made man"). The context of the last phrase unambiguously insists on it, however: "Quis hanc valeat altitudinem investigabilem vestigare et inscrutabilem perscrutari, secundum quam Deus *hominem temporalem*, ante quem nemo unquam hominum fuit, non mutabili voluntate in tempore condidit et genus humanum ex uno multiplicavit?" (Who could search out this unsearchable depth, scrutinize this inscrutable depth according to which God, with an unchanging will, established in time a *temporalized man* before which no man was, and made the human species out of just one a multitude?) (ibid.).

11. *Commentaries on the Psalms* 84, 8, *PL* 37, 1073. See: "vocantem me invocarem te" (I called you, you who had called me) (*Confessiones* XIII, 1, 1, 14, 424).

12. And again, with other temporalizations: "fecisti me et *oblitum* tui non *oblitus* es . . . *priusquam* essem, tu eras, nec eram, cui praestares ut essem" (you made me, and even *forgetful* of you, you did not forget me . . . and *before* I was, you were, and I was not there for you to grant being to me) (XIII, 1, 1, 14, 424). "O *tardum* gaudium meum!" (O my *delayed* joy!) (II, 2, 2, 13, 334). For that matter, those who object to the creation of the world without seeing that of time are also characterized by belatedness, "pleni sunt vetustatis" (puffed up with oldness) (XI, 10, 12, 14, 290).

13. See "*differabam* 'de die in diem' vivere in te, et non *differebam* quotidie in memet *ipso* mori" (I *deferred* "from one day to the next" [Ecclesiastes 5:8], living in you, but I did not daily *defer* dying in myself) (VI, 11, 20, 13, 560). Or: "Et putaveram me propterea *differre* 'de die in diem' contempta spe saeculi te solum sequi . . ." (And I had thought that if I *deferred* "from one day to the next" [Ecclesiastes 5:8] following you, you alone, with contempt for the hopes of the world,

this was because . . .) (VIII, 7, 18, 14, 44). Note however sometimes a positive oc-currence: "amor utiliter *differendus*" (*Soliloquia* I, 13, 23, *BA* 5, 72).

14. We find a striking, but unfortunately untranslatable, parallel in the *Commentaries on the Psalms* 102, 16: "Frater, non *tardes* converti ad Dominum. Sunt enim qui praeparant conversionem et *differunt*, et fint in eis vox corvinas *cras, cras*. Corvus de arca missus, non est reversus. Non quaerit Deus *dilationem* de voce corvina, sed *confessionem* in gemitu columbino. Missa columba, reversa est. Quamdiu *cras, cras*? Observa ultimum *cras*; quia ignoras quid sit ultimum cras, sufficat quod vixisti usque ad hodiernum peccator" (*PL* 37, 1330). Untranslatable is the word *cras*, because to its obvious meaning, *tomorrow*, is added the onomatopoeia of the cry of the crow (what we say as *caw*), meaning thereby no doubt to oppose this harsh explosive to the dove that, having been sent from the Ark to see if land had emerged following the Flood, returned. The intention is unambiguous: always putting off conversion until tomorrow is equivalent to crying *caw, caw*, therefore to refusing it (so cried the anticlerical faction of 1905, it seems, at the passing of the Catholic processions). Even by risking a double translation (with a more contemporary equivalent), one does not render this play on words: "My brother, do not *delay* your conversion to God. There are those who prepare for it and *defer* it, and they end up saying *tomorrow, tomorrow / Caw, caw*. The crow sent from the ark did not return. God does not ask for the *delay* in the voice of the crow but the *confession* from the sighing of the dove. The dove was sent, but it, it came back. Will it go on for a long time, this *tomorrow, tomorrow / Caw, caw*? Pay attention to the last *tomorrow/caw*. Because you do not know when it will be, this last *tomorrow/caw*, let it suffice that the sinner has lived until today."

15. Plotinus, *Enneads* 3.7.1; and Husserl, *The Phenomenology of the Internal Time-Consciousness* (Husserliana 10:4–5 [English trans., 21–22]). See also Simplicius (*In Aristotelis Physicorum librorum Commentarium*, ed. H. Files [Berlin, 1892], 695). A collection of medieval and modern readings of *Confessiones* XI is more than outlined in Flasch, *Was ist Zeit?* 160–95, 27–75.

16. Wittgenstein, very much to the point, cites these "manifestissima et usitatissima" as an example of the real difficulty in philosophy: confronting the obscure evidence of ordinary language (*Philosophische Untersuchungen*, §436, 1:417 [English trans., 109e]). Elsewhere, when commenting on the Augustinian formulation of time, he shows that the impossibility of *saying* what we nevertheless *know*, time, offers a privileged case of "the sense [in which] logic is something sublime":

> Not, however, as if to this end we had to hunt out new facts; it is, rather, of the essence of our investigation that we do not seek to learn anything *new* by it. We want to *understand* something that is already in plain view. For *this* is what we seem in some sense not to understand. [Here is the citation of the

aporia in *Confessiones* XI, 14, 17.] This could not be said about a question of natural science ("What is the specific gravity of hydrogen?" for instance). Something that we know when no one asks us, but no longer know when we are supposed to give an account of it, is something that we need to *think* (*besinnen*). (And it is obviously something which for some reason it is difficult to think.) (§89, ibid., 291 [English trans., 36e (modified)])

17. Husserl, *The Phenomenology of the Internal Time-Consciousness*, 21 (though he obviously does so *also*).

18. See another analysis of the *where/ubi* accorded to the present: "*Ubi* sunt deliciae vestrae, propter quas ambulatis per vias pravas? Non dicimus *ubi* erunt, cum haec vita transierit, sed modo *ubi* sunt? Cum hesternum diem hodiernus abstulerit, et hordiernum crastinus ablaturus sit, quid eorum quae diligitis non transcurrit et transvolat? Quid non fugit pene antequam capitur, cum ex ipso hodierno die nulla possit vel hora contineri? Ita enim secunda excluditur a tertia, sicut prima exclusa est a secunda. Ipsius horae unius, quae praesens videtur, nihil est praesens: omnes enim partes ejus et omnia momenta fugitura sunt" (*Where* are your delights, on account of which you go your wicked ways? We do not say *where* will they be, since this life will pass, but only *where* are they [now]? Since the day of yesterday was taken away by that of today, as that of tomorrow will take away that of today, what is it, in all that you love, that will not flee and fly away? Is there something that has not already very nearly passed away even before you have grasped it, as soon as one cannot even keep an hour of the day of today? The second hour is eliminated by the third, as the first was by the second. Of this hour itself, which [alone] seems present, nothing is [in the] present; for all its parts and all its moments are fleeting) (*Sermon* 157, 4, 4, *PL* 38, 861).

19. This description, which reduces the temporal flux to a delay (*mora*) ceaselessly vanishing, also and without a doubt first of all has a biblical version, the commentary on Psalm 38:5: "Et numerum dierum meorum qui est" (*Vetus Latina*). The reduction, in this exegesis, goes from *dies* to *dies hodiernus*, then to *hora*, then to *momentum*, and finally to *est* itself. But this *ipsum est* is still composed of three syllables, the second of which I reach only once the first has passed, and so on, such that nothing remains, not even the delay of a letter: "Cum dicis ipsum *Est*, certe una syllaba est, et momentum unum est, et tres litteras syllaba habet; in ipso ictu ad secundam hujus verbi litteram non pervenis, nisi prima finita fuerit; tertia non sonabit, nisi cum et secunda transierit. Quid mihi de hac una syllaba dabis? Et tenes dies, qui unam syllabam non tenes?" (When you say even just this *est* itself, it is only one syllable and one moment, and just three letters; [but] you cannot even touch the second letter of this word without the first having [already] terminated; and the third will not sound out except when the second will have passed. What can you give me of this simple syllable? And you will take hold of the days, you who cannot even hold a single

syllable?) Consequently, even the most simple word, *est*, cannot persist in the slightest present; but *est* is precisely *est* of *to be*; therefore it is *to be* that cannot *be*. "*Est* illud simplex quaero, *Est* verum quaero, *Est* germanum quaero, *Est* quod est in illa Jerusalem sponsa Domini mei, ubi non erit mors, non erit defectus, non erit dies transiens, sed manens, qui nec hesterno praeceditur, nec crastino impellitur" (I seek this pure and simple *is*, the true *is*, the authentic *is*, the one that is in this Jerusalem that is the bride of my Lord, where death will not be, nor lack, nor the passing day, but the day staying, that no yesterday precedes nor any tomorrow presses ahead" (*Commentaries on the Psalms* 38, 7, *PL* 36, 419). The aporia of present time, its im-*mora*-lity, poses a crisis for the being of the instant, the *est* of the *nunc*. Far from consecrating the primacy of presence by the privileging of the present, the aporia of present time defers, from the outset and forever, the advent of any presence equal to itself. Saint Augustine theorizes differ*a*nce and destroys Being in presence. Another commentary pushes the decomposition all the way to the letter in the syllable: "Dum syllabus loquor, si duas syllabas dicam, altera non sonat, nisi cum illa transierit; ipsa denique una syllaba, si duas litteras habet, non sonat posterior littera, nisi prior abierit. Quid ergo tenemus de his annis!" (While I am saying syllables, in the case when I say two of them, the latter does not sound if the former has not already passed; and in the final analysis, this first syllable, if it has two letters, the last does not sound so long as the first has not passed. What then will we say when it is a question of years!) (*Commentaries on the Psalms* 76, 8, *PL* 36, 976).

20. *Physics* 4.10.217b33.

21. "What is composed of nonbeings seems not to be able to participate in οὐσία" (*Physics* 4.10.218a2–3).

22. *BA* 14, 307, unfortunately translates "sentimus intervalla" as "we perceive the intervals," "sentiendo metimur" as "we measure them by perceiving them," and "tempus sentiri et metiri potest" as "it can be perceived and measured." That is a misreading, for Saint Augustine endeavors to *sense* in the immediacy of immanence what we precisely cannot *perceive* in intentional ecstasy—time as passage.

23. See the suggestions of A. Solignac in *BA* 14, 586, and the research of J.-F. Callahan, "Basil of Caesarea: A New Source for St. Augustine's Theory of Time," *Harvard Studies in Classical Philology* 63 (1958): 437–54; "Gregory of Nizza and the Psychological View of Time," *Atti del XII Congressio internazionale di filosofia*, vol. 9 (Florence, 1960); and *Augustine and the Greek Philosophers* (Villanova, 1969). But why not simply think of the "man inflated with a monstrous pride" (*homo immanissimo typho turgidus*) mentioned in *Confessiones* VII, 9, 13, 13, 608? He would have transmitted, through "certain platonic books" (*per quidem Platonicorum libri*) (for example, Plotinus, *Enneads* 7.7), the doctrine of time as κίνησις, or κινουμένον, or more generally, κινήσεώς τι, a doctrine common to Plato (*Timaeus* 39c–d; see R. Brague, *Quatre études sur le temps chez Platon et*

Aristote (Paris, 1982¹); Aristotle obviously; and Chrysippus (see *Stoicorum veterum fragmenta*, ed. J. von Arnim [Stuttgart (1902¹), 1968], 3.2.14.492). Let us note that Basil of Caesarea also criticized Eunomius precisely for having defined time on the basis of the movement of the stars (*Against Eunomius* I, 21, *PG* 29, 557).

24. "What is composed of nonbeings seems unable to participate in *ousia*" (Aristotle, *Physics* 4.10.218a2–3).

25. Ibid., 4.10.218b9.

26. Ibid., 4.11.219b1.

27. "Quaero utrum motus ipse sit dies an mora ipsa, quanta peragitur, an utrumque" (*Confessiones* XI, 23, 30, 14, 320).

28. See: "iste spatium temporis in silentio memoriaeque commendans" (this man confiding the space of time silently to his memory) (XI, 27, 36, 14, 334).

29. See also: "Cum enim movetur corpus, tempore metior, *quamdiu moveatur*, ex quo moveri incipit donec desinat" (When the body moves, I measure it by time, *as long as it is moving*, starting from the moment when it begins until the moment when it ends) (XI, 24, 31, 14, 322).

30. In opposition to God, for man, "ejus intentio de cogitatione in cogitationem transit" (his intentionality passes from thought to thought) (*De civitate Dei* XI, 21, 35, 92ff.). For him, "intentio ad agendum praesentis est temporis, per quod futurum in praeteritum transit" (intentionality bears on the present time, across which the future passes to the past) (*De immortalitate animi* III, 3, 5, 176).

31. Likewise, God "non enim more nostro ille vel quod futurum est prospicit, vel quod praesens est aspicit, vel quod praeteritum est respicit" (does not do as we do: he does not foresee what arrives, he does not observe what is present, and he does not look back upon what is past) (*De civitate Dei* XI, 21, 35, 92).

32. *Confessiones* XI, 27, 35, 14, 330, citing Saint Ambrose: "Deus creator omnium (2 Maccabees 1, 24) / Polique auctor, vestiens / Diem decoro lumine / Noctem saporis gratia" (*Hymni* I, 2, v 1, in *Sancti Ambrosii Episcopi opera: Hymni Inscriptiones. Fragmenta*, ed. G. Banterle [Milan 1994], 42). Though the name of the author is not mentioned, this is an homage paid to Saint Ambrose, who has played a decisive role ever since the somewhat failed encounter reported in *Confessiones* V, 12, 23, 13, 506.

33. Translating *pronuntio/renuntio* by *declamation/proclamation* (as *BA* 14, 331) inverts the temporalities by putting the *pro*-clamation after the *re*-sumption. For what it's worth, despite the displacement that *reclaim* imposes, it should be noted that—*nuntiare* is recovered exactly in—*clamer* and therefore authorizes the parallelism of the two terms.

34. Two texts from *De musica* comment, to the same effect but with less detail, on the same verse from Ambrose's hymn: (a) *De musica* VI, 2, 2 asks if, in pronouncing "Deus creator omnium," "istos quattuor iambos, quibus constat, et tempora duodecim, ubique esse arbitraris?" (these four iambs of which it consists and

the twelve times, where do you think they are found?). Is it in physical extension, in the sensation of the listener, or in the act of pronunciation? Or else: "in memoria quoque nostra" (also in our memory) (*BA* 7, 360)? In fact, they are found everywhere, but the rhythms are found only in memory, *genus numerorum in memoria* (VI, 3, 4, 7, 366). Cognition, which always amounts to cognizing temporally, therefore means *re*cognition: "talis agnitio, *re*cognitio est et *re*cordatio" (VI, 8, 22, 7, 408). Is this a matter of reproductive memory, or what I have here translated as *re*clamation? (b) "Sed ego puto, cum ille a nobis propositus versus canitur 'Deus creator omnium,' nos eum et occursoribus illis numeris audire, et recordabilibus recognoscere et progressoribus pronuntiare" (But I suppose that when one sings the verse that we are proposing, "Deus creator omnium," we begin by hearing it thanks to the arriving rhythms, then we recognize it by those returning to memory, and finally we pronounce them by those that advance toward us) (VI, 9, 23, 7, 410). (c) Another reference to this verse insists on its truth (signified), more than on the manner of hearing it or singing it (signifying) (*De musica* VI, 17, 57, *BA* 7, 472).

35. *Commentaries on the Psalms*, respectively 44, 4, *PL* 36, 496 and 99, 5, *PL* 37, 1272.

36. As J. J. O'Donnell ventures to affirm: "His famous description of time as a *distentio animi* cannot be a definition, but is, rather, a metaphor" (O'Donnell, *Augustine: Confessions*, 3:289).

37. Also: "Quoniam sensus manifestus, brevi syllaba longam metior eamque *sentio* habere bis tantum" (Inasmuch as the sensation is manifest, I measure the long syllable by the short and *I sense* that it counts as two of them" (XI, 27, 35, 14, 330). It is about the affect we already saw: "Affectionem, quam res *praetereuntes* in te [sc. anima mea] faciunt, et cum illae praeterierint, manet, ipsam metior praesentem" (It is the affect, which the passing things produce in you and which remain once passed, that I measure [because it remains] present to it) (XI, 27, 36, 14, 332).

38. Plotinus, *Enneads* 3.7, respectively §§2–3, 8, and 9–10. See W. Beierwaltes, introduction to *Plotinus: Uber Ewigkeit (Enneade* 3.7) (Frankfurt, 1967).

39. Plotinus, *Enneads* 3.7.11.41. See P. Ricoeur, *Temps et récit*, 1:34ff. (English trans., 1:27ff.).

40. Plotinus, *Enneads* 3.13.65 and 3.13.67. Here I follow G. O'Daly: "Plotinus' approach is quite different. . . . Whatever it may hold in principle, Augustine does not behave very platonically in practice in *Confessions*. His method is rather empirical: he considers time as a fact of everyday experience, as a practical problem. This has rather liberating consequences" (*Augustine's Philosophy of Mind* [Berkeley, 1987], 152). Ricoeur says nothing different (*Temps et récit*, 1:41ff. [English trans., 1:29ff.]).

41. For example, "animus meus": *Confessiones* XI, 22, 28, 14, 314; XI, 27, 34, 14, 328; XI, 27, 36, 14, 332.

42. *Homilies on Ecclesiastes* VI (τὸ δίαστημα τοῦ χρόνου) and VIII (ὁ αἰὼν διστηματικόν τι νόημα), *PG* 44, 700c and 752d. On these texts, in addition to H. U. von Balthasar, *Presence and Thought. An Essay on the Religious Philosophy of Gregory of Nyssa* (San Francisco, 1995); and J. Daniélou, *L'Être et le temps chez Grégoire de Nysse* (Leiden, 1970); see also T. P. Vergehen, "*Diastema* and *diastasis* in Gregory of Nyssa," in *Gregory of Nyssa and Philosophy*, 2nd Colloque International, 1972 (Leiden, 1978); and the classic works of J.-F. Callaghan, esp. *Augustine and the Greek Philosophers*, chap. 3.

43. G. Madec assembled the relevant texts perfectly in *Saint Augustin et la philosophie*, chap. 12, in particular p. 95.

44. Aristotle, *Physics* 4.11.219a5.

45. Ibid., 4.14.223a21–28. The argument, a difficult one, can be reconstituted in this way: certainly time, understood as the decompositive accounting of before and after, is not possible without the soul, which alone decomposes and counts. But the very thing that is in each moment time, its "substrate"—namely, movement—that very thing happens without the soul, for in the natural world it changes and moves without the soul. Whence the at least implicit conclusion that time, if it evidently is not carried out without decomposition (therefore without the soul), is not equal to it, according to what it *is in each moment*. I am following the interpretation advanced by R. Brague, *Quatre études sur le temps chez Platon et Aristote*, 144; and the notes of W. D. Ross, *Aristotle: "Physics"* (Oxford, [1936¹], 1966⁴), 611.

46. Some of these have been collected in particular in Flasch, *Was ist Zeit?* esp. 92ff. See also U. Duchrow, "Der sogenannte psychologische Zeitsbegriff Augustins im Verhältnis zur physikalischen und geschitlichen Zeit," *Zeitschrift für Theologie und Kirche* (1967), who insists on the contradiction between *distentio animi* and the time of the creation of the world.

47. *Confessiones* XI, 30, 40, 14, 340. See the excellent response to Flasch by N. Fischer, "Distentio animi: Ein Symbol der Entflüchtigung des Zeitlichen," in *Die "Confessiones" des Augustins von Hippo: Einführung und Interpretationen zu den 13 Büchern*, ed. N Fischer and C. Meyer (Freiburg, 2004); see also N. Fischer, *Augustins Philosophie der Endlichkeit: Zur systematischen Entfaltung seines Denkens aus der Geschichte der Chorismos-Problematik* (Bonn, 1987).

48. There is even less contradiction between these texts from *Confessiones* XII and those of *Confessiones* XI as the latter opens, just after the aporia of time, with this same argument: "Si nemo ex me quaerat scio; si quaerenti explicare velim, nescio: fidenter tamen dico scire qui, si *nihil* praeteriret, non esset praeteritum tempus, et si *nihil* adveniret, non esset futurum tempus, et si *nihil* eset, non esset praesens tempus" (If nobody asks me, I know it; if I want to explain it to whoever asks me the question, I do not know. But nonetheless, I can say with confidence that I know that if there was nothing that

passed, there would not be past time; if there was nothing that came, there would be no future time; and if there was nothing present, there would be no present time) (XI, 14, 17, 14, 300). This *[non]nihil*—how are we to understand it? This could mean *here* only the *mens* itself, not inasmuch as "psychological" and "intramental" reality in opposition to the "physical" and "extramental" world but as the first and least contestable occurrence of the *creatura*, in fact as its most radical figure, since it conditions the knowledge of the change of all the other *creaturae*.

49. As for the opposition between the subjectivity of time (as pure form of intuition) and the objectivity of the phenomena that it determines in the world (the objects of experience), it is surprising to see that a number of principals to the debate take it as a given, indisputable and obvious, while Kant demonstrated perfectly and definitively its inanity (see *Critique of Pure Reason*, "Transcendental Aesthetic," §7, A 36–47/B53–58, Ak. A. IV, 39ff.). A little bit of philosophy never hurts in the examination of conceptual texts, something the critics seem to forget.

50. C. Romano, *L'événement et le temps* (Paris, 1991), 121, 123. This objection thus nullifies that of Ricoeur: "The major *failure* [my emphasis] of the Augustinian theory of time is that it is unsuccessful in substituting a psychological conception of time for a cosmological one, despite the undeniable progress this psychology represents in relation to any cosmology of time. The *aporia* [my emphasis] lies precisely in the fact that while this psychology can legitimately be added to the cosmology, it is unable to replace cosmology, as well as in the further fact that neither concept, considered separately, proposes a satisfying solution to their unresolvable disagreement" (*Temps et récit*, 3:19 [English trans., 3:12]). I. Bochet indicated, with all good intentions, the limits of this reading; see his *Augustin dans la pensée de Paul Ricœur* (Paris, 2003), 44ff.). It could be there was neither disagreement, failure, nor aporia.

51. I resume a lexicon I used in my *Le visible et le révélé* (Paris, 2005), 91ff. The treatment of creation as event, whose advent temporalizes the *distentio animi* itself, was highlighted by R. Jurgeleit: "Dem Zeit als Dauer kann freilich erst mit dem ersten *Ereignis überhaupt* einsetzen. Dies ist für Augustinus die Schöpfung, von der in der Bibel berichtet wird. Dieser Bericht kann vergegenwärtigt werden, d. h. der Hörer oder Leser des Alten Testaments kennt die Schöpfung als das erste Ereignis" ("Die Zeitbegriff und die Kohärenz des Zeitlichen bei Augustinus," *Revue des études augustiniennes* 34 [1988]: 209–29).

52. *Sein und Zeit*, §82, 436 (English trans., 486 [modified]). This criticism takes place under cover of a discussion of Hegel's doctrine of time, but the Augustinian determination of time as *distentio animi* (XI, 26, 33, 14, 326) is cited, with those of Aristotle, Hegel, and Kant, under the heading "ordinary conception of time" (§81, 427). As often is the case, Heidegger puts Augustine forward

as his opponent at the precise moment when he resumes Augustine's analysis against Aristotle.

53. *Sein und Zeit*, §68, 347 (English trans., 398).

54. Flasch puts this quite nicely: "*Distentio* appears on one hand as our life and on the other hand as an evil" (*Was ist Zeit?* 398). Likewise Ricoeur: "*Distentio animi* no longer provides just the 'solution' to the aporia of the measurement of time. It now expresses the way in which the soul, deprived of the stillness of the eternal present, is torn asunder" (*Temps et récit*, 1:50 [English trans., 1:27]).

55. Which I have done up until now, just as *BA* 14 ("distention," 327, 339); O'Donnell (*distentio, Augustine: Confessions*, 3:289ff., *distention*, 295ff.); and Flasch (*distentio, Was ist Zeit?* 381ff., 398ff.).

56. J.-L. Chrétien has indicated this point quite precisely: "Contrary to what is written about Saint Augustine in a peremptory and professorial tone by those authors who have read, and poorly, only a few pages of the *Confessions*, and repeat afterward those who have read nothing, the *distentio* does not characterize the essence of human time in general, but only the time of man the sinner" (*La joie spacieuse: Essai sur la dilatation* [Paris, 2007], 46).

57. The Vulgate reads: "Fratres, ego me non arbitror comprehendisse: unum autem: quae quidem retro sunt, obliviscens, ad ea vero, quae ante sunt, extendens me ad destinatum persequor, ad bravium supernae vocationis Dei in Christo Jesu."

58. See, on spaces: "Quando Deum ubique praesentem, et non spatiis *distentibus* quasi aliqua mole vel *distentione* diffusum, sed ubique totum, cogitare te *extendis*, averte mentem ab omnibus imaginibus corporum" (When you *extend* [*extract*] your thoughts to thinking omnipresent God present everywhere without spreading out into *distanced* spaces as if like some mass or by a *distantiation*, turn your mind from all images of bodies) (*Letter* 187, 13, 41, *PL* 33, 848). And, for times: "neque enim   variatur affectus sensusque *distenditur*" (for, [your] affection does not change, nor does it *distract* [your] feeling) (*Confessiones* XI, 31, 41, 14, 343).

59. See also other strategic uses of Philippians 3:13 in the *Confessiones*, which, without explicitly mentioning the opposition *distentio/extensio*, have treated temporality. For example: IX, 10, 23, 14, 114ff. (the contemplation at Ostia): "Conloquebamur ergo soli valde dulciter et 'praeterita obliviscentes in ea quae ante sunt extenti' quaerebamus inter nos apud *praesentem* veritatem, quod tu es" (We were speaking one to another very sweetly and "forgetting passed things, stretched out toward those to come," we were seeking together the *present* truth, that you are); XI, 30, 40, 14, 340: "Videant itaque nullum *tempus* esse posse sine creatura et desinant istam vanitatem loqui. *Extendantur* etiam 'in ea quae ante sunt' et intelligant te *ante omnia tempora aeternum* creatorem omnium temporum neque ulla tempora tibi esse coaeterna nec ullam creaturam, etiamsi est aliqua supra

tempora" (Let them see that there can be no *time* without creatures and then cease to speak vainly. *Let them also tend* "toward the things that are before them" and understand that you are *before all times* the eternal creator of all the times, that no time is coeternal with you and that no creature either, even if it was above the times); XII, 16, 23, 14, 378: "*recordans* Hierusalem *extento* in eam sursum corde"; XIII, 13, 14, 14, 448 (Heavenly Church). But also *Commentaries on the Psalms* 38, 8, *PL* 36, 419; or 39, 3, *PL* 36, 434; or 72, 5 *PL* 36, 917 ("Ad patriam supernae promissionis Dei"); and 80, 14 *PL* 36, 1040 ("'in ea quae ante sunt,' id est in veritatem *extensus*"); or else 149, 8, *PL* 37, 1954 ("*Extendit* se ipse: tetigit Christus et sonavit dulcedo veritatis").

60. See the highly relevant commentary of P. Agaësse: "The words *intentio* and *extensio* are therefore a bit like synonyms. . . . In opposition, *distentio* characterizes the state of dispersion and corresponds to the Plotinian διάστασις, scattering in a non-unified time" (note in *BA* 16, 589ff.). The same opposition is found in J. M. Quinn, "Four Faces of Time in St. Augustine," *Recherches augustiniennes* 26 (1992): 181–231.

61. J. J. O'Donnell: "The punning between *intentus, extentus,* and *distentus* is only possible in Latin" (*Augustine: Confessions,* 3:290). I note that even this "kunstvolle Spiel" (Flasch, *Was ist Zeit?* 397) can be transposed into French and English.

62. *Commentaries on the Psalms* 83, 4, *PL* 37, 1058.

63. *Commentary on the First Epistle of Saint John* IV, 6, *PL* 35, 2008–9. See also: "Antequam perveniamus ad unum, multis indigemus. Unum nos *extendat,* ne multa *distendant* et abrumpant ab uno. 'Ergo, inquit, non me arbitror apprehendisse unum autem quae retro oblitus, in ea quae ante sunt *extentus.*' Non *distentus,* se *extentus.* Unum enim *extendit.* Multa *distendunt,* unum *extendit.* Et quamdiu *extendit*? Quamdiu hic summus. Cum enim venerimus, colligit, non extendit" (Before we reach the one, we have need of multiple things. The one *extends* us [by extraction, drawing us out], so that multiplicity does *not distend* us and separate us from the one. "Truly," says Saint Paul, "I do not believe myself to have understood anything, except just this: forgetting all that is behind me, I *tend* toward what is before me" [Philippians 3:15]). Not *distended,* but *tended* (*by extraction*). For the one *makes for tension.* The multiplicity of things *distend;* the one *puts into tension.* And for how long a time does he *put us in tension*? As long as we remain here. When we will have arrived, he will gather, without *extending* (*Sermon* 255, 6, 6, *PL* 38, 1189). See the wise comments of E. P. Meijering, *Augustin über Schöpfung,* 103ff.

CHAPTER 6

1. There are, of course, exceptions: "Sed sic est Deus per cuncta diffusus, ut non sit qualitas mundi; sed substantia *creatrix mundi,* sine labore regens, sine

onere continens mundum" (But God is so diffused through all things that he is not a quality of the world, but substance *creator of the world*, which he directs effortlessly and contains without weight) (*Letter* 187, 14, *PL* 33, 837). But God also creates the heart (*Letter* 166, 26, *PL* 33, 731). When in other places he uses the term *mundus* (world), Saint Augustine intends it in the Johannine sense: "Mundus enim appelatur non solum ista fabricata quam fecit Deus, caelum et terram, mare, visibilia et invisibilia, sed habitatores mundi mundus vocantur; quomodo domus vocatur et parietas et inhabitantes" (We call *world* not only this fabrication made by God, the heavens and the earth, the sea, visible and invisible things, but the inhabitants of the world are also called world, just as we call house the walls and also those who live in it) (*Commentary on the First Epistle of Saint John* II, 12, *PL* 35, 1995). See:

> Quid est "mundus factus est per ipsum"? Caelum, terram, mare et omnia quae in eis sunt, mundus dicitur. Iterum alia significatione *dilectores* mundi mundus dicuntur. . . . Sed qui non cognoverunt? Qui *amando* mundum dicti sunt mundus. *Amando* enim habitamus corde: *amando* autem hoc apellari meruerunt quod ille, ubi habitabant. Quomodo dicimus: mala ista domus aut bona est illa domus, non in illa quam dicimus malam, parietes accusamus, aut in illa, quam dicimus bonam, parietes laudamus, sed malam domum, inhabiantes malos; et bonam domum, inhabiantes bonos. Sic et mundum, qui inhabitant *amando* mundum. Qui sunt? Qui *diligunt* mundum, ipsi enim corde inhabitant in mundi. Nam qui non *diligunt* mundum, carne versantur in mundo, sed corde inhabitant caelum.
>
> What does it mean: "Through him the world was made"? Heavens and earth, the seas and all that is found therein, are called world. But there is an additional meaning: those who love the world are called the world. . . . But who are those who do not know this? Those who, *loving* the world, were also named world. For it is by *loving* that through the heart we dwell; they have in effect deserved, *by loving*, to be called with the very name of what they inhabit. In the same way when we say that this house is bad or that that one is good, we are not accusing the walls of the one that we call bad, nor praising those of the one that we call good; but in the bad, the inhabitants are bad; in the good, the inhabitants good. In this way we call *world* those who inhabit the world *by loving it*. Who are they? Those who *love* the world; for it is they who are inhabitants of the world by their heart. Those who do not *love* the world are found there carnally, but by their heart they reside in the heavens. (*Commentary on the Gospel of Saint John* II, 11, *PL* 35, 1394)

In this sense one cannot, as Heidegger does, comment on the latter text by saying that "'World' means: being in its totality as the definitive How in accordance with which human Dasein positions and holds itself with respect to being" (*Vom Wesen des Grundes*, *GA* 9:145 [English trans., 57]). The world defines not being as being, even as a whole, but the (ontic, if you will) whole *of what I love*, of being as I love it (possibly in the place of God); for I dwell only to the measure of my love. Or rather: to be sure I dwell only by thinking, but I think in the radical sense only as I love, since in the end I know only by loving (see above, Chapter 3, §§20–21).

2. Heidegger, *Sein und Zeit*, §6, 24, 38–40 (English trans., 46 [modified]). I am risking the neologism *creatureness* in order to avoid the pleonasm *being-created* [*être-créé*] used in the French translation by Martineau.

3. Heidegger, *Sein und Zeit*, §20, 92, 34–35, then 24–26 (English trans., 125 [modified]). Heidegger is here criticizing Descartes. His criticism explicitly understands *ens creatum* in terms of *Vorhandenheit*, whose connection to creation, in its theological sense, remains entirely undetermined (at least as much so as the meaning of Being according to Descartes).

4. The strange ambiguity in Heidegger's formulation has not been commented upon often enough: does creation (creature status; creatureness, therefore) truly emerge with "ancient thought" in general or, since the Greeks seem to know nothing of it, with Christian theology alone? And if the latter, why attribute to it the eminently Greek characteristics of presence, *Gegenwart, Anwesenheit* (*Sein und Zeit*, §6 25, 19–24 [English trans., 47])? My question becomes even less avoidable when it is seen that Heidegger is here critiquing Descartes, whom it is difficult to consider Greek or a Christian theologian.

5. Heidegger, *Einfuhrung in die Metaphysik*, §1, *GA* 40:9 (English trans., 6–7 [modified]).

6. Heidegger, "Was ist Metaphysik?" *Wegmarken, GA* 9:122 (English trans., 112 [modified]).

7. Heidegger, "Einleitung zu: 'Was ist Metaphysik?'" *Wegmarken, GA* 9:382 (English trans. in *Pathmarks*, 290 [modified]).

8. Heidegger, *Sein und Zeit*, §20, 92, 18 (English trans., 125).

9. *Commentaries on the Psalms* 128, 5, *PL* 37, 1691. Only the vices (lust, greed, etc.) cannot praise God because, being nothing themselves, they do not bear the trace of any good creation. In contrast, even the wicked man, who was created and remains, inasmuch as still real, good, can wind up praising: "Non laudant ista, quia non ipse illa fecit. Laudant ibi homines Deum; hominis creator Deus est" (These things, they do not praise him because he did not make them. Here, in contrast, men praise God; for God is creator of Man) (ibid.).

10. See: "Quid est 'Confessio ejus est in terra et caelo?' Qua ipse confitetur? Non, sed qua illum omnia confitentur, omnia clamant; omnium pulchritudo quodam modo vox ejus est, confitentium Deum. Clamat caelum Deo: Tu me fecisti, non ego. Clamat terra: Tu me condisti, non ego. Quomodo clamant

ista? Quando considerantur, et hoc invenitur; ex tua consideratione clamant, ex tua voce clamant . . . . Id est, confiteris ei de rebus terrenis, confiteri ei de rebus caelestibus" (What is this "His confession is on the earth and in the heavens"? Would this be the confession by which he would confess himself? No, but rather that by which all things confess him, all acclaim him; the beauty of all that which confesses God is in a certain way the voice of confession. The heavens proclaim to God: "It is you who made me, not myself." The earth proclaims: "It is you who established me, not myself." How do they proclaim this? When one considers them [correctly], one finds out: they proclaim it through your consideration, they proclaim it through your voice; . . . that is to say, confess God for the things of the earth, confess him for the things of the heavens) (*Commentaries on the Psalms* 148, 15, *PL* 37, 1946ff.).

11. It is within this framework that one must consider (and seriously) the rules posed for the discussion, confrontation, and possible covalidation of the different hypotheses for interpreting scripture in general (and the *caelum caeli* in particular) in the second section of *Confessiones* XII (14.17–32.43). The agreement of the exegeses and even the exegetes, despite their differences (when they are found to be mutually legitimating), constitutes an essential condition for recognizing creation (precisely *creatureness*, to say exactly the creature status of the things seen). Praise can come only from the community of believers.

12. I should note that here it is not a matter of the moral defect of a place, my heart, not yet purified, denounced in other texts. "Invocas Deum, quando in te vocas Deum. Hoc est enim illum invocare, illum in te vocare, quodam modo eum in domum cordis tui invitare. Non autem auderes tantum patrem familias invitare, nisi nosses ei habitaculum praeparare. Si enim tibi dicat Deus: Ecce invocasti me, venio ad te, quo intrabo, tantae sordes conscientiae tuae sustinebo? Si servum meum in domum tuam invitares, nonne prius eam mundare curares? Invocas me in cor tuam, et plenum est rapinis" (You invoke God when you call him into yourself. For that is what it means to invoke him: to call him into yourself, to invite him in some fashion into the house of your heart. Now you would not dare to invite even the father of your family if you had not prepared a lodging for him. But if God says to you: "Behold, you called me, I come unto you, where will I enter? If you invite my servant into your house, wouldn't you take care first to clean it? You called me to come into your body, and it is full of rapaciousness") (*Commentaries on the Psalms* 30, 2, *PL* 36, 249).

13. See: "et exclamaverunt voce magna: 'Ipse fecit nos' . . . responsion[ibus] caeli et terrae et omnium . . . dicentium 'Non sumus Deus' et 'Ipse fecit nos'" (and cried out with a loud voice: "He, he alone made us" . . . the responses of heaven and earth and of all things . . . saying: "We are not God" and "He, he alone made us") (X, 6, 9, 14, 156). Or: "Ecce sunt caelum et terra, clamant, quod facta sint; mutantur enim atque variantur. Quidquid autem factum non est et

tamen est, non est *in eo* quicquam, quod ante non erat: quod est mutari atque variari. Clamant etiam, quod se ipsa non fecerint" (Behold heaven and earth, which say that they were made; they change and vary. Everything that was not made but which nevertheless is does not give *place* for anything whatsoever that was not there beforehand: which is what is called changing and varying. They cry aloud, too, that they did not make themselves) (XI, 4, 6, 14, 280).

14. When it takes on a positive sense, it is always a matter of the very *here* (*ibi*) of God or of a *here* seen from God's point of view, which becomes acceptable for us only eschatologically: "*Ibi* esse nostrum non habebit mortem, *ibi* nosse nostrum non habebit errorem, *ibi* amare nostrum non habebit offensionem" (*Here*, no more death for our being, *here* no more error for our knowledge, *here* no more offense done to our love) (*City of God* XI, 28, 35, 122).

15. See *Vetus Latina: Die Reste der altlateinischen Bibel*, by P. Sabatier, newly collected and edited by Erzabtei Beuron (Freiburg, 1951), 2:2–6.

16. *Ève*, in *Œuvres poétiques complètes*, ed. F. Porché (Paris, 1967), 936.

17. *De natura boni* XVIII, 1, 454. See: "materies informis corporalium formarum capax ab eis ὕλην appellaretur" (*Contra Faustum* XXI, 4, *PL* 42, 39).

18. See: "nec intelligis, cum Deus dicitur *de* nihilo fecisse quod fecit, non dixit aliud quia *de* seipso non fecit. . . . *De* nihilo est ergo, quod non est *de* aliquo" (you do not understand that when it is said that God made what he made *with* nothing, nothing other than this is being said: he did not make it *with* himself. . . . That is made *with* nothing which is not made *with* something" (*Contra Julianum* V, 31, *PL* 45, 1470). In other words God created starting from and with the stuff of the only imaginable contrary to him, nothingness: "Ei ergo qui summe est, non potest esse contrarium nisi quod non est" (Nothing can be contrary to him who exists supremely, except what is not) (*De natura boni* XIX, 1, 456).

19. See the study by J. Pepin, "Recherches sur le sens et les origines de l'expression *caelum caeli* dans le livre XII des *Confessions* de saint Augustin," *Archivum Latinitatis Medii Aevi (Bulletin du Cange)* 23, no. 3 (1953); repr. in *Ex Platonicorum Persona: Etudes sur les lectures philosophiques de saint Augustin* (Amsterdam 1997), as chapter 6, "Le platonisme judéo-chrétien d'Alexandrie et l'exégèse augustinienne du 'ciel du ciel.'" He comes to several conclusions: (a) other biblical bases (Deuteronomy 10:14; Amos 9:6; Psalm 113:24, but also Psalm 67:34 and 148:4); (b) the origin of the theme in Philo, *De Opifice Mundi* §35; and esp. Saint Ambrose, *Expositio Psalmi* 118, 8: "Unde et caelum purius et defaecatius ad omni labe peccati est, longeque remotius ab illo de quo scriptum est 'Sicut volatilia caeli'" (Matthew 6:26)" (*CSEL* 62:127); (c) its posterity (Prosper of Aquitaine, *Expositio in Psalmos* 118, 16 *PL* 51, 329); (d) its plurivocity (formless matter of the intellectual creature, of the visible world, and the formed being of the invisible creature by opposition to the physical sky); and, above all, (d) its ambiguous status including both "intellectual creature near in dignity to the divine Word," but

which also "inasmuch as it turns away from Wisdom . . . lives wretchedly in uniformity, but . . . receives counsel by turning toward it" (216). See also H. Armstrong, "Spiritual or Intelligible Matter in Plotinus and St. Augustine," *Augustinus Magister*, 1:277–83; and A. Solignac, *BA* 14, 592ff.

20. See: "spiritualem vel intellectualem illam creaturam semper faciem Dei contemplantem" (this spiritual and intellectual creature who is always contemplating the face of God) (XII, 17, 24, 14, 380).

21. Or *casta civitas tua* (XII, 15, 20, 14, 372).

22. *Confessiones* XII, 16, 23, 14, 378. This wonderful text melds Psalm 122 (the ascent to Jerusalem) and Philippians 3:13 (see above, Chapter 5, §36 and Chapter 7, §47).

23. I am here taking up an illuminating hypothesis put forward by J. J. O'Donnell (see *Augustine: Confessions*, 3:250ff.).

24. I am following the reconstitution of the text attempted by J. J. O'Donnell (*Augustine: Confessions*, 3:344ff.) on the basis of Beuron, *Vetus Latina: Die Reste der altlateinischen Bibel*, 16–17, 26.

25. The Vulgate says either *in species suas* (Genesis 1:21) or *secundum species suas* (Genesis 1:24) or *juxta species suas* (Genesis 1:25), as well as *secundum genus suum* (Genesis 1:21) or also *in genere suo* (Genesis 1:24, 25).

26. *De Genesi ad litteram* III, 12, 20, *BA* 48, 242ff. Farther along, the same text observes that in order to create man, God does not say *fiat*, but passes into the plural: "Faciamus hominem ad imaginem et similitudinem nostram) (III, 19, 29, *BA* 48, 258), indicating in this way not only the Trinity but also the direct implication of God, which no longer harbors the neutrality of (efficient) causality and abstract omnipotence.

27. Certainly, in this same text, Saint Augustine hopes that we will not say "Hominem vero non imaginem, sed ad imaginem" (ibid.), arguing on the basis of the authority of 1 Corinthians 11:7: "Man should not cover his head, for he is the image and glory of God" (doubtless, for that matter, wrongly, because this is about ἀνήρ/*vir*, not *homo* and because our question concerns not so much its image status as the likeness of this image). But he concedes at least that even if man is not always reducible to the *ad imaginem*, this restriction never applies to the Son, "imago aequalis Patri." Concerning the importance of this *ad*, see the note "L'homme à l'image," in *BA* 15, 589; H. Somers, "Image de Die: Les sources de l'exégèse de saint Augustin," *Revue des études augustiniennes* 7 (1961): 105–25; P. Hadot, "L'image de la Trinité dans l'âme chez Victorinus et chez saint Augustin," *Studia Patristica* 6 (1962): 410–24; and R. A. Markus, "*Imago* and *similitudo* in Augustine," *Revue des études augustiniennes* 10 (1964): 125–43.

28. *De civitate Dei* XI, 2, *BA* 35, 36. This is indeed a case of a reflection on *ad imaginem*: "Cum enim homo rectissime intellegatur, vel si hoc non potest, saltem credatur factus *ad* imaginem Dei" (ibid.).

29. "In its proper sense, however, the distinction of being an image belongs only to man," says quite beautifully Etienne Gilson, *Introduction à l'étude de saint Augustin*, 288 (English trans., 219). But in a sense still more radical than he seems to suppose: not because man *is* the image but because he appears *in, according to, by reference to* the unimageable and thus bears his image.

30. *Commentary on the Psalms* 42, 6 *PL* 36, 480.

31. These terms are very nearly confirmed by the *Confessiones*: "Trinitatem omnipotentem quis intelliget? Et quis non loquitur eam si tamen eam? . . . Vellem ut haec tria cogitarent homines in se ipsis. . . . sed dico autem haec tria: esse, nosse, velle. Sum enim et scio et volo: sum sciens et volens, et scio esse me et velle, et volo esse et scire" (Who understands the omnipotent Trinity and who can speak of it, if indeed it is it of which he speaks? . . . I would like for men to think in themselves these three things. . . . I will say them, these three things: being, knowing, willing. For I am and know and will: I am knowing and willing, and I know myself being and willing, and I will being and knowing) (XIII, 11, 12, 14, 442).

32. *De Trinitate* XIV, 8, 11, 16, 374.

33. Ibid., 12, 18, 16, 386.

34. Ibid.

35. *De moribus Ecclesiae Catholicae et de moribus Manichaeorum* I, 4, 6, *BA* 1, 144.

36. Levinas: "The face is signification, and signification without context. . . . In this sense one can say that the face is not 'seen.' It is what cannot become a content, which your thought would embrace, it is uncontainable, it leads you beyond" (*Ethique et infini: Entretien avec Philippe Nemo* [Paris, 1982], 90–91 [English trans., 86–87]).

37. Nietzsche, "als das 'abschätzende Tier an sich,'" *Zur Genealogie der Moral* II, §8 (English trans., 70).

38. Heidegger, "Was ist Metaphysik?" in *Wegmarken*, *GA* 9:118 (English trans., 108).

39. Heidegger, *Brief über den "Humanismus,"* 342 (English trans., 210).

40. Gregory of Nyssa, *On the Making of Man* XI, 3, *PG* 44, col 156b (English trans., 396–97 [modified]). See also the same teaching in, among others, Basil of Caesarea, *Against Eunomius* III, 6, *PG*, 29, col. 668bff.; as well as Jean Chrysostom, *On the Incomprehensible Nature of God* V.

41. *Confessiones* X, 5, 7, 14, 150 (see above, Chapter 2). This citation of 1 Corinthians 2:11ff., which we saw was diverted from its obvious sense in Saint Paul, returns to it again *in fine* within the frame of a complete response to the question of what we are: "Quomodo ergo scimus et nos 'quae a Deo donata sunt nobis'? Respondetur mihi, quoniam quae per ejus Spiritum scimus etiam sic 'nemo scit nisi Spiritus Dei'" (How then do we too know "the things that God has given

us"? The response given to me is this: the things that we know by the Spirit, even in this way, "nobody knows them except the Spirit of God") (XIII, 31, 46, 14, 512). What we know of ourselves, since that too, comes to us as a gift, we know only inasmuch as the Spirit knows it in us and for us. We are *ego*, but of a *cogito* that is displaced, by reference, *unto* the image and resemblance of the incomprehensible. I think myself in another thought besides my own, more mine than whatever I myself might think myself.

42. *Confessiones* X, 5, 7, 14, 152, which cites at the end Psalm 89:8.

43. *Letter* 157, 2, 9: "Anima quippe velut pondere, amore fertur quocumque fertur. Jubemur itaque detrahere de pondere cupiditatis quod accedat ad pondus caritatis, donec illud consumatur, hoc perficiatur" (The soul, wherever it goes, is taken there by its love as by a weight. Let us strive then to shake off the weight of desire so as to add to the weight of charity, to the point that the first is consumed and the latter completed) (*PL* 33, 677).

44. *De Trinitate* XI, 11, 18, 16, 210.

45. Aristotle, *Physics* 4.8.214b12–16.

46. Iamblichus uses this distinction to explain that the νοῦς can descend if it goes toward the body but ascend if it goes toward the intelligible (according to Simplicius, *Commentary of the "Categories," Commentaria in Aristotelem Graeca*, vol. 8, ed. C. Kalbfleisch [Berlin, 2007], 128, l, 32–35). See the evidence collected by D. O'Brien, "'Pondus meum, amor meus' (Conf., XIII, 9, 10): Augustin et Iamblique," *Revue d'histoire des religions* 4 (1981): 423–28; and *Studia Patristica* 16 (Berlin, 1985); see also R. J. O'Connell, *Imagination and Metaphysics in St. Augustine* (Milwaukee, 1968), 4–16; as well as J. J. O'Donnell, *Augustine: Confessions*, 3:356ff. This rapprochement (as also with Aristotle and Plotinus) still remains highly approximate, since it concerns neither love nor even weight but quantities in the incorporeal (ἐν τοῖς ἀσωμάτοις).

47. "Terrena et humida [partes] suopte nutu et suo *pondere* ad pares angulos in terram et in mare *ferantur*, reliquae duae partes, una ignea, altera animalis, ut illae superiores in medium locum mundi *gravitate ferantur* et *pondere*, sic hae rursus rectis lineis in coelestem locum *subvolent*, sive ipsa natura superiora appetente, sive quod a gravioribus leviora natura repellantur" (*Tusculanes* I, 17, 40). See also: "Inde est indagationata initiorum et tanquam seminum . . . unde terra et quibus librata ponderibus, quibus cavernis maria sustineantur, qua omnia delata *gravitate* medium mundi locum semper *expetant*, qui idem infimus in rotundo" (*Tusculanes* V, 24, 69, 48 and 496).

48. *De quantitate animae* XXII, 37, BA 5, 302.

49. *Commentaries on the Psalms* 29, 2, 10, PL 36, 222.

50. *De civitate Dei* XXII, 11, 1, 37, 602. Likewise: "Sed necesse est, *inquiunt*, ut terrena corpora naturale *pondus* vel in terra tenat, vel cogat ad terram et ideo in caelo esse non possint" (It is necessary, *they say*, that the natural *weight* of earthly

bodies either maintains them on the earth or forces them toward the earth and that therefore they cannot be in the heavens) (ibid., XIII, 18, 35, 298).

51. See a commentary on this verse in *De Genesi ad litteram* IV, 3, 7, 14, *BA* 48, 288–98; and *De Genesi contra Manicheos* I, 16, 25–26, *BA* 50, 212ff. (and the note on p. 515).

52. Virgil, *Bucolics* 2.65, ed. F. Plessis and P. Legay (Paris, 1903), 14.

53. *Commentary on the Gospel of John* XXVI, 4, *PL* 35, 1608. See "amandi trahitur" (26, 5, *PL* 35, 1609).

54. See 2 Corinthians 4:17, on which Saint Augustine offered little commentary.

55. *De musica* VI, 11, 29, *BA* 7, 424.

56. *Letter* 55, 10, 18, *PL* 33, 212ff. See also: "Et est pondus voluntatis et amoris, ubi apparet, quanti quidque in appetendo, fugiendo, praeponendo postponendoque pendatur" (And in the weight of the will and of the soul appears what is at issue in what one seeks, what one flees, what one prioritizes, and what one postpones, and its price) (*De Genesi ad litteram* IV, 4, 8, *BA* 48, 290). Or: "Et ordinem aliquem petit aut tenet, *sicut* sunt pondera vel collocationes corporum, *atque* amores aut delectationes animarum" (And [every creation of God] asks for and possesses a certain order, the loves and pleasure of souls *as well* as the weight and placement of bodies) (*De Trinitate* VI, 10, 12, 15, 498).

57. *De civitate Dei* XI, 28, 35, 122.

58. Ibid., 26, 35, 84.

59. *De libero arbitrio* III, 1, 2, 6, 326.

60. *Sermon* 344, 1, *PL* 39, 1512. See: "*pondere* superbiae meae in ima decidebam" (the *weight* of my pride makes me fall lower) (*Confessiones* IV, 15, 27, 13, 454). And: "et non stabam frui Deo meo, sed rapiebar ad te decore tuo moxque deripebar abs te *pondere meo* et ruebam in ista cum gemitu; et *pondus* hoc consuetudo carnalis" (and I did not remain stable in the enjoyment of you, but I was ravished unto you by your beauty; then all at once I was hoisted away far from you [dragged] by my own *weight*, and I collapsed in grief among the things around me; and this *weight* was the habit of the flesh) (VII, 17, 23, 13, 626). This confirms: "*pondere* malae suae consuetudinis" (beneath the *weight* of bad habit) (*De Genesi contra Manicheos* II, 22, 34, 50, 352). And one more time: "Amant enim requiem, sive piae animae, sive iniquae; sed qua perveniunt ad id quod amant, plurimae nesciunt. . . . Nam sicut corpus tam diu nititur *pondere* sive deorsum versus sive sursum versus, donec ad locum quo nititur veniens conquiescat . . ., sic animae ad ea quae amant propterea nituntur ut perveniendo requiescant" (*Letter* 55, 10, 18ff., *PL* 33, 212ff.).

61. *De Trinitate* VIII, 2, 3, 16, 32. See: "tanta vis amoris, ut ea quae cum amore diu cogitaverit, eisque curae glutino inhaeserit, attrahat secum etiam cum ad se cogitandum quodam modo redit" (so great is the strength of love that what it [the spirit] has, for a long time, thought lovingly and that to which it is stuck in caring

about it, it *draws it along* with it in some fashion [even] when it turns back toward itself in order to think itself) (*De Trinitate* X, 5, 7, 16, 134).

62. *Commentary on the Gospel of John* VI, 20, *PL* 35, 1435.

63. *Confessiones* X, 28, 39, 14, 208. See above, Chapter 4, §2.

64. *Commentaries on the Psalms* 86, 3, *PL* 37, 1 (respectively 1102 and 1103).

65. *Commentaries on the Psalms* 121, 1 *PL* 37, 1618.

66. Ibid.

67. *Commentaries on the Psalms* 31, 2, 5, *PL* 36, 260.

68. *Sermon* 34, 1, 2, *PL* 38, 210. This transcendental and unconditioned character of love was seen perfectly by Jaspers: "The *universality of love*: In human life, Augustine finds nothing in which there is no love. In everything that he is, man is ultimately will, and the innermost core of will is love. Love is a striving for something I have not (*appetitus*). . . . Everything a man does, even evil, is caused by love. . . . There is no excuse that would permit him not to love" (*Augustinus*, 51 [English trans., 95 (modified)]).

69. Anders Nygren, *Den kristna kärkkstanken genom tiderna: Eros und Agape* (Stockholm, 1932), vol. 1 (English trans., 494). Seeing as well this point and expressing it in the same terms, Arendt credits it to Saint Augustine: "Charity and covetousness differ only by the object they intend, not by *how* they intend it" (*Le concept d'amour . . .* , p. 40).

70. Nygren, *Den kristna kärkkstanken genom tiderna* (*Agape and Eros*, 210 and 451 respectively).

71. Ibid. (*Agape and Eros*, 460). Nygren goes on: "The impulse toward this deepening [in Augustine's doctrine of love] came, *without doubt*, from the New Testament, but *not from it alone*. What Augustine found in the New Testament would never have been *enough* by itself to give love the place it holds for him. It was only because he came to Christianity by way of Neoplatonism that he became aware of the centrality of love in Christianity" (ibid. [my emphasis]). A truly peculiar vision of things is called for to think that Saint Augustine first had the experience of love in reading books, and above all those of philosophers, without imagining that his conception could have come from the things themselves. Later on, commenting on a text that shows precisely that every "ecstasy" (Neoplatonic or not) *fails* ("aciem figere *non* evalui" [*Confessiones* VII, 17, 23, 13, 628]) if it claims to do away with the mediation of Christ, Nygren acknowledges finding no foothold for his thesis but obviously does not hesitate to maintain it: "True, in certain respects this differs from the Neoplatonic tradition, and in particular the ecstatic absorption in God is lacking; *yet it is impossible to doubt* that the entire scheme of this ascent is determined by the Eros motif" (*Agape and Eros*, 467 [my emphasis]). In other words the argument can be summed up in this way: the text cited has nothing Neoplatonic about it; *therefore*, it is indubitable that it is thoroughly Neoplatonic. It is remarkable that this sort of sophistry or, more simply (for it isn't even a matter of a ruse or

of ignorance), that this contempt for the texts could enjoy so long an authority. See the critical account of Holte, *Béatitude et sagesse,* 207ff.).

72. *Homilies on the First Letter of John* II, 8, *PL* 35, 1992; *De civitate Dei* XIV, 28, 35, 464.

73. *Commentaries on the Psalms* 90, 1, 8. One can also oppose the desire for the contingent, for the *passing* ("nihil aliud est cupiditas, nisi amor rerum transuentium" [desire is nothing other than love of things that pass] [*De diversis quaestionibus LXXXIII* 33, *BA* 10, 98]), to love as such, which loves what does not pass and for itself: "Nihil aliud est amare, quam propter se ipsam rem aliquam appetere" (To love is nothing other than to seek a thing for itself) (*De diversis quaestionibus LXXXIII* 35, 1, also citing the "radix omnium malorum cupiditas" from 1 Timothy 6:10).

74. *De diversis quaestionibus LXXXIII* 35, 2; and *Sermon* 53, 1: "Quomodo enim non erit ibi caritas, cum nihil caritas, quam dilectio? Ipsa autem fides definita est 'quae per dilectionem operatur' (Galatians 5:6)" (*PL* 38, 359). Similarly: "Ipsa vero dilectio sive caritas (nam unius rei est utrumque nomen)" (Dilection itself or charity [for both names count for one and the same thing]) (*De Trinitate* XV, 18, 32, 16, 510).

75. *Sermon* 349, 3, *PL* 39, 1529.

76. *De doctrina christiana* III, 10, 16, *BA* 11, 258.

77. *De Trinitate* VIII, 3, 4, 16, 32, with the excellent commentary of P. Agaësse: "There is thus a superiority of *bonum* to *esse*" (*BA* 16, 586).

78. *Commentary on the First Epistle of John* VII, 8, *PL* 35, 2033. See on this point the analysis by J. Gallay, "*Dilige et quod vis fac*: Notes d'exégèse augustiniennes," *Recherches de science religieuse* 43, no. 4 (1955): 545–55.

79. A surprising text perfectly justifies a rapprochement with Kant, since it asks how one can distinguish the betrayal (*traditio*) of Judas handing Christ over to death from the Father (*traditio* again) handing his Son over to the world: "Qui Filio proprio non pepercit, sed pro nobis omnibus tradidit" (Romans 8:32)? He answers by asking us to judge according to the intentions: "Diversa ergo intentio diversa facta fecit" (The difference in intentions makes for the difference in acts). How to judge the intentions? By considering the wills: "Videtis quia non quid faciat homo considerandum est, sed quo animo et voluntate faciat" (See that you must not consider what a man does, but the will and spirit in which he does it). But again, how to judge wills? According to the criteria of charity: "Tantum valet caritas. Videte quia sola discernit, videte quia facta hominum sola distinguit" (So valuable is charity that it alone, mark you well, discriminates, that it alone, mark you well, distinguishes the works and deeds of men) (*Commentary on the First Epistle of Saint John* VII, 7, *PL* 35, 2032). On this criterion see G. Combès, *La charité d'après saint Augustin* (Paris, 1934), esp. the appendix on the natural virtues without charity.

80. *Commentary on the First Epistle of Saint John*, X, 7, *PL* 35, 2059, and II, 8, *PL* 35, 1193. See also: "Habere autem *caritatem*, et facere malum, non potest" (To have charity and do evil, that cannot happen) (VII, 6, *PL* 35, 2032).

81. One can even extend this univocity to a certain carnal charity, a spontane-ous one between animals: "Nonne videmus etiam in multus animantibus et ir-rationalibus ubi non est spiritualis caritas, sed carnalis et naturalis, exigi tamen magno affectu de uberibus matris lac a parvulis" (*Commentary on the First Letter of Saint John* IX, 1, *PL* 35, 2045). See also *Sermon* 90, 10, *PL* 38, 566.

82. *De civitate Dei* XIV, 7, 1, 35, 370–72. We find in St. Ambrose a sketch of the Augustinian exegesis of this passage when he opposes *dilectio* and *amor* to the benefit of the latter. While the former would designate only "*animi caritas*" (charity of spirit), the second would also include "quemdam aestum conceptum corporis ac mentis ardore" (some warmth conceived by the ardor of the body and mind) (*Commentary on the Gospel of Luke* X, 176, *PL* 15, 1848). See an excellent commentary by H. Petré, "C*aritas,*" *Étude sur le vocabulaire latin de la charité chrétienne* (Louvain, 1948 [thesis of 1941, Paris]), 79–91. On the originality of the position here taken by Saint Augustine in opposition to previous authors, see P. Agaësse (in *Commentaire de la première épître de saint Jean, Sources chrétiennes* [Paris: CERF, 1961], 75:35); and G. Bardy (note to "Amour et charité," in *BA* 35, 529ff.). Inversely, *dilectio* can sometimes take on a negative meaning in the scrip-tures themselves, as in Psalm 10:6 and 1 John 2:15.

83. *Commentary on the Gospel of John* CXXIII, 5, *PL* 35, 1968, which, just like the *Homilies on the First Letter of John* VIII, 5, *PL* 35, 2038, lays out the same ex-egesis as *De civitate Dei*. Nygren, a very reliable guide *a contrario*, comments: "he tries to prove that there is no difference between amor and Caritas" (*Agape and Eros*, 557). We should be more confident about Saint Francis de Sales: "In con-trast, Saint Augustine, having given better consideration to the usage of the word of God, shows clearly that the name love is no less sacred than that of dilection and that both sometimes signify a holy affection and also other times a depraved passion, adducing in support several passages from scripture" (*Traité de l'amour de Dieu* I, 14, 394).

84. *Commentary on the First Letter of Saint John* II, 8, and II, 14, *PL* 35, 1195 and 1197.

85. There is, therefore, an ambiguity in seeking the place outside of oneself, "Quaerebam te *foris* a me" (I sought you outside myself) (VI, 1, 1, 13, 514)—an uncertain step, because if I must indeed seek an other than myself, it could be that this other (and this first place) is not found outside myself but in me. One would thus commit the inverse error of Husserl (in *Cartesian Meditations* §69, Husserliana 1:183; see above, Chapter 2, §15n p. 348n68 and n69), when, in order to play interiority off against exteriority, without seeing that the nonplace dis-qualifies them both, he truncates the text of *De vera religione* XXXIX, 72: "Noli

foras ire, in te *ipsum* redi, in interiore homine habitat veritas; *et si tuam naturam mutabilem inveneris, transcende et teipsum. Sed memento cum te transcendis, ratiocinantem animam te transcendere. Illuc ergo tende, unde ipsum lumen rationis accenditur*" (Do not go outside, enter into you *yourself*; the truth resides in the most interior of man; *and if you found your mutable nature, transcend yourself too. But remember that when you transcend yourself, you also transcend your reasoning soul. Direct yourself therefore toward the point from which the rational light shines*) (*BA* 8, 130). Husserl (who curiously omits the *ipsum*) keeps from Augustine's text only what in fact amounts to a citation of Plotinus: "ἄναγε ἐπὶ σαυτὸν καὶ ἰδὲ, return into yourself and see" (*Enneads* I.6.9), as was rightly observed by N. Fischer, "Sein und Sinn der Zeitlichkeit im philosophischen Denken Augustinus," *Revue des études augustiniennes* 33 (1987): 205–34. It is necessary to return into oneself, or rather *toward* oneself, but so as to exit oneself at once: "Redi *ad* te: sed iterum sursum versus cum redieris ad te, noli remanere in te. Prius ad his quae *foris* sunt redi ad te, et deinde redde te ei qui fecit te" (Return *toward* yourself: but, again, when you return toward yourself by reascending toward the heights, do not remain in yourself. First, return from the things that are *exterior* to you toward yourself and next offer yourself to he who made you) (*Sermon* 330, 3 *PL* 39, 1457). In fact, the truly interior man is not the ego but the Christ who dwells in him: "Ille autem qui consulitur, docet, qui 'in interiore homine habitare dictus est Christus'" (The one whom we consult, the one who teaches, the one about whom it is said that "he dwells in the inner man, the Christ" [Ephesians 3:16–17]) (*De Magistro* XI, 38, 6, 102).

86. *Confessiones* III, 6, 11, 13, 382. See: "omni luce clarior, sed omni secreto interior, omni honore sublimior" (clearer than all light, but more inward than every secret, more sublime than all honor) (IX, 1, 1, 14, 72). "Rursum, cum ad illum, quantum possum, ingressus fuero, interiorem mihi et superiorem invenio" (Again, having proceeded toward him as far as possible, I find him more inside myself and higher) (*Commentary on the Psalms* 134, 4, *PL* 37, 1740). And "cum sit ipse [Deus] nullo locorum vel intervallo vel spatio incommutabili excellentique potentia et interior omne re, quia in *ipso* sunt omnia, et exterior omni re, quia ipse est ante omnia" (since God, without any spatial or temporal interval, but by the excess of his immutable power, is at once more inside each thing, because all things are in him, and more outside each thing, because he is before them all) (*De Genesi ad litteram* VIII, 26, 48, *BA* 49, 82).

87. *Homilies on the First Letter of John* II, 14, *PL* 35, 1997.

88. *Commentaries on the Psalms* 70, s. 1, 1, *PL* 36, 874.

89. See Jean-Luc Marion, *Being Given: Toward a Phenomenology of Givenness*, trans. Jeffrey L. Kosky (Stanford, 2002), §26; see also Chapter 2, §15 (above).

90. *De libero arbitrio* III, 16, *BA* 6, 410. See also: "Neque omnino potuit nisi Deus omnipotens esse talium creator animarum, quas et non dilectus faciat, et

diligens eas reficiat, et dilectus ipse perficiet; qui *et non existentibus* praestat ut sint" (Absolutely nobody, outside omnipotent God, could be the creator of souls such as he makes them while not being loved by them, remakes them by loving them, and perfects them in being beloved; he who gives being *even to those who do not [yet] exist*) (III, 20, 56, *BA* 6, 430). In *Confessiones* VII, 21, 27, the verse 1 Corinthians 4:17 becomes an argument for the theory of knowledge: "Et coepi et inveni, quidquid illac verum legeram, hac cum commendatione gratiae tuae dici, ut qui videt non 'sic glorietur, quasi non acceperit' non solum id quod videt, sed etiam ut videat—'Quid enim habes quod non accepit?'" (And I began to discover that all the truth that I read there [in the Platonists] was found here [in the scriptures] with the recommendation of your grace, to the effect that he who sees "does not glorify himself as if he had not received" not only what he sees but also the very fact of seeing—"what have you that you have not received?") (13, 638).

91. *De Trinitate* V, 15, 16, 15, 460ff., and XV, 19, 36, 16, 522.

CHAPTER 7

1. The point was contested by R. Mortley, *From Word to Silence*, vol. 2, *The Way of Negation, Christian and Greek* (Bonn, 1986), but should no longer be after V. Lossky, "Les éléments de 'théologie négative' dans la pensée de saint Augustin," *Augustinus Magister*, 1:575–81; and D. Carabine, "Negative Theology in the Thought of St. Augustine," *Recherches de théologie ancienne et médiévale* 59 (1992): 5–22.

2. *De Trinitate* VI, 7, 8, 15, 488.

3. *Confessiones* I, 4, 4, 13, 278.

4. See my own explanation of this in "In the Name: How to Avoid Speaking of It," in Jean-Luc Marion, *In Excess: Studies of Saturated Phenomena*, trans. Robyn Horner and Vincent Berraud (New York, 2002), chap. 6, §2.

5. *Confessiones*, I, 1, 1, 13, 272. Citation composed of Psalm 47:1, 144:3, and 95:4. The latter receives an illuminating commentary here: "Ergo quid diceret? Quoniam 'magnus Dominus et laudabilis nimis.' Quid enim dictura est lingua parva ad laudandum magnum? Dicendo 'nimis,' emisit vocem et dedit cogitationi quod sapiat; tanquam dicens: Quod sonare non possum, tu cogita; et cum cogitaveris, parvum erit. Quod cogitatio nullius explicat, lingua alicujus explicat? 'Magnus Dominus, et laudabilis nimis.' Ipse laudetur, ipse praedicetur, ejus gloria nuntietur et aedificatur domus" (And what then would the Prophet be saying? That "The Lord is great and praiseworthy par excellence." For what can a tiny tongue say to praise he who is great? In saying "par excellence," it emits a sound and gives thought to meditate; as if it said: think what I cannot utter; and when you will have thought it, you will see that it is

not a great-thing. What the thought of no person explains, whose tongue will explain it? "Great is the Lord and praiseworthy par excellence." Let him be praised, him and him alone, let him be glorified, him and him alone; let his glory be proclaimed and his house will be built) (*Commentaries on the Psalms* 95, 4, *PL* 37, 1230).

6. *Confessiones* XIII, 33, 48, 14, 516. Observe one difference: the first praise came only from man ("aliqua portio creaturae tuae" [a portion of your creation]), while the last rises from all the works.

7. *Sermon* 117, 3, 5, *PL* 38, 663. See also: "Si comprehenderis, non est Deus" (*Sermon* 52, 6, 16, *PL* 38, 360).

8. *De Trinitate* XV, 2, 2, 16, 422. This text can be seen as the source of Pascal: "Take comfort, you would not seek me if you had not found me" (*The Mystery of Jesus*, 314), by way of St. Bernard: "Sed enim in hoc est mirum, quod nemo te quaerere valet, nisi qui prius invenerit. Vis igitur inveniri, ut quaereris, quaeri, ut inveniaris. Potes quidem quaeri et inveniri, non tamen praeveniri" (*De diligendo Deo* VII, 22, *PL* 182, 987).

9. *Letter* 130, 15, 28, *PL* 33, 505.

10. Saint Augustine, for that matter, always denied that God could be determined by substance (οὐσία as first acceptation of ὄν): "Manifestum est Deum abusive substantiam vocari, ut nomine usitatiore intelligatur essentia, quod vere et proprie dicitur; ita ut fortasse solum Deum dici oporteat essentiam" (It is manifestly an abuse to call God a substance, in such a way that one means by that the more usual name *essence*, which is said truly and properly, so that perhaps God alone is rightly called *essence*) (*De Trinitate* VII, 5, 10 [citing *Exodus* 3:14], 15, 538). For "nihil in eo [Deo] secundum accidens dicitur, quia nihil ei accidit; nec tamen omne quod dicitur, secundum substantiam dicitur. In rebus enim creatis atque mutabilibus, quod non secundum substantiam dicitur, restat ut secundum accidens dicatur. . . . In Deo autem nihil quidem secundum accidens dicitur, quia nihil in eo mutabile" (nothing in God is said according to the accident because nothing happens to him accidentally; but all that is said is not said of the substance. For in created and mutable things, which are not said according to substance, they can only be said according to the accident. . . . But in God nothing is said according to the accident because in him nothing is mutable) (*De Trinitate* V, 5, 6, 15, 432). It is therefore necessary, rigorously, not to speak of *substantia* with regard to God but possibly of *essentia*: "substantia, vel, si melius dicitur, essentia Dei" (the substance, or to say it better, the essence of God) (III, 10, 21, 15, 318, as well as V, 2, 3, 15, 428). For a text that makes an exception (*De Trinitate* VI, 7, 8, 15, 488), see below, p. 390n18.

11. Respectively E. Zum Brunn, "L'exégèse augustinienne de 'Ego sum qui sum' et la 'métaphysique de l'Exode'" (in *Dieu et l'être: Exégèses de l'Exode 3.14 and de Coran 20.11–24*, ed. E. Zum Brunn (Paris, 1978), 142; G. Madec, *Saint Augustin et*

la philosophie: Notes critiques (Paris, 1996), 39; D. Dubarle, *Dieu avec l'être: De Parménide à Saint Thomas: Essai d'ontologie théologale* (Paris, 1986), 173 (originally appearing as "Essai sur l'ontologie théologale de saint Augustin," *Revue des études augustiniennes* 16 [1981]: 197–288); and E. Gilson, *L'être et l'essence* ([1948¹], 1962²), 45. Despite the care, which is, I think, a bit excessive, that the first three take to distinguish themselves from the last with regard to "the metaphysics of Exodus," it remains obvious that they agree on the nomination of God as Being.

12. See M. Harl, "*Exode*, 3, 14 chez les Peres grecs des quatre premiers siècles," in Brunn, *Dieu et l'Être*, 87–106.

13. *De civitate Dei* VIII, 11 (no doubt an allusion to *Timaeus* 27d), which concludes from this that Plato was not unaware of the book of Exodus, "illorum librum expertem non fuisse" (34, 270–72). See another echo of this argument: "Sed haec omnia terrena, volatica, transitoria, si comparentur illis veritati, ubi dictum est 'Ego sum qui sum,' totum hic quod transit, vanitas dicitur" (But all these earthly, aerial, and passing things, once compared to this other truth, where it is said "I am He who is," all that passes here is called vanity) (*Commentaries on the Psalms* 143, 11, *PL* 37, 1863; and *De vera religione* XLIX, 97, 8).

14. *Commentary on the Gospel of John* XXXVI, 6, *PL* 35, 1679. See the reading by A.-M. La Bonnardière of the forty-seven Augustinian commentaries on Exodus 3:14, reproduced in Brunn, *Dieu et l'être*, 164.

15. *De Trinitate* I, 1, 2, 15, 90. See also, with the same intention, *Commentaries on the Psalms* 49, 14, *PL* 37, 575, and 82, 14, *PL* 37, 1055.

16. *Confessiones* XIII, 31, 46, 16, 514. I am following the text of Knöll and Skutella, which the *BA* copies. Here J. J. O' Donnell (*Augustine: Confessions*, 3:411) refers to saint Paul in terms of *De Magistro* V, 14: "Ergo, ut ea potissimum auctoritate utamur, quae nobis carissima est, cum ait Paulus apostolus: 'Non erat in Christo *est et non*, sed *est* in illo erat' [1 Corinthians, 1:19], non opinor, putandum tres istas litteras, quae enuntiamus cum dicimus *est*, fuisse in Christo, sed illud potius quod istis tribus litteris significatur" (Therefore, out of preference for using an authority that is very dear to us, when the apostle Paul says: "in Christ there was no *yes/is and no*, but there was only *yes/is*," I do not think that what was in Christ was these three letters that we pronounce when we say *yes/is*, but what they signify" (6, 48). This text is the basis for Gilson's entire interpretation, "Notes sur l'être et le temps chez saint Augustin," *Recherches augustiniennes* 2 (1962): 205–23. As early as 1932, he assimilated this formulation, though nonbiblical, to "the divine name that God Himself announced" (*L'esprit de la philosophie médiévale* [Paris, 1932¹; here cited according to 1943²/1969, 53n2] [English trans., 53]). C. J. Vogel, privileging *Est est*, goes so far as to conclude that "it is by God himself that the philosophical notion of absolute Being is acknowledged and confirmed as expressing his essence" ("'Ego sum qui sum' et sa signification pour une philosophie chrétienne," *Revue des sciences religieuses* 4 [1961]: 337–55, 354). See

another substantive use of *est*: "Discute rerum mutationes, invenies *fuit* et *erit*; cogita Deum, invenies *est*, ubi *fuit* et *erit* esse non possit" (Dissect the variations of things and you will find *it was* and *it will be*; think God and you will find neither *it was* nor *it will be*) (*Commentary on the Gospel of John* XXXVIII, 10, *PL* 35, 1680). Yet this sort of redoubling can also be extended to the good: "Est enim est, sicut bonorum bonum, bonum est" (He is in effect *is*, just as the good among the goods [is] good) (*Commentaries on the Psalms* 134, 5, *PL* 37, 1741).

17. *De libero arbitrio* III, 7, 20, 6, 362. The rest of the text also speaks of "id quod summe est."

18. *Sermon* 7, 7, *PL* 38, 66. See also: "Deus . . ., cui profectio *ipsum esse*, unde essentia nominata est, maxime ac verissime competit. Quod enim mutatur, non servat *ipsum esse*" (God . . ., who in the truest sense comes forward as *Being itself*, from whom essence draws its name. What changes does not preserve *Being itself*" (*De Trinitate* V, 2, 3, 15, 428). And: "Deus vero multipliciter quidem dicitur magnus, bonus, sapiens, beatus, verus et quiduid aliud non indigne dici videtur. . . . et non est ibi aliud beatum esse, et aliud magnum, aut sapientem, aut verum, aut bonum, esse, aut omnino *ipsum esse*" (God is said in many ways, [as] great, good, wise, happy, true, and all that seems worthy of being spoken of him. . . . And, in this case [sc. God's], to be happy is not another thing than to be great or wise or true or good or, quite simply, than Being itself) (*De Trinitate* VI, 7, 8, 15, 488).

19. *De moribus Ecclesiae Catholicae et de moribus Manichaeorum* I, 14, 24, 1, 172.

20. *De immortalitate animi* VII, 12, *BA* 5, 190.

21. Saint Thomas Aquinas, *Summa Theologiae* Ia, respectively q. 13, a. 11, resp., and q. 12, a. 2, resp. See *Summa Theologiae*, Ia, q. 3, a. 4, resp.; *Contra Gentes*, II, 54.

22. D. Dubarle, *Dieu avec l'être*, 203. We should be surprised not only at the casual treatment of Saint Thomas, who "judged it good to nuance" Saint Augustine by imposing on him retrospectively the *substantiality* of God (despite the Augustinian critique of substance), but especially at what the Augustinian *ipsum esse* is supposed to signify: "the highest taking place in fullness that, of itself, without needing anything other, it posits itself as a unified and self-sufficient self" (ibid.).

23. J. Maritain, "La sagesse augustinienne," *Mélanges augustiniennes publiés à l'occasion du XVème anniversaire de saint Augustin* (Paris, 1931), 405, 1 (my emphasis). The cited text is obviously "Deus nihil aliud dicam esse, nisi idipsum esse" (*De moribus Ecclesiae Catholicae et de moribus Manichaeorum* I, 14, 24, 1, 172). Gilson, who cites this text with approval in *L'esprit de la philosophie médiévale* (53), declared, in the same collection and with the same tone: "However, if we admit that a religion must be expressed by a master, and if we inquire as to what *metaphysician* [sic] can be considered the model and the norm of a *Catholic philosophy*

[*sic*], who else but Saint Thomas could we choose, Him and nobody else, not even Saint Augustine?" ("L'avenir de la métaphysique augustinienne," 379).

24. "Ipsa enim natura, vel substantia, vel essentia, vel quolibet alio nomine apellandum est *idipsum quod* Deus est, quidquid illud est, corporaliter videri non potest" (For this nature itself, or substance, or essence, or by whatever other name one calls *that itself* which is God, whatever he is, that cannot be seen corporeally) (*De Trinitate* II, 18, 35, 15, 268). The sequence lists, but *so as to disqualify*, the usual ontico-ontological nominations, so as to deny them with the same blow as all material nomination (neither more nor less inadequate than they are) and to intend, by a mere designation, in fact empty, the thing itself, *idipsum*.

25. *Confessiones* IX, 10, 24, 14, 116 (I am correcting *id ipsum* with *idipsum*, following J. J. O'Donnell, *Augustine: Confessions*, 1:113). The same terms are found in the *Commentaries on the Psalms* 121: "Jam ergo, fratres, quisquis erigit aciem mentis, quisquis deponit caligem carnis, quisquis mundat oculum cordis, elevet et videat *idipsum*" (For here, my brothers, whoever raises the sharpness of his mind, deposes the darkness of the flesh, purifies the eye of his heart, rises up and sees *that itself*" (121, 5, *PL* 37, 1622). As we will see, this is not by chance.

26. *Confessiones* XII, 7, 7, 14, 352 (I reestablish the third *idipsum*, according to the manuscripts and the Maurists, with J. J. O'Donnell, *Augustine: Confessions*, 3:308, contra Skutella and *BA*).

27. This is the case for the last two texts cited, *Confessiones* IX, 10, 24 and XII, 7, 7, in *BA* 14, 117 and 353 (E. Tréhorel and G. Bouissou, trans.). The two major English translators do the same (R. Chadwick, *St. Augustine: Confessions* [Oxford, 1991]; and M. Boulding, *The Confessions*, [New York, 1997]). For *Confessiones* IX, 10, 24, Chadwick offers "towards eternal Being" (171) and Boulding "towards that which is" (227). And for *Confessiones* XII, 7, 7, Chadwick translates: "the selfsame *very being itself*" (249: here there are, in fact, two translations juxtaposed, the first one of which is written in the text of Augustine, the other only in the mind of the translator); and Boulding: "Being itself" (315). Both leave out the third occurrence. The same happens in other languages. For example, if Labriolle renders XII, 7, 7 almost correctly ("le même, le même," the third being left out [*Confessions* (Paris, 1926¹), 2:7]), he commits the error in the case of IX, 10, 24 ("vers l'Être lui-même" (10); translation cited by P. Henry, *La vision d'Ostie: Sa place dans la vie et l'œuvre de saint Augustin* [Paris, 1938], 9, an imprecision that bodes ill for the scientificity of the arguments in favor of "Plotinian ecstases"). And if H. U. von Balthasar renders XII, 7, 7 perfectly ("sondern Derselbe, Der-selbe, Derselbe" [*Die Bekenntnisse*, 321]), he misses IX, 10, 24 ("zum 'Wesenhaften'" [229]).

28. Boulding, *The Confessions*, 217, and *BA* 14, 91. But Chadwick here translates correctly with *the selfsame* (*St. Augustine: Confessions*, 169).

29. Respectively *BA* 14, 375; and Boulding, *The Confessions*, 323 (see "not *Being itself*" [Chadwick, *St. Augustine: Confessions*, 25]).

30. I am reestablishing *id ipsum* (*BA* 14, 444) as *idipsum* (following J. J. O'Donnell, *Augustine: Confessions*, 1:188). Respectively *BA* 14, 445; Chadwick, *St. Augustine: Confessions*, 280; and Boulding, *The Confessions*, 350.

31. This is proven clearly by *De Trinitate* I, 8, 17, 15, 132: "nondum intellexerat eo quoque modo *idipsum* se potuisse dicere 'Domine, ostende nobis te et sufficit nobis'" (he [Philip] had not yet understood that he could say the *same thing* by saying: "Lord, show yourself to us and that would be enough") (here correctly translated by "in the same manner," *BA* 15, 133). Or else *Confessiones* XII, 17, 25: "ex nihilo cuncta facta sunt, quia non sunt *idipsum* quod Deus," to be understood simply as "all things were made out of nothingness because they are not *the same thing* as God." This becomes, however, "de rien toutes les choses ont été faites, car elles ne sont pas l'*être même* comme Dieu" (*BA* 14, 382–83), or "because they are not *Being itself* as God is" (Chadwick, *St. Augustine: Confessions*, 258) or "they are not *Being-Itself* like God" (Boulding, *The Confessions*, 325).

32. G. Madec "risks the 'Identical,'" thereby correcting Solignac (*Le Dieu d'Augustin* [Paris, 2000], 129; see 403n1). Brunn also: "you are the identical" (*Dieu et l'être*, 158).

33. *Confessiones* I, 6, 10, 13, 290 and its translation (*BA* 13, 291).

34. A. Solignac, translating a fragment of the *Commentaries on the Psalms* 121, 5, in a note consecrated to *Idipsum* in *Confessiones*, *BA* 13, 550 (my emphasis). Once again, the *technical* is a dutiful child, masking one's incomprehension or rather overinterpretation. See the well-placed criticism of G. Madec (402n1), who imagines, however, "a passion for Being that Augustine wants to make the Christian people share" (*Saint Augustin et la philosophie*, 75). One might hope that he had other passions with a higher priority to share, to begin with the passion for the Passion.

35. For example, M.-F. Berrouard: "Augustine who had meditated on this word [*idipsum*] from the time of his retreat at Cassiciacum (*Confessiones* IX, 4, 11), compares it to the revelation at Horeb (Exodus 3:14) and *interprets* it as the expression of the mystery of the *Being itself* of God" (in an otherwise helpful note on the "*Idipsum*" of *BA* 71 [Paris, 1993], 845). As for D. Dubarle, he does not hesitate to "say not 'God is Being,' but 'God is Being itself' *ipsum esse* or [!] *id ipsum*," "even if it means having recourse to the *convenience* of the expression '*ipsum esse*—Being itself,' or else '*Idipsum*—that (Being) itself'" (*Dieu avec l'être*, respectively pp. 201 and 200 [my emphasis]). The *convenience* gains what exactitude loses.

36. See my study "Saint Thomas d'Aquin et l'ontothéologie," *Revue thomiste* 95, no. 1 (January 1995): 31–66 (repr. as "Thomas Aquinas and Onto-theo-logy," in *Mystics: Presence and Aporia*, ed. Michael Kessler and Christian Sheppard [Chicago, 2003]).

37. Perhaps one could take here in a positive sense Lacan's warning: "This *I am who I am* by which God asserts his identity to Being prompts a pure absurdity,

when it is God who speaks to Moses before the burning bush" (*Des-noms-du-Père, séminaire 1963*, 78).

38. This is according to the *Vetus Latina* used by Saint Augustine. By contrast, the translators who follow the Hebrew all correct the ending. Hence the Vulgate "Hierusalem quae aedificaris ut civitas, cujus participatio ejus simul"; or Lemaitre de Sacy, who follows the Vulgate: "Jerusalem, which is being built as a city, and about which all parties are in perfect unity"; and *Le Bible de Jérusalem*: "Jerusalem, built as a city, where everyone together makes one body," which sees in it, in a note, only the "symbol of the unity of the chosen people," therefore of the Church (Paris, 1961), 779.

39. *De Trinitate* II, 18, 35, 15, 268 (or "non sunt idipsum quod Deus" [*Confessiones* XII, 17, 25, 14, 382]).

40. *De Trinitate* III, 10, 21, 15, 318.

41. "This *misreading* counts for us as a very lovely exegesis that draws *idipsum* near not only to Exodus 3:14, but also to the 'metaphysics of Exodus'" (Brunn, "L'exégèse augustinienne de 'Ego sum qui sum' et 'la métaphysique de l'Exode,'" 158 [my emphasis]). Not only is there no misreading, but the "lovely exegesis" in question tends entircly to *distance* as much as possible Exodus 3:14 from any "metaphysics of Exodus." J. Swetnam, in an otherwise helpful article ("A Note on *idipsum* in St. Augustine," *Modern Schoolman* 30, no. 4 (1952–53): 328–31), also is guilty of a misreading when he supposes one in the Augustinian exegesis: "it seems that St. Augustine did not perceive the real meaning of the phrase because of the extremely literal nature of the version he possessed."

42. *Commentaries on the Psalms* 121, 5, PL 37, 1621–22.

43. "Jam ergo angelis et in angelo Deus dicebat moysi quaerenti nomen suum *Ego sum qui sum. Dices fillis Israël: Qui est misit me ad vos.* Esse nomen est incommutabilitatis. Omnia quae mutantur desinunt esse quod erant et incipiunt esse quod non erant. Esse verum, esse sincerum, esse germanum non habet nisi qui non mutatur" (*Sermon* 7, 7, PL 38, 66). J. Pépin argues very clearly in this direction: "Da due brani emerge che, per Agostino, *idipsum* significa innanzitutto identità, immutabilità, permanenza; poiché sono i caraterri dell'essere, il termine designerà l'essere in possesso di questi carrateri, *ma non; l'essere primo intuitu*; non traduerrei petanto l'essere', preferendo l''identico' o l''immutabile.' Del resto, *idipsum* non indica, in senso stretto, l'Essere, ma Dio *in quanto Bene* immutabile" (in *Sant'Agostino, Confessioni: Testo criticamente riveduto e apparati scritturistici a cura di Manlio Simonetti* [Milan, 1997], 5:181). And citing *De vera religione*, 21, 41: "*idipsum* id est naturam incommutabilem" (*that itself*: to wit, immutable nature" [8, 80]; and *De Trinitate* III, 8: "*Idipsum* quippe in hoc loco illud summum et incommutabile bodum intelligitur, quod Deus est" (*That itself* in this case [Psalm 121:3] is understood as this supreme and unchangeable good, which is God) (15, 282).

44. *De Trinitate* V, 2, 3, 15, 428. See Exodus 3:14 justifying "Est enim vero solus, quia incommutabilis" (*De Trinitate* VII, 5, 10, 15, 538).

45. This is according to the opposition found in *De Trinitate* II, 5, 9, 15, 204. This visibility of *idipsum* would even contradict another declaration: "audeo fiducialiter dicere, nec Deum Patrem, nec Verbum ejus, nec Spiritum ejus, quod Deus unus est, per id quod est atque *idipsum* est, ullo modo esse mutabilem ac per hoc multo minus esse visibilem" (I dare say with confidence: neither God the Father, nor the Word, nor his Spirit, which is the one God, is in any way, by that which he is and *the thing itself* that he is, mutable and, on that account, still less visible) (*De Trinitate* III, 10, 21, 15, 318). For in Christ, where the Son "ipse se exuit" (*De Trinitate* IV, 13, 17, 15, 382), God becomes mutable in order to be made visible.

46. *Commentaries on the Psalms* 121, 5, *PL* 37, 1621ff. (the four moments of which I have commented on).

47. See: "Deus autem hoc est quod est, ideo proprium nomen sibi tenuit *Ego sum qui sum*. Hoc est Filius dicendo 'nisi credideritis quia ergo sum;' *ad hoc* pertinet et *tu quis es? Principium*" (God is that which is; consequently, he has most properly the name *I am who I am*. This is the Son saying: 'If you do not believe that I am'; to which is referred also *and you who are you? The Principle*) (*Commentary on the Gospel of Saint John* XXXIX, 8, *PL* 37, 1685; or else XL, 3, *PL* 37, 1687). In fact, it should even be said that between Exodus 3:14 and John 8 and 12, the mediator is Philippians 2:6–11.

48. This is emphasized by G. Madec ("Christus, scientia et sapientia nostra," *Recherches augustiniennes* 10 [1975]: 77–85); and D. Dubarle: "in Saint Augustine, the event of the burning bush, far from being limited to a teaching about what one might wish to call 'the metaphysics of Exodus'—a theologic metaphysics to be sure, but one limiting itself to the ontology of the *Ego sum qui sum*—, already belongs, in anticipation, . . . to Christology, about which the New Testament and in particular the Gospel of Saint John will permit a full explanation" (*Dieu avec l'être*, 197).

49. *Confessiones* XII, 7, 7, 14, 352.

50. *Sermon* 7, 7, which cites Exodus 3:14 and comments: "Esse, nomen est incommutabilitatis. Omnia enim quae mutantur, desinunt esse quod erant et incipiunt esse quod non erant. Esse verum, esse sincerum, esse germanum non habet nisi qui non mutatur" (Being, this is the name of immutability. For all the things that change cease to be what they were and begin to be what they were not. True Being, authentic Being, originary Being has nothing, except what does not change) (*PL* 38, 66).

51. "Ontological difference" is meant here in the sense of *Sein und Zeit* (difference of the ways of Being), not in the later sense (difference of Being and beings), according to the distinction made in my *Reduction and Givenness: Investigations*

of Husserl, Heidegger, and Phenomenology (Evanston, IL: Northwestern University Press, 1998), chap. 4.

52. *De civitate Dei* XII, 2, 35, 154.

53. Ibid., VIII, 11, 34, 272.

54. *Confessiones* IX, 4, 11, 14, 90.

55. Ibid., XII, 17, 25, 4, 382.

56. *De vera religione* XXI, 41, 8, 80. See an explanation of *Ego sum qui sum* in solely temporal terms (ibid., XLIX, 97, 8, 166–68). There remain, of course, less clear-cut texts, such as *De Trinitate* V, 2, 3, 15, 428 (already cited). Or: "Nam sicut omnino tu es, tu sis solus, qui es imcommutabiliter et scis incommutabiliter et vis incommutabiliter" (For, just as you are absolutely, you are the sole who is immutably, who knows immutably, and who wills immutably" (*Confessiones* XIII, 16, 19, 14, 458). On these texts and their relative ambiguity see Brunn, "L'exégèse augustinienne de 'Ego sum qui sum' et la 'métaphysique de l'Exode,'" 144–46.

57. *Commentaries on the Psalms* 146, 11, *PL* 37, 1906.

58. *Commentaries on the Psalms* 101, s. 2, 10, *PL* 37, 1311.

59. Gilson, *Introduction à l'étude de saint Augustin*, 26–27 (English trans., 21). This diagnosis of Saint Augustine is shared by E. Zum Brunn: "the discovery of God-Being is still only an incomplete and distant knowledge" ("L'exégèse augustinienne de 'Ego sum qui sum' et la 'métaphysique de l'Exode,'" 144).

60. Isn't this an *artifact* produced by the commentary but absent from the text? Like the "absolute Being" supposedly found in *Confessiones* VII, 10, 16 (according to G. Madec, *Saint Augustin et la philosophie*, 39), where, in contrast, there appears the intrinsic connection that connects eternity to charity and not to Being: "O aeterna veritas et vera caritas et cara aeternitas!" (*BA* 13, 616).

61. *Le Thomisme: Introduction à l'étude de saint Thomas d'Aquin* (Paris, 1945), 195, 196, 75, and 127 (English trans., 135, 136, 49, and 87).

62. Ibid., 196 (English trans., 136).

63. *De civitate Dei* VIII, 1, *BA* 34, 230.

64. E. Gilson, *L'esprit de la philosophie médiévale*, 51 (English trans., 51). And if one softens it by saying: "Certainly the identification of God and Being is the common possession of Christian philosophers as Christian. But the agreement of Christians upon this point did not prevent philosophers from being divided on the interpretation of the notion of Being" (*Le Thomisme*, 123 [English trans., 84]), it would be necessary rather to say that Christian thinkers diverge about Being only inasmuch as they see it first *as Christians*, on the basis of another authority.

English Translations Cited

Following is a list of English translations of works cited in the text of this book. Ancient and medieval texts have been translated in accordance with the intentions reflected in Jean-Luc Marion's own rendering of them into French. Standard English editions would have been greatly modified in almost every case in order to capture Marion's sense. Interested readers can find these passages easily enough since they are cited according to a standard reference format. Suggestions about Marion's reasons for offering his own translations of Augustine, rather than using standard versions, can be found in his foreword, as well as in Chapter 7.

Arendt, Hannah. *Leibesbegriff bei Augustin*. Translated as *Love and St. Augustine*. Edited by Joanna Vecchiarelli Scott and Judith Chelius Stark (Chicago: University of Chicago Press, 1996).

Balthasar, Hans Urs von. *Herrlichkeit*, 2. Translated by Andrew Louth, Francis McDonagh, and Brian McNeil as *Studies in Theological Style*. Vol. 2 of *The Glory of the Lord: A Theological Aesthetics* (New York: Crossroad, 1984).

Bergson, Henri. *La pensée et le mouvant: Essais et conférences*. Translated by Mabelle Andison as *The Creative Mind* (New York: Greenwood Press, 1968).

Descartes, René. *Œuvres de Descartes*. Translated by John Cottingham, Robert Stoothof, Dugald Murdoch, and Anthony Kenny as *The Philosophical Writings of Descartes*. 3 vols. (Cambridge, UK: Cambridge University Press, 1984–91).

Gilson, Etienne. *Introduction à l'étude de saint Augustin*. Translated by L. E. M. Lynch as *The Christian Philosophy of St. Augustine* (New York: Random House, 1960).

———. *L'esprit de la philosophie médiévale*. Translated by A. H. C. Downes as *The Spirit of Medieval Philosophy* (New York: Charles Scribner's Sons, 1940).

———. *Le Thomisme: Introduction à l'étude de saint Thomas d'Aquin*. Translated by L. K. Shook as *The Christian Philosophy of St. Thomas Aquinas* (New York: Octagon Books, 1988).

Gregory of Nyssa. *On the Making of Man.* In *Nicene and Post-Nicene Fathers.* Ser. 1. Vol. 5, *Gregory of Nyssa Dogmatic Treatises.* Edited by Philip Schaff and Henry Wace (New York: Christian Literature, 1893).

Heidegger, Martin. *Brief über den "Humanismus."* Translated by Frank A. Capuzzi, in collaboration with J. Glenn Gray, as "Letter on Humanism." In *Basic Writings.* Edited by David Farrell Krell (New York: Harper & Row, 1977).

———. *Einführung in die Metaphysik.* Translated by Ralph Mannheim as *An Introduction to Metaphysics* (New Haven: Yale University Press, 1959).

———. "Einleitung zu 'Was ist Metaphysik?'" Translated by Walter Kaufmann as "Introduction to 'What Is Metaphysics?'" In *Pathmarks.* Edited by William McNeill (Cambridge: Cambridge University Press, 1998).

———. *Grundprobleme der Phänomenologie.* Translated by Albert Hofstadter as *The Basic Problems of Phenomenology* (Bloomington: Indiana University Press, 1981).

———. *Identität und Differenz.* Translated by Joan Stambaugh as *Identity and Difference* (New York: Harper & Row, 1969).

———. *Metaphysische Anfangsgründe der Logik.* Translated by Michael Helm as *The Metaphysical Foundations of Logic* (Bloomington: Indiana University Press, 1984).

———. *Phänomenologie des religiösen Lebens.* Translated by Matthias Fritsch and Jennifer Anna Gosetti-Ferencei as *The Phenomenology of Religious Life* (Bloomington: Indiana University Press, 2004).

———. *Prolegomena zur Geschichte des Zeitbegriffs.* Translated by Theodore Kisiel as *History of the Concept of Time: Prolegomena* (Bloomington: Indiana University Press, 1985).

———. *Sein und Zeit.* Translated by John Macquarrie and Edward Robinson as *Being and Time* (San Francisco: Harper & Row, 1962).

———. *Vom Wesen des Grundes.* Translated by Terrence Malick as *The Essence of Reasons* (Evanston, IL: Northwestern University Press, 1969).

———. "Vom Wesen der Wahrheit" Translated by John Sallis as "On the Essence of Truth." In *Basic Writings.* Edited by David Farrell Krell (New York: Harper & Row, 1977).

———. "Was ist Metaphysik?" Translated by David Farrell Krell as "What Is Metaphysics." In *Pathmarks.* Edited by William McNeill (Cambridge: Cambridge University Press, 1998).

Henry, Michel. *C'est moi la Vérité: Pour une philosophie du christianisme.* Translated by Susan Emanuel as *I Am the Truth: Toward a Philosophy of Christianity* (Stanford: Stanford University Press, 2003).

Husserl, Edmund. *Cartesianische Meditationen.* Husserliana 1. Translated by Dorion Cairns as *Cartesian Meditations* (The Hague: Martinus Nijhoff, 1960).

———. *Die Idee der phänomenologie.* Husserliana 2. Translated by William P.

Alston and George Nakhnikian as *The Idea of Phenomenology* (Dordrecht: Kluwer, 1990).

———. *Logische Untersuchungen*. Translated by J. N. Findlay as *Logical Investigations*, 2 vols. (London: Routledge and Kegan Paul, 1970).

———. *Zur Phänomenologie des inneren Zeitbewusstseins*. Husserliana 10. Translated by James S. Churchill as *The Phenomenology of Internal Time-Consciousness* (Bloomington: Indiana University Press, 1964).

Jaspers, Karl. *Augustinus*. Translated by Ralph Mannheim as *Plato and Augustine*. Vol. 1 of *The Great Philosophers* (San Diego: Harcourt Brace, 1962).

Kant, Immanuel. *Kritik der reinen Vernunft*. Translated by Norman Kemp as *Critique of Pure Reason* (New York: St. Martin's, 1965).

———. *Religion innerhalb der Grenzen der Blossen Vernunft*. Translated by Theodore M. Greene and Hoyt H. Hudson as *Religion Within the Limits of Reason Alone* (New York: Harper, 1960).

Levinas, Emmanuel. *Autrement qu'être ou au-delà de l'essence*. Translated by Alphonso Lingis as *Otherwise Than Being, or Beyond Essence* (Dordrecht: Kluwer, 1991).

———. *Ethique et infini: Entretien avec Philippe Nemo*. Translated by Richard A. Cohen as *Ethics and Infinity* (Pittsburgh: Duquesne University Press, 1985).

———. *Le temps et l'autre*. Translated by Richard A. Cohen as *Time and the Other and Additional Essays* (Pittsburgh: Duquesne University Press, 1987).

Lyotard, Jean-François. *La confession d'Augustin*. Translated by Richard Beardsworth as *The Confession of Augustine* (Stanford: Stanford University Press, 2000).

Marion, Jean-Luc. *De surcroît: Etudes sur les phénomènes saturés*. Translated by Robyn Horner and Vincent Berraud as *In Excess: Studies in Saturated Phenomena* (New York: Fordham University Press, 2004).

———. *Dieu sans l'être*. Translated by Thomas A. Carlson as *God Without Being* (Chicago: University of Chicago Press, 1991).

———. *Etant donné: Essai d'une phénoménologie de la donation*. Translated by Jeffrey L. Kosky as *Being Given: Toward a Phenomenology of Givenness* (Stanford: Stanford University Press, 2002).

———. *Le phénomène érotique*. Translated by Stephen E. Lewis as *The Erotic Phenomenon* (Chicago: University of Chicago Press, 2008).

———. *Le visible et le révélé*. Translated by Christina Gschwandtner as *The Visible and the Revealed* (New York: Fordham University Press, 2008).

———. *L'idole et la distance*. Translated by Thomas A. Carlson as *The Idol and Distance* (New York: Fordham University Press, 2001).

———. *Questions cartésiennes*. Translated as *Cartesian Questions: Method and Metaphysics* (Chicago: University of Chicago Press, 1999).

————. *Questions cartésiennes II.* Translated by Christina Gschwandtner as *On the Ego and on God: Further Cartesian Questions* (New York: Fordham University Press, 2007).

————. "Saint Thomas d'Aquin et l'ontothéologie." Translated by B. Gendreau, R. Rethy, and M. Sweeney, revised and completed by the author, as "Thomas Aquinas and Onto-theo-logy." In *Mystics: Presence and Aporia.* Edited by Michael Kessler and Christian Sheppard (Chicago: University of Chicago Press, 2003).

————. *Sur le Prisme Métaphysique de Descartes.* Translated by Jeffrey L. Kosky as *On Descartes' Metaphysical Prism* (Chicago: University of Chicago Press, 1999).

Montaigne, Michel de. *Essais* Translated by Donald M. Frame as *The Complete Works of Montaigne* (Stanford: Stanford University Press, 1957).

Nietzsche, Friedrich. *Der Wille zur Macht.* Translated by Walter Kaufmann and R. J. Hollingdale as *The Will to Power* (New York: Vintage, 1968).

————. *Zur genealogie der moral.* Translated by Walter Kaufmann as *On the Genealogy of Morals* (New York: Vintage, 1969).

Nygren, Anders. *Den kristna kärkkstanken genom tiderna. Eros och Agape.* Translated by Philip S. Watson as *Agape and Eros* (Philadelphia: Westminster Press, 1953).

Pascal, Blaise. *De l'art de persuader.* Translated by Emile Cailliet and John C. Blankenagel as "The Art of Persuasion." In *Great Shorter Works of Pascal* (Philadelphia: Westminster Press, 1948).

————. "The Mystery of Jesus." In *Pensées.*

————. *Pensées.* Translated by A. J. Krailsheimer (New York: Penguin, 1966).

Ricoeur, Paul. *Temps et récit,* vol. 1. Translated by Kathleen McLaughlin and David Pellauer as *Time and Narrative,* vol. 1 (Chicago: University of Chicago Press, 1984).

————. *Temps et récit,* vol. 3. Translated by Kathleen Blamey and David Pellauer as *Time and Narrative,* vol. 3 (Chicago: University of Chicago Press, 1988).

Rimbaud, Arthur. *Œuvres complètes, "La Pléiade."* Translated by Wallace Fowlie as *Complete Works, Selected Letters* (Chicago: University of Chicago Press, 2005).

Rousseau, Jean-Jacques. *Confessions.* Translated by Christopher Kelly as *The Confessions.* In *The Collected Writings of Rousseau.* Vol. 5. Edited by Christopher Kelly, Roger D. Masters, and Peter Stillman (Hanover, NH: University Press of New England, 1995).

Spinoza, Baruch. *Ethica.* Translated by Samuel Shirley as *Ethics.* In *Ethics, Treatise on the Emendation of the Intellect, and Selected Letters* (Indianapolis: Hackett, 1992).

Wittgenstein, Ludwig. *Philosophische Untersuchungen.* Translated by G. E. M. Anscombe as *Philosophical Investigations* (Oxford: Blackwell, 2001³).

———. *Vermischte Bemerkungen.* Translated by Peter Winch as *Culture and Value* (Chicago: University of Chicago Press, 1980).

———. *Zettel.* Translated by G.E.M. Anscombe as *Zettel.* Edited by G. E. M. Anscombe and G. H. von Wright (Berkeley: University of California Press, 1967).

Index locorum

CONFESSIONES

Index nominum

Cultural Memory in the Present

Andrew Herscher, *Violence Taking Place: The Architecture of the Kosovo Conflict*

Hans-Jörg Rheinberger, *On Historicizing Epistemology: An Essay*

Jacob Taubes, *From Cult to Culture*, edited by Charlotte Fonrobert and Amir Engel

Peter Hitchcock, *The Long Space: Transnationalism and Postcolonial Form*

Lambert Wiesing, *Artificial Presence: Philosophical Studies in Image Theory*

Jacob Taubes, *Occidental Eschatology*

Freddie Rokem, *Philosophers and Thespians: Thinking Performance*

Roberto Esposito, *Communitas: The Origin and Destiny of Community*

Vilashini Cooppan, *Worlds Within: National Narratives and Global Connections in Postcolonial Writing*

Josef Früchtl, *The Impertinent Self: A Heroic History of Modernity*

Frank Ankersmit, Ewa Domanska, and Hans Kellner, eds., *Re-Figuring Hayden White*

Michael Rothberg, *Multidirectional Memory: Remembering the Holocaust in the Age of Decolonization*

Jean-François Lyotard, *Enthusiasm: The Kantian Critique of History*

Ernst van Alphen, Mieke Bal, and Carel Smith, eds., *The Rhetoric of Sincerity*

Stéphane Mosès, *The Angel of History: Rosenzweig, Benjamin, Scholem*

Pierre Hadot, *The Present Alone Is Our Happiness: Conversations with Jeannie Carlier and Arnold I. Davidson*

Alexandre Lefebvre, *The Image of the Law: Deleuze, Bergson, Spinoza*

Samira Haj, *Reconfiguring Islamic Tradition: Reform, Rationality, and Modernity*

Diane Perpich, *The Ethics of Emmanuel Levinas*

Marcel Detienne, *Comparing the Incomparable*

François Delaporte, *Anatomy of the Passions*

René Girard, *Mimesis and Theory: Essays on Literature and Criticism, 1959-2005*

Richard Baxstrom, *Houses in Motion: The Experience of Place and the Problem of Belief in Urban Malaysia*

Jennifer L. Culbert, *Dead Certainty: The Death Penalty and the Problem of Judgment*

Samantha Frost, *Lessons from a Materialist Thinker: Hobbesian Reflections on Ethics and Politics*

Regina Mara Schwartz, *Sacramental Poetics at the Dawn of Secularism: When God Left the World*

Gil Anidjar, *Semites: Race, Religion, Literature*

Ranjana Khanna, *Algeria Cuts: Women and Representation, 1830 to the Present*

Esther Peeren, *Intersubjectivities and Popular Culture: Bakhtin and Beyond*

Eyal Peretz, *Becoming Visionary: Brian De Palma's Cinematic Education of the Senses*

Diana Sorensen, *A Turbulent Decade Remembered: Scenes from the Latin American Sixties*

Hubert Damisch, *A Childhood Memory by Piero della Francesca*

José van Dijck, *Mediated Memories in the Digital Age*

Dana Hollander, *Exemplarity and Chosenness: Rosenzweig and Derrida on the Nation of Philosophy*

Asja Szafraniec, *Beckett, Derrida, and the Event of Literature*

Sara Guyer, *Romanticism After Auschwitz*

Alison Ross, *The Aesthetic Paths of Philosophy: Presentation in Kant, Heidegger, Lacoue-Labarthe, and Nancy*

Gerhard Richter, *Thought-Images: Frankfurt School Writers' Reflections from Damaged Life*

Bella Brodzki, *Can These Bones Live? Translation, Survival, and Cultural Memory*

Rodolphe Gasché, *The Honor of Thinking: Critique, Theory, Philosophy*

Brigitte Peucker, *The Material Image: Art and the Real in Film*

Natalie Melas, *All the Difference in the World: Postcoloniality and the Ends of Comparison*

Jonathan Culler, *The Literary in Theory*

Michael G. Levine, *The Belated Witness: Literature, Testimony, and the Question of Holocaust Survival*

Jennifer A. Jordan, *Structures of Memory: Understanding German Change in Berlin and Beyond*

Christoph Menke, *Reflections of Equality*

Marlène Zarader, *The Unthought Debt: Heidegger and the Hebraic Heritage*

Jan Assmann, *Religion and Cultural Memory: Ten Studies*

David Scott and Charles Hirschkind, *Powers of the Secular Modern: Talal Asad and His Interlocutors*

Gyanendra Pandey, *Routine Violence: Nations, Fragments, Histories*

James Siegel, *Naming the Witch*

J. M. Bernstein, *Against Voluptuous Bodies: Late Modernism and the Meaning of Painting*

Theodore W. Jennings, Jr., *Reading Derrida / Thinking Paul: On Justice*

Richard Rorty and Eduardo Mendieta, *Take Care of Freedom and Truth Will Take Care of Itself: Interviews with Richard Rorty*

Jacques Derrida, *Paper Machine*

Renaud Barbaras, *Desire and Distance: Introduction to a Phenomenology of Perception*

Jill Bennett, *Empathic Vision: Affect, Trauma, and Contemporary Art*

Ban Wang, *Illuminations from the Past: Trauma, Memory, and History in Modern China*

James Phillips, *Heidegger's* Volk: *Between National Socialism and Poetry*

Frank Ankersmit, *Sublime Historical Experience*

István Rév, *Retroactive Justice: Prehistory of Post-Communism*

Paola Marrati, *Genesis and Trace: Derrida Reading Husserl and Heidegger*

Krzysztof Ziarek, *The Force of Art*

Marie-José Mondzain, *Image, Icon, Economy: The Byzantine Origins of the Contemporary Imaginary*

Cecilia Sjöholm, *The Antigone Complex: Ethics and the Invention of Feminine Desire*

Jacques Derrida and Elisabeth Roudinesco, *For What Tomorrow . . . : A Dialogue*

Elisabeth Weber, *Questioning Judaism: Interviews by Elisabeth Weber*

Jacques Derrida and Catherine Malabou, *Counterpath: Traveling with Jacques Derrida*

Martin Seel, *Aesthetics of Appearing*

Nanette Salomon, *Shifting Priorities: Gender and Genre in Seventeenth-Century Dutch Painting*

Jacob Taubes, *The Political Theology of Paul*

Jean-Luc Marion, *The Crossing of the Visible*

Eric Michaud, *The Cult of Art in Nazi Germany*

Anne Freadman, *The Machinery of Talk: Charles Peirce and the Sign Hypothesis*

Stanley Cavell, *Emerson's Transcendental Etudes*

Stuart McLean, *The Event and Its Terrors: Ireland, Famine, Modernity*

Beate Rössler, ed., *Privacies: Philosophical Evaluations*

Bernard Faure, *Double Exposure: Cutting Across Buddhist and Western Discourses*

Alessia Ricciardi, *The Ends of Mourning: Psychoanalysis, Literature, Film*

Alain Badiou, *Saint Paul: The Foundation of Universalism*

Gil Anidjar, *The Jew, the Arab: A History of the Enemy*

Jonathan Culler and Kevin Lamb, eds., *Just Being Difficult? Academic Writing in the Public Arena*

Jean-Luc Nancy, *A Finite Thinking*, edited by Simon Sparks

Theodor W. Adorno, *Can One Live after Auschwitz? A Philosophical Reader*, edited by Rolf Tiedemann

Patricia Pisters, *The Matrix of Visual Culture: Working with Deleuze in Film Theory*

Andreas Huyssen, *Present Pasts: Urban Palimpsests and the Politics of Memory*

Talal Asad, *Formations of the Secular: Christianity, Islam, Modernity*

Dorothea von Mücke, *The Rise of the Fantastic Tale*

Marc Redfield, *The Politics of Aesthetics: Nationalism, Gender, Romanticism*

Emmanuel Levinas, *On Escape*

Dan Zahavi, *Husserl's Phenomenology*

Rodolphe Gasché, *The Idea of Form: Rethinking Kant's Aesthetics*

Michael Naas, *Taking on the Tradition: Jacques Derrida and the Legacies of Deconstruction*

Herlinde Pauer-Studer, ed., *Constructions of Practical Reason: Interviews on Moral and Political Philosophy*

Jean-Luc Marion, *Being Given That: Toward a Phenomenology of Givenness*

Theodor W. Adorno and Max Horkheimer, *Dialectic of Enlightenment*

Ian Balfour, *The Rhetoric of Romantic Prophecy*

Martin Stokhof, *World and Life as One: Ethics and Ontology in Wittgenstein's Early Thought*

Gianni Vattimo, *Nietzsche: An Introduction*

Jacques Derrida, *Negotiations: Interventions and Interviews, 1971–1998*, ed. Elizabeth Rottenberg

Brett Levinson, *The Ends of Literature: The Latin American "Boom" in the Neoliberal Marketplace*

Timothy J. Reiss, *Against Autonomy: Cultural Instruments, Mutualities, and the Fictive Imagination*

Hent de Vries and Samuel Weber, eds., *Religion and Media*

Niklas Luhmann, *Theories of Distinction: Re-Describing the Descriptions of Modernity*, ed. and introd. William Rasch

Johannes Fabian, *Anthropology with an Attitude: Critical Essays*

Michel Henry, *I Am the Truth: Toward a Philosophy of Christianity*

Gil Anidjar, *"Our Place in Al-Andalus": Kabbalah, Philosophy, Literature in Arab-Jewish Letters*

Hélène Cixous and Jacques Derrida, *Veils*

Andrew Baruch Wachtel, *Making a Nation, Breaking a Nation: Literature and Cultural Politics in Yugoslavia*

Niklas Luhmann, *Love as Passion: The Codification of Intimacy*

Mieke Bal, ed., *The Practice of Cultural Analysis: Exposing Interdisciplinary Interpretation*

Jacques Derrida and Gianni Vattimo, eds., *Religion*